2014

CASSELL'S COMPANION TO

EIGHTEENTH-CENTURY BRITAIN

CASSELL'S COMPANION TO

EIGHTEENTH-CENTURY BRITAIN

Stephen Brumwell and W. A. Speck

GENERAL EDITOR · DEREK BEALES

CASSELL&CO

First published in the United Kingdom in 2001 by Cassell & Co.

Distributed in the United States of America by
Sterling Publishing Co., Inc., 387 Park Avenue South, New York, NY 10016-8810

A CIP catalogue record for this book is available from the British Library

ISBN 0-304-34796-5

Designed by Gwyn Lewis
Printed and bound in Finland by WS Bookwell

Cassell & Co., Wellington House, 125 Strand, London, WC2R 0BB

FRONTISPIECE Joseph Goupy's painting (c.1735) of Robert Walpole haranguing his cabinet
© *The Fotomas Index*

Contents

General editor's introduction

Knowledge of the history of one's own country is necessary for an understanding of its present situation. Hence English, Welsh, Scottish and Northern Irish men and women have become more interested in the history of their own countries – both of the larger unit, the United Kingdom, and of the nations within it – even as the significance of these nations and their histories has apparently been diminished by the dismantling of the Empire, devolution, the development of European integration and globalization. At the same time, the richness of recent historical writing has made it more difficult than ever for the non-specialist reader to keep up-to-date with current scholarship.

For many outside Britain, too, British history must have a special appeal. Large parts of the world have been deeply influenced, for good or ill, by British rule, commerce, industry, religion and example, and by the English language and its literature.

The object of these dictionaries is to make readily accessible the necessary basic information about the history of the United Kingdom and its constituent nations together with some account of the results of historians' new research and thinking. It is intended to appeal to VI Form and University students and libraries and to the reader generally interested in British history. Each volume will be the work of one, or at most two, distinguished historians so that each book, while fulfilling the necessary functions of a work of reference, will reflect the individual approach of its author(s). I believe that the series will be found both practically useful and intellectually stimulating.

Professor Derek Beales

SIDNEY SUSSEX COLLEGE, CAMBRIDGE, 2001

Authors' introduction

The years bounded by the 'Glorious Revolution' of 1688 and the Battle of Waterloo in 1815 represent an epoch of pivotal importance for British history. Not only did the political concept of 'Great Britain' itself achieve substance through the Acts of Union with Scotland and Ireland in 1707 and 1800, but that same term gained a far greater resonance as Britain donned the mantle of leading world power.

Britain's gradual acquisition of 'greatness' during the course of what historians have dubbed the 'long' eighteenth century stemmed from a variety of converging factors. Relative political stability, dynamic economic growth, and the evolution of a financial system strong enough to take the strain of protracted global conflicts, all bequeathed Britain the stamina to emerge from the century's climactic wars ahead of her exhausted rivals.

On a more human level, Britain's rise was aided by the contributions of forceful individuals whose talents for leadership in politics, business, technical innovation, exploration, warfare and empire-building were matched by personal qualities that continue to fascinate. It is with *both* the institutional and individual aspects of this dramatic and important era in British history that this dictionary is concerned. It follows, therefore, that the reader interested in charting Britain's chequered fortunes during the Seven Years War of 1756–1763 will not only find a concise assessment of the course and significance of that conflict, but also a character sketch of the troubled and brilliant statesman widely credited with its successful management, William Pitt the Elder.

For historians armed with the benefit of hindsight, Britain's rise to Great Power status during the eighteenth century can sometimes assume a certain inevitability. Yet for those who actually lived through the turbulent years that provide the focus for this book, such a triumphant outcome can rarely have seemed so apparent. Just as the position of William III was only consolidated after bitter fighting in Scotland, Ireland and Flanders, so the Hanoverian Succession itself remained precarious far into the eighteenth century. In both 1715 and 1745, rebellions supporting the exiled House of Stuart posed serious threats to the future of the country's German-speaking rulers. Although these dynastic struggles had subsided by 1750, the long wars with France that dominated the century repeatedly raised the spectre of invasion from across the Channel: such fears were never greater than at the very end of the period, when Napoleon Bonaparte dreamed of conquering 'perfidious Albion'. Indeed, to the modern eye, much of the era's undoubted fascination stems from the fact that British prestige experienced both spectacular peaks and dismal troughs. For example, just twenty years after the Peace of Paris of 1763 had confirmed Britain's major territorial gains during the Seven Years War, she was obliged to relinquish forever the prized colonies that became the United States of America. Yet by the 1780s Britain already possessed the underlying strengths to recover from this humiliating *volte-face* and rise again as the implacable and ultimately victorious opponent of Revolutionary and Napoleonic France.

The 'limited monarchy' and balanced constitution that emerged from the 'Glorious Revolution' in 1689 permitted the evolution of a political system that would prove the envy of other European nations dominated by absolutist and reactionary regimes. While it would be anachronistic to identify the era's loose and poorly-disciplined 'parties' with their modern successors, or to equate the Georgian 'political nation' with its twenty-first-century counterpart, there are some respects in which the political world of eighteenth-century Britain can appear strikingly modern. In Sir Robert Walpole, the pre-eminent politician of the 1720s and 30s, the age produced what many historians regard as the first 'prime minister'; throughout the period political 'issues', such as policy towards the American colonies, actually mattered. In an age when MPs might speak for several hours without pause, debates could be swayed by the power of oratory. Then, as now, politicians remained vulnerable to the vagaries of public opinion. During the eighteenth century, such opinion found expression through an increasingly vocal press. In marked contrast to an age in which 'voter apathy' is an increasingly worrying phenomenon, the vigour with which all ranks of Georgian society voiced their concerns remains striking. Throughout the century those members of the 'lower orders' who fell outside the ranks of the enfranchised nonetheless proved ready to vent their feelings through direct crowd action, of which the notorious Gordon Riots of 1780 provide an extreme example. However, nowhere is the relative 'modernity' of the Hanoverian political scene more notable than in the influence wielded by the era's prolific political caricaturists, of whom James Gillray takes the crown. As an exhibition in 2001 of Gillray's work at Tate Britain in London demonstrated, his technical brilliance was allied to an unrestrained approach to subject matter that makes today's political cartoonists appear positively tame.

Gillray was of course fortunate that his career coincided with an age possessing an unusually colourful *dramatis personae*. The spindly, port-swilling William Pitt the Younger, and his great rival, the blue-jowled Charles James Fox, were gifts to Gillray's talents. Even popular heroes like Horatio Nelson were not immune from printed satire. Men like Nelson, and James Wolfe before him, became icons whose daring exploits and self-sacrifice helped to foster patriotism and 'forge' a British national identity. Yet there was another side to this tempestuous age of war and revolution: the very years when Nelson acquired an 'immortal memory' at the cost of limb and ultimately life, were also those in which the novelist Jane Austen depicted a rarified social world with an unique insight that continues to lure Hollywood scriptwriters. Here, as in the landscape gardens of Lancelot 'Capability' Brown, the poetry of William Wordsworth and the portraiture of Joshua Reynolds, Georgian Britain proved itself an influential and enduring player upon Europe's cultural stage. Eighteenth-century Britain was likewise in the very forefront of the movement through which the architectural legacy of the ancient world was adapted to uses as diverse as the remodelling of the Bank of England, the furniture of Thomas Chippendale and the pottery of Josiah Wedgwood.

Such widespread dissemination of restrained neoclassical motifs has helped to earn Britain's eighteenth century a reputation as a polite 'age of elegance'. But this surface sophistication and calm concealed an underbelly of violence and strife. The serene portraits of Gainsborough must be balanced against the gritty engravings of William Hogarth, and the Palladian glories of country mansions with the squalid rookeries of London's East End. And for all the progressiveness that would see it achieve the world's most advanced industrial economy, Hanoverian Britain also retained characteristics that recalled a darker and more brutal past. Traditional 'sports' subjected animals to appalling cruelties. As late as 1746 Jacobite rebels were beheaded, or hung, drawn and quartered before vast crowds. Long into the reign of Victoria, gentlemen duellists killed each other over trivial slights in defence of their 'honour'. Travellers who crossed London's encircling heaths after dark did so at considerable risk of robbery and violence, whilst the footpads and high-waymen who preyed upon them often ended up rotting in chains on a road-side gibbet. For the historian, as for the general reader, it is the sheer diversity of the eighteenth-century scene, as embodied by these extremes of modernity and medievalism, sophistication and brutality, that renders it such a deeply satisfying field for exploration.

It is the authors' sincere hope that readers of this book will share their own enthusiasm for an era that remains amongst the most exciting and important in Britain's past. Those readers who are inspired to search more deeply into the eighteenth century can draw upon a detailed list of 'Further Reading' that reflects the very latest scholarship. During the past fifty years the study of Britain during the 'long' eighteenth century has itself undergone nothing short of a revolution. A period once dominated by the colossal figure of Sir Lewis Namier – whose pioneering work inspired many others to explore the minutiae of high politics – has since attracted scholars with very different interests and agendas: indeed, a new generation of historians has extended the scope of scholarly inquiry into other fields – most notably social and cultural history. In consequence, what was once a neglected and unfashionable backwater of British history has been transformed into one of its most vibrant epochs. Whilst not ignoring the traditional perspectives, this book seeks to reflect the full range of this current upsurge of scholarly endeavour, and to present it in an accessible and stimulating fashion.

In researching and writing this dictionary the authors have received assistance from several quarters. In particular, they wish to thank Hallie Rubenhold for contributing the entry on 'Women'. They are also extremely grateful to Richard Milbank, Reference Publisher at Cassell and Co., for his editorial support, and to Rosie Anderson and all at Wellington House for their meticulous attention to the typescript. Both of them wish to acknowledge the role of the General Editor, Emeritus Professor Derek Beales, who made many helpful suggestions towards improving the text. In addition, they have much appreciated the unstinting assistance of Christine Cascarino in resolving problems of software compatibility. Steve would also like to offer heartfelt thanks to Laura Durnford for her unfailing support and encouragement throughout the project.

NOTE ON DATES. In the eighteenth century there were two calendars in operation in Europe: the Julian and the Gregorian. England used the Julian system until 1753 (*see* CALENDAR REFORM OF 1751) before switching to the Gregorian calendar employed on the Continent. In the text, dates for events in England and Scotland before 1753 are given in the 'old style'; those relating to Europe employ the 'new style'.

A–Z of 18th-century Britain

A

Abercromby, Sir Ralph (1734–1801), military commander who crowned a sometimes controversial army career by inflicting a decisive defeat upon the French forces at ALEXANDRIA in Egypt in 1801. The son of a Scottish laird, Abercromby was originally destined for the law. However, while he was studying at Leipzig, the example of Frederick the Great inspired a change of direction, and in 1756 Abercromby obtained a commission in the Third Dragoon Guards, serving with them in Germany during the SEVEN YEARS WAR.

Abercromby's political sympathies left him disinclined to fight against the rebellious colonists during the AMERICAN WAR OF INDEPENDENCE. However, when conflict erupted with revolutionary France in 1793, the 58-year-old Colonel Abercromby volunteered his services and was promoted to major general. Despite chronic short-sightedness that obliged him to rely upon a telescope, Abercromby served with great credit in Flanders under the duke of YORK. It was Abercromby who led the column that stormed Valenciennes that summer; the following spring he earned York's public thanks after he coolly extricated his troops from French encirclement at Tourcoing. During the winter of 1794, Abercromby led the army's rearguard during the retreat across Holland and Germany. He was one of the few officers to emerge from the debacle with his reputation intact and was chosen to command Britain's expedition to the West Indies in 1796. Despite crippling losses from malaria and yellow fever, Abercromby succeeded in capturing the main French base at St Lucia. He then recovered Grenada and St Vincent, and in 1797 took Trinidad. Unable to wrest Puerto Rico from the Spaniards, Abercromby re-embarked his entire force with great skill. Later that year he was given command in Ireland, where the unruly crown forces were inflaming an already volatile situation. Believing the discontent to be rooted in the harshness of the Protestant gentry towards their Catholic tenants, Abercromby famously informed the Irish army that its indiscipline rendered it formidable to anyone but the enemy. The rebuke offended influential members of the Dublin Parliament. Denied the support of the viceroy, Lord Camden, Abercromby resigned his command. His successors adopted repressive policies that contributed to the onset of the bloody IRISH REBELLION OF 1798.

Events in Ireland had strained Abercromby's relationship with the younger PITT; the rift widened when the general criticized preparations for a joint Anglo-Russian expedition to Holland. Nonetheless, Abercromby led the successful amphibious landing before handing over command to York. Although the campaign ended in a humiliating withdrawal, Pitt offered Abercromby a peerage for his efforts. However, considering the honour misplaced, Abercromby refused. In May 1800, through the influence of his powerful relative Sir Henry Dundas, Abercromby was appointed to command Britain's forces in the Mediterranean. Like his loyal protégé John MOORE, Abercromby excelled as a trainer of troops – the army he led to Egypt a year later made good its landing at Aboukir Bay in the face of fierce French resistance before advancing to defeat the veteran 'Army of the Orient' at the battle of Alexandria. Abercromby died from wounds sustained during the confused fighting and was buried in Malta. The victory at Alexandria ultimately led to French withdrawal from Egypt, but Abercromby's greatest legacy was the revived British army that would eventually emerge triumphant under WELLINGTON.

FURTHER READING P. Mackesy, *British Victory in Egypt, 1801: The End of Napoleon's Conquest* (1995).

Act of Settlement (1701), legislation that established the HANOVERIAN SUCCESSION. The death in the previous year of William duke of Gloucester, the only surviving child of Princess ANNE, meant that the arrangements for the succession in the BILL OF RIGHTS had failed to provide an heir to the throne after Anne herself. The Act of Settlement overlooked an estimated fifty claimants with a better hereditary claim to the crown than the elector of Hanover, but who were debarred because they were Catholics.

The act was also known as 'An Act for the further limitation of the Crown', and, in addition to the restrictions imposed on them by the Bill of Rights, it also removed or curtailed other prerogative rights of Hanoverian monarchs. They would not be allowed to appoint judges removable at royal pleasure. Instead judges would have life tenure and could only be removed by adverse votes in both Houses of Parliament. Other clauses forbade the monarch from leaving the kingdom without consent of Parliament, and excluded PLACEMEN from the House of Commons.

Fortunately for GEORGE I, these two clauses were amended in the reign of Queen ANNE.

Act of Union (1707). *See* UNION OF ENGLAND AND SCOTLAND.

Act of Union (1800). *See* UNION OF BRITAIN AND IRELAND.

Adam, Robert (1728–92), architect. He was the second of four sons of William Adam, king's mason at Edinburgh, who all followed their father's profession as architects. Robert became the most celebrated, and in 1761 was appointed joint architect of His Majesty's Works along with Sir William CHAMBERS. This recognition came after a GRAND TOUR in which he had acquired a unique knowledge of classical architecture by studying the remains of the palace of Diocletian at Split. It was followed by commissions for himself and his brother James to design houses such as Kedleston, Kenwood, Osterley Park and Syon House, and to improve the appearance of government buildings in Whitehall by giving them a characteristic NEOCLASSICAL appearance. Their most famous public building is the Old College of Edinburgh University.

In addition to architecture Robert designed interior features such as fireplaces and furniture, for example at Harewood House. The most ambitious project of the Adam brothers, the Adelphi, envisaged an elaborate development between the Thames and the Strand in London. This ran into opposition from the City of London, as well as financial difficulties, and the scheme was only saved by a lottery in 1778. Robert's reputation with the aristocracy was unaffected by this setback, and at his funeral in Westminster Abbey five peers of the realm helped to carry his coffin.

FURTHER READING G. Beard, *The Work of Robert Adam* (1978).

Addington, Henry, 1st Viscount Sidmouth (1757–1844), Pittite politician; prime minister (1801–4). Addington first entered Parliament in

1784 as a supporter of his friend William PITT THE YOUNGER. In 1789 Pitt persuaded him to take the speaker's chair, which he occupied for twelve years. The son of a court physician, he was snobbishly referred to as 'the Doctor' by his opponents. Addington supported the UNION OF BRITAIN WITH IRELAND, but disagreed with Pitt that the corollary of union was CATHOLIC EMANCIPATION, and tried to dissuade him from pursuing it. When Pitt insisted and resigned upon the king's objection, George III asked Addington to form a government.

Addington was prime minister from 1801 to 1804. His ministry was popular at first, and in 1802 signed the treaty of AMIENS with the French; but when it became clear that the treaty would provide no more than a breathing space, Addington was criticized for lulling the country into a false sense of security. He turned to Pitt for help, but Pitt's terms were not attractive to him, and for a while they were estranged. When war resumed, Addington's unpreparedness for it was also criticized. Pitt openly opposed him, and in 1804 Addington resigned.

When Pitt succeeded as prime minister, Addington at first went into opposition. In 1805, however, the two men were reconciled and Addington was raised to the peerage as Viscount Sidmouth, joining the cabinet for a few months. On Pitt's death Sidmouth became a member of the MINISTRY OF ALL THE TALENTS. After that ministry fell, Sidmouth was out of office until 1812, when he served briefly under PERCEVAL before becoming home secretary in Lord LIVERPOOL's government. He held that post for ten years, in which time he earned a reputation for reactionary views, severity and repression.

FURTHER READING P. Ziegler, *Addington* (1965).

Addison, Joseph (1672–1719), Whig politician and essayist. Addison was the son of Lancelot Addison, a high-church dean of Lichfield. Like his father he went to Queen's College, Oxford, although he showed such promise as a writer of Latin poetry that he obtained a demyship (foundation scholarship) at Magdalen College. He later became a fellow of Magdalen, and kept the fellowship until 1711. Unlike his father he was a staunch WHIG, and earned the notice and patronage of Charles Montagu, future earl of HALIFAX, a member of the Whig JUNTO, and, at the time (1695), chancellor of the exchequer. Addison published a poem 'To the King', dedicated to Halifax's Junto colleague Lord SOMERS, and a Latin poem on the treaty of RYSWICK in 1697, dedicated to Halifax himself.

Halifax obtained for his protégé a pension of £300 a year, which Addison used to pay for a tour of France, Italy , Switzerland, the Holy Roman Empire and the Netherlands, undertaken in the years 1699 to 1703. After his return he published 'A Letter from Italy to … Lord Halifax' (1703) and *Remarks on several parts of Italy* (1705). These display a conventional English Protestant's objections to 'popish superstition' and its association with absolute power and poverty. Addison's own religious views, although outwardly Anglican, were inclined towards DEISM – as is implied in his hymn 'The spacious firmament on high', which argues for the existence of God (the 'Great Original') from the design of the universe.

As a leading Whig poet, Addison was the obvious choice to write a eulogy of the duke of MARLBOROUGH's victory at BLENHEIM in 1704, which he did in 'The Campaign'. This captured the imagination with its vivid image of Marlborough as an avenging angel flying over the battlefield, just as a hurricane had flown over England the previous year:

> So when an angel by divine command
> With rising tempests shakes a guilty land;
> Such as of late o'er pale Britannia past
> Calm and serene he drives the furious blast;
> And, pleas'd the Almighty's orders to perform,
> Rides in the whirlwind and directs the storm.

After the publication of the poem Addison was appointed commissioner of appeals. The following year he was made undersecretary to the secretary of state for the south, a post he held until 1709, when he went to Ireland as secretary to the lord lieutenant.

Although 'The Campaign' had made him famous as a poet, and although he had tried his hand as a librettist with the opera *The Fair Rosamond* in 1707, Addison really came into his own as an essayist. He contributed essays to Richard Steele's *Tatler* from 1709 to 1711, and then collaborated with Steele in producing the SPECTATOR from 1711 to 1712. The latter periodical purported to portray the members of the 'Spectator Club'. These included an archetypal country gentleman, Sir Roger de Coverley, depicted as a Tory knight from Worcestershire. Addison's urbane style became a model for later writers, being admired even by Jane AUSTEN. It reflects the good-tempered, sociable author who joined the KIT CAT CLUB and held court at Button's COFFEE HOUSE. Although both these institutions were exclusively Whig, Addison contrived to keep on good terms with Jonathan SWIFT even when the latter went over to the Tories in 1710 and he himself lost office.

Addison's detachment from partisan politics is most discernible in his tragedy *Cato*, produced in 1713; both Whigs and Tories claimed that its basic theme upheld their values. When the Whigs came to power in 1714 Addison was restored to his office as undersecretary, and then to membership of the BOARD OF TRADE. His restraint and moderation were again displayed during the JACOBITE RISING of 1715, when he started to publish a political newspaper, the *Freeholder*, to uphold the Hanoverian cause, causing some to complain that instead of blowing a trumpet to rouse loyalists against the rebels he played on a flute. Even though Addison's fictional Tory country gentleman, Foxhunter, is a much coarser character than Sir Roger de Coverley, he was still handled with kid gloves. Indeed Macaulay claimed that Foxhunter was 'the original of Squire Western', the bluff, irascible foxhunting countryman in Fielding's *Tom Jones*, and that he was drawn 'with a delicacy of which Fielding was altogether destitute'.

In 1717 Addison was made secretary of state, although he had to retire the following year on grounds of ill health, receiving a pension of £1500 a year. In the last years of his life he fell out with his old friend Steele, largely over financial disagreements. Their estrangement took a political turn in 1719 over the Peerage Bill, a measure aimed at freezing the numbers of the hereditary nobility and only making new creations to replace extinct lines (*see* LORDS, HOUSE OF). Addison defended the bill in the *Old Whig*, while Steele attacked it. They were unreconciled when Addison died on 17 June 1719.

FURTHER READING R. Otten, *Joseph Addison* (1982).

agriculture. Agricultural productivity almost doubled between 1650 and 1800. For the first half of that period, when POPULATION levels were stagnant or growing slowly, this produced an agricultural surplus that went for export. In the latter half of the period, as the population began to grow rapidly, it helped to feed the increased numbers.

This striking increase in agricultural productivity can be attributed to a variety of causes. The weather cannot be ignored, for there seems to be little doubt that wheat prices were mainly affected by a run of good harvests in the second quarter of the 18th century after indifferent or even bad summers in the first. The incidence of poor harvests increased after mid-century, with particularly extreme dearths in 1756–7, 1766–7, 1772, 1782–3, 1795–6, 1800–1 and 1812–13.

The effect of poor harvests was partly offset by an increase of the area under cultivation, which expanded by some 20% between 1700 and 1800. Enclosure, whereby common land was divided up as private property and separated by boundaries such as hedges or ditches, had also helped to improve productivity. How much land had been enclosed by 1700 is unknown, with estimates varying from between a quarter to a half of all land under cultivation. While the Midlands still retained open fields, much of the northeast, southeast and southwest had been enclosed. How much is uncertain. The uncertainty is due to the existence of various methods of enclosing land. One was by common agreement, another was by enrolment in Chancery, whereby the owners of the majority of the land involved registered their agreement to enclose with the court, a third was by act of Parliament. Of these methods only parliamentary enclosure has left anything like a systematic record. Between 1750 and 1830 about 4000 acts were passed. In the reign of George I some 7268 ha (17,960 acres), under George II 129,007 ha (318,778 acres), and between 1760 and 1815 some 2.8 million ha (7 million acres) were enclosed by statute.

The enclosure movement peaked during the REVOLUTIONARY AND NAPOLEONIC WARS; indeed, no less than 43% of English enclosure acts were passed between 1793 and 1815. Enclosure was stimulated by rising grain prices. Such inflation stemmed from a combination of dismal harvests and disruption resulting from the 'economic warfare' by which Napoleon hoped to cripple British trade: the emperor's 'Continental System' attempted to prevent British goods from entering European ports, thereby prompting Britain to retaliate with its own ORDERS IN COUNCIL. The lure of vast wartime profits encouraged farmers to bring all available land under cultivation. Despite this enhanced investment in agriculture, the increase in grain imports during the French wars suggests that food production failed to satisfy the demands of a rising population.

Merely erecting a fence or wall, digging a ditch or growing a hedge round land does not automatically improve it. However, the improving landlord or farmer could experiment far more easily with crops if they were not grown in scattered strips, or with breeding animals if they did not have to mingle with his neighbours' beasts on the common pasture. Enclosure made for more rational division of the land, and this in turn helped to make farming more efficient.

This was certainly the case in Scotland, where enclosures helped in the reduction of run-rig farm-ing, which had hindered agricultural improvement. In the run-rig system, land was generally divided for husbandry into an outfield, used mainly for oats, which surrounded an infield, where other crops were grown. Infields were divided into 'rigs', not unlike the strips of English open fields, except that they were farmed by groups of farmers rather than by individual families. Run-rig husbandry produced barely enough for subsistence, and in the 1690s harvest failure in Scotland, unlike in England, actually led to famine. After 1700 conditions slowly improved. The UNION OF ENGLAND AND SCOTLAND in 1707 stimulated the cattle trade, since the sale of black cattle to England became a foundation of the Scottish economy. Consequently much arable land was converted to pasture, a process that led to many evictions and much discontent. In the 1720s so-called 'Levellers' made their appearance in the Lowlands. Nevertheless the process continued, and the production of beef for the English market became a staple of Scottish agriculture, although there are signs after 1760 of livestock owners turning from cattle to sheep, in order to meet an increasing demand for wool for England's textile industry. Meanwhile arable farming improved as landlords – inspired by the Society of Improvers in the Knowledge of Agriculture (created in 1723) – encouraged the abolition of run-rig and the introduction of enclosures.

Both in Scotland and in England, enclosure facilitated better drainage, more rigorous crop rotation and more effective use of fertilizers. Although all these developments can be discerned before 1700, they did not become widespread until after 1750. A variety of reasons led to their extension. In some instances improving landlords, like Thomas COKE of Holkham and 2nd Viscount TOWNSHEND of Rainham in Norfolk, took the lead and insisted that tenants adopt the new methods.

Elsewhere farmers were the innovators. Jethro TULL, for instance, an Oxfordshire farmer, invented a seed drill in 1700 that improved methods of sowing. His more celebrated practice of 'horse-hoeing husbandry' was much less influential. It sprang from an obsession with hoeing that Tull picked up from a study of French viniculture, and was really impractical for most forms of British agriculture. Robert BAKEWELL, a Leicestershire farmer, made the first significant advances in the scientific breeding of animals, with experiments with horses, cattle and sheep. He was most successful with sheep, producing the Leicester variety, with which by 1770 he could make 3000 guineas a season from letting his rams to other breeders. Such experiments were partly responsible for the improvements in the weight of cattle and sheep in the 18th century, which increased by about a quarter between 1732 and 1795.

Other individuals prominent in the movement to improve agricultural productivity were William Marshall and Arthur YOUNG. Marshall, land agent to Sir Harbord Harbord in Norfolk, published *Minutes of Agriculture* in 1780. Young published *Annals of Agriculture* in 1783, the first of 47 volumes. Together they were instrumental in setting up the Board of Agriculture in 1793, of which Young became secretary. Under the presidency of Sir John Sinclair, the Board set out to survey every county. Although provided with a grant by the government, it did not function as a ministry but as a semi-private club of enthusiasts. In 1821 its grant was stopped after the Board advocated protection for agriculture against the free-trade policies of Lord LIVERPOOL's administration. The Board was wound up in 1822.

FURTHER READING G.E. Mingay (ed.), *The Agricultural Revolution. Changes in Agriculture, 1650–1880* (1977); M. Overton, *Agricultural Revolution in England: The Transformation of the Agrarian Economy 1500–1850* (1996).

Aix-la-Chapelle, treaty of (1748), treaty that brought an end to the War of the AUSTRIAN SUCCESSION. As far as Britain was concerned it also finally ended disputes over the succession to the British crown. The house of Hanover was internationally recognized as the legitimate ruling family, and Charles Edward STUART, the 'Young Pretender' who had invaded Britain in 1745, was barred from France. The treaty stipulated the mutual return of conquests, the British surrendering Cape Breton in North America in return for French gains in INDIA. The *asiento*, the right given to British merchants to trade with the Spanish empire by the treaty of UTRECHT in 1713, was renewed for four years.

Albemarle, Arnold Joost van Keppel, 1st earl of (1669–1718), courtier and military commander. Keppel accompanied William of Orange as a page of honour during his invasion of England in 1688. He subsequently became a favoured confidant of the king: he rose to groom of the bedchamber in 1691, and was appointed master of the robes four years later. As William's constant companion in peace and war, the handsome and charming young Keppel helped to fuel persistent rumours of the king's homosexuality. Jealousy at Keppel's apparent monopoly over William's royal patronage surfaced in Parliament; a similar unease among Englishmen at the influence of foreign 'aliens' would later manifest itself against the Hanoverian cronies of George I.

Despite such criticisms, Keppel continued to enjoy the king's favour: in 1696 he was made earl of Albemarle, and in the following year gained the rank of major general. William placed immense trust in Albemarle. During his final days he sent him with instructions to his deputy at the Hague, and, as William lay dying, it was to Albemarle that he handed the keys to his private cabinet. Following William's death in 1702 Albemarle returned to Holland, where he assumed his seat in the States General and accepted the rank of general in the Dutch army.

During the War of the SPANISH SUCCESSION Albemarle continued his old master's struggle against the ambitions of Louis XIV. Albemarle proved himself a capable commander of cavalry, and enjoyed the confidence of the duke of MARLBOROUGH. He participated in the allied victories of RAMILLIES and OUDENARDE, and distinguished himself during the siege of Lille. Albemarle's military services and winning personality secured the favour of Queen Anne. At her death the States General despatched him to Hanover to congratulate the elector on his accession as George I, thereby establishing Albemarle and his family as servants of the new ruling dynasty.

Alexandria, battle of (21 March 1801), engagement which marked the first decisive defeat of a French army by British troops during the REVOLUTIONARY AND NAPOLEONIC WARS. Following NELSON's destruction of the French Mediterranean fleet at the battle of the NILE in 1798, Napoleon's 'Army of the Orient' remained stranded in Egypt, while Bonaparte himself returned to France to consolidate his position. In 1800 Sir Ralph ABERCROMBY was given command of Britain's 14,000 troops in the Mediterranean and set about transforming this polyglot and dispirited force into a fighting machine capable of ousting the French from Egypt.

On 8 March 1801, part of Abercromby's force overcame French defences to mount a successful amphibious assault upon Aboukir Bay. Marching inland, the British displaced a force that sought to contest their advance at Mandara on 13 March. The decisive clash of the campaign followed soon after on 21 March when French infantry and cavalry attempted to dislodge Abercromby's army from its defensive positions at Alexandria. During a fierce encounter, the well-trained British infantry outfought the famed veterans of Napoleon's Italian campaigns. British victory was achieved at considerable cost – casualties included Abercromby himself, who was mortally wounded during the battle. The vanquished suffered even more heavily. Indeed, the bloody outcome of Alexandria broke the French resolve to fight on; their remaining forces surrendered and were repatriated and Egypt was restored to the Turks. Coming after the military humiliations of the 1790s, Abercromby's victorious Egyptian campaign went far in restoring the morale of the British army.

Almanza, battle of (25 April 1707), decisive engagement near Valencia during the War of the SPANISH SUCCESSION. A combined English, Dutch and Portuguese army commanded by the French Huguenot Lord Galway was badly defeated by a much larger force of French and Spanish troops led by an English exile, the duke of BERWICK.

The outnumbered allies at first attacked with considerable success, but the collapse of the Portuguese on their right flank placed the remainder of Galway's army under increasing pressure. A brigade of British infantry commanded by Brigadier General George WADE fought particularly stoutly, but proved unable to stave off defeat. The outcome of the battle turned the tide against the allies' attempts to win Spain for their candidate, the archduke Charles of Austria, and consolidated the position of the Bourbon claimant, Philip V.

American colonies 1763–1776. At the end of the SEVEN YEARS WAR in 1763 the British government determined to assert its sovereignty over its American colonies, which on the continent included Canada and Florida as well as the 13 that became the USA. A proclamation was issued in 1763 for the governance of these new territories. It also forbade further expansion west of the Alleghenies, and an army was stationed in North America to police this measure. The colonists were expected to pay for this force. Consequently, in the following year Parliament passed a Sugar Act to raise revenue from the colonial trade with non-British sugar-producing islands in the West Indies. In 1765 this was followed by a STAMP ACT taxing such items as newspapers and legal documents.

It had long been predicted that the expulsion of the French from the continent east of the Mississippi would lead the colonies to desire the relaxation rather than the tightening of the imperial connection. The reaction to these policies was therefore predictable. There were protests at the passing of the Sugar Act, although the fact that Parliament's right to regulate colonial trade had been long accepted somewhat blunted their impact. The Stamp Act, however, was a different proposition, since the British government had never taxed the colonies directly before. The reaction was therefore much more solid. Nine colonies sent representatives to a Stamp Act Congress in New York to protest against the act on the grounds that it was unconstitutional to tax the colonists without their own consent. They claimed that they should only be taxed by their own assemblies. The Congress also subscribed to a prohibition on the use of British imports until the act was repealed. Elsewhere more violent action was taken. Distributors of the hated stamps were intimidated to prevent them from taking up their posts, while in Boston the house of the lieutenant governor of Massachusetts, Thomas Hutchinson, was sacked.

A change of ministry in Britain from the administration of George GRENVILLE to that of the marquess of ROCKINGHAM eased the tension. Rockingham's government repealed the act, although it stood by the principle that the king in Parliament was sovereign over the colonies by passing the Declaratory Act, which affirmed Parliament's right to pass legislation affecting America 'in all cases whatsoever'. The constitutional issues at stake were therefore clearly defined. Britain claimed the sovereignty of the king in Parliament over its American colonists, while the latter insisted on the sovereignty of the people. In practice, however, both backed off from the implications of the disagreement. The Rockingham ministry was reluctant to exercise the theoretical sovereignty claimed by the Declaratory Act, while most colonists rested content with the repeal of the Stamp Act.

Tension rose again in 1767, when the chancellor of the exchequer Charles TOWNSHEND raised duties on American imports. He was responding to the distinction between external and internal taxes allegedly made by colonists when they reluctantly accepted the Sugar Act but resisted the Stamp Act. But colonial objections now appeared to any attempt to impose taxes in the colonies by a Parliament in which they were not represented.

Opposition to the Townshend duties took the form of embargoes on British imports, although the degree to which they were effective differed from port to port. Boston and New York made serious efforts, whereas Philadelphia dragged its heels. When the incoming prime minister Lord NORTH dropped all the duties except that on tea in 1770 most of the resistance collapsed.

A crisis in the relationship between Britain and the colonies nevertheless seemed to be imminent in that year, which witnessed the clash between civilians and soldiers known as the Boston Massacre. Troops stationed in Boston opened fire on a crowd that was taunting them, and some six men were killed. The withdrawal of the troops from Boston itself, and the trial of those accused of firing the fatal shots, averted a violent outcome to the crisis at the time. Indeed, the next three years are known as a 'period of quiet'. The British press virtually stopped reporting colonial affairs, and outside New England there was relative calm. Only in Massachusetts and Rhode Island was there friction, which showed that the controversy had not died down in those colonies. In Massachusetts the governor had a debate with the General Court about the locus of sovereignty in the British empire – a debate that revealed the fundamental difference between the two sides. In Rhode Island in 1772 a customs boat, the *Gaspee*, was attacked and burned down to the waterline. Elsewhere the drawing back from confrontation suggests that the final clash between Britain and the colonies was not inevitable, or at least that it might not have occurred when it did.

The calm was shattered by a crisis in another part of the empire – INDIA. The EAST INDIA COMPANY ran into financial difficulties as a result of its having to administer a subcontinent following the conquest of India during the Seven Years War. In order to bail it out Lord North got Parliament to pass a Tea Act allowing the Company to ship tea directly to the American colonies. There the tea would have to pay the Townshend duty, North refusing advice to drop it at the time. The result was inevitable: importation of the tea was violently resisted. In 1773 men disguised as Mohawk Indians boarded the Company's ship in Boston and emptied the tea into the harbour.

The reaction of the British government to the 'Boston Tea Party' precipitated the final showdown. North in fact overreacted with the so-called 'Intolerable Acts'. These punished not only the inhabitants of Boston but people throughout Massachusetts for the actions of a handful of insurgents. The closing of Boston harbour and the remodelling of the constitution of the colony were the responses of a minister exasperated by the whole of New England rather than by its principal port. North made a mistake that strategists in the forthcoming war were to repeat in its opening stages. He clearly thought that the trouble was largely confined to the northeastern colonies, and that these could be separated from the others. The establishment of inter-colonial 'committees of correspondence' soon proved how wrong he was. It was also unfortunate that, coincidentally with the Intolerable Acts intended to coerce Massachusetts, the government passed the Quebec Act. This not only gave French Catholics in Canada full citizenship, but also included a whole swathe of the Ohio area within Canadian boundaries, effectively placing the colonists there more firmly under the jurisdiction of the British crown.

The combination of 'popery and arbitrary power' proved as potent in 1774 in America as it had done in 1688 in England. The Quebec Act was now also found intolerable. The first Continental Congress assembled in Philadelphia, and, declaring the Intolerable Acts to be 'unconstitutional', resolved on a non-importation and non-exportation agreement until they were repealed. At this stage the majority were in favour of a return to the previous position, although a vocal minority were already demanding independence. This did not become the majority view until after the outbreak of hostilities at Lexington and Concord in 1775.

The 'shots that rang round the world' concentrated minds wonderfully. Thomas PAINE articulated the new mood in *Common Sense* in 1776. To demand a return to the harmonious relationship that had existed between the mother country and the colonies before the reign of the tyrannical GEORGE III was a reasonable negotiating stance, but an inadequate war aim. Now that war had broken out men could not be asked to fight and die for that end. Only independence was worth dying for. That was the common sense of Paine's pamphlet. By July it had become the opinion of the majority in Congress who signed the Declaration of Independence. The war had now become the AMERICAN WAR OF INDEPENDENCE.

FURTHER READING P. Maier, *From Resistance to Revolution: Colonial Radicals and the Development of American Opposition to Britain 1765–1776* (2nd edn 1991); K. Perry, *British Politics and the American Revolution* (1990).

American War of Independence (1775–83), conflict between Britain and the American colonists, resulting in American independence. The French, Spanish, and Dutch, all joined in against the British, helping to ensure American victory.

On a hot October afternoon in 1781, the British garrison of YORKTOWN, Virginia, marched out to surrender to a besieging Franco-American army. According to tradition, the redcoats' regimental bands played a popular tune called 'The World Turned Upside Down'. The choice of music reflected the scale of Britain's humiliation: for all its massive wealth and prestige, Europe's most powerful state had proved unequal to the task of subduing its rebellious American colonies.

The simmering political crisis between mother country and colonies (*see* AMERICAN COLONIES BEFORE 1776) had first boiled over into armed confrontation in the spring of 1775, as Boston's British garrison tested the resolve of the surrounding rebel militias. Skirmishes at Lexington and Concord, followed by the bloody battle of Bunker Hill, indicated that the rebellion was likely to prove serious. As patriot forces massed in Massachusetts, Britain's commander in chief in North America, Sir William HOWE, evacuated his troops northwards to the naval base at Halifax, Nova Scotia. Reinforced from Britain in 1776, Howe attacked the Middle Colonies; by taking New York, he hoped to isolate New England from the southern rebels. Congress's commander in chief, George Washington, took a beating, and the rebellion threatened to collapse. Washington nonetheless recovered, and in December 1776 and January 1777 launched raids on Trenton and Princeton that surprised British outposts and boosted patriot morale.

Howe struck next at the revolutionary capital of Philadelphia. The British secured their objective, scoring victories at Brandywine and Germantown. While Howe was preoccupied with Washington, a second British expedition, under General John BURGOYNE, advanced from Canada. Burgoyne's force became mired in the wilderness, and in October 1777 was obliged to surrender at SARATOGA to a rebel army under General Horatio Gates. News of the disaster prompted France to join the colonists; this development, followed by the intervention of Spain in 1779 and the Dutch Republic in 1781, transformed the conflict from colonial rebellion into world war. In the coming years, fighting flared as far afield as the Channel Islands, Gibraltar, the Caribbean, India and West Africa. Without allies of its own, Britain had its resources stretched to the limit.

While Washington's army endured the harsh winter of 1777–8 at Valley Forge, Howe's successor as British commander in chief, Sir Henry CLINTON, decided to concentrate upon New York, from where troops could be despatched to protect the West Indies. Washington followed, and at Monmouth, New Jersey, the armies clashed. Although indecisive, the battle proved that Congress's Continental Army could face the redcoats in open battle.

Stymied in both the northern and Middle Colonies, Britain now turned south. Initially this strategy worked well: Georgia was taken, and in 1779 a Franco-American attack upon Savannah

was bloodily repulsed. In May 1780 Clinton captured Charleston in South Carolina, along with its garrison of more than 5000 men. Britain's successful run continued that summer when Gates, the victor of Saratoga, was drubbed at Camden by CORNWALLIS. Yet at the very moment when British troops were poised to strike north, the tide turned. In October 1780, a royal force was destroyed at King's Mountain, while in early 1781, another British contingent met defeat at Cowpens. The rebels' general in the south, Nathanael Greene, employed a cautious strategy to grind down the outnumbered British. Although beaten by Cornwallis at the hard-fought battle of Guilford Court House, Greene escaped to fight another day. Baffled and harassed, Cornwallis withdrew to Virginia. Exploiting temporary naval superiority, a Franco-American force trapped Cornwallis in the Yorktown peninsula. Although peace was not declared for another two years, the fall of Yorktown marked the end of major fighting. Britain finally recognized the independence of the United States at the treaty of VERSAILLES in 1783.

Historians probing the causes of British defeat have emphasized not only the determination of a hard core of American patriots to maintain the struggle, but also the daunting scale of the military problem confronting the mother country. In 1775 Britain lacked the soldiers to subdue America, and was obliged to hire Hessian mercenaries to bolster its army; this manpower problem was exacerbated after the French intervention required the diversion of troops to other fronts. British politicians cherished a policy of quelling the rebellion by harnessing those colonists sympathetic to King George III. Such loyalists may have numbered one-fifth of the white population, but Britain's unrealistically high hopes of them played havoc with a strategy that was already muddled and inconsistent. Bourbon involvement placed a heavy strain upon the Royal Navy, and failure to maintain naval supremacy only served to heighten another problem that dogged British efforts to crush the rebellion. Unable to rely upon local supplies, the redcoats were obliged to look across the Atlantic for logistical support. Without command of the seas, this 5000-km (3000-mile) lifeline proved precarious. Hence British commanders were frequently unable to accumulate sufficient supplies to mount the prolonged offensives necessary to defeat the elusive patriot forces.

Technically, Britain could have maintained the struggle even after Yorktown; indeed, its resilience was demonstrated by Admiral RODNEY's victory over France's West Indies fleet at the battle of the Saints in 1782. However, after six years of warfare, public opinion was turning against a conflict that appeared increasingly futile. The struggle with the American colonists was never universally popular in Britain, perhaps because it was too much of a civil war: such attitudes are today reflected in the fact that no British regiment numbers victories from the American war amongst its official battle honours.

FURTHER READING S. Conway, *The War of American Independence, 1775–1783* (1995); D. Higginbotham, *The War of American Independence: Military Attitudes, Policies, and Practice, 1763–1789* (1971); P. Mackesy, *The War for America, 1775–1783* (1964).

Amherst, Jeffery, 1st Baron (1717–97), general. As commander in chief of British forces in North America from 1758 to 1763 Amherst orchestrated the final conquest of French Canada.

Amherst began his lengthy army career in 1735 in the regiment commanded by one of Britain's leading soldiers, Sir John LIGONIER. Their association was to prove crucial for Amherst's advancement. During the War of the AUSTRIAN SUCCESSION Amherst served in Europe as Ligonier's aide-de-camp, and was present at the battles of DETTINGEN and FONTENOY.

At the outset of the SEVEN YEARS WAR in 1756 Colonel Amherst was given administrative responsibility for a large contingent of Hessian mercenaries in British pay; in this role he was present at the battle of Hastenbeck in July 1757 when the

duke of CUMBERLAND was defeated by the French. Later that year Ligonier succeeded the disgraced Cumberland as Britain's commander in chief, and used his influence with George II to secure Amherst's promotion to 'Major General in America' in command of the expedition destined to attack the crucial French stronghold of Louisbourg on Cape Breton. Amherst's troops cooperated with a powerful fleet commanded by Admiral Edward BOSCAWEN. Following a hazardous amphibious assault in June 1758, Amherst subjected Louisbourg to a methodical siege. On 26 July the battered fortress surrendered; it was Britain's first major success of the war, and contributed to Amherst's selection as commander in chief in America.

PITT's plans for 1759 instructed Amherst to assault Canada from the south, while Major General James WOLFE attacked Quebec. After months spent assembling men and supplies from the British colonies or 'provinces', Amherst opened his campaign in mid-June. Although the French swiftly abandoned the key posts of TICONDEROGA and Crown Point, Amherst proved reluctant to push forward without ships capable of dominating Lake Champlain, and instead consolidated his position. Amherst finished the job in the following summer, when he led the largest of three armies that converged upon Montreal.

From his headquarters at New York Amherst subsequently helped to stage the British expeditions against Bourbon possessions in the Caribbean. In 1763 he faced the challenge of containing the dangerous Indian war associated with the Ottawa chief Pontiac. Indeed the general's thrifty policies towards the Native North Americans, which denied the tribes the gifts to which they had grown accustomed, probably contributed to their uprising. In November, having deployed the troops at his disposal, Amherst sailed for England with the outcome of the war still undecided.

Amherst proved reluctant to return to the continent where he had made his reputation. In 1775, as hostilities with the colonists loomed, GEORGE III asked him to take command in America; he refused the offer, and demurred again when it was repeated in 1778. As commander of forces in Britain, Amherst was responsible for the bloody suppression of the GORDON RIOTS in 1780. Dismissed at the fall of Lord NORTH's ministry, the elderly Amherst resumed an ineffective command during the opening years of the war with Revolutionary France. Cautious rather than dashing, his talents as a soldier lay in the careful organization of operations.

FURTHER READING R. Whitworth, 'Field Marshal Lord Amherst, a military enigma' in *History Today* IX (1959), 132–7.

Amiens, treaty of (1802), treaty between Britain and France that provided a brief period of peace in the REVOLUTIONARY AND NAPOLEONIC WARS. After a decade of war with Revolutionary France the warring powers were exhausted. Austria signed the treaty of Luneville with France in 1801. The following March Britain signed the treaty of Amiens, hoping to end hostilities. To this end Britain ceded all conquests except those in Ceylon (Sri Lanka) and the West Indies. But peace was short-lived, lasting just over a year before war again broke out in May 1803.

Anglesey, Henry William Paget, 1st marquess of. *See* PAGET, LORD HENRY WILLIAM, 1ST MARQUESS OF ANGLESEY.

Anne (1665–1714), queen of England and Scotland (Great Britain from 1707) and Ireland (1702–14). Anne was the second daughter of James duke of York, the future James II, by his first wife Anne Hyde. She was brought up as an Anglican, and in 1683 married the Protestant GEORGE PRINCE OF DENMARK. In the Revolution of 1688 she deserted her father and fled to Nottingham with the bishop of London. At the REVOLUTION SETTLEMENT of 1689 she accepted the BILL OF RIGHTS, which gave WILLIAM III precedence over her for the throne in the event of the death

of his wife MARY, Anne's elder sister. Consequently she did not become queen until William died in 1702. By then she was prematurely aged, the result of 17 pregnancies of which only 6 came to full term. All her children died young, the last, William duke of Gloucester, in 1700. This necessitated the ACT OF SETTLEMENT, which provided for the succession of the house of Hanover on Anne's death.

At her accession Anne announced her adherence to the Church of England, and declared that her heart was entirely English, which was a thinly veiled snub to the late Dutch king. She cultivated an Elizabethan image, deliberately inviting comparisons between her reign and that of the last woman to rule England alone. In some respects it was a glorious era, crowned by MARLBOROUGH's victories against the French in the War of the SPANISH SUCCESSION and by the Act of UNION OF ENGLAND AND SCOTLAND in 1707, which brought into being the United Kingdom of Great Britain. Moreover, Anne herself deserves some of the credit for these achievements. She ruled as well as reigned, attending weekly cabinet meetings, and even the occasional debate in the House of Lords.

Anne initially backed Marlborough up to the hilt, dismissing Tory ministers who opposed his influence over her counsels. But as he turned increasingly to Whig support for the war effort – egged on by his wife Sarah, duchess of MARLBOROUGH, the Queen's confidante – Anne resisted, her Stuart obstinacy coming to the fore. As long as she was committed to the war she could do little more than put up a rearguard action against Whig encroachments, and her stamina even for this was broken by the death of her husband in 1708. Between 1708 and 1710 her ministry was almost entirely in Whig hands.

But by 1710 Anne was persuaded that the Whigs were deliberately prolonging the war for their own ends, and became determined to negotiate a peace with Louis XIV. This policy reduced her dependence on Whig support and on the duchess of Marlborough, whose influence over her had waned long before. Advised by Robert

HARLEY, she turned more and more to the Tories, until by the autumn of 1710 her ministry was almost entirely Tory. A general election held at that time procured her new ministers a Tory majority. They proceeded to negotiate the treaty of UTRECHT of 1713, bringing the war to an end, but on terms that were regarded as treacherous by Britain's allies. Among the powers they had alienated was the electorate of Hanover, which boded ill for Tory fortunes when Anne died.

On the rock of the succession the Tory government split. Harley, now earl of Oxford and 'prime minister', stood staunchly by the Hanoverian succession. However, Henry St John, Viscount BOLINGBROKE, kept the option of a Stuart restoration open as the only hope for the Tory party in the next reign. Anne herself was put under severe stress by these tensions, but although she dismissed Oxford in 1714 she did not commit herself to the cause of her half-brother, James Francis Edward STUART, the Old Pretender. On her deathbed she gave the treasurer's staff not to the Jacobite Bolingbroke but to the Hanoverian Charles TALBOT duke of Shrewsbury, thus ensuring the peaceful accession of GEORGE I.

FURTHER READING E. Gregg, *Queen Anne* (1980); G. Holmes, *British Politics in the Age of Anne* (1987).

Anson, George (1697–1762), naval commander. Anson joined the NAVY as a volunteer in 1712. He was commissioned in 1716 partly through his family connection with Lord Chancellor Macclesfield, who was his uncle. Between 1724 and 1735 he was stationed in North America, cruising between the Carolinas and the Bahamas on police duty against pirates and other interlopers in colonial trade. During these years he acquired property and slaves in Charleston, South Carolina. From 1737 to 1739 he performed similar policing duties off the coast of Africa and in the West Indies.

In 1739 Anson was recalled to take command of an expedition to the Pacific. There were difficulties in equipping it owing to the priorities given to other naval commitments on the outbreak of war with Spain, and the expedition did not sail until September 1740. It was manned by raw recruits and pensioners from Greenwich Hospital previously invalided out of service. Of the six ships that sailed, only three got round Cape Horn and made it to the island of Juan Fernandez. Most of the men had perished by then, and those who survived were put on board Anson's own ship, the *Centurion*, which alone continued the voyage. They continued across the Pacific to Macao, a Portuguese possession in China, the first visit there by a ship of the Royal Navy. They then sailed to Manila to intercept a Spanish ship bound for Acapulco. The ship was captured, a prize worth £500,000. The *Centurion* then sailed back to England by way of the Cape of Good Hope, arriving at Spithead in June 1744. The treasure taken from the Spanish ship was paraded through London on 32 wagons, accompanied by those of Anson's own crew who had returned with him.

The circumnavigation of the world was the high point of Anson's naval career. He subsequently served as a member of the Admiralty Board, as a junior lord from 1744 to 1751, and as first lord from 1751 to 1762, apart from a brief break in 1756–7. Traditionally he has been credited with transforming the navy after a period of neglect into the fighting force that helped Britain defeat the French on three continents during the SEVEN YEARS WAR. Recent historians have shown that the navy was not unduly neglected in the years between the War of the SPANISH SUCCESSION and the War of the AUSTRIAN SUCCESSION. Moreover, the administration of the navy was not significantly reformed during Anson's stint at the Admiralty Board. Nevertheless he emerged as the dominant figure there, and he inspired the navy to some of its greatest achievements.

FURTHER READING F.B. Stitt, 'Admiral Anson at the Admiralty, 1744–62' in *Staffordshire Studies* IV (1991–2), 35–76; G. Williams, *The Prize of all the Oceans: The Triumph and Tragedy of Anson's Voyage around the World* (1999).

Anti-Jacobin, the, a journal published by George CANNING and others between November 1797 and July 1798. It was supported by the government and sought to counter the views of those who sympathized with the Revolution, stigmatizing them as muddle-headed and unpatriotic. One of its chief butts was the poet SOUTHEY.

antiquarianism. Interest in antiquities, which had always been a pursuit of individuals, also became a collective activity after the GLORIOUS REVOLUTION. Previously the Stuarts had presided over a remarkable era of antiquarian scholarship, when such luminaries as Sir Robert Cotton, Sir William Dugdale and Anthony Wood had collected medieval manuscripts and published many of them in such tomes as Dugdale's *Monasticon* and his *Antiquities of Warwickshire*. The only body which coordinated antiquarian research was the College of Heralds, established in the Middle Ages to investigate the genealogies of armigerous families through local visitations. Dugdale was a member of the College, and conducted some of the last visitations to be undertaken in the late 17th century. After 1689, however, the state began to take an interest in antiquarian activities. William III commissioned Thomas Rymer to collate all the treaties which his predecessors had negotiated. These were published in 17 volumes, the printing of which alone cost £10,615 12s 6d. In 1702 an act of Parliament arranged for Sir Robert Cotton's collection of books and manuscripts to be housed in a public library. In 1706 Sir Christopher Wren designed the first Cottonian library, and the following year an act acquired the contents for the public. The projected library, however, was never built, and the Cottonian collection was housed in a ruinous building which experienced a disastrous fire in 1732. This stimulated the movement for the permanent preservation of the collection, which led to the establishment of the BRITISH MUSEUM in 1753.

Meanwhile individuals had organized themselves collectively into the Society of Antiquaries, which was founded in 1707 and received a royal charter in 1717. At first, much of their activity was concerned with the antiquities of Britain. Thus Browne Willis, who played a leading part in getting the society its charter, collected materials on the history of Buckinghamshire, and the antiquities of boroughs and cathedrals. They were also relatively amateur and prone to misinterpreting their finds. For example, Dr John Woodward, a professional physician who indulged in geological as well as antiquarian pursuits, became notorious for his claim that a shield he had acquired was of much greater antiquity than was the case, for which he was much ridiculed. Dr Woodward's shield was a *cause célèbre* in the growing sophistication of antiquarian scholarship.

Whereas it had previously been devoted primarily to the study of British antiquities, interest in classical antiquity grew in the 18th century. In 1732 the Society of Dilettanti was launched, its members being especially interested in the archaeology of ancient Greece. The noblemen and gentry who went on the GRAND TOUR brought back coins, sculptures and other relics of ancient Rome, for which they sometimes created entire galleries in their country houses, as at Holkham Hall, Woburn Abbey and Nostell Priory. This growing interest in the classical world was catered to by the earl of BURLINGTON in his publications on the excavations at Herculaneum in 1738 and Pompeii in 1748, and reached its apogee in Edward GIBBON's *The Decline and Fall of the Roman Empire* (1776–88). The most spectacular import of classical sculptures was that of the marbles from the Parthenon by Lord Elgin between 1803 and 1812, which were purchased for the British Museum in 1816 (*see also* ELGIN MARBLES).

FURTHER READING J.M. Levine, *Dr Woodward's Shield: History, Science and Satire in Augustan England* (1977).

apprentice boys, group of Protestant apprentices who resisted the surrender of Londonderry to Catholic forces in 1688 during the WILLIAMITE

WARS OF SUCCESSION. When troops loyal to James II led by the earl of Antrim invested Londonderry in December 1688, many of the city's governors were prepared to hand the city over to them. But 13 apprentices shut the gates and thereby signalled the start of the siege, which was not raised until 28 July 1689. Their action came to symbolize the resistance of Protestants loyal to WILLIAM III to Catholic supporters of James II. It was apparently re-enacted on the anniversary of the raising of the siege as early as 1692. In the 1790s such re-enactments, involving the Orange Order, became annual events.

Aram, Eugene (1704–59), linguistic scholar and convicted murderer. Aram was a schoolmaster in Knaresborough, Yorkshire, from 1734 to 1745. He acquired a sufficient knowledge of languages to form the basis of a comparative European dictionary. In 1745 he suddenly left the town about the time that an associate, Daniel Clark, disappeared. In 1758 Aram was arrested in King's Lynn, where he had become a schoolmaster, and charged with Clark's murder. A witness attested that he had killed Clark and buried him in St Robert's Cave in Knaresborough. Aram put up a skilful defence at York Assizes, but was found guilty and executed. His case attracted considerable attention, and his career inspired Bulwer-Lytton's novel *Eugene Aram* (1832), which asserted his innocence.

Arbuthnot, John (1667–1735), physician and writer, the originator of the character of John Bull. Arbuthnot was born in Arbuthnott, Scotland, where his father was minister in the Episcopal church. He studied mathematics at Aberdeen and medicine at St Andrews, where he took a degree in 1696. He then moved to London, where he published an *Essay on the usefulness of mathematical learning* in 1700. He became a fellow of the ROYAL SOCIETY in 1704.

The following year Arbuthnot became physician extraordinary to Queen ANNE, allegedly as a result of successfully curing her husband when he was taken ill at Epsom, although Arbuthnot had attended the queen since 1703. In 1709 he became a physician in ordinary to her majesty, and SWIFT considered him to be her favourite when he became acquainted with Arbuthnot in 1710. That year Arbuthnot published a paper in the *Philosophical Transactions* of the Royal Society on the slight majority of female births to male births, arguing that it was providential.

Arbuthnot's most famous work, *Law is a bottomless pit* (1712), was an allegory of international relations in western Europe in the War of the SPANISH SUCCESSION. In this allegory, Britain is represented by John Bull, a successful tradesman rather than the farmer of later times. Bull is bullied by Lewis Baboon, representing the French, and bamboozled by Nicholas Frog, representing the Dutch. Arbuthnot was a member of the Brothers' and SCRIBLERUS clubs of Tory writers, contributing to the polemical pamphlets of the last four years of Anne's reign and to the more enduring satires that make up the *Memoirs of Martinus Scriblerus*.
FURTHER READING R.C. Steensma, *Dr John Arbuthnot* (1979).

architecture. Macaulay observed that, if the England of 1685 could be recreated for the readers of his *History* in 1848, they would scarcely recognize one building in ten thousand. Although as usual he exaggerated the differences between late Stuart and Victorian England, there can be little doubt that the architectural face of the country was dramatically altered during the 18th century, at least with regard to secular and vernacular building. Ecclesiastical architecture was less drastically affected, but nevertheless experienced significant developments.

The country houses of the landed classes bore the most striking brunt of architectural changes in the countryside. Some of the most famous country houses were built during the century. The BAROQUE mansions of BLENHEIM PALACE and CASTLE HOWARD were designed by Sir John VANBRUGH in its opening decades. Vanbrugh, like most architects at the start of the century, was an amateur rather than a professional, his true profession being the army (he was also a playwright). The GOTHIC extravaganzas of STRAWBERRY HILL and Fonthill Abbey were later constructed by Horace WALPOLE and William Beckford (the son of the radical politician William BECKFORD). Other great country houses were transformed from their original appearance in accordance with prevailing fashions, such as the addition of PALLADIAN wings to STOWE and Wentworth Woodhouse. Between 1745 and 1770 James Paine, who was clerk of the works at Nostell Priory, effected alterations to many houses in the north of England, including Alnwick Castle, CHATSWORTH and Kedleston. In many cases – as at Fonthill – an earlier house was pulled down to make way for a new one, such as Beningbrough Hall near York. The owners of these houses wished to be isolated from their neighbours, and built huge walls around the perimeter of their estates to hide their private lives from prying eyes. Sometimes this was taken to the length of removing neighbouring houses that were considered too close to the family home. Thus the earl of Oxford had a whole village demolished and rebuilt at a distance from his seat at Hardwicke in Cambridgeshire. The cottages that they had constructed represented the elite eye's view of what the deserving poor deserved; examples include the almshouses built by such philanthropists as John Howard and Robert Sutton in many towns.

The elite also built town houses for themselves. The example was set by the aristocrats who frequented London to attend Parliament or the 'season'. Thus the Churchills owned Marlborough House in Pall Mall, designed by Sir Christopher WREN, as well as Blenheim Palace in Oxfordshire, while Sir Robert WALPOLE built a place for himself and his mistress in Chelsea to supplement his country house at Houghton in Norfolk. One of the most opulent town houses was Norfolk House, built for the duke of Norfolk in St James's Square around 1750. With its classical facade, and

reception rooms arranged round a central staircase, it served as the model for aristocratic town houses in the second half of the 18th century. St James's Square was a very fashionable address, at the heart of the new development between it and Hanover Square that DEFOE described as being almost a distinct city in its own right.

Elite demand led to the provision of buildings in other TOWNS, such as town houses, ASSEMBLY ROOMS, and theatres. Thus BATH's development under John Wood senior and John Wood junior made it *the* 18th-century architectural experience. EDINBURGH was similarly transformed during the century, with the addition of its carefully planned New Town. Civic pride was also reflected in buildings. Many towns built town halls like that at Brackley in Northamptonshire, constructed thanks to the beneficence of the earl of Bridgwater. Others improved their local markets with permanent structures where business could be carried on; examples include the pavilion at Beverley and the piece hall at Halifax.

The closing decades of the 18th century witnessed the onset of several large-scale government building projects. Amongst the most prestigious of these was the Thames-side administrative complex of Somerset House in London, which was undertaken by Sir William CHAMBERS between 1775 and 1796. Although the outbreak of war with France in 1793 halted the commission of most such major government buildings, a notable exception was the ambitious re-modelling of the BANK OF ENGLAND by Sir John Soane (1753–1837) from 1788 to 1833. Like Chambers and Robert ADAM, Soane was influential in promoting and perfecting the elegant and restrained NEOCLASSICAL style: drawing inspiration from the architectural legacy of ancient Greece and Rome, the movement had a profound impact on British architecture throughout the long reign of GEORGE III.

While all this building activity was transforming the secular architecture of Britain, the country had to rely on its stock of medieval and early modern churches. For this was not a great century for church building, despite the completion of St Paul's by Wren in 1710 and such jewels as James GIBBS's St Martin-in-the-Fields. A scheme to build fifty new churches in London foundered, and only about twelve were constructed in the event, although some – such as St George's in Bloomsbury, designed by Nicholas HAWKSMOOR – are outstanding. Besides the construction of Anglican churches, this was also an age of chapel building. The TOLERATION ACT of 1689 allowing DISSENTERS to worship in their own conventicles set off a spate of activity constructing Baptist, Independent and Presbyterian places of worship. By 1710 well over 300 had been built. Some of these, such as the Presbyterian meeting house in Friar Gate, Derby, built in 1698, were substantial structures.

Religious bodies were also concerned with the provision of education. Anglicans had a monopoly of the English UNIVERSITIES of Oxford and Cambridge. Both experienced considerable architectural activity in the 18th century. Oxford saw the complete rebuilding of Queen's College, mainly by Hawskmoor, as well as his Gothic alterations to All Souls, while Gibbs designed the Radcliffe Camera. Gibbs was also responsible for the Fellows' Building at King's College and the Senate House in Cambridge. In Scotland the Presbyterians dominated the four ancient universities. These also saw significant construction in this period, most notably the Old College in Edinburgh, designed by Robert ADAM. Many English dissenters, denied entry to Oxford and Cambridge, studied for degrees in Scotland. South of the border they built their own academies, such as Stoke Newington, which Defoe attended, and Warrington, where Joseph PRIESTLEY taught.

SEE ALSO BURLINGTON, 3RD EARL OF; LANDSCAPE GARDENING; NASH, JOHN.

FURTHER READING M. Girouard, *Life in the English Country House* (1978); J. Summerson, *Architecture in Britain: 1530–1830* (1983).

Argyll, John Campbell, 2nd duke of (1678–1743), distinguished army officer and leading Scottish politician. His military career included outstanding action under MARLBOROUGH at the battles of RAMILLIES, OUDENARDE and MALPLAQUET. His political career began in 1703 when he was made a privy councillor, and in 1705 he became lord high commissioner of the Scottish Parliament. His advocacy of the UNION OF ENGLAND AND SCOTLAND earned him the title of earl of Greenwich. He quarrelled with Marlborough in 1709, disagreeing with the duke's bid to be made captain general for life. This quarrel endeared him to Robert HARLEY, who sent him to Spain as commander in chief. He was, however, estranged from the Harley ministry when he felt that its policy on promotions in the army favoured JACOBITES.

Argyll's support for the Protestant succession led GEORGE I to make him commander in chief in Scotland in 1714. He was thus in charge of the forces there that were challenged by the earl of MAR in the JACOBITE RISING of 1715. On 13 November they engaged in the battle of Sheriffmuir, which both afterwards claimed to have won. A draw, however, was as good as a defeat for Mar, and when Argyll marched against his position at Perth, where the Pretender had joined the rebels, the Jacobites withdrew to Montrose. Mar and the Pretender embarked there for France, ending the rebellion.

Afterwards Argyll had a chequered political career. His support of the prince of Wales led to his dismissal from all offices in 1716, though he was reinstated in 1719. Thereafter he generally supported the ministry until 1737, when he went into opposition after disagreeing with WALPOLE's draconian measures for punishing Edinburgh for the PORTEOUS RIOTS, even though Argyll had commanded the garrison there at the time. His electoral influence in Scotland was so formidable that at the general election of 1741 the results there went against the government and severely weakened Walpole's position in Parliament.

On Walpole's fall, Argyll was again made commander in chief, but resigned his offices shortly afterwards, apparently piqued that he was not given a more important role in the new ministry. GEORGE II said of his ambition, 'I did not know but the duke of Argyll wanted to be king himself.' The Jacobites hoped to gain his support, and the Pretender personally sent him a letter, but Argyll rebuffed their approaches. He died in 1743, a loyal Hanoverian.

FURTHER READING J.S. Shaw, *The Management of Scottish Society, 1707–1764* (1983).

aristocracy. The term aristocracy carries two meanings. It can refer simply to the nobility, those peers whose hereditary titles enabled them to sit in the House of Lords. Or it can also encompass the landed elite, those landowners of broad acres and tenant farms who dominated the countryside and represented the single largest social category in the House of Commons. The first is a narrow legal definition, the second a broad economic distinction. The peerage per se was limited on average to about 180 men until it began to be expanded in the last two decades of the 18th century. Together with the substantial country gentlemen they formed a class of about 2% of the population. It is in the second sense that historians use the term to describe those who dominated the county militias and the commissions of the peace (*see* JUSTICES OF THE PEACE) and who nominated the knights of the shires who represented the counties in the Commons. These positions effectively controlled the countryside and gave them a substantial influence in Parliament.

At the top of the peerage were the dukes, who shared the same status as the king's sons other than the eldest, the prince of Wales. Below them were the marquesses, earls, viscounts and barons. Some peers were fabulously wealthy. The duke of NEWCASTLE's annual revenues realized about £32,000 in the reign of George I. Lord Foley was alleged to have left assets worth £28,000 a year in 1766 plus £500,000 in the funds. Such noblemen ranked in wealth with the German princes of the Holy Roman Empire, and indeed the 1st duke of MARLBOROUGH actually was a prince of that empire with a principality in Mindelheim. His palace at BLENHEIM rivalled the noblest private houses in Europe. Other stately homes were almost as palatial, such as Chatsworth, rightly called the 'palace of the Peak', and Castle Howard, the 'palace of the North'. The inhabitants of these houses were among the richest of the subjects of the Hanoverians. Other peers were much less wealthy. Lord Willoughby of Parham had estates in Lincolnshire worth only £150 a year. Some Scottish peers were even more penurious. The 5th earl of Kellie was alleged to have less than £15 a year to live on. Nevertheless they shared the dignity and privileges of the peerage. In one respect they were more privileged than the European aristocracy, for noble descent went only to the eldest son, and this kept the British peerage much smaller than its continental counterparts. On the other hand, apart from the right to sit in the House of Lords and to be tried by their peers, they had few privileges that distinguished them legally from non-noble elements in society. Unlike the continental nobility they were not exempt from taxation.

The peerage were conscious of their status in society to the point of considering themselves as a class above the mass of the people below them. Indeed in many ways they became almost a caste in the 18th century, entrance to which was very restricted. Although the attempt to 'freeze' their numbers by the Peerage Bill in 1719 failed (*see* LORDS, HOUSE OF), the Hanoverians did not make many new creations, in fact scarcely enough to make up for extinctions until after 1783.

Economically the peers were indistinguishable from the country gentlemen. The latter were only below the peers in status, which is why many historians put the nobility and the landed gentry together when using the term aristocracy. Most of this landed elite derived their income from rents paid by tenant farmers on their estates, although this was not always the sole source of revenue. Exploitation of mineral resources – in Cumberland, Durham and Northumberland for example –

was an extension of landowning activities, and could be very lucrative. Coal-owners such as Sir James Lowther of Whitehaven and George Bowes of Durham were among the richest men of the century.

The great landowners attended the winter season in London and the summer season in BATH, or later in the century other spas that became fashionable, such as Scarborough. They sent their sons to Oxford or Cambridge after privately educating them at home, and completed the education of the eldest with the GRAND TOUR, which was at the height of its fashion in the 1730s and 1740s. While the eldest son would inherit the estate, daughters and younger sons had to be provided for. Younger sons could be permitted to marry daughters from social circles outside the family's; for example, in HOGARTH's *Marriage à la mode* Lord Squanderfield's heir marries a merchant's daughter, with tragic consequences. But daughters had to marry the sons of aristocrats or the family would lose face. This could be expensive. It cost the earl of NOTTINGHAM £32,000 to endow his daughters, all but one of whom married peers' sons, and she married a baronet. Younger sons could be allowed to go into the professions, but again it was thought to be demeaning to put them into trade. Providing younger sons with a profession could be as costly as endowing a daughter: in around 1750 a premium to a reputable London lawyer to take on a younger son as a clerk could cost over £600.

There were few restrictions on acquiring a country estate, although many great estates were subject to a legal arrangement called a 'strict settlement' or 'entail' which made it difficult or impossible for heirs to sell off land and hence restricted the land market. Hence entry into the peerage by the purchase of landed property appears to have been relatively rare in this period. The hegemony of the aristocracy was so entrenched then that some historians see the 18th as 'the aristocratic century'.

SEE ALSO ELECTORAL SYSTEM.

FURTHER READING J. Cannon, *Aristocratic*

Century: The Peerage of Eighteenth-Century England (1984); J.M. Rosenheim, *The Emergence of a Ruling Order. English Landed Society 1650–1750* (1998).

Arkwright, Richard (1732–92), inventor and industrialist. The son of a Lancashire labourer, Arkwright was a self-made man who rose from being a barber's apprentice to become one of the richest entrepreneurs of the Industrial Revolution. Others also devised mechanical means of spinning cotton thread: for example, Thomas Highs, who designed a device that anticipated the 'frame' machine patented by Arkwright. Arkwright's machine spun cotton into thread strong enough to make a warp, whereas earlier machine-made thread, such as that produced by James Hargreaves's spinning jenny (*see* TEXTILES), was only strong enough for weft.

The capital needed to take out the patent and to implement mass production took Arkwright into partnership with John Smalley, David Thornley, Samuel Need and Jedediah Strutt. Several frames were installed in Arkwright's first factory in Nottingham, powered by horses. Finding that water power was more effective, Arkwright moved his mill in 1771 to Cromford in Derbyshire, where the machines became known as water frames. By then he had spent some £12,000 on machinery, and found returns on the investment slow, because cloth produced entirely from cotton warp and weft was subject to a double duty by an act of Parliament, in order to protect British manufacturers from Indian calicoes. Arkwright persuaded Parliament to exempt his process from the act in 1774. In 1775 he took out another patent for a machine that performed all the tasks of carding, drawing, rolling and spinning. Thereafter he increased production considerably, and sold the patent for his water frames to other manufacturers.

The impact of cheap mass-produced thread on domestic spinning was dramatic, and in 1779 some of those adversely affected attacked one of Arkwright's mills at Chorley in Lancashire. This provoked him to make the Cromford mill impregnable to attack. Finding that his machines were being pirated by other mill owners he took court proceedings against them in 1781, but lost because he had not fully patented his invention. In 1785 he successfully defended his patents in the Court of Common Pleas, only to have his right to them overturned again in King's Bench. He nevertheless profited greatly from his own mills in the Midlands, the north of England and Scotland. Arkwright crowned his career with a knighthood in 1786, and in 1789 was made high sheriff of Derbyshire. His acceptance into society led him to build a substantial Georgian residence, Willersley Castle, near Cromford. When he died his funeral at Matlock was witnessed by over 2000 people.

FURTHER READING R.S. Fitton, *The Arkwrights – Spinners of Fortune* (1989); R.L. Hills, *Richard Arkwright and Cotton Spinning* (1973).

armed neutrality. In 1780, at the height of the AMERICAN WAR OF INDEPENDENCE, Catherine II of Russia made a declaration of 'armed neutrality' which advertised that Russia was willing to deploy force in defence of neutral states whose ships carried naval stores to Britain's enemies. Russia's lead was soon followed by Sweden and Denmark, whilst Holland, Prussia and Austria all joined in 1781: it was a manifestation of international disapproval that has been seen as a diplomatic low point for Hanoverian Britain.

Yet more than prestige was a stake – as a maritime power, Britain's survival depended upon the Royal Navy's capacity to deny supplies to its enemies. Armed neutrality also added the United Provinces to Britain's official opponents in the war against America and the Bourbons. Although obliged by treaty to aid Britain if required, the Dutch had maintained a neutral stance throughout the conflict and continued to ferry naval stores to France. Dutch adherence to the pact would have required the other signatories to resist British assaults upon Dutch shipping. In an effort to prevent this development, Britain declared war in late 1780 after the United Provinces rebuffed its formal request for assistance: this pre-empted official Dutch participation in the armed neutrality and thereby made it possible to avoid open hostilities between the existing signatories and Britain.

The issue of armed neutrality surfaced again in 1800 when Britain faced France during the REVOLUTIONARY AND NAPOLEONIC WARS. A Northern Confederation composed of Russia, Prussia, Denmark and Sweden declared their armed neutrality in the conflict. By denying Britain's right to search merchant vessels the declaration threatened to disrupt the Royal Navy's crucial blockade of France. The second armed neutrality foundered in 1801 after Britain's defeat of the Danish fleet at COPENHAGEN, combined with the assassination of Tsar Paul of Russia, caused the collapse of the Confederation.

army. In 1689 WILLIAM III harnessed the military and financial resources of his new kingdom to contest the continental ambitions of his archrival, the 'Sun King' Louis XIV. William's intervention in Europe triggered the onset of a 'second Hundred Years War' with France. That struggle – which would range from the lowlands of Flanders to the volcanic islands of the Caribbean, and from the frozen forests of North America to the sun-scorched plains of INDIA – only terminated in 1815, with the final defeat of Napoleon. The long road to WATERLOO witnessed the rise of Britain from third-rate state to leading world power. It also saw the growth of the British army from a puny and despised force to a formidable and renowned fighting machine.

During the Dutch Wars of Charles II in the 1660s and 1670s, England's army had mustered just 20,000 men. By the mid-1690s, when William III campaigned in the Low Countries, that figure had already reached more than 93,000. In 1813, at the height of the REVOLUTIONARY AND NAPOLEONIC WARS, there were no fewer than 250,000 regular British soldiers under arms. These figures represent wartime peaks of manpower; once the fighting was over, Britain's army was inevitably axed to the bare minimum required for home defence and the protection of a growing number of overseas possessions.

Such rapid demobilizations reflected widespread antipathy towards the military. While British soldiers might enjoy a momentary popularity in the wake of such famous victories as BLENHEIM, CULLODEN or WATERLOO, the redcoat was more usually viewed with suspicion or hostility by his civilian countryman. To educated men who followed political debate, a large standing army posed a threat to English liberties; in the hands of a despot, such soldiers could easily become the storm troops of tyranny. Lingering suspicion of the military surfaced during the ritualized debates surrounding the annual passage of the MUTINY ACT, by which Parliament permitted the army's continued existence. It was this ingrained fear of professional soldiers that obliged the Hanoverians to maintain a separate military establishment in Ireland, in a bid to conceal the true size of their forces. (*See also* STANDING ARMY CONTROVERSY.)

People lower down the social scale had their own reasons for disliking the soldiery. Before the barrack-building programmes of the 1790s, soldiers were commonly billeted amongst a resentful populace. Another factor underlay the army's unpopularity. In an age lacking a professional police force, soldiers ultimately maintained law and order. Whether waging guerrilla warfare with gangs of smugglers or quelling a starving mob, the redcoated infantryman or dragoon was the ultimate defender of the state.

Throughout the 'long 18th century', soldiering in the lower ranks remained a low-caste occupation. Gregory KING in 1688 and Joseph MASSIE in 1759 both placed the income of the 'common soldier' below that of the unskilled labourer. Savage discipline and hard service likewise rendered the army an unattractive option for all save the most desperate or adventurous of the 'lower orders'. Hence, while the British army was technically a volunteer force, it was occasionally necessary to use other methods to fill the ranks. 'Press Acts' were enforced to conscript the unemployed, while criminals were sometimes offered enlistment as an alternative to their original punishment. The duke of WELLINGTON's notorious verdict upon the fruits of such policies – the 'scum of the earth ... enlisted for drink' – has long served to colour the popular image of the Georgian soldier. However, while the army mustered its fair share of hard cases, such miscreants were balanced by a core of steady, reliable soldiers whose recruitment stemmed from economic factors. The introduction of short-service wartime enlistments in the 1750s and 1770s, and an influx of volunteers from the militia during the Napoleonic Wars, fostered a genuine esprit de corps in many regiments.

Britain's officers hailed from the upper regions of the social scale. Embracing both aristocrats and humbler members of the emerging 'middle classes', all were expected to behave as 'gentlemen'. While the bulk of commissions were purchased for set fees, a significant minority were earned by merit alone. Similarly, although frowned upon by many senior officers, promotion from the ranks was by no means unknown. The occasional presence of blunderers who were plainly unfitted for high command has overshadowed the fact that most officers advanced by long service and acquired a professional outlook. Despite the ferocity of army discipline, a growing number of officers exhibited a paternalistic attitude to their soldiers – a trend encouraged by the spread of Enlightenment values and epitomized by men such as Sir John MOORE.

In the Royal Artillery, the British army possessed a highly efficient corps of gunners; by contrast, its engineers remained lamentable, resulting in bungled siege operations that proved costly in both blood and gold. Britain's cavalry regiments enjoyed a reputation for dash and swagger, but were difficult to control in action. The real strength of the British army lay in the humble redcoated infantryman. From Blenheim to Waterloo the redcoat carried the smooth-bore flintlock musket and bayonet, and under the leadership of men such as MARLBOROUGH, WOLFE and Wellington, he employed both with considerable effect. Even in defeat, as at FONTENOY in 1745, the discipline and courage of the redcoat earned admiration. As the protracted struggle with the Bourbons expanded into a truly global conflict, the army cooperated with a powerful Royal NAVY to mount amphibious operations such as the capture of Havana in 1762. The British soldier was also required to adapt to irregular conditions very different from the European warfare for which he had been trained. Campaigning in North America – conducted at first against the French and their Native American allies, and later against the rebellious colonists themselves – saw the evolution of the 'thin red line' and the light-infantry skills that were destined to prove a battle-winning combination during the PENINSULAR WAR.

By the dawn of the 19th century the British army's uniquely varied experience had forged an organization with a keen sense of regimental tradition (encouraged by the introduction of county affiliations in 1782), allied to a distinctive tactical ethos. These traits underpinned the remarkable success of the army that ejected Napoleon's legions from Portugal and Spain and back onto French soil. As Wellington himself was obliged to admit, with such troops he could 'go anywhere, and do anything'.

SEE ALSO MILITIA.

FURTHER READING S. Brumwell, *Redcoats. The British Soldier and War in the Americas 1755–1763* (2001); D. Chandler and I. Beckett (eds.), *The Oxford Illustrated History of the British Army* (1994); J.A. Houlding, *Fit for Service: The Training of the British Army 1715–1795* (1981).

Ashby vs. White (1701–4), legal case involving voting rights, which also had wider political ramifications. In 1701 Matthew Ashby, a cobbler of Aylesbury, Buckinghamshire, sued William White and three others at the county assizes. The four had all been constables of the town in 1698, and Ashby accused them of denying him the right to vote in the general election held in that year, despite his being legally qualified to do so.

Judgment was found in his favour, and he was awarded £5 damages.

This was a victory not only for Ashby, but also for the WHIG Lord Thomas WHARTON, who had financed the action, which was aimed primarily against the Tory Sir John Pakington, who had appointed the constables. Wharton and Pakington were thus engaged in a struggle for control of a parliamentary borough, a struggle that spilled over into national politics.

Pakington persuaded the constables to appeal to the Court of Queen's Bench. The hearing took place in 1703. Of the four justices, the lord chief justice, Sir John Holt, upheld the decision of the assizes, arguing that a legal right, such as that of voting, ought to have a legal remedy. But the other three found for White and his colleagues on the grounds that the sole jurisdiction over franchise disputes in parliamentary elections lay with the House of Commons.

Wharton moved for a writ of error to reverse the judgement in the House of Lords. In January 1704 the Whig-dominated upper house found in favour of Ashby, while the Tory minority protested that this usurped the jurisdiction of the Commons. The dispute thus caused a clash between the two Houses of Parliament. The Tory majority in the lower house upheld that chamber's right to be sole judge of electoral disputes on 15 January 1704 by 215 votes to 97. The Lords retaliated by passing resolutions protesting against the Commons' decision. Parliament was then prorogued.

During the recess a heated exchange of pamphlets kept the controversy alive. So did an action brought at the Buckinghamshire assizes against White by five more Aylesbury men who accused him of denying their votes. When the next session began in October 1704 these men were summoned to the Commons and sent to Newgate prison for breach of privilege. Wharton reacted by getting four Whig lawyers to apply to Queen's Bench for a writ of habeas corpus. Again the justices were divided, Holt denying that either House of Parliament had any power to imprison other than their own members, while his three colleagues maintained that the commitment of the Aylesbury men by the Commons could not be set aside by the court. When the Commons learned that supporters of the Aylesbury men had applied for a writ of error to the Lords, they voted all four lawyers who had pleaded for a writ of habeas corpus guilty of a breach of privilege, and ordered them into the custody of the sergeant at arms. The Aylesbury men themselves were also transferred from Newgate into his custody. The Lords retaliated by resolving that the Commons had assumed an unconstitutional jurisdiction over private citizens. A conference between the two Houses failed to resolve the deadlock. It was only ended when Queen Anne prorogued Parliament, closing the session. This caused the jurisdiction claimed by the Commons to lapse, and the Aylesbury men were released.

The return of a Whig majority to the Commons at the ensuing general election meant that the dispute was not revived. The right of the Commons to judge the franchise in any constituency was never again challenged. At the same time the right of an individual voter to have his qualification to vote adjudged by inferior courts was never again disputed by the lower house.

FURTHER READING E. Cruickshanks, 'Ashby v. White: the case of the Aylesbury men 1701–4' in C. Jones (ed.), *Party and Management in Parliament 1660–1784* (1984).

asiento, term used to describe a contract granted by the kings of Spain to supply slaves to their American colonies. *Asiento* was a jealously guarded privilege, which the French Guinea Company acquired for ten years in 1701 when the Bourbons succeeded to the throne of Spain. In 1713 it was extended to Britain in the treaty of UTRECHT, which allowed the British to send one ship a year for 30 years to three designated ports in Spanish America. It has been estimated that this permitted them to ship some 4500 slaves annually across the Atlantic from West Africa to Spanish colonies. This disappointed expectations of vast profits, and,

although the contract was modified in Britain's favour in 1717, returns to the South Sea Company, which was set up to exploit the trade, remained modest. Many British merchants evaded the strict terms of the contract, becoming illegal interlopers in the Spanish slave trade. This led to reprisals which were to culminate in the War of JENKINS'S EAR in 1739 and the withdrawal of the *asiento* by Spain. It was renewed at the treaty of AIX-LA-CHAPELLE in 1748 but effectively lapsed in 1750.

assembly rooms. Whereas country houses were the foci of entertainment for the elite in rural areas, in TOWNS 'assemblies' generally provided amenities for balls, card games, drinking, gambling and other amusements. The gentry and leading citizens of provincial towns would subscribe to the building of assembly rooms. At one time York had two, one for the Tories and one for the Whigs, a reflection of how the rage of party polarized people even in their leisure pursuits. When the rage calmed down, the citizens of York made do with one. Subscriptions were also required of those frequenting assembly rooms, in order to restrict admission to the polite.

By 1750 assembly rooms were already a focal point for fashionable society in the provinces, and at least 60 towns and spa resorts possessed such facilities by 1770. As the novels of Jane AUSTEN indicate, assembly rooms fulfilled a crucial social function by offering the perfect environment for flirtation and courtship.

association movement. *See* PARLIAMENTARY REFORM.

Astell, Mary (1666–1731), writer on WOMEN's issues. Astell was born in Newcastle upon Tyne, but moved to London in 1686. Her most celebrated work was *A Serious Proposal to the Ladies for the Advancement of their True and Greatest Interest* (1694), which proposed that they retreat to a secular nunnery. She supported the subordination of wives to husbands in *Some Reflections upon Marriage* (1700).

Atterbury, Francis (1662–1732), high-church bishop of Rochester, credited with JACOBITE leanings. Atterbury was educated at Westminster School and Christ Church, Oxford, where he stayed as a tutor after graduation. He was there when James II began to infiltrate Oxford colleges with Catholics. Atterbury defended Anglicanism against Roman Catholicism in a celebrated tract in 1687. After the GLORIOUS REVOLUTION he became a chaplain to Queen MARY, and after her death emerged as the leader of the high-church clergy in the CONVOCATION CONTROVERSY.

In 1704 Atterbury became dean of Carlisle and a thorn in the flesh of the low-church Bishop Nicolson. At the time of the trial of Dr SACHEVERELL in 1710 he was widely credited with writing the doctor's defence speech. In 1711 he became dean of Christ Church, and two years later received simultaneously the deanship of Westminster and the bishopric of Rochester.

In 1714, after ANNE's death, Atterbury wrote a pamphlet in anticipation of a general election: *English Advice to the freeholders of England*. In this he claimed for 'the church party' that they would make 'no alteration of the constitution in church and state', and for the Whigs 'an entire and thorough revolution'. At that time it seems he was not a Jacobite, and he attended the coronation of GEORGE I. But when it became clear that the high-church principles for which he stood had been superseded by the triumph of the low-church party, he despaired and made overtures to the exiled Stuart court.

How far he was involved in actively promoting a JACOBITE RISING was disputed at the time, and has been debated ever since. His defenders argue that the government twisted the evidence against him. Thus his friend SWIFT satirized the methods used to incriminate him in *Gulliver's Travels* when he described the cryptographers in Lagado reading in a letter 'our brother Tom has just got the piles' and seeing in it an anagram of 'resist; a plot is brought home; the tower'. A bill of pains and penalties was carried through both Houses of Parliament, stripping him of his clerical offices and sentencing him to banishment. In 1723 he went to Calais, and after spending some time in Brussels eventually moved to Paris, where he did temporarily enter the Pretender's service. On his death his body was brought back to England and buried in Westminster Abbey.

FURTHER READING G.V. Bennett, *The Tory Crisis in Church and State: the career of Francis Atterbury, Bishop of Rochester* (1975).

Augsburg, War of the League of. *See* NINE YEARS WAR.

Augustan Age, term applied by contemporaries to the reign of GEORGE II, from the conceit that the king's name was George Augustus, and from the fact that his reign was a golden age for English literature, with writers such as GAY, POPE and SWIFT flourishing just as Latin authors such as Horace, Ovid and Virgil had under the emperor Augustus Caesar.

Others claimed that it was inappropriate, partly because where Augustus presided over the efflorescence of literature as a patron, the court of George II signally failed to patronize the major literary figures of Hanoverian England. Indeed, Sir Robert WALPOLE was known as 'the poet's foe'. Looking back in 1759, Oliver GOLDSMITH gave 'An Account of the Augustan Age in England' in *The Bee*, dating the period from around 1690 to 1740. Modern literary scholars adopted the expression but used it to describe a longer period spanning the era from Dryden to JOHNSON. In recent years, the term has fallen out of favour. Yet, just when the term no longer seemed applicable to literature, historians began to appropriate it for their own use. Again the period covered by the expression is elastic, and can be stretched from the 1680s to the 1760s. 'The Augustan Age' can be used as a convenient alternative to the clumsy 'late Stuart and early Hanoverian era'.

Austen, Jane (1775–1817), novelist. Austen was the daughter of a Hampshire clergyman in whose rectory at Steventon she lived until 1800. She then spent five years in Bath, and when her father died she moved to Southampton. In 1809 she settled in Chawton, remaining there for the rest of her life.

Austen's novels, regarded by many as among the greatest in the English language, were mainly written in Steventon and Chawton. The plots revolve around the strategies adopted by minor gentry and professional families to ensure good marriages for their daughters. They have thus aroused comment that they do not address the social and political concerns of a country enduring the upheavals of the Industrial and French revolutions. But while the plots concern a few families in southern villages, and therefore are remote geographically from the economic changes in the industrial north, their themes are relevant to the ideological debates surrounding the revolutionary politics of the times.

Thus *Sense and Sensibility* (1811), the first of Austen's novels to be published, contrasts the rational political discourse of conservatives with the emotional appeal of the radicals. In *Mansfield Park* (1814) the Bertram family is a microcosm of a society torn between traditional and liberal values. Austen sided with the conservatives in these disputes. The eponymous heroine of *Emma* (1815–16) is nearly led astray by the antisocial antics of Frank Churchill, an alien intruder into a harmonious society, only to be brought back to her social obligations by Mr Knightley. But while her heroines uphold the social order, they do not accept male hegemony. Jane Austen was a feminist in her insistence that such women as Emma, and Elizabeth Bennett in *Pride and Prejudice* (1813), should be acceptable as the equals of the men they marry. She herself never married, and died in Winchester at the age of 42.

FURTHER READING M. Butler, *Jane Austen and the War of Ideas* (1987); D. Nokes, *Jane Austen* (1997).

Australia. Australia had been discovered by the Dutch in the 17th century, but remained largely unvisited by Europeans until the voyages of Captain COOK in the late 18th century. In 1770 Cook sailed along the coast of what he named New South Wales, and established a base at Botany Bay. It is from proposals to establish a convict colony at Botany Bay that Australia's origins as an outpost of the British empire can be traced.

Botany Bay was named in honour of the botanists who had sailed aboard the *Endeavour* on its voyage of exploration. Sixteen years later one of those same scientists, Sir Joseph BANKS, promoted Botany Bay as the obvious location for the first British settlement in New South Wales.

Plans to colonize Australia had been discussed as early as 1779, at the height of the AMERICAN WAR OF INDEPENDENCE, but the scheme foundered on grounds of cost, and the absence of any obvious economic benefit to Britain. However, by the mid-1780s Britain's desire to counter Dutch and French interests in the Pacific combined with a more pressing domestic issue to place New South Wales back on the agenda. Since the early decades of the 18th century Britain's American colonies had provided the destination for thousands of felons sentenced to TRANSPORTATION as an alternative to the gallows; American independence subsequently placed this traditional dumping ground off limits. In the absence of prisons designed to accommodate offenders, Britain had instead experimented with floating 'hulks'. The inadequacy of this response was only underlined by the customary postwar rise in crime levels (*see* CRIME AND PUNISHMENT). Under these circumstances, proposals for a penal colony at Botany Bay gained increasing support.

The 'First Fleet' of eleven vessels sailed from Spithead in the spring of 1787 carrying 756 adult convicts; surprisingly, only 33 died during the outward voyage of eight months. Upon arrival at

Botany Bay in January 1788 the settlers encountered a very different environment from the fertile paradise depicted by Banks. Governor Arthur Phillip was so unimpressed with the suggested location that he promptly decided to look elsewhere. Phillip was drawn to the superb harbour of Port Jackson, and eventually sited his settlement at Sydney Cove. Although preferable to the original destination of Botany Bay, the new choice remained far from perfect, and the colony's early days amounted to a grim struggle for survival. The Europeans initially proved incapable of living off the land, and the failure of the Second Fleet to materialize with supplies in 1789 heightened the crisis. The hard-pressed settlement was succoured when the long-awaited flotilla duly appeared in 1790, and by the time that Governor Phillip departed in 1792 the colony had spread inland. The number of convicts and their guards soon rose to 2500, and by the closing years of the century their numbers were being augmented by an influx of free settlers. In addition, Port Jackson became an established rendezvous for whalers and sealers.

Although initial contacts with the Aborigines were largely peaceable, relations between the Europeans and natives rapidly degenerated. Phillip's instructions to treat the Aborigines with humanity were ignored by the settlement's tough populace of sailors and convicts, and native suspicion of the newcomers was only heightened when a devastating smallpox epidemic swept through the Sydney area in 1789.

For those responsible for British law enforcement, transportation to Australia had proved a successful innovation; unlike felons exiled to America, those 'bound for Botany Bay' rarely returned to their old haunts, as the distances involved were simply too great. But while Australia became a favoured destination for opponents of Britain's ruling hierarchy during the troubled opening decades of the 19th century, the institution of transportation was itself soon overtaken by the emergence of PRISONS as the state's preferred form of secondary punishment.

FURTHER READING R. Hughes, *The Fatal Shore: A History of the Transportation of Convicts to Australia, 1787–1868* (1987).

Austrian Succession, War of the (1740–8), a

war between Austria and Prussia, in which Britain sided with Austria, while France and Spain sided with Prussia. Britain's involvement in this untidy and indecisive conflict marked its first military intervention on the European continent since the days of Marlborough. A war that is chiefly remembered in Britain for the dramatic and tragic JACOBITE RISING of the '45 in fact embraced a far wider struggle, ranging from the modern Czech Republic to Belgium, and from North America to India.

When hostilities between GEORGE II and Louis XV of France were formally declared in 1744, Britain had already been at war for five years. The onset of fighting with Spain in 1739 ended an era in which the pacific prime minister, Sir Robert WALPOLE, had endeavoured to keep Britain clear of costly and disruptive strife. Walpole's stance avoided British entanglement in the War of the Polish Succession earlier in the decade, despite fears that France was becoming the dominant continental power. It required a rising tide of anti-Spanish sentiment, centred upon the issue of colonial trade and fuelled by dubious atrocity stories, to trigger open conflict.

Popular support for war with the old Bourbon enemy was initially vindicated when British sea power secured Porto Bello (in present-day Panama) in November 1739. Subsequent expeditions against Spanish America in 1741–2 all ended in costly failures. When the dispiriting outcome of these West Indian campaigns became apparent, the so-called War of JENKINS'S EAR had already been swamped by European developments. The death of the Holy Roman emperor Charles VI in October 1740 left the scattered Habsburg domains in the uncertain grip of the young Maria Theresa; the resulting crisis offered opportunities to acquire territory at Austria's expense that Spain, Prussia and France all proved unable to resist.

As Austria reeled under assault from all quarters, Britain succoured its traditional continental ally by raising subsidies for the defence of its far-flung domains. However, the neutrality of George II's beloved electorate of Hanover was only bought at the high price of supporting Charles Albert of Bavaria, France's own nominee for Holy Roman emperor. A discredited Walpole was forced from office in 1742, and for the following two years British foreign policy was orchestrated by the king's favourite, Lord CARTERET; his key diplomatic priority was the construction of a coalition strong enough to counter a resurgent France. Maria Theresa was accordingly persuaded to accept Prussia's annexation of Silesia, so securing Frederick II of Prussia's withdrawal from the conflict and allowing Austrian forces to concentrate upon attacking Bavaria. Finally repudiating the neutrality of his electorate, George II now led the motley 'Pragmatic Army' to victory at the battle of DETTINGEN in 1743.

Despite this triumph, Carteret was ousted in 1744 at the insistence of the PELHAM brothers and their parliamentary supporters; his elaborate plans had backfired when the Habsburg recovery prompted Frederick II to invade Bohemia, a development that ultimately pushed Austria to seek aid in the arms of France.

For Britain, 1745 proved the crisis year of the war. In Flanders, the young duke of CUMBERLAND proved no match for the wily Marshal Saxe, and suffered defeat at the battle of FONTENOY in May. Although the Austrian Netherlands now lay open to the French, Cumberland was recalled to counter a Jacobite invasion aimed at toppling his father from the throne. Before that rebellion was crushed at Culloden in April 1746, Brussels was in French hands. Cumberland duly returned to Flanders, but was again outgeneralled by his old antagonist.

Britain's setbacks in Europe had been offset by developments across the Atlantic. In 1745, as warfare raged in Europe, a joint Anglo-American force captured the key French base of Louisbourg on Cape Breton. This unexpected success delighted those rising politicians such as William PITT THE ELDER who believed that Britain should free herself from continental commitments and instead adopt a BLUE-WATER POLICY aimed at eradicating rival colonies. The capture of Louisbourg, bolstered by subsequent British naval victories, ensured that when peace was negotiated at AIX-LA-CHAPELLE in 1748, France was obliged to evacuate Belgium in return for regaining Canada's bulwark. The peace of 1748 proved precarious: none of the war's participants viewed it as anything more than an armed truce. This pessimistic stance was justified eight years later upon the outbreak of the SEVEN YEARS WAR.

FURTHER READING M.S. Anderson, *The War of the Austrian Succession, 1740–1748* (1995).

Aylesbury men. *See* ASHBY VS. WHITE.

B

Bage, Robert (1728–1801), 'Jacobin' novelist. Bage was born into a Quaker family in Derby, and in 1751 acquired a paper-making business near Tamworth, which he kept until his death. In 1765 he went into partnership in an iron works; this failed in 1779, leaving him in debt. To retrieve his finances he took to writing novels, the first, *Mount Heneth*, appearing in 1781. Three others appeared in the 1780s, but it was not until after the French Revolution that he produced the two that are regarded as his best, the JACOBIN NOVELS *Man as he is* (1792), and his last work, *Hermsprong; or man as he is not* (1796).

Bakewell, Robert (1725–95), agricultural improver. Bakewell was born in Leicestershire, the son of a tenant farmer whose farm he took over on his father's death in 1760. He experimented with improving the breed of livestock, first cattle and then, more successfully, sheep. His Leicester breed of sheep became world-renowned. He also devoted efforts to improving animal husbandry in other ways, such as developing new types of fodder. Other farmers whom he interested in such projects joined his Dishley Society to disseminate knowledge of scientific breeding.

Although he made money from hiring out his rams to stud he failed to make a fortune, and went bankrupt in 1776.

ballads. Whether printed or transmitted orally through song, ballads represented an influential cultural phenomenon in 18th-century Britain. Traditional folk ballads recounting the exploits of legendary heroes such as Robin Hood, and popular topical ballads sold as cheap printed 'broadsides', both provided the inspiration for more literary efforts by established poets keen to exploit their narrative power.

Although many ballads enjoyed only a short life span, others that caught the popular imagination endured for centuries. For example, the powerful ballad relating the last words and testimony of Jack Hall, who was hanged for housebreaking in 1707, later surfaced as a 'turn' in the Edwardian music hall, having been kept alive through oral transmission in the intervening period. Similarly, a song celebrating the gallant conduct of Admiral BENBOW in 1702 circulated orally for a century before becoming a popular subject for broadsheet publication. Topical ballads can sometimes shed interesting light upon their subjects. For example, *The Soldier's Praise of Duke William* (1746) provides accurate details of the tactics employed at the battle of CULLODEN, while *The Lads of Virginia* (*c*.1770) bewails the causes and consequences of TRANSPORTATION to America: it is the lure of 'buxom lasses' that leads the doleful narrator into highway robbery before being 'lagged to Virginia'.

During the 18th century, ballad selling was a well-organized business. The ballad-monger bought broadsheets directly from the printing house, then sung and sold them on the streets. Although ballads were often sung to a limited range of familiar tunes, their subject matter was constantly changing: in 1689 the London ballad printer William Thackery had more than 300 titles in stock. The importance of ballads and their singers is apparent from the regularity with which they appear in the art and literature of the era. For example, a bawling female ballad singer dominates the bustling foreground of William HOGARTH's engraving of the *Idle 'Prentice's Execution* at Tyburn, with the ragged figure's appearance suggesting that ballad-mongers often inhabited the lower rungs of society.

In the 1640s, singers of ballads that criticized Parliament had risked a flogging. More than a century later, anti-establishment ballads could still attract the wrath of the powerful – in 1763 two women were sent to a 'house of correction' for singing scurrilous political ballads in front of Lord BUTE's house in South Audley Street. As the poet John GAY warned in 1716, the crowds such hawkers attracted also provided a tempting prey for pickpockets:

> Let not the ballad singer's thrilling strain,
> Amid the swarm thy lis'ning ear detain,
> Guard well they pocket, for these syrens stand,
> To aid the labours of the diving hand.

For Gay, a rifled pocket would have been a small price to pay for the boost that such ballads gave to his own flagging career. His *Beggar's Opera* (1728) – the runaway theatrical success of the century – exploited the mass appeal of the folk and broadside ballad. Gay's triumph prompted a flurry of interest in 'ballad operas' that combined spoken dialogue with popular songs. Although the ballad opera boom lasted barely a decade, ballads continued to attract the attention of the literary community throughout the 18th century: Coleridge's *The Rime of the Ancient Mariner* (1798) provides an example of their importance to the LAKE POETS. Georgian Britain also saw a steady growth of scholarly interest in the collection and preservation of historical ballads: Thomas d'Urfey's *Pills to Purge Melancholy* (1719–20) and PERCY's *Reliques of Ancient English Poetry* (1765) were particularly influential. The trend culminated with Walter Scott's *Border Minstrelsey* (1802), a collection that embraced both genuine ballads and Scott's own interpretations of the genre. Ballad selling declined in the closing decades of the 19th century, although the ballads themselves live on.

FURTHER READING R. Palmer, *A Ballad History of England from 1588 to the Present Day* (1979).

Bangorian controversy, argument concerning the power of the church. In 1716 Benjamin HOADLY, the low-church bishop of Bangor, published a sermon entitled *A Preservative against the Principles and Practices of the Nonjurors both in Church and State*. In it he defended the government's right to deprive the NONJURORS among the clergy of their livings after the GLORIOUS REVOLUTION of 1688. Hoadly did so by arguing that the church was subordinate to the state – a stance encapsulating the doctrine of ERASTIANISM. He also alleged that the clergy's claims of jurisdiction over the laity were unfounded. This offended moderate churchmen as well as high-church clergymen, among them Edmund GIBSON, bishop of London; Gibson's *Codex Juris Ecclesiastici Anglicani* (1713) had systematized ecclesiastical law, which he was convinced was binding on laymen.

Hoadly set out to clarify his views on the power of the church over its members in a sermon preached before GEORGE I on 31 March 1717. Taking as his text 'Jesus answered, my kingdom is not of this world', he came to the conclusion that Christ 'had left behind him no visible, humane authority; no vicegerents, who can be said properly to supply his place; no judges over the consciences or religion of his people'. It followed from this that the church had no absolute authority over its members whatsoever.

The *Preservative* had raised a storm, but the sermon produced a hurricane. At issue were two divergent views of the Church of England and its jurisdiction. To Hoadly the church was a voluntary association of sincere believers, and as such was on a par with other congregations of Christians, whereas to his opponents it was the one true church. Whereas to the bishop of Bangor its form of government was the most convenient, his opponents argued that episcopacy was sanctioned by divine right and upheld by the apostolic succession. What Hoadly had done was to apply LOCKE's political theories, which he himself had popularized, to the church. This raised the whole question of the relationship between the state and the church. Was the church superior, independent, or subordinate to the state? His theory produced an avalanche of refutation, more pamphlets appearing in the Bangorian controversy than in the SACHEVERELL affair. The debate went on long after the Bangorian controversy itself had subsided, the most important contribution to it being William WARBURTON's *The Alliance between Church and State*, published in 1736.

Bank of England, England's reserve bank. In return for a charter permitting it to operate for 21 years, it was set up by act of Parliament in 1694. It loaned the government £1,200,000 at a rate of interest of 8%, guaranteed by Parliament. The original investors numbered 1268, most of them inhabitants of London and the Home Counties. The charter was periodically renewed, and in 1708 the Bank was given the monopoly of joint stock banking in England. From 1697 to 1826 no other joint-stock bank was allowed to operate in England. The Bank was also the leading issuer of notes, with a monopoly upon the larger denominations. Until 1797 it was obliged to exchange these for gold, but thereafter the obligation was relaxed until 1821.

Throughout the 18th century the Bank's position at the hub of the nation's financial system permitted it to exert an immense influence on the evolution of banking in general. Besides acting as official government banker and assuming the role of 'central' bank, it also supervised other banks. **SEE ALSO** FINANCIAL REVOLUTION.

Banks, Sir Joseph (1743–1820), explorer and patron of the sciences. The son of a wealthy Lincolnshire landowner, Banks was educated at Harrow, Eton and Oxford, where he demonstrated a precocious interest in botany. On the death of his father Banks inherited considerable wealth, but eschewed the conventional GRAND TOUR around Europe in favour of a more taxing itinerary – in 1766 he joined the ship's company of HMS *Niger* on a voyage to Newfoundland and Labrador. An assiduous collector of plants and insects, Banks returned with an impressive array of specimens. His growing reputation, coupled with the influential backing of Lord SANDWICH at the Admiralty, helped to gain him a berth on Captain James COOK's famous first Pacific voyage of 1768–71. During the course of the expedition Banks continued his researches in Tahiti, New Zealand and Australia. It was in honour of Banks and the other scientists aboard the *Endeavour* that Cook named the site of the future penal colony BOTANY BAY. Banks returned to England to great public acclaim, although this adulation may have led him to inflate his own importance with the Admiralty. Efforts to browbeat the navy into upgrading the scientific role of Cook's second voyage of exploration led to friction and ensured that he did not accompany Cook aboard the *Resolution* when she sailed in 1772. Denied this ambition, he instead financed his own relatively minor expedition to Iceland.

Banks's well-publicized discoveries attracted the attention of GEORGE III, who in 1773 appointed him overseer to the Royal Gardens at Kew. Further honours followed and in 1778 he was elected president of the ROYAL SOCIETY, an office he held until his death more than 40 years later. As a leading patron of the sciences, Banks was increasingly called upon to advise the government upon a range of issues. In 1786 it was Banks who advocated Botany Bay as a suitable destination for British criminals sentenced to TRANSPORTATION; although his own assessment of the area's fertility proved over-optimistic, he continued to champion the interests of the fledgling colony of New South Wales. Another example of Banks's quasi-official role is provided by his promotion of breadfruit as a staple for Britain's West Indian possessions; it was this scheme that led to the famous mutiny on the *Bounty* after Captain BLIGH was sent to gather the plant on Tahiti.

Banks maintained a firm belief that science should be harnessed for the greater good of mankind. To this end he encouraged links between British and foreign scientists, and became a leading member of the Royal Institution, which was founded in 1799 with the aim of employing scientific research to relieve poverty. Banks was made a baronet in 1781 and a knight of the Bath in 1795. Besides collecting and classifying of a wide range of animals, plants and minerals, he was also a connoisseur of rare books and manuscripts. He bequeathed much of his collection to the British Museum.

FURTHER READING P. O'Brian, *Joseph Banks: A Life* (1993).

banks and banking. The BANK OF ENGLAND was one of many banks in Britain during the 18th century. The Bank of Scotland was incorporated in 1695, and was given the monopoly of issuing Scottish notes. It survived several liquidity crises until 1716, when as a result of being suspected of Jacobitism it lost its monopoly. In 1727 a rival, the Royal Bank of Scotland, was established. Whereas north of the border there was no restriction on the establishment of banks and branches, in England an act of 1708 restricted the number of branches to six. In the early 18th century, most banks were centred in London, and were private family firms arising from the practice of goldsmiths and other financiers lending money to creditors. Thus the Hoares, a family of goldsmiths, established a bank in Anne's reign. By 1725 there were about 25 private banks in the capital, a number which increased to around 70 by 1800. Meanwhile a network of country banks was established, which grew from about 12 in 1750 to 119 in 1784, 370 in 1800 and 660 by 1813. A postwar slump saw some of these country banks collapse, so that by 1816 they numbered 575.

Barbauld, Anna Laetitia (*née* Aikin) (1743–1825), poet and woman of letters. The daughter of a teacher who taught at Warrington Academy, she was herself well educated, acquiring French, Italian, Latin and Greek. She published her first volume of poems in 1773 and, with her brother, a collection of essays in the same year. In 1774 she married the Reverend Rochemont Barbauld, a Presbyterian minister from a Huguenot family. After their marriage they moved to Suffolk where Mr Barbauld became a nonconformist minister. There they ran a successful boys' school. In 1785 the Barbaulds left Suffolk and, after a year spent touring France, settled in London, where Mr Barbauld died in 1808 in a hospital for the insane.

Following the death of her husband, Anna devoted herself to literature, editing classic novels and writing poetry. A poem she wrote on the prospects facing England in 1811 provoked a highly critical review from Robert Southey, and she never published another. She enjoyed a wide range of literary acquaintances, including Joseph PRIESTLEY, Hannah MORE, Sir Walter Scott and William Wordsworth. Today she is seen as an early feminist, notably for her poem 'The Rights of Woman', in which she urged women to 'Make treacherous Man thy subject, not thy friend'.

baroque, style of ARCHITECTURE of the 17th and early 18th centuries, characterized by ornate decoration, dramatic effects and a sense of movement.

The architecture that cultural historians label baroque is usually associated with the ecclesiastical buildings of the Counter-Reformation, such as the Gesú in Rome and Melk monastery on the Danube. Its application to buildings in Protestant

England is therefore open to question. Nevertheless it has been applied to such churches as St Paul's Cathedral and to such country houses as Beningbrough Hall in Yorkshire, BLENHEIM PALACE in Oxfordshire and Seaton Delaval Hall in Northumberland. Other structures such as Queen's College Chapel in Oxford and the Naval College at Greenwich are also regarded as baroque in some circles. St Paul's Cathedral is perhaps the most closely attuned to the continental mode of the baroque. Clearly influenced by, although not modelled on, St Peter's in Rome, it offers a more restrained English version of baroque exuberance.

Beningbrough, built for the Bourchier family by Thomas Archer in the reign of Queen Anne, has been described as having a 'Baroque axial plan' as its 'most noticeable feature'.

> The front and garden doors are in line so that one can see right through the short axis of the house into the light beyond. The internal doorways, connecting rooms together, are also aligned, giving an enfilade effect of long vistas through many rooms. This gives a transparent effect to the internal spaces of the hall, the eye travels through the rooms of the building giving that sense of movement which is a prerequisite of Baroque architecture. (Jane Hatcher, 'Beningbrough hall preservation and renewal' in *York Georgian Society Report*, 1980, p. 13).

The house has several Italianate features, which may have been suggested by John Bourchier, the original owner, who had toured Italy before commissioning the building of his new house. Sir John VANBRUGH was building CASTLE HOWARD not far away about the same time, and his designs might have had some impact on Beningbrough too, as craftsmen worked on both. Certainly Vanbrugh's ideas for Blenheim and Seaton Delaval are models of English baroque.

barrier fortresses, a line of citadels in the Spanish (subsequently Austrian) Netherlands (now Belgium and northern France). During the War of the SPANISH SUCCESSION the Dutch were anxious to be granted command of these fortresses to act as a barrier between themselves and the French in case of further attacks from France.

In 1709, in order to keep the Dutch in the war, 2nd Viscount TOWNSHEND – on behalf of the Whig government in Britain – negotiated the 'Barrier treaty', which guaranteed to obtain for the Dutch a chain of nine fortresses, including Lille, Namur, Tournai, Valenciennes and Ypres, and a further ten were they to be taken by the allies from the French. In return the Dutch undertook to guarantee the Hanoverian succession, if necessary by sending up to 6000 troops to assist in suppressing any JACOBITE RISING.

These arrangements with the Dutch were resented by the Tories, who undertook to review them when they came to power in 1710. SWIFT led the attack on them with his *Remarks on the Barrier Treaty* (1712), which concluded that the treaty was a 'wild bargain'. The House of Commons then repudiated it, and in its place a second treaty was negotiated in 1713, reducing the number of fortresses to be held by Dutch garrisons to half those enumerated in the Townshend treaty. Thus Lille and Valenciennes were removed from the list.

In 1715 a third treaty was negotiated between Britain, the Dutch Republic and the Austrian Habsburgs (to whom the former Spanish Netherlands had been ceded in the treaty of UTRECHT in 1713). The Dutch were now to hold seven barrier fortresses in the Austrian Netherlands, and to garrison Dendermonde jointly with the Austrians. The Austrians were to pay three-fifths of the costs of the 35,000 troops to be garrisoned in the barrier fortresses, while Britain undertook to supply 10,000 men and 20 warships to assist in the defence of the barrier should it be attacked.

Barrow, Sir John (1764–1848), explorer and naval administrator. Barrow was born near Ulverston in Lancashire, where he attended the Town Bank

Grammar School. There he showed precocious ability at mathematics, which led to his becoming a teacher of the subject at a school in Greenwich. He gave private lessons to the son of Sir George Staunton, who recommended him to Lord Macartney to accompany him as a secretary on an expedition to China. After returning to England, Barrow again went with Macartney to South Africa, where he was responsible for mapping previously uncharted terrain, travelling over 1600 km (1000 miles) in the process. He planned to settle in Cape Town, but had to leave for England after the signing of the peace of AMIENS in 1802. When Melville (*see* DUNDAS, HENRY) became first lord of the Admiralty in 1804 Barrow was appointed as one of the secretaries under him. He continued as an Admiralty secretary until 1845, with a brief break between 1806 and 1807. In this role he initiated an ambitious programme of Polar and African exploration.

Bath, spa town in southwest England, the archetypal 18th-century city. Its heyday in the age of Beau Nash, master of ceremonies for 56 years from 1705, saw it at its height of fashion as a health spa and gambling centre, which made its social life such a notable feature of the era.

Leisure was too akin to idleness to be pursued purely for its own sake, and so spas became venues for its pursuit – and Bath became the queen of spas. This was largely due to the architectural transformation that the city enjoyed during the century. In Anne's reign the queen went there for her health rather than for recreation, and the amenities were unremarkable. But in the course of a few decades a new pump room and theatre were built, while the architects John Wood and his son John after him virtually rebuilt the city. The father built the Assembly Room in 1728, and the son added the Upper Rooms in 1771. John senior developed Queen Square between 1729 and 1736, and John junior completed the Georgian development with the Circus in 1766. In the 1790s a new and bigger pump room was built.

All this development was made possible by the availability of stone quarries, of which Ralph Allen was the most conspicuous owner. Allen, whose PALLADIAN mansion built by the elder Wood dominated the town, constructed a railway using horse-drawn trucks to bring stone from Combe Down to the heart of Bath. When the river Avon was made more navigable in 1727 other building materials, such as timber from Scandinavia, also became readily available. This encouraged many genteel families not only to visit the spa for the season from autumn to spring, but to settle there in town houses. As a result the population expanded from about 3000 to 35,000 over the century.

FURTHER READING R.S. Neale, *Bath: A Social History 1680–1850* (1981).

Bathurst, Allen, 1st Earl (1684–1775), Tory peer. Bathurst was ennobled as Baron Bathurst in 1712 as one of the twelve peers created to give the Tory government a majority in the House of Lords. He remained a prominent Tory peer throughout the reigns of the first two Georges. POPE dedicated an epistle to him extolling his traditional taste, in contrast to the allegedly corrupt taste of the ruling Whig oligarchy. Apart from a brief spell as captain of the band of pensioners between 1742 and 1744, Bathurst remained in opposition until the accession of George III, when he received a pension of £2000 a year. In 1772 he was elevated to an earldom.

Battle of the Books, name given by Jonathan SWIFT to the quarrel between the ancients and moderns, in which the supporters of the superiority of classical antiquity were ranged against exponents of modern accomplishments and progress. The battle began in England with the publication in 1692 of Sir William Temple's essay on *Ancient and Modern Learning*, in which he claimed that the ancients were superior to the moderns in every branch of art, literature and science. He gave a hostage to fortune when he used as an illustration of this thesis the 'Letters of Phalaris', and inspired the Hon. Charles Boyle to publish an edition of

them – for Richard BENTLEY was able to demonstrate that the letters were in fact spurious, a task he took on with particular zeal since Boyle's preface wrongly accused him of acting insolently as royal librarian. The battle was as much about breeding as about scholarship, for the Christ Church wits of Oxford rallied to Boyle's defence against a man 'bred among the peasantry'. This attitude even informs Swift's mock epic 'Battle of the Books' published in *A Tale of a Tub* in 1704. The verdict of contemporaries on the outcome was mixed, but that of posterity is unanimous that Bentley won.
FURTHER READING J. Levine, *The Battle of the Books* (1991).

Beckford, William (1709–70), radical politician. Beckford was born in Jamaica where his father was governor. The Beckfords were immensely wealthy sugar planters on the island, and the estate passed to William on the death of an elder brother in 1735. Meanwhile he had gone to England to be educated at Westminster School, and to set up in London as a merchant. He settled in Wiltshire where he acquired a country seat, Fonthill. Beckford was returned as member of Parliament for Shaftesbury in 1747. At the next general election in 1754 he was chosen as one of the members for the City of London, for which he was returned again in 1761 and 1768. He also served as lord mayor of London in 1762 and 1769. Politically he was associated with PITT THE ELDER and the expansion of the British empire in the SEVEN YEARS WAR. Later he supported John WILKES's stance for the freedom of the press and the rights of the electors of Middlesex. His son William (1759–1844), the author of the Gothic novel *Vathek* (1786), turned Fonthill into a Gothic palace.

Beggar's Opera. *See* GAY, JOHN.

Bell, Henry (1767–1830), Scottish inventor, the first to apply steam power successfully to a sea-going vessel. Born near Linlithgow, he was apprenticed to a millwright. In 1791 he established the engineering firm of Bell and Paterson in Glasgow, where he experimented with developing a steam engine that would propel a vessel. After several abortive attempts, he succeeded in 1812 with the *Comet*, a steamship that worked as a ferry between Glasgow and Greenock until 1820.

Benbow, John (1653–1702), admiral. A Shropshire lad of humble origins, Benbow ran away to sea as a boy. He rose through hard experience in the merchant service to become master of his own ship. According to an early account of his life, Benbow's craft was attacked, whilst on passage to Spain by Moorish, 'Barbary Corsairs'. The pirates were repulsed and fled, leaving 13 of their number dead behind them. At Benbow's orders their heads were severed and pickled in a tub of brine. When he landed at Cadiz, Benbow's grisly haul impressed the Spanish authorities. His bloody exploit was brought to the notice of James II of England, who offered him a naval command.

Benbow's rise continued after the GLORIOUS REVOLUTION. He was prominent during the naval campaigns of the NINE YEARS WAR, playing important roles in the battles of Beachy Head in 1690 and La Hogue in 1692. Benbow was promoted to admiral in 1696. Five years later, as a fresh war loomed, WILLIAM III sent him to the Caribbean to await an opportunity to attack France's colonies. By the summer of 1702, when news of the outbreak of the War of the SPANISH SUCCESSION reached the West Indies, the French had assembled superior naval forces in the area. Most of these vessels were designated to escort a fabulous treasure fleet bound from Vera Cruz to Spain. Meanwhile, a smaller squadron under the French admiral Du Casse was sent to disrupt Anglo-Dutch traders along the 'Spanish Main'. Benbow gave chase to Du Casse, and in August caught up with his quarry. Benbow's command outgunned the opposition, but in the running fight that followed, four of his seven ships held back from the fight. The behaviour of the laggard captains has never been fully explained – Benbow was a 'tarpaulin' admiral whose spectacular rise from lowly origins may have excited their jealousy and animosity. On 24 August, the sixth day of the engagement, Benbow's right leg was shattered by a chain shot. Nothing daunted, the admiral ordered his ship's carpenter to rig a cradle on the quarter-deck so that he could continue to direct the battle. At the urging of Captain Kirby of the *Defiance*, Benbow subsequently called a council of war and abided by its recommendation to break off the action. Back at Port Royal, Jamaica, Benbow had the reluctant captains tried by court martial. Two of them, Kirby and Wade, were sentenced to death for cowardice and disobedience. They were sent home in disgrace and shot when they reached Plymouth in April 1703.

Months before Wade and Kirby faced the firing squad, Benbow had already succumbed to his wounds. Although his last fight ended in defeat, the bluff admiral's indomitable courage made him a hero. 'The Death of Admiral Benbow' became one of the most popular of all 18th-century BALLADS. And as the opening scenes of Robert Louis Stevenson's wonderful seafaring yarn *Treasure Island* remind us, 'brave Benbow' likewise remained a favourite image on the sign boards of coastal inns.

Bengal. *See* INDIA.

Bentham, Jeremy (1748–1832), philosopher, jurist and reformer, generally regarded as the founder of utilitarianism. Bentham was born in London and educated at Westminster School and Queen's College, Oxford. He then entered Lincoln's Inn, where he was called to the bar. Instead of practising law, however, he wrote on jurisprudence. In 1776 he published a *Fragment on Government*, a critical commentary on BLACKSTONE's *Commentaries on the Laws of England*. This brought him to the attention of Lord SHELBURNE, who invited him to stay at Bowood.

It was at Bowood that Bentham wrote his *Introduction to the Principles of Morals and Legis-lation*, which developed the principle of utility. This maintained that the ultimate object of government should be to procure the greatest happiness of the greatest number. To this end the law should be used not simply to punish, since that increased unhappiness, but to use punishment in order to deter people from antisocial behaviour and to reform those who were not deterred. The reforming aspect of penal practice was the basic idea behind his project to make prisons into 'Panopticons', where the activities of prisoners could be monitored by managers. Attempts to implement such reformatories were unsuccessful. Bentham was not initially a radical, being proud of his Tory ancestry. But his utilitarianism led him to become an advocate of PARLIAMENTARY REFORM and ultimately of democracy.

FURTHER READING J. Dinwiddy, *Bentham* (1989).

Bentinck, William. *See* PORTLAND, WILLIAM BENTINCK, EARL OF.

Bentinck, William Henry Cavendish. *See* PORTLAND, WILLIAM HENRY CAVENDISH BENTINCK, 3RD DUKE OF.

Bentley, Richard (1662–1742), classical scholar. Bentley was educated at Wakefield Grammar School and St John's College, Cambridge. He then became tutor to a son of Bishop Stillingfleet, accompanying his charge to Oxford. There he added an appendix to an edition of the chronicle of John Malelas published by the Sheldonian Press in 1691. It immediately earned him the reputation of being the leading classical scholar in England. In 1692 he was invited to deliver the first Boyle lectures, and in 1694 was appointed as royal librarian at St James's. It was in this capacity that he became embroiled in the so-called BATTLE OF THE BOOKS. In 1700 he became master of Trinity College, Cambridge, and spent most of the rest of his life quarrelling with the fellows. He nevertheless found time to publish editions of *Horace* (1711),

Terence (1726) and *Manilius* (1739), which secured him an international reputation as the greatest classical scholar of the age.

Beresford, John (1738–1805), Anglo-Irish politician. He was prominent in Irish politics from his appointment as a revenue commissioner in 1770 to his death. He represented Waterford in the Irish Parliament from 1760 to 1801, and at Westminster after the UNION OF BRITAIN AND IRELAND. He was so powerful that Lord Fitzwilliam, who became lord lieutenant of Ireland in 1795, claimed that he was 'virtually king of Ireland'. His resistance to Fitzwilliam's policy of conciliation with the Catholics led to the latter's withdrawal and to PITT's policy of union.

Berkeley, George (1685–1753), philosopher and cleric. Berkeley was born in Ireland and educated at Kilkenny School and Trinity College, Dublin, where he became a fellow in 1707. He was inspired by LOCKE's *Essay concerning Human Understanding* to speculate on the same problem, which led him to the conclusion that to exist is either to perceive or be perceived. Thus he concluded that 'the visible world has no absolute existence, being merely the sensible expression of supreme intelligence and will'. The principal exposition of his theory was developed in his *Treatise concerning the principles of human knowledge*, published in 1710.

In 1713 Berkeley went to England and became acquainted with such writers as ADDISON, STEELE and SWIFT. He accompanied the earl of Peterborough on an embassy to Italy as his chaplain from November 1713 to August 1714. Arriving back in England shortly after Queen Anne's death he found himself suspected of being a JACOBITE through his Tory associations. Receiving no preferment, he returned to Italy in 1716, staying until 1720. There he finished the second part of his *Treatise*, but lost the manuscript and never published the complete work.

On the occasion of his second return from Italy Berkeley found England undergoing the crisis of the SOUTH SEA BUBBLE, and wrote an *Essay toward preventing the ruin of Great Britain*, which denounced luxury. POPE introduced him to Lord BURLINGTON, on whose recommendation he went to Ireland as chaplain to the lord lieutenant, the duke of GRAFTON. In 1724 Berkeley's financial circumstances improved when he received the lucrative deanery of Derry and a legacy from Esther Vanhomrigh, Swift's 'Vanessa'. For the next ten years he devoted himself to a project to educate the American colonies in the principles of the Church of England, even projecting a college in Bermuda for this purpose. Although this was abortive, he went to America himself, settling in Rhode Island as a farmer from 1729 to 1731. There he wrote *Alciphron; or the minute philosopher*, an attack upon the doctrines of Bernard MANDEVILLE and the 3rd earl of SHAFTESBURY. He then decided to leave all his books to Yale University and to return to England.

After spending the years 1732 to 1734 in London, Berkeley returned to Ireland as bishop of Cloyne. He devoted most of the rest of his life to his bishopric, earnestly recommending to his family and friends the benefits of tar water as a panacea for all ills. He retired in 1752 and spent his last months in Oxford, where his son was at Christ Church. On his death he was buried in the cathedral there.

FURTHER READING K.P. Winkler, *Berkeley: An Introduction* (1989).

Berwick, James Fitzjames, 1st duke of (1670–1734), one of the most distinguished soldiers of his generation. As the illegitimate son of James duke of York and Arabella Churchill he was the nephew of the foremost general of the age, John Churchill duke of MARLBOROUGH – although fate decreed that his own talents should always be employed in a rival cause.

Fitzjames was born and educated in France. In 1685, when his father succeeded to the throne as James II, Fitzjames was sent to gain military experience in Hungary under Charles of Lorraine.

Despite his youth he soon demonstrated the courage and sober leadership that was to characterize his subsequent career. Created duke of Berwick in 1687, Fitzjames was appointed governor of the strategically important town of Portsmouth. When the invasion of William of Orange obliged James II to abandon his kingdom, Berwick joined his father in France, where he played a leading role in organizing Bourbon backing for the Stuarts. When French troops invaded Ireland on James's behalf, Berwick was prominent in raising recruits amongst the Catholic Irish. Following service at the siege of Derry, Berwick displayed conspicuous bravery during the battle of the BOYNE: although thrown from his horse and trampled in the melee, Berwick fought on until just 16 of his 200 Life Guards remained un-wounded. Berwick briefly held command of James's troops in Ireland, but when Patrick Sarsfield surrendered at Limerick he returned to France. (*See also* WILLIAMITE WARS OF SUCCESSION.)

During the NINE YEARS WAR, Berwick maintained the fight against William III in the fresh theatre of Flanders. He served as a volunteer under Marshal Luxembourg, and in 1692 was present when William's Anglo-Dutch army was defeated at the bloody battle of STEENKIRK. In the following year Berwick was promoted to lieutenant general in the army of Louis XIV; although captured by the English during the confrontation at Neerwinden, he was swiftly released.

At the onset of the War of the SPANISH SUCCESSION in 1702, Berwick once again campaigned in the Low Countries. He then led a French contingent in support of Philip V, the Bourbon claimant to the throne of Spain, and in the Iberian peninsula his cautious tactics shielded Philip's kingdom from superior Anglo-Portuguese forces. Berwick had become a naturalized Frenchman in 1703, and this qualified him to accept the marshal's baton he was offered three years later. In 1707 he returned to Spain, and concluded a careful campaign by shattering the allied army of the Huguenot Lord Galway at ALMANZA; it was a significant victory, not least because it was won by an exiled Englishman leading French troops against Britons commanded by a Frenchman.

Almanza earned Berwick fame and honours. In 1709 he was recalled from the peninsula to defend France's eastern frontiers from the imperial forces of Prince Eugène of Savoy, and Berwick achieved this objective through the cautious defensive campaigning that had become his trademark. Following the treaty of UTRECHT, Berwick demonstrated little enthusiasm for the efforts of his half-brother James – 'the Old Pretender' – to restore the Stuart fortunes in Britain; by contrast, he actually supported the maintenance of the new English alliance. It is nonetheless intriguing to speculate upon the outcome of the sporadic Jacobite invasion attempts if the vastly experienced Berwick, rather than the lacklustre James, had represented the legitimate figurehead of the Stuart cause.

Berwick took the field for France once more when the War of the Polish Succession erupted in 1733, and was given command of the army destined to oppose his old enemy Eugène. In the summer of 1734, after crossing the Rhine, Berwick laid siege to Philipburg. While making his regular rounds of inspection the elderly marshal was decapitated by a cannon ball. Berwick's sudden death ranked as a national disaster for France, and he was buried with honours in Paris.

Bewick, Thomas (1753–1828), wood engraver. Bewick was born in Ovingham, Northumberland. His engravings were used to illustrate his books, the most renowned appearing in *Gay's Fables* (1779), *Select Fables* (1784), *A History of British Birds* (1797–1804) and *Aesop's Fables* (1818). His blocks, many of which survive (including his superb 'Chillingham Bull'), are among the finest woodcuts ever produced in Britain.

Bill of Rights (1689), a statute declaring the rights and liberties of the subject, limiting the power of the crown and settling the succession.

The CONVENTION PARLIAMENT of 1689 passed a Declaration of Rights that condemned James II for illegal use of the royal prerogative. It listed some twelve allegedly unlawful activities, including the use of the royal prerogative to suspend statute laws in general and to issue dispensations to individuals to prevent them from being prosecuted for breaches of the penal laws, and raising a standing army in time of peace. Although some of these claims, especially the last, were dubious, they clarified the legal position thereafter. Thus standing armies in time of peace were declared to be illegal without consent of Parliament (*see also* STANDING ARMY CONTROVERSY).

The Declaration also laid down the future succession to the crown. It set aside the claim of James II, ignored that of his son James Francis Edward STUART, born in June 1688, and settled the succession on the children of WILLIAM III and MARY, then on those of Princess Anne, Mary's sister, and then on any children William might have by a future wife in the event of Mary dying before him. It also declared that no Catholic or spouse of a Catholic could be king or queen of England. In December 1689 the Declaration was changed into the Bill of Rights, by the first Parliament to be elected under William and Mary.

SEE ALSO REVOLUTION SETTLEMENT.

FURTHER READING L. Schwoerer, *The Declaration of Rights* (1981).

Birmingham, one of the most important towns in the Midlands, long before it became a parliamentary borough in 1832. Its importance was largely due to its position at the centre of a metal-manufacturing district producing ironware of all kinds, from toys to guns. In the 1750s Taylor's button and enamelled snuffbox business boasted around 500 employees, while Matthew Boulton's Soho factory employed nearly 1000 workers in the 1770s. However, most metalwork was produced in small artisanal workshops. Birmingham's population grew from around 9000 in 1700 to 50,000 in about 1780. By the middle of the century

it could be described as 'London in miniature'.

SEE ALSO LUNAR SOCIETY; PRIESTLEY, JOSEPH.

bishops. The incumbents of the 26 bishoprics of the Church of England in the 18th century have not on the whole had a good press since R.H. Tawney described them as 'servile appendages of a semi-pagan aristocracy'. They owed their translations from one see to another more to active service on the Whig side in parliamentary elections, and to voting for the government in the House of Lords, than to exemplary piety or to theological scholarship. Indeed, they were more likely to publish pamphlets in defence of the ministry than treatises in defence of the faith. Their time was largely spent in London, attending ministerial levees or debates in the upper house, rather than in their dioceses, taking care of souls, ordaining priests or confirming the laity. All in all, they did not present themselves as an exemplary episcopate.

Critics who accused them of being careerists singled out some for especial condemnation. Benjamin HOADLY, who climbed the episcopal ladder from Bangor to Winchester via Hereford and Salisbury, was the chief whipping boy of those who castigated the bishops for failing in their spiritual duties. He only visited Bangor once, and never set foot in Hereford. Bishops who did not visit their dioceses could ordain those who were prepared to travel to London for the laying on of hands, but they could not confirm *in absentia*. More scandalous in this respect than Hoadly was Lancelot Blackburne, archbishop of York from 1724 to 1743, who, in the whole of that time, did not conduct any confirmations.

However, it would be a mistake to judge the 18th-century episcopate by these notorious examples. Hoadly was exceptional, and in any case was so physically disabled that he had to walk on crutches, making visitations difficult, so that his lack of mobility cannot be attributed to his indifference. As a pamphleteer he was a doughty champion of an erastian view of the relationship between church and state (*see* ERASTIANISM). Alongside

Hoadly there were bishops who did not neglect their spiritual duties. Not all ordinands had to go to London to be ordained. Of the 388 clergymen ordained in Devon and Cornwall between 1689 and 1792 only 26 had to travel to the capital for the laying on of hands. Nor was confirmation always neglected. William Nicolson found when he became bishop of Carlisle in 1702 that there had been no confirmations in that diocese since 1684, a reflection on the practice of the late 17th century rather than that of the 18th. He himself confirmed 5449 during his first visitation.

The difference between the pre- and post-GLO-RIOUS REVOLUTION bishops was that the latter were obliged to attend the House of Lords every year, whereas their predecessors had not. It is significant that one of the best sources for debates in the upper house during the first decade of the 18th century is the parliamentary diary kept by Bishop Nicolson. Thus the 18th century was a peculiar era in which, in addition to their spiritual tasks, the bishops had to undertake arduous political duties at Westminster. In the circumstances they performed both duties remarkably well. Unlike the hereditary peers whom they joined on the bishops' bench, many of them were not from landowning families but were from professional or business backgrounds. They thus leavened the Upper House with a plebeian rather than a patrician element.
FURTHER READING P. Virgin, *The Church in an Age of Negligence* (1989); J. Walsh, C. Haydon and S. Taylor (eds.), *The Church of England c.1689–1833* (1993).

Blackstone, Sir William (1723–80), jurist. Blackstone was the first Vinerian professor of English law at Oxford University, and the lectures he gave there were published as *Commentaries on the Laws of England* (1765–9). In it he developed the classical case that the English polity was a limited monarchy in which the forces of the crown, the House of Lords and the House of Commons acted as checks and balances on each other (*see* CONSTITUTION).

Blake, William (1757–1827), poet and artist. He was born in London, and his parents were DIS-SENTERS, although of what denomination is unknown. That they probably did not belong to a particularly radical sect is suggested by the fact that he was baptized in St James's Church, Piccadilly. He was apprenticed to an engraver, and made his living primarily from making engravings both of his own and other people's works.

Blake devised a style of relief etching that incorporated illustration and text, a device that makes *Songs of Innocence* (1789) and *Songs of Experience* (1794) immediately recognizable as his. Although the poems in these works have a simple rhyming scheme and deceptively accessible themes, they also convey profound notions that anticipate Blake's later enigmatic and prophetic poems. For Blake was a radical sectarian. He enrolled himself in the Swedenborgian church in 1789, although he later parted from it. His prophecies *Europe* and *America* are couched in mythical, almost mystical, visionary language. In part this was because at the time the authorities were sensitive to political predictions and tried to suppress them (*see* BROTHERS, RICHARD) – and Blake's sympathies with the American and French revolutions roused their suspicions of his loyalty.

Today Blake is regarded as an early Romantic, criticizing the ENLIGHTENMENT for its valuing of reason over the imagination, and lamenting the impact of manufacturing upon society.
FURTHER READING P. Ackroyd, *Blake* (1995); E.P. Thompson, *Witness Against the Beast* (1993).

Blathwayt, William (*c.*1649–1717), moderate Tory politician, who was secretary at war from 1686 to 1704, and commissioner of trade from 1696 to 1707. As secretary at war he served both James II and WILLIAM III. William was particularly well inclined towards him on account of his knowledge of foreign languages, and Blathwayt accompanied the king on campaign in the Low Countries. As an original member of the BOARD OF TRADE set up in 1696 he was closely involved in its colonial policies, and took a leading part in attempts to take the charter and proprietary colonies into royal control.

In 1686 Blathwayt married Mary Wynter of Dyrham Park, Gloucestershire, and through his marriage acquired that estate together with electoral influence in nearby Bath, which he represented in Parliament from 1693 to 1710. His alterations to Dyrham Park transformed it into a magnificent mansion in which he entertained Queen ANNE when she visited Bath in 1703.

However, this did not prevent Blathwayt's dismissal from the secretaryship at war in 1704, when his patron, the earl of NOTTINGHAM, ceased to be secretary of state. Blathwayt retained his commission on the Board of Trade for three more years, when the encroachment of Whigs prised even moderate Tories like himself from office. Blathwayt's Toryism was so moderate, indeed, that he is best considered as a court politician, one of those civil servants whose first allegiance was to themselves and the monarch rather than to a party.

FURTHER READING S. Webb, 'William Blathwayt, imperial fixer' in *William and Mary Quarterly* XXV (1968), 3–21; XXVI (1969), 373–415.

Blenheim, battle of (13 August 1704), engagement during the War of the SPANISH SUCCESSION in which a Franco-Bavarian army led by Marshal Tallard was beaten by the forces of the grand alliance commanded by the duke of MARLBOROUGH. The battle resulted from allied efforts to protect the territories of the Austrian Habsburgs against invasion by the elector of Bavaria. In response to this threat, Marlborough led an Anglo-Dutch contingent on a remarkable 400-km (250-mile) march from Flanders to the Danube; his audacious strategy, which was kept secret from wary Dutch politicians who might have vetoed the unorthodox plan, proved brilliantly successful. On 10 June, Marlborough rendezvoused with an imperial Austrian force led by Prince Eugène of Savoy. It marked the beginning of an influential friendship between the two outstanding generals of the age.

After capturing the Schellenberg fortress on 2 July, the allied troops proceeded to devastate the elector's territories. A battlefield confrontation finally followed on 13 August at the Bavarian village of Blenheim, near the Danube. The elector's troops had united with French contingents under Marshals Tallard and Marsin; the 60,000-strong Franco-Bavarian army occupied a strong defensive position anchored upon three villages and screened the Nebel stream. The 56,000 allies ranged against them included some 9000 Britons: the remainder comprised a motley array of imperialists, Prussians, Hanoverians, Dutch, and Hessian and Danish mercenaries. Marlborough's men endured a prolonged cannonade before Eugène's troops were ready to attack the enemy's left wing. The duke's British battalions, under the command of the fire-eating Lord John 'Salamander' Cutts, were sent against Blenheim itself; the ensuing struggle for possession of the fortified village absorbed major French reinforcements, so weakening Tallard's centre. After the allied infantry and artillery rebuffed a French cavalry charge, Marlborough and Eugène countered with a devastating advance of their own. The French centre crumbled, obliging the beleaguered garrison of Blenheim to surrender.

An exhausted Marlborough scribbled the first report of the victory on the back of a tavern bill; sent to his wife Sarah, the note swiftly passed to Queen ANNE. It was, as Marlborough wrote, 'a Glorious Victory'. In defeat, the Franco-Bavarians lost 30,000 men killed, wounded, missing and captured. More significantly, Blenheim shattered the French reputation for invincibility and ended Louis XIV's expansionist ambitions; it also marked the first major continental success for English troops since Agincourt in 1415.

Blenheim Palace, vast and imposing country house built by the duke of MARLBOROUGH. In 1704, in gratitude for Marlborough's victory at Blenheim, Queen ANNE granted to him and his family in perpetuity the manor of Woodstock in

Oxfordshire, and Parliament voted money for the erection of a palace on the land. Sir John VAN-BRUGH was the principal architect, and he designed the building to resemble a citadel, as a reminder of Marlborough's military successes. The duchess of MARLBOROUGH took against the idea and the architect from the start, objecting that it was a grim, uninhabitable palace and preferring Marlborough House in London's Pall Mall, which she commissioned Sir Christopher WREN to build. The military grimness of the BAROQUE palace was later in the century softened by the addition of statues to the roof, and above all by the lake added to the grounds by Capability Brown (*see* LANDSCAPE GARDENING).

Bligh, William (1754–1817), naval officer and colonial administrator. He is best remembered for his ill-fated captaincy of the *Bounty*, whose crew, led by Fletcher Christian, mutinied in April 1789. The ship was on course from Tahiti, where it had spent several months gathering breadfruit, to the West Indies, with a view to planting the cargo there. The mutiny occurred because the crew regretted leaving the tropical island, where they had enjoyed the hospitality of the local people, and resented Bligh's harsh discipline. The mutineers set Bligh and 18 men adrift in an open boat. Without any charts, he managed to sail 5789 km (3618 miles) to Timor in the East Indies.

This was but one epic episode in a long career, which began with Bligh accompanying COOK on his second voyage round the world, and ended with his promotion to the post of vice admiral. Bligh's reputation as a strict disciplinarian has been questioned, some attributing it to Christian's accomplices who used it to justify their mutiny. But he was notoriously a martinet, and was deposed from the governorship of New South Wales in 1808 by subordinates who resented his harshness.

FURTHER READING G. Dening, *Mr Bligh's Bad Language: Passion, Power and Theatre on the Bounty* (1992).

Bloody Code, term applied by some historians to the penal statutes that added to the number of capital offences in the 18th century. It has been estimated that some 50 crimes were punished by the death penalty in 1700, and about 200 by 1800. It was regarded as paradoxical that when reformers on the continent influenced by the ENLIGHTENMENT were urging more liberal criminal codes and citing Britain as an example of an enlightened regime, the British were in fact resorting more and more to capital punishment even for comparatively trivial offences such as stealing a handkerchief worth more than one shilling. Yet at the same time the actual number of executions fell, partly because of the alternative of transportation and partly through the reluctance of juries to condemn people to death for relatively trivial offences.

SEE ALSO CRIME AND PUNISHMENT.

FURTHER READING V.A.C. Gatrell, *The Hanging Tree: execution and the English people, 1770–1868* (1994).

bluestocking, name given in the mid-18th century to any of the ladies who pursued literary and scholarly activities in London in the houses of Mrs Montagu, Mrs Ord and Mrs Vesey. It was particularly associated with the group who met at Elizabeth MONTAGU's salon. Indeed the term was first used by her in a letter of 1756, which referred jokingly to the fact that the eccentric Benjamin Stillingfleet wore them. Gentlemen wore expensive white silk stockings, whereas blue dyed hose were cheap. Thus it originated as a term for men who cultivated intellectual friendships with women. Later by association it was applied to female intellectuals such as Elizabeth Carter, translator of Francesco Algarotti's *Sir Isaac Newton's Philosophy explained for the use of Ladies* (1739) and *The Works of Epictetus* (1758). When Fanny BURNEY satirized intellectual women of the 'Esprit Club' in her play *The Witlings* in 1779, Mrs Thrale noted in her diary that she had been advised not to do so 'for fear of displeasing the female wits – a formidable body, and called by those who ridicule them, The Bluestocking Club'.

FURTHER READING S.H. Myers, *The Bluestocking Circle* (1990).

blue-water policy, strategy that emphasized Britain's pre-eminence as a sea power rather than as a land power. Its advocates stressed that in times of war Britain's contribution should mainly be to deploy her navy to protect merchant shipping and to support combined operations with land forces. They deplored the commitment of English resources to fight major wars in continental Europe, and even to engage as a principal in military operations.

Under the later Stuarts this attitude was largely adopted by the Tories, in opposition to Whig enthusiasm for combating Louis XIV on the continent with large armies, whether led by WILLIAM III in the NINE YEARS WAR or by the duke of MARLBOROUGH in the War of the SPANISH SUCCESSION. Under the Hanoverians it took the form of criticism, by backbench Whigs as well as by Tories, of the alleged policy of putting the interests of the electorate of Hanover before those of Britain. They were particularly concerned to protect British colonial commerce. These critics urged the priority of trade in British foreign policy, clamouring for war with Spain in the 1730s and demanding more effort in extra-European theatres in the War of the AUSTRIAN SUCCESSION and the SEVEN YEARS WAR.

Board of Control, body set up in 1784 to administer the government of INDIA. After the conquest of huge swathes of territory in the subcontinent during the SEVEN YEARS WAR the government of India had become a pressing problem. Previously the British involvement with India had been largely the concern of the EAST INDIA COMPANY, which maintained a number of factories there. But the Company ran into difficulties attempting to administer a territorial rather than a commercial empire. A scheme to take the government of India out of the Company's hands and to lodge it in a board elected by and responsible to the House of Commons – rather than being appointed by the crown – offended GEORGE III, and led to the downfall of the FOX–NORTH coalition in 1783. When William PITT THE YOUNGER became prime minister he created the Board of Control by the India Act of 1784; this body took over responsibility for the government of India, but left trade and patronage in the hands of the Company. It also avoided the dubious constitutional innovation of having it answerable to the Commons rather than to the crown.

Board of Trade, body established by Parliament in 1696 as 'the Board of Trade and Plantations' to replace other ad hoc bodies in the administration of colonial affairs. In the years immediately after its establishment it was the single most important body dealing with the colonies. Thus the appointment of governors was largely in the hands of the Board. It also tried to make all colonies directly subordinate to the crown by eliminating proprietors.

This last objective was realized with the reduction of New Jersey to a crown colony in 1702, but attempts to take the proprietorship of Pennsylvania and Delaware from William PENN were unsuccessful. This was partly because other agencies continued to exercise jurisdiction over the colonies, such as the Admiralty and the secretaries of state. In the War of the SPANISH SUCCESSION the duke of MARLBOROUGH also nominated colonial governors, insisting on military men. By the end of Anne's reign the initiatives of the Board were weakening. In 1715 the colony of Maryland, which had been taken over by the crown, reverted to the proprietorship of Lord Baltimore. The later reduction of the Carolinas from proprietary to crown colonies owed little to the Board. During the years of 'salutary neglect' under WALPOLE the most important agent dealing with the colonies was the duke of NEWCASTLE as secretary of state.

In 1748 the 2nd earl of HALIFAX became president of the Board of Trade, and remained in that office until 1761, apart from an interval between

June 1756 and October 1757. Halifax retrieved for the Board the direction of colonial affairs, especially in America. However, the appointment of a secretary of state for the colonies in 1768 heralded the end of the Board's role in colonial affairs. It was abolished in 1782 following the effective loss of the American colonies, which became the United States of America. The Board was revived in 1786 by the younger PITT, and continues to exist today.

SEE ALSO CARY, JOHN.

Bolingbroke, Henry St John, 1st Viscount

(1678–1751), Tory politician. St John entered parliament in 1701 and quickly made his mark as a high-church Tory. He was a staunch supporter of the Occasional Conformity Bills of 1702 and 1703 (*see* OCCASIONAL CONFORMITY ACT). His considerable talent as a debater led Robert HARLEY to befriend him, and in 1703–4 he became a Harleyite. Thus, when his patron was made secretary of state in 1704, St John was appointed secretary at war. He proved a faithful supporter of the ministry now led by the 'triumvirs' – the duke of MARLBOROUGH, Lord Treasurer GODOLPHIN and Secretary Harley. His loyalty to his 'master', as he called Harley, was such that when the latter resigned in 1708 St John also left office with him. His failure to find a seat in the Commons at the general election held later in the year, however, led to an estrangement between them.

When Harley engineered the ministerial revolution of 1710 he initially meant to bring St John back in his former post as secretary at war. It was only late in the making of the changes that he promoted him to a secretaryship of state. The younger man resented this, and took out his resentment by leading Tory backbenchers in their harassment of the ministry early in 1711, with the aim of making more changes in favour of high-churchmen. When Harley became earl of Oxford that year – whereas St John was only elevated to the peerage as a viscount in 1712 – he blamed the prime minister. In fact it was Queen Anne who was reluctant to

bestow more honour upon him, since she disapproved of his well-deserved reputation as one of the leading rakes of the age.

The rivalry between Bolingbroke, as St John was now known, and Oxford became one of the more serious issues in the fraught politics of Anne's last four years. Bolingbroke was much more ready to sell out to France in the treaty of UTRECHT than was his rival, and even more prepared to open the option of a restoration of James Francis Edward STUART, the Old Pretender. Consequently, when George I succeeded and the Whigs became triumphant at court and in Parliament, Bolingbroke feared for his life. He fled to France and entered the service of the Pretender, thereby giving credence to the propaganda that the Tories were JACOBITES. He quickly became disillusioned with the Pretender's cause, however, and left his service to angle for the restoration of his title and estates, which had been confiscated by Act of Attainder. It took him until 1723 for him to receive a pardon and to recover all his rights except that of attending the House of Lords.

Debarred from participating in parliamentary debates, Bolingbroke took up his pen against the ministry of Sir Robert WALPOLE. Thus he collaborated with William PULTENEY by contributing to the *Craftsman*, the main organ of the opposition during the decade following its launch in 1726. His most celebrated contributions were 'Remarks on the History of England' and 'A Dissertation upon Parties'. Bolingbroke returned to France disillusioned in 1735, and stayed there until 1744. He made occasional visits to England, on one of which in 1738 he made the acquaintance of the prince of Wales, which inspired him to write *The Idea of a Patriot King*. Although he did not publish this until 1749, it circulated in manuscript and in a limited edition by POPE. His posthumous publications on philosophy revealed him as a freethinker, which startled many who had been convinced that he was a staunch Anglican.

FURTHER READING H.T. Dickinson, *Bolingbroke* (1970).

Boscawen, Edward (1711–61), admiral. A younger son of Viscount Falmouth, Boscawen bolstered his aristocratic Whig origins by establishing a formidable reputation as a hard-fighting naval officer. He first went to sea at the age of 14, and made his name during VERNON's celebrated conquest of Porto Bello in 1739. In 1744 he won the nickname 'Old Dreadnought' after the ship he commanded during a bloody encounter with a French vessel. Boscawen sustained a shoulder wound during Edward HAWKE's combat off Cape Finisterre in 1747; the injury may have contributed to the characteristic lopsided stance that earned him the additional sobriquet of 'wry-necked Dick'. As the youngest admiral in the navy, Boscawen was sent to command in the East Indies, where he mounted a skilful withdrawal from Pondicherry.

In 1755, as a fresh war loomed between Britain and France, Boscawen was ordered to intercept French reinforcements for Canada, but owing to fog the bulk of the convoy reached its destination unmolested. During the following year Boscawen presided over the court martial that sentenced Admiral BYNG to death for his failure to safeguard MINORCA. In 1758 he commanded the naval forces in the successful combined operation against the key French fortress of Louisbourg on Cape Breton.

By the summer of 1759 Boscawen was deployed in the Mediterranean; his object was to prevent the Toulon squadron from uniting with the French fleet at Brest poised to invade England. When the squadron under Admiral de la Clue finally emerged and gave Boscawen the slip, he set off in dogged pursuit. The chase ended in Lagos Bay, Portugal, where Boscawen attacked and inflicted heavy casualties, earning the thanks of Parliament and a pension of £3000 a year. Boscawen was a rigid disciplinarian, although his celebrated fighting spirit was matched by genuine concern for the welfare of his crews. 'Old Dreadnought' maintained his Cornish connections, serving as MP for Truro from 1742 until his death.

Boston Massacre. *See* AMERICAN COLONIES BEFORE 1776.

Boston Tea Party. *See* AMERICAN COLONIES BEFORE 1776.

Boswell, James (1740–95), Scottish writer, known for his biography of Samuel JOHNSON. Boswell was born in Ayrshire, and educated in Edinburgh and Glasgow. In 1762 he visited London, where he became acquainted with the leading literati of the day. He met Dr Johnson on 16 May 1763, and struck up a long-lasting friendship with him. They accompanied each other on a tour to the Highlands and Western Isles in 1773, which both described in print, although Boswell's account was not published until 1785, soon after Johnson's death. In 1791 Boswell's *Life of Johnson* appeared, and after its appearance it rapidly acquired its reputation as the greatest biography in the English language.

Boswell's own life has attracted attention following the publication of his journals by the Yale University Press. The public life of their author was that of a respectable lawyer, who went to Utrecht in 1763 to acquire a knowledge of civil law so that he could practise at the Edinburgh bar and go on circuit in Scotland. He did not, however, have an outstandingly successful legal career, and attracted few briefs. The explanation is partly to be found in his private life, as revealed in his journals. Released from the strict surveillance of his family and the social controls of Scotland into the urban jungle of Hanoverian London, the young Boswell indulged in a dissolute social life of drunkenness and fornication, punctuated by remorse and efforts at control that never lasted long. Nevertheless he paints a picture of himself as at bottom a hero with an essentially good heart.

This has misled some biographers into accepting his own account of himself at face value. Yet Boswell, in his frank and confessional journals – so explicit that some Victorian descendant was driven to weed them – did not tell the whole truth even to himself. His treatment of his wife is a case in point. His many infidelities can perhaps be overlooked, not least since she herself apparently forgave them. But his insistence on fulfilling his own ambitions in London, at the expense of her physical comfort when she was obviously terminally ill, was – however much remorse he expressed about it – hardly heroic. Boswell's biographer has a problem reconciling his subject with the image he tried to create of himself. The adoption of a gauche persona was an invaluable strategy for writing both the *Journal of a Tour to the Hebrides* and the biography of Johnson, and it is clear that Boswell also projected to the Doctor a false image of himself as a naïve Scot, an image that is markedly at odds with the sharp intelligence of the observations he made about his subject.

FURTHER READING F. Bradley, *James Boswell: The Later Years* (1984); F.A. Pottle, *James Boswell: The Earlier Years* (1966).

Botany Bay. *See* AUSTRALIA.

Boulton, Matthew (1728–1809), industrialist. He was one of the leading iron manufacturers of BIRMINGHAM, setting up his Soho works there in 1762. He went into partnership with James WATT to apply steam power to the works, investing considerable capital in the project before it began to realize a profit. He was also a leading light in the LUNAR SOCIETY, which often met at his house to discuss topics of scientific and intellectual interest.

Bounty, HMS. *See* BLIGH, WILLIAM.

Bourbon, the family name of the kings of France, whose relatives also ruled in Spain, Naples and Sicily during the 18th century.

Bow Street runners, officers of the Bow Street magistrates' court in London, who from 1749 to 1829 were charged with the pursuit and apprehension of criminals.

The 'crime wave' that preoccupied men of property in the wake of the War of the AUSTRIAN SUCCESSION proved responsible for countermeasures that were destined to lay the foundations of Britain's modern police force. In London, the offensive against crime was led by the novelist Henry FIELDING and his equally remarkable blind half-brother John. Henry, who wrote the influential *Inquiry into the Causes of the Late Increase in Robbers*, served as chief magistrate for Westminster until his sudden death in 1754; John, the energetic 'blind beak', occupied the same position until 1780.

In contrast to those pundits who called for even harsher punishments to deter criminals, the Fielding brothers instead believed that the answer to rising crime levels lay in more effective methods of law enforcement. The Fieldings argued that time-honoured methods of combating crime, which centred upon the notoriously unreliable 'charlies' of the watch and the often unenthusiastic parish constables, were incapable of coping with increasingly violent and sophisticated criminals. Instead, they advocated the establishment of a reliable and active police force prepared to wage vigorous war upon crime. The Fieldings' vision remained highly controversial: a professional police force suggested the sinister absolutist regimes characteristic of continental Europe, and was therefore considered to be incompatible with traditional 'English liberties'.

Despite deep-seated opposition to their proposal, the Fieldings secured sufficient secret-service funds to permit the formation of a fledgling squad of 'runners', based at the Bow Street magistrates' office. The first half-dozen runners were former parish constables paid a guinea a week, plus a bounty for every criminal they apprehended. As professional thief-takers the Bow Street runners developed techniques perfected by the century's arch-criminal Jonathan WILD, whose exploits had earlier inspired one of Henry Fielding's novels. Although little more than licensed bounty-hunters, the Bow Street runners soon made a noticeable impact upon street crime in the capital. They also established a reputation for dogged determination in pursuit of their prey, operating far beyond the limits of the capital, and proving ready to tackle criminal gangs with pistol and cutlass.

During his lengthy magistracy, John Fielding campaigned to expand the scope of the runners and place them on a permanent footing, and in 1772 he produced a 'General Preventative Plan' that proposed a truly national police force. Although Fielding did not live to see his dream become reality, the effectiveness of the runners was recognized in 1792 when seven more offices on the Bow Street model were established throughout London. In addition, the London-based runners could be called in to deal with serious crime throughout the country. By the end of the 18th century they represented an increasingly accepted antidote to crime. In 1801, for example, a pair of runners tracked four highwaymen who had committed a robbery at Shooters Hill near Woolwich; enlisting the assistance of soldiers from the nearby barracks they cornered the gang, who were captured and later executed.

Although not without their critics, the Bow Street runners paved the way for a professional police force. Their lead was followed by the establishment of Sir Robert Peel's Metropolitan police in 1829, and the national adoption of police forces in 1856.

SEE ALSO CRIME AND PUNISHMENT.

FURTHER READING J.M. Beattie, *Crime and the Courts in England, 1660–1800* (1986).

Boyle, Richard, 3rd earl of Burlington. *See* BURLINGTON, RICHARD BOYLE, 3RD EARL OF.

Boyne, battle of the (1 July 1690), engagement during the WILLIAMITE WARS OF SUCCESSION between an Anglo-Dutch army led by WILLIAM III and a Franco-Irish army commanded by James II. The battle took place on the banks of the river Boyne west of Drogheda in Ireland. The decisive defeat of James ensured that William would conquer Ireland, a task accomplished by 1692. Even now, 12 July is a red-letter day for the Orange Order, while King Billy on his white horse with the slogan 'Remember 1690' is a popular symbol with Ulster Protestants.

Bray, Thomas (1656–1730), the presiding genius over the establishment of the SOCIETY FOR PROMOTING CHRISTIAN KNOWLEDGE in 1699 and its offshoot the SOCIETY FOR THE PROPAGATION OF THE GOSPEL in 1701. In the interval between the two societies being launched he visited Maryland at the request of Anglicans there to assist in the creation of parishes.

Bridgeman, Charles. *See* LANDSCAPE GARDENING.

Bristol, city and port of southwestern England. At the start of the 18th century it was the third largest city of England after London and Norwich, but by 1750 had risen to rank second to the capital in terms of population, with about 50,000 inhabitants.

By the early 19th century, however, although Bristol had grown, it had been eclipsed by MANCHESTER and LIVERPOOL. Liverpool also outstripped Bristol as a port during the 18th century, especially in the SLAVE TRADE. The UNION OF ENGLAND AND SCOTLAND in 1707 admitted Scots into the commerce of the British empire, and this produced a geographical realignment of merchant shipping routes that benefited northern ports. For a while the northwestern port of Whitehaven enjoyed a brief boom, while Glasgow became a major entrepôt for imperial goods.

The result was the relative decline of Bristol, although it remained important as a destination for such products as tobacco and sugar destined for domestic and, through re-export, European markets. It also retained its importance as a regional capital for southwest England and even much of south Wales. Its significance as a centre of bourgeois culture is apparent in the development of the elegant suburb of Clifton, in the foundation of the first provincial hospital in 1735 and in the establishment of its Library Society in 1773.

Britain. Following the UNION OF ENGLAND AND SCOTLAND in 1707, England and Scotland were merged into Great Britain, and officially became South and North Britain respectively. The fact that the English never accepted the expression 'South Britain', and the attempt to foist the northern label upon the Scots eventually failed, indicates the strength of traditional identities on both sides of the border.

Nevertheless there was an attempt to inculcate British national sentiment under the Hanoverians. Thus the ARMY, NAVY and the empire became British immediately. Later the BRITISH MUSEUM, albeit housed in London, expressed this endeavour, as perhaps did the *Encyclopaedia Britannica* – first published in Edinburgh in 1772. But such attempts were from the top down. There was little positive identification with the new concept from the mass of the population. On the contrary, anti-Scottish feeling increased during the century in England, reaching its peak in the Wilkite agitation of the 1760s: John WILKES's infamous publication, *The North Briton*, was meant to refer to the Scots in general and Lord BUTE in particular.

Under the early Hanoverians national identity was mostly negative, in the sense that Britons were anti-French and anti-Catholic. The patriotic song 'Rule Britannia', with words by James Thomson and music by Thomas Arne, reflects these sentiments. It was first performed in the masque *Alfred* in 1740, at a time of rapidly increasing hostility towards France. Although the anti-French element was if anything exacerbated by the REVOLUTIONARY AND NAPOLEONIC WARS, the decades of warfare also brought about a positive national sentiment. **FURTHER READING** L. Colley, *Britons: Forging the Nation 1707–1837* (1992).

British Museum, institution established in London in 1759 by a trust that acquired Montagu House in Bloomsbury to house the Cotton, Harley and Sloane collections. A bill to charge for admission was defeated in 1784. The Royal Library, mainly of GEORGE III's books, was added in 1822.

Britons. *See* BRITAIN.

'broad-bottom administration', nickname inspired by Lord CHESTERFIELD and given to the ministry formed in 1744. After the accession of the house of Hanover in 1714, and especially after the suppression of the JACOBITE RISING of 1715, the Tories were proscribed. Thus they were effectively purged from positions in the administration, from the cabinet and royal household to the commissions of the peace (*see* JUSTICES OF THE PEACE) in the localities. As long as Sir Robert WALPOLE was prime minister the proscription was complete.

On Walpole's fall, however, there was a jockeying for position between rival politicians to replace him, the two main factions being led by the duke of NEWCASTLE and his brother Henry PELHAM, and Lord CARTERET. To outflank Carteret the Pelhams appealed to Tories for support, offering them posts in a 'broad-bottom administration'. Their negotiations led to the inclusion in the ministry by 1744 of such Tories as Sir John Hinde Cotton and John Philipps. The experiment was, however, short-lived. Philips resigned within six months, and Cotton was dismissed in 1746. Nevertheless, it spelled the end of proscription of Tories in the shires, where Tory justices were admitted to the commissions of the peace for the first time since 1716. The idea of a broad-bottom administration survived, being applied to the PITT–Newcastle ministry.

Brothers, Richard (1757–1824), prophet. Brothers was born in Newfoundland and later went to England, where he enrolled in the Royal Navy as a midshipman at the age of 14. He rose to be a lieutenant, but in 1783 was discharged on half pay. He continued to receive his half pay until 1790, when his reluctance to take the oath required for payment led to it being refused. His explanation for his refusal revealed that he entertained religious scruples over oath-taking not unlike those of the Quakers. Shortly afterwards, it became clear that his religious beliefs demonstrated an unorthodoxy that betrayed symptoms of mania.

In May 1792 Brothers wrote to the king and to ministers that he was going to attend Parliament to warn members that God had informed him that the time was come to fulfil the prophecy in chapter 7 of the Book of Daniel. In 1794 he published *A Revealed Knowledge of the Prophecies and Times* in two parts. One prophecy was that he was to be revealed as the prince of the Hebrews and ruler of the world on 19 November 1795. On 4 March 1795 he was arrested for treasonable practices and confined as a criminal lunatic. He was released in 1806, and the treason charge was dropped. Brothers attracted several disciples while in confinement, and continued to be a prophet until his death, although he seems to have avoided making further political prophecies.

Brown, Lancelot 'Capability'. *See* LANDSCAPE GARDENING.

Bruce, James (1730–94), Scottish explorer. He was born in Stirlingshire. Bruce came to the notice of Lord HALIFAX, who had him appointed as consul in Algiers in 1763, with a view to examining and recording antiquities in the desert. During the mid-1760s Bruce accomplished this task with the help of an Italian draughtsman.

In 1768 Bruce went to Egypt hoping to trace the source of the Nile, and to this end he proceeded to Gondar, the capital of Abyssinia, the first Briton – preceded by very few Europeans – to arrive there. He ingratiated himself with the authorities, who assisted him in his expedition to the source of the Blue Nile, which he reached in November 1770. It took him two years trekking back through hostile terrain to reach Aswan. He then returned to Britain by way of France. At home his account of his travels was widely disbelieved, and he received very little recognition for them in his lifetime. But, though he undoubtedly embellished his story, its essence was subsequently verified.

Brummell, George (1778–1840), leading regency dandy. The son of Lord NORTH's private secretary, George 'Beau' Brummell compensated in style for what he lacked in wealth or influence. Whilst still in school at Eton, he was already demonstrating the seemingly effortless poise that was to provide the mainstay of his reputation. Brummell's ready wit and elegance gained him the influential friendship of George, the prince of Wales and future GEORGE IV; he was given a commission in the prince's own regiment, the 10th Light Dragoons, but soon left the army to follow his true calling as the uncrowned king of the bucks and beaux.

Although fastidious about his own personal appearance and hygiene, Brummell disdained the sartorial excesses of the foppish 'Macaronis'. In reaction to men such as the perfumed, painted and satin-clad Sir Lumley 'Skiffy' Skeffington, Brummell advocated an understated but supremely elegant approach to male fashion. The attention that Brummell devoted to tying his cravat became legendary. The prince of Wales regularly called upon Brummell simply to watch him dress; it was rumoured that Brummell once reduced 'Prinny' to tears by criticizing the cut of his coat. Amused at his own fame and influence, Brummell did nothing to discourage the legends that accumulated around him, revealing, for example, that the polish employed to give his boots their superlative shine was made from the finest champagne. Yet there was clearly more to Brummell than his immaculate exterior, and he retained the friendship of such discriminating hostesses as the duchess of York.

At his peak, Brummell wielded an influence that Byron believed exceeded Napoleon's. However, the Beau's fortunes began to turn in 1811 following a rift with the regent; this was compounded by a run of bad luck at the gambling tables that Brummell characteristically blamed upon the loss of a lucky sixpence. Yet two years later Brummell coined one of the most famous retorts of the era. With three other friends, Brummell decided to give a lavish ball at the Argyle Rooms. When the regent arrived he shook hands with two of the hosts, but deliberately snubbed both Brummell and William 2nd Baron Alvanley. Brummell then called out in a voice that cut through the throng, 'Alvanley. Who's your fat friend?' The jibe left the vain and portly regent mortified.

By 1816, mounting gambling debts obliged Brummell to flee from his creditors. On decamping to Calais he left a message on his dressing table that encapsulated the essence of his glory days. It read: 'starch is the man!' Brummell served briefly as consul at Caen, but his final years were blighted by poverty and declining health. In a twist of fate that was truly tragic, the man whose spotless appearance and well-honed wit had once made him the toast of London, ended his days insane and unkempt in a French asylum.

FURTHER READING H. Cole, *Beau Brummell* (1977).

Brunswick, house of, alternative name for the house of Hanover, whose heads were also dukes of Brunswick-Wolfenbüttel. *See* HANOVERIAN SUCCESSION.

Bubble Act (1720), legislation that declared companies without a charter to be illegal. Its purpose was to remove competition for investment from the South Sea Company, and the act closed down many companies that had mushroomed in that year of speculation (*see* SOUTH SEA BUBBLE). Joint-stock companies were required to have a statute authorizing their activities, and this severely restricted the formation of such companies until the act was repealed in 1825.

Burdett, Sir Francis (1770–1844), radical politician. Burdett entered Parliament in 1796 and immediately became known as a leading supporter of PARLIAMENTARY REFORM and an opponent of PITT THE YOUNGER's repression of radicals. In 1802 he was returned as a radical for Middlesex, although his return was successfully challenged by a defeated candidate, and Burdett was himself defeated at the subsequent by-election. He stood

successfully for the county in 1805 but was defeated in 1806. He was then returned for Westminster, a constituency he represented for the next 30 years. He was a leading critic of the duke of York, implicating him in the sale of commissions in the army. In 1810 he was imprisoned for breach of parliamentary privilege.

Burgh, James (1714–75), political reformer and writer. Burgh was born in Scotland and educated at St Andrews. He went to London where he was employed by a publisher, and then became an usher at a school in Marlow, where he wrote *Britain's Remembrancer* to celebrate the suppression of the JACOBITES in the '45. In 1747 he set up an academy at Stoke Newington where he taught and published until 1771. In his last years he wrote his most famous work, *Political Disquisitions*, published in three volumes in 1774 and 1775. In them he objected to the dominance of the landed interest in Parliament and called for more representation for merchants, which he felt could be achieved by a reform of the electoral system that greatly expanded the electorate.

Burgoyne, John (1723–92), general and playwright. Reputedly the illegitimate son of Lord Bingley, John Burgoyne courted controversy in 1751 when he eloped with Lady Charlotte Stanley, the daughter of the influential earl of Derby. The young lovers were obliged to spend a period of exile in Europe, but reconciliation followed and Burgoyne's powerful in-laws ultimately smoothed his chosen path in the army. At the outbreak of the SEVEN YEARS WAR in 1756 Burgoyne purchased a captaincy in the cavalry. During the campaign in Portugal he won plaudits as a dashing commander of light dragoons, a role in which he was depicted in a striking portrait by REYNOLDS. Burgoyne also wrote manuals that recommended an enlightened attitude towards military discipline: this humane stance gained him the enduring affection of his soldiers who dubbed him 'Gentleman Johnny'. When not gambling or writing for the stage, Burgoyne proved a vocal member of Parliament: he was elected for Midhurst in 1761, and subsequently for Preston. In the Commons, Burgoyne opposed the repeal of the STAMP ACT and was a prominent critic of the Indian career of Lord Robert CLIVE.

In 1775, at the onset of the AMERICAN WAR OF INDEPENDENCE, Burgoyne held the army rank of major general. Sent across the Atlantic with generals William HOWE and Henry CLINTON, he became an advocate of tough measures against the rebellious colonists. It was Burgoyne who devised the ambitious plan to strike against New England from Canada, and persuaded Lord George Germain (*see* SACKVILLE, LORD GEORGE) to let him command the operation. The subsequent advance down the Hudson Valley began promisingly enough with the capture of TICONDEROGA, but ultimately met fierce resistance that led to Burgoyne's surrender at SARATOGA in October 1777. As his troops marched off into captivity, Burgoyne returned home making unsuccessful demands for the court martial he believed would clear him of any responsibility for the debacle. Burgoyne now employed his oratory in the service of the parliamentary opposition led by his friend Charles James FOX. At the fall of NORTH's ministry in 1782, he was rewarded with the post of commander in chief in Ireland. Burgoyne remained an active playwright and in 1786 achieved widespread acclaim for his comedy *The Heiress*.

FURTHER READING G.A. Billias, 'John Burgoyne, Ambitious General' in G.A. Billias (ed.), *George Washington's Opponents: British Generals and Admirals in the American Revolution* (1969).

Burke, Edmund (1729–97), Anglo-Irish ROCKINGHAMITE Whig politician and political theorist, regarded as one of the founders of modern conservatism. The son of an Irish attorney, Burke was educated first by a Quaker schoolmaster, then studied at Trinity College, Dublin, and later at the Middle Temple. He married the daughter of an Irish Catholic in 1756. Burke began his career as a writer, editing *The Reformer* in Dublin after graduating in 1748. In 1756 he published *A Vindication of Natural Society*, and in 1757 *A Philosophical Enquiry into the origin of our ideas on the Sublime and the Beautiful*. The *Enquiry* attempted to provide an objective basis for aesthetic criticism, arguing that ideas of the sublime and the beautiful could be accounted for on the pleasure/pain principle: the sublime inspired awe, and the beautiful pleasure. From 1759 to 1789 he was chief editor of *The Annual Register*, although he was assisted in his editorial duties after he entered the House of Commons in 1766.

Burke's political career was distinguished by his opposition to alleged repression at home and abroad. He attacked ministerial attempts to control Parliament in *Thoughts on the Cause of the Present Discontents* (1770). When his patron, the marquess of ROCKINGHAM, became prime minister in 1782, Burke carried a measure aimed at reducing the crown's influence by curtailing its powers of patronage. He championed the causes of Irish Catholics, American colonists and Native North Americans against the British government and its agents. His letters and speeches on these issues did not prepare his Whig colleagues for his denunciation of the FRENCH REVOLUTION in *Reflections on the Revolution in France* (1790).

Yet, as he argued in *An Appeal from the New to the Old Whigs* (1791), he had remained faithful to the principles of the GLORIOUS REVOLUTION. To him this meant the maintenance of the sovereignty of the king in Parliament against rival theories of the sovereignty of the king alone on the one hand or of the people on the other. Thus, while opposing any increase in the influence of the crown, Burke had consistently resisted encroachments by the electorate. He refused to receive instructions from his constituents when elected at Bristol in 1774, and had little time for the advocates of parliamentary reform. By upholding the sovereignty of the king in Parliament the Glorious Revolution had preserved English liberty; by asserting the sovereignty of the people the French Revolution was destroying liberty in France.

FURTHER READING C.C. O'Brien, *The Great Melody: A Thematic Biography of Edmund Burke* (1992); F.P. Lock, *Edmund Burke: Vol. I. 1730–1784* (1999).

Burlington, Richard Boyle, 3rd earl of (1695–1753), the presiding genius of the PALLADIAN movement in architecture. Burlington succeeded to his title at the age of nine and spent several years in Italy in his teens, where he acquired an admiration for the architect Andrea Palladio (1508–80). On his return to England he transformed Burlington House along Palladian lines, although these have now been largely obliterated since it became the home of the ROYAL ACADEMY. Chiswick House, however, has been preserved virtually intact as a model of the style. Burlington was the patron of William Kent (*see* LANDSCAPE GARDENING), and included GAY, POPE and SWIFT among his literary associates; Pope dedicated an epistle to him as the arbiter of taste. In politics Burlington was a Tory, although allegations that he was also a Jacobite have not been substantiated.

Burnet, Gilbert (1643–1715), Whig cleric and historian. Burnet was educated at Aberdeen University and in Amsterdam, and became one of Charles II's chaplains. His early career was in Scotland, where he was an ordained minister and, from 1669, professor of divinity at Glasgow University. Finding himself harassed by his former patron, the earl of Lauderdale, he left for London in 1674, where he was made chaplain to the Rolls chapel by the master. He displayed an exceptionally broad tolerance of Presbyterianism, episcopacy and even Roman Catholicism. But, having associated with those who had plotted Charles II's death in 1683, he went temporarily to France.

In November 1684, after his return from France, Burnet preached a sermon against popery in the Rolls chapel, for which he was dismissed from the chaplaincy. He again left for the continent, travelling through France, Italy and Switzerland to the Netherlands. He was favourably received by the prince and princess of Orange – the future WILLIAM III and Queen MARY – at the Hague. James II was so incensed by this that he issued warrants for Burnet's arrest for alleged treason and even, according to Burnet himself, had a contract out for his assassination. In 1688 Burnet set sail with the prince of Orange, whose Declaration he had penned. When they landed in Torbay the prince asked him, 'Well, Doctor, what do you think of predestination now?'

After Burnet became bishop of Salisbury in 1689 he took pains to justify the GLORIOUS REVOLUTION as providential intervention in mundane affairs. In 1698 he published an *Exposition of the Thirty-nine Articles of the Church of England*, in which he argued that the ambiguities of the articles allowed for divergent interpretations. For this he was censured by the high-church party in the Convocation of 1701. Their champion, Dr SACHEVERELL, also attacked him in his notorious sermon of 1709.

Although Burnet had been tutor to Queen ANNE's son the duke of Gloucester between 1699 and 1700, and although he was an advocate of the scheme known as 'Queen Anne's Bounty', Anne never gave him any preferment during her reign, and he died in 1715 still bishop of Salisbury. Burnet is chiefly remembered as a historian, publishing a *History of the Reformation* in three volumes between 1679 and 1714, and writing a celebrated *History of my own Time*, which appeared posthumously in two volumes, the first in 1723 and the second in 1734. In its terse, dry style, it sought to vindicate the part played by the Whigs and William of Orange in late-Stuart politics.

Burney, Frances ('Fanny') (1752–1840), woman of letters. She was the daughter of the music historian Charles Burney, and a close friend of Dr JOHNSON. She became second keeper of the queen's robes in 1786, a post she held until 1791. In 1793 she married a French army officer, Alexandre d'Arblay.

Fanny kept a diary that is a major source for the activities of the court while she was in the queen's service, documenting the onset of GEORGE III's 'madness'. She also wrote plays, none of which succeeded, and novels which brought her fame. By far the most successful was her first, *Evelina*, published in 1778. Royalties from her novels were a vital source of income for the d'Arblays: those from *Camilla* (1796) brought in enough to provide a house for them, appropriately called Camilla Cottage.

FURTHER READING K. Chisholm, *Fanny Burney: Her Life* (1998).

Burns, Robert (1759–96), Scottish poet. Burns was not the 'heaven-taught ploughman' of legend but the son of a smallholder in Ayrshire who was able to give him a rudimentary education and to pay a tutor, who taught him English and even French literature. On his father's death in 1784 Burns himself farmed at Mossgiel near Mauchline. He was extremely sociable, being a founding member of the Tarbolton Bachelors' Club in 1780 and becoming a freemason in 1781. In 1786 he impregnated Jean Armour, and married her two years later. In 1786 he also published *Poems chiefly in the Scottish Dialect*, which immediately attracted attention and earned him an invitation to Edinburgh. He became an excise officer and abandoned farming to move to Dumfries in 1791, where he died.

Burns's politics ran the gamut from JACOBITISM to JACOBINISM. He wrote or adapted about thirty Jacobite songs, including 'Charlie he's my darling'; his Jacobitism was not merely sentimental but an expression of Scottish independence in the only form it could take under the Hanoverians. Thus he deplored the UNION OF ENGLAND AND SCOTLAND and famously characterized the Scottish commissioners who negotiated it as 'a parcel of rogues in a nation'. He considered that the union had ended a long and proud tradition of Scottish independence, which he traced back to the days of Robert Bruce in 'Scots wha' hae wi' Wallace bled'. He also seems to have equated Scottish independence before 1707 with liberty, and this links his nostalgic Jacobitism with his more progressive

Jacobinism. One of the many poems recited at Burns Night suppers every 25 January betrays his enthusiasm for the French Revolution:

> It's coming yet for a' that
> That man to man the warld o'er
> Will brothers be for a' that.

Burns was accused in 1792 of joining in the singing of the French revolutionary song 'Ça ira' ('that will come'). This was a serious charge, especially since he was a government official in the excise service. He excused his behaviour on the grounds that he was drunk at the time, which is plausible enough since he seems hardly ever to have been sober. Nevertheless the revolutionary sentiment is surely expressed in 'It's coming yet'. Not that it is necessary to look for any political message in order to enjoy Burns's poems. Many of them, such as 'My love is like a red red rose' and 'Ye banks and braes of Bonny Doon', live on long after his death, making him perhaps the most popular poet in the language.

FURTHER READING R. Bentman, *Robert Burns* (1987).

Bute, John Stuart, 3rd earl of (1713–92), politician and prime minister (1762–3). He was born in Edinburgh and educated at Eton. He succeeded his father as earl in 1723, and in 1736 married Mary, the daughter of Edward and Lady Mary Wortley MONTAGU, the match bringing him lucrative estates in Yorkshire. He entered Parliament as a representative peer of Scotland in 1737, but was not elected at subsequent elections under GEORGE II.

Bute moved to London after the '45 JACOBITE RISING and made the acquaintance of FREDERICK PRINCE OF WALES, who appointed him as one of the lords of his bedchamber in 1750. Following the death of the prince in 1751 Bute became groom of the stole and tutor to the future GEORGE III, and was reputed to be the lover of Frederick's widow – George's mother. The story of Bute filling the young prince's head with unconstitutional notions of kingship was a WHIG myth. In fact the future king was imbued by his tutor with ideas of ruling as a limited monarch in accordance with the principles of the REVOLUTION SETTLEMENT.

At the accession of George III in 1760, Bute acquired great influence over ministerial appointments, himself becoming secretary of state in 1761 and again a representative peer of Scotland. PITT THE ELDER resigned in 1761, having failed to persuade the cabinet to declare war on Spain. Bute now became virtual prime minister, presiding over a policy of making peace with France to end the SEVEN YEARS WAR; and the following year *The* duke of NEWCASTLE also left the ministry, Bute replacing him as first lord of the Treasury.

The treaty of PARIS, signed in 1763, was highly unpopular following the successes of the war, which Bute's many opponents felt should have brought Britain more concessions from France than were accorded. These sentiments were most vociferously expressed by John WILKES in *The North Briton*, the title of which indirectly targeted Bute as a Scot. Indeed the prime minister suffered from the Scoto-phobia exploited by the opposition until he felt unable to face his critics, and he resigned after the peace was concluded.

Bute nevertheless continued to influence the king during the ministry of his successor, George GRENVILLE, until the new prime minister protested and elicited from George a promise not to allow Bute to advise him. Although the king apparently kept this promise, the opposition continued to accuse Bute of being an *éminence grise* for many years thereafter. Bute finally retired from politics in 1780, when he declined to stand in the general election as a candidate for one of the 16 Scottish seats in the House of Lords.

FURTHER READING K. Schweizer (ed.), *Lord Bute: Essays in Re-interpretation* (1988).

Butler, James, 2nd duke of Ormonde. *See* ORMONDE, JAMES BUTLER, 2ND DUKE OF.

Butler, Joseph (1692–1752), Anglican cleric, noted for his opposition to DEISM. He was edu-

cated as a DISSENTER but converted to Anglicanism and completed his education at Oxford. In 1732 he was appointed to the lucrative living of Stanhope in County Durham. There he wrote the *Analogy of Religion, Natural and Revealed, to the Constitution and Course of Nature*. When this was published in 1736 it was received as the profoundest contribution to the deist controversy in the 18th century. Butler argued that natural and revealed religion, so far from being distinct and independent sources of evidence for the truth of Christianity, mutually support each other. Queen CAROLINE was sufficiently impressed by the *Analogy* to appoint Butler to be her clerk of the closet. When she died in 1737 he was promoted to the bishopric of Bristol, from which he was translated to Durham in 1750.

Byng, John (1704–57), naval commander. An admiral's son, Byng entered the NAVY in 1718 as an able seaman and rose in the service to command several ships, becoming commander in chief in the Mediterranean by 1747. In 1756 he was given the same command and ordered to proceed with a fleet to the defence of MINORCA. When he arrived there he found the island occupied by French forces, and engaged an enemy fleet defending them. Failing to effect an attack he withdrew to Gibraltar, and was subsequently court-martialled for negligence. He was found guilty and, although the court recommended mercy, the king declined to reprieve him. He was shot on his own quarter-deck in Portsmouth on 14 March 1757 – 'to encourage the others', as Voltaire sardonically observed.

Byrom, John (1692–1763), poet and hymn writer. He was born near Manchester and educated at Merchant Taylor's School and Trinity College, Cambridge. After Cambridge he went to Montpellier to study medicine, but although he was called 'Doctor' by his friends he never took a degree in the subject. On his return to England in 1718 he taught a system of shorthand that he had

invented. In 1724 he became a fellow of the ROYAL SOCIETY and published on shorthand in the *Philosophical Transactions*. In 1740 he inherited family property in Manchester and settled there. Although he was a notorious JACOBITE, Byrom declined to support the Young Pretender when he arrived in the town in 1745. His Jacobitism is a feature of his poetry, which includes the lines:

> God bless the king, God bless our faith's
> defender,
> God bless – no harm in blessing – the
> pretender;
> But who pretender is, and who is king,
> God bless us all! – that's quite another thing.

He also wrote hymns, of which the Christmas carol 'Christians awake' is the best known.

Byron, George Gordon, 6th Baron (1788–1824), one of the leading poets of the ROMANTIC MOVEMENT. He was the son of Captain George Byron by his second wife, Catherine Gordon. When her husband abandoned her she returned to her native Aberdeen, taking her son with her. In 1796 his uncle, the 5th Baron Byron, died childless, so that young George inherited the title and the estate of Newstead Abbey in Nottinghamshire. After Harrow and Trinity College, Cambridge, he returned to Newstead, where he dissipated himself until his mother upbraided him, and at the age of 21 he left for the continent. After two years touring, mainly in the Mediterranean, he returned to Newstead to find that his mother had just died. In 1812 he made his maiden speech in the House of Lords, defending the LUDDITES.

That year also saw the publication of *Childe Harold's Pilgrimage*, which – unlike Byron's earlier volume of poems, *The House of Idleness* (1807) – was well received. Even the *Edinburgh Review*, which had ridiculed the first collection with such scorn that Byron had been moved to retaliate with *English Bards and Scotch Reviewers*, found something to praise in it. Indeed *Childe Harold* announced the arrival of a major poet, and Byron was lionized. His handsome if somewhat effeminate features made him much sought after by women, of which he took every advantage.

In 1815 Byron married Annabella Milbanke, the daughter of a Durham country gentleman. But the marriage was a disaster despite the birth of a daughter, Ada. Lady Byron was convinced that her husband was having an incestuous relationship with his half-sister Augusta, his father's daughter by his first wife. Recently unearthed evidence leaves little doubt that her suspicions were well founded. When she left him and the story broke, Byron was disgraced. He left England permanently in 1816.

Initially Byron settled near Lake Geneva, where he scandalized even Shelley with his debauchery. One of the company, Jane Clairmont, finding herself pregnant by him, returned to England where their daughter Allegra was born. Byron meanwhile had gone to Italy, where he found similarly dissolute companions, including the count and countess Guiccioli, with whom he set up a *ménage à trois* in their palace in Ravenna. There he composed his greatest work, *Don Juan*. He also became involved with Italian liberals, one of whom was the countess's brother. When their activities became known to the Austrian authorities they were obliged to leave Ravenna and move to Livorno. There Byron became aware of a committee in London sympathetic to Greek nationalists in their struggle against the Turks. He arranged to represent the committee in Greece, and went there only to die, probably of malaria, in 1824. His death transformed him into the Romantic hero of Byronic legend.

FURTHER READING P. Grosskurth, *Byron* (1997).

C

cabinet, inner circle of senior government ministers. Although the expressions 'cabinet', 'cabinet council' and 'inner cabinet' were used of meetings of ministers in the 18th century, this does not mean that there was such a thing as cabinet government. On the contrary, it could be claimed that there was a movement towards less and less formal consultation between prime ministers and their colleagues as the period progressed.

Under WILLIAM III and ANNE there were regular meetings of bodies known as 'the lords of the committee' and 'the cabinet council'. It seems that the lords of the committee comprised the same ministers as the cabinet, save that the monarch was not present. By Anne's reign this had become formalized in weekly meetings of both bodies. The lords of the committee – comprising such ministers as the lord treasurer, the secretaries of state, the lord high admiral, the lord chancellor, the lord steward and even the archbishop of Canterbury – dealt with urgent business, usually to do with the war effort. Thus the secretary at war, or the paymaster of the forces abroad, would be called in to answer questions pertaining to the maintenance of armies in the field. Decisions would be taken on these matters, which would then be laid before the cabinet council with the queen present.

After Anne's death these arrangements were not sustained. Although the cabinet council continued as a body, including the chief ministers of state, it did not conduct the main business of the ministry. Sir Robert WALPOLE announced on GEORGE II's accession that he was 'against having the cabinet; no good ever came from them'. Instead he held meetings of an inner cabinet of which he and the two secretaries were the core, while other ministers attended on an ad hoc basis.

Such inner cabinets continued to meet under Walpole's successors. There was only a limited sense of collective responsibility, for ministers were often individually appointed by the king and not selected by the prime minister. At times, prime ministers stood up to the monarch, to insist on the appointment of supporters to ministerial posts, or on the dismissal of opponents. There were several such incidents in the century, the most critical arising in times of war, when the ministry was relatively strong. Thus crises over ministerial appointments arose in 1708, 1744, 1745, 1756–7 and 1782.

The long wars against France between 1793 and 1815, coupled with George III's incapacity, increased the powers of the prime minister and the cabinet. By 1800 the monarch usually accepted the unanimous advice of the cabinet. In 1812 the regent gave the cabinet the choice of prime minister.

Calcutta. *See* INDIA.

calendar reform of 1751. Until the 16th century western Europe employed the Julian calendar. By the time Gregory XIII became pope in 1572, this was ten days out of phase with the solar year, largely because each centennial year had been regarded as a leap year. To correct this the Gregorian calendar, named after the pope, was devised. It added ten days to the Julian calendar, and thereafter sought to keep pace with the solar year by making only every fourth centennial year a leap year.

Since this was a 'popish' measure, much of Protestant Europe, including England, declined to adopt it and continued to use the Julian calendar. The year 1600 was a leap year in both calendars, so that England remained only ten days behind the continent throughout the 17th century. In 1700, however, the Julian calendar added a leap day, while the Gregorian did not, so that thereafter England was eleven days behind: thus when it was 12 June in Paris it was 1 June in London. To make matters even more complicated the Julian calendar began the year on 25 March, while the Gregorian started it on 1 January, so that 12 January 1751 in Paris was 1 January 1750 in London. The two calendars with their different dates were distinguished as 'old style' and 'new style'.

To rectify this situation an act was passed in May 1751 that provided for the elimination of the eleven days between 3 and 13 September 1752, so that 2 September was to be followed by 14 September. The new year in 1753 was to open on 1 January. The resultant outcry – 'Give us back our eleven days' – was not entirely a superstitious reaction, since the change necessitated nice calculations about rents, leases, debts and wages as well as of saints' and holy days.

Camden, Charles Pratt, 1st Earl (1714–94), judge and politician. He was a close friend of PITT THE ELDER, in whose administration of 1757–61 he served as attorney general. In 1761 he became lord chief justice of the Court of Common Pleas, and presided over the case brought by John WILKES against the secretary of state's office for false arrest under a GENERAL WARRANT. Pratt, a judge of liberal principles, had no problem finding for the plaintiff, and declared general warrants (warrants in which those who were to be apprehended were not named) to be illegal. In 1765 he was ennobled as Baron Camden and made speeches in the House of Lords against the Stamp Act and the Declaratory Act. In his view the American slogan 'no taxation without representation' was entirely justified.

When Pitt, then earl of Chatham, formed a government in 1766, Camden became lord chancellor. He supported the ministry even when he disagreed with its colonial policies, but protested at its suppression of Wilkes, for which he was dismissed in 1770. He opposed Lord NORTH, supporting Chatham's stance against the government's attitude to the American colonies. Camden was appointed president of the council by Lord ROCKINGHAM, declined to serve under the FOX–NORTH coalition, but again became president of the council in the ministry of PITT THE YOUNGER in 1784. Two years later he was promoted to the earldom of Camden. During the debates on the REGENCY CRISIS in 1788 he determined that the queen's marriage had effectively naturalized her as a British subject, making her eligible to serve as a regent. His long-held view that jurors in libel cases should judge whether the matter complained of was libellous, as well as the fact of its publication, was embodied in the Libel Act of 1792.

Campbell, John, 2nd duke of Argyll. *See* ARGYLL, JOHN CAMPBELL, 2ND DUKE OF.

Camperdown, battle of (11 October 1797), British naval victory in the REVOLUTIONARY AND NAPOLEONIC WARS in which a squadron commanded by the veteran Admiral Adam Duncan inflicted a decisive defeat upon the fleet of Revolutionary France's Dutch satellite, the Batavian Republic. The action occurred some 24 km (15 miles) off the Dutch coastal village of Camperdown. Duncan's squadron of 16 ships of the line encountered an equal number of Dutch vessels.

A Scotsman of huge physique, Duncan was also an immensely experienced officer, whose service embraced the siege of Havana in 1762 and both reliefs of Gibraltar during the AMERICAN WAR OF INDEPENDENCE. In 1797, as commander of the North Sea Squadron, Duncan had faced the challenge of containing the Dutch fleet – an operation that was hindered by the dangerous mutiny at the Nore (*see* NAVAL MUTINIES OF 1797).

At Camperdown, Duncan adopted an approach that won the admiration of Horatio NELSON. His daring strategy of attacking the enemy's line of battle at right angles involved enduring the enemy's broadsides before his own gun crews could reply; in addition, because the Dutch possessed ships of shallower draught, Duncan also ran the risk of running aground if he proceeded too far inshore after puncturing their formation. The hotly contested engagement that followed rekindled memories of the great Anglo-Dutch naval clashes of the previous century. Duncan's aggressiveness and tactical skill resulted in overwhelming victory. Although Duncan's ships took a pounding, none was lost; by contrast eleven Dutch ships was captured, included both flagships.

While Duncan's victory had demonstrated many of the same qualities that were to gain fame for Nelson, Camperdown attracted relatively little publicity; as far as the British public were concerned, the French, not the Dutch, were the real enemy. Yet the success was important, not least because it demonstrated the continued efficiency and loyalty of the North Sea Squadron in the wake of the worrying Nore mutiny; it also eliminated the danger of Dutch naval support for a projected French invasion of Ireland. Duncan's leadership and skill was recognized through the award of the title of Viscount Duncan of Camperdown.

canals. Conveying freight by water was much cheaper than carrying it by road. Thus it cost about £2 to transport a ton of merchandise overland from Liverpool to Manchester, a journey that by river cost twelve shillings. Fortunately Britain was equipped with an extensive system of navigable rivers. There were 1100 km (700 miles) of natural, navigable waterways in England, which with improvement by engineers were increased to 1600 km (1000 miles) by 1700, and 2200 km (1400 miles) by 1760. But the most dramatic exploitation of navigable waterways came with the construction of canals in the second half of the 18th century.

The first was the Sankey Brook canal in Liverpool, initiated by an act of Parliament in 1755. The most renowned was undertaken in 1759 by James Brindley, who engineered a canal to take the duke of Bridgwater's coal from his mines at Worsley into Manchester. When the Worsley canal was completed in 1761 it so lowered the cost of transporting coal from the duke's mines that he was able to halve its price in Manchester.

Such economies were a big attraction to investment in canals. Brindley led the way, backed by Bridgewater, constructing a canal linking Manchester with Liverpool by 1767. They were followed by joint-stock companies, which raised enough money to create a network of canals, even though they cost £3000 a kilometre (£5000 a mile) to construct. Canals built by such companies included the Forth and Clyde canal, begun by John SMEATON in 1768, and the Trent and Mersey, completed in 1777, which with subsidiary canals eventually linked the manufacturing districts of the Midlands with the northern ports of Liverpool and Hull.

The subsequent construction of the Grand Junction canal enhanced communications between London and England's heartlands. By 1816, which saw the completion of the Leeds–Liverpool, canals not only connected all the main ports and manufacturing areas but had also spread to service the southern agricultural regions of Britain.

FURTHER READING C. Hadfield, *British Canals*

(1969); J. Rule, *The Vital Century: England's Developing Economy, 1714–1815* (1991).

Canning, George (1770–1827), politician, foreign secretary (1807–9, 1802–07) and Tory prime minister (1827). Canning was always regarded as an outsider because his mother was an actress, even though he had a brilliant career at Eton and Christ Church, Oxford. His youthful political inclinations were to the WHIGS, but the course of the French Revolution turned him into a Burkean conservative.

When Canning became a member of Parliament in 1794 he enlisted with the Pittites, becoming undersecretary of state in 1796. He was one of the principal contributors to the ANTI-JACOBIN journal, from 1797 to 1798. Not only was he a witty writer, but he was acknowledged as one of the great orators of the age. In 1800 he was made paymaster general, but resigned when PITT THE YOUNGER quit over CATHOLIC EMANCIPATION, which Canning also supported. On Pitt's return to office in 1804 he was made treasurer of the navy. After Pitt's death, Canning consciously assumed his mantle. Canning declined to join the MINISTRY OF ALL THE TALENTS, but accepted the post of foreign secretary under PORTLAND. In this post he masterminded the capture of the Danish fleet in 1807.

Canning quarrelled over strategy with the secretary at war, Lord CASTLEREAGH, to the extent of demanding his dismissal, which came about in 1809 after Canning and Castlereagh had fought a duel, in which the former was wounded in the leg. When Portland resigned in October, Canning left office, and in 1814 left England, not returning until 1816. Then he accepted the post of president of the BOARD OF CONTROL for INDIA in Lord LIVERPOOL's ministry. He was thus a minister at the time of the Tory reaction to radical agitation, which qualifies assessments of him as a 'liberal Tory' in the 1820s.

FURTHER READING P. Dixon: *George Canning: Politician and Statesman* (1976).

Cape St Vincent, battle of (14 February 1797), British naval victory over the Spanish during the REVOLUTIONARY AND NAPOLEONIC WARS. In late 1796, as the armies of the French revolutionary regime swarmed through Italy, the Royal Navy was obliged to withdraw from the Mediterranean, where it no longer possessed secure bases. Britain's Mediterranean Fleet was commanded by Admiral Sir John Jervis, who employed GIBRALTAR as a base from which to blockade the Atlantic ports of France's new ally, Spain. Jervis's subordinates included Commodore Horatio NELSON, who was assigned the task of evacuating British troops from Corsica.

On Valentine's Day 1797, a powerful Spanish fleet was intercepted by Jervis off Cape St Vincent while on passage from Cartagena to Cadiz. Jervis deployed 15 warships against 27 more heavily armed Spanish vessels. The Spanish fleet soon fell into disorder and became divided. In an effort to prevent the enemy from reuniting, Nelson took his ship, the 74-gun *Captain*, out of the British line of battle without orders. Although representing a technical breach of discipline, the importance of Nelson's action in heading off the enemy was recognized by Jervis, who signalled other ships to his aid; they included the *Excellent*, commanded by Nelson's staunch friend Captain Cuthbert COLLINGWOOD. After two Spanish vessels – the 80-gun *San Nicholas* and the more formidable three-decker *San Joseph* of 114 guns – collided in the subsequent fighting, Nelson led his men aboard the first, then used her as a springboard from which to capture the larger vessel. This spectacular feat was subsequently celebrated as 'Nelson's patent bridge for boarding First Rates'. Despite the odds against them, Jervis's men proceeded to capture two more Spanish vessels.

The battle gave early notice of the Royal Navy's ascendancy over the Spanish 'Grand Fleet'. Nelson, who sustained a rupture during the action, was compensated with a knighthood and his first taste of popular acclaim. Jervis gained the title earl of St Vincent.

capital punishment. *See* CRIME AND PUNISH-MENT.

caricatures. The later Georgian era was the 'golden age' of British political caricature. A tradition rooted in the propaganda broadsides of the English Civil War and nurtured during the first half of the 18th century finally reached its apogee during the long reign of GEORGE III.

Satirical prints had enjoyed an upsurge in popularity from the 1720s in consequence of the growing opposition to Sir Robert WALPOLE. Visual antiministerial propaganda surfaced in popular journals, illustrated ballads and as individual prints, and productions varied from crude woodcuts to fine engravings. Regardless of quality, such graphic images remained unfettered by government censorship, and they therefore provided a forum for popular expression that would have been unthinkable under the more authoritarian regimes across the Channel.

By mid-century, this lively native tradition of visual social commentary was beginning to absorb elements of caricature. The art of caricature had originated in Italy, where painters such as Pier Leone Ghezzi created humorous portraits of acquaintances by emphasizing their salient features. Some of those British artists who flocked to Florence and Rome in search of inspiration imbibed the genre. For most visiting artists caricature was an amusing sideline, although Thomas Patch (1725–82) specialized in grotesque group portraits of wealthy followers of the GRAND TOUR. While William HOGARTH's heavily satirical paintings and engravings had an undoubted impact upon the subsequent development of British caricature, the artist himself was at pains to draw a distinction between his own work and the output of men like Ghezzi. Indeed, in his 'Characters and Caricatures', reproduced on the subscription ticket for his *Marriage à la Mode* engravings, Hogarth sought to demonstrate that, while 'character' resulted from careful observation, 'caricature' was mere exaggeration.

At the very time when Hogarth was dismissing such foreign imports, a native tradition of political portrait caricature was emerging. One of its first exponents was the aristocratic George Townshend (1724–1807), a prominent soldier who was also a keen amateur artist. Even while serving as a brigadier at the siege of Quebec in 1759, he amused himself by producing waspish sketches of his lanky superior, General James WOLFE. Townshend had already directed his talents against other influential figures, including his former commanding officer, the duke of CUMBERLAND, whose rotund physique offered an obvious target. Although poorly executed by later standards, Townshend's attacks upon Cumberland and the NEWCASTLE–FOX ministry established important precedents: they represented deliberate attempts to provide caricatures of known politicians, and their impact was increased by the circulation of prints of them.

The prices of prints, which were sold 'plain' for sixpence and coloured for a shilling, placed them beyond all but an elite market. However, they reached a wider audience through display in print-shop windows, where crowds regularly gathered to inspect the latest releases.

The volatile British political scene of the 1760s gave fresh impetus to the satirical print. King George III's favourite Lord BUTE provided the butt for a wave of scurrilous attacks that employed a range of visual puns, while John WILKES was quick to harness the power of the printed image in his propaganda war with the government. In the provinces, an interest in caricature was kept alive by Lancashire's John Collier, better known as 'Tim Bobbin'. His 1773 collection, *Human Passions Delineated*, featured more than '120 Figures, Droll, Satirical, and Humourous'.

By the closing years of the AMERICAN WAR OF INDEPENDENCE the increased volume of satirical political prints was matched by a skilful deployment of caricature at the hands of James GILLRAY. With his technical brilliance, fertile imagination and ability to respond swiftly to topical themes, Gillray paved the way for the modern political cartoon. He provides a counterpoint to his friend Thomas ROWLANDSON, whose own interest in caricature centred upon a sardonic but sensitive observation of the contemporary social scene.

Gillray represented the high-water mark of British political caricature. Although his tradition was inherited and upheld into the reign of GEORGE IV by George Cruikshank (1792–1872) – the son of Gillray's competitor Isaac Cruikshank – the satirical etching rapidly lost its cutting edge. During the age of Peterloo the genre was increasingly replaced by mass-circulation shilling pamphlets aimed at ordinary workers. Many of these pamphlets were illustrated with woodcuts by Cruikshank, thereby providing at least some degree of continuity with the traditions of the previous century.

FURTHER READING D. Donald, *The Age of Caricature: Satirical Prints in the Reign of George III* (1996).

Caroline of Ansbach (1683–1737), queen consort of GEORGE II. She was born in Ansbach, the daughter of the margrave of Brandenburg-Ansbach. In 1696 she was orphaned, and the elector of Brandenburg became her guardian. She moved to Berlin, where her guardian's wife Sophia Charlotte, daughter of the electress Sophia of Hanover, took charge of her education. She was introduced to Leibniz, a frequent guest of Sophia Charlotte's. They encouraged her to resist marriage to the Archduke Charles, Habsburg claimant to the Spanish inheritance, on the grounds that it would require her conversion to Catholicism. Instead she married George Augustus, son of the future GEORGE I, in 1705.

Caroline accompanied her husband to London after he became prince of Wales, and took his side when George I quarrelled with him in 1717. She even tolerated the prince of Wales's mistresses, who included her own lady of the bedchamber, Mrs Howard. Although Mrs Howard became Lady Suffolk on the accession of George II, Caroline ensured that she did not influence the new king's choice of advisers. Thus the queen connived at Sir Robert WALPOLE's successful attempt to outmanoeuvre Sir Spencer COMPTON in the crisis over the premiership at the outset of the reign, and she remained one of Walpole's firmest supporters throughout later crises. As queen she cultivated relations with leading churchmen such as BERKELEY, BUTLER, CLARKE and HOADLY. She even had some say in the appointment of bishops. Her death from the complications of an umbilical rupture devastated George II. When she urged him on her deathbed to marry again he replied, 'No, I shall have mistresses.' 'That's no obstacle,' she replied. Her wit and intellect were always more than a match for his dull intelligence.

Carteret, John, 2nd Earl Granville (1690–1763), politician. At the age of five he succeeded to the barony of Carteret. He was educated at Westminster School and Christ Church, Oxford, where he acquired a deep and lasting knowledge of the classics in the original languages. He entered the House of Lords after his 21st birthday, although his first recorded speech was not until 1716.

In the Whig schism of the following year Carteret sided with STANHOPE and SUNDERLAND against 2nd Viscount TOWNSHEND and WALPOLE. He then went on a diplomatic mission to Scandinavia in which he succeeded in persuading the warring powers in the Northern War to enter negotiations. He also obtained concessions for British merchant ships in the Baltic. In 1721 he became secretary of state for the north. There ensued a struggle for power between him and his supporters on the one hand and Townshend and Walpole on the other.

Walpole overcame his rival when he got the duke of NEWCASTLE to replace him as secretary of state and persuaded the king to send Carteret to Ireland as lord lieutenant. There he had to deal with the aftermath of WOOD'S HALFPENCE, in which he was helped by his friendship with SWIFT, the chief critic of the copper coinage in the guise of the 'Drapier'. Carteret was reappointed to the lord lieutenancy of Ireland on the accession of GEORGE II, but was dismissed in 1730. Although he was offered another position, he preferred to go into opposition.

Carteret associated with William PULTENEY throughout the 1730s, and when Walpole finally fell, Carteret became secretary of state again. He made it his business to go with the king to Hanover in 1743. While on the continent he witnessed George II fighting at the battle of DETTINGEN from the safety of a coach. His closeness to George, cemented by his knowledge of German, led his critics to accuse him of preferring Hanoverian interests to those of Britain. The duke of Newcastle complained that his 'chief view in all that he proposes to do, is the making court to the king by preferring Hanoverian considerations to all others'. PITT THE ELDER openly attacked him in the Commons as 'an execrable, sole minister, who had renounced the British nation and seemed to have drunk of the potion described in poetic fictions, which make men forget their country', a charge with added venom in view of Carteret's well-known partiality for the bottle.

These attacks were somewhat unfair, for Carteret in fact had a much wider vision of Britain's role in Europe than that of a handmaiden to Hanover. He was anxious to restore British prestige on the continent to a position that it had not enjoyed since the days of his mentor Stanhope. Like Stanhope he fancied himself as the arbiter of Europe, and sought to build up a system of alliances that would guarantee the integrity of Austrian hereditary territories against Prussian and French aggression. He envisaged a grand alliance of Austria, Britain, the Dutch Republic, Hanover and Savoy such as had contained French aggression during the War of the SPANISH SUCCESSION. He took a step towards achieving this ambition by negotiating the treaty of Worms in 1743. Bourbon successes in Italy forced Austria to accept this treaty with Savoy and Britain in which Carteret committed Britain to extend subsidies to both countries. The Pelhams were appalled, Newcastle because Savoy fell within his sphere of interest as

secretary for the south, Henry PELHAM because of the fiscal commitment he would have to honour as first lord of the Treasury. Carteret's arrogance further salted the wounds, and they marked Carteret down for destruction.

Their chance came in 1744, when the shadow boxing that had marked the military engagements and diplomatic moves between the various forces aligned in the War of the AUSTRIAN SUCCESSION ended, and real fighting broke out when France declared war on Britain and Hanover in March, and on Austria in May, followed by an invasion of the Austrian Netherlands. Although French pressure on the Netherlands was partly relieved by an Austrian invasion of Alsace, this had to be called off when Prussia attacked Bohemia. These disasters for Austria and her allies caused them to look for Dutch assistance, but this was not forthcoming, largely because George II would not commit Hanover to the war as a principal.

The Pelhams became convinced that this reluctance was due to Carteret, and that in order to bring in the Dutch he must go. They therefore delivered an ultimatum to the king on 1 November 1744. Its gist was that either Earl Granville, as Carteret had become in October, should be dismissed, or they would resign. George protested and tried to negotiate with other politicians, but eventually had to yield to the Pelhams' demands. Granville left the ministry. George had given in with an ill grace, and continued to show preference for Granville. This led to another showdown with the Pelhams, this time in February 1746 in the middle of the '45 JACOBITE RISING. When the king refused to appoint William Pitt as secretary at war the ministers resigned. George turned to the earl of Bath and Granville to form a ministry but, although they tried, it only lasted 24 hours. Granville and Bath had no alternative but to resign, although after the fiasco it was observed that 'Lord Granville is as jolly as ever, laughs and drinks; owns it was mad, and that he would do it again tomorrow.'

In fact Granville never got the chance again to form a ministry, although he did return to office in 1751 as president of the council. He refused to help out Newcastle when he ran into difficulties in 1756, saying that 'You are now being served as you and your brother served me.' And in 1761 he stood up to Pitt when the Great Commoner talked of being 'responsible to the people', observing that ministers were responsible to the king.

FURTHER READING B. Williams, *Carteret and Newcastle* (1966).

Cartwright, Edmund (1743–1823), inventor and industrialist, the younger brother of John CARTWRIGHT. He was educated at Oxford and ordained a clergyman, obtaining a living in Leicestershire in 1779, and becoming prebendary of Lincoln in 1786. After a visit to Richard ARKWRIGHT's mill at Cromford he worked on a power loom, which he patented in 1785. He took out further patents after improving the machine in 1786, 1787 and 1790. In 1787 he installed his looms in a mill in Doncaster, where he also devised a wool-combing machine, patented in 1789. It was alleged to do the work previously done by 20 workers, and wool-combers petitioned the House of Commons against it. The application of steam to the power loom also threatened the livelihoods of hand-loom weavers. When a Manchester mill owner acquired some power looms his mill was burned down.

Cartwright never made much money from his invention, and at one time was bankrupt. He himself retired to the south of England and the service of the duke of Bedford. But the introduction of his machines in Bradford made a fortune for one mill owner, and led to Cartwright being lionized there.

Cartwright, John (1740–1824), political radical and reformer, the older brother of Edmund CARTWRIGHT. He was known as Major Cartwright from his commission in the Nottinghamshire militia of 1775. Before that, however, he had been an officer in the navy, rising to the rank of deputy commissary of the vice-admiralty court in Newfoundland. He declined to serve in the AMERICAN WAR OF INDEPENDENCE because of his sympathies with the rebellious colonists.

Instead Cartwright turned his attention to PARLIAMENTARY REFORM, publishing a tract *Take your Choice* in 1776, which advocated the secret ballot, universal manhood suffrage and equal electoral districts. He supported these radical proposals not so much by an appeal to natural rights as by a historical argument that claimed that Englishmen had enjoyed these constitutional liberties under the Anglo-Saxon kings, particularly Alfred, and that they had been usurped by the Normans. In 1780 he founded the Society for Constitutional Information. Although he stood for Parliament himself in his native Nottinghamshire, he was unsuccessful. He went on to campaign tirelessly for reform, travelling the country until an advanced age. To consolidate his reforming activities he founded Hampden Clubs, named after the parliamentary hero John Hampden (1594–1643) who was killed in the Civil War. His efforts earned him the title of 'the Father of Reform'.

Cary, John (d. 1720), Bristol merchant who contributed to the debates leading to the establishment of the BOARD OF TRADE in 1696. His main contribution was *An Essay on the state of England in relation to its trade, its poor and its taxes for carrying on the present war against France* (1695). Discrete parts of this tract, for example on the East India trade and Cary's proposals for the poor, were published separately, while the whole went through several editions, including French and Italian translations, between 1695 and 1745. Cary's tract provoked considerable interest at the time, John LOCKE praising it as 'the best discourse I ever read on that subject'. Cary's views were taken seriously by the Board of Trade when it was launched in 1696. One of Cary's proposals for the poor was the setting up of workhouses, a recommendation he himself implemented in Bristol in 1697. This proved to be so successful in reducing the poor rate that it was adopted by other towns, until a general act was passed in 1723 to permit their establishment.

Castle Howard, vast country house near Malton in Yorkshire. One of the most striking buildings in Britain, Castle Howard stands as a monument to the extraordinary architectural partnership of Sir John VANBRUGH and Nicholas HAWKSMOOR. Charles Howard 3rd earl of Carlisle expended a total of £78,240 2s. 10d. upon the extensive buildings and sprawling landscaped gardens that bear his name. Built largely between 1701 and 1712, the huge house engulfed the North Yorkshire hamlet of Henderskelfe, and continues to dominate the surrounding countryside.

Carlisle had called upon the talents of his friend Vanbrugh after the project's original architect, William Talman, proved troublesome. It was Vanbrugh's first architectural commission, and he recruited the assistance of the experienced Hawksmoor, who had previously worked with Sir Christopher WREN. Although the exact nature of the professional relationship between Vanbrugh and Hawksmoor remains the subject of debate, the pair undoubtedly represented a formidable team: the combination of Vanbrugh's architectural designs and Hawksmoor's inspired interpretations of them yielded spectacular results at both Castle Howard and BLENHEIM PALACE.

The main buildings of Castle Howard were executed in a monumentally BAROQUE style. Distinctive features include the entrance courtyard with its curving flanking arms, the spectacular south front, and the imposing entrance hall, topped by a tower and the first substantial dome to feature in British domestic architecture. Both Vanbrugh and Hawksmoor designed buildings independently of each other for the grounds. Vanbrugh's Temple of the Four Winds, built on a commanding knoll between 1726 and 1728, derives from Palladio's famous Villa Rotonda; this inspiration serves as a reminder that Vanbrugh was more in tune with changing architectural trends than such 'PALLADI-ANS' as Colen Campbell and Lord BURLINGTON appreciated. Hawksmoor's Mausoleum (1729–42) represents a contrasting vision of classical architecture, and he defended his design against the criticisms of Burlington, who felt that the pillars were arranged too closely together.

Castle Howard's extensive grounds feature mock fortifications, including an archway and towers. The gardens provide panoramic vistas, and contain statues suggestive of heroic themes. They also reveal the beginnings of a fresh approach to LANDSCAPE GARDENING, incorporating irregular features that diverge from the symmetrical designs of the typical baroque garden: for example, the Terrace Walk follows a curving course from house to temple, while Wray Wood is full of winding paths. Such features suggest that Vanbrugh had anticipated the coming trend for the picturesque and 'romantick'. The glories of Castle Howard more recently reached a worldwide audience when they formed the backdrop for an acclaimed television adaptation of Evelyn Waugh's *Brideshead Revisited*.

FURTHER READING C. Saumurez Smith, *The Building of Castle Howard* (1990).

Castlereagh, Robert Stewart, Viscount (1769–1822), Anglo-Irish politician, chief secretary for Ireland (1798–1801), secretary of state for war (1805–6, 1807–9) and foreign secretary (1812–22). He acquired the title Viscount Castlereagh in 1796 when his father became an earl. In 1816 his father was elevated to marquess, and on his father's death in 1821 Castlereagh became 2nd marquess of Londonderry.

Castlereagh was born in Ireland, and, after attending St John's College, Cambridge, was elected as a member for County Down to the Irish Parliament in 1790. There he supported the extension of the franchise to Roman Catholics, a vote that was recalled to his embarrassment in his later reactionary days. He also sat in the British Parliament from 1794 to 1798, when he resigned in order to take up the post of chief secretary to the lord lieutenant of Ireland. In that capacity he presided in Dublin Castle in the absence of the lord lieutenant throughout the IRISH REBELLION OF 1798. His insistence on the use of regular troops rather than the Irish militia ensured the suppression of the uprising. Afterwards he became the chief promoter of the UNION OF GREAT BRITAIN AND IRELAND as the only way to avoid Irish independence. He steered the bill through the Irish Parliament with a mixture of persuasion and bribery that secured its passage in June 1800. When he failed to persuade the king to accompany the union with CATHOLIC EMANCIPATION he resigned his post.

Castlereagh continued to advise on Irish affairs, however, and in 1802 returned to office under Addington as president of the BOARD OF CONTROL for India. In that post he displayed such a grasp of foreign as well as of Indian affairs that PITT not only kept him on as president but appointed him secretary of state for war in 1805. When he sought re-election for County Down after obtaining this post he was defeated, and had to be returned to the House of Commons for an English seat.

Castlereagh was at the war office under Pitt and PORTLAND, although not under GRENVILLE. He pursued a policy of active intervention against the Napoleonic empire. Thus he encouraged the opening up of the Iberian theatre under WELLINGTON, a strategy that eventually yielded dividends. He also promoted the expedition to Walcheren to capture Flushing and Antwerp in 1809, which ended in disaster and his dismissal. His dismissal was also connected in ways that remain obscure with a duel that Castlereagh fought with CANNING, whom he accused of double-dealing over ministerial appointments.

Castlereagh remained in opposition until 1812, when he became foreign secretary and leader of the House of Commons. As foreign secretary Castlereagh orchestrated the coalition against Napoleon, exhibiting great diplomatic skills, above all in 1814 when he went to the continent as minister plenipotentiary. His achievement in holding together the allies in the treaty of Chaumont in March of that year led to Napoleon's abdication. Castlereagh represented Britain at the Congress of Vienna (1814–15), where he found it more

difficult to get the allies to agree to the peace settlement than it had been keeping them together in the war effort. When Napoleon escaped from Elba and renewed the war Castlereagh was again in his element. Britain played a key role in the final defeat of the emperor at WATERLOO and in the treaty of Vienna of 1815.

After the war Castlereagh's reputation steadily declined as he became identified with the repressive measures taken by LIVERPOOL's government against radicals. As leader of the House of Commons he had to introduce such bills as that for suspending habeas corpus in 1817, since the home secretary, Lord Sidmouth – who was primarily responsible for enforcing it – sat in the Lords. Castlereagh thus became the prime target of radical resentment. Shelley singled him out as one of the chief perpetrators of the Peterloo massacre in his *Mask of Anarchy*. 'I saw Murder on the way – / He had a mask like Castlereagh.' Castlereagh was so unpopular that crowds cheered at his funeral following his suicide in 1822.

FURTHER READING J.W. Derry, *Castlereagh* (1976).

Catholic emancipation. The long-running problem of the status of Catholics within a Protestant kingdom came to a head after the UNION OF BRITAIN AND IRELAND in 1800. Prime Minister William PITT THE YOUNGER wanted to give Irish Catholics full citizenship, removing all statutory restrictions on their rights – for example, allowing them to stand for Parliament, which the Test Act of 1678 prevented. GEORGE III, however, refused to grant this concession, arguing that it would violate his coronation oath to protect the constitution in church and state. The king held out and Pitt resigned. The issue, however, refused to go away and polarized the political debate between those who insisted that the constitution was essentially Protestant, and those who urged that to keep a majority of the Irish out of full participation would jeopardize the stability of the realm. It was not resolved until Catholic Emancipation was conceded in 1829.

Catholics. The number of Roman Catholics in 18th-century Britain is impossible to determine with any accuracy. The best estimates suggest that they were around 1.2% of the population in 1700, and that, while their numbers probably increased as the century progressed, the increase was not in line with the rise of the overall number of inhabitants, so that by 1800 they probably constituted less than 1%. Moreover, the increase occurred in the lower ranks of society, principally from the influx of Irish immigrants. Catholic noble and gentry families, the traditional mainstay of Catholicism, declined, and with them the number of priests.

It has been suggested that the Catholics were similar to any other nonconformist sect, and while there is much to make this view compelling, there were too many differences for it to be convincing. They certainly shared some characteristics of the DISSENTERS, for example, their loose non-parochial organization, the important role played by the laity, and their strength in areas where Anglicanism was weak. But they were a much more international body than most Protestant sects, and would not condone any communication with them. Moreover, in the early 18th century they were still regarded as a threat by Protestants, and the penal laws remained on the statute book. They were rarely enforced, however, except in years of JACOBITE RISINGS. Indeed there was much fraternization between Catholics and Protestants in the upper ranks of society. This trend was encouraged by the formation of the 'Catholic Committee' in 1782. In the later 18th century the political elite relaxed its anti-Catholic stance, and even introduced measures of relief, tolerant measures such as the Catholic Relief Act of 1778 allowing Catholics to hold commissions in the army. Such relaxations, however, were unwelcome among the lower orders, where fears of 'popery' still endured. Thus the Catholic Relief Act precipitated the GORDON RIOTS of 1780.

FURTHER READING E. Duffy, *Peter and Jack: Roman Catholics and Dissent in 18th-century England* (1983).

Cato's Letters, series of tracts attacking corruption, written by John TRENCHARD and Thomas Gordon, a Whig writer notorious for his anti-clericalism. The *Letters* first appeared weekly in the *London Journal* in 1720, and were later published in four volumes. They initially attacked those responsible for the SOUTH SEA BUBBLE, calling for the punishment of the governor and directors of the South Sea Company. They went on to develop a critique of corruption that informed 'Country' ideology (*see* COUNTRY PARTY) and opposition to the government through the ministry of WALPOLE and beyond. American critics of GEORGE III's ministers used the thesis of *Cato's Letters* to expose what they considered to be a conspiracy to undermine the liberties of Englishmen. The essence of this thesis is encapsulated in the 18th letter, entitled 'The terrible tendency of public corruption to ruin a state exemplified in that of Rome and applied to our own'.

Cavendish, Georgiana, duchess of Devonshire. *See* DEVONSHIRE, GEORGIANA CAVENDISH, DUCHESS OF.

Cavendish, Henry (1731–1810), scientist. Cavendish was the grandson of the 2nd duke of Devonshire. He was educated at Peterhouse, Cambridge, but left without taking a degree. He then settled down to live as a recluse on Clapham Common, where he conducted mathematical and scientific experiments. He was principally renowned for his discoveries about the properties of gases in the atmosphere, on which subject he read a paper to the Royal Society in 1766 and published *Experiments on Air* in 1784. Thereafter he made no further discoveries about the atmosphere, but did give a paper to the Royal Society in 1795 on the density of the earth. On his death he left a fortune of £1,175,000.

Cavendish, William, 4th duke of Devonshire. *See* DEVONSHIRE, WILLIAM CAVENDISH, 4TH DUKE OF.

censorship. Control of the PRESS had been a major concern of the Stuarts. The Restoration Parliament passed a Licensing Act whereby all publications had to be submitted to an official censor before being printed. Thus religious sermons and tracts had to be given the *imprimatur* of a bishop, legal disquisitions required the approval of the lord chancellor, while works of history had to be submitted to a secretary of state. However, the Licensing Act never became permanent, having being passed only for a specified period. It lapsed temporarily between 1680 and 1685, and permanently in 1695. Thereafter there was no pre-publication censorship, though authors, printers and booksellers (publishers) remained subject to the draconian laws of libel, until these were amended by the LIBEL ACT in 1792. Censorship of the THEATRE was introduced in 1737 by a Licensing Act which obliged playwrights to submit their scripts to the lord chamberlain before they could be performed. This came about as a result of increasingly vehement attacks from the stage – such as the notorious *Festival of the Golden Rump* (1736) – upon the royal family and the leading ministers. The powers of the lord chamberlain's office to censor plays survived beyond the immediate motive of political censorship until the 1960s, being exercised latterly to remove material deemed to be morally offensive.

census. In the 18th century it was generally believed that populousness reflected a nation's well-being. A large and growing population was held to be healthy for a country's economy and its ability to wage war. The British were reluctant to gauge the exact number of Britons, however, on the grounds that a census would be an interference with liberty. A proposal to enumerate the population failed to be approved by Parliament in 1753 largely on these grounds. It was left to other countries, such as Sweden and the United States of America, to lead the way. The needs of defence, however, led to adult males being identified for service in the militia after 1757 and in the armed forces in 1798. This paved the way for the first official census of England, Scotland and Wales in 1801. It numbered the British population at 10,777,600. Thereafter there were decennial censuses in Great Britain. The first four were conducted by John Rickman (1771–1840), a pioneer statistician. He attempted to project the population figures back from 1801, using information provided by clergymen from parish records. The figures he extrapolated have been superseded by those provided in E.A. Wrigley and R. Schofield, *The Population History of England and Wales 1548–1871: A Reconstruction* (1989).
SEE ALSO POPULATION.

Chambers, Sir William (1726–96), public architect of the late 18th century. He was born in Sweden of Scottish parents. After studying architecture in France and Italy, he began his career at Kew Gardens in 1757. His most important publication, a *Treatise on Civil Architecture*, appeared in 1759. The following year Chambers was appointed along with Robert ADAM as 'joint architects of his Majesty's works', and in 1769 he was made comptroller of the Board of Works. He was elected a fellow of the ROYAL SOCIETY in 1776, and became the first treasurer of the Royal Academy in 1778. By 1782 he was surveyor general. His main public commission was to build Somerset House, between the Strand and the Thames in London, for government offices.
SEE ALSO ARCHITECTURE; LANDSCAPE GARDENING.

charity. The 18th century prided itself on being 'an age of benevolence'. Whereas in the previous century individual benefactors had been in the forefront of charitable endeavour, establishing almshouses and endowing hospitals and schools, now collective efforts were prominent, with subscriptions being raised for charitable purposes. There was even a Charitable Corporation, which lent small sums to enable journeymen to set up their own enterprises, although this collapsed in 1732 owing to the fraudulent practices of its administrators. Other endeavours, such as the charity-school movement, were more successful. Charity-school classes promoted the teachings of the Church of England; this strong religious component – which aimed to counter the influence of rival doctrines – was bolstered by basic instruction in reading, writing and arithmetic. A largely urban phenomenon, the free charity schools provided a model for the SUNDAY SCHOOLS that emerged after 1780.

Typical of the institutions set up by subscription were the Marine Society to get poor boys off the streets and into the navy, and the Magdalen Hospital to free penitent prostitutes from their dependence on bawds and pimps and place them in domestic service. The Marine Society was founded in 1756 and within three years had raised nearly £25,000 from its subscribers. The Magdalen, founded in 1758, had a very eminent list of fashionable subscribers. These institutions provided a model for later collective endeavours such as the Society for the Relief of the Infant Poor in London (1769) and the Philanthropic Society (1788). How far these initiatives reflected genuine philanthropy or were motivated by less worthy instincts, such as the pride and vanity of individuals, or the collective anxieties of the upper and middle classes about the socially disruptive potential of the destitute, was much discussed by contemporaries and still informs historical debate.

SEE ALSO CORAM, THOMAS; HANWAY, JONAS; HOSPITALS; SOCIETY FOR THE PROMOTION OF CHRISTIAN KNOWLEDGE; SOCIETY FOR THE PROPAGATION OF THE GOSPEL IN FOREIGN PARTS.

Charlotte Sophia, princess of Mecklenburg-Strelitz (1744–1818), queen consort of GEORGE III, whom she married in 1761 within hours of meeting him for the first time. It seems nevertheless to have been a love match, the couple setting an example of matrimonial constancy unique in the Hanoverians. They also had 15 children. Charlotte played no part in British politics, except when used as a pawn by PITT THE YOUNGER in the REGENCY CRISIS of 1788. Her devotion to her husband through the traumas of his illness and the agonies of the Regency was truly exemplary.

Chatham, William Pitt, 1st earl of. See PITT, WILLIAM, THE ELDER, 1ST EARL OF CHATHAM.

Chatsworth, the Derbyshire home of the Cavendishes, dukes of Devonshire, rightly regarded as the 'Palace of the Peak'. Designed by William Talman between 1687 and 1688, it virtually replaced an Elizabethan mansion with a building on massive lines. It has been suggested that it was one of the models for 'Timon's villa' in POPE's *Epistle to Lord Burlington* – those country houses that Pope and others regarded as monuments to the bad taste of the Whig oligarchs of Walpolian England. Certainly the Emperor Fountain, which shoots a jet of water up to 12 m (40 feet) high, is the prime example of the misuse of water – 'in useless columns tost' – that the poet satirized in his *Epistle to Lord Bathurst*. When Celia FIENNES visited the house in 1697 there were even more water effects, but these were largely replaced by Capability Brown (*see* LANDSCAPE GARDENING) in the early 1760s, when the formal gardens that so impressed Fiennes were also swept away and the whole park landscaped. About the same time James Paine added a new wing to the north and stables to the northeast.

Chatterton, Thomas (1752–70), poet. Chatterton was born in Bristol, the son of a charity-school teacher who died before he was born. His father had been sexton of St Mary's Redcliffe, acquiring from the church fragments of medieval manuscripts, which his mother, a dame-school teacher, used as scraps of paper for household purposes. Chatterton was slow to learn, and his mother regarded him at the age of six as 'little better than an absolute fool'. But he became fascinated by the manuscript fragments, and learned to read in order to decipher their meaning. He then made rapid progress, became an insatiable reader, and was entered at the Bluecoat School as a scholar. At the

age of ten he published a poem, 'The Last Epiphany or Christ coming to Judgement'.

The interest in the Middle Ages aroused by the manuscripts led Chatterton to write poems in a medieval style, which he passed off as originals by a 15th-century monk, Thomas Rowley. The first of these was written in 1765, although none were published until after his death. In 1767 Chatterton started an apprenticeship with a Bristol attorney. He was so exploited by his employer that he threatened suicide. This led to his being released from his apprenticeship. He then went to London hoping to set himself up as a professional writer. He failed to obtain recognition, and eventually committed suicide on 24 August 1770. After his death he was taken up by the Romantics as the 'marvellous boy'. Robert SOUTHEY published a subscription edition of his works in 1803, while Shelley sang his praises in *Adonais*, and Keats dedicated *Endymion* to him.

FURTHER READING L. Kelly, *The Marvellous Boy* (1971).

Chesterfield, Philip Dormer Stanhope, 4th earl of

(1694–1773), politician and diplomat, also remembered for his epigrammatic and urbane *Letters to his Son*. As a member of Parliament from 1715 until he succeeded to the peerage on the death of his father in 1726, Chesterfield showed an inclination to support the Whigs in power. Thus he denounced the Tory authors of the treaty of UTRECHT in his maiden speech, and in 1722 supported an increase in the armed forces, for which he was rewarded with the post of captain of the gentlemen pensioners in 1723. He resisted WALPOLE's overtures, however, rejecting the offer of the Order of the Garter in 1725 as 'one of the toys Bob gave his boys'. The prime minister retaliated by depriving him of his post.

On the accession of George II the new king made Chesterfield a lord of the bedchamber and a privy councillor. Walpole was reluctant to have him made a minister, and so he was sent as ambassador to the Hague from 1728 to 1732. While

there he helped to negotiate the second treaty of Vienna in March 1731 by which Britain guaranteed the succession of Maria Theresa to the Habsburg territories. He also met Mlle du Bouchet, by whom he had a son who was to be the recipient of the posthumously published *Letters*. Described by Dr Johnson as teaching 'the manners of a dancing master and the morals of a whore', the *Letters* were nonetheless prescribed to would-be gentlemen for many generations afterwards, and became widely known and admired.

Although Chesterfield had been reconciled with Walpole sufficiently to accept the Garter at last in 1730 and to become lord steward, he opposed the excise scheme in 1733 (*see* EXCISE CRISIS), for which he was dismissed from the stewardship. He compounded his offence by marrying Petronilla von Schulenberg, the daughter of George I by his mistress the duchess of Kendal, for which he was barred from court. Their marriage was one of convenience, for they lived next door to each other and Chesterfield openly kept a mistress, Fanny Shirley. In 1737 Chesterfield made his most renowned parliamentary speech, in opposition to the Licensing Bill which obliged playwrights to submit their plays to the lord chamberlain's office for permission to perform them. Although this and other sallies against Walpole failed to secure their immediate objectives, they amounted to a sustained and vigorous opposition that contributed to the fall of the prime minister.

For some time Chesterfield remained *persona non grata* to George II, who tried to deny the former's wife a legacy left by George I to her mother when she died in 1743. Chesterfield sued the crown for the amount due, until the king settled out of court for £20,000. Chesterfield continued to oppose the new ministry, particularly in the press, where he used the pseudonym 'Geoffrey Broadbottom'. Thus the name of the BROADBOTTOM ADMINISTRATION was inspired by him, and he was included in it as lord lieutenant of Ireland in 1745. The new prime minister Henry PELHAM insisted on his appointment, even though the king expostulated that 'he should have nothing'.

Chesterfield was resident in Dublin throughout the '45 JACOBITE RISING, offering sterling support to the government in both Ireland and Britain. In 1746 he returned to England to assume the post of secretary of state, though he resigned in 1748 in protest at the duke of NEWCASTLE's resistance to negotiations for peace with France. He never held office again, though he continued to attend the House of Lords until increasing deafness led him to stop attending in 1755. His one great contribution to legislation was his support of the CALENDAR REFORM OF 1751.

FURTHER READING C. Franklin, *Lord Chesterfield: His Character and Characters* (1993).

children. The 18th century has been seen as creating a 'new world' for children. Instrumental in the alleged change were the views of John LOCKE expressed in *An Essay concerning Human Understanding* (1690). This challenged the notion of original sin by arguing that there were no innate ideas, the mind at birth being a blank sheet upon which information derived from experience was entered, and then processed by reason. It followed that, instead of breaking the child's will, parents and educators should inculcate experiences conducive to socially acceptable behaviour. This more liberal approach made childhood a different state from that known previously. Indeed the notion of the years between infancy and adolescence being a distinct stage in development is seen as a concept arising from this new approach. Hence the publication of books aimed specifically at children during the 18th century. John Newbury is held to have launched the publication of such literature with *A Little Pretty Pocket-Book* (1744).

The extent to which these trends did alter attitudes towards children, however, is debatable. They probably had little if any impact on the offspring of the labouring poor. If anything their lot got worse as the exploitation of child labour became more extensive, the most notorious example being

that of the chimney sweeps (*see also* INDUSTRY). Despite the protests of such figures as the poet William BLAKE and a statute aimed at the control of the trade in 1788, young boys continued to be used to sweep the narrow, twisting flues of the ever-increasing rows of terraced houses, which were the most conspicuous signs of the growth of towns in the latter half of the century. The middle-class occupants of those houses, however, might have treated their own children more liberally than the 'middling sort' had earlier, as ideas on child rearing trickled down from the upper classes. It was at the level of the aristocracy and gentry that the new notions probably had most impact.

SEE ALSO EDUCATION.

Chippendale, Thomas (1718–79), furniture designer and maker. He was the son of a joiner in Otley, in the West Riding of Yorkshire, and learned the craft of making furniture from his father. By 1750 he had established his own workshop in London. His furniture was advertised in *The Gentleman and Cabinet-Maker's Director* (1754), one of the first trade catalogues for furniture. It attracted orders that made him the most famous furniture maker of the century. Some of his best work is preserved in Harewood House and Nostell Priory in his native county. He is particularly celebrated for his hooped-back chairs.

SEE ALSO FURNITURE.

Churchill, John, 1st duke of Marlborough. *See* MARLBOROUGH, JOHN CHURCHILL, 1ST DUKE OF.

Churchill, Sarah, 1st duchess of Marlborough. *See* MARLBOROUGH, SARAH CHURCHILL, 1ST DUCHESS OF.

Church of England. The established church was central to the life of 18th-century England. The monarch, as supreme governor of the church 'insofar as the law of Christ allows', was not obliged to conform to the church until after the ACT OF SETTLEMENT of 1701 came into operation on the accession of GEORGE I in 1714. Previously there had been no such requirement, and the anomaly of a Roman Catholic king in James II's reign had produced friction, while WILLIAM III, as a lax member of the Dutch Reformed Church, had also provoked criticism. Queen MARY and her sister ANNE were the only pious Anglicans to wear the crown since the reign of Charles I.

In theory too, office holders under the crown had to be in communion with the Church of England, according to the Test Act of 1673, as had members of corporations under the Corporation Act of 1661. Neither statute was repealed until 1828, so that England was in the view of some historians a 'confessional state'. In practice there were so many exceptions to this rule for Protestant DISSENTERS that others maintain that the Church of England was partially disestablished in 1689 with the passing of the TOLERATION ACT.

It has been claimed that the Church of England in the 18th century slept the sleep of the comfortable. Its BISHOPS have been accused of being careerists who neglected their duties. Against this it has been asserted that they were no more lax in their discipline than their predecessors under the later Stuarts, but that the requirement to attend Parliament and sit on the bench of bishops in the House of Lords was a major constraint on the time they could devote to their dioceses. Since Parliament met in annual session after 1689 – whereas before its meetings had been sporadic – this was a call on them that previous bishops had not found to be so irksome. The inferior clergy have also been much criticized for such practices as pluralism and non-residence. There were about 10,000 parishes in England and Wales whose ministers were meant to minister to the needs of their parishioners, performing and registering baptisms, marriages and burials. Yet many parishes had no resident minister, being in the care of poorly paid curates. Again the poverty rather than the cupidity of clergymen has been cited as the principal cause of pluralism and non-residence (*see* QUEEN ANNE'S BOUNTY). Insofar as the Church

of England lost touch with the people, this was an institutional rather than a personal failing.

The growth of population and its redistribution into manufacturing towns put a strain on the parochial system. It was difficult to provide for the masses, since new parishes required an act of Parliament. Against this, however, it has been pointed out that there was no such restriction on the building of chapels of ease (churches built to serve those living at a distance from a parish church), but while some new parish churches were constructed, there was not as much effort put into church building as there might have been. The most notorious failure to provide new churches came when an opportunity was presented to build fifty new ones in London by an act of Parliament of 1712. In the event only about a dozen were constructed. This represented a failure of the will, which did mean that when others such as the METHODISTS tried to fill the gap the Church of England had only itself to blame.

SEE ALSO BANGORIAN CONTROVERSY; CONVOCATION CONTROVERSY; EVANGELICAL REVIVAL; FEATHERS TAVERN PETITION.

FURTHER READING J. Walsh, C. Haydon and S. Taylor (eds.), *The Church of England c.1689–1833* (1993).

Church of Scotland, the established church in Scotland, originally founded along Presbyterian lines in the 16th century. During the 17th century attempts by the Stuarts to impose bishops and a prayer book upon the Scottish church – 'the kirk' – provoked resistance. In the GLORIOUS REVOLUTION the Presbyterians sided with William of Orange, and in the Settlement of 1689 episcopacy was abolished. The bishops and their supporters set up a separate Episcopal Church of Scotland. The Scottish Toleration Act of 1712 was passed in an attempt to protect Episcopalians from the intolerance of Presbyterians.

In the UNION OF ENGLAND AND SCOTLAND in 1707 the independence of the Presbyterian Church was recognized, clauses in the statute frustrating any attempt to interfere with its establishment.

When an act was passed by Parliament in 1712 to restore lay patronage to the Scottish church, complaints were raised that this violated the guarantees in the Act of Union, for the right of lay patrons to appoint ministers to church livings had been abolished in the Revolution. With the abolition of the Scottish Parliament in 1707, the general assembly of the kirk to some extent replaced it as the only representative body able to articulate Scottish sentiments.

The general assembly became involved as arbiter in a number of disputes that racked the kirk for the rest of the century. One of the first was the so-called 'marrow' controversy. This was started by the publication in 1718 of a new edition of *The Marrow of Modern Divinity*, first published in 1645. It originally contributed to the puritan debate over the covenant of works and the covenant of grace, and argued that the second had completely superseded the first. This position was denounced by an act of the assembly in 1720 as antinomianism, the belief that faith and the grace of God can release individuals from their obligation to obey the moral law. Twelve ministers entered a protest against the act, for which they became known as the twelve apostles or marrowmen.

One of the marrowmen, Ebenezer Erskine, led a secession from the Church of Scotland in 1733, in protest at an act of the assembly that confirmed the rights of patrons over those of congregations. The seceders formed an associate presbytery, which had enough members by 1744 to establish an associate synod. At its first meeting, however, dissensions among the seceders over the terms of the 'burgher oath' became manifest. The oath of burgesses in Edinburgh, Glasgow and Perth pledged them to uphold 'the true Protestant religion presently professed within this realm and authorized by the laws thereof'. To some this was to swear to maintain the established church from which they had just seceded. In 1746 these dissenters in turn seceded from the associate synod to set up the general associate synod. The rival bodies became known as the burgher

and anti-burgher synods. The two were not reunited until 1820.

FURTHER READING C. Brown, *The Social History of Religion in Scotland since 1730* (1987).

civil list, moneys voted by Parliament for the support of the royal family and household. The distinction between the crown's domestic finances and the state's was unknown before the GLORIOUS REVOLUTION. Royal revenues from crown lands and other assets, together with taxes voted by Parliament, were supposed to pay for the living costs of the royal family and the expenditure on such organs of state as the army and the navy. During the reign of WILLIAM III the traditional distinction between 'ordinary' and 'extraordinary' expenditure was converted into the private finances of the king and the public finances of the state, Parliament voting him £700,000 per annum in 1698 for his 'ordinary' expenses. This became known as the civil list. It was voted at the start of a new reign and could become a political issue. Thus in 1727 a generous grant to the incoming GEORGE II helped WALPOLE, who had engineered it, to retain his post as prime minister. The resort to Parliament by the spendthrift prince of Wales in GEORGE III's reign in order to clear his debts caused embarrassment both to his family and to his political allies.

Claim of Right (1689), the Scottish equivalent of the BILL OF RIGHTS. It was passed by the Convention of Estates that met in Edinburgh in 1689.

The Claim of Right was much more radical than its English counterpart, claiming that James VII had converted the constitution from 'a legal, limited monarchy to an arbitrary, despotic power'. By his 'inverting all the ends of government' he had 'forfaulted' the throne, a forfeiture that included his son and the heirs of both. As with the Bill of Rights, appended to it was a list of the king's actions that were declared illegal. Similarly the crown was offered to WILLIAM and MARY. The most controversial clause in the Claim was that which abolished episcopacy in Scotland (*see* CHURCH OF SCOTLAND).

Clapham sect, EVANGELICAL group. It was so named after the residence in Clapham of a number of evangelicals, also known as 'saints', who attended Holy Trinity Church, Clapham, during the incumbency of its rector John Venn from 1793 to 1813. These included Zachary Macaulay, Henry Thornton, Hannah MORE and William WILBERFORCE. Macaulay, father of the Whig historian Thomas, had experienced slavery at first hand in Jamaica, and in 1793 became the first governor of Sierra Leone, the African colony for free slaves. He settled in Clapham High Street in 1803 and there produced the *Christian Observer*, the main Evangelical organ, which campaigned for the abolition of the slave trade. Along with Thornton and Wilberforce, Macaulay devoted himself to this cause, and the ending of the slave trade in 1807 owed much to their efforts.

Clarke, Samuel. *See* DEISM.

Clarkson, Thomas (1760–1846), campaigner for the abolition of the SLAVE TRADE. As a graduate student at St John's College, Cambridge, Clarkson won a prize essay on the slave trade. When he published the essay it brought him to the attention of Granville SHARP, William WILBERFORCE and others engaged in the enterprise. He became a member of a committee for the suppression of the slave trade in 1787.

Whereas most of the committee members were Quakers, Clarkson himself – although sympathetic to the Friends, and author of a life of William PENN – remained an Anglican. He was indeed a deacon in the Church of England, and preached sermons and published tracts against slavery itself as well as the slave trade. In 1789 he even went to France to try to persuade the French revolutionary leaders to outlaw slavery in their colonies. His industry in travelling through England to draw attention to the issue contributed to the breakdown of his health in 1794, and he had to retire from active involvement in the campaign for nine years.

Shortly after his return, the efforts of those who had agitated for the abolition of the slave trade were crowned with success when an act of Parliament was passed to suppress it in 1807. Clarkson then devoted himself to the abolition of slavery in the British empire, which was accomplished in 1833.

class. Since the Industrial Revolution it has become common to discuss social structure in terms of three classes: upper, middle and lower. Although the term 'class' was used occasionally to describe social categories in the 18th century, it was not generally employed to mean a horizontal stratum, but rather 'type', as in a class of battleship. More usual were analyses in terms of 'ranks' and 'degrees'. Thus Gregory KING in the 1690s drew up a famous table ranking society into 26 groups, ranging from temporal and spiritual lords at the top to 'vagrants as gypsies, thieves, beggars etc' at the bottom.

King himself divided the population into two categories, dividing those whom he claimed were increasing the wealth of the country from those allegedly decreasing it. This was a rather idiosyncratic division based on his calculations of income and expenditure per family, which led him to claim that over a quarter of the population were dependent upon charity, public or private, to subsist. While the data on which he reached this conclusion are suspect, it has been largely substantiated by investigations into the incidence of poor relief. It does appear that, at times of dearth at least, maybe 1 million people were officially paupers. This substratum of the population can too easily be ignored in considerations of class structure in the 18th century.

Another substratum hidden in King's calculations consisted of domestic servants, whom he subsumed under the household units. Yet domestic service was one of the biggest employers of labour, especially of female labour, in the century, and such servants need to be added to the labourers who formed the bulk of the unskilled workers in the period. They did not form part of a working class at that time, for urbanization and industrialization had not yet brought into being a proletariat. Contemporaries referred to labourers and servants collectively as 'the lower orders'.

Contemporaries also grouped categories above this level into 'the middling sort', increasingly referred to as the 'middle classes' or even, more rarely, 'the middle class'. This middle class was a rather elastic concept, which could be stretched to include craftsmen at the bottom and professional men such as lawyers and the clergy at the top. As the century progressed these emerged as a much more cohesive grouping, different from the mass of the labouring poor below them and the ARISTOCRACY above them.

FURTHER READING R. Porter, 'English society in the 18th century revisited' in J. Black (ed.), *British Politics and Society from Walpole to Pitt 1742–1789* (1990).

Cleland, John (1710–89), novelist and writer. Cleland acquired the reputation of being a pornographer after the publication in 1748 and 1749 of the two parts of his *Memoirs of a Woman of Pleasure*, better known as the eponymous tale of *Fanny Hill*. After attending Westminster School, Cleland went into the service first of the Levant Company and then of the EAST INDIA COMPANY, serving them in Smyrna and Bombay respectively. He left India under a cloud and returned to Europe. His attempts to set up in business failed and he was imprisoned for debt in the Fleet. It was while in prison that he began to write his erotic novel. The publication of the first part does not seem to have provoked criticism, but the appearance of the second was used to arraign him before the privy council. The motive, however, was as much political as moral, for Cleland had entered a controversy over the merits of executing Bosavern Penlez for riotous behaviour in 1749. Rioters had destroyed a brothel in a court just off the Strand, and Penlez had been arrested as their leader. The government justified his execution on the grounds that the riot presented a serious threat to property. Opponents of the severity used against Penlez claimed that an attack on a brothel was more deserving of commendation than condemnation, and that Penlez had been made a scapegoat, the evidence against him – that of the brothel keeper and his wife – being tainted. Cleland entered the debate on 7 November 1749 with a tract *The Case of the Unfortunate Bosavern Penlez*. He sympathized with the 'harmless unthinking lad' who had unfortunately got caught up in the sacking of the brothel after having had too much to drink. The very next day Cleland was hauled before the council to answer for the publication, not of the tract, but of *Fanny Hill*. At least one privy councillor sympathized with him, however, for Lord Granville procured for Cleland a pension of £100 a year. This and the profits from the printing of *Fanny Hill* in one volume in 1750 made him financially independent. His next and last novel was *Memoirs of a Coxcomb* (1751). Thereafter he devoted himself to plays and newspaper articles and in the 1760s turned his attention to linguistic studies.

FURTHER READING W.H. Epstein, *John Cleland: Images of a Life* (1974).

Clinton, Henry (1738–95), general who became commander in chief of British forces during the AMERICAN WAR OF INDEPENDENCE. A capable and experienced soldier, Clinton had the misfortune to inherit the unenviable task of subduing Britain's rebellious American colonists. Born in Newfoundland, where his father was the governor, Clinton served in the New York militia before returning to England and joining the Coldstream Guards. He participated in the victorious German campaigns during the closing phase of the SEVEN YEARS WAR, winning a reputation as a gifted officer. Steady promotion followed, and by 1772 Clinton was a major general. In 1775, at the outbreak of the American war, Clinton was despatched to fight against the rebels, and soon earned promotion to lieutenant general. After witnessing the blood bath at Bunker Hill, he served in the south and New York before replacing Sir William HOWE as commander in chief in 1778.

Clinton's assumption of command coincided with a period of changing strategy: the entrance of France into the conflict prompted the London government to place increased emphasis upon safeguarding British possessions in the Caribbean. In consequence, it was decided to concentrate the army at the port of New York, from where the West Indies could be swiftly reinforced. Clinton's withdrawal from Philadelphia was handled with great skill, but the evacuation of the revolutionary capital and deflection of forces from the mainland theatre only served to hearten the rebels.

The campaign of 1779 proved more encouraging to British arms. Clinton's efforts now concentrated upon the south, and notable successes resulted. In 1780 the rebels received their worst defeat of the war at Charleston, while Clinton's vigorous subordinate CORNWALLIS went on to score further victories at Camden and Guilford Courthouse. However, Clinton's apparent conquest of the south was deceptive, as the British army lacked the resources to keep what it had won. In the spring of 1781, when Cornwallis was cornered at YORKTOWN by a superior Franco-American force, a lack of naval superiority prevented Clinton from sending relief in time. The fall of Yorktown marked the effective end of the war. Clinton resigned soon after and returned home to bear the brunt of criticism for Britain's defeat. He ended his days as governor of Gibraltar.

Clive, Catherine ('Kitty') (1711–85), actress. She was the daughter of an Irish lawyer, William Raftor, who fled to France after fighting for James II at the battle of the Boyne. He went to London in the reign of Queen ANNE, and was given a royal pardon. Kitty early hankered after the stage, and obtained a part in a tragedy produced by Colley Cibber at Drury Lane when she was 17. Her singing voice was more noted than her acting ability, and Cibber cast her in the role of Phillida in his ballad opera *Love in a Riddle* in 1729. Her talents as a singer and an actress made her ideal for comedies and farces, as audiences discovered with

her portrayal of Nell in Charles Coffey's *The Devil to Pay: or the wives metamorphosed* in 1731. Shortly afterwards she married, and then separated from, George Clive, a barrister. Although she played roles in plays of dubious taste she was also engaged by HANDEL as Delilah in the first production of his *Samson* in 1742. Kitty was an actress in GARRICK's company at Drury Lane from its start in 1746 until her retirement from the stage in 1769. She then moved to a house at Strawberry Hill, a gift of Horace WALPOLE. He wrote an epitaph for her, describing Kitty as 'the laughter-loving dame'.

Clive, Robert (1725–74), soldier and colonial administrator. Clive was a Shropshire lad, being born near Market Drayton. When he was 18 he went to INDIA as a clerk in the EAST INDIA COMPANY. After the outbreak of war with the French in the subcontinent he enlisted and obtained a commission, distinguishing himself at the siege of Pondicherry.

Clive remained in service following the peace of 1748, helping to build up alliances with Indian princes to offset those of the French leader Dupleix. In 1751 this rivalry led the two sides to set up different candidates for the principality of the Carnatic. When Dupleix besieged Trichinopoly, where the British claimant was based, Clive occupied Arcot, forcing Dupleix to invest that town too. He held out against the French for nearly two months before relief came and Dupleix was defeated. Clive remained on active service for another two years, when sickness forced him to return to England.

On his recovery Clive went back to India as lieutenant colonel and governor of Fort St David. In 1756 as the SEVEN YEARS WAR began, the French and their Indian ally Siraj-ud-Daula took British factories in the Deccan and Calcutta. Clive recaptured Calcutta in January 1757 and defeated Siraj at the battle of PLASSEY in June. When news of this victory reached the East India Company in London they made Clive governor of Bengal. His first governorship lasted until 1760, when he returned to England. There he was treated as a conquering hero, or as Pitt put it, 'a heaven-born general'. He was elected MP for Shrewsbury, a seat he retained for the rest of his life. In 1762 he was made Baron Clive of Plassey in the Irish peerage, and two years later became a knight of the Bath.

In the same year, 1764, Clive was appointed once again by the Company as governor of Bengal. There he embarked on a programme of eradicating corruption in the civil service and the army; his efforts, although they reformed the administration, made him many enemies. His enemies accused him in turn of corruption, charges that he vigorously rebutted in the House of Commons on his return from India. In the ensuing parliamentary inquiry into his conduct he uttered the celebrated words: 'By God, Mr Chairman, at this moment I stand astonished at my own moderation!' Although the committee uncovered evidence that Clive had benefited considerably from native gifts, the House resolved without dividing that he had rendered 'great and meritorious services' to the state. Despite this acclaim Clive, who had suffered all his life from depression, was plunged into despair by the proceedings against him. Recourse to opium failed to raise his spirits, and he committed suicide on 22 November 1774.

FURTHER READING J. Lawford, *Clive: Proconsul of India* (1976).

clubs. The 18th century was the first age of clubs. They flourished above all in London after the GLORIOUS REVOLUTION of 1688, when the guarantee of annual sessions of Parliament brought MPs and their entourages to spend a season in the capital. Members for particular counties, such as Cornwall and Yorkshire, met together for annual feasts. Such gatherings were social rather than political, with MPs of both parties attending. Other organizations composed of politicians, however, were more partisan. Thus the Whigs formed the KIT CAT CLUB and the Tories the Board of Brothers and the Cocoa Tree. Another political club was the Rump Steak, membership comprising those politicians who had been publicly spurned by GEORGE II.

Clubs were instigated for social as well as political purposes. The idea of a club inspired the most celebrated periodical of the age, the *SPECTATOR*, which was formed around a fictitious club whose members included Sir Roger de Coverley and Sir Andrew Freeport. Dr JOHNSON presided over the Literary Club in London. Gambling rather than literature was the *raison d'être* of Brooks's and White's, where the scions of aristocratic houses won, and lost, fortunes in a night's play. Other clubs were formed in the provinces, the most famous being the Lichfield Lunar Society and the Spalding Gentlemen's Club.

Club membership spread below the level of the gentry, with box clubs being joined by workmen who contributed to a box as a form of insurance. By mid-century the London Society of Gentlemen Tailors had 40 such clubs, whose activities were coordinated by a grand committee. These benefit clubs preceded the friendly societies. By the 1790s artisans were also joining political clubs such as the London and Sheffield CORRESPONDING SOCIETIES.

SEE ALSO COFFEE HOUSES; HELL FIRE CLUB; OCTOBER CLUB; SCRIBLERUS CLUB.

FURTHER READING P. Clark, *British Clubs and Societies, 1580–1800: The Origins of an Associational World* (2000).

Coalbrookdale. *See* DARBY, ABRAHAM.

Cobbett, William (1762–1835), radical journalist. The son of a Surrey farmer, Cobbett was an autodidact. In 1783 he enlisted in a regiment that was posted to Canada until 1791. On his return he supported demands for an increase in soldiers' pay in terms that the authorities considered to be advocating mutiny, and he was obliged to flee abroad, at first to France and then to Philadelphia. When Joseph PRIESTLEY was feted there after his arrival in 1794, Cobbett published a tract criticizing him for denigrating England, and praising the English constitution. This made his reputation on both sides of the Atlantic. His controversial views, however, led to prosecutions for libel, and he left Pennsylvania, initially for New York and then for England, where he arrived in 1800.

In January 1802 Cobbett issued the first *Political Register*, which he was to continue to publish for the rest of his life. The early weekly issues supported the government. Cobbett particularly admired PITT THE YOUNGER, but was disillusioned with what he called 'Pitt's system' when the impeachment of Lord Melville, formerly Henry DUNDAS, revealed that it rested on corruption. Cobbett then turned his journal into a sustained critique of a system that kept corrupt aristocrats and borough-mongers in power and denied the people their natural rights. Thus he denounced the aristocracy as 'a prodigious band of spungers', and the Establishment as 'the Thing'. He was convinced that taxation went to sustain a vast parasitic caste, and that public extravagance would ultimately bring the country to ruin.

An article on corporal punishment in the army led to Cobbett being tried in 1810 and imprisoned for two years. This experience did not temper the radicalism expressed in his *Political Register*. On the contrary, in November 1816 he brought out a twopenny edition aimed at 'the journeymen and labourers of England, Wales, Scotland and Ireland'. The resulting sale alarmed the government, and Cobbett, fearing he would be prosecuted for sedition, fled to the United States in 1817, where he stayed for two years. The difference in his politics between his first and second sojourns in America can be measured by the fact that while he was a journalist in Philadelphia he had attacked Thomas PAINE, whereas when he returned to England in 1819 he brought back with him Paine's mortal remains.

Back in England Cobbett entered the fray over the Queen Caroline affair as one of her staunchest supporters. Throughout the 1820s he undertook tours of Britain, which he recounted in his *Rural Rides*, published in 1830. In 1831 he was acquitted of a charge of inciting agricultural labourers to riot. After several abortive attempts to enter Parliament he finally succeeded in 1832 when he was returned for Oldham.

FURTHER READING R. Williams, *Cobbett* (1983).

Cobham's Cubs. When Sir Richard Temple, Viscount Cobham, was deprived of his military commission in 1733 for opposing Walpole's excise scheme (*see* EXCISE CRISIS), he went into opposition and grouped around him a number of younger politicians. These included George GRENVILLE, George LYTTELTON and William PITT. They held together as a political connection into the 1750s, being known variously as the 'Cobhamites', 'the Grenville cousins' and 'the cousinhood'.

coffee houses. Coffee along with chocolate and tea entered the English diet from the mid-17th century. By 1700 all three commodities were available to customers in specialist outlets, the most popular by far being coffee houses, of which there were some 80 in 1663 in London alone, a number that had grown to 650 by 1714. Taking in Westminster and the suburbs, the total was probably nearer 2000.

By the 18th century some of the coffee houses catered for particular customers. For instance, there were at least a dozen that attracted Welsh visitors to the capital. Garraway's and Jonathan's in Exchange Alley were frequented by so many stockbrokers that they rivalled the Royal Exchange in the trade in stocks. Lloyds became a forum for shipping news, from which its insurance interests developed. Others were notorious for their political partisanship. The Cocoa Tree and Ozindas were Tory establishments, while Button's and the St James were Whig.

From the start there were coffee houses in the provinces. Oxford and Cambridge quickly followed London, Bristol had four by 1666 and York could boast one by 1669. *Ursa Major and Minor*, a tract published in 1681, claimed that there were coffee houses in 'most of the cities and boroughs of the nation'.

It was observed that all ranks of society mingled in coffee houses. In 1701 John Houghton claimed that 'Coffee houses make all sorts of people sociable. The rich and poor meet together, as also do the learned and the unlearned.' Women too both ran and frequented them.

One reason for the popularity of coffee houses was that, at a penny a bowl, coffee was cheaper than ale. Another was that customers could also read newspapers and gossip about their contents. Ned Ward observed in 1720 that

> Ev'ry cobbler quits his Awl
> And twice a day for coffee leaves his stall
> Purely to read, or if he can't to hear
> What wonders we have done this present
>   year.

Indeed it was because of their dissemination of news that they played a crucial part in the development of the PUBLIC SPHERE. By the early 19th century the coffee house was in decline. The availability of affordable newspapers, the growing popularity of tea, and the rise of the private club all contributed to the demise of an institution that had previously fulfilled a crucial social function.
FURTHER READING S. Pinkus, '"Coffee politicians does create": Coffeehouses and Restoration Political Culture' in *Journal of Modern History*, LXVII (1995), 807–834.

Coke, Thomas (1752–1842), agricultural improver. Coke of Holkham in Norfolk was a prominent Whig member of Parliament for that county from 1776 to 1832, with only two breaks. The first occurred in 1784 when he stood down rather than risk defeat through his association with the FOX–NORTH coalition. In 1806 his election was declared void and he was elected for Derby at a by-election. Although he succeeded to one of the greatest aristocratic estates and was frequently offered a peerage, he declined to accept one until 1837, when he became earl of Leicester. However, it is as an agricultural enthusiast rather than as a politician that he is chiefly remembered. He introduced scientific sheep and cattle breeding and crop rotation onto his own farms, and insisted that his tenants adopted his methods on theirs. The resulting improvements reputedly caused a tenfold rise in his rent roll, although in reality the increase was more modest.
FURTHER READING R.A.C. Parker, *Coke of Norfolk* (1975).

Coleridge, Samuel Taylor. *See* LAKE POETS.

Collingwood, Cuthbert (1750–1810), naval officer, who, as commander of Britain's Mediterranean Fleet after Trafalgar, did much to consolidate the famous victory of his lifelong friend Horatio NELSON.

A native of Newcastle upon Tyne, Collingwood joined the Royal Navy as a boy volunteer during the SEVEN YEARS WAR. Collingwood and Nelson began their enduring friendship when both were serving as lieutenants in the West Indies. Although he shared Nelson's courage and unswerving zeal for the service, the burly and outwardly reserved Collingwood provided a marked contrast in physique and temperament. Unlike Nelson, Collingwood lacked influential connections; promotion therefore came slowly, and he did not secure a captaincy until he was 30.

Collingwood participated in Richard HOWE's morale-boosting victory of the 'Glorious First of June' over France in 1794, although he failed to share in the subsequent allocation of honours. Three years later he played an even more conspicuous role at CAPE ST VINCENT, where he gave vital support to Nelson's lone strike against the disordered Spanish fleet. Although he missed his old friend's great victory at the battle of the NILE, Collingwood – who was promoted to admiral in 1799 – served as second in command at TRAFALGAR on 21 October 1805. Nelson's dependence upon 'dear Coll' was not misplaced: it was Collingwood, in the *Royal Sovereign*, who spearheaded the attack on the Franco-Spanish fleet, engaging the powerful *Santa Anna* and attracting heavy fire from other vessels. He assumed command of the battered but victorious fleet upon Nelson's death that afternoon, and struggled to hold it together during the ensuing week of gales.

Collingwood gained the title of baron for his exploits at Trafalgar, and continued at the head of Britain's Mediterranean Fleet during the gruelling and unglamorous years of attrition and blockade that followed in the wake of that epic encounter. Exhausted by his punishing duties, Collingwood died at sea in March 1810, just a day after his ship finally sailed for England. Baron Collingwood, First Admiral of the Red, was buried in St Paul's Cathedral within hailing distance of his devoted comrade Nelson.

Collins, Anthony. *See* DEISM.

Colquhoun, Patrick (1745–1820), Scottish merchant and reformer. Colquoun was born in Dumbarton, prospered as a merchant trading with Virginia, and became lord provost of Glasgow in 1782. Re-elected the following year he founded the Glasgow Chamber of Commerce, of which he was the first chairman. He moved to London in 1789. When the metropolitan magistracy was reformed in 1792 he became one of the new police magistrates. His experiences led him to publish pamphlets on such subjects as the licensing of public houses, poor relief and, most famously, a *Treatise on the Police of the Metropolis, explaining the various crimes and misdemeanours which are at present felt as a pressure on the community, and suggesting remedies for their prevention.* This first appeared in 1795 and had gone through seven editions by 1806. He continued to publish pamphlets and to take practical measures to improve the policing of the city and to relieve and educate the poor. His last major work was his *Treatise on the wealth, power and resources of the British Empire* (1814). Although its data are flawed it is still a useful source of social and economic information.

Combination Acts, statutes against combinations of workmen whose aim was to press for higher wages and better conditions. Such acts began to be placed on the statute book in the 1720s. These were consolidated into an act of 1799 that banned all combinations. The ban on all forms of wage bargaining was lifted in 1800 in an act that allowed for arbitration over wages and appeals by manufacturers or workers to magistrates.

commerce. The commercial revolution of the 17th century, which reoriented British trade from Europe to the Atlantic, gathered increasing momentum in the 18th. Indeed, the 18th century saw Britain emerge as the foremost overseas trading nation.

This spectacular growth of commerce was intimately related to the steady rise of the British EMPIRE. For example, territorial expansion in INDIA was initially driven by a desire to safeguard lucrative markets and sources of raw materials; as the extent of Britain's colonies increased, so did the range and value of these raw materials and the size of overseas markets for British manufactured goods. By the 1770s West Indian sugar and its by-products accounted for 25% of imports, while the proportion of goods exported across the Atlantic rose from 11% to 42% between 1700 and 1775.

From the 1650s onwards, Britain's growing colonial commerce was regulated through the passage of NAVIGATION ACTS that sought to enforce protective polices reflecting mercantilist theories (*see* MERCANTILISM). With the continuing expansion of trade during the course of the 18th century, such restrictive legislation itself came under increasing attack from those economists who favoured free trade. The rise in Britain's overseas commerce during the 18th century caused trade to expand by nearly 2% per annum. In the century's last two decades, however, this annual growth in trade more than doubled to about 4.9%. The sharp upturn in trade was largely due to continental Europe's demand for British manufactures and goods originating from Britain's burgeoning colonies. During the REVOLUTIONARY AND NAPOLEONIC WARS, this growth was severely disrupted by Napoleon's 'continental system' aimed at crippling Britain's economy. Indeed, warfare generally exerted a similarly detrimental effect on overseas trade, the only exception to this rule being the SEVEN YEARS WAR, when hostilities failed to halt the expansion of commerce.

It has been calculated that by 1740 something like half the world's commerce was already conducted by British ships. This merchant marine consisted largely of private traders. Although trading companies such as the EAST INDIA COMPANY, the Levant Company and the Royal African Company continued to operate into the 18th century, the great expansion in Atlantic commerce was undertaken by independent merchants. After 1694, the African Company was forced to allow such merchants to exploit the SLAVE TRADE, which was technically its monopoly, by payment of fees. Although the company successfully resisted an attempt to open the trade to all in 1712, its efforts to retain its monopoly were eventually unavailing. In 1750 the joint stock was dissolved. Thereafter the slave trade was opened up. The thriving 'Atlantic economy', of which this commerce in slaves formed an important part, boosted the significance of ports on Britain's western coastline such as LIVERPOOL, BRISTOL and Glasgow.

Expansion of overseas trade during the course of the 18th century was paralleled by the growth of domestic commerce. Especially significant was the trade in agricultural produce required to feed a rising POPULATION that was increasingly centred upon manufacturing TOWNS. Much domestic commerce was conducted by sea, for example, the coastal trade in transporting coal from Newcastle to LONDON. During the course of the 18th century, internal trade was enhanced by improvements in ROADS along with the dramatic expansion of CANALS that ultimately linked the major manufacturing centres of the north and Midlands with each other, the capital and all the leading ports. Growing British commerce – both overseas and domestic – underpinned the development of INDUSTRY, banking and insurance, and consolidated the position of London as Europe's leading financial centre.

FURTHER READING M.J. Daunton, *Progress and Poverty: An Economic and Social History of Britain, 1700–1850* (1995); R. Davis, *The Rise of the Atlantic Economies* (1973).

Commons, House of, lower chamber of the British Parliament. The House of Commons in the 18th century was theoretically held to be an equal estate along with the crown and the House of LORDS in the CONSTITUTION. But to what extent it was actually on the same level as the other two is a matter of dispute. Many historians have assumed that it was already superior to the others. Thus the official *History of Parliament* has published surveys that deal entirely with the lower house. However, it has been much criticized for this, and recently decided to include the House of Lords in its remit.

Critics of the concentration on the Commons argue that the monarchy was still strong, while the Lords were actually superior. The monarch could influence the composition of the Commons, directly in some constituencies – for example, in the so-called Treasury boroughs – and indirectly by giving MPs places under the crown (see PLACEMEN). Some contemporaries actually argued that such tactics could create a majority in the House, reducing the legislature to dependency upon the executive. Historians, however, are generally agreed that the Commons never became a rubber stamp of the king and his ministers.

Nevertheless many historians claim that the Lords remained the more important of the two Houses. They point out that most ministers either were peers or were ennobled, indicating their awareness of where the power lay. Against this, the precedent set by Sir Robert WALPOLE, who chose to remain a commoner throughout his premiership, suggests that he was aware of the crucial importance of the lower house. After he fell in 1742, through failing to control a majority in the Commons, the longest-serving prime ministers of the century, Henry PELHAM, Lord NORTH and William PITT THE YOUNGER, all sat in the lower house. It was after all responsible for finance. Money bills could only originate there, the role of the Lords being limited to either accepting or rejecting them. Taxation played an essential part in the development of the fiscal-military state, which was such a vital element in British political history in the century. Thus its control of the purse strings in the last analysis made the Commons more important than the Lords.

The Commons was also called 'the representative of the people', being regarded as the democratic element in the constitutional trinity. How far it represented 'the people' in practice was a matter of much dispute at the time, and has remained so ever since. Palpably not all adult males, let alone any females, were enfranchised at the time by the prevailing ELECTORAL SYSTEM. If anything the proportion of adult males who enjoyed the vote actually declined over the period. Yet even in the early 18th century it was obvious that the majority of the Commons by no means reflected the majority of votes cast in a general election. This was made starkly clear in 1734 when Walpole's supporters were heavily defeated in constituencies where a popular protest could be made against his excise scheme (*see* EXCISE CRISIS), but he nevertheless procured a parliamentary majority, because of the number of members returned for small boroughs where the outcome was such a foregone conclusion that no contests occurred.

SEE ALSO PARLIAMENTARY REFORM.

FURTHER READING P.D.G. Thomas, *The House of Commons in the Eighteenth Century* (1971).

Commonwealthmen, strictly speaking, advocates of a republic, though in the 18th century, as Professor John Pocock has observed, 'English republicanism, wherever we meet it, takes the experience of a central monarchy and a unitary realm for granted.' Thomas Gordon, one of the leading Commonwealthmen, claimed in *CATO'S LETTERS* that 'Our own constitution is the best republic in the world, with a prince at the head of it.' This was because mixed or limited monarchy, which was the essence of the CONSTITUTION, was regarded by Commonwealthmen as having sufficient popular checks on the monarch to satisfy republican principles. It was also perhaps because they realized that the idea of a republic without a king had been discredited by the actual experience of one during the Interregnum of the mid-17th century.

Prominent commonwealthmen included Thomas Hollis (1720–74) and his friend Thomas Brand (1719–1804), who benefited from his will and adopted his surname – becoming Brand Hollis, and Robert Molesworth (1656–1725). In *An Account of Denmark* (1694), Molesworth tried to explain how the Danish constitution had been changed from constitutional to absolute monarchy. He concluded that only the constant vigilance of the concerned citizen could prevent a similar process occurring in England. Molesworth's idea was to adapt the classical republican notion of civic virtue to the circumstances of 18th-century Britain. Other Commonwealthmen were sceptical about relying upon virtue to sustain the liberties of the subject, since human nature was too susceptible to corruption. They sought a constitutional mechanism which would offset the inevitable tendency of a polity to become corrupt, and found it in an adaptation of the theories of Machiavelli and the political theorist James Harrington (1611–77), for which they have been regarded as 'neo-Harringtonians' as well as Commonwealthmen. The notion of a balanced CONSTITUTION, in which the various elements of monarchy, aristocracy and 'democracy' offset each other, seemed to offer a better safeguard of liberty than reliance on virtue alone. These ideas, developed along genuinely republican lines, found their ultimate expression in the checks and balances of the American Constitution of 1789.

FURTHER READING J.G.A. Pocock, *The Machiavellian Moment: Florentine Political Thought and the Atlantic Republican Tradition* (1975); P. Rahe, *Republics Ancient and Modern: Classical Republicanism and the American Revolution* (1992); C. Robbins, *The Eighteenth-Century Commonwealthman* (1959).

comprehension, term applied to attempts to modify the liturgy of the CHURCH OF ENGLAND in order to accommodate some DISSENTERS within it. There was no way that Baptists, Independents or Quakers could be comprehended within the established church, but some Presbyterians were prepared to consider it if three of the thirty-nine Articles were dropped, episcopal ordination was not required and other modifications of Anglican observance were made. The last attempt at such an accommodation was during the REVOLUTION SETTLEMENT of 1689. But Convocation failed to make the necessary concessions, and Prebyterians had thus to become subject to the TOLERATION ACT, which was meant to cater for sects that were not interested in comprehension.

SEE ALSO CONVOCATION CONTROVERSY.

Compton, Henry (1632–1713), cleric who was instrumental in initiating the GLORIOUS REVOLUTION. Compton was educated at Queen's College, Oxford, and commenced a military career, obtaining a commission, before deciding to enter the church, for which purpose he attended Cambridge University in 1661. In 1669 he was made a canon of Christ Church Cathedral in Oxford, and became bishop of that diocese in 1674. The following year he was appointed dean of the Chapel Royal and bishop of London. He was admitted into the privy council and entrusted with the religious education of the duke of York's daughters MARY and ANNE. In view of the suspicions aroused by the duke's Catholicism, Compton took pains to ensure that they became staunch Anglicans.

After James's accession as king in 1685 Compton's stand against his Catholicizing policy led to his being dismissed from the Chapel Royal and suspended from his see of London. In 1688 he was one of the seven who invited William of Orange to invade, and following the invasion he accompanied princess Anne to Nottingham. After the Revolution he presided over the coronation of WILLIAM and MARY. His disappointment at twice being overlooked by William when Canterbury became vacant led him to side more and more with the Tories. This suited Anne when she became queen, and he once more found himself in royal favour, becoming lord almoner in 1702 and a commissioner of trade and plantations in 1705. This appointment to the BOARD OF TRADE was due to the responsibility of the bishopric of London for the affairs of the Anglican church in the colonies.

Compton, Spencer, 1st earl of Wilmington (1673?–1743), Whig politician. Compton was a member of Parliament for the borough of Eye in Suffolk from 1698 to 1710. He became chairman of the committee of privileges and elections, and in 1707 treasurer to GEORGE PRINCE OF DENMARK. At the general election of 1710 he failed to find a seat through having been a manager at the trial of Dr SACHEVERELL, but was returned for East Grinstead in 1713, and for that borough and Sussex in 1715 and 1722, choosing to sit for the county. He was chosen speaker of the House of Commons in 1715 and again in 1722, combining the post with that of paymaster after 1722.

Compton became closely attached to the prince of Wales, and when the latter became king on the death of George 1 in 1727, Compton was favoured by him over Sir Robert WALPOLE. For a brief period after GEORGE II's accession it looked as though Compton would become prime minister, but he showed a total incapacity to manage the Commons and was easily outmanoeuvred by Walpole. In compensation he was made Baron Wilmington in 1728. Two years later he was promoted to an earldom and became lord privy seal, and shortly after lord president of the council. He opposed Walpole in 1739 over the growing threat from Spain, and on the prime minister's fall joined in the struggle for power, becoming first lord of the Treasury. But he presided over the ministry only technically, staying in that position until his death.

Constable, John (1776–1837), artist who ranks alongside TURNER as a major British landscape painter of the early 19th century. A miller's son, Constable was born at East Bergholt, Suffolk. Like GAINSBOROUGH and the Norwich-born John Crome (1768–1821), Constable drew inspiration both from the Dutch landscape painters of the 17th century and the East Anglian countryside around him. In common with his contemporary Turner, Constable studied in the schools of the ROYAL ACADEMY.

With the backing of WEST, Constable devoted his efforts to the painting of landscapes. Like Turner, the young Constable was heavily influenced by the innovative technique of the watercolorist Thomas Girtin (1775–1802). He soon developed a distinctive style of his own, and by 1808 was working up studio pictures based upon sketches made rapidly in the open air. Although particularly associated with the river Stour in his native Suffolk, Constable roamed throughout southern England to produce canvases such as *Weymouth Bay* (1816), a seascape encapsulating his belief that the sky should provide the 'chief organ of sentiment' in any landscape painting.

Constable's efforts received relatively little recognition in Britain during his own lifetime, and he did not become a full member of the Academy until 1829. His *Haywain* (1821) nonetheless created a sensation and earned a gold medal when it was exhibited at the Paris Salon in 1824. With his bold brushwork and handling of colour, Constable has been widely regarded as a major influence upon the Impressionists. The tranquil *Haywain* remains amongst the best known of all English paintings, and has, quite unfairly, led to Constable's being branded as the blinkered champion of an idealized rural community. In fact, Constable was acutely aware of the social tensions that underlay the countryside's picturesque surface; *Salisbury Cathedral from the Meadows* (1831), with its dark and stormy sky, provides a more appropriate record of his attitudes on the eve of the Great Reform Act.

FURTHER READING M. Rosenthal, *Constable: The Painter and his Landscape* (1983).

constitution. Britain notoriously has no written constitution. But there was a consensus about Britain's polity for most of the 18th century, and this consensus was that mixed or limited monarchy had been secured by the GLORIOUS REVOLUTION. Britain was first and foremost a monarchy, and the crown still stood at the centre of government. In law all appointments of ministers, judges, bishops, army officers and other key posts were made by the crown, and in practice monarchs exercised this authority, especially over commissions in the armed forces.

But there were practical limitations on the powers of monarchs. While they could appoint judges, they could not – after the ACT OF SETTLEMENT of 1701 came into force in 1714 – do so at pleasure, only on the basis of good behaviour, and judges could only be removed by a resolution passed by both Houses of Parliament. The prerogative of appointing ministers at pleasure also depended, although less formally, on their being able to control a parliamentary majority. Hence the notion that the constitution was one of limited or mixed monarchy.

In such a polity the three powers of the crown, the LORDS and the COMMONS had been brought into equilibrium. Thereby the pure, classical forms of monarchy, aristocracy and democracy were mixed, and held each other in check. Furthermore the balance ensured that the disadvantages of each could be avoided. The tendency of monarchy to degenerate into tyranny could be offset by the Lords and the Commons combined; that of aristocracy towards oligarchy by the king and Commons; and that of democracy towards anarchy by the crown and Lords. Sir William BLACKSTONE summed up this consensus in his *Commentaries on the Laws of England* thus:

> Herein indeed consists the true excellence of the English government, that all parts of it form a mutual check upon each other. In the legislature the people are a check upon the nobility, and the nobility a check upon the

people … while the king is a check upon both, which preserves the executive power from encroachments. And this very executive power is again checked and kept within due bounds by the two houses.

Although Blackstone argued that the constitutional equilibrium was a self-regulating mechanism, others disagreed. Critics of the executive complained that it sought to overtip the balance in its favour by undermining the independence of the two Houses of Parliament, through the systematic use of its patronage to corrupt a majority of peers and MPs. These critics sought, however, to reduce the crown's capacity to subvert parliamentary independence by such measures as place bills to curtail the practice of promoting members of Parliament to posts in the administration (*see* PLACEMEN). They also sought to eliminate corrupt electoral practices that allowed the executive to influence the outcome of elections in small boroughs.

Such campaigns aimed at restoring the alleged pristine purity of the REVOLUTION SETTLEMENT rather than at reforming the constitution. Even the Wilkites, the most radical of the executive's critics before the 1780s, called themselves the SOCIETY OF SUPPORTERS OF THE BILL OF RIGHTS. Thomas PAINE, however, called the BILL OF RIGHTS a 'Bill of Wrongs'. In his view 'the defect lies in the system. The foundation and the superstructure of the government is bad.' Paine and other radicals, such as Joseph PRIESTLEY and Richard PRICE, took issue with Edmund BURKE on the alleged perfection of the constitution. They felt that an opportunity had been missed in 1689 to put it onto more acceptable foundations. Thus Protestant DISSENTERS could have been given full citizenship, instead of being barred from office-holding by the Corporation and Test Acts.

Religion indeed played a major part in the debate on the constitution, for it was still regarded as being 'in church and state'. Thus it is significant that many of the clergy who took part in the campaign leading to the FEATHERS TAVERN PETITION became involved in campaigns for PARLIAMENTARY REFORM after its failure. At bottom, agitation for reform arose over a disagreement about the locus of sovereignty. Where reformers like Paine insisted on the sovereign power of the people, conservatives like Burke upheld the sovereignty of the king in Parliament. During the period of the French Revolution the cause of popular sovereignty made little headway in Britain, and reform had to await a less turbulent era.

SEE ALSO ELECTORAL SYSTEM; REVOLUTION SETTLEMENT.

controverted elections, elections whose outcomes are disputed by the defeated candidate. Between 1604, when the House of Commons finally wrested adjudication of parliamentary elections from the crown, until 1868, when it was placed in the courts, defeated candidates who wished to protest against the return of sitting members on the grounds of electoral irregularities did so by petitioning Parliament.

After 1672, whenever Parliament met, the Commons would decide to hear such petitions either by setting up a committee of privileges and elections, or by simply having them heard at the bar of the House. In theory the committee was a judicial body impartially judging the merits of a case. There were various grounds on which a candidate might appeal for jurisdiction in a controverted election, although by and large they can be divided into two categories: disputes arising from the franchise; and those concerning the conduct of an election.

Although the right to vote in the counties had been established in the 15th century as residing in those possessing freeholds to the value of 40 shillings a year, the heterogeneous nature of the borough franchise was a fruitful source of contention. Above all, those boroughs where some sort of residential qualification was required afforded most occasions for the Commons to determine the right to vote. Rival candidates would dispute the precise qualification in such boroughs, for example, one side insisting that it lay in all resident householders, while the other contended that it was confined to those who paid church and poor rates.

Disputes about the conduct of elections were more frequent, and could involve counties as well as boroughs. Thus defeated candidates could petition on the grounds that the returning officer had acted partially in favour of those returned, or they could complain that the sitting members had been in breach of the laws against bribery and treating at elections.

In practice the Commons decided these petitions upon political rather than on judicial grounds. Throughout the 17th century the prevailing majority blatantly used petitions from unsuccessful candidates who would vote with them to unseat sitting members who sided with the minority. The polarization of the House into parties under the later Stuarts ensured that a Tory majority would unseat Whig members and replace them with petitioning Tories, and vice versa. By the 18th century this had developed into a fine art. As Sir Richard Cocks noted in his diary on 25 February 1702 about a decision taken by the committee of privileges and elections, '[it] is certainly the most corrupt Court in Christendom, nay in the world'.

Because the procedure for hearing election petitions was in practice a machinery for increasing the majority of the party that had been victorious at the polls, some pains were taken to ensure that that party controlled the procedure. The political rather than the judicial nature of the trials of petitions was most blatant if they were heard at the bar of the House rather than in committee, and decisions on where to hear them were taken by the majority in the Commons on the sole grounds of party advantage. A hearing at the bar decided the issue on the spot, whereas decisions taken in committee had to be endorsed by the House, giving the opposition a second chance to rally its forces to reverse a close vote. By and large the prevalent party would order hearings at the bar of petitions from leading members of their own

side or against leading members of the other side, and refer to the committee less crucial petitions from their own side and almost all those from the other side. The majority of petitions ordered to be tried at the bar were actually heard, whereas most of those referred to the committee were either withdrawn or not heard at all.

The session of 1708–9 was particularly notorious in this respect. The Whig majority in the Commons ordered all petitions to be tried at the bar, and did not even appoint a committee to hear them. As one disgruntled Tory who was replaced by a Whig after a decision at the bar put it, 'Any opposition may give a handle to a petition. No matter for the justice of it, power will maintain it.'

After 1715 when the Whigs acquired a permanent majority in the Commons the partisan nature of judging controverted elections became even more blatant. Petitions from defeated Tory candidates dwindled as they realized that even the most obvious breach of election law by their Whig opponents would be overlooked by the House. Some Whigs expressed concern at this trend, especially after the general election of 1727, when even Lord Hervey admitted that 'the manifest injustice and glaring violation of all truth in the decisions of this Parliament surpass even the most flagrant and infamous instances of any of their predecessors'. Speaker Onslow agreed that 'we should not bear this a month in any other judicature in the kingdom'.

An attempt was made in 1729 to curb some of the excesses by the Last Determinations Act. This took its name from a clause in a statute 'for the more effectual preventing bribery and corruption in the election of members to serve in parliament'. The clause stated 'that such votes shall be deemed to be legal, which have been so declared in the last determination in the House of Commons; which last determination concerning any county, shire, city, borough, cinque port or place shall be final to all intents and purposes whatsoever, any usage to the contrary notwithstanding'. This did not prevent petitioners from disputing the validity of the last determination of the Commons, necessitating a standing order in 1736 disallowing evidence concerning the legality of votes other than those so determined. Even thereafter some petitioners were prepared to call previous determinations in question. In 1737, for example, upon hearing a petition from Windsor, the House overlooked rulings of 1690 and 1697 in favour of one from 1680.

Nevertheless, the passage of the Last Determinations Act in 1729 shows that, even during WALPOLE's administration, the Commons did not totally lose sight of the principle that objective rather than subjective criteria ought to affect decisions upon controverted elections. The downfall of the prime minister in 1742 came about as a result of a decision on a petition from Chippenham going against government supporters and in favour of opposition candidates.

After the fall of Walpole the trial of election petitions never again played a central part in the political battle. For one thing the number of petitions plummeted from 99 in 1722, the highest in the century, to a mere 17 in 1747. For another they ceased to be as partisan. This prepared the ground for GRENVILLE's Election Act of 1770, which relegated decisions upon controverted elections to a select committee chosen without regard to political considerations.

SEE ALSO ELECTORAL SYSTEM; PARLIAMENTARY REFORM.

Convention of Estates, the Scottish equivalent of the CONVENTION PARLIAMENT OF 1689; *see* CLAIM OF RIGHT.

Convention Parliament, special legislative assembly that met to deal with the constitutional crisis of 1689. WILLIAM of Orange's professed aim in coming over to England in 1688 was to persuade James II to call a 'free parliament' to settle the issues raised by his style of kingship. James actually went so far as to issue writs on 28 November 1688 for a general election to be held and for

Parliament to meet on 17 January 1689. However, his flight in December – during which he threw the Great Seal into the Thames – led to the elections being countermanded.

On 24 December a body of peers in London addressed William, asking him to take upon himself the administration of the government, and 'to write circular letters to all the counties, cities and universities and cinque ports to choose Representatives to meet in a convention at Westminster on the 22nd of January next'. The prince replied 'that he could not give an answer to these addresses, till he had spoken with the gentlemen who had been formerly in the House of Commons' in the reign of Charles II, but pointedly not those who had sat in James's Parliament in 1685. On 26 December he met such members of the 'Exclusion' Parliaments of 1679–81 as were in London, together with the lord mayor, aldermen and about fifty common councillors. They agreed to make the same addresses to him as the Lords had done. William then reconvened the peers on 28 December and accepted the addresses.

The circular letters for the convention were accordingly issued, elections were held and the body met on 22 January. It was called a convention rather than a Parliament because it had not been summoned by a reigning monarch, following the precedent of 1660. It was therefore always open to the charge from JACOBITES that it was an illegal body, even though after William and MARY accepted the crown they assented to an act changing its name to a Parliament.

SEE ALSO BILL OF RIGHTS; ORMONDE, JAMES BUTLER, 2ND DUKE OF; REVOLUTION SETTLEMENT

Convocation controversy (1689–1717), debate in the CHURCH OF ENGLAND. The two Convocations were ancient assemblies of bishops and clergy of each of the archdioceses, summoned by the crown. The controversy was largely between the bishops of the upper house of the Canterbury Convocation and the ordinary clergy of the lower house.

The Anglican clergy felt that the Church of England was in danger after the GLORIOUS REVOLUTION of 1688, during which, in the view of some historians, it had been partially disestablished. Thus they saw nonconformists – allowed to worship separately by the TOLERATION ACT of 1689 – as formidable rivals for the cure of souls. They saw some of them holding office in borough corporations in defiance of the spirit of the Corporation Act of 1661; this they did by taking communion once a year in the Church of England, while the rest of the time they frequented their own conventicles (*see* OCCASIONAL CONFORMITY ACT). They saw a press – liberated from pre-publication censorship by the lapsing of the Licensing Act in 1695 – unleashing a torrent of tracts against the established church in general and its clergy in particular.

Their fears at these threats to their position, and their nostalgia for the reign of Charles II – when the church had been protected from its opponents – were superbly articulated by Francis ATTERBURY and others in *A Letter to a Convocation Man concerning the rights, powers and privileges of that body*, published in 1697. This polemical tract claimed that Convocation historically had been summoned simultaneously with Parliament, and that the failure to do so since the Revolution was unconstitutional. The argument was historically nonsense, and Convocation had really ceased to be convened since Charles II's reign, when it had abandoned its right to raise clerical taxes. But Atterbury's tract appealed to a majority of Anglican clergymen, who felt that the church had been endangered by the Revolution of 1688. The *Letter* called for the convening of Convocation to start to repair some of the damage, for instance by condemning attacks on the church in print.

When Convocation met in 1701 the majority of the representatives of the inferior clergy, elected as proctors to the lower house, supported a strong line against dissent and were called the high-church party. But a majority of the bishops in the upper house advocated leniency towards dissent and were dubbed the low-church party. The session broke up in heated debates between the two parties. These were repeated when Convocation again convened simultaneously with the election of a Tory Parliament in 1702. Between 1705 and 1710, when the Whigs were in power, Convocation was kept in continual prorogation. But it met again in 1710, when once more the high- and low-church parties clashed in angry exchanges. After the accession of the house of Hanover, and especially after the BANGORIAN CONTROVERSY, the decision was taken in 1717 to keep the body in abeyance, and it never met again in the 18th century apart from briefly in 1741.

Cook, James (1728–79), navigator and cartographer, the greatest explorer of his age. He charted many parts of the Pacific, including New Zealand and the eastern coast of Australia, hitherto unknown to Europeans.

Cook was the son of an agricultural labourer in Yorkshire. He served as an apprentice to a ship owner in Whitby, but volunteered for the Royal Navy when war broke out in 1755, and acted as pilot to the expedition against Quebec in 1759. His patron, Sir Hugh Palliser, a fellow Yorkshireman, became governor of Newfoundland, and with his encouragement he surveyed the Newfoundland coast.

Again largely thanks to Palliser, in 1768 Cook received the Royal Society's commission to captain the *Endeavour* to the Pacific to observe the transit of Venus and to discover whether the suspected great southern continent, Terra Australis, actually existed. Accompanied by the scientist Joseph BANKS, Cook sailed by way of Cape Horn, observed Venus from Tahiti, discovered New Zealand, visited Botany Bay in Australia, and returned to England in 1771 by way of the Cape of Good Hope. On his next expedition, on board the *Resolution*, he circumnavigated the world in the other direction, setting out in July 1772 and returning three years later. In the course of this voyage he sailed round Antarctica, and discovered New Caledonia, the South Sandwich islands and

South Georgia. On a third voyage to the Pacific in 1779 he was killed by the inhabitants of Hawaii.

Cook's explorations added considerably to knowledge of the earth's surface, establishing the location of many islands previously unknown to Europeans, and discounting the existence of the long conjectured Terra Australis.

FURTHER READING L. Withey, *Voyages of Discovery: Captain Cook and the Exploration of the Pacific* (1987).

Cooper, Anthony Ashley, 3rd earl of Shaftesbury. *See* SHAFTESBURY, ANTHONY ASHLEY COOPER, 3RD EARL OF.

Coote, Sir Eyre (1726–83), Anglo-Irish army officer. Coote was a tough professional soldier who played a major role in the protracted warfare that underpinned the establishment of Britain's empire in INDIA.

Coote was born at Limerick and joined the army in time to serve against the Jacobites during the '45 Rebellion (*see* JACOBITE RISINGS). In 1754 he accompanied the 39th Foot when it sailed to India; he subsequently played an important part in Robert CLIVE's decisive victory at PLASSEY in 1757. Promoted to lieutenant colonel on Clive's recommendation, Coote achieved a notable success of his own when he defeated the French-led forces of the Count de Lally at Wandewash on 22 January 1760, and his destruction of French fortunes in India was completed in the following year when he obliged Lally to surrender Pondicherry.

Coote's services won the gratitude of the EAST INDIA COMPANY and gained him immense wealth; upon his return to England in 1762 he bought the estate of West Park in Hampshire. Elected MP for Leicester in 1768, Coote returned to India in the following year as commander in chief of the troops in Bengal. However, Coote was soon at loggerheads with the Madras Council over the limits of his authority, and he returned to England via Egypt.

In 1779 Coote once again took passage to the subcontinent to serve as commander in chief under Warren HASTINGS at Calcutta. Coote's experience and leadership were to prove crucial during the wars that followed against the tenacious and skilful Hyder Ali of Mysore. In 1780 Hastings despatched Coote to the Carnatic in an effort to protect Madras from Mysore's victorious armies. With a mixed force of Europeans and native sepoy troops, Coote finally confronted Hyder Ali at Porto Nuovo on 1 July 1781. After heavy fighting Coote's outnumbered forces succeeded in dislodging the enemy from their strong position. During the months that followed Coote fought hard to consolidate his success, before failing health obliged him to hand over command to Major General James Stuart. Exhausted by his efforts and further debilitated by a stroke, Coote died at Madras in April 1783. Coote's body was returned to England and buried at Rockburne Church, Hampshire.

Although his efforts remained largely unappreciated in Britain, Coote's dogged campaigning had gone far to stabilize the Indian territories that would increasingly compensate for the loss of the American colonies. The East India Company knew this only too well, and contributed a memorial to the cantankerous, greedy, but determined soldier who had done so much to safeguard its fortunes.

FURTHER READING E.W. Sheppard, *Coote Bahadur: A Life of Lieutenant-General Sir Eyre Coote* (1956).

Copenhagen, battle of (2 April 1801), a hard-fought encounter between the British and Danish fleets during the REVOLUTIONARY AND NAPOLEONIC WARS. In 1800 the Northern Confederation of Baltic powers declared an ARMED NEUTRALITY that threatened the Royal Navy's access to vital sources of shipbuilding materials and threatened its blockade of the French coast. In retaliation a fleet was despatched to the Baltic under Admiral Sir Hyde Parker, with NELSON as his second in command.

As the Confederation had not yet assembled a joint fleet, it was decided to start the campaign by attacking the Danes. The Danish navy adopted a defensive position screening Copenhagen. Like the French at the NILE, the Danes fought at anchor, although their line was far stronger than that assaulted by Nelson three years earlier – not only were the Danes warned of their enemy's approach, but they were also protected by powerful shore defences and treacherous shoals. Nelson was placed in command of a squadron of frigates and two deckers capable of operating in such hazardous conditions, whilst Parker remained in reserve with larger vessels.

Prior to the attack, Nelson took careful soundings of the area. Despite this precaution, two British ships ran aground; the other 15 were soon heavily engaged. From Parker's position the battle appeared to be going badly and he hoisted a signal advising Nelson to disengage if necessary. Nelson ordered the signal to be acknowledged, then observed to Captain Foley: 'You know Foley, I have only one eye – I have a right to be blind sometimes.' Lifting his telescope to his blind eye he added: 'I really cannot see the signal.' By early afternoon British gunnery had gained the upper hand and the Danes accepted the offer of a truce to remove their wounded. The wily Nelson took advantage of the ensuing lull to adjust his deployments, withdrawing some ships from vulnerable positions and shifting others closer in readiness to bombard the city itself. Further negotiations led to an extended truce of 14 weeks. Soon after the battle, news arrived of the death of Tsar Paul of Russia, a development that precipitated the collapse of the Northern Confederation.

Copley, John Singleton (1738–1815), American painter. Like his countryman Benjamin WEST, Copley sought fame and fortune in London. Born in Boston, he studied in Rome before moving to England in 1775, the year of the outbreak of the AMERICAN WAR OF INDEPENDENCE, and never returned to America. Copley's experience reflected the divided loyalties resulting from that bitter conflict. In 1765, when he was already established as a

leading colonial portrait painter, he had varied his output by producing cartoons opposing the STAMP ACT. Eight years later, however, Copley's own father-in-law was the merchant due to receive the consignment of tea that provoked the Boston Tea Party of 1773. When he painted his own family in London in 1776, therefore, Copley depicted a group of loyalist exiles.

It was during the period of the American war that Copley produced some of his most important works: he combined his mastery of portraiture with a dramatic new approach to the prestigious genre of 'history painting'. For example, *Watson and the Shark* (1778) was a vivid exercise in reportage depicting a real incident at Havana in which the London merchant Brook Watson was literally plucked from the jaws of death. However, it was in 1783 that Copley unveiled his masterpiece, *The Death of Major Peirson*. Like West's painting of the death of Wolfe, Copley's canvas recalled an event from recent history, in this instance the repulse of the French invasion of Jersey just two years before. Prior to the painting's exhibition GEORGE III requested a private viewing; according to legend, he was so moved by this powerful expression of self-sacrifice and PATRIOTISM that he stood quietly contemplating the work for several hours.

Copley subsequently incurred the displeasure of the ROYAL ACADEMY, which considered that he had stooped to undignified crowd-pleasing tactics by erecting a tent in Hyde Park to display his vast depiction of the *Siege of Gibraltar* (1791). Although Copley died a bitter man, his work has been viewed as exerting a profound influence upon French Romantic painters such as Delacroix. Relatively unappreciated in his native land, he remains one of the finest of American artists.

Coram, Thomas (1668–1751), philanthropist. Born in Dorset, Coram went to New England and became a shipwright and then a merchant seaman. He returned to England in 1719, setting up as a merchant. His interest in the colonies led him to support the scheme for the foundation of

GEORGIA, of which he became a trustee, and to advocate a similar settlement in Nova Scotia.

Appalled at the abandonment and murder of newborn children in London, Coram campaigned for the establishment of a foundling hospital, which received the backing of the earl of Derby and other nobles, and received a royal charter in 1739. The Foundling Hospital was initially one of the more successful charities in mid-18th-century England, receiving grants of £3000 from the king, who was at the head of a host of distinguished subscribers. Later, however, its efficacy was questioned, as its success in rearing its inmates and finding apprenticeships for them was modest. In 1760 it was turned into a private institution. Fortunately Coram himself did not live to see its demise.

Cornwallis, Charles (1738–1805), soldier and administrator. Cornwallis was born into a prominent Whig family, and after attending Eton entered the army in 1756. He studied at the military academy in Turin, and then became aide-de-camp to the marquess of GRANBY, under whom he fought at MINDEN. In 1762 he obtained the command of his own regiment. The same year he succeeded his father as the 2nd Earl Cornwallis. He obtained office under ROCKINGHAM as lord of the bedchamber, a post he retained until 1769 when he was made a vice treasurer of Ireland. Despite his opposition to the policy of taxing the American colonies, he became constable of the Tower in 1770 and was promoted to the rank of major general in 1775. The following year he was sent to America with seven regiments to reinforce General HOWE.

Cornwallis's military reputation was enhanced by his conspicuous role in Howe's victory at Brandywine in 1777. After spending a year in England on leave he went out again to serve under CLINTON, whom he persuaded to support his strategy of a campaign in the south. Cornwallis was second in command during Clinton's successful siege of Charleston. He subsequently scored victories of his own at Camden in 1780 and

Guildford Court House in 1781 before he was ordered by Clinton to YORKTOWN. This proved a calamitous mistake. Cornwallis was left to defend a peninsula against a joint Franco-American force with no way of escape, since the French had also blocked his exit at the mouth of the Chesapeake. The result was a defeat for which Clinton (who was in New York), rather than Cornwallis, was held responsible.

Certainly Cornwallis himself was not disgraced, and in 1786 he was made governor general of INDIA. His first task was to root out corruption among the civil servants employed by the EAST INDIA COMPANY and to inspire efficiency in the army. In 1791 he took command of the forces in the third Mysore war and defeated Tipu Sultan, the main enemy of the British and their Indian allies. His achievement was recognized in 1792 when he became 1st Marquess Cornwallis. After implementing further financial and judicial reforms, some of which the Company resented as not being in its long-term interests, he returned to England in 1794.

Back at home Cornwallis became involved in the military efforts against revolutionary France, entering the cabinet as master general of the ordnance. In 1797 he was put in charge of the defences of Ireland as viceroy and commander in chief, in which capacities he suppressed the IRISH REBELLION OF 1798 and defeated a French attempt at invasion. He then advocated the UNION OF BRITAIN AND IRELAND and championed the cause of CATHOLIC EMANCIPATION, which he – like PITT – thought was a necessary corollary. When GEORGE III set himself against it Cornwallis resigned from all his posts. He was nevertheless employed in the negotiations leading to the peace of AMIENS, and in 1805 set out once again for India as governor general and commander in chief. Shortly after arriving there he died.

FURTHER READING H.F. Rankin, 'Charles Lord Cornwallis: A Study in Frustration' in G.A. Billias (ed.), *George Washington's Opponents* (1969); F. and M. Wickwire, *Cornwallis: The American*

Adventure (1970); F. and M. Wickwire, *Cornwallis: The Imperial Years* (1980).

corresponding societies, radical organizations that disseminated political intelligence and opinions. Committees of correspondence were established in the American colonies during the friction between them and the mother country in the 1760s (*see* AMERICAN COLONIES 1763-1776). In London, the Society for Constitutional Information was founded in 1780, and printed tracts that it distributed to provincial constitutional societies in places such as Manchester and Norwich.

Radical corresponding societies sprang up in the ideological ferment created by the FRENCH REVOLUTION. The London Corresponding Society was founded in 1792 by Thomas Hardy, a boot maker, who became its secretary. Its membership was largely confined to artisans. It too kept in touch with provincial societies, such as that in Sheffield. Like the Society for Constitutional Information it circulated tracts, although these, such as Paine's *Rights of Man*, tended to advocate more radical measures.

The activities of the corresponding societies were regarded as seditious by the government following the outbreak of war with France in 1793. When corresponding societies sent delegates to a 'General Convention of the Friends of the People' in Edinburgh that year it was regarded as particularly provocative. The convention was broken up and several delegates, including two from England, were brought to trial and sentenced to transportation to Australia by the ferocious Judge Braxfield.

Notwithstanding this setback, Hardy began to organize another convention to be held in London in 1794. For this he and several others were tried for treason. Although a jury acquitted them the triumph for the societies was short lived. Two acts of 1795, the Treasonable Practices Act and the Seditious Meetings Act, were aimed at crushing them out of existence. Although these measures were not immediately successful, the societies did eventually peter out in the late 1790s.

Corunna, battle of (16 January 1809), British victory in northwest Spain over French forces during the REVOLUTIONARY AND NAPOLEONIC WARS. In the autumn of 1808 Britain resumed its military intervention in the Iberian peninsula following the political storm generated by the controversial Convention of Cintra (*see* PENINSULAR WAR). Command of the British expeditionary force went to Sir John MOORE, a highly experienced officer with a formidable reputation as a trainer of troops.

In an attempt to distract the French armies from Madrid, Moore led his men into northern Spain. With the Spanish armies shattered and his own supply lines overstretched, it soon became clear that Moore's command was in danger of isolation by superior French forces. Rather than seek battle and probable destruction, he decided to preserve his army by mounting a lengthy withdrawal to the coast via the Galician mountains. Closely followed by the army of Marshal Soult, Moore led his troops on a hellish trek through the snowbound mountains.

Moore's soldiers were spoiling for a fight with the French; when denied this opportunity, the discipline of some units degenerated under the cold and fatigue. Although the rearguard maintained its order and efficiently covered the retreat, widespread drunkenness left hundreds of stragglers an easy prey to the merciless French dragoons who menaced the ragged column.

Moore's haggard redcoats finally reached the sea at Corunna, where Royal Navy ships were waiting to embark them. On 16 January 1809 Moore's 15,000 men rebuffed a series of attacks by the numerically superior French army.

Moore was mortally wounded by cannon fire, but lived long enough to learn of his army's victory. His troops were successfully evacuated, although the appalling condition of the survivors caused widespread shock when they landed in England.

cotton. *See* TEXTILES.

countess of Huntingdon's Connexion. *See*
METHODISM.

counties. There were 40 counties in England, 12 in
Wales and 33 in Scotland in the 18th century. They
were basically administrative units, with a sheriff
appointed by the crown and a shire town where
the assizes were held. Some larger counties had
more than one central authority or location. Thus,
although there was a high sheriff for the whole of
Yorkshire, this was an honorary post, and each of
the three ridings had its own sheriff. They also had
their own centres where the assizes met, that for
the West Riding meeting at Wakefield. Other counties also had more than one county town, for example Sussex was divided into East and West Sussex,
with centres at Lewes and Chichester. Each county
also had a lord lieutenant or royal representative,
whose position gave opportunities for patronage
and who commanded the MILITIA.

The shires were more than merely administrative areas. Local loyalties were attached to them,
and people still used the word 'country' to mean
county. All counties were parliamentary constituencies. To be returned to Parliament as a
'knight of the shire' gave a member a higher status
than that of a representative of a borough. In all
English and Welsh counties the electorate consisted of those adult males who possessed a freehold worth 40 shillings a year.

In addition to the ancient shires, several cities
were also counties in their own right. Thus
Kingston upon Hull, Newcastle upon Tyne, York,
Bristol and London were both cities and counties.
They had their own sheriffs and assizes, and 40-
shilling freeholders as well as the freemen of the
city voted for their MPs.

Country party, term that, along with 'COURT
PARTY', predates the labels TORY and WHIG. In the
later 17th century the Country party emerged as
the collectivity of all those opposed to the government in Parliament. Thus the opposition to the
ministry of the earl of Danby in the 1670s was so
described. During the Exclusion Crisis of 1679–81,
however, Parliament and the electorate became
divided more on the new lines of Tory and Whig.
After the GLORIOUS REVOLUTION the Country and
Court labels survived as the major division in politics until the accession to office of the JUNTO
Whigs in the mid-1690s.

The unprecedented phenomenon of a Whig
ministry, and the inevitable compromises that
power entailed, disillusioned many of their backbench supporters. These claimed that Whig principles established in the Revolution had been
eroded by the growth of a STANDING ARMY and the
systematic use of patronage to create a bloc vote
of PLACEMEN in the House of Commons. Led by
Paul Foley and Robert HARLEY these backbenchers
combined with Tories to form a new Country party
in the Commons.

This new grouping elected commissioners of
public accounts to enquire into government expenditure, and spearheaded attacks on the placemen
and the standing army. They achieved success in
reducing the army to a nominal 7000 by 1698 and
by including in the ACT OF SETTLEMENT of 1701
a clause that would have eliminated placemen from
the House of Commons completely had it come
into effect. This was the greatest victory of the new
Country party. It was, however, repealed by the
government in the Regency Act of 1706. Although
this move was resisted by both Tories and opposition Whigs, they did not manage to combine
their forces against it into a sustained opposition
to the government.

By then loyalty to the Tory and Whig parties
was too strong to allow the formation of a united
Country party. Although the term continued
to be used in the 18th century – for instance to
describe Tories and dissident Whigs opposed to Sir
Robert WALPOLE and later to Henry PELHAM and
his brother the duke of NEWCASTLE – these opposition groupings rarely held together cohesively
enough to justify the use of the term in the sense
of a body of politicians in Parliament uniting their
voting strength in a sustained opposition to the

ministry. While they could be relied upon to vote against the standing army and placemen, when traditional issues – especially concerning religion – arose that divided politicians along Whig and Tory lines, their temporary alliance on 'Country' issues generally disintegrated. Only in the EXCISE CRISIS of 1733 did they hold together long enough to be recognizable as a party united on a major issue against the 'Court'. Eventually, during the ministry of the elder Pitt and the duke of Newcastle, the term 'Country party' fell into disuse. However, traditional 'Country' concerns were embraced by the constitutional reform movements that emerged during the political crises of the 1760s and 1770s. Elements of the 'Country' agenda, including a suspicion of ministerial corruption and aristocratic patronage, influenced Christopher WYVILL and supporters of the widespread association movement (*see* PARLIAMENTARY REFORM).

Court party, term applied to those members of Parliament who consistently upheld the ministry when the House divided. The hard core of the Court party consisted of those MPs who were PLACEMEN, holding offices of profit in the administration together with their seats in the House. They were joined by the adherents of the politicians who composed the ministry of the day.

Although the royal purse was tiny compared with the resources of foreign rulers, the monarch's court remained throughout the period perhaps the most important focus of upper-class society. The households of the monarch, consorts and royal princes employed altogether hundreds of people and the major offices were keenly sought after. So were the awards – peerages, baronetcies and knighthoods – the distribution of which the monarch supervised. Royal patronage was assiduously cultivated by artists, musicians and writers since the monarch's approval could bring both prestige and financial reward.

Because the monarch continued to exercise real influence over the appointment of politicians and churchmen, the royal court also retained a serious political function. However, the term 'Court party' was misleading in that the choice of ministers was never completely in the monarch's hands and at times could be beyond his control; standing in one or other house of Parliament was likewise essential to any major politician and on rare occasions credibility with the public could also be decisive.

The first systematic attempt to build up a Court party is generally held to have been undertaken by the earl of Danby in the 1670s. This was shattered by the Popish Plot and the Exclusion Crisis, which raised issues transcending those of government and opposition. The next major effort was made by the JUNTO in the 1690s. Again this came to grief when the issues of religion and the succession surfaced at the end of the decade, realigning politicians upon WHIG and TORY lines. The votes of the 120 or so placemen in the Commons became less and less predictable.

Although this realignment polarized Parliament well into the 18th century, the term 'Court party' came increasingly into use during WALPOLE'S long ministry to define those who supported the prime minister. He increased the number of placemen in the Commons to around 150, while their voting behaviour became more constant. Under the Pelhams – Henry PELHAM and his brother the duke of NEWCASTLE – this bloc of votes became known as the 'OLD CORPS'.

The Court party that had sustained the Whig ministries of the first two Georges disintegrated in the opening years of GEORGE III's reign, which resulted in the 'Massacre of the Pelhamite Innocents'. Some of those who upheld the various ministries from that of Lord BUTE to the fall of Lord NORTH's in 1782 were called 'the King's Friends'. A remodelled Court party formed under PITT THE YOUNGER, reinforced by the defection of Whigs led by the duke of Portland from the opposition to the ministry in 1794.

Cowper, William (1731–1800), evangelical poet. Born in Berkhamsted, Hertfordshire, where his father was rector, Cowper was educated at West-minster School and the Middle Temple. He was entered for an examination for a clerkship in the House of Lords, but preparation for it unnerved him to the point of a nervous breakdown, the first of several bouts of severe depression that he suffered from all his life.

After his recovery Cowper spent some time in Huntingdon where he lodged with the Unwins, an evangelical family. On the death of Mr Unwin in 1767, Cowper moved with Unwin's widow Mary to Olney in Buckinghamshire at the invitation of its evangelical minister John NEWTON. Newton had been appointed by Lord DARTMOUTH, a member of the countess of Huntingdon's Connexion (*see* METHODISM), and Cowper shared with them the strict Calvinist doctrine of salvation by the unearned gift of grace preached by George WHITE-FIELD. In collaboration with Newton, Cowper composed the *Olney Hymns*, and while writing them he became convinced that he was damned, a conviction that drove him mad for two years. During this period he lived with Newton, and his recovery was helped by gifts of hares, which he kept in the house as pets.

After regaining his senses Cowper never wrote hymns again, but turned to secular poetry instead. His evangelicalism is implicit throughout his poems, becoming most explicit in those that deplored the SLAVE TRADE. Cowper's most cele-brated poem was *The Task*, published in 1785. It was suggested to him by 'a lady fond of blank verse [who] gave him the SOFA for a subject'. In it he gave 'some account of myself', which included the famous line 'I was a stricken deer'. The passage in which he develops this view of himself anticipates in some respects Wordsworth's *Prelude*.

FURTHER READING D. Cecil, *The Stricken Deer* (1929).

Crabbe, George (1754–1832), poet. Crabbe was born in Aldeburgh, Suffolk, which provided the setting for his two most celebrated poems, *The Village* and *The Borough*. He served an appren-ticeship to local doctors and set up his own medical practice. It did not flourish, however, and he decided to seek a career as a poet, having published some verse, including *Inebriety* (1775), whose opening lines echoed Pope's *Dunciad*: 'The mighty Spirit and its power which stains / The bloodless cheek, and vivifies the brains / I sing.'

In 1780 Crabbe went to London, where he published *The Candidate* and sought a patron. Having been refused by Lord Thurlow he was taken up by Edmund BURKE, who invited him into his home at Beaconsfield and persuaded the pub-lisher Dodsley to publish Crabbe's *The Library* and to give Crabbe the profits. He also introduced Crabbe to Dr JOHNSON and the painter Joshua REYNOLDS, while Thurlow repented his former dis-missal and gave him £100. Burke convinced Crabbe that he should become a clergyman, and after he was ordained procured him the post of chaplain to the duke of Rutland in 1782.

The following year Crabbe published *The Village*, a realistic corrective to GOLDSMITH's idyllic representation of rural life in *The Deserted Village*: 'I paint the Cot / As Truth will paint it and as Bards will not.' It led Robert SOUTHEY to describe Crabbe as 'an imitator, or rather an antithesizer, of Goldsmith'. After *The Newspaper* (1785) Crabbe published no more poems until 1807, when *The Parish Register* appeared. It was followed in 1810 by *The Borough*, which included the moral tale of the murderer Peter Grimes; the composer, Ben-jamin Britten, was to use this as the original for his opera. In 1814, following the death of his wife, Crabbe moved to Trowbridge, where he spent the rest of his life. There he published *Tales of the Hall* in 1819, the last of his works to appear in his life-time, although an edition of his *Poetical Works*, including some posthumous verse, came out two years after his death.

FURTHER READING R.L. Chamberlain, *George Crabbe* (1965).

Creech, Thomas (1659–1700), classical scholar. Elected a fellow of All Souls, Oxford, in 1683,

Creech was renowned for his translations from the classics, of which the most famous was his Lucretius. Disappointed in love and desperately short of money, he hanged himself in June 1700.

cricket. *See* SPORT.

crime and punishment. Crime and punishment together evoke some of the most enduring popular images of 18th-century Britain. The lone highwayman awaiting his prey on some desolate heath, the canny smuggler unloading contraband wares under the very nose of the revenue man, and the creaking gibbet with its ghastly burden, are all scenes familiar from literature and cinema alike.

Yet this romantic legacy reflects the very real impact of law-breaking upon Hanoverian society. As the unprecedented popularity of John GAY's *Beggar's Opera* demonstrated, a sometimes obsessive interest in crime and its perpetrators remained characteristic of rich and poor alike. Just as men of property demanded ever harsher measures to combat the depredations of footpads and pickpockets, so humbler folk provided an avid audience for the chapbooks and BALLADS that embroidered the exploits and dying speeches of such star criminals as Jack Sheppard and Dick TURPIN. More recently, 18th-century crime has proved equally alluring for scholars, whose researches have resurrected the subject as a fertile and ideologically charged field of social history.

Elite society's morbid fear of the criminal underpinned a dramatic strengthening of the century's notorious 'BLOODY CODE' of justice. During the course of the 'long 18th century' the number of so-called 'hanging offences' rose from 50 to more than 200, the threat of the gallows being employed to counter a perceived assault upon the twin bastions of property and authority. In 1751, when he published his influential *Inquiry into the causes of the late increase in robbers*, the novelist Henry FIELDING argued that contemporary crime levels reflected the poor's desire to share the conspicuous wealth of their betters. Indeed, the century's 'consumer

revolution' flooded the market with portable and disposable luxury goods calculated to tempt both casual and organized criminals.

However, modern historians of crime have demonstrated that many indictments stemmed less from envy than a gut reaction to hunger. Regional studies reveal a close relationship between crime and economic conditions. With much of the population hovering perilously close to the subsistence level, even a slight rise in the price of bread could tempt the desperate to steal. Particularly striking was the increase in serious property offences accompanying the termination of the era's great wars. Scholars have concluded that the armed services temporarily absorbed the young labouring men who provided the bulk of the criminal classes, only to disgorge them upon a postwar economy, where the prospects for honest toil were poorer than ever. Peacetime therefore witnessed an upsurge in such serious offences as highway robbery.

Recent research into Georgian crime has also emphasized the extent to which certain activities deemed 'criminal' in the eyes of officialdom enjoyed widespread support amongst the population in general. Smugglers, poachers and wreckers were tolerated by the rural communities within which they operated; such acceptance reflected both extensive local involvement in such time-honoured practices, and the violence and intimidation that they frequently involved. In the absence of a professional police force, many remote regions were quite literally beyond the law; it required unusually vicious crimes – like those committed by the Hawkhurst gang of Sussex smugglers in 1747 – to trigger concerted crackdowns by the authorities.

Given its role as a rapidly expanding centre of population and wealth, London naturally provided a magnet for criminal activity, ranging from casual street theft of wigs and watches to systematic pilfering of sugar and tea from the port's wharves. Although the extent of the capital's 'criminal underworld' should not be exaggerated, London hosted increasingly sophisticated malefactors such as Jonathan WILD, the infamous 'Thief-Taker General'. A former Wolverhampton buckle-maker, Wild graduated from pimp and strong-arm man to head a sprawling criminal empire based upon the receiving of stolen goods. Wild ended his days at Tyburn in 1725, execrated by the mob because of his policy of informing against his own henchmen.

Yet for those sentenced to hang for less odious crimes, the Calvary-like procession from Newgate to the triple tree at Tyburn offered a last opportunity to demonstrate courage and bravado before an appreciative and sympathetic audience. The carnival atmosphere of 'Tyburn Fair', immortalized in HOGARTH's stark engraving of the 'Idle 'Prentice's' execution, caused grave concern to those who believed that public hanging should instead provide a grim warning to potential criminals. In the opinion of Henry Fielding, execution was concerned less with punishment of the individual than the 'terror of the example' to others. Such attitudes go far to explain why, despite the growth in capital offences between 1688 and 1815, many of those sentenced to death escaped the ultimate penalty. In addition, with the extension of the 'Bloody Code' to relatively minor counts of theft, reluctant juries sometimes responded by undervaluing the worth of the goods concerned. Reprieves and royal pardons likewise ensured that the full weight of the law fell largely upon the notorious or unlucky.

In the final quarter of the 18th century, this picture was transformed through the growing use of imprisonment as a punishment in its own right (*see also* PRISONS). The role of incarceration had previously proved insignificant; the prison reformer John HOWARD's survey of English and Welsh gaols in 1776 reported just 653 inmates – the majority debtors or those on remand. However, from the mid-1770s increasing use of imprisonment was accompanied by the growing belief that confinement could exert a reforming influence upon criminals. The timing of this change reflected the closure of the rebellious American colonies to the thousands of felons who, like DEFOE's fictional

Moll Flanders, had been transported across the Atlantic since 1718 (*see* TRANSPORTATION). The colony of Botany Bay in AUSTRALIA opened a fresh dumping ground from 1787, yet the hiatus since the onset of American independence had allowed the concept of imprisonment as a sanction midway between corporal and capital punishment to take root. On the eve of the Victorian era, as the 'Bloody Code' was finally diluted, the country's gaols were absorbing an ever-growing population of reprieved felons.

SEE ALSO PIRACY.

FURTHER READING D. Hay, P. Linebaugh and E.P. Thompson (eds.), *Albion's Fatal Tree: Crime and Society in Eighteenth-Century England* (1975); P. Linebaugh, *The London Hanged: Crime and Civil Society in the Eighteenth Century* (1991); F. McLynn, *Crime and Punishment in 18th-century England* (1991).

Crompton, Samuel (1753–1827), inventor who helped transform the spinning process in the TEXTILE industry. Employed as a spinner by his widowed mother at their home near Bolton in Lancashire, he improved on Hargreaves's spinning jenny, making a machine that could spin thread fine enough to make muslin. He called this machine a 'spinning mule', as it was a cross between ARKWRIGHT's water frame and the spinning jenny (jenny being a female donkey). His machine enabled a muslin industry to grow in Britain where previously the fabric had been largely imported from the east.

Crowley, Sir Ambrose (1658–1713), early industrialist. Crowley was an iron manufacturer at Winlaton near Newcastle upon Tyne, and the *Law Book* of his firm is a major source for historians studying industrial organization and relations in the late Stuart period. Crowley lived in London, serving as sheriff in 1707.

Culloden, battle of (16 April 1746), final victory of the Hanoverian forces over the JACOBITES in the '45 JACOBITE RISING, fought on Drummossie moor near Inverness. The respective armies were headed by the duke of CUMBERLAND and Charles Edward STUART. Cumberland's men numbered about 9000 and Charles's about 5000. Contrary to myth the 9000 were not all English nor the 5000 all Scots. There were many Scottish troops in Cumberland's ranks, and some French soldiers in the Pretender's. The Jacobites were not only outnumbered, but also outclassed in weapons, being themselves often dependent upon broadswords and shields while their enemies had muskets and bayonets and above all artillery. Fire power soon reduced the moor to a killing field. The Jacobites took the onslaught for several minutes before advancing. Although their right wing reached the front line of the Hanoverian army, they were forced to retreat. Charles fled the field and eventually escaped to France. Some 2000 Jacobites were slain, compared with only about 300 casualties on the Hanoverian side. It was a decisive battle, ending all prospects of a Stuart restoration.

Cumberland, William Augustus, duke of

(1721–65), army commander, the younger son of GEORGE II and Queen CAROLINE. He fought at the battles of DETTINGEN, where he received a leg injury, and FONTENOY, where he commanded with distinction. Afterwards he was recalled from the continent to lead the army formed to combat the JACOBITE RISING of 1745. His savage repression of the Highlanders after the battle of CULLODEN earned him the nickname of 'the Butcher'. He fought at Laffeldt in 1747 and at Hastenbeck in 1757, but was stripped of his command that year for signing the convention of Kloster-Zeven, which virtually handed Hanover to the French. As this was a virtual capitulation, George II repudiated and recalled his son. Cumberland then retired from active service. Politically he was an Old Corps Whig, and when GEORGE III sought a replacement for George GRENVILLE in 1765 Cumberland recommended the marquess of ROCKINGHAM, the heir to the Walpole and Pelham Court Whig tradition. He died shortly after the appointment of the first Rockingham administration.

FURTHER READING W.A. Speck, *The Butcher: The Duke of Cumberland and the Suppression of the '45* (1995); R. Whitworth, *William Augustus, Duke of Cumberland: A Life* (1993).

D

Dalrymple, John, 2nd earl of Stair. *See* STAIR, JOHN DALRYMPLE, 2ND EARL OF.

Darby, Abraham (1677–1717), iron master and industrialist. Darby was apprenticed by his father, a Quaker farmer, to a Birmingham malt-mill maker. Darby himself set up in that business in 1698. In 1704, following a visit to the Netherlands, he established the Baptist Mills Brass Works at Bristol, employing Dutch craftsmen. He then experimented with ways of substituting cast iron for brass in certain products, but when these proved costly his associates refused to incur the expense of further experiments. He therefore withdrew from the Bristol concern and in 1709 moved to Coalbrookdale in Shropshire where he leased a furnace. There he discovered how to smelt iron ore using coke rather than charcoal, a process he patented in 1709.
SEE ALSO INDUSTRY.

Darien scheme, disastrous scheme to establish a Scottish colony in Central America. In 1695 the Scottish Parliament passed an act incorporating the Company of Scotland trading to Africa and the Indies. The object of this company was to found a colony on the isthmus of Panama, then known as Darien. This colony, called New Caledonia, was intended to give Scots the opportunity to catch up with other European nations in the colonization of the New World. Darien was so strategically placed that a settlement there could effectively combine eastern and western commerce in the way that the Panama canal was to do two hundred years later. The scheme was so attractive to investors that most Scots with any liquid capital subscribed to it.

Unfortunately, other European nations objected. Spain in particular complained that the company's activities violated its claim to the isthmus, and put pressure on WILLIAM III to cancel its privileges. English merchants also feared Scottish competition in the Atlantic trade and voiced their objections. Potential subscribers in England were forbidden to invest in the company.

Nevertheless, the company raised enough to launch an expedition to Darien in 1698, taking 1200 settlers there. Despite friction with Spanish officials in Central America, the town of New Edinburgh was settled, and in 1699 more colonists were sent out by the company. But disease had ravaged New Edinburgh and it had been abandoned, and the new arrivals found a deserted settlement. Although they started to resettle Darien, disease again took its toll. When a Spanish expedition arrived to besiege the colony, it was abandoned once more, this time finally. The loss was resented by the Scots, who blamed the English as much as, if not more than, the Spaniards. Many Scots had been bankrupted by the failure of the venture. The

Darien scheme loomed large in the negotiations that led to the UNION OF ENGLAND AND SCOTLAND in 1707.

FURTHER READING J. Prebble, *The Darien Disaster* (1968).

Dartmouth, William Legge, 2nd earl of (1731–1801), politician. Legge inherited his title on the death of his father in 1750. He opposed the BUTE and GRENVILLE administrations formed after the accession of George III, and became president of the Board of Trade in the first ministry of Lord ROCKINGHAM in 1765. He resigned the following year on the fall of the ministry, and was out of office until 1772, when he was again appointed president of the Board of Trade in NORTH's government. He also acted as secretary of state for the colonies between 1772 and 1775, and as such was heavily involved in colonial policy, at a time when relations between the mother country and her North American colonies were rapidly deteriorating.

While there seemed a chance of avoiding hostilities Dartmouth advocated a conciliatory approach, but was overruled by the king and cabinet, and was replaced by the more bellicose Lord George SACKVILLE in 1775. He thereupon was appointed to the post of lord privy seal. After war broke out, however, Dartmouth took a strong line towards American resistance to British rule, speaking against conciliation and arguing for military suppression of the rebellious colonies. Dartmouth resigned on the fall of Lord NORTH in 1782, but returned to office as lord steward in the FOX–North coalition. When Pitt came to power, Dartmouth lost office and left public life. He was a prominent member of the countess of Huntingdon's Connexion, a sect of Calvinist METHODISTS, and nominated John Newton to the living at Olney. Newton's neighbour, the poet William COWPER, praised Dartmouth as 'one who wears a coronet and prays'.

Darwin, Erasmus (1731–1802), physician and thinker, whose innovative ideas on a range of subjects were usually presented in verse. He was the grandfather of Charles Darwin, and himself speculated about evolution. Darwin attended Cambridge and Edinburgh universities, where he studied medicine. He settled as a physician first in Nottingham and then in Lichfield. There he made the acquaintance of the savants who formed the LUNAR SOCIETY. He also planted a botanical garden there which he celebrated in his poetry. Later he moved to Derby where he founded a philosophical society in 1784. As a minor poet he achieved some fame. The second part of his *Botanic Garden* praised the use of steam, predicting that it would 'drag the slow barge or drive the rapid car; or on wide-waving wings expanded bear the flying-chariot through the fields of air'.

Davy, Sir Humphry (1778–1829), chemist and inventor. Born in Cornwall, Davy was educated at Truro Grammar School before being apprenticed to a surgeon. He then entered Thomas Beddoes's Pneumatic Institute at Bristol, a hospital renowned for its use of gas in the treatment of lung disorders. There he experimented with nitrous oxide – 'laughing gas' – which he introduced to his acquaintances, including the poets COLERIDGE and SOUTHEY, as a recreational drug. In 1801 he became a lecturer in chemistry at the Royal Institution and earned renown as a teacher. He was elected a fellow of the Royal Society in 1803, becoming president in 1820. His experiments were very wide-ranging, and in 1807–8 he discovered the chemical elements potassium, sodium, calcium, barium, magnesium and strontium. He is perhaps best remembered for the 'Davy safety lamp', perfected in 1815, which protected miners from fire damp.

FURTHER READING H. Hamilton, *Humphry Davy* (1966).

Declaration of Rights. *See* BILL OF RIGHTS.

Declaratory Act (1720), legislation passed by the British Parliament declaring that the Irish House of

Lords could not hear appeals, which could only be made to the British House of Lords. In 1719 the Irish House of Lords had claimed that it was the final court of appeal in Ireland, and that appeals could not be made from it to the British House of Lords. In 1782 the second ROCKINGHAM ministry repealed the act, giving the Irish Parliament the full powers enjoyed by the British. This situation was ended when the Act of UNION abolished the Irish Parliament in 1801.

Declaratory Act (1766), legislation passed by the British Parliament declaring its right to legislate for the colonies 'in all cases whatsoever'. Thus the sovereignty of the king in Parliament was asserted over the colonists. The act followed the repeal of the STAMP ACT by the first ROCKINGHAM ministry (*see* AMERICAN COLONIES 1763–1776).

Defoe, Daniel (1660–1731), novelist, journalist and government agent. Defoe was the son of a DISSENTER and grew up in London, being educated at the dissenting academy at Stoke Newington. In 1684 he married Mary Tuffley and set up as a haberdasher in partnership with his wife's family. In 1692, however, he became bankrupt. He succeeded then as a tiler, and began to write on economic concerns, his *Essay upon Projects* appearing in 1697. He continued to publish tracts on business activities, his last major publication being *The Compleat English Tradesman*, which appeared in 1726–7.

Defoe's successful entry into journalism under WILLIAM III encouraged him to write on politics, and in 1701 he published *The True-born Englishman*, a poem satirizing English xenophobia by pointing out what a mongrel breed the English were. He attracted considerable attention with this poem, of which he was so proud that he signed other works as being by 'the author of the True-born Englishman'. He also became embroiled in the party strife of the year when he took the side of the Whigs, championing their mobilization of public opinion against the Tory majority in the

Commons. Indeed he helped to mobilize it himself by taking the side of the Kentish petitioners, who were subject to parliamentary censure for petitioning the Commons to drop their squabbles and unite behind the need for war against France. Thus he published *Legion's Memorial* and *A New Satyr on the Parliament*.

Defoe's gift for satire backfired on him, however, when he published *The Shortest Way with the Dissenters* in 1703. In it he mimicked the views of high-church clergymen like Henry SACHEVERELL, reducing them to their logical conclusion, which was the eradication of dissent. Unfortunately for Defoe it was taken as a serious high-church tract. He was found guilty of seditious libel, pilloried and imprisoned.

The secretary of state, Robert HARLEY, procured his release, and thereafter Defoe worked for the government. His thrice-weekly *Review of the Affairs of France* was an organ of ministerial propaganda for ten years. He also undertook a tour of constituencies prior to the 1705 general election, and went to Scotland as a government spy at the time of the UNION OF ENGLAND AND SCOTLAND. These travels contributed much of the information that appeared in *A Tour through the whole island of Great Britain*, published between 1724 and 1727.

At the accession of the house of Hanover, Defoe was initially discredited as a hack for the disgraced Tory ministry of the last four years of Anne's reign. But he redeemed his reputation and wrote for the incoming Whig administration. His *Journal of the Plague Year* (1722) was partially intended to justify draconian measures taken by the government as a precaution against a threatened renewed outbreak of the plague.

Meanwhile, Defoe had found a new outlet for his writing talents in *The Adventures of Robinson Crusoe* (1719), now widely regarded as one of the earliest English novels. It was such a success that he followed it up with a sequel, and in 1722 with *The Fortunes and Misfortunes of Moll Flanders* and *The History of Colonel Jacque*. He was one of the first writers to make a career out of writing in a new age when the PRESS and a market for NOVELS first came into their own.

FURTHER READING P. Backscheider, *Daniel Defoe: His Life* (1989); P. Earle, *The World of Defoe* (1977).

deism and deists, philosophical position that denies revelation and insists on unaided reason alone as the basis of faith. This led deists to deny the doctrine of the Trinity as being irrational. They were thus accused of Arianism (the belief that God the father was superior to Christ or the Holy Spirit) and Socinianism (which denied the deity of Jesus).

In the first half of the 18th century it was the deists who appeared to present the most serious threat to Christian orthodoxy. The deists denied the revelation of scripture, and in place of revealed religion they advocated natural religion. Thus they argued that such doctrines as eternal life and a judgement after death could be deduced from observing nature with the help of reason, and thus did not require revelation. The deism that they advocated denied the divinity of Christ and the doctrine of the Trinity, which they claimed were not susceptible to rational explanation and were based on scriptural authority alone. Such leading deists as John Toland, Samuel Clarke, Anthony Collins and Matthew Tindal wrote tracts that the orthodox felt obliged to repudiate.

John Toland (1670–1722) was born in Ireland and raised as a Catholic, but converted to Protestantism and completed his education in Glasgow, Edinburgh and Leiden. Shortly after his return to England he published *Christianity not Mysterious* (1696), an attack on such 'mysteries' as the doctrine of the Trinity, for which he was in turn attacked as a Socinian. He went back to his native Ireland, but found his work even more notorious there, where it was burned by the common hangman in Dublin. Retreating to England he sought protection from sympathetic patrons, and found them in Robert HARLEY, the duke of Newcastle and the 3rd earl of SHAFTESBURY. It was under Harley's influence that he wrote *The Art of*

Governing by Parties (1701) and accompanied the earl of Macclesfield when he took the ACT OF SETTLEMENT to Hanover. He was abroad again from 1707 to 1710, but back in England he contributed pamphlets to the SACHEVERELL controversy. By then he had toned down his deism and professed to be an orthodox Anglican.

Samuel Clarke (1675–1729), after graduating from Caius College, Cambridge, where he distinguished himself by his knowledge of Newton's theories, became chaplain to the bishop of Norwich. His reputation as a philosopher led to his being invited to give the Boyle lectures in 1704–5. These caused controversy, Clarke being accused of advocating deism by high-church critics. His low-church supporters, however, regarded him as a champion of orthodox Christianity against its sceptical critics. He was introduced to Queen Anne, who made him a chaplain and in 1709 appointed him to the rectory of St James's Westminster. The publication of his *Scripture Doctrine of the Trinity* in 1712, at the height of the high-church reaction, was bound to get him into trouble. It was presented to Convocation for censure in 1714, but the charge was dropped when Clarke denied that he was an Arian. After the accession of the house of Hanover he became acquainted with CAROLINE OF ANSBACH, wife of the prince of Wales and future queen. She encouraged him to correspond with Leibniz on philosophical problems.

Antony Collins (1676–1729) was a friend of John LOCKE in the latter's final years, and was influenced by the views he had expressed in the allegedly deist *The Reasonableness of Christianity* (1696). Collins's first foray into polemical writing was an attack on Samuel Clarke's view of the immortality of the soul on Lockeian grounds. In 1709, however, he joined the deist controversy with *Priestcraft in Perfection*, in which he criticized revealed religion as a system designed to empower priests, and cited as an example of priestly usurpation the twentieth of the Thirty-nine Articles of the Anglican Church. This maintains that 'the Church has power to decree rites and ceremonies, and authority in controversies of faith'. His most notorious tract was *A Discourse of Freethinking* (1713), which SWIFT ridiculed in an alleged commentary rendering Collins's tract 'in plain English for the use of the poor', and accusing him of denying the Trinity in order to justify immorality. An even more effective attack on orthodoxy from a deist point of view was Collins's *Discourse on the grounds and reason of the Christian religion*, which WARBURTON claimed was one of the more plausible contributions to the literature of deism.

Matthew Tindal (1657–1733) was educated at Oxford, becoming a law fellow at All Souls in 1678. In 1685 he was admitted as an advocate in Doctor's Commons. During the reign of James II he converted to Catholicism, but went back to the Church of England in April 1688. After the GLORIOUS REVOLUTION his legal advice was sought on such subjects as whether ships manned by sailors loyal to James II could be deemed to be engaged in piracy. He published pamphlets from a Whiggish, low-church viewpoint, but none made a stir until the appearance in 1706 of his *The Rights of the Christian Church asserted against the Romish and all other priests who claim an independent power over it*. This attack on priestcraft revealed Tindal as a leading champion of the deist cause, and provoked a storm of refutation from high-churchmen. Tindal's tract was so notorious that the House of Commons ordered it to be burned along with Dr SACHEVERELL's sermon in 1710. Tindal played a part in the controversy raised by the Doctor in that year, publishing pamphlets attacking the high-church point of view. After the accession of George I he contributed to the pamphlet war raised by the Whig schism. But his political writings attracted little attention in comparison with his deist effusions. His last publication, however, which appeared in 1730, roused as much controversy as *The Rights of the Christian Church*. This was the classic statement of 18th-century deism, summed up in the very title, *Christianity as old as the Creation, or the Gospel a Republication of the Religion of Nature*. It marked the high-water mark of the deist controversy, which Toland had begun with his *Christianity not Mysterious* and which was effectively ended by Joseph BUTLER's *Analogy* (1736).
FURTHER READING J.A.I. Champion, *The Pillars of Priestcraft Shaken* (1992).

Despard, Edward (1751–1803), soldier, colonial administrator and conspirator. Born in Ireland, Despard served as an army officer in the West Indies with some distinction. In 1783 he was put in charge of the contingent of log cutters allowed by the treaty of Paris to exploit the forests of the Yucatán peninsula. His rule was criticized as harsh and eventually he was recalled to England, although no charges were pressed. His treatment by the authorities left him bitter, and in 1802 he became involved in a seditious plot to seize the Tower of London and assassinate the king with the help of disaffected soldiers, mostly Irish. When this was discovered he was arrested, tried for treason, found guilty and executed.

Dettingen, battle of (27 June 1743), engagement in Germany during the War of the AUSTRIAN SUCCESSION in which the 'Pragmatic Army' of Britain and its allies routed a superior French force.

During the summer of 1743 the allied army – originally led by the experienced earl of STAIR – came under the personal command of GEORGE II himself. On 27 June 1743 French troops commanded by Marshal Noailles succeeded in trapping the combined British, Austrian and Hanoverian forces in a dangerous bottleneck: hemmed in by the river Main on the left and wooded hills on the right the allies had little option but to press forward. Luckily for them the impetuous duke of Grammont advanced from his strong defensive position in the village of Dettingen to give battle in the open.

The last English monarch to lead his troops into battle in person, King George had a lucky escape when his frightened horse ran away with him. Eventually dismounting safely, he spent the rest of the battle encouraging his men on foot.

During the confused combat that followed, both sides revealed their lack of discipline, but the French were eventually put to flight by superior allied musketry. Relieved at that events had gone so well, George decided against sending his cavalry in active pursuit.

Dettingen was Britain's first continental victory since the glorious days of MARLBOROUGH. However, the genuine celebrations it prompted soon subsided amidst grumbles that the king was unduly biased towards his own Electoral troops. The cautious George subsequently proved reluctant to exploit his success by mounting a vigorous campaign against the French; after his advice was repeatedly ignored, the exasperated Lord Stair resigned in disgust.

Devonshire, Georgiana Cavendish, duchess of

(1757–1806), celebrated society hostess. The daughter of Lord Spencer of Althorp, Georgiana married the 5th duke of Devonshire when she was just 17. Although not beautiful, she was glamorous and striking. She became an arbiter of taste, leading the fashions of the day with ever more outlandish and expensive outfits. She also gambled heavily and took several lovers, including Earl Grey and the prince of Wales. This lavish and liberal lifestyle was accompanied by a concern for politics that led her, in the traditions of the Spencers and Cavendishes, to espouse the Whigs. Thus she notoriously canvassed for Charles James FOX in the Westminster election of 1784, her efforts generating many hostile and even obscene prints. She also had literary interests and talents, which brought her to the notice of Dr Johnson and led to the publication of some verse.

FURTHER READING A. Foreman, *Georgiana, Duchess of Devonshire* (1998).

Devonshire, William Cavendish, 4th duke of

(1720–64), politician, briefly prime minister in 1756–7. He became MP for Derbyshire at the age of 21 on the family's electoral interest in the county. He married the daughter of the earl of Burlington, and acquired the Londesborough estates in East Yorkshire and Lismore Castle in Ireland when his father-in-law died without male heirs in 1753. The following year he became lord lieutenant of Ireland. When a ministerial crisis arose in 1756 through PITT's refusal to serve under the duke of NEWCASTLE, and the king's reluctance to ask Pitt to form a ministry, the issue was resolved by the appointment of Devonshire as first lord of the Treasury and technically prime minister, although Pitt as secretary of state was effectively premier. This arrangement lasted only six months, until Newcastle replaced Devonshire as first lord and the latter was given the post of lord chamberlain. He left the ministry along with Newcastle in 1762 in the 'massacre of the Pelhamite innocents'. Within two years he was dead at the age of 44.

Diplomatic Revolution

(1756), major shift in European alliances, particularly bringing together France and Austria, which had been enemies for 250 years. During the War of the AUSTRIAN SUCCESSION (1740–8) Britain allied with Austria against France and Prussia, whereas in the SEVEN YEARS WAR (1756–63) Britain allied with Prussia against France and Austria. This was known as the Diplomatic Revolution, since it represented not just a temporary realignment of powers but a significant change in the pattern of alliances that had been established by the War of the SPANISH SUCCESSION (1701–13), when Britain and Austria, along with the Dutch Republic, had formed the backbone of the Grand Alliance against France. It also aligned Protestant against Catholic Europe, with the major exception of Portugal.

dissenters,

Protestants who did not conform to the CHURCH OF ENGLAND. In the 18th century the term was usually employed in preference to 'nonconformists'. In the early 18th century the most important dissenting sects were the Presbyterians, the Congregationalists, the Baptists and the Quakers. The Presbyterians were originally closest to the Church of England but were opposed to bishops, objected to some of the thirty-nine Articles and disliked many Anglican ceremonies. Their chapels were organized into local synods and a national assembly. Congregationalists, otherwise known as Independents, formed themselves into so-called 'gathered' churches of 'covenanted' members which controlled their own affairs with no national organization. The Baptists repudiated infant baptisms, believing that adults when baptized experienced regeneration. Quakers were organized into the Society of Friends. They had no ministers, believing the 'inner light' inspired all Friends. They were distinguished also by their pacifism. In 1715 dissenters probably numbered about 350,000. Although only about 7% of the population, they appeared more formidable to Anglicans than their numbers seemed to warrant.

The Church of England became alarmed at the number of chapels that were licensed under the TOLERATION ACT of 1689 for dissenting worship. Dissenters also formed a considerable proportion of the electorate, especially in larger towns, in which they tended to be concentrated. It is possible that they made up as much as a quarter of the urban electorate. At first, Quakers could not vote, as they refused to take the oaths of allegiance that the returning officers could administer to voters, because of their refusal to swear. In 1696, however, Parliament passed the Affirmation Act, allowing them to affirm rather than swear. Initially this was a temporary measure, which had to be re-enacted from time to time. In 1722, however, it finally became permanent. Fear of the electoral influence of dissenters largely accounts for the OCCASIONAL CONFORMITY ACT of 1714.

By the time the Occasional Conformity Act was repealed in 1719 dissent no longer seemed to pose the threat it had done since the Glorious Revolution. This was partly because the most numerous sect, the Presbyterians, were seriously divided over the issue of UNITARIANISM. In 1719 their differences emerged at the Salters' Hall conference in London, when a majority of delegates refused to subscribe to the doctrine of the Trinity. The schism in Presbyterianism led to a sharp decline in their numbers. The Congregationalists, who were strong in Wales and the Welsh borders in 1700, also declined in numbers before 1750, when they numbered about 15,000, but recovered by 1800, when they had about 35,000. Baptists too experienced decline in the first half of the century and growth in the second. The New Connection General Baptists were founded in 1770, and the Baptist Missionary Society in 1792. It was not until the rise of METHODISM, and the secession of Wesleyan Methodists from the Church of England to form the nucleus of what became known as 'new dissent', that the Anglicans again felt threatened from dissenters outside their own ranks.

SEE ALSO DODDRIDGE, PHILIP; FEATHERS TAVERN PETITION; PRIESTLEY, JOSEPH.

FURTHER READING G. Rupp, *Religion in England 1688–1791* (1986); M.R. Watts, *The Dissenters*, two vols. (1978, 1995).

Dodd, William (1729–77), clergyman and felon. Dodd was ordained in 1751 and became chaplain of the Magdalen Hospital for penitent prostitutes shortly after its opening in 1758. He was a fashionable preacher and was appointed chaplain to the king in 1763, which opened the way to lucrative livings including Charlotte Chapel in Pimlico, named after the queen. He had tried his hand as an author before becoming a clergyman, and renewed his career as a writer in 1760 by editing *The Christian Magazine* and contributing to other journals.

When Dodd's wife, Mary Perkins, whom he had married in 1751, received a legacy of £1500 and won £1000 in the lottery the couple began to live in a style that earned him the title of 'the macaroni parson'. They overreached themselves when Mrs Dodd wrote to the lord chancellor's wife offering money to procure him the living of St George's Hanover Square. He was struck off the list of royal chaplains and she was dubbed 'Mrs Simony'.

Their extravagant lifestyle incurred serious debts, to settle which Dodd offered a bond for

£4200 to a stockbroker in the name of Lord Chesterfield, to whom he had acted as tutor. That he had forged Chesterfield's signature was discovered, and Dodd was brought to trial and found guilty of forgery. Despite enormous pressure for a reprieve, orchestrated by Dr JOHNSON, the king refused to commute the death sentence and Dodd was hanged on 27 June 1777.

Doddridge, Philip (1702–51), dissenting minister. Doddridge was educated at dissenting schools at Kingston on Thames that his grandfather had established, and St Albans. When he decided to become a nonconformist minister he went to Kibworth Academy in Leicestershire, and became minister there in 1723. In 1729 he was appointed as the first tutor at a new academy in Market Harborough. Later that year he accepted the ministry of an Independent congregation in Northampton.

Doddridge's publications in defence of nonconformity earned him a national reputation as an advocate of uniting the various strands of DISSENTERS. Although he described himself as a Calvinist 'in all important points', he avoided theological questions that had divided dissenters, for example the issue of the Trinity. Such disagreements had caused the decline of dissent, which he was anxious to arrest. His own range of contacts was wide, embracing the MORAVIAN Count Zinzendorf, the Methodists John WESLEY and George WHITEFIELD, and archbishop Herring. His *Family Expositor* in six volumes, the first of which appeared in 1739, was popular with people of several religious persuasions. His hymns were also widely admired and sung. He never enjoyed good health, and in 1751 he went to Lisbon to try to recover from the lasting effects of a severe cold, but died there.

Dodington, George Bubb (1691–1762), politician. Dodington was a flamboyant character, a patron of poets, and also a place-hunter of the most sycophantic type, whose *Diary* records the workings of the patronage system that greased the machinery of politics in the 18th century. He was born George Bubb, and added the name of Dodington when he inherited an estate from his uncle George Dodington in 1720. He completed the house that his uncle had started to build at Eastbury in Dorset, employing VANBRUGH as architect.

Dodington sat as MP for Bridgewater from 1722 to 1754. His electoral interests at Weymouth and Melcombe Regis were also influential enough to return his candidates to Parliament. He began as a supporter of WALPOLE, and was made a lord of the treasury in 1724. In the 1730s, however, he associated with dissident Whigs, leading to his dismissal from the treasury commission in 1740. He became treasurer of the navy under Henry PELHAM in 1744, but again intrigued with opposition Whigs, this time associated with FREDERICK PRINCE OF WALES, and was again dismissed in 1749. He featured prominently in Frederick's political schemes, but expectations of further promotion were thwarted by the prince's death in 1751.

Dodington recovered from this blow by mending fences with the duke of NEWCASTLE; he was appointed to the treasurership of the navy again in 1755, only to lose it again when PITT came into office the following year. To his credit Dodington defended Admiral BYNG when it was not popular to do so. He attached himself to the REVERSIONARY INTEREST, and when GEORGE III became king he was ennobled as Baron Melcombe. He did not, however, enjoy office again, dying in 1762.

drama. In 1698 Jeremy Collier, a NONJUROR, published his *Short View of the Prophaneness and Immorality of the English Stage*. It is usually regarded as a diatribe against Restoration comedies, such as William Wycherley's *The Country Wife* (1675), which were not so much suggestive as outright explicit in their bawdy eroticism. But it also attacked Whig dramatists, whom Collier accused of undermining deference for the social hierarchy by portraying peers and country gentlemen as ignorant boobies, and clergymen as corrupt time servers. Many leading dramatists of his day, such as Susannah Centlivre, Colley Cibber, William Congreve, Nicholas Rowe and John VANBRUGH, were Whigs whose plays depicted such stock characters as country gentlemen – who in real life were the backbone of the Tory party – as unlettered clowns.

The Short View is generally held to have been effective, and to have been instrumental in bringing about the transition from Restoration to 'sentimental' comedy. Certainly there is a more refined wit and less crude social comment in later plays such as Richard STEELE's *The Tender Husband* (1705) and *The Conscious Lovers* (1722). These paved the way for the farces of Arthur Murphy and such sparkling comedies as GOLDSMITH's *She Stoops to Conquer* (1773) and SHERIDAN's *The Rivals* (1775) and *The School for Scandal* (1777).

Tragedy too was toned down for a more sensitive audience. Dryden began the trend by modifying Shakespeare's *Antony and Cleopatra* into *All for Love* (1678). Political themes such as patriotism informed many tragedies in the century. ADDISON's *Cato* (1713) was probably the most produced play in the whole period. The 'patriots' associated with FREDERICK PRINCE OF WALES included dramatists like James THOMSON, whose tragedies *Agamemnon* (1738), *Edward and Eleanora* (1739) and *Tancred and Sigismunda* (1745) upheld 'patriot' ideals. His most famous play, written with David Mallet, the masque *Alfred* (1740), included 'Rule Britannia', for which Thomas Arne wrote the music. One of the more popular tragedies of the period was the Scottish dramatist John Home's *Douglas* (1756). When it was first produced in 1756 a Scot in the audience was heard to shout 'Whaur's yer Wullie Shakespeare noo?'

Shakespeare himself had had many editions of his works published during the century, including those edited by POPE (1725) and JOHNSON (1765), but was generally criticized for his lack of classical restraint and formal structure. However, he made a comeback in his supposed bicentenary year, 1769, when David GARRICK – the most famous actor-producer of the century – launched an extravagant

'Shakespeare Jubilee' in Stratford-upon-Avon, and with it the cult of 'Bardolatry'.

Although the period between 1780 and 1815 has often been viewed as a barren era for British drama, it nonetheless generated a spate of plays inspired by the prevailing mania for GOTHIC literature and architecture. Works such as George Colman's *The Iron Chest* (1796) and 'Monk' Lewis's *The Castle Spectre* (1797) fed audiences a diet of mystery and melodrama that provided ample scope for spectacular sets, atmospheric music and ingenious special effects.

SEE ALSO THEATRE.

Duck, Stephen (1705–56), poet. Born in Wiltshire, Duck became a farm labourer. He began to write poems contrasting the idyllic representations of farm labourers in pastoral poetry with the harsh reality. This brought him to the notice of Queen CAROLINE, who made him a yeoman of the guard in 1733. His *Poems on Several Occasions* (1736) included 'The Thresher's Labour', and thereafter he was known by his many critics as 'the thresher poet'. He entered the church and after ordination became minister at Byfleet in 1753. Duck committed suicide in 1756.

duelling. During the course of the 'long 18th century', many hundreds of educated Britons fought duels to the death in defence of an 'honour code' that owed more to the 'Gothic' past than the increasingly 'Enlightened' present. As contemporary newspapers testify, duelling among members of the male governing classes remained common into the early Victorian era. One contemporary authority on duelling, James Gilchrist, recorded no fewer than 172 such encounters during the reign of George III alone; as Gilchrist's tally omits several notorious duels, this total undoubtedly underestimates the real scale of a phenomenon that embraced fiery young bucks and level-headed politicians alike.

Originating in Renaissance Italy and spreading to France, duelling first took root in England during the Jacobean period. Alarmed by the death toll among his courtiers, the pacific James I issued a proclamation against duelling, and Charles I and Cromwell likewise sought to halt the lethal craze. Duelling returned with the Restoration. Charles II shared his predecessors' disapproval of 'affairs of honour', but did little to curb them; he certainly failed to match Louis XIV's ruthless efforts to eradicate the confrontations that decimated France's touchy *noblesse d'épée*.

While British duelling never lacked critics, it nonetheless enjoyed widespread acceptance among those elites for whom honour remained paramount; indeed, in the opinion of the historian Jonathan Clark, its prevalence proved 'the survival and power of the aristocratic ideal as a code separate from, and ultimately superior to, the injunction of law and religion'. In common with that other aristocratic trait of reckless gambling, duelling demonstrated contempt for the 'prudent, rational, calculating values' associated with the middle and lower classes. The elite's confident stance was bolstered by the judiciary. Under the law, a duellist was guilty of affray; a duel resulting in death carried a count of manslaughter against the victor if fought in 'hot' blood, but murder if – as was usually the case – the fatal meeting occurred after tempers had cooled. However, as murder carried the death penalty, juries were notoriously reluctant to convict duellists of the more serious crime. According to 'The British Code of Duel', provided that the encounter had been conducted fairly in keeping with the 'laws of honour', acquittal was customary. In the eyes of duelling's critics, it was the unlikelihood of punishment for duelling that underpinned its continuing popularity.

Duelling was endemic in Britain's armed services, where boredom and heavy drinking sparked frequent quarrels. In the claustrophobic atmosphere of the regimental officers' mess or man-o'-war's wardroom, a careless word all too often led to events taking on a dreadful momentum of their own, with neither party prepared to back down for fear of losing 'reputation'. For while an officer

who fought a duel breached the Articles of War, the man who refused a challenge was guilty of the far more serious crime of cowardice. The Georgian army proved a nursery for serial duellists like 'Fighting Fitzgerald' and 'Tiger Roche'. Dismissed on a false charge of theft, Roche first challenged his accuser and then the officer he believed to have informed against him; recovering from wounds sustained on that occasion, Roche proceeded to 'call out' and fight his former colonel. Like civilian juries, courts martial proved reluctant to convict the officer duellist who had 'killed his man' in fair fight. For example, when Captain Lieutenant Peter Van Ingen of the Royal American Regiment fatally wounded a brother officer at New York in 1761 after a row during supper, the accused told the court: 'no one could have acted otherwise than I did ... I have comported myself like a gentleman, a man of honour, and like one not unworthy of the commission with which His Majesty has been pleased to distinguish me.' Van Ingen was honourably acquitted.

The British duelling movement gained momentum from changes in armament. From the late 17th century the deadly but unwieldy rapier was ousted by the far handier and equally effective 'small sword'. Fencing masters established schools to teach the science of swordsmanship to genteel clients. Dexterity with the blade required arduous practice, giving the skilled swordsman an obvious advantage in any encounter. By contrast the pistol, which began to oust cold steel as the duelling weapon of choice from the 1750s onwards, offered a fairer alternative; although some confirmed duellists devoted many hours to improving their marksmanship, the customary distance of twelve paces between the antagonists helped to level the odds against the tyro.

In theory at least, duelling was governed by a strict etiquette covering both the grounds for dispute and the conduct of the resulting duel. The 'Irish Code Duello', adopted at Clonmel Assizes in 1777, included 26 distinct rules. For example, if swords were employed, the duellists were to engage 'till one is well blooded, disabled or disarmed; or until, after receiving a wound and blood being drawn, the aggressor begs pardon'. The Irish Code recognized that duelling was a serious business; in consequence, 'no dumb-shooting or firing in the air [is] admissable in any case. The challenger ought not to have challenged without receiving offence; and the challenged ought, if he gave offence, to have made an apology before he came to the ground.'

Real duels did not always match the formal courtesies specified by the rule books. Indeed, one of the most notorious duels of the period, that fought between Lord Mohun and the duke of Hamilton in 1712, proved a savage affair that ended up involving the 'seconds' supposedly enlisted to ensure fair play and claimed the lives of both principals. Again, when SHERIDAN fought the bellicose Captain Matthews – having already faced him once in defence of his future wife's reputa-tion – the duel soon degenerated into an ugly brawl. As the pair struggled on the ground, Matthews stabbed the unarmed Sheridan five times before employing his sword hilt like a knuckle-duster to pulverize the helpless play-wright's face.

Duels frequently stemmed from trivial causes. In April 1803, Captain Macnamara of the Royal Navy killed Colonel Montgomery after an argument in Hyde Park regarding the latter's dog. Both Macnamara and Montgomery had previously served bravely against revolutionary France; at a time of national emergency such veterans would have been better employed fighting the common enemy than each other. Duelling had posed a far greater risk to the country's good in 1798, when the prime minister, PITT THE YOUNGER, felt obliged to accept a challenge from the MP George Tierney after harsh words were exchanged in the House of Commons regarding naval manning levels. In a year of invasion scares and Irish rebellion, the king was not the only citizen to register shock at such irresponsibility. Luckily for protagonists and nation alike, the resulting meeting with pistols on Putney Common proved bloodless. By contrast, wrangling between CASTLEREAGH and CANNING over the distribution of ministerial posts in 1809 led to a notorious duel that left the latter seriously wounded.

FURTHER READING D.T. Andrew, 'The Code of Honour and its Critics: The Opposition to Duelling in England 1700–1850' in *Social History* V (1980), 409–434; J.C.D. Clark, *English Society, 1688–1832: Religion, ideology and politics during the ancien regime* (2nd edn, 2000).

Dundas, Henry, 1st Viscount Melville (1742–1811), Scottish, Pittite politician, who for 30 years was the most powerful man in Scotland, managing the government's interest there with considerable effectiveness.

Dundas was a leading Scottish lawyer who in 1766 was made solicitor general for Scotland, and was promoted to the post of lord advocate in 1775. Entering Parliament as member for Midlothian in 1774, he emerged as a vigorous opponent of any leniency towards the rebellious American colonies. He retained his post of lord advocate through the ROCKINGHAM and SHELBURNE ministries, but lost it under the FOX–NORTH coalition.

When PITT THE YOUNGER formed his ministry in 1783 Dundas became treasurer of the navy. He had shown an interest in Indian affairs, chairing a committee to investigate them in 1781 and presenting a bill for the government of India to the Commons that was superseded by Fox's notorious measure in 1783. This interest led to his appointment to the BOARD OF CONTROL in 1784, of which he was effectively the manager, even though he did not become president until 1793. He became a defender of Warren HASTINGS, whom he called 'the saviour of India'.

Dundas was elected MP for Edinburgh in 1790. He served as home secretary from 1791 to 1793, when he became secretary of war, a post he resigned when Pitt left office in 1801. He continued to support the government, using his influence in the Scottish elections of 1802 to help return almost all the members for Scotland as ministerialists. His loyalty led to his elevation to the peerage as Viscount Melville.

When Pitt formed a ministry in 1804 Dundas became first lord of the Admiralty. The following year he resigned as a result of an inquiry into his conduct as treasurer of the navy that led to charges of his misusing funds. The House of Commons voted to impeach him, but the House of Lords found him not guilty. However, he never held office again. His downfall disillusioned many who had believed in the probity of the younger Pitt and his ministerial colleagues.

FURTHER READING M. Fry, *Henry Dundas* (1993).

Dunk, George Montagu, 2nd earl of Halifax.

See HALIFAX, GEORGE MONTAGU DUNK, 2ND EARL OF.

Dunning's motion (6 April 1780), motion intro-

duced in the House of Commons by John Dunning, a ROCKINGHAMITE MP, 'that the influence of the crown has increased, is increasing and ought to be diminished' (often misquoted as 'the power of the crown'). The *power* of the crown over parliament could be exercised by using the prerogative to prorogue or dissolve the Houses, or to make peers. The *influence* of the crown was less direct, extending to the appointment of Lords or MPs to posts in the administration ranging from the great offices of state to pure sinecures. Dunning was referring to the latter. The resolution passed by 233 votes to 218.

Dunning's success was more symbolic than real, for attempts to follow it up were frustrated until the marquess of ROCKINGHAM formed a ministry in 1782, when some measures to reduce the influence of the crown over the Commons, for example BURKE's Economical Reform Act, were carried (*see* PARLIAMENTARY REFORM).

E

East India Company, company that in theory monopolized British trade with the East Indies (INDIA and the Spice Islands of the Malaya archipelago), and in practice became the virtual ruler of India in the course of the 18th century.

The East India Company was first granted a charter by Queen Elizabeth in 1600, and became a joint-stock company. Although rivals were active as interlopers, and some were even licensed by the crown, the Company retained the monopoly of trade with the Far East until 1698, when a second East India Company was launched. In some respects these developments were due to the party strife of the times, the old company being regarded as largely Tory and the new one as Whig. Supporters of the two fought at the polls in the general election of January 1701. By 1709, however, their rivalries were subsumed in common support of the war effort, and they merged into the United East India Company, which gave the government £2 million in return for confirmation of its privileges (*see also* FINANCIAL REVOLUTION).

For most of the 18th century the Company was engaged in exchanging goods between Britain and India. Since there was an adverse balance of trade – demand for Indian produce in Britain being far greater than demand for British manufactures in India – the gap was made up by the export of bullion, although this violated MERCANTILIST principles. After the middle of the century the Company became more and more involved in the government of INDIA.

SEE ALSO CLIVE, ROBERT; COMMERCE; HASTINGS, WARREN.

FURTHER READING P. Lawson, *The East India Company 1600–1857* (1993).

economical reform. *See* PARLIAMENTARY REFORM.

Eden treaty (1786), commercial treaty with France, negotiated by William Eden. The treaty was based on tariff cuts by both the British and the French, giving each 'most-favoured nation' status. It was held that Britain was more favoured than France, and gave PITT's ministry a reputation for sound economic policies.

Edgeworth, Maria (1767–1849), Anglo-Irish novelist. She was the daughter of Richard Lovell Edgeworth by his first wife, who died in 1773. Her eccentric father married again three months later, and when his second wife died in April 1780 he married her sister in December. Upon her death in 1797 he married for the fourth time in 1798. By his four wives he had 22 children, and Maria spent much of her life helping to bring them up. The Edgeworths had property in both England and Ireland. After spending time in each country, they settled down on their Irish estate at Edge-worthstown in 1782.

Maria was devoted to her father, and began her literary career in partnership with him, producing *Letters to Literary Ladies* and children's books. Even her first and most successful novel, *Castle Rackrent*, was read and approved by him before its publication in 1800. After his death in 1817 she completed his *Memoirs*. Although she wrote other popular novels, including *Belinda* (1801), none was more celebrated than *Castle Rackrent*. In the central character of Thady Quirk she created a plausible Irish steward whose very voice echoes the rhythms and figures of speech of a genuine Irish peasant. This creation was a major literary feat, and it made her more successful than any other novelist of the age, including Jane AUSTEN, until the publication of Scott's Waverley novels.

Edinburgh, capital city of Scotland. Edinburgh underwent a transformation in the 18th century. Politically it was changed from the capital of a still independent Scotland to the status of little more than a provincial town. Culturally, however, it developed into the 'Athens of the North'. In 1700 the city was still confined to the 'Old Town', the site of the university, the High Kirk of St Giles and the Scottish Parliament. It was a rabbit warren of tenement buildings and closes, notorious for its unsanitary and smoky conditions, which led to the town being dubbed 'Old Reekie'. By 1800 the Scottish Parliament had been lost since the UNION OF ENGLAND AND SCOTLAND in 1707, but the 'New Town'– a magnificent example of classical architecture and urban planning – had been gained. The transformation symbolized the change from political to cultural capital.

The loss of the Parliament and of the Scottish privy council led many of the elite to migrate to London seeking the patronage of the British government. The vacuum left by their departure was largely filled by the professional and business classes. They created a lively social and intellectual life centred on clubs such as the Easy Club and the Philosophical Society, founded in 1737, which stimulated the SCOTTISH ENLIGHTENMENT.

In 1752 proposals were made to create a new town alongside the medieval core of old Edinburgh, and these plans were implemented by the architect James Craig in 1767. The North and South Bridges were constructed to join the New and Old Towns. Then the original development was thought to be too much of a grid, and so curves and crescents were introduced, and Charlotte Square was redesigned on a grander pattern in the 1780s by Robert Adam. By the end of the century the population numbered 83,000.

education. There was no system of education in 18th-century England. Instead there was a wide variety of educational provision, from teaching in the home, which was the lot of almost all girls (*see* WOMEN), to boarding at private schools, which catered for the sons of the aristocracy and gentry and even the prosperous middle classes. Between them were schools run by private individuals, many of them women or 'dames', parish schools, charity schools and endowed grammar schools. The 700 or so grammar schools which existed in 1815 ranged from those located in towns such as Bradford in Yorkshire, which catered to the sons of the trading and professional classes, to the nine great 'public' schools attended by the scions of the aristocracy, of which Eton, Harrow, Westminster and Winchester were the most famous.

What proportion of the population attended such schools is unknown. Most children probably had little or no education before becoming domestic servants in the case of girls, or servants in husbandry – farm labourers – in that of boys. Education for a trade was for most boys provided by apprenticeship, which catered not only for trades but even for some professions. The provision of schooling might have improved during the course of the century, spearheaded by the charity-school movement and the growth of dissenting schools and academies. But it still had a long way to go to catch up with the system of education in Scotland, where the provision of schooling at parish level was far more extensive. In addition, an emphasis upon the teaching of Latin provided able Scottish boys from even the most humble backgrounds with the qualifications necessary to attend university.

The application of pedagogic principles to schoolteaching was much influenced by John LOCKE's *Some Thoughts concerning Education* (1693). Locke's ideas were particularly influential in the 18th century, when many gentry, and even middle-class, families followed the precept that a child's mind was a blank slate at birth, and that therefore the data to be written on it were crucial to a child's development. Thus these families adopted Locke's view that individual tutors were more likely to inculcate beneficial impressions than were schools.

Concern about the standard of teaching in schools led to the introduction of innovative methods by educationists such as Joseph Lancaster and Andrew Bell. Lancaster set up a school in London in 1798 offering free education on the monitor principle. This he set out in *Improvements in Education* in 1803. The following year the British and Foreign School Society was launched, adopting his methods. Andrew Bell introduced the Madras system, so called because he had developed it in India, where the more advanced pupils taught those at an earlier stage. Bell became superintendent of the National Society for Promoting the Education of the Poor in the Principles of the Established Church, founded in 1811. Such initiatives did something to improve the provision of education for schoolchildren.

Improvement cannot be claimed for the English UNIVERSITIES, however, which seem to have declined in both the quantity of students and the quality of tuition. They were also, along with the grammar and public schools, accused of retaining a medieval curriculum of classical literature and philosophy, at a time when scientific knowledge was expanding and there was a growing demand

for more practical subjects. Oxford appears to have deserved this reputation more than Cambridge, where the traditional curriculum was largely replaced by Newtonian natural philosophy, where the study of mathematics had primacy. But the Scottish universities and continental institutions were so much more advanced, especially in medicine, that many preferred to attend them. DISSENTERS, who were barred from the Anglican universities anyway, led the way in the modernization of the syllabuses in their own academies, from which many went to the universities of Edinburgh and Leiden. Glasgow and Edinburgh universities became the centres of the SCOTTISH ENLIGHTENMENT.

SEE ALSO CHARITY; LITERACY; SUNDAY SCHOOLS.
FURTHER READING G. Sutherland, 'Education' in F.M.L. Thompson (ed.), *The Cambridge Social History of Britain, 1750–1950,* Vol. 3 (1990).

electoral system. During the 18th century there were 269 constituencies for England and Wales, most of which returned two members to Parliament, where there were 513 English and Welsh representatives. To these were added 45 members for Scotland in accordance with the terms of the Act of Union of 1707, all of whom were returned from single-member constituencies. After 1800 a further 100 MPs sat at Westminster to represent Ireland. Clearly this distribution did not reflect the relative populations of the three countries; if it had, there would have been something like a ratio of five English and four Irish seats for every Scottish seat (*see* POPULATION). Instead this distribution of seats was held to be roughly equivalent to the relative tax burdens borne by each country (*see* UNION OF ENGLAND AND SCOTLAND and UNION OF BRITAIN AND IRELAND).

It was notorious, however, that the English constituencies were not distributed proportionally to the incidence of taxation. On the contrary, there were far fewer seats for the highly taxed Home Counties than there were in the relatively lightly taxed south and west. Thus the county of

Cornwall alone had 44 seats, only one less than the whole of Scotland after 1707. This was because representation had not been devised on a single occasion but had evolved gradually over several centuries. The notion that the 40 counties should each have two representatives – or knights of the shire as they were known – had some basis in rationality, though when Wales was incorporated in the 16th century it was only allowed one member per county.

However, the distribution of the remaining MPs into borough constituencies defied any rational scheme. It had come about as the result of interactions between power brokers at the centre and in the localities, in which local magnates had been able to use their clout at court to obtain representation for boroughs within their spheres of influence. This process came to an end with the enfranchisement of Durham and Newark under Charles II, after which the list of English constituencies remained fixed until the 19th century.

If the pattern of parliamentary boroughs was haphazard, so was the franchise within them. Although there was a national qualification for the vote in the counties, fixed by statute in the 15th century, there was no such arrangement for other constituencies. The qualification for the franchise in the shires was the possession of a freehold worth 40 shillings a year. When this measure had been enacted it was meant to restrict the county electorates to quite substantial property-holders. By the 18th century, however, inflation had reduced the value of a 40-shilling freehold to the level where quite small proprietors could exercise the right to vote. Since there were no electoral registers before 1832 it is difficult to estimate how many freeholders could vote in counties, but it is generally accepted to have been between 200,000 and 250,000.

By contrast, except in those boroughs where the franchise was restricted to the corporation, it is almost impossible to gauge the extent of the electorate. This was because the right to vote varied almost from borough to borough. The universi-

ties of Cambridge and Oxford were unique in enfranchising those of their graduates who were masters of arts. The remaining boroughs can be divided into four broad categories, one being the corporations. In some the franchise was attached to properties known as burgages. In others it pertained to the freemen. In yet others it involved some kind of residential qualification, such as being an inhabitant householder who paid the church and poor rates, sometimes known as scot and lot. The franchise could even descend lower than this to those who could maintain themselves independently of charitable provision, such men often being referred to as potwallers or potwallopers, because they were able to boil their own pot, in other words they were self-sufficient. There were even mixtures of these franchises in some towns and cities. For instance in those boroughs that also enjoyed the status of counties, such as York, the 40-shilling freeholders voted for the borough members, and not for the knights of the shire for Yorkshire, along with the freemen of the city. The result was a bewildering array of franchises involving an unknowable number of voters. At most, however, it cannot have been much more than 50,000. These together with the county voters came to roughly 300,000.

Thus the electorate comprised about a quarter of adult males in 1700, whereas by 1800 – when the total population had nearly doubled – the proportion enjoying the franchise had dropped to perhaps 15% of men over 21. Since there were many more boroughs than counties, this inevitably meant that the electorates in most were tiny in comparison with the thousands of 40-shilling freeholders who had the right to vote in the vast majority of English counties. Some boroughs – about a third – had under 100 voters, while perhaps a third again had between 100 and 500. This left a third with over 500, but only a handful could count their electorates in four figures. Among this handful was London, where membership of the livery companies conferred the franchise, the voters numbering at least 8000.

The small boroughs were susceptible to the patronage of local magnates. A country house on the outskirts of a parliamentary constituency with fewer than 100 voters – such as Ickworth, Lord Hervey's seat near Bury St Edmunds, where only the 36 members of the corporation could vote – exerted an enormous influence on the behaviour of the voters. The entire corporation was entertained at Ickworth, gifts were presented to the town hall, and eventually the Herveys came to control the returns for both Bury's seats. In small burgage boroughs patrons acquired control by purchasing the burgages. Thus the earl of Burlington came to own most of the properties that conferred the right to vote in Knaresborough, and consequently nominated its two members. Such boroughs were known as 'pocket boroughs'. There were also complaints about the unrepresentative nature of small decayed boroughs (known as 'rotten boroughs') early in the period, Defoe being especially scathing about some in his *Tour through the whole island of Great Britain*. But it was not until the later 18th century that a sustained campaign for their reform came into being (*see* PARLIAMENTARY REFORM).

Before the later 18th century the growth of oligarchy had not eroded the general belief that the electoral system ensured the representation of the people at large. Indeed, in the period of the TRIENNIAL ACT (1695–1715) and of the bitter party struggle under William III and Anne, there were frequent contests even in the smaller boroughs. Thus the Herveys had to contend with the Davers family for control of Bury St Edmunds. Lord Hervey eventually triumphed because he was a Whig while Sir Robert Davers was a Tory, and the efforts of the Whigs to exert control over small boroughs were backed by the court after the accession of the house of Hanover (*see* PARTIES). Before that the struggle between Tory and Whig rivals resulted in contested elections in most boroughs.

Following the passage of the SEPTENNIAL ACT in 1716 the incidence of contests declined. This was partly due to the inability of Tory patrons to compete with their Whig opponents, especially when the level of expenses rose as the return on the investment – a seat for an average of six years rather than the two years that had been the case before 1716 – became much more attractive. The decline was not immediate, for it was not until the general election of 1734 that it became obvious that the court-backed Whig oligarchy could gain a majority of seats owing to its control of small boroughs. After 1734, however, the numbers of contested elections slumped sharply, from a peak of over a third of all constituencies to a trough in the 1740s, 1750s and 1760s of under 15%.

Even in the central decades of the 18th century, however, electoral activity did not atrophy to the point where general elections were totally controlled by the oligarchy. Although the majority of small boroughs had succumbed by then, and the cost of contesting the counties had become so formidable that few knights of the shire faced a contest, there was still vigorous electioneering in larger boroughs which remained impervious to control by local magnates. Elections in and around London were particularly lively, with the 'independent electors of Westminster' living up to their name.

The result was the emergence of two electoral systems towards the end of the century. One was the system that the reformers attacked, symbolized by notoriously rotten boroughs like Old Sarum, which had no inhabitants but which returned two members to Parliament. Along with these could be counted the 45 Scottish constituencies, which had tiny electorates, most of them dependent upon aristocratic patrons who nominated their representatives. Such notorious examples tend to be regarded as typical of the unreformed electorate. But side by side with this were the larger constituencies, which upheld the notion that the House of Commons was ultimately the representative of the people.

SEE ALSO CONTROVERTED ELECTIONS.

FURTHER READING F. O'Gorman, *Voters, Patrons and Parties: The Unreformed Electoral System of Hanoverian England 1734–1832*

(1989); J.A. Phillips, *Electoral Behaviour in Unreformed England: Plumpers, Splitters and Straights* (1982); W.A. Speck, 'The Electorate in the First Age of Party' in C. Jones (ed.) *Britain in the First Age of Party 1680–1750* (1987).

eleven days. *See* CALENDAR REFORM OF 1751.

Elgin Marbles, sculptures from the frieze and pediments of the Parthenon in Athens, brought back to England by Thomas Bruce 7th earl of Elgin. Elgin went as ambassador to Constantinople in 1799. He hired a team of artists to draw the classical monuments of Athens, Greece then being part of the Turkish dominions. In 1801 he received permission for scaffolding to be erected round the Parthenon, so that moulds could be made of the sculptures in the frieze and pediments. Alarmed at their deterioration over the centuries, and especially under the Turks, he negotiated for their sale to himself, along with other ancient sculptures. He then undertook to transport them to England.

The first attempt was abortive, the vessel carrying them sinking off Cerigo in 1803. The marbles were, however, retrieved and shipped to England. Over the next nine years many more crates were sent from Greece, 80 arriving in 1812 alone. Meanwhile, Elgin had made his way back home after being detained by the French en route. There was much criticism of his exploit in removing the marbles from Greece, some saying it was an act of vandalism. Elgin put them on display to disarm his critics, and then sold them to the British Museum so that they could be viewed by the public. An act of Parliament was passed to pay him £35,000 for this purpose. This did not silence the criticism, which continues to this day.

FURTHER READING C. Hitchen, *Imperial Spoils: The Curious Case of the Elgin Marbles* (1987).

Emmet, Robert (1778–1803), Irish nationalist. The younger brother of Thomas Addis Emmet, secretary of the Society of United Irishmen, Robert was, like his brother, educated at Trinity College, Dublin, and then became involved in the Irish nationalist movement. Neither took part in the IRISH REBELLION OF 1798. But whereas Thomas did not get himself implicated in violence, Robert led an armed uprising in Dublin in 1803. When it was suppressed he fled the city, but was caught and brought to trial. His execution led to his being immortalized as an Irish martyr. The celebrated words spoken by Emmet at his treason trial have been frequently quoted by Irish nationalists and republicans as a patriotic statement of faith.

> Let no man write my epitaph; for as no man who knows my motives dare now vindicate them, let not prejudice or ignorance asperse them. Let them rest in obscurity and peace! Let my memory be left in oblivion, my tomb uninscribed, until other times and other men can do justice to my character. When my country takes her place among the nations of the earth, then, and not till then, let my epitaph be written.

empire. The term 'British empire' typically recalls the Victorian heyday of imperial dominion, when classroom maps showed swathes of the world's surface coloured red. Yet key territorial gains were made by Britain during the course of the 18th century and by 1815 the framework for further expansion was already firmly in place. Indeed, from the 1760s onwards it was becoming increasingly common for commentators to regard Britain's scattered and disparate overseas possessions as constituting a wider entity, or 'British empire'. It was in this period, following Britain's triumph over France in the SEVEN YEARS WAR, that the term first appeared in print. Britain soon after lost possession of its long-established colonies along the eastern seaboard of North America, but gains elsewhere – particularly in INDIA – more than compensated for this setback.

The so-called 'second British empire' was more extensive than the first. During an age of exploration in which British seamen such as James COOK played a prominent role, the Union Jack was being raised over ever more far-flung territories; within five years of the humiliating defeat in America, Britain's first Australian colony had been founded at Botany Bay (*see* AUSTRALIA) and a foothold in Africa established at Sierra Leone. By 1815, at the close of the long REVOLUTIONARY AND NAPOLEONIC WARS, an underlying shift in empire from west to east was apparent – the formal acquisition of Cape Colony and Ceylon from the Dutch, in 1795 and 1802 respectively, helped to secure the sea route to Indian possessions that now constituted the prized 'jewel' in Britain's imperial crown.

Britain's rise to major international power between 1688 and 1815 stemmed largely from its successful efforts to acquire territory overseas. Such impressive expansion was itself the result of a desire to *protect* the growing trade networks that provided much of Britain's wealth and power. In the early days of English colonization, expansion into new territories was typically motivated by commercial gain rather than imperial ambition – interest focused upon trade not territory. Colonial possessions not only provided raw materials for domestic consumption, but also offered ready markets for goods produced in England. From the Cromwellian era of the mid-17th century onwards, when colonial trade first began to expand, the state began to regulate this extensive and growing commerce. NAVIGATION ACTS were passed to discourage foreign competition and to ensure that England itself derived the maximum benefit from colonial trade.

During the course of the 18th century, Britain's trading patterns underwent a dramatic transformation; the traditional emphasis upon Europe gave way to the so-called 'Atlantic Economy'. Britain's own burgeoning range of manufactured goods was exported in exchange for raw materials that grew increasingly varied as British overseas possessions expanded. Whereas manufactured goods had represented a third of Britain's imports in 1700, by the 1770s they had dropped to less than 10%. The prime imports were now produce and raw materials such as tea and silk from India and the East Indies, and sugar, tobacco, coffee and rice from the Americas. The same period saw Britain emerge as the major European distributor for American tobacco and cotton cloth from India; indeed, at this time around one half of all British exports were actually *re*-exports.

The 'first British empire' had centred upon the Americas. English colonization of North America began in the early 17th century with the establishment of tiny settlements in Virginia and Massachusetts Bay. After an unsteady start, natural expansion boosted by steady immigration from Europe saw the American mainland colonies grow to represent a key segment in Britain's trading jigsaw. Not only did the dynamic continental colonies generate a wide range of raw materials, but their rapidly expanding population provided a major market for Britain's own manufactures. It was the growing awareness of the economic importance of these colonies that led Britain to divert considerable resources towards the destruction of French power in North America. By the defeat of France in 1763, Britain not only gained Canada, but also a theoretical sovereignty over the vast wilderness stretching west to the Mississippi. Within 20 years of this victory, the AMERICAN WAR OF INDEPENDENCE had forced Britain to relinquish the 13 colonies, which emerged as the United States of America. However, Britain retained control of territory north of the Great Lakes and, equally significantly, soon re-established commercial links with its former colonial possessions.

British interest in America was not restricted to the mainland. The islands of the Caribbean also exerted a powerful attraction for traders. The English presence in the West Indies was a consequence of attempts to establish bridgeheads on the margins of Spain's South American empire. In the 1620s, Englishmen withdrawing from an unsuccessful bid to settle in the Amazon lowlands, instead relocated to the islands of St Kitts, Nevis and Barbados. In 1655, England's Caribbean possessions were augmented by the capture of Jamaica from Spain. These English West Indian island colonies had originally attracted settlers interested in the cultivation of tobacco. However, the emergence of sugar cane as the staple crop led to the evolution of new plantation societies based upon slavery (*see* SLAVE TRADE): tobacco was usurped by sugar, and poor white settlers gave way to enslaved blacks from Africa. Although small in terms of land mass, the islands generated valuable cash crops and were backed by a powerful and vocal merchant lobby in Britain. Throughout the 18th century Britain fought hard to protect its West Indian possessions, and to acquire more territory at the expense of France. By 1800, it is estimated that these islands generated about one-third of all Britain's trade. In the 1790s, during the wars with France, Britain therefore sent the bulk of its army to the Caribbean. Interest in the West Indian islands slackened in the early 19th century when their economic importance declined and the gradual abolition of slavery undermined the viability of the plantation system.

British expansion in Africa was strictly limited during the 18th century; the so-called 'scramble for Africa' amongst the European powers was a phenomenon of the late 19th century. The limited British presence in West Africa during the Georgian era initially resulted from the steady demand for slaves to toil in the West Indies and the North American mainland colonies of Virginia, Georgia and South Carolina. In consequence the English established trading stations or 'factories' in isolated forts along the West African coast. Like other European powers, Britain was only able to purchase slaves because powerful and independent native rulers were interested in supplying them in exchange for trade links that enhanced their own political influence. Slavery was also a factor in the foundation of Britain's first African colony of Sierra Leone. This resulted from the efforts of the abolitionist Granville SHARP to establish a homeland for freed black slaves living in Britain; settled in the late 1780s, it became a crown colony in 1808.

Whilst expansion in Africa was insignificant during the 18th century, the reverse was true of developments upon the Indian subcontinent. Although trade alone motivated the first Englishmen in India, by the middle years of the 18th century the EAST INDIA COMPANY was harnessing European firepower and discipline to accumulate territory at the expense of local rulers. Mounting concern over the changing nature of the company's activities led the British government to impose regulatory legislation in 1773 and 1784. Such intervention indicated a growing desire to bring Britain's sprawling and diverse colonies under a more effective authority than that represented by the BOARD OF TRADE: this trend became more pronounced when the volatile revolutionary climate of the 1790s heightened metropolitan fears of colonial insurrection. The office of secretary of state for war and the colonies was first established in 1801, and the opening decades of the 19th century saw the Colonial Office playing an increasingly important role in the formulation of imperial policy.

British ascendancy in India was only established after protracted warfare against powerful and determined native opponents; such conflict serves as a reminder that British imperialism was all too often based upon coercion. Although representative governments with elected legislatures characterized Britain's older colonies and were gradually extended to the former possessions of rival European powers, the non-white inhabitants of new crown colonies fared very differently; despite British efforts to retain existing customs and legal systems, such peoples were subject to more authoritarian regimes. The British empire forms an emotive subject that continues to attract detractors and apologists alike. British imperial rule could indeed appear benevolent when set beside that of other European colonial powers, and sometimes went hand in hand with such genuinely humanitarian causes as the abolition of slavery; however, it should not be forgotten that its primary objective remained the exploitation of subject territories for the economic gain of the mother country.

FURTHER READING P.J. Marshall (ed.), *The Oxford History of the British Empire: Vol. II, the Eighteenth Century Empire* (1998).

enclosures. *See* AGRICULTURE.

Enlightenment, the. The concept of the Enlightenment is generally applied to continental Europe in the 18th century, and particularly to France, being associated with the *philosophes* or 'lumières' whose work was enshrined in Denis Diderot's *Encyclopédie*. However, although the Enlightenment is often viewed as an overwhelmingly continental phenomenon, it undoubtedly derived inspiration from Britain. Thinkers in both England and Scotland, where a distinctive SCOTTISH ENLIGHTENMENT has been recognized, likewise drew upon intellectual developments across the Channel. Indeed, until the 1790s, when many Britons recoiled from the excesses of the FRENCH REVOLUTION, there was a steady interchange of ideas between English and continental thinkers and writers.

The Enlightenment's disciples possessed diverse views but shared a common belief 'that things can change and should change'. They were united by a determination to look critically at traditional practices and beliefs and to explore fresh intellectual possibilities, especially through observation and experimentation. Many of the writers involved were strongly anti-clerical, wishing to assert the right of laymen to pronounce on questions of morality and metaphysics which the church had hitherto tried to monopolize. They sought to replace the church's preoccupation with preparation for the hereafter with an emphasis upon working for earthly happiness and improvement.

Enlightened thought clearly owed much to such influential Englishmen as the philosopher John LOCKE, who has been dubbed 'the father of the Enlightenment', and the scientist Isaac NEWTON: their contribution, along with the views of the DEISTS, placed England in the very vanguard of intellectual exploration at the dawn of the 18th century. The relaxation of ecclesiastical control and censorship after the GLORIOUS REVOLUTION of 1688 enabled their writings to be read and discussed in England with little danger of prosecution. In Roman Catholic countries by contrast, where the church, and especially the Jesuits, still exercised strict censorship, all these works were officially condemned; anyone reading them risked severe punishment.

It was in France that the most effective attack upon the control of the Catholic Church was mounted by the prominent *philosophes* Montesquieu (1689–1755) and Voltaire (1694–1778). These authors looked to Britain and the Netherlands as model states where a degree of religious toleration, representative government and a relatively free press prevailed.

Down to the 1740s, the continental Enlightenment was therefore often a matter of lauding Britain as an example to be imitated by absolutist Catholic regimes. This emphasis is apparent from the writings of both Voltaire and Montesquieu. Banished from France in 1726, Voltaire came to London where he stayed for more than two years, immersing himself in English culture. The most notable product of this period was Voltaire's anonymous *English Letters*, first written and published in English in 1733, followed a year latter by a French edition (*Lettres philosophiques*). In this immensely influential work Voltaire praised Britain's system of government, its religious toleration and the achievements of Bacon, Newton and Locke. Montesquieu also visited England, and in 1748 published *The Spirit of the Laws*; this brilliant attempt at comparative analysis of constitutions is best known for Montesquieu's praise of 'the separation of powers' – executive, leglislative and judicial – which he discerned in Britain's system of government.

Diderot's *Encyclopédie* had initially been planned as a translation of the Scottish *Chambers' Encyclopaedia* (1728). However, the 17-volume edition that appeared between 1751 and 1765 was essentially a new work reflecting the views of the *philosophes* and their sympathizers. The *Encyclopédie* became a standard work in England as elsewhere: it thereby inaugurated an era in which continental thought exerted a profound impact upon English intellectuals, so reversing the trend that had dominated during the first half of the 18th century. For example, Jeremy BENTHAM drew upon the penal theory of Beccaria, while Horace WALPOLE, Edward GIBBON and Lord SHELBURNE were among those writers and intellectuals who benefited from their contacts with the French *philosophes*.

A strong case has recently been made for a recognizable 'English Enlightenment' that went far beyond the work of Locke and Newton and combined with its Scottish counterpart to form a true 'British Enlightenment'. It has been argued that this was less a movement than a state of mind. While the search for the 'truth' has been criticized by postmodernists as lacking any objectivity, the examination of any proposition to determine whether or not it could be shown to be untrue – which has been called 'clearing away the rubbish' – was a characteristic of enlightened method which was as objective as any human enquiry can be. Authority, whether of the Bible or of the classics, was challenged as a touchstone of truth. It was not rejected out of hand but subjected to rigorous empirical analysis. This rational enquiring approach extended to almost all spheres of enquiry, from astrology to zoology. It is evident not only in politics and religion but also in gardening and medicine. It inculcated a scepticism about metaphysical explanations of reality such as pervades, for instance, Gibbon's historical investigations. Above all, it encouraged a questioning of authoritarianism as well as of authority, developing a liberal-minded individualism.

SEE ALSO SCOTTISH ENLIGHTENMENT.

FURTHER READING D. Outram, *The Enlightenment* (1995); R. Porter, *Enlightenment: Britain and the creation of the modern world* (2000).

enthusiasm, a feeling of religious ecstasy defined by Dr JOHNSON in his *Dictionary* as 'a vain confidence of divine favour or communication'. His derogatory definition expressed the conventional wisdom that it was a delusion in an individual of being divinely inspired. Jonathan SWIFT ridiculed it as fanatical frenzy in *A Tale of a Tub* (1704), which associated it with Puritans and DISSENTERS. It was later attributed to METHODISTS. George Lavington, bishop of Exeter, one of the most doughty opponents of the Methodists, accused them of 'pretence and enthusiasm'. WESLEY retaliated by denying that all who claimed to be inspired were deluded, and asserting that true inspiration was to be revered rather than reviled. By the end of the century 'enthusiasm' had largely dropped its pejorative overtones and acquired its modern meaning.

Equiano, Olaudah (1745–97), former slave. He was born in West Africa, where he was enslaved in 1755 and taken to the West Indies. The following year he went to England where he was taught to read and write. He remained a slave, employed mainly on ships trading with the Caribbean, until 1766, when he purchased his freedom for £40. For several years he continued to be a mariner, taking part in an expedition to the Arctic in 1773. He published his autobiography in 1789 as the *Interesting Life of Olaudah Equiano*. It proved to be a best seller, and influential propaganda in the campaign to abolish the SLAVE TRADE. In 1792 he married an English wife, Susannah Cullen, by whom he had two daughters. They lived in Soham, Cambridgeshire, where he died in 1797.

Equivalent, the, financial settlement accompanying the UNION OF ENGLAND AND SCOTLAND. When the union came about in 1707 the new British government expunged the national debt of Scotland. The sum proposed to pay off the debt – much of it owing to shareholders in the ill-fated DARIEN SCHEME – was fixed at the precise figure of £398,085 10s. 0d. Since Scots after the union were to take over their share of the burden of the

British national debt, this money was known as 'the Equivalent'.

Erastianism, the view, generally held by 18th century politicians and by many Anglicans, that the church should be subordinate to the state. The term was named after Thomas Erastus (1524–83).

Erskine, John, 11th earl of Mar. *See* MAR, JOHN ERSKINE, 11TH EARL OF.

evangelical revival, religious revival affecting many Protestants in the 18th century. 'Evangelical' was a term employed to describe anybody, Anglican or DISSENTER, who stressed salvation and the need for conversion or individual regeneration to assure it. Thus it came to be used of the early METHODISTS and of other Anglican churchmen, such as Henry Venn, curate of Clapham and vicar of Huddersfield, in the middle of the 18th century.

The 'revival' not only involved English sects, but was also an international phenomenon encompassing Pietists in Europe and the Great Awakening in the American colonies. Indeed the MORAVIANS, led by Count Zinzendorf, were active on both sides of the Atlantic and played a role in the English revival. Benjamin Ingham, an early adherent of John WESLEY, became a Moravian, and in 1744 leased to them the settlement at Fulneck near Pudsey in Yorkshire. Though he later separated from them and had his own following of Inghamites, the Moravians remain at Fulneck to this day.

By the later 18th century, however, evangelicalism became a recognizable movement in the CHURCH OF ENGLAND. It was initially associated with Charles Simeon, a Cambridge don and vicar of Holy Trinity from 1783 until his death. Simeon influenced many ordinands at the university, who became known as Simeonites. Another prominent figure in the evangelical revival was John Venn, the son of Henry, who became rector of Clapham in 1792. He influenced a group that became known as the CLAPHAM SECT.

Evangelicals were also involved in missionary work, founding the London Missionary Society in 1795, the Church Missionary Society in 1797 and the British and Foreign Bible Society in 1804. Their missionary activities were not directed entirely abroad. In many ways the Proclamation Society, set up in 1787 in response to a royal proclamation against vice, was a mission to fellow countrymen. Like the earlier Societies for the Reformation of Manners it advocated moral reform, but unlike its predecessors, which confined their efforts to reforming the lower orders, the Proclamation Society sought reformation from the top down. The outbreak of the war with France in 1793 renewed their zeal, as the French were seen as enemies to Christianity. Hannah MORE, another member of the Clapham sect, urged the elite to suppress vice as a weapon in the campaign against revolutionary principles. She also opposed radicalism in her *Cheap Repository Tracts*, which sold an estimated 2 million copies from 1795 onwards.
FURTHER READING M.A. Noll, D.W. Bebbington and G.A. Rawlyk (eds.), *Evangelicalism: Comparative Studies of Popular Protestantism in North America, the British Isles, and Beyond, 1700–1900* (1994).

excise crisis (1733), political crisis that threatened the ministry of Sir Robert WALPOLE. In 1733 Walpole introduced a scheme to replace the customs duties on the import of tobacco and wine with inland duties on these commodities. On being imported they were to be stored in bonded warehouses, paying an excise on being removed for sale in Britain. He hoped thereby to save over £200,000 per annum previously lost to the customs service by smuggling. The scheme provoked an uproar in Parliament and in the country. Fifty-four constituencies petitioned against it, largely on the grounds that an increase in excise surveillance would be a breach of liberty, since inspectors could search premises without notice, and cases brought against those accused of flouting the excise regulations were tried in courts without juries. Walpole was taken aback by the vehemence of the objections, which caused his majority to be eroded to the point where his control of the Commons was in jeopardy. He therefore withdrew the scheme, though it was used against him and his supporters in the general election of 1734.

FURTHER READING P. Langford, *The Excise Crisis. Society and Politics in the Age of Walpole* (1975).

exploration. Knowledge of the surface of the globe was increased considerably in the late 18th century by intrepid explorers who risked their lives in their efforts to answer previously unanswered questions. Three men were outstanding in these endeavours. James BRUCE solved the riddle of the source of the Blue Nile (the source of the main White Nile wasn't found till the later 19th century) while Mungo PARK tried to reach the source of the Niger. Above all, James COOK added more to geographical knowledge than any other man in the century.

Many other notable individuals were involved in exploration. At the end of the 17th century William Dampier had circumnavigated the globe, visiting Australia and discovering the islands of New Ireland and New Britain. Another circumnavigation was made in the 1740s by George ANSON. Navigation was made much easier when John Harrison's marine chronometers enabled LONGITUDE to be established with accuracy. On his first voyage Captain Cook used one of Harrison's chronometers to great effect. On that voyage Cook was also accompanied by the scientist Sir Joseph BANKS, who was subsequently involved in sponsoring other expeditions, such as that of Mungo Park. Meanwhile, Sir John BARROW explored in China and South Africa, and was later responsible for several notable expeditions to Africa and the polar regions, a particular aim being the discovery of the Northwest Passage, which Cook had failed to find in his final voyage to the Pacific. In the 1790s and 1800s Matthew Flinders (1774–1814) charted the whole coastline of Australia and Tasmania, considerably adding to European knowledge of the Pacific region.

FURTHER READING J. Brose, *Great Voyages of Discovery: Circumnavigators and Scientists, 1764–1843* (1985).

F

Feathers Tavern petition (1772), petition to
Parliament by Anglican clergymen asking to be
relieved from subscribing to the Thirty-nine Articles. The petition was drawn up at the Feathers
Tavern in London.

Many Anglican clergymen were uneasy about
subscription to all of the Thirty-nine Articles of
the Church of England. Their views were expressed
by Francis Blackburn, rector of Richmond, Yorkshire, in *The Confessional; or a full and free Enquiry
into the right, utility and success of establishing confessions of faith and doctrine in Protestant Churches*.
The first edition appeared in 1766, the second in
1767 and the third in 1770. In 1772 some two
hundred of the clergy who espoused Blackburn's
views drew up the Feathers Tavern petition, and
when it was defeated in the Commons by 217
votes to 71, several who had signed it left their
livings. They included John Jebb and Christopher
WYVILL, who thereafter channelled their energies
into PARLIAMENTARY REFORM.

Fenwick, Sir John (*c*.1645–97), JACOBITE conspirator. He had pursued a military career under
Charles II and James II and represented Northumberland, his native county, in Parliament in their
reigns. After the Glorious Revolution he was not
returned to the Commons, but turned instead to
plotting the restoration of James II. Although he

denied it, he was implicated in the plot to assassinate William III in 1696. When he was apprehended trying to escape to France after the
discovery of the plotters, he accused leading figures in the government of being Jacobites. They
struck back by bringing a bill of attainder against
Fenwick into Parliament. Although it passed both
Houses there were strong minorities opposed to
this arbitrary procedure. Nevertheless, after the bill
received the royal assent Fenwick was executed.

Ferguson, Adam (1723–1816), social philosopher, one of the leading figures of the SCOTTISH
ENLIGHTENMENT. After serving as a chaplain in a
Gaelic-speaking Scottish regiment, the Black Watch
(in which capacity he was present at the battle of
FONTENOY), and as librarian of the Faculty of Advocates, Ferguson became professor of natural philosophy at Edinburgh University in 1759. Five
years later he was appointed to the chair of pneu-
matics (sic: mental) and moral philosophy at Edinburgh. His *Essay on the History of Civil Society*
published in 1767 went through several editions
and reached a wide audience. With this and the
publication of his lectures he made a significant
contribution to moral philosophy.

Fielding, Henry (1707–54), novelist, playwright
and journalist. He was also chief magistrate of

Westminster, and in this capacity was instrumental in the formation of the BOW STREET RUNNERS.

After leaving Eton, Fielding went to London and began his writing career as a playwright, producing *Love in several masques* in 1728. Other plays followed, including *Tom Thumb, Pasquin* and *The Historical Register for the Year 1736*, which provoked the WALPOLE ministry to pass the Licensing Act (*see* THEATRE). He then turned to journalism, editing the *Champion* with James Ralph from 1739 to 1741. Later he wrote *The True Patriot* (1745–6), *The Jacobites' Journal* (1747–8) and the *Covent Garden Journal* (1752). Besides writing for periodicals he also wrote tracts, among which was *A proposal for making effectual provision for the poor* (1753).

But it is as a writer of NOVELS that Fielding is best remembered. His first novel, *Shamela*, a burlesque of Samuel RICHARDSON's *Pamela*, appeared in 1741, to be followed by *Joseph Andrews* in 1742. The *Miscellanies* of 1753 included 'The Life of Mr Jonathan Wild the Great'. *Tom Jones*, his greatest achievement as a writer, was first published in 1749. After completing his last novel, *Amelia*, his health broke and he went to Lisbon, where he died. *The Journal of a Voyage to Lisbon* was published posthumously.

This impressive output, written over 25 years and extending to so many genres, has raised questions about Fielding's consistency. In his politics he sometimes supported the COUNTRY PARTY and at other times the COURT PARTY. In his novels he frequently took a sympathetic view of the poor, whereas in his tracts he advocated harsh measures towards them. To some extent these ambiguities can be resolved chronologically. For much of Walpole's ministry Fielding sided with the opposition, whereas under the Pelhams he went over to the ministry. The patronage of the 4th duke of Bedford was crucial here, obtaining for him a place on the commission of the peace (*see* JUSTICES OF THE PEACE) for Middlesex and Westminster in 1747. Yet, while this might explain the apparent shift in Fielding's attitudes, it does not explain them away.

For both Court and Country sentiments can be found in his earlier plays, and similarly liberal and reactionary views of the poor coexist in his writings after 1747. Although Fielding's ideology will always provoke debate, there can be no question that he was never a Tory, let alone a Jacobite, but at bottom a Whig.

FURTHER READING M.C. and R.R. Battestin, *Henry Fielding: A Life* (1989).

Fiennes, Celia (1662–1741), travel writer. She belonged to a staunchly parliamentary and Presbyterian family, and was herself a Whig and a DISSENTER. She made several journeys round England between 1682 and 1712, recording them for her family. The accounts of her travels remained in manuscript until 1888, and were therefore not available to Macaulay, who would have found them invaluable for the third chapter of his *History of England*. For they have been mined by social and economic historians ever since, especially following their publication unabridged in 1947.

FURTHER READING C. Morris (ed.), *The Illustrated Journeys of Celia Fiennes* (1982).

Financial Revolution, term used by historians to sum up those measures introduced to underwrite the wars against Louis XIV in the periods 1689–97 and 1702–13. These wars, and those that followed during the remainder of the 'long' 18th century, required revenues on a quite unprecedented scale. Moreover, the taxes voted by Parliament, although initially adequate for war finance, took time to reach the Treasury. Meanwhile allies and the armed forces had to be paid and equipped, necessitating the anticipation of revenues. The government therefore resorted to loans secured on the various taxes, at first short term but increasingly long term, until a national debt came into being, which depended on faith in the regime's ability to pay the interest. This system of public credit was enshrined in the BANK OF ENGLAND established in 1694. In return for its privileged financial status the Bank lent £1,200,000 to the Treasury. In 1709 an act of Parliament increased its capital to £4,402,343 and allowed it to lend another £2,900,000.

Other corporations were also involved in the new financial machinery. The EAST INDIA COMPANY was frequently tapped for loans in return for the confirmation of its privileges. During the 1690s, when there were two East India companies vying for the government's favours, the state received substantial sums from this source. Thus in 1698 when the 'new' East India Company was incorporated, it lent £2 million to the government, and in 1708, just before the rival concerns joined to form the United East India Company, a further sum of £1,200,000 was advanced.

In 1711 the financial mechanism was completed with the launching of the South Sea Company, which incorporated the state's short-term creditors and transformed some £9 million of debt into the new corporation's stock (*see* SOUTH SEA BUBBLE). These links between the state and the City created a fiscal-military complex that underpinned Britain's newly acquired great-power status and permitted the nation to sustain major conflicts culminating in the REVOLUTIONARY AND NAPOLEONIC WARS.

SEE ALSO   BANKS AND BANKING; FISCAL-MILITARY STATE.

FURTHER READING   P.G.M. Dickson, *The Financial Revolution* (1967); D.W. Jones, *War and Economy in the age of William III and Marlborough* (1989).

Finch, Daniel, 2nd earl of Nottingham. *See* NOTTINGHAM, DANIEL FINCH, 2ND EARL OF.

fiscal-military state, term used by historians to characterize the financial and administrative apparatus that evolved in Britain to meet the strain of prolonged bouts of warfare between 1689 and 1815. During those 126 years open conflict occupied no fewer than 66. Moreover, there were periods of uneasy truce between the NINE YEARS WAR and the War of the SPANISH SUCCESSION, and again

between the War of the AUSTRIAN SUCCESSION and the SEVEN YEARS WAR – 13 years in total – in which the government sought to maintain its armed forces in readiness for renewed conflict.

The maintenance of a military capability was thus an overriding priority for much of the 'long' 18th century. Both the ARMY and the NAVY grew with every conflict to peak during the REVOLUTIONARY AND NAPOLEONIC WARS. Spending on the armed forces, and the servicing of debts arising from warfare, is estimated to have accounted for an average of between 75% and 85% of annual central government expenditure throughout much of the 18th century. The impact of protracted warfare becomes apparent when it is appreciated that total government spending rose from £49 million during the course of the Nine Years War, to more than £160 million in the Seven Years War, and in excess of £1600 million during the culminating French wars of 1793–1815.

The state's growing fiscal requirements were met by the creation of a machinery of public credit underpinned by taxation in the FINANCIAL REVOLUTION. These developments brought into being what has since been dubbed the 'fiscal-military state'.

FURTHER READING   J. Brewer, *The Sinews of Power: War, Money and the English State 1688–1783* (1989).

Fitzjames, James, 1st duke of Berwick. *See* BERWICK, JAMES FITZJAMES, 1ST DUKE OF.

Fitzroy, Henry, 3rd duke of Grafton. *See* GRAFTON, HENRY FITZROY, 3RD DUKE OF.

Flaxman, John (1755–1826), NEOCLASSICAL sculptor, designer and book illustrator, William Blake's 'Dear Sculptor of Eternity'. Flaxman was born in York but brought up in London, where his father manufactured models and casts for sculptors. He showed a precocious skill at drawing copies of these and making his own designs, winning prizes from the Society of Arts at the ages of

12 and 15. He then entered the Royal Academy Schools, where he met William BLAKE, with whom he formed a life-long friendship.

In 1775 Flaxman began to make patterns for WEDGWOOD pottery, including classical friezes, at which he showed unusual skill. He also earned fame as a designer of church monuments, his first commission being one for the poet Thomas CHATTERTON at St Mary's Redcliffe in Bristol, executed in 1780. He spent the years 1787 to 1794 in Italy, where he accepted commissions for copies of famous classical works of sculpture, including an enormous *Fury of Athamus* for Frederick Hervey earl of Bristol, the notorious bishop of Derry, to exhibit in his house at Ickworth. Following his return Flaxman settled down in London, and earned commissions that kept him busy for the rest of his life. Among the more celebrated are the memorials to Lord Mansfield in Westminster Abbey and Sir Joshua Reynolds in St Paul's Cathedral. The Royal Academy appointed him its first professor of sculpture in 1810.

FURTHER READING D. Bindman (ed.), *John Flaxman* (1979).

Flood, Henry (1732–91), Anglo-Irish politician. Flood was born in Ireland and educated at Trinity College, Dublin, and Christ Church, Oxford. He entered the Inner Temple with a view to becoming an English lawyer, but then returned to Ireland where he was elected to the Irish Parliament. There he emerged as a leader of the patriot opposition to the government in the 1760s, demanding reforms similar to those advocated by the COUNTRY PARTY in England. When Lord George Townshend became lord lieutenant in 1767 some concessions were made to these demands, including the passing of an Octennial Act, requiring a general election to be held at least once every eight years. Pressure was kept up on Townshend, even when he prorogued Parliament for over a year, by means of a popular paper, *The Freeman's Journal*, to which Flood contributed.

In 1772 Townshend was recalled. Flood then made overtures to the government, which were rewarded by his appointment as vice treasurer of Ireland from 1775 to 1781. His spell in office identified him with the repressive measures against the colonies and by implication against Ireland. Though his increasing criticism of these measures led to his removal, he failed to regain his former popularity with the opposition, even though he joined the Volunteer movement: initially a loyalist military response to the threat of French invasion during the crisis posed by the AMERICAN WAR OF INDEPENDENCE, the Volunteers had swiftly adopted a political agenda aimed at enhancing the powers of the Irish Parliament. Flood, nonetheless, played a prominent role in the campaign that brought Ireland legislative independence in 1782. He was never reconciled with GRATTAN, though, who challenged him to a duel after a bitter exchange. In the Volunteer convention of 1783 Flood supported an extension of the franchise, but not to Catholics. He left Ireland to enter the British House of Commons, where he distinguished himself by offending all parties. Failing to find a seat in 1790 he returned home to Ireland, where he died soon after.

Fontenoy, battle of (11 May 1745), engagement in the Austrian Netherlands between an Anglo-Dutch army and the French during the War of the AUSTRIAN SUCCESSION. While attempting to break the siege of Tournai, the duke of CUMBERLAND, commander of the allied army, decided to attack Marshal Saxe's larger French army, which was established in a strong defensive position at Fontenoy, under the eyes of Louis XV. Although Cumberland's command included contingents of Austrian and Dutch troops, the brunt of the fighting was sustained by his British and Hanoverian infantry. The duke's generalship proved uninspiring, but the courage and discipline of his redcoats was beyond reproach and came close to gaining the victory.

Swept by murderous artillery fire from the flanks and rear, the British battalions advanced to the very heart of the French position. As they breasted the slope and came face to face with the waiting French Guards, an extraordinary incident ensued: Lord Charles Hay stepped forward from the British ranks, swept off his hat and drank a toast to his opponents, expressing the hope that they would stand their ground and not run away as they had at DETTINGEN! Voltaire tells how Hay then invited the French to fire first. Bizarre as it seems today, Hay's request made sense at the time: in 18th-century warfare, the side that held its own fire until the last possible moment enjoyed an immense tactical advantage. Indeed in the close-range confrontation that followed, British fire-power punched a gaping hole in the French line.

The outcome of the battle teetered in the balance, but was finally swayed in Saxe's favour after a ferocious counterattack by the 'Wild Geese' – the Irish brigade of JACOBITES in French service. Under increasing pressure from French cavalry and infantry, Cumberland's battalions slowly retreated the way they had come. Both armies had suffered heavily, and Cumberland's crippling casualties left him unable to prevent the fall of Tournai.

Fox, Charles James (1749–1806), politician, the leading Whig member of the House of Commons, where he sat from 1768, when he was only 19, until his death at the age of 57. He was the third son of Henry FOX. He was foreign secretary in 1782 and 1806.

Fox served twice as a lord of the admiralty between 1770 and 1774, when Lord NORTH dismissed him for his obstructive behaviour to the ministry in the Commons. Although he was never a ROCKINGHAMITE, he allied with them in opposition to Lord North's American policies. When Lord ROCKINGHAM formed his second administration on the fall of North in 1782 he appointed Fox foreign secretary. During Rockingham's ministry Fox became associated with economical reform, though he did not then support PARLIAMENTARY REFORM. The unexpected death of ROCKINGHAM led to a struggle for the succession between Fox and LORD SHELBURNE, which the latter won.

Fox then went into opposition, and allied himself with his former enemy Lord North to defeat Shelburne in the Commons. These tactics, and above all the formation of the Fox–North coalition ministry in 1783, gave him a reputation for pure opportunism. But some sort of coalition was an inevitable consequence of the structure of politics at the time, and the issue that had previously divided the partners in the Fox–North coalition was removed with the recognition of the independence of the United States. The Fox–North ministry proceeded without the support of the king, who marked it down for destruction. His opportunity arose when Fox proposed a reform of the government of India that gave the Commons – rather than the crown – control of patronage in the subcontinent. George III made his opposition to the bill known in the House of Lords, where it was thrown out. The coalition was then dismissed and replaced by the ministry of PITT THE YOUNGER.

Fox protested that the king's actions were unconstitutional, and that a ministry should have the confidence of the Commons. Pitt certainly was not able to control the lower house, and was defeated in several divisions, including one of no confidence. But when the king dissolved Parliament and held a general election in 1784 a majority was returned to uphold Pitt in power. Fox protested that the dissolution violated a convention, that the Parliament elected in 1780 should be allowed to sit for the maximum period permitted by the Septennial Act of 1716; but this was pure sophistry. He also claimed that the government owed its majority to the machinations of the crown. Though royal influence helped Pitt to win in 1784, his government was also more popular than the Fox–North coalition. Fox himself nearly lost his election for Westminster, while so many of his supporters were either defeated or declined to stand that they were known as 'Fox's Martyrs'.

In opposition again, Fox finally associated himself with the cause of Parliamentary reform. He was also prominent in the dissenting campaign to repeal the Corporation and Test Acts. He became the inseparable companion of the prince of Wales. Their rakish social life of gambling, drinking and womanizing made the pair notorious. Fox also hoped that their friendship would be politically useful, and that when the king died and the prince became George IV he would bring in a Whig ministry. The opportunity seemed to arise sooner than expected in 1788, not because George III died, but because he became mentally unbalanced to the point where a regency seemed to be necessary. Fox, who was in Italy at the time, rushed back to England to exploit the situation. He badly mishandled it, partly because he was suffering from dysentery contracted on his travels. To the surprise even of his own supporters, whom he had not consulted, he argued in the Commons that the prince should be given full regal powers during his father's incapacity. Pitt outmanoeuvred him by pointing out that this was scarcely consistent with Whig principles, and also by delaying tactics that gave the king time to recover. When he did recover, the king swore he would never appoint Fox to any ministerial post again.

Fox played into the king's hands by opposing the war with France, which made him deeply unpopular. The war also led to a split in the Whig party in 1794, which left Fox with only about sixty supporters in the Commons. Their devotion to him testified as much to his capacity for friendship as to his political leadership. For much of the period 1797–1802 Fox did not attend Parliament. George III kept his word about refusing to appoint Fox again in 1804 when he declined to make him foreign secretary, partly because he supported CATHOLIC EMANCIPATION. After Pitt's death in January 1806 the king gave in, but Fox's enjoyment of the foreign secretaryship was shortlived, for he died that September. He lived long enough, however, to realize that the abolition of the SLAVE TRADE, which he had advocated, would succeed.

SEE ALSO LIBEL ACT.

FURTHER READING L.G. Mitchell, *Charles James Fox* (1992).

Fox, Henry (1705–74), politician, the father of Charles James FOX. After wasting his substance in riotous living on the continent, Fox returned to England and entered Parliament in 1735. In the Commons he supported WALPOLE's ministry and was rewarded with the post of surveyor general of the works in 1737. During the PELHAM administration he was a lord of the Treasury from 1743 to 1746, when he became secretary at war, largely at the recommendation of his political patron, the duke of CUMBERLAND. Fox defended Cumberland vehemently against attacks made upon him during the debates on the Regency Bill in 1751. In 1753 he led the attack on Hardwicke's marriage bill. His opposition was attributed to his having himself clandestinely married Lady Georgiana Caroline Lennox in 1744, a marriage that proved to be a great success.

On the death of Henry Pelham the duke of NEWCASTLE offered to bring Fox into the cabinet as secretary of state, but without the usual control of secret-service money, a condition he refused to accept. Though he continued as secretary at war, he was not a loyal supporter of the ministry, often combining with PITT THE ELDER to criticize its measures. Newcastle bought him off in 1755 by giving him a seat in the cabinet, the leadership of the Commons and later a secretaryship of state. He resigned in 1756, however, balking at defending the loss of Minorca.

Following the negotiations that led to the Pitt–Newcastle ministry in 1757, Fox became paymaster general, a post he held until 1765. It was regarded as the most lucrative in the government, especially in time of war, when vast sums went through the paymaster's office which were not audited until after peace was made. Fox used it to retrieve a parlous financial situation brought on by his own extravagance. It also sealed his reputation for corruption. When Lord BUTE – who had come into office promising to eliminate corruption from government – brought Fox into his cabinet in 1762, it gave Edmund BURKE the occasion to condemn him for hypocrisy. Fox used his position to eliminate the supporters of Newcastle from the administration in what became known as the 'Massacre of the Pelhamite Innocents'. In 1763 Fox was elevated to the peerage as Baron Holland. As Lord Holland he made little impact in the upper house. An attempt to reconcile himself with the Whigs was repudiated with scorn by ROCKINGHAM. Investigations into his accounts as paymaster were blocked by the king. He died at Holland House, where he had lived since 1749, making it one of the great social centres of 18th-century London.

France. Throughout the 'long' 18th century Englishmen eyed their neighbours across the Channel with a baffling mixture of undisguised suspicion and sneaking admiration. The first of these sentiments dominated, and was fuelled by an intense rivalry that regularly erupted into bouts of open warfare. Between the Glorious Revolution and the battle of Waterloo, France represented a remarkably consistent opponent to British ambitions: this colonial and commercial competition endured despite the upheavals that marked the end of the *ancien régime*. Just as the territorial ambitions of the Bourbon Louis XIV had appeared to threaten English liberties at the onset of the 18th century, so the sprawling Napoleonic empire revived similar fears 100 years later. So ingrained was this bleak perspective upon Anglo-French relations that as late as 1854, when the old antagonists were themselves fighting as allies in the Crimea, Britain's commander Lord Raglan habitually referred to his Russian foes as 'the French'.

During much of the period, Britain and France were officially at war with each other: the NINE YEARS WAR (1689–97) was followed by the War of the SPANISH SUCCESSION (1702–13), the War of the AUSTRIAN SUCCESSION (1740–8), the SEVEN YEARS WAR (1756–63), the AMERICAN WAR OF INDEPENDENCE (1778–83) and the REVOLUTIONARY AND NAPOLEONIC WARS (1793–1801 and 1803–15). For many of the intervening years – with the debatable exception of the Anglo-French alliance of 1716–31 – relations between the two powers remained strained. Some historians refer to the period between 1689 and 1815 as the second Hundred Years War. Repeated conflicts generated deep-seated animosities and ultimately developed a momentum of their own; for example, France's intervention against Britain on behalf of the rebellious American colonists in 1778 was largely motivated by a desire to avenge its humiliating defeat in the Seven Years War. Such lingering resentments also operated at a more personal level: the Marquis de Lafayette, who volunteered for service with the American rebels during the War of Independence, was the son of an army officer killed by British artillery at MINDEN in 1759. For Georgian Britons, France was undoubtedly the enemy *par excellence*. Hatred for the French was encouraged by press coverage of such 'war crimes' as the 'massacre' of Anglo-American troops by French-led Native American warriors at Fort William Henry in 1757 – an incident immortalized in James Fenimore Cooper's *The Last of the Mohicans*; it is significant that enthusiasm for the subsequent war with America increased markedly after French involvement transformed what had been an unpopular 'civil war' into a legitimate conflict against the traditional foe.

At a popular level, prolonged international rivalry whipped up a vigorous spirit of Francophobia. Syphilis had long been known as 'the French disease', and French workers who settled in London were vilified for taking the bread from the mouths of natives. Such sentiments underpinned the Haymarket Theatre disturbances in 1738 when press opposition to the employment of French comedians culminated in a full-scale riot. Cartoons depicted the English lion mauling the Gallic cockerel, while sturdy London butchers or fishwives bloodied the noses of effeminate French fops. The symbolic contrast between the roast beef of old England and the thin soup of France was portrayed at mid-century in Hogarth's *Calais Gate*, and much the same theme proved equally popular half a century later when GILLRAY contrasted a portly beef-eating Englishman with a scrawny sans culotte – shown relishing a meagre meal of raw onions – in his *French Liberty: British Slavery* of 1792.

Ideological differences likewise served to maintain anti-French feeling. Louis XIV's persecution of the Huguenot Protestant minority reinforced ingrained suspicions of Catholicism; in popular terms, the superstitious credulity of the French was linked with political intolerance and the poverty epitomized by 'wooden shoes'. Anti-Catholicism proved a recurring theme in the British press, while voyeuristic accounts of the sexual peccadilloes of French priests enjoyed a ready readership. During the Seven Years War, when Britain allied with Protestant PRUSSIA, the conflict was often portrayed in terms of a crusade against 'popery'.

Yet alongside such negative images of the French, very different attitudes to the old enemy could coexist. In seafaring communities from Cornwall to Essex, where smuggling was a way of life, cross-Channel contacts were frequent and cordial. For the members of metropolitan polite society in particular there was much to admire in French culture. Parisian manners, fashions and hairstyles set the standards to be matched, while French cooks, valets and masters of fencing and dance remained in heavy demand. And for those wealthy young Englishmen who rounded off their education with a protracted GRAND TOUR of Europe, the sophisticated galleries, salons and brothels of Paris were as much a feature of the itinerary as the picturesque ruins of Rome.

Educated Frenchmen likewise found much to admire when they looked across the Channel. British advances in manufacturing and agriculture sparked widespread interest. The famed English constitution, and the liberties theoretically enjoyed by Englishmen of all classes, were lauded by such intellectual heavyweights as Montesquieu. The *philosophes* Voltaire and Rousseau both visited England, as did Montesquieu, and maintained close contact with eminent British thinkers. French books enjoyed healthy sales in Britain, while the output of British authors found an avid readership across the Channel. And, just as wealthy Britons mimicked French elite culture, so the upper classes of *ancien régime* France adopted the clothing and customs of their British counterparts. In the years between 1763 and the crisis of 1789, the French aristocracy adopted horse racing with passion, and commissioned portraits of themselves in the hunting dress of the bluff and hearty English squirearchy.

Despite such evidence of mutual admiration, the relationship between Britain and France remained overwhelmingly antagonistic throughout the 18th century. The stereotypes created and reinforced during these long years of commercial and imperial rivalry were destined to blight relations for a further century, until the emergence of a belligerent and unified Germany created a new and common enemy.

FURTHER READING J. Black, *Natural and Necessary Enemies. Anglo-French relations in the 18th century* (1986); G. Newman, *The Rise of English Nationalism: A Cultural History, 1740–1830* (1987).

Fraser, Simon, 11th Baron Lovat (*c*.1667–1747), Scottish JACOBITE and chief of the clan Fraser, who paid the price for a lifetime of cynical political intrigue when he was beheaded for high treason on 9 April 1747. Fraser, who may have been as old as 79 when he finally went to the block, died in consequence of his support for the failed JACOBITE RISING of Prince Charles Edward STUART. It was a fitting end to a lengthy career in which Fraser's loyalties had frequently flitted between the Hanoverian and Jacobite camps.

Following a classical education at Aberdeen, Fraser was soon exploiting the opportunities offered by the disputed succession to the thrones of England and Scotland, dividing his time between London and the court of the exiled James II at St Germain. With the onset of the War of the SPANISH SUCCESSION in 1702, Fraser pledged his assistance to Louis XIV of France; in the following year he sought to ingratiate himself through a plot to foment rebellion in the Highlands – a gambit that led to his imprisonment in Paris on suspicion of double-dealing. Despite his reputation for duplicity, Fraser enjoyed the fierce loyalty of his clansmen, and they followed him when he backed George I during the crisis of the 1715 rebellion. Fraser was rewarded with a full pardon and the rent of the sprawling Fraser estates.

Despite such favour, Fraser was all too soon attracted towards the Jacobite camp during the Spanish-backed attempt of 1719, and was subsequently obliged to justify his conduct to the Hanoverians. In the wake of the failed rebellion Fraser attempted to win their favour by offering to recruit companies of Highlanders to police the troubled region. The plan was greeted with scepticism by the authorities, but the suggestion provided the germ for the future 'Black Watch' regiment.

Fraser obtained the full recognition of his title in 1733, but this failed to still his restlessness. With the arrival of the Young Pretender in 1745, Fraser decided to mobilize his clan for the Jacobites. Under Simon's son, the master of Lovat, they fought at Falkirk and CULLODEN. Following Prince Charles's defeat, the elderly Fraser went into hiding. Too old and fat to evade Cumberland's dragnet, he tried to hide in a hollow tree, but was soon captured at Loch Morar in the western Highlands.

Shortly before his execution, the corpulent Fraser was painted by William HOGARTH: his unrepentant gaze represents one of the artists's most powerful studies of character. As newspapers reported, Fraser met his death with superlative courage. So many people flocked to Tower Hill that a stand collapsed, and some twenty spectators died of their injuries – a circumstance that would no doubt have given the 'old fox' grim satisfaction. The Fraser family fortunes were eventually restored by the pardoned master of Lovat, who led a regiment of Highlanders under General WOLFE at Quebec.

Frederick prince of Wales (1707–51), eldest son of GEORGE II and CAROLINE OF ANSBACH. He was born in Hanover, where he stayed until 1728, then joined his parents in England. In 1729 he was made prince of Wales. Relations between the prince and the king and queen were strained, his mother frequently expressing the wish that her son was dead. They quarrelled particularly over his choice of a wife, quarrels that seemed to be resolved when he married Augusta of Saxe Gotha in 1736. But the failure of George II to increase the prince's payment from the civil list from £50,000 to £100,000, which the king himself had enjoyed as prince of Wales, perpetuated the quarrel.

The birth of a son the following year led to an open breach, with the prince taking elaborate steps to prevent his mother being present at the occasion. Frederick set up a rival court at LEICESTER HOUSE and attracted to it politicians opposed to his father's favourite, Sir Robert WALPOLE. The prince played a part in the downfall of the prime minister, using his electoral interest in Cornwall in the general election of 1741 against ministerial candidates. The possibility of a reconciliation with his father was dashed on the subject of the prince's allowance, however, and he continued in opposition.

During the JACOBITE RISING of 1745, while his younger brother the duke of CUMBERLAND was actually besieging Carlisle Castle, Frederick was reduced to bombarding an icing-sugar model of it with sugar plums. After the rebellion was crushed the government cashed in on its popularity by dissolving Parliament in 1747, a year earlier than was necessary under the SEPTENNIAL ACT. The prince was caught on the hop and, unprepared for the polls, the Leicester House candidates fared badly. His political associates nevertheless drew up elaborate plans to form a ministry in the event of the death of the elderly George II. Unfortunately for them their hopes were dashed when Frederick himself died suddenly and unexpectedly in 1751.
SEE ALSO REVERSIONARY INTEREST.

Freemasonry, male-only secret society espousing the principles of brotherly love, charity and faith in a supreme being. The origins of freemasonry have been obfuscated by masonic claims of ancient ancestry for the movement. But it apparently emerged in Scotland under the Stuarts, and became established in England after the Revolution of 1688. The first regular meetings of lodges date from 1691. Freemasonry flourished in the early 18th century, the first grand lodge being established in 1717, while the first constitution was adopted in 1723. Although associated with DEISM, and paradoxically with Jacobitism (*see* JACOBITES), it was not regarded as being subversive to Christianity in Britain – unlike continental freemasonry, which was condemned by the pope in 1738. Lodges associated themselves into a national organization in 1802.

French and Indian War, name given by Americans to the fighting in North America during the SEVEN YEARS WAR.

French Revolution. The French Revolution is commonly considered to have begun with the successful attack of a Paris mob on the Bastille fortress on 14 July 1789. Initially it promoted a constitutional government which adopted a pacific foreign policy. But in 1792 the regime became expansionist and anti-religious and put King Louis XVI on trial. He was executed in January 1793. War was declared on Britain soon afterwards. During the 'Terror' of 1793–4, hundreds of clergy, aristocrats and others were guillotined. A more moderate regime followed, giving way to the rule of Napoleon. The impact of the French Revolution on Britain varied over time. At first it was greeted with enthusiasm by radicals such as Richard PRICE, a dissenter whose *Discourse on the Love of our Country* on 4 November 1789 argued that it promised a better outcome for France than the GLORIOUS REVOLUTION of 1688 had held out for Britain. This provoked Edmund BURKE to riposte with his *Reflections on the Revolution in France* (1790), in which he claimed that whereas the Glorious Revolution had preserved the traditional institutions of England, the French Revolution threatened to destroy those of France.

Thomas PAINE in turn replied to Burke with *The Rights of Man*, part one of which appeared in 1791, to be followed by a second part in 1792. Despite their suppression, and the prosecution of Paine for seditious libel, cheap editions featuring extracts of both were circulated around CORRESPONDING SOCIETIES, discussion groups in London and some provincial towns. The fact that these were attended largely by craftsmen alarmed the authorities, especially when they sent delegates to a 'General Convention of the Friends of the People' in Edinburgh in 1793. Since Britain went to war with revolutionary France in that year, the fraternal greetings sent to French politicians by the convention could be construed as treason. The Scottish judiciary responded by sentencing delegates found guilty of abetting the enemy to transportation to Australia. Charges brought against English radicals, however, resulted in their acquittal.

The government of PITT THE YOUNGER, strengthened by the addition of some Whigs led by the duke of PORTLAND, embarked on a policy of repressing British 'JACOBINS'. In 1794 the habeas corpus act was suspended, and in the following year public meetings were banned unless approved by magistrates. The policy of suppression proved to be effective, there being few signs of radical activity for the rest of the period of the wars with revolutionary France. It also proved popular, most Britons rallying to the government in the 1790s. In 1792 associations to defend 'liberty and property' sprang into existence (*see* REEVES, JOHN). Although the government encouraged their formation, they also represented a spontaneous reaction. Paine was burnt in effigy on 25,000 occasions during the decade.

Only in IRELAND was there genuine support for the regime in France. The French responded by attempting a landing in Bantry Bay in 1796 and by encouraging the IRISH REBELLION OF 1798. Pitt was converted to the view that the only safe solution was to incorporate Ireland into the United Kingdom with the Act of Union of 1800 (*see* UNION OF BRITAIN AND IRELAND).

FURTHER READING H.T. Dickinson (ed.), *Britain and the French Revolution* (1989).

friendly societies, organizations for mutual insurance against sickness and unemployment, and to provide pensions for widows in case of death. Friendly societies first came into being in the 17th century. They flourished in the 18th century, and by 1793 there were 7200 societies with a total of 648,000 members. That same year, an act was passed for their encouragement, which became known as 'Rose's Act' owing to the fact that it had been introduced into Parliament by George Rose. A Registrar of Friendly Societies was appointed in 1795. Rose's Act sought to distinguish friendly societies, which were regarded as peaceful and respectable, from allegedly subversive artisan organizations that were being supressed at the time. Thus they were exempted from taxation and their funds were safeguarded from fraudulent officers. They consequently thrived, their membership numbering 704,350 by 1803 and 861,657 by 1815.

Friends of the People. *See* SOCIETY OF THE FRIENDS OF THE PEOPLE.

furniture. From the restrained elegance of the 'Queen Anne' style to the ROCOCO splendours of Thomas CHIPPENDALE and the inspired NEOCLASSICISM of Robert ADAM, the 18th century marked a golden age for British furniture design. Furniture makers flourished: more than 50,000 of them were active between the Restoration and the opening of Victoria's reign.

By time of the accession of Queen Anne in 1702, English cabinet makers already possessed skills comparable with the best of their foreign rivals. In the opening decades of the 18th century

such craftsmen were given ample scope for their talents as wealthy Whigs commissioned high-quality furniture to fill their BAROQUE and PALLADIAN mansions. Just as the multitalented William Kent is associated with innovation in architecture and landscape gardening at this period, so his name remains linked with the contemporary revolution in furniture design. In keeping with their surroundings, such pieces were executed on a monumental scale, and often mimicked stonework or sculpture.

Alongside the heavily decorated furniture of the elites, the first two decades of the century saw the refinement of functional domestic furniture: this more modest 'Queen Anne' style was characterized by use of veneered walnut, a smaller size, and less extravagant ornamentation. Just as the monumental pieces of the aristocracy complemented their grandiose settings, so this lighter and more restrained walnut furniture was well suited to the smaller town houses of the emerging 'middling' classes. Both styles remained popular until the 1740s, when the growing availability of mahogany, combined with the popularity of French rococo decorative forms, led to new fashions.

The fluid and fanciful forms of the rococo gave great scope to the skilled woodcarver. Furniture makers responded with elaborate designs. Some of the most inspired of these were showcased in the Yorkshireman Thomas Chippendale's catalogue, *The Gentleman and Cabinet-Maker's Director* (1754). This featured more than 270 designs spanning the gamut of domestic furniture, and became the blueprint for a distinctively English interpretation of the rococo in furniture. Rococo designs also adapted well to the taste for Chinese features – 'chinoiserie' – that emerged at mid-century. The same period witnessed the resurgence of medieval-style details in the furniture commissioned by devotees of the 'GOTHIC revival'.

From the 1760s a reaction against rococo decorative styles followed Robert Adam's advocacy of neoclassical motifs. George Hepplewhite's *The Cabinet-maker and Upholsterer's Guide* (published in 1788, two years after his death) was also influential in promoting the neoclassical in furniture design. The revolution in taste pioneered by Adam had a major impact throughout the decorative arts; his formal yet delicate designs, drawing upon ancient prototypes, were soon adopted by furniture makers. Men like Chippendale, who had excelled at the rococo, proved equally adept with the neoclassical: new designs reflecting these changing tastes were already incorporated in the third edition of Chippendale's *Director* (1762). This speedy response offered striking evidence of Chippendale's versatility, particularly as he had been unable to visit Italy and Greece to study such classical designs in person.

Furniture produced by Chippendale in the 1770s included outstanding examples of marquetry work, which may have been undertaken by specialists who contracted their skills to recognized makers. Despite the superb levels of craftsmanship involved, Georgian furniture often originated in large workshops capable of handling a wide range of commissions. The firm established in London by William Linnell and his son John catered for more than a thousand clients, while Chippendale deployed an extensive workforce to meet demand for his furniture, which was available in 'standard', 'refined' or 'luxury' versions to suit the patron's taste or purse.

FURTHER READING G. Beard, 'The Decorative and Useful Arts' in B. Ford (ed.), *Cambridge Guide to the Arts in Britain. Volume 5: The Eighteenth Century* (1992).

G

Gainsborough, Thomas (1727–88), portrait and landscape painter, best known for compositions that achieve a graceful harmony between both genres. Unlike most contemporary artists, Gainsborough came from a rural background; in contrast to the gritty, turbulent and overwhelmingly urban canvases of HOGARTH, his works often reflect a calmer and more idealized vision of the mid-Georgian era.

Born in Sudbury, Suffolk, Gainsborough went to London in 1740 and studied figure painting at the St Martin's Lane Academy. He taught himself landscape painting, drawing inspiration from the great Dutch artists of the 17th century, particularly Ruisdael. By 1748, when he returned to his native Suffolk, Gainsborough was already established as an accomplished landscape painter. He worked in Ipswich for a decade, painting portraits for profit and landscapes for pleasure. These years produced several works in which the figures of his sitters were posed against extensive and naturalistic rural backdrops. Among the most memorable of such hybrid paintings is that of *Mr and Mrs Andrews* (*c*.1750) – a definitive image of the country gentry and their landed estates.

For all their modern celebrity, in Gainsborough's lifetime such paintings were regarded as provincial eccentricities. Gainsborough instead adapted his distinctive style to the conventional life-size portrait. Moving to Bath in 1759, he remained there as a painter of fashionable society for the next 14 years. Gainsborough's sojourn in the West Country secured his reputation and witnessed a dramatic transition in his style: visits to such great country houses as Wilton brought him into contact with the works of Van Dyck, and led to an enhanced technique apparent in portraits of such society beauties as *Mary, Countess Howe* (*c*.1765) and the *Hon. Mrs Graham* (1775–6). Unlike his great contemporary REYNOLDS, who frequently delegated drapery painting to assistants, Gainsborough executed entire canvases in his own highly distinctive hand, often applying paint in an unconventional fashion that anticipated the impressionists.

Just as Gainsborough modified his portraiture after acquaintance with the works of Van Dyck, so the influence of Rubens led to a maturing of his landscapes. Unlike his earlier renderings of a recognizable Suffolk countryside, which suggest Gainsborough's role as a precursor of CONSTABLE, his later landscapes reflect the artificial and idealized ROCOCO style reminiscent of the French artist Watteau. Despite a continued interest in landscape, which led him to visit the Lake District in his later years, contemporary tastes ensured that this aspect of Gainsborough's output remained relatively unappreciated in his lifetime.

Gainsborough was invited to become a founding member of the ROYAL ACADEMY in 1768. Subsequent dissatisfaction with the Academy's approach to hanging his pictures led him to exhibit in his own London studio instead. Gainsborough is often depicted as an arch-rival of Reynolds, although they differed too widely in temperament and approach for such comparisons to have much meaning. Reynolds outlived Gainsborough, and in one of his celebrated *Discourses* generously praised the latter's key role in the development of a distinctively 'British' school of painting.

FURTHER READING E.K. Waterhouse, *Gainsborough* (1958).

game laws, series of acts passed between 1671 and 1830 with the aim of confining the killing of game – hares, pheasants and partridges especially – to those with landed estates worth more than £100 a year. These game laws were widely resented since wild animals were regarded as common property. There was consequently considerable evasion of them by poachers. Contrary to some perceptions of the law in the 18th century, poaching was not a felony. It should not be confused with deer stealing, which was regarded as theft of private property since most deer in England were bred in deer parks. Stealing from such parks was a criminal offence punishable by death. Poaching was punished by a fine or, if the accused could not pay, corporal punishment.

FURTHER READING P.B. Munsche, *Gentlemen and Poachers: The English Game Laws 1671–1830* (1981).

gardens. *See* LANDSCAPE GARDENING.

Garrick, David (1717–79), the most famous actor of the 18th century, who was responsible for bringing the THEATRE to the centre of Georgian England's cultural stage, when acting had previously been considered a low-grade activity.

Garrick spent his youth in Lichfield, where he began an enduring and valuable friendship as a pupil of Samuel JOHNSON. In 1737 Garrick joined Johnson on his journey to find fame in London. After dabbling in law and the wine importation business, Garrick gained widespread fame when he took to the stage, and his performance as Richard III in 1741 created a sensation. It was merely the first of many celebrated roles that mesmerized audiences accustomed to the wooden acting of his contemporaries.

Garrick's versatility as an actor won him acclaim for tragic and comic roles alike, although his impact upon the theatre went far beyond performance. In 1747 he became the manager of Drury Lane Theatre, and from this position he was to exert a powerful influence on the London theatrical scene for the following three decades. Garrick pioneered many modern theatrical techniques, and was influenced by innovations he encountered during a continental tour from 1763 to 1765. Besides his emphasis upon naturalistic interpretation of character, he introduced modifications in both theatre and stage design and lighting, experimented with historically 'accurate' costumes and encouraged professionalism among companies by insisting upon regular rehearsals.

As an actor-manager Garrick also demonstrated a curiously modern appreciation of the importance of publicity. His most famous performances were captured by HOGARTH and REYNOLDS, while his own patronage of the young Johann ZOFFANY resulted in a series of paintings that gained wider circulation as engravings.

Besides writing his own plays and staging those of contemporaries, Garrick demonstrated a keen interest in preserving classics from the past. He performed a particularly important role in reviving the neglected works of Shakespeare, although he often took considerable liberties with the texts in an effort to tailor them to his own conception of the audience's expectations. His obsession with the Bard culminated in an elaborate 'Shakespeare Jubilee' at Stratford-upon-Avon in 1769. Despite dismal weather, Garrick's well-oiled publicity machine ensured that it proved one of the century's most influential cultural events. Garrick's retirement in 1776 generated interest across Europe, and his fame and popularity earned him burial in Westminster Abbey.

FURTHER READING A. Kendall, *David Garrick* (1985).

Gay, John (1685–1732), minor poet and friend of POPE and SWIFT who achieved overnight celebrity when he wrote *The Beggar's Opera*. Combining popular songs with comedy and biting satire, Gay's creation became the most popular theatrical work of the 18th century. Although rejected by Colley Cibber, the manager of Drury Lane Theatre, *The Beggar's Opera* was an immediate success when John Rich produced it at Lincoln's Inn Fields. Gay's spoken dialogue was punctuated by an array of folk tunes and popular songs drawn from Britain and France, and these were arranged by the established German composer Johann Pepusch. The first performance, on 29 January 1728, triggered a record-breaking run that went some way to recouping the financial losses that Gay had earlier sustained as a result of the SOUTH SEA BUBBLE.

The Beggar's Opera achieved the rare feat of appealing to all classes of society. Set against the backdrop of Newgate Prison, Gay's ballad opera exploited the contemporary fascination with the criminal underworld to present a satire whose targets ranged from Italian opera to corrupt statesmen. The central characters Macheath and Peachum were thinly veiled portraits of the popular highwayman Jack Sheppard and the notorious 'thief-taker' Jonathan WILD, both of whom had recently ended their days on the gallows at Tyburn, and *The Beggar's Opera* suggested that the methods of the prime minister, Sir Robert WALPOLE, had much in common with those employed by such predators. A pivotal moment in the play's third act formed the subject of several important paintings by HOGARTH.

Despite its great popularity, *The Beggar's Opera* did not escape criticism from those who considered it a crude and dangerous glamorization of crime, and Gay's sequel of 1729, *Polly*, was banned by the lord chamberlain. A life-long sufferer from asthma, Gay died soon after. The enduring appeal of his most celebrated work was demonstrated when Brecht adapted its satirical approach for *The Threepenny Opera*.

general warrants, warrants that did not name the persons to be apprehended in the pursuit of the authors, printers and publishers of alleged libels. Such warrants were issued by the secretaries of state for the south, whose responsibilities included those assumed by the home secretary when the Home Office was set up in 1782. They based their right to issue such general warrants on the powers given to their predecessors by the Licensing Act of 1662, even though this had lapsed in 1695. John WILKES challenged the general warrant under which he was arrested in 1763 as the author of *The North Briton* number 45. He successfully sued the undersecretary who had arrested him under the warrant in the Court of King's Bench, and in 1768 also prosecuted the secretary, Lord HALIFAX, who had issued it. The Wilkes cases established the illegality of general warrants.

SEE ALSO CAMDEN, CHARLES PRATT, 1ST EARL.

Gentleman's Magazine, The, monthly periodical – the first to describe itself as a magazine – that was launched in January 1731 and survived until 1914. It was far and away the most successful of all the magazines that appeared in the 18th century. Its circulation is estimated at more than 10,000 per issue. Edward Cave, its founder, was the son of a Rugby shoemaker, and had had experience as a journalist on various provincial and London newspapers before he decided to set up on his own. Cave signed himself 'Sylvanus Urban', indicating a desire to appeal to both town and country, and indeed the first issue was subtitled *Trader's Monthly Intelligencer*. This subtitle was replaced by *Monthly Intelligencer*, which was itself dropped later.

Initially the magazine was a distillation of the news, particularly of politics and international affairs. Samuel JOHNSON contributed to it after 1738, and got round the prohibition on reporting parliamentary debates by the transparent device of recounting fictitious discussions in the senate of Lilliput. But the magazine also commented on the manners of the times, published poems and reviewed books. Gradually original materials submitted to the magazine superseded the digests of other publications, which probably accounts for its survival where competitors perished.

FURTHER READING E.A. Reitan, *The Best of the Gentleman's Magazine* (1987).

George I (1660–1727), elector of Hanover (1698–1727) and king of Great Britain and Ireland (1714–27). George succeeded Queen ANNE by virtue of the ACT OF SETTLEMENT (1701) and the Act of Union (1707; *see* UNION OF ENGLAND AND SCOTLAND; HANOVERIAN SUCCESSION). The house of Hanover had been chosen because of its Protestantism, George himself being a Lutheran who had married the Protestant Sophia Dorothea of Celle. The asset of his marriage turned to a liability, however, when he divorced his wife for adultery and kept her under house arrest until her death, while he himself openly consorted with mistresses.

Although he had known for 13 years that he would rule the English, George had made little or no attempt to learn their language, and communicated with his ministers largely in French. Those ministers were overwhelmingly Whig, since George distrusted the Tories, whom he accused of betraying the Grand Alliance in the treaty of UTRECHT and of favouring his rival, James Francis Edward STUART, the Old Pretender. George's poor English restricted his ability to conduct business, though the notion that by 1718 he had ceased to attend the cabinet is incorrect – he retained an interest in cabinet concerns, especially those involving military or foreign affairs.

George had been elector of Hanover since 1698 and showed a preference for his electorate, which he visited as often as he could. Such visits were made easier by the repeal in 1715 of a clause

in the Act of Settlement that prevented the Hanoverian monarchs from leaving England without the consent of Parliament. The first visit occurred in 1716, after the crushing of the JACOBITE RISING of 1715 had made his throne secure. The visit fomented arguments between those ministers George took with him, STANHOPE and SUNDERLAND, and those like 2nd Viscount TOWNSHEND and WALPOLE whom he left behind. The latter particularly objected to the use of British resources to achieve Hanoverian objectives in the Baltic. Their quarrel resulted in the Whig schism that ended the two-party system that had begun to emerge under Anne: George retained the services of Stanhope and Sunderland, while Townshend and Walpole went into opposition.

The following year George's son George Augustus – the future GEORGE II – fell out with the ministry and set up a rival household to his father at Leicester House. This became a focus for opposition politicians until father and son were reconciled in 1720. Townshend and Walpole came back into the ministry, and fortunately for them this was after the decisions had been taken that led to the SOUTH SEA BUBBLE. They thus escaped involvement in the scandal that threatened the dynasty, since George I and his household as well as leading ministers like Sunderland were implicated in it. The king survived partly because Walpole's efforts to screen the major culprits from investigation were successful, and partly because the Pretender failed to exploit the situation for his own advantage. When he did stir up followers like Francis ATTERBURY to plot on his behalf in 1722 it was too late.

By then the obstacles to the advancement of Townshend and Walpole had been removed with the deaths of Stanhope and Sunderland. George had come to rely on his ministers even more than on Hanoverian advisers such as Bernstorff and Bothmar, who had been prominent earlier in the reign. He could now leave England for Hanover without causing major political upheavals. It was on such a visit that he had a stroke and died at Osnabrück in 1727.

FURTHER READING R. Hatton, *George I: Elector and King* (1978).

George II (1683–1760), king of Great Britain and Ireland (1727–60) and elector of Hanover. George was known to Britons as a soldier who had fought gallantly at the battle of OUDENARDE in 1708 before he accompanied his father GEORGE I to England in 1714. The pacific policy of WALPOLE meant that he was unable to display his martial qualities again until 1743. Then he led his troops into battle, the last British king to do so, at the battle of DETTINGEN in 1743. Although he did not fight in it, being 73 when it began in 1756, the SEVEN YEARS WAR reached its apogee in the 'wonderful year' of 1759, when British arms achieved their greatest successes of the century. George II was perhaps first and foremost a soldier-king. Certainly his notorious dislike, verging on hatred, of his elder son FREDERICK, and his adulation of his younger son, William Augustus duke of CUMBERLAND, was fuelled by his military ideals. Frederick to him was a wimp, while Cumberland was 'the martial boy'.

Although he had to yield control over his rights of political patronage to his ministers, George rigorously retained it over appointments in the armed forces. It was the fact that ministers had to keep the confidence of the Commons as well as the crown that led George to complain that he was 'in toils' to them. The first occasion of this dependence is often claimed to have been at the very outset of the reign, when he tried to make Spencer COMPTON his prime minister, but had to concede the leadership of the ministry to Walpole because of the latter's greater parliamentary skills. However, the incident seems to have arisen not because the king wanted to drop Walpole, but because he was anxious to demonstrate where the power ultimately lay. For at the end of the day the king's support was indispensable to ministers. Although they could bring pressure to bear on him to sack men he liked but they did not, as the PELHAMS did in 1744 and again in 1746 when they procured the dismissal of CARTERET, they could not stay in power

for long unless he showed that they enjoyed his confidence.

Walpole gained George's favour partly because he cultivated the support of the queen, CAROLINE OF ANSBACH. Caroline was the most cultivated consort of a Hanoverian monarch, being something of a BLUESTOCKING. She was shrewd enough to ensure that her unlettered husband made her views his own. Her death in 1737 was undoubtedly a blow to Walpole. It was of course an even bigger blow to George, who undoubtedly loved her and sobbed bitterly at her deathbed. His reply to her advice that he should marry again, 'No, I shall have mistresses', might not have been the most tactful, but was surely well intentioned. The fact that Frederick went into open opposition in the same year as his mother's death was another source of grief to the king, who had quarrelled with his own father. But where he had been reconciled to George I, Frederick remained irreconcilable until his own death in 1751. While this quarrel could have seriously weakened the dynasty, the final defeat of the JACOBITES at CULLODEN in 1746 considerably strengthened it and the ministry of Henry Pelham. When Pelham died in 1754, George II said, 'Now I shall have no more peace.'

George's prediction became true in an unintended sense when war broke out in North America that very year, and engulfed Europe two years later. It was also true of the king's relations with the politicians, for the outbreak of war enabled PITT THE ELDER to outmanoeuvre the duke of NEWCASTLE, Pelham's successor, and force himself on the king as prime minister despite George's objections. But the spectacular successes of 1759 reconciled the irascible king to his maverick premier. The following year he died of a stroke while sitting on his water closet.

FURTHER READING J.H. Plumb, *The First Four Georges* (1956); C. Trench, *George II* (1973).

George III (1738–1820), king of Great Britain and Ireland (1760–1820) and elector of Hanover. George was the grandson of George II and the son of FREDERICK PRINCE OF WALES and his wife Augusta of Saxe Coburg. He was the first British monarch to be born in his kingdom since the accession of the house of Hanover, and boasted that he 'gloried in the name of Briton'. He even referred to Hanover as 'that horrid electorate'. Yet, though he flirted with an English heiress, he married in 1761 CHARLOTTE of Mecklenburg Strelitz, a German princess.

The decision to marry Charlotte was, however, on the advice of his tutor, Lord BUTE, whose every word the young king had followed through his adolescence. Bute indeed was alleged by Whig politicians and historians to have imbued George with unconstitutional notions, stressing the prerogative rights of the crown over its dependence upon Parliament. Ever since the influential Oxford historian Sir Lewis Namier (1880–60) exploded the Whig myth it has been accepted that Bute's lessons in the constitutional duties of the monarchy were unexceptionable. In practice, nevertheless, if not in theory, George did play a role in politics that had not been enjoyed by his immediate predecessors. He acted as his own first minister, dispensing with the services of the duke of NEWCASTLE, who had presided over the victories of the SEVEN YEARS WAR, and replacing him with Bute, who was largely a figurehead rather than a premier. When in 1763 the new ministry negotiated the peace of PARIS, bringing the war to an end, it was accused of betraying the nation's interests, conceding to the French more than was necessary after the victories gained over them. Among the more vociferous critics of the peace was John WILKES, who deplored the king's speech to Parliament on the subject in the 45th issue of his paper *The North Briton*. By 'North Briton' Wilkes meant 'Scot', and his main target was the Scottish favourite Bute. Bute was so taken aback by the ferocity of his opponents at this time that he resigned in 1763.

The king appointed George GRENVILLE to succeed Bute, but soon wished he had not done so. For although they were agreed that Wilkes should be silenced, and that the Americans should be taxed with the STAMP ACT, they disagreed on most other subjects. Grenville was resentful of the continued influence of Bute 'behind the curtain'. The king particularly resented Grenville's handling of the regency crisis in 1765. In that year George III suffered the first attack of an illness that was eventually to incapacitate him completely. While its symptoms were mental derangement the disease itself has been diagnosed as a rare physical complaint, porphyria. A Regency Act was considered necessary in case another attack made the king unfit to rule, and against George's will Grenville excluded his mother, the queen dowager, from the list of regents before the bill was presented to Parliament. The prime minister's clumsy handling of a delicate matter affecting the royal family led George to dismiss him.

Instead of turning to Bute for advice the king turned to his uncle the duke of CUMBERLAND. This was a sign not only that Bute's influence was rapidly waning – though the former favourite continued to be suspected of undue influence for years to come – but that the king was desperate. He had not previously sought help from the 'Butcher of Culloden', who anyway advised him to take in the heirs of the Newcastle Whigs, now led by the marquess of ROCKINGHAM. The Rockingham administration, though it lasted long enough to repeal the Stamp Act, was short-lived. In 1766 George turned to the man who had led the most successful ministry since Walpole's, the elder PITT. Unfortunately Pitt's second ministry was a fiasco. The prime minister's mental stability, always precarious, gave way, and his inability to conduct affairs led to his resignation in 1768. This left the duke of GRAFTON at the head of the ministry. Grafton's ineptitude led him to be ridiculed in some of the most vitriolic satires of the century, the *Letters of JUNIUS*. Clearly here was not a man to shield the king from the Whig clans.

By this time, however, the generation of politicians that had dominated politics under George II was being steadily removed by death. When Grafton resigned in 1770 the political world was very different from that which George III had inherited a decade before. By now too he had found his ideal prime minister in Lord NORTH, who became a personal friend of the king and enjoyed the support of the Commons. Until he lost that support twelve years later North provided the stable government that George had been seeking since his accession. In that respect the year 1770 was as much of a turning point as 1760 had been.

North eventually fell because of the loss of the American colonies. George III was personally held to be responsible for the measures leading to colonial resistance, according to the American Declaration of Independence. While the charge that he deliberately designed to erect a tyranny over the colonists is unwarranted, he himself accepted on declaring war that the die was cast, and that they must either submit to him or become independent. The fact that they had achieved their independence was brought home to him by the defeat of British troops at YORKTOWN in 1781. George III would have carried on the conflict – he was always more hawkish than his prime minister – but the House of Commons had no stomach for further fighting. George actually drafted a declaration of abdication and even of voluntary exile, but then thought better of it. In 1783 he recognized the independence of the United States, and in 1785 received John Adams as the first American ambassador to the court of St James's. 'I was the last to consent to the separation,' he told his excellency, 'but the separation having been made ... I say now that I would be the first to meet the friendship of the United States as an independent power.' (*See also* AMERICAN COLONIES 1763–1776; AMERICAN WAR OF INDEPENDENCE.)

The two years that followed the fall of Lord North were characterized by political instability such as had marked the opening years of the king's reign. Once again the king was in the toils of factions. Rockingham formed a second ministry, which pushed through measures to reduce the crown's influence over the Commons. But its stay in power was short-lived, for Rockingham died a few months after taking office. Lord SHELBURNE and Charles James FOX struggled for the leadership, a contest that the king decided by making Shelburne chief minister. Fox then went into opposition and shocked the political world by joining with North, formerly his bitter enemy, to work for Shelburne's removal. They contrived to do this by getting the House of Commons to pass a vote of no confidence. This manoeuvre succeeded, resulting in the formation of the most remarkable of George III's ministries, the Fox–North coalition. George was the most shocked at this outcome, and once again contemplated abdication. Eventually, however, he was able to bring about the defeat in the House of Lords of a major measure concerning India that the coalition had put forward (*see* BOARD OF CONTROL). This was the most intrusive intervention in parliamentary politics of any 18th-century monarch since Queen Anne had created twelve peers at a stroke in 1712. The king let it be known that any lord who supported the India Bill would be regarded as his enemy. Though Fox protested that it was unconstitutional, this tactic allowed the king to remove the coalition and to ask PITT THE YOUNGER to form a ministry.

At first Pitt could not command a majority in the Commons, but early in 1784 Parliament was dissolved and a general election was held. This was the ultimate answer to those who held that the king could not appoint a minister who lacked the confidence of the Commons, for the influence of the crown was sufficient in many small constituencies to ensure a majority for the prime minister. On this occasion, however, even in large constituencies Pitt's supporters prevailed. George III was more popular than Charles James Fox. His popularity was to increase as he entered the later years of his reign.

These later years were clouded by the renewed onset of the illness that made him incapable of conducting business. In 1788 it was so severe that he had to be restrained in a straitjacket, and again a Regency Bill was introduced to provide for the government of the kingdom while he was incapacitated. The opposition tried to secure extensive powers for the prince of Wales (the future GEORGE IV). Pitt stonewalled in the Commons, hoping the king would recover. Eventually George did get better, and, on learning of the opposition's tactics over the Regency Bill, he determined never to employ them in his service.

During the 1790s the king largely withdrew from administration, leaving the day-to-day government to his trusted prime minister Pitt. The decade was marked by war with revolutionary France, which broke out in 1793 (*see* REVOLUTIONARY AND NAPOLEONIC WARS). French attempts to exploit Irish discontent led Pitt to pass the Act of Union with Ireland in 1800, which brought 100 members representing the island to Westminster (*see* UNION OF BRITAIN AND IRELAND). The prime minister thought that a logical corollary to this was to give Catholics in Ireland relief from the penal laws (*see* CATHOLIC EMANCIPATION). George III, who felt that it was his duty to uphold the constitution in church and state, was convinced that this would be a betrayal of his coronation oath and refused to go along with it. Pitt consequently resigned in 1801.

The episode brought on another bout of the king's illness. He was afflicted with it again in 1804. On both these occasions he recovered. But in 1810 there came the final, permanent onset of the illness, necessitating a regency that was to last through the next decade, until the king's death ended his remarkable 60-year reign. Those years had seen the monarchy first weakened, especially by the loss of the American colonies, and then strengthened, despite or even because of the king's illness. His obvious sincerity, devotion to his wife, and dislike of corruption led him to rise above the political strife to become a symbol of national unity.

FURTHER READING J. Brooke, *King George III* (1972); L. Colley, 'The Apotheosis of George III: Loyalty, Royalty and the British Nation 1760–20' in *Past and Present* (1984), 94–9; R. Pares, *George III and the Politicians* (1953).

George IV (1762–1830), king of the United Kingdom of Great Britain and Ireland (1820–30), prince regent (1811–20) during the final illness of his father, GEORGE III.

After a strict upbringing and rigorous education George was given a separate establishment in 1780. He immediately used his independence to pursue pleasure. In the company of Charles James FOX he acquired the reputation of a rake. He gambled at White's, drank heavily and womanized, to the scandal of his upright parents. These activities ran up huge debts, which his Whig friends liquidated when the ROCKINGHAM ministry came to power in 1782. On attaining his majority he entered the House of Lords and supported the Whigs. Thus he canvassed for Charles James Fox in the Westminster election of 1784. By then George was again heavily in debt, but this time there was no friendly government to bail him out. His irate father refused to help, and he had to retrench until PITT THE YOUNGER finally agreed to a grant to pay off his debts in 1787. George immediately embarked on ostentatious extravagance, including the building of the Brighton Pavilion.

The prince was at Brighton in 1788 when news came of George III's illness. In the ensuing debates over the need for a regency, the prince and Fox were blatantly opportunist, insisting on full regal powers while the king was incapacitated. When the king recovered, their opportunism proved counterproductive.

Although George had gone through a form of marriage ceremony in 1785 with a widow, Mrs Fitzherbert, this had never been recognized by the king, and was in breach of the Royal Marriages Act. George therefore felt free to marry Princess Caroline of Brunswick in 1794. The marriage was doomed from the start: when he first met Caroline the prince complained of faintness and demanded a glass of brandy. Soon after the birth of Charlotte, their first and only child, George sought a separation and even made a will leaving what little he would have after the settlement of his debts to Mrs Fitzherbert, his 'true wife'.

Nevertheless, as a result of his marriage he was reconciled with his father, and again received parliamentary assistance to repair his precarious financial position. Even so he had to be assisted again in 1803.

When George III succumbed to insanity permanently in 1811 the prince was made regent, at first with restrictions on his prerogatives, but by 1812 with full regal powers. The Whigs, who expected to take office on his becoming regent, were disappointed when he refused to dismiss the ministers appointed by his father. During the Regency the capital was transformed with buildings designed by NASH, and Regent's Park and Regent Street survive as monuments to his extravagance and taste.

FURTHER READING C. Hibbert, *George IV, Regent and King* (1973); E.A. Smith, *George IV* (1999).

George prince of Denmark (1653–1708), the husband of Queen ANNE, whom he married in 1683. George is usually regarded as a nonentity. Charles II opined that he had 'nothing in him' whether 'drunk or sober', while James II, on hearing that George had joined the Revolutionaries in 1688, dismissed him with '*Est-il possible?*' Anne certainly regarded his abilities too highly when she tried to get him accepted as commander in chief of the allied armies in 1702, so that he had to be fobbed off with the grandiloquent but empty title of generalissimo. Her appointment of him as lord admiral was also ambitious, and uniquely he had to be assisted by an Admiralty Council, which did the real work.

But George was not without merit. As a Lutheran he was staunch for the Protestant cause. His own Protestantism had been the main reason why he had not been elected king of Poland in the 1680s, and why after 1688 he was totally behind the Revolution and the HANOVERIAN SUCCESSION. He was embarrassed when his wife made him support the OCCASIONAL CONFORMITY BILL in 1702, telling the Whigs 'my heart is vid you', and relieved when the following year she took him off to Windsor before the vote on the second bill in the House of Lords. His conduct of naval affairs was rightly criticized in Parliament in 1708 following disasters at sea for the merchant marine. But he was a pillar of strength to his wife, and his death in 1708 devastated the queen, who went into mourning for the maximum period and temporarily withdrew from public life.

Georgia, the last colony to be planted by Britain on the North American seaboard. It was launched by James OGLETHORPE and Lord Egmont, who named it after George II. They persuaded Parliament to pass an act in 1732 setting up a trust that would manage the settlement in the colony of debtors released from jail for the purpose. Initially there were to be no slaves imported into it, not because of any ideological aversion to slavery but through fears that they might threaten the colonists, especially if encouraged to do so by the Spanish authorities in nearby Florida. Such considerations were provoked by the experience of South Carolina where there was a black majority, and where the Stono rebellion in 1738 was indeed fomented from Florida. The strategic issue was paramount, since relations with Spain were strained and the establishment of Georgia was regarded as one of the provocations that led to the War of JENKINS'S EAR in 1739. However, the realities of rice cultivation along the Savannah river made the removal of the prohibition inevitable, and slavery was established in the first decade of settlement. In 1752 the trust was wound up and Georgia became a crown colony.

Gibbon, Edward (1737–94), historian of the Roman empire. Gibbon was the son of a Hampshire landowner. After his mother's death he was brought up by his aunt, Catherine Porten, who he claimed in his *Autobiography* was 'the true mother of my mind'. She supplied the education he was denied because of ill health at Westminster School and through donnish indolence at Magdalen

College, Oxford. His conversion to Catholicism ended his college career, and his father sent him to stay with a Calvinist minister in Lausanne. His host reconverted him and then 'wisely left me to my Genius'.

Gibbon's wide range of reading of ancient and modern authors equipped him to defend the former against their neglect by the latter in his first work, *Essay on the Study of Literature* (1761), which was partly written in Lausanne in 1758 and finished in England in 1759. After three years' service as an officer in the Hampshire militia, Gibbon again visited the continent, passing through France, Switzerland and Italy. Back in England he published a journal for the year 1767, *Literary memoirs of Great Britain*, to which he contributed an essay on George LYTTELTON's *Henry II*. His next publication, *Critical Observations on the sixth book of the Aeneid* (1770), was an anonymous attack on Bishop Warburton's assertion that Virgil's theme was an allegory and not a fable.

Gibbon lived in Hampshire until his father's death in 1772, and for the next decade was active in both political and literary circles. He served as member of Parliament, and in the debates over America 'supported with many a sincere and silent vote the rights, though not, perhaps, the interest of the mother country'. His support of the government resulted in his becoming a lord commissioner of trade and plantations, a post he held until 1782 when the BOARD OF TRADE was abolished. Meanwhile he had become a leading light in Samuel JOHNSON's Literary Club. After abandoning a plan to write a history of Switzerland, he completed the first three volumes of *The Decline and Fall of the Roman Empire*, which were published in 1776. The last three volumes appeared in 1788. He died in London in 1794 after spending the last ten years of his life in Lausanne.

The contribution of Gibbon's philosophy, intellect and style to the study of history was immense. In his controversial explanation, in *The Decline and Fall of the Roman Empire*, of the progress of Christianity, Gibbon dismissed the conventional attribution of it to Providence in a paragraph, while two celebrated chapters (15 and 16) were devoted to a completely secular interpretation of the church's success.

FURTHER READING J.W. Burrow, *Gibbon* (1985).

Gibbons, Grinling (1648–1721), England's most famous woodcarver. Gibbons was born in Rotterdam, but moved to London with his English father before he was 20. He himself took a house in Deptford, where in January 1671 John Evelyn found him at work on a woodcarving of Tinteretto's *The Crucifixion*. Evelyn was so impressed by his craftsmanship that he introduced Gibbons to the court. Charles II made him his master carver in wood, and Gibbons worked at Windsor Castle from 1677 to 1682. Although operating as a sculptor, Gibbons was at his best when carving soft lime wood or oak; indeed, in his fluent and intricate renderings of flowers, fruit, sea shells and cherubs' heads he easily surpassed the work of contemporary rivals. In 1693 Gibbons succeeded Henry Phillips as 'master sculptor and carver in wood' to the crown.

The naturalism that characterizes Gibbons's woodcarving is in marked contrast to the stiffness of his work in marble and bronze. His 1707 monument in Westminster Abbey to Admiral Sir Cloudesley SHOVELL attracted little praise, while the more accomplished statue of James II off Trafalgar Square (1686) may represent the efforts of Gibbons's partner Arnold Quellin. In William III's reign Gibbons was employed by WREN on the new St Paul's Cathedral, and in Anne's reign at Hampton Court. He received commissions from many provincial noblemen to decorate their houses with his characteristic carvings of flowers, fruit, game and grain; among the more outstanding examples are those at Chatsworth.

Gibbs, James (1682–1754), Scottish architect. Gibbs was of Catholic parentage, and studied at the Scots College in Rome. There, instead of preparing for the priesthood, he studied architecture, taking full advantage of the BAROQUE environment. On his return to Britain he was commissioned as a surveyor for the 50 new Anglican churches projected by an act of 1711. In the event only twelve were built, one of them being Gibbs's St Mary-le-Strand, very much in the WREN tradition. Later he designed St Martin-in-the-Fields, a compromise between the baroque and the classical. His most famous commissions outside London were the Fellows' Building of King's College and the Senate House at Cambridge, and the Radcliffe Camera at Oxford. He also disseminated his ideas in print, particularly in *A Book of Architecture* (1728) and *Rules for drawing the several parts of Architecture* (1732).

Gibraltar. The craggy fortress of Gibraltar was the rock upon which Anglo-Spanish relations foundered throughout the 18th century. Possession of Gibraltar had been a matter of national pride for Spain since its capture from the Moors in 1462. During the Georgian era the Rock acquired similar significance in the eyes of Englishmen. Indeed, Gibraltar exerted an influence upon diplomacy out of all proportion to its size or strategic importance. Above all, Britain's refusal to surrender Gibraltar became a key factor behind the continuance of the 'Family Compact' that united the Bourbon powers of France and Spain against Britain. Gibraltar's role in souring relations with Spain was notorious: George III condemned it as a 'proud fortress', capable of causing war or, at the very least, 'a constant lurking enmity'.

For an objective destined to stir such strong passions, Gibraltar had fallen into British hands with surprising ease: during the War of the SPANISH SUCCESSION, an Anglo-Dutch force under Admiral Sir George Rooke captured the stronghold in the summer of 1704 after a siege of just one day. Bourbon troops maintained a fruitless blockade throughout the following winter. By the treaty of UTRECHT in 1713, Britain retained possession of both Gibraltar and MINORCA. While the importance of the latter island as a Mediterranean naval base was readily acknowledged, British statesmen remained less certain of Gibraltar's merits; the relative value placed upon them was indicated in 1757, when PITT THE ELDER proposed returning Gibraltar in exchange for Spanish assistance in recapturing Minorca from the French. Pitt's initiative was neither the first nor last occasion during the 18th century when a British politician sought to relinquish the Rock. However, the unpopularity of a surrender for British public opinion had been indicated as early as 1720, when rumours that the Whig minister James STANHOPE intended such a move prompted widespread protest.

The significance of Gibraltar in foreign affairs was demonstrated most clearly in 1779, when Britain was fighting against both France and its own rebellious American colonies in the AMERICAN WAR OF INDEPENDENCE. Spain joined the war against Britain on France's pledge to continue the struggle until Gibraltar was regained. A dramatic four-year blockade of the Rock's garrison followed. The crisis of the 'Great Siege' came on 13 September 1782, when the governor, General George Augustus Elliot, employed 'red-hot shot' to destroy the Spanish floating batteries. Admiral Richard HOWE's relieving fleet arrived soon after. Elliot earned a knighthood, while Gibraltar's role as a symbol of British defiance against the odds was reinforced. The importance of Gibraltar for Spanish war aims was underlined by secret negotiations with Britain aimed at gaining the Rock in exchange for withdrawal from the conflict.

Equally significantly, though Britain was ready to return Gibraltar in 1782, the peace settlement at the treaty of VERSAILLES excluded any such requirement – so fostering continued Anglo-Spanish hostility and bolstering the Bourbon alliance. Despite such friction, it was only in the latter half of the 19th century, with the opening of the Suez Canal, that Gibraltar acquired its full strategic significance for Britain as a base en route to the east.

FURTHER READING S. Conn, *Gibraltar in British Diplomacy in the 18th century* (1942).

Gibson, Edmund (1669–1748), LOW-CHURCH cleric. Gibson graduated from being a fellow of Queen's College, Oxford, to the bishopric of London, which he held from 1720 until his death. As bishop he was WALPOLE's adviser on spiritual matters, and became known as the prime minister's 'pope'. He especially advised on ecclesiastical appointments, and ensured that as far as possible no high-churchman was preferred.

But Gibson was no Whig timeserver. Indeed he quarrelled with Walpole in 1736 on the question of jurisdiction over tithes. The government backed a bill to prohibit cases involving compulsory collections from being heard in the ecclesiastical courts, confining them to the justices of the peace in the localities. The bill thus sided with those who objected to the payment of tithes, particularly Quakers, against tithe owners, including the clergy. The bill passed the Commons, but was defeated in the Lords when the bishops who usually supported the ministry defected. Gibson was a renowned champion of ecclesiastical jurisdiction, having published a classic defence of it in 1713 in his *Codex Juris Ecclesiastici Anglicani*, which earned him the nickname of Dr Codex. His opposition to the tithes bill cost him the archbishopric of Canterbury, which became vacant in 1737 on the death of William WAKE. He was offered it in 1747, but declined.

Gilbert's Act (1782), legislation that enabled parishes to combine to establish common workhouses for juvenile or elderly paupers. Thomas Gilbert (1720–98), MP for Lichfield, promoted several measures to amend the POOR LAWS, of which this was the only one to reach the statute book.

Gillray, James (1756–1815), political caricaturist. The son of a veteran of FONTENOY, Gillray trained at the ROYAL ACADEMY and possessed the skills of a professional engraver. By the mid-1780s, Gillray had decided to devote his efforts exclusively to caricature. From 1791, when he entered into partnership with the West End printseller and publisher Hannah Humphrey, until he succumbed to madness in 1811, Gillray produced a constant barrage of highly original prints. Gillray's talents fed upon an era of violent political upheaval that was peopled by a colourful cast of characters including such diverse politicians as PITT THE YOUNGER and Charles James FOX, national heroes like NELSON and the arch-enemy Bonaparte. Gillray produced memorable – and instantly recognizable – caricatures of them all. One of his most famous creations was 'Little Boney', a diminutive jack-booted tyrant that reputedly reduced Napoleon to impotent rage. Alongside his depictions of the famous, Gillray created memorable grotesque caricatures of paranoid English JACOBINS and plundering United Irishmen.

The excesses of the FRENCH REVOLUTION inspired Gillray's most striking compositions: he reacted to news of the September Massacres of 1792 with a ferocious depiction of a family of cannibalistic sans-culottes. The possible consequences of successful French invasion formed the themes for equally powerful prints. Besides their clear propaganda messages, Gillray's works often demonstrated great invention and a complexity of design that indicates a debt to contemporary history painting. *The Apotheosis of Hoche* (1798) is an extraordinary depiction of the late revolutionary general ascending above the bodies of his victims while strumming a guillotine-shaped lyre. So effective were Gillray's creations that in 1794 the revolutionary Committee of Public Safety commissioned Jacques-Louis David to retaliate: the efforts of the great French neoclassical artist were not a success. By 1797 the Tories were paying Gillray an annual pension of £200 to deflect his attacks from their own leaders and policies. Britain's royal family was less fortunate: the stolid GEORGE III and his thrifty Queen CHARLOTTE were frequent targets, along with the excesses of their debauched eldest son, George prince of Wales.

FURTHER READING D. Hill (ed.), *The Satirical Etchings of James Gillray* (1976).

Gin Acts (1729, 1736, 1743, 1751), four statutes designed to control if not to eradicate gin drinking in London and other large towns, which was perceived to be a serious social problem in the early 18th century. Gin drinking was prevalent because it was cheaper than other intoxicants, costing only one penny per dram. The first act, passed in 1729, put a duty on the drink, and obliged retailers to pay £20 for a licence. This was repealed in 1733. A second act in 1736 imposed a duty of £1 per gallon on spirits, and increased the cost of a licence to £50. It provoked serious riots at the time, but was largely ineffective. The third actually reduced the duties in 1743, but attempted to control the trade by restricting the number of retailers granted licences. This approach led in 1751 to the last act, further reducing the number of licensed dealers in spirituous liquors. This appears to have satisfied contemporaries that a problem graphically illustrated in William HOGARTH's *Gin Lane* had been brought under control. In fact an increase in the market price of spirits led to a fall in the consumption of gin.

Glencoe, glen in the western Highlands of Scotland, notorious as the site of a massacre of members of the clan Macdonald in 1692.

In an attempt to detach Scots from the JACOBITE cause the government in Edinburgh issued a proclamation offering a pardon to those who would swear allegiance to WILLIAM III and MARY by 31 December 1691. Those who refused would be regarded as traitors. The chief of the Macdonalds of Glencoe failed to take the oaths in the prescribed time. The authorities decided to make a terrible example of their refractoriness. William III gave his approval to a scheme to extirpate the Macdonalds. Glencoe was occupied by a regiment raised by Archibald Campbell earl of Argyll and commanded by another Campbell. After twelve days of feigned fraternization with their Macdonald hosts, at 5.00 a.m. on 13 February 1692 these troops massacred all the members of the clan they could lay their hands on. Many managed to escape,

though of these some died from exposure in the cold wintry weather. The homes of the Macdonalds were pillaged and burned. A letter from a participant in the massacre to the government in London stated that 'there are enough killed for an example and to vindicate public justice'. A commission of inquiry set up by the Scottish Parliament in 1695 held Sir John Dalrymple, secretary of state, responsible. William III dismissed Dalrymple, but also granted him immunity from any further action. The massacre was regarded as particularly shocking because of the breach of the Highland custom of hospitality, and the affair was a major propaganda coup for the JACOBITES.

FURTHER READING P. Hopkins, *Glencoe and the End of the Highland War* (1986).

Glorious First of June (1794), name given to the battle in the approaches to the English Channel during the REVOLUTIONARY AND NAPOLEONIC WARS in which Admiral Richard HOWE inflicted a crushing defeat on the French fleet.

Glorious Revolution (1688), the upheaval in which the Catholic James II was ousted from the throne, and replaced by the Protestant WILLIAM III (William of Orange) and MARY. The first recorded use of the term 'glorious revolution' was by John Hampden, who used the expression on 18 November 1689 when he was testifying before a committee of the House of Lords investigating the Rye House Plot. Ever since then the events of 1688 have been regarded as 'glorious', at least by critics of James II and supporters of William of Orange who supplanted him. William succeeded in doing so partly because James had made himself unpopular with his subjects and partly because William arrived in England with sufficient troops to pose a considerable military threat to his rival.

James alienated himself from his countrymen by trying to obtain complete religious toleration for fellow Roman Catholics. This involved not only attempts to repeal the penal laws and Test Act but also the appropriation of colleges at Oxford and

Cambridge as seminaries to train Catholic priests. Thus Catholics became heads of Sidney Sussex College in Cambridge and University College in Oxford, and in Oxford the fellows of Magdalen College who protested against James's choice of a president sympathetic to Catholics were dismissed. Had James succeeded he would have put the Roman Catholic Church on a legal par with the Church of England as by law established.

Anglicans resisted the king's attempt to subvert the restrictive legislation against Catholics in the only Parliament to meet in the reign, which was prorogued in November 1685 just six months after being elected. At the polls a majority of Tories had been returned, whom the king hoped would cooperate with his aims. They objected, however, to his retention of Catholic officers in the army raised over the summer to defeat the rebellion of the duke of Monmouth, Charles II's illegitimate, Protestant son. James had achieved this by issuing the Catholic officers with dispensations from the Test Act, which obliged officers under the crown to take communion in the Church of England. Tory ministers continued in office, but became increasingly uncooperative with the king, who dispensed with their services early in 1687. Thereafter he decided to ally with former Whigs and dissenters in order to achieve his objectives. In July 1687, therefore, James dissolved Parliament, determined to call another that would be more amenable. This he hoped to achieve by a thorough remodelling of the constituencies. Although the process still had a considerable way to go when James called it off on learning of William's intention to invade in 1688, contemporaries were convinced that it could succeed. Indeed, fear of a packed Parliament was probably the biggest single cause of the Revolution – the 'Immortal Seven' who invited William to invade also urged him to call a 'free' Parliament.

William was sufficiently encouraged by the invitation to enlist a large army to invade England. He was further persuaded by the birth of a son – James Francis Edward STUART – to James and his second wife, Mary of Modena, in June 1688. This would perpetuate the Catholic dynasty and set aside the claims of William's own wife, Mary, James's daughter by his first wife. William was determined to protect Mary's inheritance, even to the point of urging an inquiry into the rumour that the infant prince of Wales was a supposititious child. Hearing of William's intended descent upon England James panicked and reversed his measures. Thus he reinstated the fellows of Magdalen College, Oxford, and restored the parliamentary constituencies to their situation before his remodelling.

But this only served to give James a reputation for vacillating, especially when he relaxed the reversal following the abandonment of William's first expedition due to adverse weather conditions. James thought that this showed that Providence was still on his side. However, William was able to relaunch his task force and land in Torbay on 5 November 1688. From there he set out to intercept James's army on Salisbury Plain. But James panicked after his high command went over to William, and retreated to London without engaging with his enemy. William pursued him there, and was close to the capital when James tried to escape to France. Unfortunately for them both he was intercepted at Faversham by Kentish sailors and had to be rescued by sympathizers in London. His return to the capital was a great embarrassment to William, who placed his father-in-law under house arrest in Rochester, from where on 24 December 1688 James managed to escape to France.

Meanwhile William had been invited by a number of peers and gentlemen to take upon himself the administration of the government until such time as a Parliament could be elected. Writs went out for an election and a CONVENTION PARLIAMENT met on 22 January 1689. This body was principally responsible for the REVOLUTION SETTLEMENT.

FURTHER READING W.A. Speck, *Reluctant Revolutionaries: Englishmen and the Revolution of 1688* (1988).

Godolphin, Sidney Godolphin, 1st earl of
(1645–1712), politician, who was lord treasurer in
1685–8, 1700–1 and 1702–10. Godolphin entered
the king's service in 1662 as a page of honour, and
was returned to Parliament in 1668 as member for
the family borough of Helston in Cornwall. During
the 1670s he was employed on a variety of diplomatic missions, the usual way in which Charles II
got his courtiers to serve their political apprenticeships. In 1678 he sold the post of groom of
the bedchamber, which he had held since 1672,
and purchased the mastership of the robes. His
first experience of the Treasury, which was to
become his forte, came in 1679 when he was appointed one of its commissioners. Although he
voted for the second Exclusion Bill – which sought
to disbar Charles's Catholic brother James from
the succession – he was allowed to remain in office.

During the Tory reaction of Charles II's last
years Godolphin became secretary of state and then
first lord of the Treasury. Before Charles II died
he elevated Godolphin to the peerage as Baron
Godolphin of Rialton. James II, however, distrusted him for his support of exclusion and on his
accession removed him from the Treasury. When in
1687 James broke with the earl of Rochester,
whom he had made lord treasurer, he put the Treasury into commission again and appointed Godolphin a commissioner. After William of Orange
invaded in 1688 the king sent Godolphin down
to Hungerford as one of three lords chosen to treat
with the prince. Godolphin was one of the last
courtiers to stay loyal to James II, and in the
CONVENTION PARLIAMENT voted for a regency to
administer the country, the tactic of most of the
late king's supporters.

Nevertheless, when the new king, William III,
appointed a Treasury commission, Godolphin was
named as one of the commissioners. In 1690
Godolphin resigned and went temporarily into
retirement, probably for personal reasons. His
absence irked the king, and at the end of the year
William persuaded him to return. He served as
Treasury commissioner until 1696, crucial years

in the FINANCIAL REVOLUTION and the formation
of the FISCAL-MILITARY STATE. He made way for
the encroaching Whig ministers to whom the king
had turned in the mid-1690s. When William
sought to renew his relations with the Tories in
1700 Godolphin made a comeback, and once again
sat on the Treasury commission. He resigned in
1701 in protest at the king's 'snap' dissolution of
Parliament.

On the accession of ANNE, Godolphin came
into his own as lord treasurer. During the War of
the SPANISH SUCCESSION he played a crucial role
in managing the finances needed to sustain the
sinews of war. Politically too his part was so vital
that he and MARLBOROUGH became known as the
'duumvirs'. Their ministry lasted from 1702 to
1710. Although both had been reckoned Tories
in the late 17th century, in the early 18th they are
best considered as 'managers' or brokers for the
crown's influence over the political parties. Thus
they moved steadily from dependence on high-
church Tory colleagues to working with moder-
ates of both parties and finally with JUNTO Whigs,
in order to get the queen's business through Parliament. This produced friction with Anne, who
considered that they were reducing her prerogative by insisting upon appointments of men she
did not like, such as the Junto, and the removal of
men she did like, such as Robert HARLEY. Harley
persuaded her that she was a prisoner of the Junto
and that she could be freed from them and from
the management of the duumvirs.

Godolphin set in motion the process that led to
his own removal when he agreed to the impeachment of Dr SACHEVERELL. The high-church
preacher had particularly antagonized the lord
treasurer in his notorious sermon of 5 November
1709 by including 'wily Volpones' among the 'false
brethren' he castigated; Godolphin's nickname
was 'Volpone'. The trial backfired on the ministry,
producing a huge Tory reaction that Harley skil-
fully exploited to remove the ministers and replace
them with his own nominees. He found it particularly difficult to remove Godolphin, for whom

Anne had a genuine regard. But he persuaded her that the lord treasurer had undermined her prerogative of dissolving Parliament by opposing its dissolution in cabinet. In August Godolphin was dismissed, though the pill was sweetened with a substantial pension. Anne's regard for Godolphin lasted until his death in 1712. Bishop Burnet paid tribute to him by observing that 'he was the man of the clearest mind, the calmest temper and the most uncorrupt of all the ministers of state I have ever known'.

Godwin, William (1756–1836), political philosopher and novelist. The son of a DISSENTING minister, Godwin was educated at Hoxton Dissenting College. He became a dissenting clergyman, but abandoned the ministry in 1783 after his faith was undermined by rationalism.

In response to the French Revolution, Godwin published *An Enquiry concerning the principles of political justice* in 1793. To Godwin monarchy and aristocracy were both pernicious, and he argued against 'legislative and executive power'. However, he was no leveller, but a meritocrat who felt that monarchy, so far from rewarding genuine merit, promoted sycophantic defenders of the hereditary principle. That was why he was even more critical of aristocracy, with its privileges and wealth. In place of the existing social system he advocated a society based on small communities, more like a parish than a nation. In these the individual would be educated to see that antisocial behaviour was irrational. The few who refused to curb their irrational impulses would have their behaviour monitored, and ultimately controlled, by their neighbours. Thus Godwin's utopian, proto-anarchist scheme ultimately depended upon an optimistic view of human nature, which he believed could be curbed by reason. In 1794 Godwin worked out his critique of existing society in a JACOBIN NOVEL entitled *Caleb Williams: or, Things as they are.*

Godwin's private life was marked by tragedy. He married Mary WOLLSTONECRAFT in 1797, who died giving birth to their daughter Mary in the same year. In 1801 he married a widow, Mrs Clairmont, but their marriage did not turn out to be a happy match. His later novels and plays were also unsuccessful. In 1813 his daughter Mary eloped with the poet Shelley. He was not reconciled to this until the couple married in 1816. That year Fanny Godwin, the illegitimate daughter of his first wife, committed suicide, and in 1822 he was declared bankrupt. His last years were relieved by his appointment to the post of yeoman usher of the exchequer in 1833. In this capacity he presided over the burning of exchequer tallies; the fire got out of hand and led to the burning down of the old House of Commons.

FURTHER READING P.H. Marshall, *William Godwin* (1984).

Goldsmith, Oliver (1730–74), Anglo-Irish playwright, poet and novelist. Goldsmith was born in Ireland and educated at Trinity College, Dublin. Although he was a prodigal student, he graduated BA and went to study medicine at Edinburgh and Leiden. He failed to graduate with a degree in medicine, however, dropping out of his studies to be an itinerant musician. By 1756 he was in London taking temporary employment as an apothecary and a schoolmaster. He also contributed to journals such as *The Bee* and the *Public Ledger*, in which he published 'Chinese Letters', an early version of *The Citizen of the World*, which appeared in 1762. It made his reputation as an author, and he gained admission to Samuel JOHNSON's Literary Club.

Goldsmith's novel *The Vicar of Wakefield* was published in 1766. Charles Primrose, the vicar, has two daughters, one of whom marries Sir William Thornhill and the other Thornhill's nephew. The two Thornhills represent the contrast between the ideal of the country gentleman and its debasement, for Sir William is in every way a deserving figure, while Mr Thornhill is a dyed-in-the-wool villain. Primrose himself represents a middle-class professional man who looks to the crown to protect his type from an unholy alliance of an unscrupulous aristocracy and a venal electorate.

Unscrupulous landlords are the villains of Goldsmith's poem *The Deserted Village* (1770), which deplores the impact of enclosure on rural life, depopulating the fictional village of Auburn and forcing its inhabitants to emigrate. Economic historians have queried the reality of the poem, maintaining that depopulation was rarely the result of enclosure in England, and arguing that Goldsmith might have been recalling Irish experiences. Yet he himself claimed that he had witnessed the events described in his poem within a day's walk of London. Goldsmith became celebrated as a playwright in his later years, his most famous play, *She Stoops to Conquer* (1773), still being frequently staged.

FURTHER READING S.H. Woods, *Oliver Goldsmith: A Reference Guide* (1982).

Gordon riots (2–8 June 1780), anti-Catholic riots in London, inspired by Lord George Gordon (1751–93). The spasm of violence that gripped London for six days during the summer of 1780 represented 18th-century Britain's worst breakdown of law and order. By the time the rioting subsided on 8 June, several of London's prisons had been gutted, along with numerous chapels, Catholic-owned properties and the homes of prominent magistrates. It is estimated that some 1000 men, women and children may have lost their lives – shot by the troops, crushed by falling debris, or burned alive as they lay stupefied with looted liquor. Another 26 people found guilty of participation in the disorder were subsequently hanged.

The episode that provided a dramatic backdrop for Dickens's *Barnaby Rudge* originated in an expression of popular opposition to what was perceived as the NORTH ministry's growing sympathy for Britain's Roman Catholics. Traditional hostility towards 'papists' was harnessed by the ambitious but unstable MP for Ludgershall, Lord George Gordon, son of the 3rd duke of Gordon. A former naval officer who was vociferously opposed

to the war against the rebellious American colonists, Gordon became the leader of resistance against the government's Catholic Relief Act of 1778. Designed to attract Catholic manpower for Britain's hard-pressed army, the act offered various limited concessions to those taking an oath of allegiance. The act was initially applied only to England and Ireland; suggestions that it should be extended to Scotland were dropped after they sparked serious rioting in Glasgow and Edinburgh.

During 1779 Gordon's parliamentary speeches employed increasingly inflammatory language, and his targets included the king himself. Many believed Gordon to be mad. As his contemporary Charles Turner observed, Gordon possessed 'a twist in his head, a certain whirligig which ran away with him' at the mere mention of religion. Whatever his mental state, Gordon's rantings tapped into a rich vein of anti-papist sentiment. Britain was at war with Catholic Bourbon powers; in addition, the effort to raise recruits for the army was seen as an unacceptable use of 'popery' against the Protestant American colonists – a group who continued to enjoy considerable support amongst the opposition.

As leader of the Protestant Association, Gordon proved capable of mobilizing major support. On 2 June 1780 Gordon called a mass meeting at St George's Fields, London, with the intention of presenting a 'Protestant Petition' to Parliament. Instead of the anticipated 20,000 marchers, no fewer than 60,000 gathered, and by the time they reached Westminster their ranks had been swollen by criminal elements. Worried at the size of the crowd, Parliament refused to consider Gordon's petition. London's magistrates failed to meet the crisis with the necessary resolution, and, rather than disperse, some of the marchers soon got out of hand. To cries of 'No Popery!' they embarked upon a comprehensive programme of destruction. In most instances the targets of the rioters were carefully chosen – indeed, fire engines were employed to ensure that blazes did not spread to neighbouring properties. As George Rudé has emphasized, the crowd's wrath was directed at property rather than persons, and it is significant that all those who died during that turbulent week were rioters. Contrary to the picture later painted by government informers, the Gordon rioters were not inspired by French or American agents, or dominated by professional criminals: Professor Rudé concluded that they represented a 'fair cross section of London's working population' whose reactions reflected deep-seated hostilities towards wealthy Catholics and foreigners.

The Bank of England also suffered repeated assaults, and its defenders included Alderman John WILKES, who later claimed to have shot two of the rioters. Although initially feeble, the government's reaction to the rioting eventually hardened, with GEORGE III playing a key role in restoring order. Frustrated by the inaction of his magistrates, the king called a privy-council meeting, which authorized the army to employ all necessary force without first obtaining the permission of the civil authorities. Thousands of regular troops and militia swamped the capital, and their uncompromising riot-control tactics soon quelled the disturbances.

As instigator of the riots, Lord George Gordon was tried for treason. He was acquitted after it was argued that he had never intended a violent outcome, and had indeed done his best to curb the excesses of his adherents. Subsequently convicted of libel, Gordon ended his years in Newgate Prison, rebuilt after its destruction in the riots of 1780.

FURTHER READING I. Gilmour, *Riot, Risings and Revolution. Governance and Violence in 18th-Century England* (1992); G. Rudé, *The Crowd in History* (1964).

Gothic, term applied both to the 18th-century revival of the medieval Gothic style in architecture, and to a genre of novels characterized by terror and the supernatural, often in mock-medieval settings such as ruins, castles and monasteries.

When Jane AUSTEN wrote *Northanger Abbey* in 1798, she was lampooning the mania for 'Gothic' novels that gripped the imaginations of

her less rational contemporaries. Austen's satire targeted those readers who craved the delicious thrills provided by melodramatic narratives of medieval magic and mystery; indeed, Austen's gullible heroine, Catherine Morland, harbours a passion for crumbling ruins that is second only to her love for Henry Tilney.

The Gothic novel had been born in 1765 with the publication of Horace WALPOLE's *Castle of Otranto*. Walpole's book offered an antidote to the often moralizing tone of many contemporary novels, and it spawned a host of imitators. These pandered to the tastes of their readers by providing such exciting fare as forbidding strongholds, secret passages, ghosts and walking portraits, and these ingredients were often set against a backdrop of picturesque and dramatic mountain scenery. During the closing years of the 18th century, the genre's best sellers included *The Monk* (1796) by Matthew Lewis (1775–1818), and *The Mysteries of Udolpho* (1794) by Ann Radcliffe (1764–1823); both feature in the pages of *Northanger Abbey* (1818).

Such literary efforts fed into a growing fascination with the medieval past that would soon be indulged further by the historical romances of Sir Walter Scott. The Georgian identity with a long-lost world could surface in unexpected places. For example, in 1778 British army officers in Philadelphia staged a medieval-style tournament to honour the retirement of their commander in chief, Sir William HOWE. By the time Howe's subordinates staged their fanciful display of knight errantry, this interest in the Gothic had also manifested itself through the conscious adoption of a medieval style in architecture.

The so-called 'Gothic revival' had originated in England during the first half of the 18th century, and gained increasing publicity from 1750 onwards. Having invented the Gothic novel, it was apt that Horace Walpole should likewise play a leading role in promoting the revival of interest in Gothic architecture through the remarkable medieval-style mansion of STRAWBERRY HILL that he created at Twickenham between 1750 and 1790. Just as Walpole's pioneering tale of the supernatural had offered a striking contrast to the rational efforts of many Georgian novelists, so the studied asymmetry of neo-Gothic buildings such as Strawberry Hill represented an alternative to the prevailing penchant for carefully balanced 'classical' architecture. Men of learning could detect merit in both forms but, as Walpole observed, while an appreciation of the classical required taste, the Gothic demanded passion.

The Gothic revival took inspiration from the splendours of England's medieval past, still visible in the surviving structures of the great cathedrals and abbeys. Details such as pinnacles, quatrefoils, buttresses, battlements, oriel windows and ogee arches were all characteristic of Gothic architecture, and would be adopted by the revivalists. Particularly influential was the distinctively English 'perpendicular' style that was held to represent the apogee of Gothic in the 14th and 15th centuries. During the Tudor and Stuart eras the Gothic tradition had never totally died, not least because architects and masons required a familiarity with its forms to maintain Britain's substantial legacy of medieval buildings. It was to meet this demand that Batty Langley issued his *Ancient Architecture Restored and Improved* in 1741–2, although, to the horror of later purists such as Walpole, this manual mixed Gothic and classical details.

Alongside the restoration of existing medieval buildings, the early 18th century saw the construction of new structures that reflected Gothic influence. For example, the leading architect John VANBRUGH – best known for his baroque masterpiece of Castle Howard – built a very different castle for himself at Blackheath in 1717, featuring asymmetrically placed towers and castellations. Another leading baroque architect to demonstrate a familiarity with the Gothic style was Vanbrugh's collaborator Nicholas HAWKSMOOR. Hawksmoor applied this familiarity from 1715, when he designed All Souls College to harmonize with the existing medieval structures of Oxford; later in his

career, in 1743, he completed the west towers of Westminster Abbey that had been left unfinished at the death of Henry III in 1272.

As with PALLADIANISM, the trend for Gothic buildings was fostered by the enthusiasm of a close-knit group of gentlemen – amateurs who combined a taste for antiquarian scholarship with an interest in architecture. Revived Gothic buildings had first surfaced on a relatively small scale in the form of 'temples' and 'pavilions' included as points of interest within landscaped gardens. Such grounds had themselves provided an inspiration for the Gothic movement when William Kent overturned the strict formalism of the French baroque garden in favour of a more naturalistic approach (*see* LANDSCAPE GARDENING). Horace Walpole noted that such irregular designs could be transferred to architecture. As Walpole's admiration for Kent suggests, the Palladian and Gothic styles could coexist. For example, in 1741 a large Gothic temple was begun in the garden of the neoclassical STOWE House, Buckinghamshire. The temple's architect was James GIBBS, whose best-known work was the classically inspired church of St Martin-in-the-Fields.

Gothic's disciples included Sir Roger Newdigate, who from 1748 clothed the Tudor heart of Arbury Hall in Warwickshire with a Gothic skin that was closely based upon medieval prototypes. The drawing room employed plaster-work tracery modelled upon the spectacular perpendicular Gothic of Henry VII's chapel in Westminster Abbey, while the chimney piece was derived from a tomb in the Abbey. Newdigate's efforts at Arbury extended over half a century, and his attention to detail was only equalled by Horace Walpole's Strawberry Hill, the first Georgian house to feature Gothic design 'through and through'.

Walpole's influential labour of love provided inspiration for the greatest Gothic-revival architect of the late Georgian era, James Wyatt (1746–1813). Although Wyatt undertook NEOCLASSICAL commissions throughout his career, his fame rests upon Gothic foundations. As Wyatt's obituary in the *Gentleman's Magazine* noted, 'his genius revived in this country the long forgotten beauties of Gothic architecture'.

Wyatt's reputation was more controversial than this tribute suggests. Appointed surveyor general to the crown in 1769, Wyatt was charged with the restoration of medieval cathedrals. He assumed this task with considerable ruthlessness, and his swingeing work at Salisbury led the antiquarian John Carter to brand him 'Wyatt the Destroyer'.

Wyatt's major Gothic projects included Lee Priory in Kent, generously described by Walpole as 'a child of Strawberry prettier than the parent'. However, it was with Fonthill Abbey in Wiltshire that Wyatt reached his greatest heights, both literally and figuratively. The project began in 1769 and was undertaken for William Beckford, the eccentric son of the celebrated lord mayor of London and author of the Gothic novel *Vathek* (1786). Built upon a cruciform plan with a soaring octagonal tower, Fonthill created a sensation. Although the original jerry-built tower collapsed, it was reconstructed in time for a gala party for Horatio NELSON in 1800. Beckford's illustrious guests on that glittering occasion included Benjamin WEST, the president of the Royal Academy, who considered Fonthill to be 'magical'. Fonthill offered a convincing recreation of medieval architecture on a massive scale. The entrance alone was 9 m (30 feet) high, and Beckford heightened the dramatic effect by employing a dwarf as a doorman. Although little now remains of Beckford's obsession, the building had an undoubted influence, which was disseminated through a succession of heavily illustrated publications.

Before 1800 the Gothic revival in architecture was chiefly associated with the homes of its wealthy British adherents, but in the 19th century, the style was applied to a wide range of public and ecclesiastical buildings throughout the English-speaking world.

FURTHER READING M. Aldrich, *Gothic Revival* (1994).

Grafton, Henry Fitzroy, 3rd duke of (1735–1811), politician; prime minister (1767–70). Grafton emerged as prime minister by default when PITT THE ELDER, Lord Chatham, proved incapable of fulfilling the role through illness.

The relationship between Grafton and Chatham was odd in many ways. Grafton was identified with the Old Corps Whigs who opposed BUTE and had come into office in the first ROCKINGHAM administration as secretary of state. But he resigned in April 1766 because Rockingham refused to appoint Chatham to a post in the ministry. When Chatham himself formed a ministry in July – taking the unusual post of lord privy seal – Grafton re-entered government as first lord of the Treasury.

When Chatham's health collapsed in 1767, Grafton had to take over such problems as the American reaction to the Townshend duties and the election of John WILKES as member for Middlesex in 1768. He was also pilloried in the *Letters of JUNIUS*. To add insult to injury Chatham marked his return to politics by criticizing his former colleague. Grafton could take no more and resigned in 1770, to be replaced by Lord NORTH. He served North as lord privy seal from 1771 to 1775, and was appointed to the same post in the second Rockingham administration from 1782 to 1783. Though he lived until 1811 he never enjoyed high office again.

Granby, John Manners, marquess of (1721–70), dashing cavalryman and skilful general, who played a key role in Britain's victorious German campaigns of the SEVEN YEARS WAR.

As elder son of the duke of Rutland, Granby was born to the privileged lifestyle of the landed aristocracy. Educated at Eton and Trinity College, Cambridge, Granby secured a seat in Parliament while barely out of his teens and retained it until his sudden death at the age of 49. In 1745 Granby raised a regiment to counter the JACOBITES, and went on to serve in Flanders during the later campaigns of the War of the AUSTRIAN SUCCESSION.

In 1759 Lieutenant General Granby fought in Germany under the command of Ferdinand of Brunswick. Although George SACKVILLE's hesitancy at MINDEN prevented Granby's troopers from transforming the French defeat into a rout, the British cavalry soon had its chance of glory. Granby inherited Sackville's command, and at Warburg in 1760 he led his men bareheaded in a spectacular and victorious charge. Under Granby's leadership the British contingent contributed to further successes at Emsdorff, Vellinghausen and Wilhelmstal – victories that helped to justify Pitt's famous boast that Canada was won in Germany.

At the peace of 1763 Granby was created master of the ordnance, and three years later became commander in chief. A hard drinker and heavy gambler, he was more at home in the saddle than behind a desk. In addition, the decade's volatile political situation was not to Granby's taste. Ridiculed by the waspish Horace WALPOLE, Granby was also made a target in the first of JUNIUS's letters to be printed in the *Public Advertiser*; it was Sir William Draper's response in defence of Granby that triggered the mystery scribe's subsequent printed onslaught against the first minister, the duke of GRAFTON.

Granby's military exploits earned him a popular celebrity that was enhanced by his distinctive physical appearance: in an age when most men of his class wore wigs and three-cornered hats, Granby flaunted his baldness – a habit that led poets and journalists to draw flattering comparisons with Caesar and Charles XII of Sweden. REYNOLDS painted Granby's portrait on several occasions, while his likeness was reproduced more widely on souvenir jugs and teapots. In 1765 Edward Penny produced a canvas depicting Granby giving alms to a sick soldier, and the resulting mezzotint enjoyed great popularity, out-selling even the print of Benjamin WEST's famous *Death of Wolfe*. As Penny's painting indicated, Granby was noted for benevolence towards his men: this included helping his former NCOs establish themselves as publicans, and in consequence Granby's

ruddy countenance and glistening pate are still commemorated in numerous inn signs.

grand tour. In the years between the Restoration and the French Revolution the education of the English gentleman frequently included a leisurely 'grand tour' of Europe. Itineraries varied according to the dictates of fashion, the changing political situation and personal whim, but the 'classic' tour began with a sojourn in Paris, followed by visits to Rome, Florence, Naples and Venice. Other major cities – including Amsterdam, Berlin, Dresden, Prague, Vienna and Geneva – also attracted their share of visitors, but only the most adventurous penetrated into Russia or the domains of the Ottoman Empire.

The popularity of the grand tour after 1714 coincided with the rise of Britain's consumer society, and was encouraged by the growing availability of travel literature. Despite the hazards posed by bandits, wolves, fleas and rutted roads, Georgian Britain's upper and middle classes became so addicted to overseas travel that British envoys and ambassadors were often overwhelmed by itinerant countrymen seeking hospitality. The volume of visitors typically slackened during the 18th century's periodic bouts of warfare, only to intensify at the end of hostilities.

At its most protracted, the grand tour could consume three years. It was often undertaken by wealthy males in their late teens or early twenties under the supervision of an educated and supposedly respectable tutor known as the 'bear leader'. Critics of the phenomenon believed that such youths were too callow to benefit from the educational possibilities of the tour, and also raised objections to the lavish expenditure involved as they rambled across Europe in gentlemanly style. Other criticisms focused upon moral concerns: while intended to refine the accomplishments of the elite by improving linguistic skills and widening intellectual horizons, such excursions undoubtedly provided opportunities for gambling, drinking and sexual dalliance.

Although many tourists possessed their own specific interests and agendas, the classical and Renaissance heritage of Italy exerted a particular lure. Travellers were drawn to the ruins of Rome and the newly excavated remains of Pompeii and Herculaneum, while the volcanic activity of Vesuvius provided an exciting and picturesque bonus. First-hand acquaintance with Italy's art and architecture had a significant impact upon British cultural trends: in architecture, it served to disseminate the influential cults of PALLADIANISM and NEO-CLASSICISM; returning connoisseurs likewise spread a taste for Italian painting and founded important collections. The steady stream of visitors to renowned cultural centres also provided a ready market for local artists: Rome's Pompeo Batoni made his reputation painting the portraits of more than 150 British tourists, while Canaletto thrived upon the production of souvenir views of Venice; others were commissioned to paint copies of Renaissance masterpieces. In Florence, the expatriate Thomas Patch commemorated the grand tourists and their hosts in caricature conversation pieces.

Always vulnerable to political upheaval, the grand tour faced more serious disruption during the prolonged European warfare that followed the French Revolution, and its traditional flavour was subsequently transformed after improvements in transport expedited travel across Europe.

FURTHER READING J. Black, *The British Abroad: The Grand Tour in the Eighteenth Century* (1992).

Granville, John Carteret, 2nd Earl. *See* CAR-TERET, JOHN, 2ND EARL GRANVILLE.

Grattan, Henry (1746–1820), Anglo-Irish politician. A key figure in Ireland's struggle for legislative independence from the Westminster Parliament, Grattan gained a legendary reputation for devotion to his country.

Educated at Dublin's Trinity College, Grattan was called to the bar in 1772 and entered the Irish House of Commons three years later. Grat-

tan's integrity and rousing rhetoric gained him the leadership of those Irish MPs who were committed to severing the links with London. The onset of Grattan's political career had coincided with the outbreak of war between Britain and her rebellious American colonists, and Grattan and his followers exploited the crisis atmosphere of the war years to further their own political aims. A series of concessions were obtained, culminating in the granting of legislative independence in 1782. Grattan's efforts on Ireland's behalf earned him a gift of £50,000 from the Irish Parliament.

The closing decades of the 18th century represented the peak of Ireland's Protestant ascendancy, a 'golden age' brought to a bloody end by the IRISH REBELLION OF 1798. Grattan's faction had split from the Irish Parliament in the previous year, and although Grattan was elected once more in 1800, all his oratory failed to stave off the subsequent Act of Union that abolished that institution (*see* UNION OF BRITAIN AND IRELAND).

Despite his own position at the centre of Ireland's privileged Protestant establishment, Grattan was a life-long campaigner for concessions towards Ireland's Catholic majority. The Act of Union had been expected to smooth the path towards CATHOLIC EMANCIPATION. When George III refused his consent, Grattan used his position as MP for Dublin to mount a dogged but unsuccessful pursuit of a goal that would only be achieved in 1829, nine years after his death. In 1806 Grattan declined an invitation from his friend Charles James FOX to join the MINISTRY OF ALL THE TALENTS. Although opposed to the Anglo-Irish union, Grattan proved a loyal supporter of the war against France. He died in London, and is buried in Westminster Abbey.

FURTHER READING G. O'Brien, *Anglo-Irish Politics in the Age of Grattan and Pitt* (1987).

Gray, Thomas (1716–71), poet, best remembered for his melancholy and moving *Elegy written in a Country Churchyard*. At the age of nine Gray was sent to Eton, where he forged a lasting friendship

with Horace WALPOLE, and his schooldays proved the happiest period of his life. In 1739, following study at Peterhouse, Cambridge, Gray joined Walpole on the GRAND TOUR, and his encounter with the physical remains of ancient Rome reinforced his early love of Latin verse. Much of Gray's English poetry was written in 1742, the year in which he returned to Cambridge. Finding Peterhouse too rowdy for comfort, Gray later transferred to Pembroke, where the environment proved more conducive to his secluded regime of study.

Published by Walpole in 1750, Gray's *Elegy* created a sensation. Its outstanding quality was acknowledged by Samuel JOHNSON, whose general assessment of Gray in his *Lives of the Poets* had been notably cool. With its sombre warning that 'the paths of Glory lead but to the grave', the *Elegy* struck a chord with contemporaries, and is one of the few poems of the age to remain popular today. According to legend, General James WOLFE recited Gray's *Elegy* during the tense hours before the battle of Quebec, announcing that he would rather have written those lines than capture the city itself.

Little of Gray's other poetry enjoyed such universal acclaim. For example, Gray's dense *Pindaric Odes* of 1757 met a mixed reception; they baffled readers like Oliver GOLDSMITH, who considered them 'terribly obscure' and complained to BOSWELL: 'We must be historians and learned men before we can understand them.' Gray fought shy of public duties: he shunned an offer of the poet laureateship, and, although appointed regius professor of modern history at Cambridge by the duke of Grafton in 1768, he never delivered a lecture there.

FURTHER READING M. Golden, *Thomas Gray* (1964).

Grenville, George (1712–70), politician; prime minister (1763–5). Grenville entered the Inner Temple in 1729 after being educated at Eton and Oxford, and was called to the bar in 1735. 'Mr Grenville thought better of the wisdom and power of human legislation than in truth it deserves,'

Burke was later to claim of his career as a lawyer. 'He conceived, and many conceived along with him, that the flourishing trade of this country was greatly owing to law ... and not quite so much to liberty.'

At the general election of 1741 Grenville was returned as MP for Buckingham, a seat he held until his death. He took part in the opposition to WALPOLE, and enjoyed office under Henry PELHAM. In his early years in Parliament, Grenville became a prominent member of the political faction known as COBHAM's CUBS. In 1744 he became a lord of the Admiralty, and in 1747 a lord of the Treasury. On Pelham's death in 1754 he became treasurer of the navy, but was dismissed the following year for supporting PITT THE ELDER's criticism of the government's foreign policy. He returned to office with Pitt in 1756, only to resign again when NEWCASTLE ousted the Great Commoner. Finally, when the Pitt–Newcastle ministry was formed, Grenville was appointed treasurer of the navy once more. He retained that post even after Pitt resigned in 1761, and became secretary of state in 1762. BUTE, however, stung by Grenville's criticism of the treaty of PARIS, got him to exchange his secretaryship of state with Lord HALIFAX, who was first lord of the Admiralty.

On Bute's resignation in 1763, Grenville succeeded him as first lord of the Treasury and chancellor of the exchequer. As a condition of becoming prime minister he insisted upon tight control of patronage. Grenville's ministry introduced measures for the administration of the North American colonies, which had been rendered necessary by the vast increase in their extent following the SEVEN YEARS WAR. The Currency Act of 1764 extended to the southern colonies the controls over the issues of paper currency that had already been applied to New England in 1751. The Sugar Act in the same year halved the duties imposed on foreign sugar by the Molasses Act of 1733, but made it clear that they would be collected to raise a revenue. The Mutiny Act of 1765 regulated the discipline of the troops kept on foot in the colonies in peacetime.

Finally, the STAMP ACT provided for raising duties on all legal documents, newspapers and other items in the colonies. This was the most controversial measure, which became the principal focus of American resistance to the Grenville programme. He announced it a year ahead of its introduction, apparently to give the colonists time to prepare for it. When he introduced it he insisted upon Parliament's right to tax the colonies, even though they were not directly represented in the Commons. Many Englishmen did not vote in elections but, he insisted, like the colonists, they were virtually represented in Parliament. Although this argument was to be vociferously repudiated in America, the Stamp Act passed the Commons with scarcely any opposition. (*See also* AMERICAN COLONIES 1763–1776.)

It was not his American policy but his clumsy handling of a Regency Bill that led to Grenville's downfall in 1765. In that year GEORGE III suffered the first signs of illness severe enough to call in question his ability to govern, and a bill was introduced to provide for regents in the event of his total incapacity. For some reason Grenville left out the king's mother from the bill, and when George recovered he took umbrage at this and dismissed the prime minister. In opposition Grenville vigorously defended his passing of the Stamp Act against the moves to repeal it. In 1770, just before his early death he was identified with an act to take the jurisdiction over disputed elections away from the House of Commons at large, and to place it with a select committee that would handle such disputes more objectively.

FURTHER READING P. Lawson, *George Grenville: A Political Life* (1984).

Grenville, William (Wyndham), 1st Baron Grenville

(1759–1834), politician, foreign secretary (1791–1801) and prime minister (1806–7). He was the third son of an earlier prime minister, George GRENVILLE.

Grenville entered Parliament as member for Buckingham at a by-election in 1782. The following year he was appointed paymaster general in the administration of PITT THE YOUNGER, his cousin. He became knight of the shire for Buckinghamshire at the general election of 1784. In September of that year he became a member of the newly created BOARD OF CONTROL for India, and in 1786 was nominated vice president of the committee on trade. The House of Commons chose him as its speaker in 1789 by 215 votes to 144. Later in the year he resigned the speakership and his other offices upon becoming home secretary. He was returned as member for Buckinghamshire at the general election of 1790, but on the day Parliament met he was ennobled as Baron Grenville. Thereafter he became the government's chief spokesman in the House of Lords.

In 1791 Grenville became foreign secretary, a post he held for ten years. His foreign policy was one of implacable hostility to France after war broke out in 1793. He believed that the French Revolution was a threat to every other government in Europe. When Pitt sought to suppress its supporters in Britain, Grenville was an enthusiastic advocate of the measures aimed at their repression, moving in the Lords the suspension of the Habeas Corpus Act and the passing of the Treasonable Practices Act and the Seditious Meetings Act. In 1800 he moved the passing of the Act of Union with Ireland (*see* UNION OF BRITAIN AND IRELAND). It was as a consequence of this becoming law that he and Pitt resigned in 1801, when the king refused to countenance CATHOLIC EMANCIPATION. Yet when Pitt replaced ADDINGTON in 1804, Grenville refused office under him unless Charles James FOX was offered a post too. Pitt took umbrage at this insistence, which ended their political partnership.

On Pitt's death Grenville succeeded as prime minister, presiding over the MINISTRY OF ALL THE TALENTS. Its greatest achievement was the abolition of the SLAVE TRADE in the British empire. The ministry fell when Grenville again pressed the king to grant concessions to Catholics by opening up a career in the armed services to them. The king refused and Grenville resigned. He never held office again.

FURTHER READING P. Jupp, *Lord Grenville, 1759–1834* (1985).

Grenville-Temple, Richard, 2nd Earl Temple (1711–79), politician. He added his mother's maiden name, Temple, to his own when he inherited his title from her in 1752. He was the brother of George GRENVILLE, and brother-in-law of PITT THE ELDER, whose lead he took in politics until Pitt became earl of Chatham and formed a ministry in 1766.

He was first lord of the Admiralty 1756–7 and lord privy seal 1759–61. Resigning with Pitt in 1761, he opposed BUTE and supported John WILKES's critique of the ministry in *The North Briton*. He even opposed his own brother George Grenville, though he joined with him in opposition to the ROCKINGHAM ministry. In 1766 he quarrelled with Chatham and subsequently wrote pamphlets critical of Chatham's administration. Though he was reconciled with Chatham when the prime minister stood down in 1768, he continued to oppose GRAFTON, and was wrongly suspected of being the author of the *Letters of JUNIUS*. He retired from politics on his brother George's death in 1770.

Grey, Charles, 2nd Earl (1764–1845), Whig politician. He entered the House of Commons in 1786 as a member for his native county of Northumberland. He immediately associated with the WHIGS led by Charles James FOX and espoused PARLIAMENTARY REFORM. In 1792 he was instrumental in setting up the Society of Friends of the People, and in 1797 introduced a reform bill into Parliament. This measure would have restored the TRIENNIAL ACT, extended the franchise to ratepayers and redistributed many constituencies. When it failed, the Foxites, including Grey, seceded from the Commons for three years. They remained in opposition after their return until the formation of the MINISTRY OF ALL THE TALENTS in which Grey first became lord of the Admiralty, and then on the death of Fox succeeded him as foreign secretary and as leader of the Whigs. In 1807 his father, the 1st Earl Grey, died and he became the 2nd earl. The impetus of reform faltered during the long wars against France. Grey continued to champion the cause after 1815, however, and it was under his premiership of the Whig administration of 1830–34 that the great Reform Act of 1832 was passed.

Grimshaw, William. *See* METHODISM.

Grub Street, derisory collective term for hack writers. There was a real Grub Street in early modern London, located in Moorfields, a dubious area associated with criminals, prostitutes and other raffish elements. By the mid-18th century it was also inhabited, according to Dr JOHNSON, 'by writers of small histories, dictionaries and temporary poems' such as himself. By then it had become a metaphor, through association with the lowlife of Moorfields, for hack writing by journalists and others who published anything they could sell. The term was thus employed by authors such as POPE and SWIFT – who considered themselves to be above such professional scribblers – to characterize bad writing.

H

Halifax, Charles Montagu, 1st earl of (1661–1715), Whig politician and poet. Montagu was educated at Westminster School and Trinity College, Cambridge, of which he became a fellow. At Westminster he gained a reputation as an author of epigrams, and at Cambridge his poem on the death of Charles II attracted the attention of the earl of Dorset, who invited him to London. In 1687 he collaborated with Matthew PRIOR in the writing of *The Hind and the Panther transvers'd to the story of the Country Mouse and the City Mouse*, a satire on Dryden. He continued to write poems, which led Addison to flatter him as 'the greatest of English poets'. He also acquired the reputation of being a Maecenas to younger authors such as POPE and SWIFT, despite deciding to enter the political arena as a Whig.

That decision led Montagu in 1688 to support the invitation to William of Orange to come to England, and on his arrival Montagu raised troops to secure Northamptonshire for the prince. He sat in the CONVENTION PARLIAMENT and subsequent Parliaments as a Whig, and in 1692 became a commissioner of the Treasury. His financial abilities lay behind the act creating the BANK OF ENGLAND in 1694. This was much criticized by COUNTRY PARTY Whigs, who identified Montagu as a member of the JUNTO. Later that year he became chancellor of the exchequer, and as such he presided over the

RECOINAGE of 1696. In 1697 he became first lord of the Treasury. Then the attacks on the Junto began to tell, and in 1699 he resigned both the chancellorship of the exchequer and the first lordship of the Treasury. In 1700 he purchased the auditorship of the exchequer and was ennobled as Baron Halifax.

The following year Halifax was subject – along with his Junto colleagues – to the attempted impeachment by the Tory majority in the Commons for his part in the king's negotiation of the second partition treaty. However, the Whig majority in the House of Lords dropped the proceedings. When Anne succeeded in 1702 she struck Halifax along with his Junto colleagues off the privy council, an unusual and vindictive act. In 1703 the Tories in the Commons attacked him once again by accusing him of irregularities in his conduct as auditor of the exchequer, and once again the Whigs in the Lords got him off the hook. The Tories then pressed charges before the attorney general, who found there was no case to answer.

Halifax was appointed a commissioner of the UNION OF ENGLAND AND SCOTLAND in 1706. Alone of the Junto he failed to get high office in the following years, and by 1710 was even intriguing with HARLEY. During the last four years of Queen Anne's reign, however, he resumed his opposition to the Tory ministry along with his fellow Whigs, and was rewarded by George I with the office of first lord of the Treasury and promotion in the peerage to the earldom of Halifax.

Halifax, George Montagu Dunk, 2nd earl of

(1716–71), politician. He was the son of George Montagu, the nephew of Charles Montagu, 1st earl of HALIFAX. He was educated at Eton (1725–32) and Trinity College, Cambridge, where he matriculated in 1734. His student days were not wasted, for he earned a reputation of being an 'extremely brilliant' scholar. He succeeded to the earldom of Halifax on his father's death in 1739, and in 1741 he married Ann Dunk, born the daughter of William Richards of Tongues in Hawkhurst, Kent. Richards had inherited the estate of Sir Thomas Dunk, ironmonger and sheriff of London (1709–10), on condition that he and his heirs took the surname Dunk. His daughter, who was only 16 at the time of her marriage to Halifax, was allegedly worth £110,000. On his marriage Halifax also took the name of Dunk, which seems to have been a condition of the match, even signing his name 'Dunk Halifax' thereafter. It was also apparently a condition that he had some connection with commerce, which he fulfilled by becoming a freeman of London. His connection with the City seems to have made him popular with the merchants of London.

Although he was a Whig, Halifax was opposed to WALPOLE, and was one of those peers who snubbed the former prime minister when he took his place in the upper house as earl of Orford. In 1742 Halifax was rewarded for his opposition to the court with the post of lord of the bedchamber in the household of FREDERICK PRINCE OF WALES, which he held until 1744 when he went over to the PELHAMS. When the JACOBITE RISING broke out in 1745 Halifax was one of the noblemen who volunteered to raise a regiment, and he was made a colonel on 4 October. Although Halifax never heard a shot fired in anger, he rose to become a lieutenant general by 1759.

Meanwhile Halifax had also become one of the leading figures in the ministry. On 7 October 1748 he became president of the BOARD OF TRADE, and remained in that office until 21 March 1761, apart from an interval between June 1756 and October 1757. Until Halifax's appointment the Board of Trade had steadily lost its influence over colonial policy to other agencies of government, notably the secretaries of state for the south. Thus, for example, nominations of colonial governors in North America and the West Indies, which had originally been part of the Board's remit when it was established in 1696, had been assumed by the secretary's office since the 1720s.

Halifax was determined to retrieve for the Board the direction of colonial affairs, especially in America. To achieve this he wished to become a member of the cabinet as president of the Board, but although the duke of NEWCASTLE attempted to persuade the king to admit him the request was refused, apparently as a result of the duke of Bedford advising against it. Bedford, who had previously been Halifax's patron, objected to his rapprochement with the Pelhams and warned GEORGE II that it would be detrimental to the royal prerogative to allow the authority of the secretary over the colonies to be ceded to the president of the Board of Trade.

Nevertheless, Halifax did succeed in appropriating some of the powers assumed by the secretaries. Thus in March 1752 an order in council placed the nominations of colonial governors in the hands of the Board. Halifax injected a new dynamism into the Board's activities, and attempted to reclaim powers that had slipped to the colonial assemblies in the era of 'salutary neglect'. Not for nothing was he referred to as 'the Father of the Colonies'. He even tried to obtain a separate secretariat for the colonies, which would have given him a seat in the cabinet, an issue on which he resigned from the presidency of the Board of Trade in 1756 when the attempt failed. In 1757 he at last obtained entry to cabinet meetings, but the outbreak of the SEVEN YEARS WAR meant that he was unable to implement schemes to assert ministerial authority over the American colonies. The only lasting impact he had on them was that his name was perpetuated in the town of Halifax in Nova Scotia. When such schemes as he had suggested were implemented after the war he was no longer president, and others, notably George GRENVILLE, were held responsible for them and their catastrophic consequences. But they owed their inspiration to his example, as Charles TOWN-SHEND, who served at the Board under him, acknowledged.

In 1761 Halifax was appointed lord lieutenant of Ireland and arrived in Dublin in October. Despite there being serious unrest in Ireland that year, with the rising of the 'Whiteboys' in Munster, Halifax proved to be popular. His popularity was enhanced by his declining to accept an increase in his allowance from £12,000 to £16,000 voted by the Dublin Parliament in February 1762, although he accepted it for his successor. This was a particularly altruistic sacrifice as during his year in Ireland he spent about £20,000. When in June 1762 he became first lord of the Admiralty Halifax was permitted to combine it with the lord lieutenancy for a year.

By September 1762, however, Halifax had been appointed secretary of state for the north, and in April 1763 he moved to the southern secretaryship. It was in this capacity that he became embroiled with John WILKES. The 45th number of Wilkes's paper *The North Briton* contained a scarcely veiled attack on the king for the speech he had made to Parliament commending the treaty of PARIS of 1763. The decision was made to prosecute him for seditious libel, and Halifax issued a warrant for the arrest of the author, printer and publishers of the paper, without naming Wilkes. Such GENERAL WARRANTS had been routinely used by previous secretaries, although they rested on a dubious legal basis. Ultimately they derived from the Licensing Act passed under Charles II to control the press, but this had lapsed in 1695. Wilkes therefore challenged their validity and brought an action against Wood, an undersecretary in Halifax's office, for damages in the Court of Common Pleas. He won and was awarded £1000. Halifax himself escaped a similar action brought by Wilkes by legal chicanery, until Wilkes was declared an outlaw and therefore could not sue him. But after the outlawry was reversed in 1768 Wilkes successfully sued the former secretary and was awarded £4000 damages in 1769.

By then Halifax was out of office, having been dismissed on the fall of Grenville's ministry in 1765. He had been approached to join the ROCK-INGHAM administration, but had refused on principle. He objected to the repeal of the STAMP ACT, claiming that 'it is not the Stamp Act that is opposed but the authority of this legislature'. In January 1770 he accepted the office of lord privy seal from Lord NORTH, and in 1771 became secretary of state again, but died shortly afterwards.

Halley, Edmond (1656–1742), astronomer. Halley was educated at St Paul's School, London, and Queen's College, Oxford, where he already displayed a precocious talent for astronomy. He left Oxford without taking a degree in 1676, and went to St Helena to study stars in the southern hemisphere. There he made the first complete observation of the transit of Mercury in 1677. On his return he was elected a fellow of the Royal Society at the age of 22. He was to publish 84 papers in its *Philosophical Transactions*, which he edited from 1685 to 1693. They covered a wide variety of scientific subjects, astronomical, geometrical, even historical. Halley became a close colleague of Sir Isaac NEWTON, and paid for the publication of his *Principia*. In 1703 he was appointed to the Savilian chair of geometry at Oxford. Queen Anne's husband George prince of Denmark set up a committee to publish Flamsteed's observations, on which Halley was a leading member. He succeeded Flamsteed as astronomer royal in 1721. Halley's most famous contribution to astronomy was his prediction that a comet observed in 1456, 1531, 1607 and 1682 would return in 1758.

When it did so on Christmas Day, 16 years after his death, it was named Halley's comet.

Handel, George Frideric (1685–1759), prolific and versatile composer, who exerted a major influence upon British music during the first half of the 18th century. He was born in Germany as Georg Friedrich Händel, and his precocious talents were soon apparent: by 1705 his first two operas had been performed in Hamburg. In his early 20s Handel undertook a protracted tour of Italy, an experience that exposed him to the leading composers and the latest musical trends.

Handel arrived in London from Hanover in 1710, and soon established his reputation with the opera *Rinaldo* (1711). The work's spectacular staging and dramatic arias made an immediate impact. Under the patronage of Lord BURLINGTON, Handel embarked upon a remarkable range of compositions reflecting genres as diverse as odes, operas, oratorios and organ concertos. His output was impressive, including more than 70 operas and oratorios. Like Henry PURCELL before him, Handel rapidly won royal favour, composing the *Utrecht Te Deum* and *Jubilate* celebrating the close of the War of the SPANISH SUCCESSION, and a *Birthday Ode for Queen Anne*.

Handel's defection from Hanover initially incurred the displeasure of the former elector, who became GEORGE I in 1714. However, Handel swiftly rehabilitated himself in the eyes of his new monarch through his *Water Music*, which also earned him a handsome pension. Handel had settled permanently in England in 1712; naturalization followed in 1727, the year that he composed four coronation anthems, including *Zadok the Priest*, for GEORGE II. Further royal commissions included the *Te Deum* for the British victory at DETTINGEN in 1743, and the widely acclaimed *Music for the Royal Fireworks* (1749) performed to mark the treaty of AIX-LA-CHAPELLE.

Although in continuing demand for such official commissions, Handel also composed for the theatre. The aristocratic Royal Academy of Music, which was formed in 1720 to promote the new Italian opera, underlay influential works including *Giulio Cesare*. Changing audience tastes – largely following the spectacular success of GAY's *Beggar's Opera* – obliged Handel to adapt his talents to the English-language oratorio, starting with *Esther* in 1732. During 1741–2 Handel visited Dublin, where he gave concerts in support of local hospitals and prisons; these featured his most popular and enduring work, *Messiah*, which raised £400 when it was first performed on 13 April 1742. The piece became more widely known through annual concerts in support of London's Foundling Hospital, and subsequently helped lay the foundations for a lasting English choral tradition. ROUBILIAC's statue of Handel as Apollo formed a centrepiece for London's popular VAUXHALL GARDENS; an indication of the composer's reputation in his adopted country is his monument by the same sculptor in Westminster Abbey. The Abbey also provided the setting for a succession of spectacular Handel festivals, to mark the composer's centenary, staged from 1784 to 1791.

FURTHER READING P.H. Lang, *George Frideric Handel* (1966); R. Smith, *Handel's Oratorios and Eighteenth-Century Thought* (1995).

Hanover, state of northwest Germany, known as the electorate of Hanover, as its rulers were hereditary electors of the Holy Roman emperor. By the ACT OF SETTLEMENT of 1701 the elector, George Lewis, succeeded in 1714 to the throne of Great Britain and Ireland as GEORGE I (*see* HANOVERIAN SUCCESSION), and through its ruling dynasty Hanover remained formally linked with Britain for more than a century. However, the dual role of the Hanoverian kings – especially the first two Georges – led to accusations that Britain's interests were being subsumed to those of the German electorate.

In June 1743 GEORGE II helped to lead the Pragmatic Army to victory over the French at DETTINGEN. Alongside the predictable wave of plaudits came sharp criticisms, for many English officers were deeply offended that their monarch had appeared upon the battlefield wearing Hanoverian – rather than British – uniform. George's choice of clothing revealed much about his own priorities in foreign affairs, and the anger of British army officers likewise reflected their countrymen's concerns about the baleful influence of what the elder PITT famously described as the 'despicable electorate'.

In an era in which monarchs still sought to play a major role in foreign policy, Hanover represented a ready focus for controversy. Just as WILLIAM III had kindled fierce opposition by harnessing British resources in the interests of his Dutch possessions, so George I and George II encountered heavy criticism for periodically placing the security of their German-speaking electorate above the needs of their English-speaking kingdom. Like William, the first two Georges generated concern and jealousy through protracted visits to their continental possessions. And, just as William had encountered criticism for his reliance upon over-mighty foreign favourites such as Keppel (see ALBEMARLE) and Bentinck (see PORTLAND, WILLIAM BENTINCK, EARL OF), so the customary xenophobia of 18th-century Englishmen fostered the suspicion that George I was paying undue heed to his undoubtedly influential countrymen Robethon and Bernstorff.

With the precedent of William III fresh before them, those Englishmen who offered the throne to the Hanoverians incorporated measures intended to restrict their royal powers. Under the Act of Settlement of 1701 the crown required Parliament's permission to wage war in defence of its foreign dominions. Another clause obliged the monarch to seek parliamentary approval before visiting his electoral possessions; deemed a personal insult to George I, this obligation was repealed when he actually succeeded in 1714. Despite determined efforts to ensure the primacy of British over Hanoverian interests, the electorate continued to influence foreign policy between 1714 and 1760. In northern Europe, the specific interests of Hanover habitually came before those

of Britain; hence George I's concerns for his electorate underpinned a substantial Royal Navy presence in the Baltic aimed at containing Russian influence following the collapse of Swedish power. More notorious was George II's cynical negotiation of a convention of neutrality for his electorate in 1741 during the War of the AUSTRIAN SUCCESSION, by which Hanover's security was bought at the humiliating price of support for Louis XV's candidate for Holy Roman emperor. Similarly, the DIPLOMATIC REVOLUTION that preceded the SEVEN YEARS WAR stemmed partly from the continuing priority given to the defence of Hanover.

The British monarchy's apparent obsession with Hanover, and the likely price in blood and gold that such interests implied, sparked regular bouts of intensive criticism. These sometimes proved capable of establishing a surface unity between diverse shades of political opinion in Britain. For example, during the opening phase of the War of the Austrian Succession in the early 1740s, the controversial issue of British subsidies to Hanover provided common ground between Tories and opposition Whigs. Distrust of the Hanoverian connection was exacerbated by a growing belief that Britain's true interests would be better served by a BLUE-WATER POLICY of colonial expansion rather than the continental entanglements that were an inevitable consequence of such territories.

Yet however unpalatable the Hanoverian connection may have been to many Britons, the inconvenient demands of the electorate were an inevitable consequence of choosing foreigners to occupy the throne of the exiled Stuarts. And while most 18th-century Englishmen viewed their monarchy's links with Hanover in an overwhelmingly negative light, historians have since suggested that the electorate could exert a beneficial influence upon the course of Britain's foreign affairs. Hanover's location left it vulnerable to attack from France and Prussia, and for France in particular the electorate offered an irresistible target. As a prized personal possession of the king of Great

Britain, a conquered Hanover represented a valuable bargaining counter that could be produced during peace negotiations to redeem colonial losses. Hanover's capacity to skew French strategy was demonstrated during the Seven Years War. In 1757 superior French armies obliged the duke of CUMBERLAND to sign the convention of Kloster-Zeven and deliver Hanover to the Bourbons. George II subsequently repudiated the armistice and, under the inspired leadership of Ferdinand of Brunswick, the so-called Army of Observation soon succeeded in inflicting severe defeats upon the French. While France frittered away its armies in European campaigns against Ferdinand and Frederick the Great of Prussia, Britain won an empire at France's expense, so lending credence to Pitt's boast that America had been conquered in Germany. By contrast, during the AMERICAN WAR OF INDEPENDENCE, when France refused to succumb to the lure of Hanover and instead deployed its resources overseas, Britain faced humiliating defeat.

The influence of Hanover upon British policies declined after 1760 when the 'patriot king' GEORGE III made a deliberate effort to assume a British identity and distance himself from the demands of his hereditary electorate. Unlike his grandfather and great-grandfather, George III never visited Hanover, and this apparent indifference did much to defuse the traditional British hostility towards the electorate. During the Napoleonic Wars, Hanover was occupied first by Prussia and then by France. At the peace of 1814 it became a kingdom and acquired extensive new territories. The Hanoverian connection with Britain was finally severed at the accession of Victoria in 1837, who, as a woman, was barred from the throne of Hanover.

FURTHER READING T.C.W Blanning, "'That Horrid Electorate' or 'Ma Patrie Germanique': George III, Hanover and the Fürstenbund of 1785' in *Historical Journal* XX (1977), 311–44.

Hanoverian succession, the course of events by which the elector of HANOVER – the future GEORGE I – and his successors became kings of Great Britain and Ireland. The Hanoverian succession came about as a result of the failure of the provisions in the BILL OF RIGHTS of 1689 to provide a successor to the crown on Queen ANNE's death. The Bill of Rights had set aside the Catholic James II and his heirs by his second wife Mary of Modena, placing the succession in WILLIAM III and MARY, then, in the event of Mary dying childless, in any heirs William might have by a second wife, and finally in the children of Anne, Mary's sister. At the time it seemed as though every contingency had been provided for. But Mary died childless in 1694, William never remarried, and in 1700 Anne's only child to survive babyhood, Prince William duke of Gloucester, died at the age of eleven. The way seemed open for a restoration of the direct Stuart line after Anne's death unless further provision was made.

The ACT OF SETTLEMENT passed in 1701 laid down that after Anne's death the crown should pass to the house of Hanover. There was a remote hereditary claim in that the dowager electress Sophia of Hanover was the daughter of Elizabeth, wife of Frederick, the elector Palatine; and Elizabeth in turn was the daughter of James I. But it is estimated that some fifty claimants had a better hereditary claim. They were ruled out because they were all Catholics, and stress was placed on the Protestant succession in the house of Hanover. Sophia died in 1714, just weeks before Queen Anne, so that her son, the elector of Hanover, became George I.

Hanway, Jonas (1712–86), philanthropist. Before devoting his energies to charitable causes, Hanway led an adventurous life as a merchant. Born in Portsmouth into a naval family, Hanway traded in Portugal and Russia, from where he made a perilous caravan journey into Persia. Hanway later published an account of his eventful travels. Arriving in London in 1750, Hanway soon took an active interest in the plight of the capital's poor, and began campaigning to alleviate it. He was a keen supporter of the Foundling Hospital, and highlighted the conditions endured by the young 'climbing boys' or chimney sweeps. He also helped to establish the Magdalen Hospital to rescue penitent prostitutes from the clutches of bawds and pimps.

At the onset of the SEVEN YEARS WAR in 1756 Hanway combined charity with patriotism when he founded the Marine Society, which sought to transform destitute boys into useful sailors. Hanway published pamphlets to attract support for his causes; these methods were clearly effective, for within three years the Marine Society had generated some £25,000 through voluntary subscription. Similar methods were employed in 1760 to promote Hanway's Society for the Encouragement of the British Troops in Germany and North America. In a matter of months this charity raised more than £7000 to provide warm clothing for soldiers and support for the widows and orphans of the global conflict.

In common with the prison reformer John HOWARD, Hanway based his proposals for reform upon exhaustive research: when seeking to expose the appalling death rate among the children of London's poor, he employed a detailed analysis of the *Bills of Mortality* to highlight the existence of black spots such as Bethnal Green and Shoreditch. Hanway's efforts earned parliamentary backing and resulted in legislation – the so-called 'Act for keeping children alive' (1762) – requiring the registration of poor children.

At times Hanway could appear eccentric and faintly ridiculous. For example, a shocking encounter with improperly clad female bathers at Southampton was sufficient to trigger a broadside against 'this reign of sea water'. Hanway's adoption of the oriental umbrella made him a focus for mockery on the streets of London, and his attack upon 'the pernicious custom of tea-drinking' prompted a bout of literary sparring with Dr JOHNSON. Despite such minor flaws, Hanway remained a hard-working philanthropist whose indefatigable efforts on behalf of the poor were recognized by a monument in Westminster Abbey.

FURTHER READING J.S. Taylor, *Jonas Hanway* (1985).

Hardwicke, Philip Yorke, 1st earl of (1690–1764), lawyer and politician, lord chancellor (1737–56). Yorke was educated at a dissenting school and after two years in a solicitor's office at the Middle Temple he was called to the bar in 1715. He entered Parliament in 1719, and represented Seaford from 1722 until 1734, when he became a peer. Hardwicke rose rapidly as a ministerial lawyer, becoming solicitor general in 1720, attorney general in 1723, lord chief justice in 1734 and lord chancellor from 1737 to 1756. He was one of the greatest of lord chancellors, his long career in Chancery enabling him to effect reforms in equity that created order out of chaos. Hardwicke was also a politician, a key element in the PELHAM and NEWCASTLE ministries. When both roles combined – as in the trials of the Jacobites arrested after the '45 JACOBITE RISING, and the legislation that sought to prevent a further uprising in Scotland – the lawyer was more evident than the Whig. He is chiefly remembered as the architect of HARDWICKE'S MARRIAGE ACT of 1753.

Hardwicke's Marriage Act (1753), statute that sought to stamp out clandestine marriages. It was promoted by the lord chancellor, the earl of HARDWICKE.

Although the proclamation of banns, or the issue of a licence from the archbishop or diocesan, were necessary legal steps towards matrimony, they did not prevent minors from marrying without the wishes or even the knowledge of their parents. This was particularly the case in London, where, it was claimed, there was a regular trade in marriages conducted by unscrupulous clergymen, particularly in the vicinity of the Fleet Prison. Horror stories were told of how young gentlemen were inveigled into wedlock by whores, and young ladies by confidence tricksters, with the connivance of the notorious Fleet parsons.

To stamp out such practices Hardwicke proposed that the consent of guardians should be made explicit in the case of minors, that residence should be established and that marriage registers, signed by the parties and by witnesses, should be kept. The bill met with some opposition in Parliament, led by Henry FOX, who had himself clandestinely married the daughter of the duke of Richmond. Fox argued that it delivered children up to the tyranny of their parents or guardians, whose choice of marriage partners was based more on material than on emotional considerations. He also claimed that it would prove a great inconvenience to the poor, placing an unnecessary obstacle in their path to wedlock, and thereby discouraging marriage and encouraging vice. Despite such objections the bill was carried and became law in June 1753.

Hargreaves, James. *See* TEXTILES.

Harley, Robert, 1st earl of Oxford and Mortimer (1661–1724), politician who rose to become effectively prime minister in the last four years of the reign of Queen ANNE. His father, a staunch Presbyterian, sent him to a dissenting school. He himself went to meeting houses until he became secretary of state in 1704. This led some Tories to distrust him later when he allied with them. Thus Francis ATTERBURY called him 'the spawn of a Presbyterian'.

At the GLORIOUS REVOLUTION Harley congratulated William of Orange on the success of his undertaking, and was returned to the CONVENTION PARLIAMENT as member for Tregoney. He became the complete House of Commons man, one of the first to grasp that it was now a permanent institution and to come to terms with the new reality of annual sessions. As John Macky noted of him, 'no man knows better the tricks of the House', a talent that was to earn him the nickname of 'Robin the Trickster'. Although he identified himself with the Whigs, during the 1690s he became disillusioned with the Whig JUNTO, accusing them of selling out in office

the principles they had upheld in opposition. This led him to combine with Tories to form what became known as the new COUNTRY PARTY, which opposed the COURT PARTY on such issues as the STANDING ARMY and PLACEMEN. By the late 1690s Harley and his supporters were little more than the Country Whig tail that wagged a Tory dog.

When William III turned to the Tories in 1700, Harley became speaker of the House of Commons. In the parliamentary session of 1701 he was among the leaders in the attack on the Junto calling for their impeachment. As speaker he piloted the ACT OF SETTLEMENT through the Commons, which transferred the crown to the house of Hanover on the death of Queen Anne. When Anne came to the throne in 1702 Harley was closely allied to her chief ministers, GODOLPHIN and the duke of MARLBOROUGH. Together they were known as 'the triumvirate'. The triumvirs were more attached to the queen than to a party, acting as brokers between her and the Tory and Whig parties. Although Anne preferred high-church Tories in her first ministerial appointments, she quickly became disillusioned with them, and by 1704 dispensed with their services. In the ministerial reconstruction that ensued Harley became secretary of state. As one of the triumvirs he played a major part in the making of the UNION OF ENGLAND AND SCOTLAND.

As the War of the SPANISH SUCCESSION continued, however, the triumvirate fell apart as Marlborough and Godolphin came increasingly to rely on Whig support for the war effort, urging the appointment of the Junto to ministerial posts. Anne, backed by Harley, resisted their encroachment. In 1708 the dispute resulted in Harley's resignation from the ministry. As long as the queen was fully committed to the war she had little choice but to acquiesce in the advice of the 'duumvirs' Marlborough and Godolphin. Two years later she was prepared to seek peace with France, and Harley returned to power as chancellor of the exchequer – effectively prime minister – presiding over a largely Tory ministry.

Harley still regarded himself as the queen's servant rather than a party man, and retained many Whigs in office. This led some Tories to demand a complete purge. They organized themselves into the 'October Club' to pressurize Harley into more Tory measures, an initiative welcomed by Henry St John (the future Viscount BOLINGBROKE), who set himself up as a rival to the prime minister. In 1711 Harley was able to fend off this threat. He launched the South Sea Company, which put the national finances on a stable footing for the first time since 1710 (*see* SOUTH SEA BUBBLE), and was rewarded by promotion to the peerage as earl of Oxford and to the post of lord treasurer. At the end of the year he also reversed a defeat in the House of Lords in a vote on the preliminaries of peace with France by getting the queen to create twelve new peers.

The making of the treaty of UTRECHT, however, was to weaken the ministry and strengthen its opponents. The Tories on whom the ministers relied in the Commons were divided over the peace. Some were prepared to accept it at any price to ease the country of the heavy taxes needed to finance the war. Others were uneasy that selling out on the allies might alienate the house of Hanover and give comfort to the Pretender, James Francis Edward STUART. The dismissal of the duke of Marlborough from his post as commander in chief and his replacement by the duke of ORMONDE – who was ordered not to engage the enemy – exacerbated these divisions in the course of 1712. In the spring of 1713 the final peace terms were accepted by Parliament, but a commercial treaty with France was defeated by a conjunction of certain Tories (the so-called 'Whimsicals') with the Whigs. These divisions in the ranks of the Tory party survived its victory at the polls in the general election held that summer. To some extent they reflected the division in the ministry between the staunchly Hanoverian Oxford and the increasingly Jacobite St John, now Viscount Bolingbroke.

In 1714 the succession became the crucial concern, following a severe illness suffered by the queen towards the end of the previous year. In April a Court motion that the succession was not in danger passed both Houses of Parliament, but by very narrow majorities. Oxford tried to wrong-foot Bolingbroke by persuading the cabinet to put a price on the Pretender's head. Bolingbroke managed to restrict the reward to £5000 at that juncture, but Oxford outmanoeuvred him in Parliament by getting the Commons to raise it to £100,000. Since Parliament was Oxford's power base against him, Bolingbroke persuaded the queen to prorogue it on 9 July. This marked his ascendancy over his rival, and on 27 July Anne dismissed Oxford. Four days later the queen died.

Oxford took his place in the meetings of the Privy Council that ensured the peaceful accession of GEORGE I. This did not prevent the Whigs from impeaching him when they came to power under the new king. Oxford spent two years in the Tower before the Whig schism enabled him to get the articles of impeachment against him dropped. He attended the House of Lords, playing a leading part, until 1719, when a decline in his health obliged him to withdraw from politics. He died on 21 May 1724.

FURTHER READING B. Hill, *Robert Harley, Speaker, Secretary of State and Premier Minister* (1988).

Harris, Howel. *See* METHODISM.

Harrison, John. *See* LONGITUDE.

Hastings, Lady Elizabeth (1682–1739), philanthropist. She was the daughter of the 7th earl of Huntingdon by his first wife, who came from Ledstone House near Pontefract, Yorkshire. Lady Elizabeth inherited the house in 1705 and lived there for the rest of her life, with her half-sisters Anne, Catherine, Frances and Margaret, daughters of her father by his second wife. She herself never married, though her beauty attracted several suitors.

Instead of devoting herself to a husband, Lady

Elizabeth devoted herself to charitable causes. Thus she established an orphanage at Ledsham and four charity schools in the West Riding. Her interest in education led her to found an exhibition at Queen's College, Oxford, for boys from twelve grammar schools in the north of England. The Hastings exhibition (it did not become a scholarship until 1922) originally included an element of chance in the form of a lottery, to leave the final choice to providence. Even Lady Elizabeth admitted that it 'may be called by some superstition or enthusiasm'.

Enthusiasm ran in the family in the form of METHODISM. Lady Betty, as she was generally known, admired the Methodists but did not become one herself. Indeed she scarcely had time to do so, for in 1738 she contracted cancer of the breast. She underwent a mastectomy at a time when there were no anaesthetics, only painkillers such as laudanum. She survived the operation, but the condition returned and she died on 22 December 1739.

Hastings, Selina, countess of Huntingdon.
See METHODISM.

Hastings, Warren (1732–1818), colonial administrator. As governor of Bengal from 1772 to 1785 Hastings became the focus for growing concerns over the manner in which British officials administered the expanding empire in INDIA. His lengthy trial for corruption ended in his acquittal.

A talented scholar, who was later to develop a keen interest in Indian art and culture, Hastings sailed for Bengal in 1750 to take up a junior appointment with the EAST INDIA COMPANY. During the coming decade, as the Company became embroiled in hostilities with both the French and native Indian rulers, Hastings played an increasingly important role in the affairs of Bengal, acting as the Company's representative at the court of the local rulers or nawabs. However, Hastings later quarrelled with the Company's council in Bengal and returned to England in 1765.

By 1769 failing funds had obliged Hastings to seek further employment in India. After service in Madras he was sent back to Bengal to oversee the Company's affairs in that province. To the subsequent consternation of many of his own countrymen, Hastings seemingly made little effort to introduce British systems of government, but instead set about ruling Bengal in a fashion that owed much to his Indian predecessors. Compared with the elected assemblies of Britain's colonies in the Americas, such methods smacked of tyranny and oriental despotism.

During the first two years of his administration in Bengal, from 1772 to 1774, Hastings sought to strengthen British rule by transferring the administrative apparatus of the province from the court of the nawab to Britain's own settlement of Calcutta. He also instigated reforms of the judicial system and attempted to rationalize the collection of taxes. In 1774, with the reorganization of the Company's affairs, Hastings was given the title of governor general, while his powers were extended to embrace other British possessions in India. However, he was also obliged to share power with four other supreme councillors. Political rivalries followed, as the new arrivals sought to discredit Hastings's rule by assembling evidence of alleged corruption. The wrangling became increasingly bitter, and Hastings actually fought a duel against his fellow councillor Philip Francis.

From 1778, after the entry of France into the AMERICAN WAR OF INDEPENDENCE transformed that colonial rebellion into a truly global conflict, Hastings was obliged to orchestrate the defence of British India against a formidable range of enemies: besides the threat of French expeditionary forces, the Company faced the powerful Mahratta confederacy of western and central India, while in the south the determined Hyder Ali of Mysore deployed his substantial army to menace Madras. Hastings rose to the challenge, and while Britain's American empire was relinquished, her embattled Indian territories were preserved and bolstered.

The draconian methods that Hastings employed to meet the wartime crisis provided fresh ammunition for his critics. When he returned to England in 1785 it was to face a wave of criticism from those who felt that he personified the unacceptable face of British rule in the subcontinent. At the urging of Edmund BURKE, Hastings was impeached. Occupying 145 days spread over more than seven years, Hastings's trial before the House of Lords offered a showcase for the oratorical fireworks of Burke and SHERIDAN and amounted to a microscopic dissection of British rule in India. When the hearing finally ended in 1795, Hastings was acquitted of all the charges against him. Although he was vindicated by the verdict, the proceedings absorbed Hastings's fortune, while the prolonged ordeal shattered his health. In retirement he followed the life of a country gentleman and scholar. Despite the outspoken criticisms of his rule in India, Hastings nonetheless demonstrated an affinity with its peoples that was all too often absent during the heyday of the empire he had done so much to consolidate.

FURTHER READING P. J. Marshall, *The Impeachment of Warren Hastings* (1965).

Hawke, Sir Edward (1705–81), admiral who inflicted a crushing defeat upon the French navy at QUIBERON BAY during the SEVEN YEARS WAR. The son of a barrister, Hawke joined the Royal Navy at the age of 14 and had reached the rank of captain by his late 20s. Following service in the West Indies during the 1730s, Hawke revealed characteristically aggressive tactics in the War of the AUSTRIAN SUCCESSION. His performance as captain of the *Berwick* at Toulon in 1744 secured his promotion to admiral. When Sir Peter Warren fell ill, Hawke was appointed to replace him as commander of the Channel Fleet. In the action off Cape Finisterre in October 1747 Hawke savaged a French convoy, accounting for all but two of the nine enemy vessels engaged. Created a knight of the Bath and vice admiral, Hawke was also returned as MP for Portsmouth.

It was during the Seven Years War that Hawke performed his most valuable service. Although the 1757 expedition to Rochefort proved a dismal failure, in the spring of 1759 Hawke began a lengthy blockade of Brest. The unprecedented operation was made possible by Hawke's meticulous planning and attention to logistics – regular revictualling ensured that his ships maintained their vigil with healthy crews. When the Brest squadron finally emerged in November, Hawke gave chase and destroyed it in an encounter that braved the hazardous weather conditions of Quiberon Bay. Hawke's celebrated victory not only scotched fears of a Bourbon invasion of Britain, but left the French navy reluctant to venture forth for the remainder of the war.

Hawke's outstanding record brought promotion to admiral of the fleet. From 1766 to 1771 he served as first lord of the Admiralty, although he enjoyed less success as a peacetime administrator than he had known as a wartime commander.

Hawksmoor, Nicholas (1661–1736), architect. Hawksmoor started his career as Sir Christopher WREN's scholar and domestic clerk. As such he was involved in the building of the new St Paul's Cathedral soon after its commencement. Wren employed him as deputy surveyor of Chelsea Hospital from 1682 to 1690. In 1691, thanks to Wren's influence, Hawksmoor became clerk of the works at Kensington Palace, a post he held until 1715. He became clerk of the works at Greenwich Hospital in 1698, and deputy surveyor in 1705. As such he was largely responsible for the construction of the hospital. In 1715 he became clerk of the works at St James's, Westminster and Whitehall, which post he resigned in 1718 on becoming secretary to the Board of Works.

Hawksmoor also took on many private commissions, including work on BLENHEIM PALACE and CASTLE HOWARD, where he designed the mausoleum. His most conspicuous buildings are in Oxford, where he rebuilt Queen's College and designed the Gothic quadrangle at All Souls, which transformed the appearance of the High Street and of Radcliffe Square. The twin towers of All Souls might have been inspired by his work on Beverley Minster between 1713 and 1717, where he helped to realign the leaning north porch, which was in danger of collapse. The magnificent towers of the minster probably influenced Hawksmoor's work on the towers of Westminster Abbey, of which he was made surveyor general on Wren's death in 1723. Hawksmoor's most famous church designs are St Mary Woolnoth, built between 1716 and 1719, and St George's Bloomsbury, built between 1720 and 1730.

Hell-Fire Club, notorious gentlemen's club. England in the 18th century was an eminently 'clubbable' society, and fraternities of various kinds catered for a wide range of groups and interests (*see* CLUBS). Of these the notorious Hell-Fire Club was distinguished by a reputation for debauchery and devil worship. Some sceptics have even questioned the very existence of the club. However, as there is ample evidence for contemporary clubs whose ceremonies were equally bizarre, some credence should be given to the enduring stories of its activities.

The most infamous of several 18th century societies revelling in the name of the Hell-Fire Club was apparently founded in the late 1750s by Sir Francis Dashwood, the colonel of the Buckinghamshire militia. Dashwood reputedly recruited a circle of twelve kindred spirits known as the Monks of St Francis, who staged orgies on the site of Medmenham Abbey; the fact that the members included the rakish John WILKES lends credence to the lurid legends of their rituals. Other luminaries linked with Dashwood's club included Bubb DODINGTON and Lord SANDWICH. It has been conjectured that when Wilkes published his obscene *Essay on Woman* he was planning to circulate it among his fellow 'Monks'. Beyond doubt is the fact that Lord Sandwich took a leading role in the condemnation of the *Essay* in the House of Lords in 1763; for informing against his erstwhile friend

Sandwich earned the unflattering soubriquet of 'Jemmy Twitcher', after the shifty character of that name in GAY's *The Beggar's Opera*.

Heritable Jurisdictions Act (1747), one of the measures passed after the suppression of the JACOBITE RISING of 1745 to try to prevent a future rebellion. The government felt that one contributory cause had been the hereditary courts of the clan chiefs, which had enabled them to force their clansmen into the rebellion because most of latter were subject to the jurisdiction of the chiefs, and could be threatened with prosecution.

The original bill distinguished three types of private court in Scotland: regalities; barons' jurisdictions; and those enjoyed by heritors of land. There were about 160 courts of regality, by no means all of them presided over by rebels — on the contrary, the greatest was owned by the duke of Argyll. The regalities were awarded compensation for their abolition. However, no compensation was awarded to baronial courts and other heritable jurisdictions such as that of hereditary sheriffs.

The Court of Sessions in Edinburgh was asked to provide a list of all heritable jurisdictions in Scotland, but refused on the grounds that to abolish them was contrary to the Act of Union, which provided for the continuance of a separate Scottish judicial system (*see* UNION OF ENGLAND AND SCOTLAND). This led most Scots to oppose the bill when it was introduced. They were joined by the Tories and even some Whigs. William Pitt stayed away from crucial debates on the bill complaining of gout.

The bill took from February to June 1747 to go through all its stages, and in the process some of the government's proposals were modified. Regalities were abolished and their jurisdictions vested in the king's courts, while heritable sheriffdoms were resumed by the crown, so that all future Scottish sheriffs were to be appointed annually, as in England. Baronial courts survived, though they could no longer try capital crimes, and their jurisdiction over lesser offences was limited to 'smaller crimes'. They continued to try civil cases where the sums involved did not exceed 40 shillings, though in arraigning tenants there was no ceiling. Clearly the government had reacted to some of the criticisms raised against the bill. Nevertheless, when it received the royal assent on 17 June 1747, the act did breach the terms of the union by bringing the judicial system of Scotland more into line with that of England.

Hervey, John, Lord Hervey (1696–1743), cynical politician and elegant man of letters whose published *Memoirs* provide an intimate portrait of the court of GEORGE II.

The second son of the 1st earl of Bristol, Hervey entered Parliament for the family borough of Bury St Edmunds in 1723. He initially sided with William PULTENEY in opposition to Sir Robert WALPOLE, but changed his allegiance when the latter retained his position as prime minister following the accession of George II in 1727. Hervey's support for the Walpolean regime was rewarded with a handsome pension, the office of vice chamberlain and admission to the Privy Council. In 1731 a printed war of words between Hervey and his old friend Pulteney led to a celebrated duel in which both men sustained wounds. Hervey also engaged in literary combat with Alexander POPE, who dubbed him 'Lord Fanny', an obvious reference to his homosexuality.

Hervey's continuing value to the ministry was recognized in 1733 when he was called to the House of Lords to bolster the ministerial ranks in the wake of the EXCISE CRISIS. Walpole prized Hervey because of the influence he wielded at court through his friendship with Queen CAROLINE. Life at court, which was punctuated by frequent rows between the royal couple and their son FREDERICK PRINCE OF WALES, provided the raw material for Hervey's entertaining *Memoirs*. Following Caroline's death in 1737 Hervey pressed Walpole for further advancement, and, despite the opposition of the duke of NEWCASTLE, he gained appointment as lord privy seal. Dismissed in July 1742 Hervey went into opposition. In 1743 he backed a proposal to dismiss the Hanoverian troops, and opposed the GIN ACT. Hervey died that summer at the age of 46; he had long suffered from poor health, which his father blamed on excessive tea drinking.

FURTHER READING R. Halsband, *Lord Hervey: Eighteenth-Century Courtier* (1974); L. Moore, *Amphibious Thing: The Life of Lord Hervey* (2000).

high church, term that appears to have come into general use around 1701, being used to distinguish the majority in the lower house of Convocation who wished to use the powers of that body to assert the privileges of the CHURCH OF ENGLAND against the perceived threat from DISSENT (*see* CONVOCATION CONTROVERSY). After the closure of Convocation under George I the term fell into disuse, but was revived in the 1790s to distinguish the more traditionalist churchmen in the Church of England from the EVANGELICALS. High-churchmen stressed the historic links between the Anglican and Catholic churches. They dwelt more on the mediation of the sacraments and ceremonies of the church than on individual salvation.

Those clergy and churchmen whose theological views were less dogmatic than either the High Churchmen or Evangelicals were sometimes called Latitudinarian, that is 'accepting the Anglican formulae but interpreting them with latitude'. The meaning of the term has been widened by some historians to denote what they see as the dominant characteristics of the 18th-century Church of England: moderation and toleration, concern with maintaining the social order, distrust of fervour or 'enthusiasm', and lack of interest in the mystical and mysterious elements of religion.

SEE ALSO LOW CHURCH.

Hillsborough, Wills Hill, 1st earl of (1718–93), politican who advocated tough measures against Britain's truculent American colonists, thereby contributing to an escalation of the imperial crisis during the decade after 1765.

Hillsborough owned extensive lands in Ireland, and controlled nine seats in the Irish Parliament. However, his political career was spent in England, where he entered Parliament for Warwick in 1741. Although he first held office in 1754 during NEWCASTLE's administration, Hillsborough began to play a more important political role following the conclusion of the Seven Years War, when he became president of the BOARD OF TRADE. Early in 1768, after the increasing importance of events across the Atlantic led to the creation of the new office of secretary of state for the American Department, Hillsborough was selected to fill the post. It was an unfortunate choice. Hillsborough's marked antipathy towards the American colonists had already attracted the wrath of the anonymous political writer 'JUNIUS'. In office his aggressive stance against the key colony of Massachusetts Bay only served to inflame a volatile situation (*see* AMERICAN COLONIES 1763–1776).

Hillsborough resigned his American post in 1772, but continued to prove a vocal opponent of any moves towards conciliation with the rebellious American colonists. In 1779 he became secretary of state for the South under Lord NORTH, relinquishing that post when the administration foundered three years later. He was created marquess of Downshire in the Irish peerage in 1789. As George III recognized, Hillsborough was notoriously tactless and devoid of judgment, and it was these traits that denied him his enduring ambition to become lord lieutenant of Ireland.

Hoadly, Benjamin (1675–1761), the most famous – or notorious – LOW-CHURCH clergyman of his day, the bugbear of such HIGH-CHURCH champions as Francis ATTERBURY and Henry SACHEVERELL.

Hoadly clashed with Atterbury in 1705 over a sermon Hoadly himself had preached on Romans chapter 13. The text, maintaining that the powers that be are ordained of God and that every man should subject himself to them, was often cited by high-church writers to justify the divine right of kings, passive obedience and non-resistance. Hoadly insisted that St Paul only advocated submission to rulers who ruled for the good of their subjects. For this he was censured by the lower house of Convocation (consisting of the ordinary clergy of the Church of England) and rebuked in print by Atterbury. The dispute between them, which also involved Offspring Blackall, the high-church bishop of Exeter, was drawn out until 1709.

In December of that year Hoadly was recommended by the House of Commons for some dignity from the queen. Anne responded by saying that she would 'take a proper opportunity to comply with their desires'. The recommendation was particularly provocative at a time when the Commons were proceeding with the impeachment of Dr SACHEVERELL. The ousting of the Whigs and their replacement by a Tory government and, after the general election of 1710, a Tory-dominated House of Commons, meant that Anne never found a proper time to gratify the Whigs' request. After her death, however, Hoadly was preferred to the bishopric of Bangor by George I in 1715. This led to the controversy in which he became involved in 1717 being described as the BANGORIAN CONTROVERSY.

In 1721 Hoadly was translated to the bishopric of Hereford, in 1723 to that of Salisbury and in 1734 to the rich see of Winchester. His rapid promotion made him the prime example of the place-seeking prelates of the 18th century who were accused of neglecting their spiritual for their political duties. He was especially vulnerable to criticism since he only once visited Bangor and never set foot in Hereford. It could be pointed out in mitigation that an adolescent illness had left him so severely disabled that he had to walk on crutches, and could only kneel to officiate in church services.

Hogarth, William (1697–1764), painter and engraver, who was a major force in the London art scene of the mid-18th century. His pictures provide some of the most vivid visual impressions of his age.

Hogarth was a Londoner through and through; born in the city in 1697, he died there in 1764. As blunt-featured as his trusty pug dog Trump, Hogarth observed his world with the sharp but cynical eye of the true Cockney. A staunch patriot who sometimes signed himself 'Britophil', Hogarth championed home-grown talent in the face of the contemporary mania for foreign artists, and poured scorn on connoisseurs who imported second-rate madonnas by the 'ship-load'.

Trained as an ornamental engraver, the young Hogarth progressed to painting via satirical prints. Drawing upon Dutch and Flemish precedents, Hogarth initially painted informal 'conversation pieces', showing his sitters in their natural social environments. His first major success, *The Beggar's Opera*, was produced in several versions in the late 1720s. Depicting a pivotal scene from John GAY's popular dramatization of London's criminal underworld, these paintings reflected Hogarth's concern with society and its moral codes.

From the early 1730s Hogarth completed successive series of paintings on contemporary themes; these highly detailed moral narratives reached a wider public through the sale of engravings. The first of these cycles, the *Harlot's Progress*, proved so popular – and was so widely copied – that Hogarth secured the passage of a copyright act protecting prints prior to the release of his next series, *The Rake's Progress*. In 1743, following a visit to Paris, Hogarth began work on a major series of paintings, *Marriage à la Mode*, which is widely regarded as his greatest achievement. Another incident-filled satirical series, *The Election*, dates from the mid-1750s. Alongside their clear 'moral' messages, such paintings often offered titillating glimpses of a brutal and licentious criminal subculture. For all their undoubted vigour and masterly technique, these works reflected a pessimistic stance, with the protagonists invariably facing a steady decline in fortune. Hogarth's world view remained too bleak for some tastes, allowing such rivals as Joseph Highmore to earn a living producing cycles of paintings featuring happier endings.

As the son of a Latin teacher who was imprisoned for debt, Hogarth possessed bitter first-hand experience of the price of professional failure. By the early 1750s Hogarth was producing engravings with the deliberate aim of steering the 'lower class of people' away from the vice and crime that could lead to poverty or the gallows. *Industry and Idleness*, along with *Beer Street* and *Gin Lane*, offered stark contrasts and simple lessons. These prints were produced as cheaply as possible to boost circulation among the target audience, with *The Four Stages of Cruelty* being issued in a crude woodcut version.

Although Hogarth failed to win widespread acknowledgement as a serious 'history' painter, he established a reputation for unpretentious life-sized portraits. Like his engravings, these held particular appeal for the emerging middle classes. Hogarth's skill as a portrait painter is nowhere better shown than in his unfinished 1759 canvas depicting his servants; probably executed as a household record, it demonstrates Hogarth's unerring ability to capture character.

The son-in-law of Sir James THORNHILL, Hogarth inherited Thornhill's painting academy in St Martin's Lane, and this became the focal point for a group of artists, such as Francis Hayman, who shared Hogarth's interests in social satire. Hogarth remained contemptuous of London's upper-class art scene – a hostility that limited his own influence and earned harsh reviews for his major study of art theory, *The Analysis of Beauty*. In his final years Hogarth considered himself a failure, but today he is regarded as one of the greatest of all English artists.

FURTHER READING D. Bindman, *Hogarth* (1981).

Holcroft, Thomas (1745–1809), playwright and novelist. Holcroft was the self-taught son of a shoemaker. At the age of 13 he was a stable boy at Newmarket, and after three years there he returned to London to work for his father. He started to contribute pieces to the press, and then entered the theatre. In 1778 his first play was performed at Drury Lane, and in 1781 a comedy was produced at Covent Garden. Both plays were only one-night productions. After visiting Paris he translated Beaumarchais's *The Marriage of Figaro*, which was performed at Covent Garden in 1784. This time the production was successful and earned Holcroft £600. His most popular play, *The Road to Ruin*, was first performed at the same theatre in February 1792.

That November Holcroft became a member of the Society for Constitutional Information, a radical CORRESPONDING SOCIETY. His radical views found expression in his JACOBIN NOVEL *Hugh Trevor*, published in 1794. The same year he was indicted along with Thomas Hardy and others on a charge of treason. Hardy's acquittal led to the charge against Holcroft being dropped. Between 1799 and 1803 he was on the continent. On his return he set up a printing business, which soon failed. He died after a long illness.

Horne Tooke, John (1736–1812), radical reformer. Horne was the son of John Horne, a poulterer patronized by FREDERICK PRINCE OF WALES. He added the name Tooke in 1782. Horne was educated at St John's College, Cambridge, and entered the Inner Temple with a view to becoming a lawyer. His father, however, wished him to pursue a clerical career, for which he was ordained in 1760. He then took up a living in Brentford.

In 1765 Horne published *The Petition of an Englishman*, a defence of John WILKES, thereby becoming involved in radical politics. When Wilkes stood for Parliament as a candidate in Middlesex in 1768, Horne was well placed at Brentford to help his campaign. The following year he took a leading part in the formation of the SOCIETY OF SUPPORTERS OF THE BILL OF RIGHTS. In 1771, however, he resigned from it, disgusted at its use of funds for paying Wilkes's debts. With those that withdrew with him he formed the Constitutional Society. The Society became embroiled with the law in 1776 for raising funds to assist the families of

Americans involved in the battle of Lexington. Horne was brought to trial in 1777 for his involvement with the subscription and sentenced to a year in prison.

By 1773 Horne was so reluctant a minister that he gave up his living and planned to resume his legal studies. When he applied to be called to the bar in 1779, however, he was refused on the grounds that he was in orders. He was to try on two other occasions, only to be turned down again. In 1780 he joined the newly formed Society for Constitutional Information (SCI), his own Constitutional Society having apparently folded. During the 1780s he supported PITT against FOX, presumably seeing in the former more chance of realizing the aims of the SCI. In 1790 he even stood against Fox at Westminster, only to be defeated. Fox then successfully sued him for his election expenses.

Horne welcomed the FRENCH REVOLUTION but refrained from advocating revolution in England. He was nevertheless tried for treason along with Thomas Hardy and others in 1794. Even after Hardy was acquitted the crown continued to press charges against Horne, but the jury found him not guilty as well. He again stood for Westminster in 1796 and was again defeated, a defeat that cost him £1000. Fortunately the expenses were paid by a wealthy supporter. Ironically for a radical reformer, Horne accepted nomination for the pocket borough of Old Sarum in 1801, only to be expelled from the House on the grounds that as a clergyman he was ineligible to sit. He then retired from politics to his house in Wimbledon, where he died.

FURTHER READING C. Bewley, *Gentleman Radical: Horne Tooke* (1998).

horse racing. In the 18th century, Britons of all classes demonstrated a passion for horse racing that fascinated foreigners and alarmed those of their own countrymen who remained immune to the lure of the turf.

By the Georgian era horse racing already

possessed a lengthy pedigree of royal patronage. Charles I had led his court on annual pilgrimages to Newmarket in Cambridgeshire, where even the onset of the Civil War failed to spoil the sport. During the Commonwealth race meetings were suppressed as a potential cover for conspirators, but at the Restoration horse racing became more popular than ever: indeed, in 1675 Charles II personally rode several winners.

During the 18th century the 'sport of kings' spread throughout society. Horse racing attracted increasing numbers of spectators, drawn from diverse social groups, who shared a love of horse flesh and gambling. The rapid growth of interest in horse racing led to the establishment of new courses: by 1730, York, Ascot and Epsom were all popular venues for the sport, and Goodwood followed in 1801. Racing's expansion prompted increasing regulation. The Jockey Club was founded in the early 1750s, a 'Racing Calendar' was introduced in 1773, and three of the 'classics' – the St Leger, the Oaks and the Derby – all date from the period 1778–80. While informal cross-country 'steeple chasing' had long formed a variant of the sport, a course incorporating fences was first introduced at Newmarket in 1794.

As the paintings of STUBBS and other sporting artists of the age reveal, aristocrats such as the 3rd duke of Richmond took an immense pride in their stables. However, the fortunes lavished on bloodstock and betting fuelled mounting concern among those who felt that the sport represented both a moral and an economic threat to society. It is significant that the second painting in Hogarth's *The Rake's Progress* of 1733–4 concentrates upon Tom Rakewell's decision to buy the racehorse 'silly Tom'; this costly acquisition is among those extravagances that soon plunge Hogarth's rake into a spiral of debt and despair.

For some men of wealth and influence, horse racing became an addiction that took priority over all other business. For example, George II's younger son, William Augustus duke of CUMBERLAND, was the proud owner of Eclipse, the most famous race-

horse of the day, and proved notoriously reluctant to abandon his first love for the world of politics; indeed, in 1765 the victor of Culloden insisted upon staging a key political meeting in his Newmarket stables. Two years earlier Newcastle had complained to Pitt that the 'Newmarket gentlemen' were so obsessed with racing 'that they hardly give themselves time to write upon any other business in a way to be understood'.

Other critics of horse racing were concerned at the promiscuous social mingling that occurred among followers of the sport. In a trend that was to be reflected in other recreations, such fears ultimately led to the segregation of spectators through the introduction of grandstands and enclosures that distanced the elite from the unruly 'lower orders'.

SEE ALSO SPORT.

hospitals. When George I came to the throne in 1714, Britain was poorly served by hospitals, but by the accession of George III in 1760 that situation had changed, as the demands of an expanding population coincided with the charitable inclinations of a rising middle class to found new hospitals both in London and in the provinces alike.

Hospitals had originated as church-run 'hospices' where accommodation was provided for the poor. The religious connection was severed by Henry VIII's dissolution of the monasteries, and in following years hospitals became an overwhelmingly secular affair. In 1700 those hospitals that did exist continued to reflect the traditional emphasis upon accommodation rather than actual treatment. For example, the 'Royal Hospitals' built for old soldiers at Dublin and Chelsea, and for sailors at Greenwich, were primarily concerned with the housing of aged or disabled veterans.

The Georgian hospital movement reflected changing attitudes to illness, as the development of scientific MEDICINE permitted a more effective response to disease and injury. Such growing optimism was manifested in a wave of foundations that offered treatment and care for the ailing poor, while wealthier patients continued to receive medical attention in the privacy and comfort of their own homes. Between 1720 and 1745 bequests and subscriptions permitted the foundation of five new hospitals in London alone. To the older institutions of St Thomas's and St Bartholemew's were added Westminster (1720), Guys (1724), St George's (1733), the London (1744) and the Middlesex (1745). By the mid-century, infirmaries had also been established at such venerable provincial cities as Bristol, Winchester, York and Exeter, and expanding industrial centres such as Leeds, Manchester and Birmingham soon followed suit. In 1800, England had some 38 hospitals. By the accession of Victoria in 1837 the total had risen to more than 100. Hospital care was increasingly supplemented by the emergence of dispensaries. Once again backed by wealthy subscribers, these diagnosed illnesses and prescribed medication for needy outpatients.

Those members of the elite and middling classes who funded the new hospitals exercised a high degree of control in return for their well-publicized benevolence. According to the size of their contribution, such benefactors enjoyed the right to admit patients of their choice from among the 'deserving poor', and they also governed the appointment of physicians and surgeons. Although treatment was free, patients were expected to abide by strict rules of behaviour. Indeed, the new hospitals were concerned with both moral and physical welfare, and few opportunities were lost to try to rid the poor of their vices and replace them with habits of piety and thrift.

For medical men themselves, the new hospitals provided important centres of learning. When Edinburgh's Royal Infirmary was established in 1729 it included accommodation for students. Patients provided the raw material upon which surgeons could practise their craft and push forward the boundaries of medical knowledge. In an age innocent of anaesthetics, surgery was necessarily restricted to such relatively short and straightforward operations as amputations and the removal of bladder stones. The incurable and infectious were usually turned away.

Alongside the general hospitals for the poor, more specialized institutions were established. In London these included several maternity wards, or 'lying-in' hospitals, while the 'locks' segregated those suffering from venereal diseases. The capital also boasted the celebrated Foundling Hospital, established by the philanthropic sea captain Thomas CORAM in 1742. Coram's foundation cared for the city's abandoned babies, an aim that appealed to the sensibilities of the age – the Foundling Hospital enjoyed the active support of HOGARTH and HANDEL, and became a major tourist attraction. Like the Foundling Hospital, the establishment of Magdalen House in 1758 marked a charitable response to an acknowledged social problem. Prompted by the proliferation of London's prostitutes, the Magdalen combined treatment with a programme of reformation intended to transform former streetwalkers into useful members of society. The Magdalen enjoyed the patronage of Queen CHARLOTTE, and by the end of the century had admitted more than 3000 women.

The treatment of the insane offered another area for specialization. Although London's Bethlehem Hospital ('Bedlam') – the ultimate destination of Hogarth's fictional rake – continued to admit voyeuristic visitors until 1770, a more enlightened approach to mental illness was embodied in the foundation of St Luke's Hospital in 1751. Widespread concern at the abuses detected in the private treatment of the mentally ill likewise led to the emergence of public asylums in several cities. Although their success was limited, these institutions attempted to harness scientific and technological advances in a more humane approach to their patients.

FURTHER READING R. Porter, *Disease, Medicine and Society in England 1550–1860* (2nd edn, 1993).

Howard, John (1726–90), a remarkable philanthropist who dedicated much of his life to the reform of PRISONS throughout Europe. Howard was a vegetarian, teetotaller and religious DISSENTER whose interest in prison reform may have originated in his own incarceration during the SEVEN YEARS WAR. He was captured by a privateer while travelling to Portugal and lodged in a noisome French gaol; upon being sent home on parole, Howard demonstrated his campaigning abilities by lobbying successfully for the release of his fellow inmates.

In 1773 Howard was appointed high sheriff of Bedfordshire, a post that gave him an insight into the grim state of local prisons. He was horrified by what he saw of prevailing conditions. Upon discovering that even prisoners who had been acquitted were often unable to secure their freedom because they could not afford to pay prison fees, Howard suggested that the gaolers should instead receive a regular salary. When his colleagues rejected this proposal, Howard embarked upon his personal crusade to end abuses within the prison system.

Howard's obsession led him to visit prisons throughout the British Isles. Given the prevalence of 'gaol fever' and his own fragile health, these investigations were undertaken at considerable personal risk. He compiled detailed dossiers of the horrors he witnessed, and his *State of the Prisons in England and Wales* (1777) was a damning indictment of the dismal state of all too many gaols, 'houses of correction' for minor offenders, and POOR LAW workhouses. Such research underpinned the 1779 Penitentiary Act, which provided for the construction of two model prisons, but the experiment foundered when the commissioners, who included Howard, proved unable to decide upon a location. Howard's indefatigable labours earned him the congratulations of the House of Commons, and he went on to extend his researches throughout Europe and the Near East, ultimately dying of typhus while on a visit to Russia.

Although the abuses that Howard identified were slow to disappear, his efforts ensured that the question of prison reform would not be ignored

when Britain increasingly turned towards imprisonment as the leading method of punishment. He gave his name to the Howard League for Penal Reform. Buried in Russia, Howard is commemorated by a statue in St Paul's Cathedral.

FURTHER READING D. L. Howard, *John Howard: Prison Reformer* (1958).

Howe, Richard, 4th Viscount and 1st Earl Howe

(1726–99), admiral, the older brother of William HOWE, and one of the most respected naval officers to emerge from the endemic warfare of the 18th century. As the son of the 2nd Viscount Howe, 'Black Dick' enjoyed influential connections, and these were matched by abilities that swiftly secured his reputation as a brave and efficient officer.

Howe first went to sea at the age of 14, gaining valuable experience on Admiral George ANSON's celebrated circumnavigation of 1740–4. In the year after his return Howe fought a crucial engagement, when he rebuffed two French ships carrying munitions for the supporters of the Young Pretender during the '45 JACOBITE RISING. Like his soldier brothers George and William, Richard Howe served with distinction during the SEVEN YEARS WAR. In 1758, after George was killed in action at TICONDEROGA, Richard became 4th Viscount Howe. He was made treasurer of the navy in 1765 and promoted to rear admiral in 1770.

In 1776, during the AMERICAN WAR OF INDEPENDENCE, Richard and William Howe exercised command of Britain's naval and land forces in North America. Alongside their military responsibilities, the brothers were also instructed to pursue peace initiatives with the rebels. This ambiguous role probably undermined the Howes' prosecution of the war at a period when a determined effort might have secured British victory. From 1778 active French support for the American rebels swung the balance of naval power against the over-stretched Royal Navy. Despite the ultimate failure to retain the American colonies, the war included notable British successes:

Howe contributed to one of the most celebrated of these when his ships broke the Bourbon blockade of Gibraltar in 1782.

At the close of the American war in 1783 Howe became first lord of the Admiralty, serving with honesty and efficiency for the next five years. He was created earl in 1788. At the resumption of hostilities with France in 1793 Howe was George III's personal choice to command the crucial Channel Fleet. The king's confidence was not misplaced: in a four-day encounter climaxing on the 'Glorious First of June' 1794, Howe inflicted heavy damage upon a French fleet escorting a grain convoy from America. A tough but fair officer, 'Black Dick's' popularity with all ranks led to his recall from retirement to negotiate with the Spithead mutineers of 1797; Howe's enormous prestige went far to defuse the crisis (*see* NAVAL MUTINIES OF 1797).

FURTHER READING I.D. Gruber, *The Howe Brothers and the American Revolution* (1972).

Howe, William, 5th Viscount Howe (1729–1814), general, the younger brother of Richard HOWE. He is best remembered as the British commander who failed to crush the rebellious American colonists during the opening years of the AMERICAN WAR OF INDEPENDENCE.

By the time he arrived in Boston in 1775, William Howe already boasted a distinguished record of army service. Tasting action in Flanders during the War of the AUSTRIAN SUCCESSION, he subsequently played a key role in Britain's conquest of Canada. A close friend of James WOLFE, Howe commanded a regiment at the siege of Louisbourg in 1758 and earned a reputation as a light-infantry specialist. Indeed, in the following summer it was Howe who led the assault up the Heights of Abraham, so paving the way for Wolfe's victory at Quebec. Following the fall of Canada, Howe returned to Europe. In 1761 he commanded a brigade at the capture of Belle Isle in the Bay of Biscay before joining the army that stormed Havana in 1762.

Howe was a long-serving member of Parliament for Nottingham. His own American service, and the colonists' respect for the memory of his elder brother George – who was killed fighting the French in 1758 – led him to oppose the government's harsh measures against Massachusetts. However, in 1775, as hostilities with the colonists loomed closer, Howe proved willing to serve in America. Impressed by Howe's combat record, the government viewed him as a vigorous replacement for the existing commander in chief, Thomas Gage. Howe was soon in action at Bunker Hill, where he led his men to a costly victory. The heavy casualties sustained on that bloody day taught Howe that the rebels were far from despicable; they may also have instilled in him the caution that dominated his own command in America.

During the winter of 1775–6 Howe made no effort to break the siege of Boston. In the following spring he evacuated his troops to Halifax. Transferring to New York in July, he waited two months for reinforcements before attacking George Washington, who used the delay to strengthen defences and discipline his troops. Howe won the subsequent battle of Long Island but failed to press home his victory with the necessary vigour, so allowing elements of Washington's army to escape. It is possible that Howe's hesitation stemmed from the fact that both he and his naval brother Richard held commissions to pursue peace negotiations.

In hindsight, the summer of 1776 offered Britain's best opportunity to win the American war. It was wasted: despite his success, Howe proved reluctant to pursue the enemy into New Jersey. Washington capitalized on this unexpected reprieve by counter-attacking at Trenton and Princeton. When Howe finally advanced in 1777, he opted for a seaborne strike at Pennsylvania. Philadelphia was captured, and victories gained at Brandywine and Germantown. However, these failed to compensate for Howe's failure to distract rebel attention from BURGOYNE's advance down the Hudson. The ensuing disaster at SARATOGA marked the beginning of the end for Britain's attempt to crush the rebellion. Sensing the coming storm of criticism, Howe offered his resignation.

Howe was personally brave and his fondness for gambling and women did nothing to diminish his popularity with his men. His officers' continuing esteem was expressed through a spectacular tournament, the 'Mischianza', staged on the eve of his departure for England. A Parliamentary inquiry failed to clear Howe's reputation. Despite his critics, Howe never lost the favour of George III, and he finally retired from the army in 1803.
FURTHER READING M.A. Jones, 'Sir William Howe, Conventional Strategist' in G.A. Billias (ed.), *George Washington's Opponents: British Generals and Admirals in the American Revolution* (1969).

Hume, David (1711–76), historian and philosopher, one of the leading figures of the SCOTTISH ENLIGHTENMENT. He was born in Edinburgh, and after studying at Edinburgh University, he tried his hand at the law and at working in a Bristol merchant's office, but found neither congenial. He then spent several years in France, where he wrote his *Treatise of Human Nature*.

As a philosopher, Hume's scepticism undermined natural as well as revealed religion, showing that the former was no more based on rational principles than was the latter. It also challenged LOCKE's view of human understanding by separating the external world from the impressions received of it by the senses. This separation led him to conclude that men can be sure of very little about their environment relying on reason alone. Hume came to similarly sceptical positions regarding reason (especially inductive reasoning), causation, necessity, identity and the self. He held that moral judgements are based on sentiment rather than reason, and that it was an error to derive moral conclusions from factual premises.

Hume was disappointed when his first essay in philosophy, *A Treatise of Human Nature*, 'fell dead-born from the press' in 1739, and though

his later philosophical writings attracted more notice – particularly in France, where he made frequent visits – he found greater fame and fortune as a historian. Indeed his *History of England*, which appeared in six volumes between 1754 and 1762, became the standard work on the subject until Macaulay replaced it in the 19th century. After spending the years 1767 to 1769 in London as an undersecretary of state he returned to Edinburgh. His death in 1776 impressed James BOSWELL because Hume did not believe in the immortality of the soul, but nevertheless faced oblivion with fortitude. Hume claimed his *History of England* made him 'not merely independent but opulent'. Today, Hume is remembered primarily as a philosopher – one of the most influential there has ever been. The great German philosopher Immanuel Kant said that it was Hume who had awoken him from his 'dogmatic slumbers'.
FURTHER READING A. Flew, *David Hume: Philosopher of Moral Science* (1986); T. Penelhum, *David Hume: An Introduction to his Philosophical System* (1991).

Huntingdon, countess of. *See* METHODISM.

Hutcheson, Francis (1694–1746), philosopher, a leading figure of the SCOTTISH ENLIGHTENMENT. Hutcheson was born in Ireland, studied at Glasgow University, then set up an academy in Dublin, before being appointed professor of moral philosophy at Glasgow University in 1729. He subscribed to the altruistic hedonism of the earl of SHAFTESBURY, and attacked the egoistic hedonism of Thomas Hobbes and Bernard MANDEVILLE. He held that humans are born with a moral sense, and his belief that moral judgements are based on feeling rather than reason influenced David HUME. He is credited with being the first to use the utilitarian expression 'the greatest happiness of the greatest number'.

Hyde, Laurence, 1st earl of Rochester.
See ROCHESTER, LAURENCE HYDE, 1ST EARL OF.

Inchbald, Elizabeth. *See* JACOBIN NOVELS.

India. At the onset of the 18th century, British power in India counted for little beyond the confines of a handful of coastal entrepôts. By the close of the Napoleonic Wars, Britain dominated the subcontinent. In the years to come, India increasingly replaced the 'first' British empire that had been lost upon the recognition of American independence, becoming the undisputed jewel in Britain's imperial crown. This transition from limited commercial presence to sprawling empire did not stem from any master plan, but was rather a reaction to the opportunities created by events. It was achieved only after the elimination of French competition, and a more protracted struggle with native rulers.

The EAST INDIA COMPANY had established its first trading footholds in India in the opening years of the 17th century. Throughout the Stuart era, the English presence remained insignificant, being restricted to the staff manning the 'factories' at Bombay, Madras and Calcutta. Concentrating upon the export of textiles, such adventurers possessed neither the interest nor the means for territorial expansion. However, in 1707, the death of the last great Mughal emperor Aurangzeb led to a breakdown of authority, allowing local rulers to carve out their own independent kingdoms.

By contrast, the European powers were slow to exploit the potential offered by the collapse of central authority. It was only in 1746 that Dupleix, the governor of the French trading base at Pondicherry, defied what remained of Mughal imperial power to capture the rival British post of Madras. Dupleix's strike represented a side show of the War of the AUSTRIAN SUCCESSION, and by the treaty of AIX-LA-CHAPELLE in 1748 Madras was duly returned.

Yet Dupleix's action had demonstrated the way in which European military intervention in local politics could lead to subsequent territorial expansion. In consequence, the French backed their own candidate for local ruler or nawab in the Carnatic, gaining extensive lands in return. This worrying development prompted British reaction. Open war erupted in 1751, and under the determined leadership of an East India Company clerk turned soldier, Robert CLIVE, Britain seized Arcot and stamped its own authority upon the region. Clive gained both fame and fortune, while Dupleix was recalled in disgrace.

In Bengal, the nawab, Siraj-ud-Daula, resented the steady commercial expansion of the East India Company, and resolved to oust the foreigners before they grew too powerful. Calcutta fell, and on 20 June 1756, British prisoners were crammed into a small room, the notorious 'Black Hole'.

Contemporary accounts claimed that all save 21 of the 146 captives suffocated during that stifling night, although modern historians reckon the toll far lower. Whatever the truth, British vengeance followed swiftly. In 1757 the Royal Navy's dominance of local waters permitted the return of Clive with sufficient reinforcements to recapture Calcutta and smash Siraj's ungainly army at PLASSEY. Clive's victory secured British control of Bengal, so providing the base from which Sir Eyre COOTE subsequently struck a mortal blow at remaining French ambitions in the Carnatic. In 1760 Coote defeated the Count de Lally in battle at Wandewash, capturing Pondicherry in the following year. At the close of the SEVEN YEARS WAR, these British gains at the expense of the French were confirmed by the treaty of PARIS in 1763.

The rise in the Company's fortunes was aided by events far to the north. There, at Panipat, the most likely successors to the Mughals – the warlike Maharatas – sustained a shattering reverse at the hands of the Afghans in 1761. Despite the spectacular gains in Bengal during the 1750s and 1760s, subsequent extension of British dominance elsewhere in India proved a painstaking process. During the global conflict triggered by the AMERICAN WAR OF INDEPENDENCE, French backing for the fiercely independent rulers of Mysore led to serious reverses for British armies; these indicated the limitations of European military methods in the face of increasingly sophisticated native forces. Indeed, in 1780 Hyder Ali overwhelmed a British detachment under Colonel William Baillie at Pollihur, and in the following year confronted the veteran victor of Wandewash, Sir Eyre Coote.

Such determined resistance was only ground down by protracted campaigns mounted during the governor generalships of Charles CORNWALLIS and Richard Wellesley between 1786 and 1805. Wellesley's brother Arthur – the future duke of WELLINGTON – played a prominent role in the operations that finally broke the resistance of Mysore and the Maharatas. Britain's generals were aided in their methodical conquests by the support of local allies keen to eliminate traditional local rivals. Of Britain's native opponents, Hyder Ali's son Tipu Sultan – the aptly named 'Tiger of Mysore' – proved particularly stubborn. Rather than surrender, Tipu chose to fight to the death at Seringapatam in 1799. Striking evidence of Tipu's enduring hatred for the British was discovered among the booty captured on that occasion – a mechanical organ, fashioned in the shape of a tiger mauling an Englishman, that emitted a piteous groaning when activated.

The steady acquisition of territory during the second half of the 18th century prompted a change in British attitudes towards India. Interest in India as a source of produce and a market for British manufactures was matched by concern at the expanding role of the East India Company. Following the military successes of the Seven Years War, the Company had gone far beyond trade to embrace the administration of justice and taxation. Such developments sparked increasing calls for control, manifested in Lord NORTH's Regulation Act of 1773, Fox's India Bill of 1783 and the younger Pitt's India Act of 1784, which established the BOARD OF CONTROL. The fears of politicians back in London likewise triggered the downfall of those buccaneering nabobs whose courage and initiative had won massive wealth in the East. In 1772 Clive himself was summoned before Parliament charged with corruption; although cleared of the allegations against him, their lingering stigma fed Clive's customary melancholy and contributed to his suicide soon after. Similarly, Britain's first governor general of India, Warren HASTINGS, was subsequently summoned home to defend his administration. Hastings was ultimately exonerated, but the experience of impeachment between 1786 and 1795 ensured that he too was left a broken man.

For all their faults, men like Clive and Hastings had mixed freely with Indian rulers, regarding them as equals and respecting their native traditions. By the era of Wellesley, Britain's growing ascendancy had encouraged some of its servants to espouse the bigotry and moral superiority that were to blight the reputation of the Victorian Raj. Such attitudes go far to explain the savagery of the mutiny that engulfed much of India upon the centenary of Clive's great victory at Plassey.

FURTHER READING L. James, *Raj* (1997); P. Lawson, *The East India Company: A History* (1993).

Industry. When the Swiss artist Philippe de Loutherbourg painted the famous iron works at Coalbrookdale in Shropshire he depicted a vortex of fire set against the night sky. Dating from 1801, de Loutherbourg's dramatic canvas represents an enduring image of Georgian industrial growth that has often been used to epitomize the elemental forces unleashed through Britain's so-called 'Industrial Revolution'.

Traditionally dated to the period between 1760 and 1830, this notion of rapid and 'revolutionary' industrial development is no longer regarded as tenable by many scholars. Economic historians have instead emphasized the gradual pace of change, and the strong existing base of localized industrial production upon which later developments were grafted. In this sense, a more appropriate visual impression of Georgian industry is provided by Joseph WRIGHT of Derby's 1772 study of a small-scale iron forge at work.

Despite such qualifications, the 'long 18th century' *did* see a transformation of Britain's economy. In 1688 the economy was overwhelmingly agricultural, with more than two-thirds of the population living on the land. By the era of the Great Reform Act a remarkable transition was already under way. The contribution of industry to growth – as measured by the gross domestic product – had overtaken that of the agricultural sector. In addition, by 1830 the number of people employed in industry was approaching the number who worked the land.

Although Britain's industrial 'revolution' clearly culminated in the Victorian era, the roots of these key changes lie in the late 18th century and earlier. In the mid-1720s, when Daniel DEFOE wrote his *Tour Through the Whole Island of Great Britain*, he commented enthusiastically upon the flourishing manufacturing he frequently encountered during his travels. By about 1750, Britain already possessed an economy that was both prosperous and expanding. To an important degree, the changes associated with the so-called 'Industrial Revolution' were themselves the latest phase of a gradual process of modernization dating back to Tudor times. While historians would not contest the key importance of the industrial growth that took place in the 19th century, it is nonetheless possible to argue that many of the conditions that permitted this spectacular expansion were themselves the products of developments occurring during the 18th century. Rapid growth rates in total industrial output only became apparent after 1800, but there had been a marked rise in specific industries from about 1760 onwards: in particular, cotton and pig iron had already experienced significant growth. Indeed, cotton imports rose from 2.3 million kilos (5 million lb) per annum in the 1770s to in excess of 30 million kilos (70 million lb) per annum during the period 1805–15. So, while it would be wrong to argue that a spectacular 'Industrial Revolution' was completed in the period before 1815, a very exceptional economic development was well under way.

A combination of factors underpinned Georgian Britain's role as the world's first industrial incubator; economic historians continue to debate their individual importance. Several underlying factors were unquestionably significant. Between 1700 and 1815, England was able to double its population, and by 1800 the country actually possessed the man-, woman- and child-power necessary for viable industrialization. The dramatic increase in population from the mid-18th century onwards has itself been seen as characteristic of an industrial society: the rise in fertility linked to lower marriage ages stemmed from a changing society in which wage labour conveyed increased independence. Again, while the population rose dramatically, the percentage engaged in agriculture fell. Up to the middle of the 18th century Britain had been able to export a surplus of grain. By 1815, Britain needed to import food to meet the demand of its ever-growing population. It was a sign of Britain's industrial progress during the later half of the 18th century that it was able to obtain this extra food through the export of its own manufactured goods. The growing population also provided a ready workforce for the expanding manufacturing industries. This workforce was attracted to urban centres such as London, Birmingham, Nottingham, Derby and Sheffield, but above all to the booming textile region of the north, a swathe embracing Leeds, Manchester, Preston and Liverpool. Yet it was not just in towns that manufacturing took place: a large industrial population was also scattered through the villages of the north, the Midlands and south Wales. Before the widespread use of steam, the cotton mills of Lancashire remained dependent upon the Pennine streams for their power. Most of these mills were concentrated far from such booming population centres as Halifax and Leeds – indeed, many occupations regarded as 'industrial' were in fact characterized by close links with agriculture. It was agricultural produce such as wool, flax and timber that provided much of the raw material for industry, while thousands of 'industrial' workers operated from their own cottages or communal village workshops. In this important sense, Georgian industrial growth was as much a rural as an urban phenomenon.

Other factors underpinned Britain's precocious industrialization, notably its rich and varied natural resources of coal, iron, tin and copper. Britain led Europe in the use of coal as an industrial fuel. Coal was already being used to smelt non-ferrous metals and to forge iron before 1700; the crucial development was the ability to smelt iron ore using coke rather than the traditional charcoal from Britain's decreasing forests. During the course of the 'long' 18th century Britain's production of coal increased tenfold, and the number of workers involved in its extraction more than tripled.

By continental standards, Britain's agricultural economy was already efficient and becoming more so as a result of improved land use and food production from the 1750s onwards (*see* AGRICULTURE). From that same period Britain's transport system underwent its own 'revolution'. The time-honoured method of transporting goods by sea or via major navigable rivers was supplemented by a network of CANALS and improved toll ROADS or turnpikes. This new transport infrastructure not only cheapened raw materials and cut the price of goods, it also brought fresh markets within reach of manufacturers.

Early industrial expansion had been hampered by inadequate financial arrangements. In the first half of the 18th century there were no country banks, and all major financial transactions had to go through London. From the 1750s onwards there was a widespread increase in the number of provincial banks: between 1780 and 1815 the number of country banks rose from less than 300 to more than 700. Local credit encouraged investment by industrial entrepreneurs.

Another distinctly British development that served to stimulate industrialization was the emergence of an identifiable 'middle class'. The early industrial capitalists – men like the steam enthusiast James WATT, the ceramics entrepreneur Josiah WEDGWOOD, and the iron-master John Wilkinson – emerged from these new 'middling orders'. Such men had the education and technical background required to generate new ideas, and the capital to back them.

In parts of Britain, landscape and climate also combined to offer favourable conditions for the manufacture of particular goods. For example, the wet and rugged valleys of the western Pennines provided the perfect setting for the production of cotton cloth, late Georgian Britain's great growth industry (*see* TEXTILES). Two factors were important here: the availability of copious water power, and a damp atmosphere that prevented the cotton from snapping.

Unlike continental Europe, which was disrupted by wars throughout the 18th century, Britain was mercifully free of such strife. After the isolated Jacobite rebellions of the '15 and '45, Britain fought its wars abroad. Not only did these foreign wars keep conflict at a distance, they also resulted in the conquest of new territories – so Britain expanded its markets along with its empire. Even the loss of the American colonies in 1783 failed to exclude the young republic as a market for British manufactures. In addition, the long bouts of warfare, particularly against France, helped to stimulate new industries. Iron, engineering, shipbuilding and textiles all helped to maintain the British war machine. For example, improved casting techniques developed at the Carron iron works at Falkirk in the Scottish lowlands provided Nelson's navy with the short-barrelled 'carronade' or 'smasher' that was used to devastating effect against the French. In marked contrast to Europe, where customs barriers and tolls hampered internal trade, there were no official restrictions upon the movement of people or goods throughout Britain. On the other hand, Britain's government took an active interest in encouraging overseas trade, and in protecting the domestic industries from foreign competition.

Although it is necessary to be wary of overemphasizing the impact of inventions, in the second half of the 18th century Britain saw growing technical innovation. In the textile industry, new spinning machines and looms increased productivity, while the iron industry benefited from such advantages as coke smelting, puddling and rolling. A new source of power emerged with the refinement of the steam engines that had been used to pump mine workings since the late 17th century, and it was the perfection of steam power that ultimately permitted the replacement of workshops by factories. However, once again change was gradual, and the factory did not emerge as the characteristic unit of production until after 1830. Indeed, the factory system only spread slowly, even in those industries, such as cotton, to which it was particularly suited. The notion of putting out work to small-scale operators, who worked from their own homes or who themselves employed a couple of workmen in a backyard shed, remained widespread.

In the traditional skilled and semiskilled trades, work patterns had often been characterized by a lack of discipline that was intolerable in the regimented factory system. Mondays were commonly given over to drinking, with the week's work crammed into four or five long days of intensive but self-imposed labour. The disciplined organization of the factory system guaranteed a wage, but the price was high, invariably requiring punishing hours of repetitive work under harsh supervision. In consequence, many of the old skilled and semiskilled workers viewed the new factories with suspicion – for these men, to become a factory worker was the ultimate degradation and loss of caste. However, Britain's rapidly expanding population meant that more children were entering the labour pool. Poor children had always been obliged to work, but with the growth of the factory system their exploitation intensified. Children, like women, provided cheap labour; they were also easier to indoctrinate into the harsh factory system than their elders. For many factory and mine workers life seemed to offer little but long hours of boring and dangerous labour, combined with the nagging fear of poverty, unemployment and the workhouse. It is this factor that some historians suggest goes a long way to explain the impact of METHODISM in the late 18th and early 19th centuries: with nothing to hope for on earth, the promise of salvation in the next world began to appear increasingly attractive.

The years between 1760 and 1820 did witness important economic developments in Britain, changes that set in motion the more dramatic industrial growth of the Victorian era. In certain sectors of manufacturing, particularly cotton and iron, and in certain geographical regions, such as Lancashire and Yorkshire, features of industry that were to prove typical of the 19th century were already surfacing in the 18th. However, it is important to remember that the pace of change throughout Britain was never uniform, and in consequence we should be wary of exaggerating the overall trend of economic growth in the late 18th century. Although enormously significant and unique in the period, industrial development in Georgian Britain was evolutionary rather than revolutionary.

FURTHER READING M. Berg, *The Age of Manufactures, 1700–1820: Industry, Innovation and Work in Britain* (1994); M. Daunton, *Progress and Poverty* (1995); J. Rule, *Vital Century: England's Developing Economy, 1714–1815* (1992).

Intolerable Acts. *See* AMERICAN COLONIES 1763–1776.

Ireland. Successive waves of settlers and conquerors from Britain, culminating in the WILLIAMITE WARS OF SUCCESSION following the GLORIOUS REVOLUTION, had gradually expanded the area owned by the British from the medieval Pale around Dublin to virtually the whole island, with the 'Scotch-Irish', mainly Presbyterians from Scotland, dominant in Ulster in the north, and the Anglo-Irish, mostly members of the Anglican Church of Ireland, elsewhere. The treaty of Limerick of 1691 left only one-seventh of the land in the ownership of the native Irish. The latter, almost all Roman Catholics, and many of them Gaelic speaking, made up the bulk of the 2 million or so inhabitants of Ireland in 1700. The Protestants were a minority of perhaps one-fifth of the total. Over the century their proportion of the population shrank in relation to the total population of Ireland, which soared to 5.3 million by 1803. The vast majority of this population was Catholic. In contrast with the 19th century, which saw successive waves of mainly Catholic emigration, the 18th century witnessed little emigration from Ireland, and most of those who did emigrate during this period were Protestants. The Protestant ascendancy maintained

control through both military and political means. Some 12,000 British soldiers were stationed in Ireland throughout the Hanoverian period, and these were augmented in times of war or civil disturbance. Ireland, though it was a kingdom distinct from England and Scotland, is often regarded as having been a British colony during this period. Certainly CATO'S LETTERS treated it as one when dealing with 'plantations and colonies'; moreover they distinguished between two sorts of settlements, 'one to keep conquered countries in subjection' and 'the other ... for trade and intended to encrease the wealth and power of the native kingdom', and put Ireland in the first category and the American colonies in the second.

Yet, despite the strong military presence there, Ireland was also treated as a dependency akin to the settlements in North America and the Caribbean. Like those, Ireland had its own assembly, the Irish Parliament. The two Houses, the Lords and the Commons, had only met fitfully in the 17th century. Charles II never summoned them again after 1662, whereas James II only convened them after his landing in Ireland in 1689. By contrast, after the reconquest of Ireland by William, the Irish Parliament met regularly every two years from 1692 to 1800. The British government, however, attempted to keep tight control of its proceedings. General elections were infrequent until the Octennial Act of 1768 required one to take place at least once every eight years. Membership both of the Lords and the Commons was restricted to Anglo-Irish Protestants, while Catholics were not even allowed to vote until 1793. Ever since 1494, Poynings Law required all bills introduced into the Irish legislature to have been previously approved by the privy council in London. Though members of the Dublin Parliament found ways round this, the long stop of legislation remained in the control of British privy councillors. In William III's reign, the English House of Lords claimed that it, and not the Irish upper house, was the ultimate court of appeal for cases initiated in Ireland, while the Westminster Parliament asserted the right to pass legislation concerning the Irish. These claims provoked indignation across the Irish Sea, most forcibly expressed in 1698 by William Molyneux in his *Case of Ireland*. The Westminster Parliament, however, insisted on its superiority and in the DECLARATORY ACT of 1720 asserted the subordination to it of the Irish legislature.

Despite the theoretical claims of the British, in practice the cooperation of the leading families of the Protestant ascendancy, who numbered about 10,000, was essential in order to secure harmonious relations between Whitehall and Dublin. The lord lieutenants of Ireland, who were appointed by the monarchs as their viceroys in their Irish kingdom, but were also ministers involved in British party politics, cultivated these leaders of the Anglo-Irish. In Anne's reign, as in England, they were divided into Tory and Whig parties. The Tory lord lieutenant, the duke of ORMONDE, worked with the Tories in the Irish Parliament to pass a Test Act in 1704 restricting officeholding in Ireland to Anglicans. When the 1st marquess of WHARTON, a Whig, went as lord lieutenant in 1709 he tried to get this act repealed in concert with the Whigs and their Ulster Presbyterian supporters, but failed. Although the Anglo-Irish were loyal to the Protestant Succession in the House of Hanover, they were also loyal to the Church of Ireland. This led many Scotch-Irish to emigrate to the American colonies under the Hanoverians. The first great migration took place in 1718. Despite the Toleration Act passed by the Irish Parliament in 1719 to placate Presbyterians, further migrations occurred in 1729 and 1739–41. The Anglicanism of the ascendancy, coupled with Protestant dread of a repeat of the Catholic counter-revolution of 1689 in the event of a Jacobite triumph, meant that Jacobite activity in Ireland was insignificant during the 18th century. Yet, while they were keenly aware of the gulf which separated them from the Catholic Irish, members of the Anglican elite, who had previously regarded themselves as English settlers, came more and more to identify themselves with Ireland. This was perhaps seen most clearly in their

resistance to WOOD'S HALFPENCE between 1722 and 1725. Jonathan SWIFT articulated their anger in the *Drapier's Letters*, the fifth of which was addressed to 'the whole people of Ireland'. CARTERET, the new lord lieutenant sent by Robert WALPOLE to deal with the crisis, coped admirably by working with 'undertakers', such as the speaker William Connolly, to manage the 'Castle interest' (as the British government's agents were known from their residence in Dublin Castle). This system survived Connolly's death in 1728 until another crisis arose between 1749 and 1755. Members of the Irish Parliament objected to the way in which surpluses on the revenue in 1749 and 1751 had been siphoned off by the British. Led by the speaker Henry Boyle, they rejected a bill appropriating the surplus in 1753. Those in the employ of the Castle who threw in their lot with the majority were dismissed, but had to be reinstated in a humiliating reversal in 1755. The Irish Commons then asserted their right to dispose of the surpluses.

The breakdown of the system of using political undertakers led to a change of policy on the part of the lord lieutenants, particularly in the lieutenancy of George, Viscount Townshend from 1767 to 1772. He sought to bypass them by building up an alternative power base using the patronage at his disposal. While this policy succeeded in making Parliament cooperative, outside unrest grew during his tenure of office. Even before he arrived in Ireland, agrarian discontent had given rise to the agitation associated with the Whiteboys in Munster in 1761 followed by the Oakboys in Ulster (1763) which had provoked a Tumultuous Rising Act in 1766. During his period of office, further disturbance occurred from the Steelboys in Ulster during the years 1769 to 1770, and riots in Dublin in 1771. After his departure from Dublin, these demonstrations became a greater threat to the British authorities with the organization of the Volunteers, first formed in 1778, who took a leaf out of the book of the American rebels. Their stance also encouraged members of the Irish Parliament led by Henry GRATTAN to demand autonomy for Ireland. When Lord ROCKINGHAM formed his ministry in 1782, he not only pledged to make peace with the Americans but also tried to pacify the Volunteers and Grattan's party by granting virtual legislative independence to Ireland. Poynings Law and the Declaratory Act were repealed. 'Ireland is now a nation,' proclaimed Grattan. Legislative autonomy was to last less than two decades, ending with the Act of Union of 1800. Catholics left out in the cold joined with Protestants who wanted complete independence to form the Society of United Irishmen in 1791. They presented so formidable a threat that the younger PITT put pressure on the Irish Parliament to pass a Catholic Relief Act in 1793, which enabled those with 40-shilling freeholds to vote in parliamentary elections, and allowed them to become members of corporations, though not of Parliament. They were even permitted to bear arms and to hold commissions in the army. These concessions failed to pacify the Society, which was suppressed in 1794. The United Irishmen then went underground to emerge in the IRISH REBELLION OF 1798. When the rebellion was crushed, Pitt decided that the only way to keep the Irish loyal was to bring about the UNION OF BRITAIN AND IRELAND. **FURTHER READING** L.M. Cullen, *The Emergence of Modern Ireland 1600–1900* (1981); Roy Foster, *Modern Ireland, 1600–1972* (1988); T.W. Moody and W.E. Vaughan, *A New History of Ireland, IV: Eighteenth Century Ireland (1691–1800)* (1986).

Irish rebellion of 1798. The bloody events that engulfed much of Ireland in the summer of 1798 resulted from a complex combination of factors, whose cause and significance remain controversial over two centuries later. What originated as a middle-class movement for constitutional change ultimately escalated into a sectarian peasant revolt as revolutionary radicalism – influenced by events in France – heightened existing tensions between a minority Protestant elite and the disadvantaged Catholic population it purported to govern. Before crown forces regained control of the country some

30,000 lives had been lost – a toll comparable to the more prolonged French 'Terror' of 1793–4.

The overthrow of the old order in France had given hope to those educated men who sought change in Ireland. In 1791 the Society of the United Irishmen was formed in Dublin and Belfast under the leadership of Wolfe TONE and Napper Tandy. The organization initially sought parliamentary reform and religious equality. Some concessions to the Catholics were made by the government, which, in the crisis of war with France, was fearful of revolution at home. But these concessions fell far short of the society's goals. In consequence the United Irishmen grew increasingly radical. In addition, despite their non-sectarian origins, they became closely linked with the 'Defenders', a Catholic rural self-defence force formed to counter the activities of the Protestant 'Peep o'Day Boys'.

By 1795 the United Irishmen had gone underground as a secret society seeking the establishment of an Irish republic. Wolfe Tone lobbied Bonaparte in the hope of securing French backing for a rising in Ireland. A substantial fleet carrying troops commanded by General Lazare Hoche gave the Royal Navy the slip and arrived in Bantry Bay in December 1796, only to discover that there was no local rising to support. The expedition was dispersed soon after by the gales of the 'Protestant Wind'. Like the old Bourbon regime in its dealings with the Jacobites, the French Directory subsequently proved reluctant to despatch military aid unless a viable rebellion was already under way; and, like the Jacobites before them, disgruntled Irishmen remained unwilling to rise without the assurance of French assistance.

Faced with outbreaks of agrarian violence and persistent rumours of rebellion, the viceroy, Earl Camden, and his Dublin government decided upon pre-emptive action to root out the conspiracy and disarm potential insurgents. In 1797 General Gerard Lake employed harsh measures in an effort to disarm Ulster. At the end of the year the brutal Lake was replaced by the capable and moderate

General Sir Ralph ABERCROMBY, who was shocked by the tense situation he encountered. Abercromby believed that the underlying cause of rural discontent lay in the harshness of the Irish gentry towards their downtrodden tenants. However, such sentiments did little to endear him to Ireland's Protestant oligarchs, while his outspoken observation that the Irish army was 'in a state of licentiousness which must render it formidable to everyone but the enemy' increased the clamour for his resignation. Having effectively disarmed the north, the government determined to repeat the exercise in the south. Before quitting Ireland Abercromby had advocated a policy of limited force to secure the government's objectives. In contrast, his successors favoured indiscriminate terror tactics calculated to force confessions and locate hidden weapons. 'Half-hangings', floggings and other tortures, including the notorious 'pitch-capping' – whereby suspects were crowned with a mixture of molten tar and gunpowder that was then ignited – all created a mood of desperation in which armed rebellion came to be seen as an increasingly attractive response to an intolerable situation.

The United Irishmen had envisaged a coordinated rising for May 1798. However, their organization had long since been infiltrated by government informers, and in March of that year 16 leading revolutionaries were arrested after agents surprised a meeting in Dublin, while others, such as the charismatic aristocrat Lord Edward Fitzgerald, took refuge in flight. In place of the planned insurrection came a succession of independent revolts. Outbreaks in Ulster and Kildare were followed by a mass rising in Wexford. The rebellion not only mobilized those fired by the ideals of the United Irishmen, but also many Catholic peasants, who were stirred into action by government repression and fear of the Protestant Orangemen. As a result, deep-seated local grudges all too often took precedence over wider political goals. The result

was a civil war mired in primitive sectarianism that was far removed from the educated Tone's vision of a united Ireland. As in France during the revolt of the Vendée, the level of violence escalated as atrocity bred counter-atrocity. The brutalities of the loyalist militia and yeomanry – many of whom were themselves Catholics – were equalled by those of the rebels.

Although the insurgents enjoyed some local successes, it was always an unequal struggle. Armed largely with home-forged pikes, the untrained rebels proved vulnerable to the disciplined musketry and artillery of the government troops. By the end of June decisive defeats at Ballynahinch in eastern Ulster and Vinegar Hill in south Leinster had broken the back of the rebellion. A small French landing at Killala Bay in Mayo in August therefore came too late to aid the Irishmen. Although the veterans of Bonaparte's Army of Italy easily routed government troops at the so-called 'Castlebar Races', they were soon after overpowered by superior British forces at Ballinamuck. The experienced soldier Charles CORNWALLIS, who had been appointed viceroy and commander in chief in June, attempted to moderate the reprisals that marked the end of the revolt. Wolfe Tone, who had been captured aboard a French warship in October, was among those sentenced to death. But he cheated the hangman by stabbing himself with a penknife.

Britain's continuing difficulties in governing Ireland ultimately led to the Act of Union of 1801. This united the parliaments of Great Britain and Ireland, and abolished the Irish Parliament in Dublin (*see* UNION OF BRITAIN AND IRELAND). The arrangement proved unsatisfactory, and the bitter memories of 1798 only served to fuel nationalist sentiment and calls for an independent Ireland.
FURTHER READING T. Pakenham, *The Year of Liberty: The Story of the Great Irish Rebellion of 1798* (1969).

J

Jacobin novels, term applied to various novels of the 1790s whose authors were positively influenced by the ideas of the FRENCH REVOLUTION. Outstanding among these writers were Robert BAGE, William GODWIN, Thomas HOLCROFT and Elizabeth Inchbald.

Robert Bage published six novels, of which the most distinguished were *Man as he is* (1792) and *Hermsprong; or man as he is not* (1796). A central feature of both is an attack upon the aristocracy. Lord Auschamp in *Man as he is* and Lord Grondale in *Hermsprong* are depicted as tyrants exploiting their privileged position in society to further their own ends at the expense of others.

This theme also informs the change in the behaviour of a principal character in Godwin's *Caleb Williams*, Falkland. In the first volume he appears as a patriarchal figure, befriending the victims of a tyrannical landlord, Tyrell. In the second volume, however, Falkland becomes a tyrant himself, harassing Caleb Williams without mercy. He abuses his privileged access to the law to destroy his victim. The explanation of this apparent character change is that Falkland, having been knocked down by Tyrell in front of an assembly of gentlemen, gets his revenge by murdering his assailant. Although at the time he manages to conceal his crime, and even has others condemned for it, Falkland's guilt is ascertained by Caleb. What made Falkland kill Tyrell was the public affront to his honour at the assembly. He is thus corrupted by the code of honour, which overcomes all other standards of morality. Once disgraced, he is ostracized from the company of gentlemen. The conclusion of all this is that the system itself is irredeemably corrupt. Moreover, as Godwin observes, Falkland 'exhibited upon a contracted scale … a copy of what monarchs are'.

Jacobin novels also attacked the church. The clergy in Thomas Holcroft's *Hugh Trevor* (1794) are particularly repellent. The bishop uses the hero's writing skills to procure preferment for himself, passing off Hugh's defence of the Thirty-nine Articles as his own, and thereby obtaining promotion to another bishopric. The inferior clergy are distinguished by their gluttony. Appalled by their greed at a banquet, Hugh observes 'poor mother church at that moment made a pitiful appearance'.

Elizabeth Inchbald (1753–1821) was primarily a playwright, but wrote two novels, *A Simple Story* (1791) and *Nature and Art* (1796), of which the latter is the more 'Jacobin'. In it the three representatives of the church, a bishop, a dean and a curate, are all shown as corrupt. The neglect of their duties is directly responsible for the tragedy that overtakes the heroine Hannah. The system, so far from punishing such ungodly churchmen, rewards them, for the dean becomes a bishop himself. Thus not only are individual clergymen denigrated as corrupt, but the church itself is depicted as an oppressive institution.

Insofar as these novels had a positive as well as a negative message, however, they were not so much Jacobin as Girondin – the novelists advocated not violent levelling, but reform.

FURTHER READING. G. Kelly, *The English Jacobin Novel: 1780–1803* (1976).

Jacobins, the more extreme grouping of French revolutionaries; the name was subsequently used by conservative elements in Britain as a derogatory label for all reformers and radicals.

The FRENCH REVOLUTION stimulated renewed calls for change within British society, inspiring Whigs to revive their campaign for PARLIAMENTARY REFORM. But a far more dramatic consequence of the upheavals across the Channel was the formation of new societies with even more radical agendas. Conservative elements were particularly alarmed by the emergence of CORRESPONDING SOCIETIES, which drew recruits from a far wider social spectrum than previous reform movements. Although committed to radical reform of Parliament and political equality for all men, the goals of such radicals fell short of social revolution. Shunning violence, British Jacobins instead pursued their objectives through debate and the dissemination of political literature. Radical views were propagated in newspapers such as the *Manchester Herald* and pamphlets, of which the most notorious was Thomas PAINE's *Rights of Man*.

Nevertheless, the government viewed the Jacobins as a serious threat and reacted with repressive policies. The corresponding societies were infiltrated with spies and informers, and their leaders prosecuted for sedition. The government also mounted a propaganda campaign of its own, which emphasized the excesses of the French revolutionaries and extolled the virtues of the established order. Such views coloured both the sophisticated arguments of the *ANTI-JACOBIN* and the didactic tracts of Hannah MORE. Political caricaturists such as Isaac Cruickshank and GILLRAY employed their skills in defence of the constitution and depicted the Jacobins as paranoid and sinister conspirators. Officially sponsored propaganda exploited the popular conservatism that manifested itself in such associations as that launched by John REEVES.

By 1799, when most societies had been banned by law, they were already in disarray – their leadership had been smashed, their propagandists gagged and their rank-and-file members intimidated. However, while government measures helped to destroy mainstream radicalism, by the late 1790s the die-hard remnants of the British Jacobins were sufficiently desperate to contemplate the treasonable revolutionary activity that their original leaders had disavowed. Such views were exported to Britain by militant members of the United Irishmen (*see* IRISH REBELLION OF 1798). By 1797 a network of United Englishmen societies was established in the northwest and the Midlands, while revolutionary groups such as the Sons of Liberty and the United Britons were formed in London. Although the evidence for political motivation remains inconclusive, PITT blamed Jacobin agitation for the dangerous NAVAL MUTINIES OF 1797. In early 1798 the government intercepted revolutionary leaders believed to be heading for France to seek aid for an insurrection; arrests across Britain followed. The Irish rebellion of 1798 was not echoed in England, although sporadic reports of revolutionary activity in the north and Midlands continued.

FURTHER READING H.T. Dickinson, *British Radicalism and the French Revolution, 1789–1815* (1985).

Jacobite risings, series of rebellions by the JACOBITES, the supporters of the restoration of the Catholic James II and his successor, the Old Pretender, James Francis Edward STUART. There were attempted risings in 1689, 1708 and 1719, but the most significant were those in 1715 and 1745–6. All ended in failure, and the HANOVERIAN SUCCESSION was secured.

Efforts to restore the senior line of the Stuart family began soon after James II's flight from England in 1688 during the GLORIOUS REVOLUTION. James's forces confronted WILLIAM III in Ireland between 1689 and 1691, but it was Scotland that was destined to become the future bastion of active Jacobitism. The beginnings for Scottish Jacobitism were inauspicious. A rising there in 1689 attracted little local support, and – although the formidable fighting potential of the Highland clansmen was demonstrated in their Pyrrhic victory at Killiecrankie – the revolt lost momentum soon after. (For more details on the fighting in Ireland and Scotland at this period, *see* WILLIAMITE WARS OF SUCCESSION.)

When James died in 1701 his son James Francis Edward became the Jacobite pretender. In 1708 he attempted to invade Scotland, and even made a landfall at Inverness. His expedition, however, was tailed by the British navy, and having put into the Firth of Forth it headed back to France round the north of Scotland. There were few signs of active support in Scotland, even though there had been considerable discontent over the 1707 UNION OF ENGLAND AND SCOTLAND for the Jacobites to exploit. However, by the death of Anne in 1714, the mood in Scotland had changed, and many Scots increasingly looked to their traditional ruling dynasty for redress. Tories excluded from high politics by the Whig ascendancy at the accession of the Hanoverian GEORGE I now contemplated extreme measures to recoup power.

Such disgruntled politicians included the earl of MAR, who ignited a large-scale rising in Scotland in 1715. He rallied substantial support, some 18 lords bringing with them 5000 men. Since the regular government troops in Scotland scarcely numbered 1500 at the start of the uprising, a determined move by Mar at this stage could have been decisive. Instead he delayed, waiting for reinforcements. This inactivity proved fatal, for while he waited the government was able to concentrate its efforts on drawing the teeth of Jacobitism in England. An act was passed empowering the king to imprison any person suspected of conspiring against him. The first arrest was made in September when an officer in the Guards was arrested for enlisting men for the Pretender. Six members of Parliament were also rounded up, including Sir William Wyndham, who was suspected of plotting a rising in the west of England, and Thomas Forster, who did lead a rising in the north with the earl of Derwentwater. Together they led about 2000 men south to Preston, where they were intercepted by Generals Carpenter and Wills and surrendered on 14 November.

Although the Hanoverian succession had triggered widespread rioting in England, few aristocratic or gentry leaders emerged to channel this discontent. With the exception of smaller outbreaks in Northumberland and Lancashire, the English Jacobites failed to rally to the cause. Despite their inaction the '15 posed a serious threat to the Hanoverian regime at a time when it rested upon precarious foundations. Its failure owed much to the lacklustre leadership of Mar, who permitted a numerically inferior pro-government force under the duke of ARGYLL to halt his advance at Sheriffmuir on 13 November. The Old Pretender himself arrived too late to revive what was undoubtedly his best opportunity to gain the crown. His position was further undermined by his failure to renounce the Catholicism that was anathema to so many Britons. James, realizing that the cause was lost, left Scotland, taking the earl of Mar back to France with him.

Friction with Britain in the Mediterranean led to Spain backing the next Jacobite rising in 1719. In a pattern destined to be repeated in coming years, the bulk of the invading armada was dispersed by storms, leaving no more than a puny secondary force to raise the Stuart standard in the Highlands. The joint Scots-Jacobite and Spanish army was soon after eliminated by government troops at Glenshiel. The Spanish component in this abortive invasion is commemorated in Sgurr nan Spainteach (peak of the Spaniards), one of the Five Sisters of Kintail.

In an era in which Britain was frequently at war with France the Jacobites offered the Bourbons a useful means of distracting their arch-rival from other fronts. The continuing importance of Bourbon support for any pro-Stuart rising ensured that the Jacobites lay dormant during the long years of Anglo-French peace that marked the Walpolean hegemony. However, the onset of the War of the AUSTRIAN SUCCESSION created a scenario in which France could once more play the Jacobite card. In 1744 Louis XV authorized a Jacobite invasion of Britain to be led by the Old Pretender's dashing son, Prince Charles Edward Stuart – Bonnie Prince Charlie. Although the original scheme was abandoned owing to unfavourable weather conditions, the 'Young Chevalier' vented his frustration by launching his own expedition in the following year.

Prince Charles landed in Scotland in July 1745 to raise his father's standard again. Although initially he only had seven supporters, within weeks he had an army of 1500 men to confront fewer than 4000 government troops under Sir John Cope. Cope assembled these men at Stirling and marched north to intercept the Jacobite forces, but found them entrenched on the Corrieyairack Pass in an impregnable position. He diverted instead to Inverness. This allowed Charles to proceed to Edinburgh, where the Jacobites took the town but not the castle. Cope meanwhile sailed his forces from Inverness to the Firth of Forth and engaged the Jacobite army at Prestonpans on 21 September. There he was routed and fled to England.

On 3 November Charles led his troops, now some 5500 strong, south to Carlisle, thus avoiding General WADE, who was stationed at Newcastle with superior forces, including 6000 Dutch soldiers. Wade tried to intercept the Jacobites but got no further than Hexham, being stranded by snow. The Jacobite army proceeded south, reaching Derby by 4 December. There was then no army between them and London, as the duke of CUMBERLAND was at Lichfield. He had been outmanoeuvred by the Jacobite General Lord George

MURRAY, who had kept him guessing that their forces were heading for Wales. On 6 December, 'Black Friday', there was widespread panic and a run on the Bank of England as news spread that the Highland host had reached Derby. Four thousand regulars who were in the capital were mobilized to protect the northern approach to the city at Finchley.

Perhaps fortunately for them they never encountered the Jacobite army, which decided on 5 December to retreat to Scotland. This was a controversial decision. Some maintain that if they had advanced they could have taken London. Others claim it was sound, since few recruits had joined them in their march through England: they had left more men to garrison Carlisle than they had recruited since. Another factor was that Cumberland was no more than a day's march away, while Wade was at Wetherby, threatening their retreat north. Cumberland chased them up the country, his most advanced troops encountering their rearguard in a skirmish at Clifton near Penrith, the last battle to be fought on English soil. The bulk of the army made it to Scotland and even defeated Hanoverian troops at Falkirk in January, only to be annihilated at CULLODEN in April 1746.

FURTHER READING J. Black, *Culloden and the '45* (1990); B. Lenman, *The Jacobite Risings in Britain 1689–1746* (1980); S. Reid, *1745. A Military History of the Last Jacobite Rising* (1996).

Jacobites, the supporters of the restoration of the Catholic James II and his successors, the Old Pretender, James Francis Edward STUART, and the Young Pretender, Charles Edward STUART. The Jacobites took their name from *Jacobus*, the Latin form of their monarch's name. There were a succession of abortive JACOBITE RISINGS between 1689 and 1746, but these failed to dislodge the HANOVERIAN SUCCESSION.

The one-sided encounter at CULLODEN that ended the Stuart cause so abruptly, and 'Bonnie Prince Charlie's' romantic ramblings in the heather before his escape to France, have bolstered the stance of those historians who view the Jacobites as anachronisms doomed to inevitable defeat at the hands of a modern and unified British state. To such scholars, Jacobitism amounted to little more than a subversive counter-culture through which discontented Tory squires, along with assorted smugglers and rioters from lower down the social scale, could vent a lingering dislike of the Whig oligarchs and their German-speaking monarchs. These historians argue that it was one thing to don a white cockade, bellow a chorus of 'The King Shall Come into His Own Again', or toast the 'little gentleman in black velvet' – a reference to the mole whose burrowing activities had allegedly caused Dutch William's horse to stumble with fatal consequences – but quite another to risk life, limb and property for the 'king over the water'. The yellowing skulls of men who had done just that in 1715 still grinned down from spikes set upon city gates and market crosses as a warning to those contemplating rebellion 30 years later.

Much scholarship has been deployed in debating the realities of the attractions of Jacobitism to the ousted TORY party, and its allure to those members of the 'lower orders' who continued to demonstrate an apparent enthusiasm for the Stuarts until the mid-18th century. By its very nature the extent of Jacobitism is difficult to document since plotters of treason rarely leave concrete evidence behind them. The degree of support for the exiled Stuarts among the Tories can only be deduced rather than documented. Certainly there were prominent Tory Jacobites such as William Shippen, Sir John Hinde Cotton and Sir Watkin Williams Wynn. These men did not become involved in rebellions, but were notoriously sympathetic to the Pretender's cause. Nevertheless the extent to which the Tory party was dedicated to the restoration of the Stuart line is much more difficult to gauge. Most Tories not only refused to rise in 1715 or 1745, but actually gave their support to the government. This suggests that Jacobitism appealed only to a minority.

However, while the extent to which English Jacobitism existed outside the fevered imaginations of government spies continues to generate controversy, there is growing recognition of the very real manner in which the continued existence of the exiled house of Stuart served to destabilize the Hanoverian regime throughout the first half of the 18th century. Indeed, if the events of 1715 and 1745 indicated that the vast majority of Englishmen were unwilling to rebel in support of Jacobite 'pretenders', they also revealed that the same men were equally reluctant to intervene on the side of the state. In a situation that recalls the sporadic dynastic conflicts of the Wars of the Roses, during both the '15 and the '45 the bulk of the population simply sat on the sidelines while relatively small rebel and government armies decided the issue on the battlefield. Such widespread apathy had permitted rapid transfers of power in both 1485 and 1688; it follows that the ultimate failure of the Jacobite attempts to regain the crown for the Stuarts should not be taken to suggest that they did not enjoy the potential for similar success.

Government reaction in the aftermath of the '15 had been relatively lenient, but in 1746 there was no such attempt to temper retribution with mercy. In the wake of Culloden hundreds of Highlanders were killed in cold blood, and many more were subsequently executed as traitors or transported to the colonies. Punitive expeditions ravaged the glens, while laws were enforced to ensure that the Highlands would never again play host to rebellion. These included bans upon carrying weapons, playing bagpipes and even wearing tartan cloth. Such steps to destroy the 'militaristic' Highland society proved indiscriminate, embracing pro-Jacobite and loyal Whig clans alike. After his brief stint as the 'Prince in the Heather', Charles Edward returned to France, where he received a hero's reception. In time the Young Pretender's well-publicized presence in France hampered attempts to broker a peace with Britain, and Louis XV – increasingly exasperated by his embarrassing guest – finally ordered his forcible ejection from the country. Charles Edward continued to blame everyone but himself for his misfortunes. He died in 1788, a brandy-sodden parody of the gallant adventurer whose exploits had once captured the imagination of all Europe.

Considering themselves betrayed by France, the clans who had traditionally provided the bedrock of the Jacobite armies never again rallied to the Stuart cause. By the mid-18th century the traditional bonds of Highland society were already dissolving as clan chiefs embarked upon the economic exploitation of their lands. Such policies would culminate in the notorious and controversial 'Highland Clearances': the introduction of sheep-farming, and the removal of crofters to participate in the coastal kelp industry, combined with voluntary emigration to depopulate much of the region. The Highland elites now sought to ingratiate themselves with the victorious Hanoverian regime by raising regiments from among their clansmen tenants to wage the government's wars across the globe. For men like Simon Fraser, who as the 'Master of Lovat' had led his clan at Falkirk, such military service to the state ultimately earned the restoration of lands confiscated after Culloden. Between 1750 and 1800 the Highlander was transformed from dangerous rebel to hero of empire. The same period had witnessed the final disappearance of Jacobitism as a viable political movement; its resurrection as romantic cult was soon to begin.

FURTHER READING M.G.H. Pittock, *Jacobitism* (1998); D. Szechi, *The Jacobites* (1994).

James III of England, title by which James Francis Edward STUART, the Old Pretender, was known by his JACOBITE supporters following the death of his father, James II, in 1701. Father and son were respectively dubbed James VII and VIII of Scotland.

Jenkinson, Robert Banks, 2nd earl of Liverpool. *See* LIVERPOOL, ROBERT BANKS JENKINSON, 2ND EARL OF.

Jenkins's Ear, War of (1739–42), conflict with Spain. From late 1740 the war became increasingly absorbed within the wider-ranging War of the AUSTRIAN SUCCESSION.

Although Captain Robert Jenkins lost his ear in a fracas with Spanish coastguards in 1731, the conflict named after the severed organ did not erupt until 1739. Historians remain sceptical of contemporary accounts that Jenkins subsequently appeared before the Commons with a jar containing his pickled ear; however, the anti-Bourbon sentiments that the case of Jenkins and other victims of Spanish 'cruelty' served to inflame are beyond doubt.

Fought primarily over issues of colonial trade, the War of Jenkins's Ear has been viewed as a precursor of the 'great war for the empire' – the SEVEN YEARS WAR – waged between 1756 and 1763. In both instances, British sea power was deployed in pursuit of a BLUE-WATER POLICY of colonial conquest; yet while the Seven Years War yielded spectacular territorial gains, the earlier amphibious expeditions against Spain's Caribbean empire ended in costly failure.

The onset of war with Spain marked the end of a lengthy period in which the prime minister, Robert WALPOLE, had sought to keep Britain aloof from international conflict. In fact, the reluctant Walpole had only been pushed into hostilities through the persistent lobbying of a powerful mercantile interest. Anglo-Spanish relations remained strained owing to Britain's possession of GIBRALTAR and the foundation of GEORGIA facing Spanish Florida. Even more contentious was the illegal trade carried out by British subjects between Spanish America and Britain's own North American and Caribbean colonies. Spain refused to ignore such smuggling and adopted harsh measures to deal with the interlopers; this tough policy gave rise to incidents such as that in which Jenkins of the *Rebecca* forfeited his ear.

British resentments came to a head in the late 1730s when a skilful parliamentary opposition, in league with the influential West Indian merchants, emphasized the paramount importance of protecting Britain's commercial interests. Anti-Spanish propaganda was reported in the press and swallowed by a populace that had forgotten the realities of war and was averse to foreigners in general and 'papists' in particular. Walpole worked feverishly to maintain peace, and the Spanish court likewise indicated a willingness to negotiate. Such conciliatory approaches foundered upon the reluctance of the South Sea Company (*see* SOUTH SEA BUBBLE) to pay its debts to Philip V of Spain and the belligerency of British public opinion.

Spain was a traditional enemy, and the prospect of a war against its wealthy New World possessions stirred patriotic memories of the swashbuckling era of Drake and Raleigh. Initially the war's course did little to disappoint popular expectations of glory and booty at the expense of the 'Dons'. In November 1739 an expedition under Admiral VERNON captured Porto Bello (in present-day Panama) and prompted widespread celebrations. However, subsequent operations against Cartagena, Cuba and Panama ended in humiliating withdrawals after British admirals and generals bickered among themselves, and tropical illnesses ravaged army and fleet alike.

Alongside its high human cost, the inglorious episode of the War of Jenkins's Ear probably damaged mercantile interests by disrupting the legitimate British trade with Spain's American empire that had been carried on through Spain itself.

FURTHER READING P. Woodfine, *Britannia's Glories: The Walpole Ministry and the 1739 War with Spain* (1998).

Jenner, Edward (1749–1823), physician who pioneered the idea of vaccination, which cured smallpox in Britain and ultimately led to its eradication across the globe.

As a pupil of John Hunter, the young Jenner studied medicine under the foremost surgeon of the age. Like his friend and mentor, Jenner founded his own methods upon careful observation and experimentation. In 1773 Jenner left London to establish a practice in his native town of Berkeley in Gloucestershire. Although Jenner's interests were wide-ranging, he devoted increasing attention to tackling the scourge of smallpox – a disease that killed many and left survivors disfigured by ugly scars. Jenner proposed the idea of inoculation against smallpox by using matter resulting from the comparatively mild disease of cowpox. Inoculation using matter produced by smallpox itself was already an established practice (it had been introduced from Turkey by Lady Mary Wortley MONTAGU), but it remained a risky and controversial procedure.

When his first scholarly paper on the subject was rejected, Jenner sought to disseminate his ideas through a privately published work entitled *An Inquiry into Cow-Pox* (1798); he followed this two years later with *A Complete Statement of Facts and Observations*. Jenner's methods were initially greeted with alarm and scorn: sceptics included the caricaturist James GILLRAY, who produced a memorable cartoon showing Jenner's patients sprouting hoofs, horns and other grotesque bovine features in consequence of his ministrations. However, the notion of 'vaccination' (from Latin *vacca*, a cow) using the cowpox virus vaccine gradually gained acceptance.

Jenner's credibility was enhanced when Parliament voted £30,000 to aid the promotion of his techniques, and leading physicians testified to their faith in the cowpox vaccine. By the close of the Napoleonic Wars, Jenner's researches had made him an international celebrity who was consulted by royalty. Jenner shunned the limelight and returned to Gloucestershire to continue work on widening the war against smallpox. The results of Jenner's work were soon apparent in Europe: his goal of ridding the world of smallpox was finally realized in 1978 when the disease was officially declared extinct.

Jewish Naturalization Act (May 1753), statute to facilitate the naturalization of Jews, for instance by dropping the words 'on the true faith of a Christian' from the oaths of allegiance and supremacy. It was in part an acknowledgement of the help that Jewish financiers had given to the public finances, which had helped to reduce the rate of interest.

At the time it aroused hardly any criticism. But before the next session of Parliament, opposition to the measure gathered strength. A petition from the City of London had been presented to Parliament protesting against the bill while it was still going through the Commons, but once it became law it was attacked throughout the country as a betrayal of the Christian religion. The chorus of complaint was orchestrated by the opposition press, which wildly exaggerated the scope of the act. Thus it was referred to as though it had not only made naturalization easier, but had actually naturalized large numbers of Jews. The more lurid literature presented visions of Britain swamped with Jews seeking to become British subjects. When Parliament reassembled the outcry was so vociferous that the PELHAM ministry reluctantly agreed to repeal the act. It was the more readily persuaded to adopt this course since a general election was due in 1754, and the unpopularity of the act threatened its supporters with defeat at the polls.

FURTHER READING T.W. Perry, *Public Opinion, Propaganda and Politics in 18th-Century England: a study of the Jew Bill of 1753* (1962).

Johnson, Samuel (1709–84), poet, critic and lexicographer, who, more than any other individual, has come to personify the spirit of 18th-century England. Yet the fame that has led generations of scholars to describe the mid-Georgian era as 'the age of Johnson' stemmed less from Johnson's own literary output than a remarkable personality that made a strong impression upon all who met him.

Dr Johnson's exterior was not prepossessing. At their first meeting in May 1763, when Johnson was a 54-year-old widower, the impressionable young James BOSWELL encountered 'a man of most dreadful appearance'. Boswell, whose 1791 *Life of Johnson* was a lasting tribute to one of the most celebrated friendships in history, provided

further unflattering details: 'He is a very big man, is troubled with sore eyes, the palsy, and the king's evil [scrofula]. He is very slovenly in his dress and speaks with a most uncouth voice.' Yet, as Boswell rapidly appreciated, Johnson's appearance was deceptive. Indeed, Boswell added: 'His great knowledge and strength of expression command vast respect and render him very excellent company. He has great humour and is a worthy man.'

At the time Boswell reported this momentous meeting at Davies's in Russell Street, Johnson enjoyed a degree of fame and financial security; in the previous year Lord BUTE had recognized his literary efforts with an annual pension of £300. For Johnson the road to success had proved long and arduous. A native of Lichfield, Johnson had been educated locally before spending a single year at Oxford. Johnson established a school in his native city but the venture soon foundered, and in 1737, in company with one of his former pupils, David GARRICK, Johnson resolved to seek his fortune in London. But while Garrick rapidly rose to dominate the London stage, Johnson faced gruelling years of toil as a GRUB STREET hack. The essence of Johnson's existence at this time is encapsulated in a line from his 1738 poem *London*: 'slow rises worth, by poverty depressed'. In that same year Johnson began to contribute parliamentary reports to the popular GENTLEMAN'S MAGAZINE.

In 1746 Johnson started work on the project that was to make his reputation. The vast *Dictionary* occupied Johnson for nearly a decade, but the result was a masterpiece of controlled prose that reflected his immense learning. While engaged upon his *Dictionary*, Johnson maintained a diverse stream of writings including a poem, *The Vanity of Human Wishes*, executed in imitation of Juvenal's satires, and regular essays published in the *Universal Chronicle* and his own periodical, *The Rambler*. The appearance of the *Dictionary* in 1755 won Johnson widespread acclaim; it was followed in 1759 by his sole novel, *Rasselas, Prince of Abyssinia*, which he penned in a single week.

Following the award of his pension, Johnson's literary output slackened, although this new financial security permitted him to complete an edition of Shakespeare that he had first considered during the early 1740s. In 1775 Johnson produced his lively account of the *Journey to the Western Islands of Scotland* that he had made in the company of his firm friend Boswell. Johnson's later works included the important biographies collected in his 1781 volume *The Lives of the Poets*.

A devout Christian, Johnson held a world-view dominated by a profound morality. Johnson sided with the NORTH administration in its unbending stance towards the rebellious American colonists, and produced pamphlets attacking the hypocrisy of men who demanded liberty for themselves while perpetuating the institution of slavery. As a child, Johnson had been touched by Queen Anne in the hope of curing his 'king's evil'; he retained an affection for the Stuarts, and expressed his Toryism in colourful broadsides against the Whigs. Some scholars have read these as evidence of Jacobitism, though they have not carried conviction.

Despite such prejudices, the gregarious Johnson enjoyed a wide circle of friends that ignored political boundaries. Indeed, Johnson's acquaintances amounted to a roll call of the mid-Georgian cultural scene: they included his old pupil Garrick, Sir Joshua REYNOLDS, Edmund BURKE and Oliver GOLDSMITH. Such luminaries gathered at the Literary Club that Johnson helped to found in 1764. Many of the conversations that ensued there were preserved in the pages of Boswell's *Life of Johnson*; in addition, Johnson's trenchant observations on a bewildering variety of subjects surface as anecdotes in the writings of many other contemporaries, so weaving his personality into the very fabric of the age.

Johnson endured a life-long struggle against poor health and black depression, but confronted both with a courage and humour that endeared him still further to his friends. He died in his beloved London, and is buried in Westminster Abbey.

FURTHER READING J. Boswell, *The Life of Dr Samuel Johnson*; J. Cannon, *Samuel Johnson and the Politics of Hanoverian England* (1994).

Junius, anonymous author of the *Letters of Junius*, which for the most part consist of arrogant, sardonic and scathing attacks upon the ministry of the duke of GRAFTON. The *Letters* appeared in Henry Sampson Woodfall's paper *The Public Advertiser* between 21 November 1768 and 21 January 1772. They were published by Woodfall in two volumes in March 1772, edited by Junius himself, who dropped the first letter and started with the second of 21 January 1769, printing 69 letters in all.

The most notorious of the *Letters*, number 35, which appeared on 19 December 1769, was addressed to the king. It concluded by reminding George III that 'while he plumes himself upon the security of his title to the crown, [he] should remember that, as it was acquired by one revolution, it may be lost by another'. But 'Junius' was no radical revolutionary. He praised the balance of the constitution, which could only be preserved by constant vigilance. The politicians he most admired were George GRENVILLE, William PITT and the marquess of ROCKINGHAM, who he hoped would replace Grafton. When in fact Lord NORTH, whose abilities he had scorned, succeeded as prime minister in 1770, the *Letters* lost much of their point, and early in North's ministry dried up.

There was much speculation at the time as to the authorship of the *Letters*, and subsequent conjecture gave rise to some sixty attributions. The case for Sir Philip Francis, though it rests almost entirely on circumstantial evidence, has been generally accepted.

FURTHER READING. J. Cannon (ed.), *The Letters of Junius* (1978).

Junto, name given to those prominent Whigs who took office in the mid-1690s: Charles Montagu earl of HALIFAX; John, Baron SOMERS; Edward Russell earl of ORFORD; and Thomas marquess of

WHARTON. To them were added in Anne's reign a fifth member, Charles Spencer earl of SUNDER-LAND. They provided the leadership of the Whig party, especially under Anne when the Whigs were more united than they had been under William. By the accession of George I their heyday was over as old age and death removed all but Sunderland from active politics.

Justices of the peace, unpaid lay magistrates who presided over non-capital offences in the localities. JPs had been appointed to 'commissions of the peace' in each county since the 16th century, and they played a growing part in local government. They were crown appointments made through the lord chancellor, generally acting on the advice and local knowledge of the lords lieutenant in the counties.

The Reverend Richard Burn, himself a JP, published a popular guide to their work in 1755, *The Justice of the Peace and Parish Officer, upon a plan entirely new, and comprehending all the law to the present time*. This two-volume work listed their various jurisdictions under more than 200 headings, two of which, 'excise and customs' and 'the poor' occupied over 200 pages apiece.

A single justice could practise summary jurisdiction on the basis of informations against offenders allegedly breaking the laws on vagrancy, drunkenness, profaneness and Sunday trading, hearing those charged and, if they were found guilty, sentencing them to a small fine or even to public chastisement. In conjunction with one other magistrate they could exercise justice in 'petty' sessions over such offenders as unlicensed alehouse keepers, unmarried mothers, and runaway servants and apprentices. Three justices could even sentence to transportation for a crime such as rick-burning. Yet more serious offences were heard in QUARTER SESSIONS, when the active magistrates on a county's commission of the peace met to hear cases presented by a grand jury of the county and determined by a petty jury of twelve.

Besides acting as judges, JPs also administered the laws covering a wide gamut of activities, such as repairing roads and bridges, licensing alehouses and implementing the poor laws. They even assumed a legislative role, making their own laws to keep the peace, for instance regulating fairs, markets and wages (*see* SPEENHAMLAND). They also appointed the 'constables of hundreds', who were responsible for maintaining law and order in the county at large.

The vast majority of JPs were country gentlemen, a hegemony strengthened by the Property Qualifications Acts of 1731 and 1744. These increased the minimum value of land from £20 a year required by a statute of 1689 to £100 per annum. The land had to be held within the county on whose commission the justice served. As the century progressed, and the duties of JPs became ever more onerous, some gentry proved reluctant to serve, and recourse was had increasingly to the Anglican clergy. In many counties the clerical justices were the most active on the commission by the end of the period.

FURTHER READING N. Landau, *The Justices of the Peace, 1679–1760* (1984).

K

Kauffmann, Angelica (1741–1807), painter. A native of Switzerland, Kauffmann made both an artistic and personal impact after she settled in London in 1766. After establishing a reputation as a child prodigy, she was persuaded to come to England by 'grand tourists' she had painted and charmed in Naples in 1763. She rapidly achieved success as a painter of mythological and historical scenes, while her vivacity and sparkling humour attracted a circle of devoted admirers, including GOLDSMITH, GARRICK and REYNOLDS.

In 1769 she was a founder member of the ROYAL ACADEMY; along with the only other female academician, Mary MOSER, Kauffmann makes an appearance as a portrait upon the wall in ZOFFANY's 1772 group picture of the Academy's original members.

Kauffmann worked in London until her marriage in 1781 to the Venetian painter Antonio Zucchi, producing many portraits and executing much decorative work for the architect Robert ADAM. After her retirement to Italy she continued to paint British sitters, and in Rome she maintained a salon that drew such celebrities as Goethe and the sculptor Canova. Although much of her work was undistinguished, Kauffmann continued to paint until her final years. Her illustrious patrons included Pope Pius VI, Joseph II and Catherine the Great.

Kentish petition, petition presented to Parliament on 8 May 1701 from the grand jury of Kent urging the Commons to 'lay aside their heats and animosities' and vote supplies 'so that his Majesty may be enabled powerfully to assist his allies before it is too late'. The House voted it 'scandalous, insolent and seditious' and ordered the five men who presented it into the custody of the sergeant at arms. Their treatment became a party affair, for the majority of members of Parliament were Tories while the petitioners were Whigs, and were held to have been encouraged in their actions by leaders of their party. One Tory called them 'tools of the late ministry'.

Their supporters visited them in prison, from which they were released when Parliament was prorogued on 4 June. Later in June an engraving was published showing the portraits of the five Kentish petitioners, with the motto 'Non Auro Patriam', implying that, unlike them, their Tory enemies had sold their country for gold. On their release they were feted at the Guildhall and feasted at Fishmongers Hall. They were accompanied in triumph back to Kent.

In January 1701 the Tories got their revenge by passing resolutions in the House of Commons condemning the petition and 'the aspersing of the last House of Commons condemning the petition and 'the aspersing of the last House of Commons or any member thereof with receiving French money, or being in the interest of France' as 'a scandalous, villainous and groundless reflection, tending to sedition'.

Keppel, Arnold Joost van, 1st earl of Albemarle. *See* ALBEMARLE, ARNOLD JOOST VAN KEPPEL, 1ST EARL OF.

Keppel, Augustus, Viscount (1725–86), naval commander who followed a distinguished seafaring career that embraced three world wars. The second son of William Anne Keppel, 2nd earl of Albemarle, Augustus Keppel first ventured to sea while still a child, and by the age of 15 he had already seen service from the Mediterranean to the Guinea coast. He subsequently survived ANSON's epic circumnavigation in the *Centurion* and played an active role in the naval operations of the War of the AUSTRIAN SUCCESSION.

As fresh hostilities with France loomed in 1754, Keppel headed the Royal Navy's presence in North America. He cooperated with Major General Edward Braddock in planning that summer's campaign, only to return to England with news of the general's defeat and death amidst the backwoods of Pennsylvania. In 1757 Keppel served on the court martial of Admiral BYNG, but was soon destined to take an important share in the events that turned the tide of the SEVEN YEARS WAR: during the following summer he commanded the squadron that captured the important French settlement of Gorée on the West African coast. Throughout the summer and autumn of 1759 Keppel served in HAWKE's command off Brest; his ship the *Torbay* spearheaded the attack upon the French fleet in the decisive victory amidst the stormy waters of QUIBERON BAY.

Keppel's share in Britain's success increased in 1761 when he commanded the naval squadron that covered the successful landing of the troops at Belle Isle in the Bay of Biscay. With the entry of Spain into the conflict, Keppel was given the rank of commodore and appointed second in command

of the naval forces sent to subdue Havana. The city fell in August 1762, yielding booty reckoned at £3 million. As Augustus's elder brother commanded the land forces at the siege, and a younger brother also served as a general officer, more than half of the prize money fell to the Keppels; this lopsided distribution of the spoils did not go unnoticed by contemporaries.

In the ensuing years of peace Keppel clashed with Lord SANDWICH, the first lord of the Admiralty. The repercussions of this feud were to prove damaging when the Royal Navy found itself stretched beyond its resources during the AMERICAN WAR OF INDEPENDENCE. Early in 1778 Keppel was promoted to admiral and given command of the grand fleet designated to prevent a union between the Brest and Toulon fleets. In June, after learning that the Brest fleet alone was superior to his own, Keppel retired to Portsmouth rather than risk defeat. In the divisive political atmosphere of the time, Keppel's strategic withdrawal was interpreted by his critics as a deliberate attempt to discredit NORTH's ministry. Suitably reinforced, the admiral ventured to sea once more in July. Although the French fleet was encountered in fog off Ushant, the resulting engagement proved inconclusive.

During the course of the action, one of Keppel's commanders, Sir Hugh Palliser, had responded sluggishly to instructions to attack, and in the mood of recrimination that followed the battle, Palliser demanded that Keppel himself be court-martialled for misconduct and neglect of duty. On 11 February 1779, after the court had considered five weeks of evidence, Keppel was honourably acquitted. Keppel's vindication was widely viewed as the victory of a brave and honourable sailor over a corrupt administration and prejudiced Admiralty. While Palliser and First Lord of the Admiralty SANDWICH were execrated, Keppel became a popular hero.

Although ordered to resign in March, Keppel used his seat in the Commons to criticize the ministry's conduct of the naval war. Upon the fall of North he succeeded his old enemy Sandwich at the Admiralty in ROCKINGHAM's administration, and was soon after raised to the peerage. His constitution shattered by hard service in the tropics, Keppel retired from public life in December 1783. He was immortalized in a dramatic and innovative portrait by REYNOLDS.

King, Gregory (1648–1712), statistician and genealogist. King entered the College of Heralds in 1677, becoming its registrar in 1684 and Lancaster herald in 1688. In 1695 he was deprived of the registrarship and charged with embezzlement. The following year he wrote his *Natural and Political Observations and Conclusions upon the State and Condition of England*. In the course of writing it he investigated the population and wealth of the country, with a view to gauging its potential to engage in the war against Louis XIV. He concluded pessimistically that the war could not be sustained beyond 1698. This conclusion sprang from his conservatism, which convinced him that the GLORIOUS REVOLUTION of 1688 had been a disaster for England socially and economically as well as politically. Hence his calculation of the 'scheme and expense of the several families of England' for the year 1688. Though this table is often reproduced and used by historians as an objective statistical analysis of England's social structure at the end of the 17th century, the pessimistic politics of its author were not taken into consideration until Geoffrey Holmes pointed them out. Yet, as Holmes demonstrated, King's politics biased his conclusions, leading him to underestimate the country's wealth. This makes his calculation of the incomes of different ranks in society almost useless, although his analysis of the structure of society remains useful.

FURTHER READING G. Holmes, 'Gregory King and the Social Structure of Pre-Industrial England' in *Politics, Religion and Society in England 1679–1742* (1986).

Kit Cat Club, Whig club started in William III's reign. Jacob Tonson, a publisher, became its secretary. It met in Christopher Cat's tavern in Shire Lane, London, and took its name from his mutton pies, known as kit-cats. In 1703 the club moved from Cat's tavern to Tonson's new house at Barn Elms, Surrey. Among its members were the JUNTO Whigs; the dukes of Grafton, Devonshire, Montagu, Newcastle, Richmond and, until his expulsion in 1710 for dealing with the Tories, Somerset; the writers Joseph ADDISON, William Congreve and Richard STEELE; the playwright and architect Sir John VANBRUGH; and the young Robert WALPOLE.

Although the Kit Cat was primarily a social club, it did have a political role too, being dedicated to the Protestant succession in the house of Hanover. Club members contributed to the construction of the Haymarket Theatre in 1705, and seats were reserved for their exclusive use free of charge. The decision to impeach Dr SACHEVERELL was probably taken at a meeting of the club. In 1711 the club raised funds to mount a pope-burning procession on 17 November, the accession day of Queen Elizabeth. However, the effigies intended for burning, which cost several hundred pounds, were apprehended by the secretary of state. In 1714 the club made contingent plans to resist a JACOBITE restoration on the death of Queen Anne. When George I succeeded peacefully their main political objective had been achieved.

By 1725 Vanbrugh could reminisce about the club, by then defunct, wishing there could be a reunion of its members. They were commemorated by portraits painted by Godfrey KNELLER, and hung at Barn Elms from which prints were made in 1733. A set of mezzotints made in 1735 is preserved in the National Portrait Gallery's exhibition at Beningbrough Hall in Yorkshire.

Kneller, Sir Godfrey (1646–1723), the foremost exponent of the English baroque portrait, who represented a formal tradition that was later challenged by the innovations of RAMSAY and REYNOLDS.

Born in Lübeck, north Germany, Kneller practised in Italy before coming to England in 1676. A dearth of native talent assisted him to establish himself at court. As a foreigner, Kneller followed precedents set by Holbein in the previous century and Van Dyck in his own. In 1688 Kneller was appointed as a principal painter to William and Mary, and he held the same office through successive reigns until his death.

Kneller's talents brought fame, wealth and honours: he was knighted in 1692, and became a baronet in 1715. Despite his alien origins, he proved keen to stimulate indigenous talent through his own academy. Although Kneller was fully capable of capturing the character of his sitters – as his series of portraits of members of the KIT CAT CLUB demonstrates – much of his work has a journeyman quality. This impression was reinforced by the ubiquitous full-bottomed wigs sported by his powerful male clients, and the fact that Kneller's busy studio employed specialized drapery artists to complete canvases after he had painted the all-important head. Kneller's death signalled the end of the era in which foreigners dominated painting at court, a trend that had already been encouraged by the decline of that institution as a focus for patronage of the arts.

FURTHER READING J.D. Stewart, *Sir Godfrey Kneller and the English Baroque Portrait* (1983).

L

Lake poets or **'Lakers'**, terms applied to the poets Samuel Taylor Coleridge (1772–1834), Robert Southey (1774–1843) and William Wordsworth (1770–1850). They earned this name by dint of living in the Lake District – Coleridge and Southey in Greta Hall, Keswick, which they rented in 1803, and Wordsworth in Grasmere.

Although the three poets were grouped together, especially by hostile critics such as Francis Jeffrey in the *Edinburgh Review*, they scarcely formed a school. Coleridge was the most intellectual, deeply influenced by the writers of the German literary revival. Whereas the other two spent the rest of their lives in the Lake District, Coleridge left early, abandoning his wife and family to the care of Southey's in 1806, and rarely returning. Southey was the most scholarly, spending his time, as he confessed, in the company of books, and writing serious biographies and histories as well as poems. Wordsworth was the greatest poet, arguably the greatest in English history.

But their affinities brought them closely together, Coleridge and Southey from their first meeting in Oxford in June 1794, and Coleridge and Wordsworth from theirs in the summer of 1795. All three shared an initial enthusiasm for the FRENCH REVOLUTION, but later became so disillusioned at its excesses that they abandoned radicalism and became reactionaries. Thus, although they initially advocated that the solution to the problems of the 'lower orders' lay in their own hands – by extension of the franchise or even revolt – they later moved to an insistence that the elite should deserve the deference of the lower orders (to whom they remained sympathetic) by practising paternalism.

Another thing they shared was that they never had to contemplate careers other than that of authors. All three benefited from the generosity of people who gave them money on which they could live in reasonable comfort. Coleridge's benefactors were Josiah and Thomas WEDGWOOD, who gave him an annuity of £100 in 1797; Southey's was Charles Watkin Williams Wynn, who settled £160 a year on him in 1796; and Wordsworth's was Raisley Calvert, who died in 1795 leaving him a legacy of £900.

When Coleridge met Southey both were students. Southey was at Balliol College, Oxford, having been refused admission to Christ Church for his schoolboy publication *The Flagellant*, an attack on corporal punishment for which he had been expelled from Westminster School. Coleridge was at Jesus College, Cambridge, but was already alienated from university life. Thus he had enlisted as a dragoon under the name of Silas Tomkyn Comberbache, a whim from which he was rescued when his brothers bought him out. Both left university without taking a degree.

In 1794 Southey returned to his birthplace, Bristol, to live on his pen and his wits. He began writing for publication, and delivered a series of twelve lectures on European history from ancient Greece to the American War of Independence. In them he boasted that he had proclaimed the 'truth and divinity' of the doctrines of Thomas PAINE. His political stance at the age of 21 was, in his own words, that of 'a republican and a leveller'. How radical he was at this stage can be gauged from his reported reaction to the news of the death of Robespierre: 'I had rather have heard of the death of my own father.' Together with Coleridge he wrote a drama, *The Fall of Robespierre*. They also devised schemes to settle a colony on the banks of the Susquehannah in Pennsylvania on principles they termed 'pantisocracy' or the rule of all, including women. However, Coleridge queried Southey's complete commitment to being a pantisocrat when he envisaged taking servants with them.

The two never made it to America but did marry sisters, Edith and Sara Fricker. Whereas Coleridge's marriage to Sara turned out disastrously, Southey's to Edith was stable. Even so his family tried to get him out of it by sending him to Spain and Portugal with his uncle from 1795 to 1796, though he thwarted their intentions by marrying Edith secretly just before his departure. While he was away his first major poem, the epic *Joan of Arc*, was published. It sold well, meriting a second edition in 1798. Southey later attributed its success to the fact 'that it was written in a republican spirit, such as may easily be accounted for in a youth whose notions of liberty were taken from the Greek and Roman writers, and who was ignorant enough of history and of human nature to believe that a happier order of things had commenced with the independence of the United States, and would be accelerated by the French Revolution'.

Wordsworth shared this early view of the momentous events in France, having experienced some of them directly after leaving Cambridge –

with a degree but without honours – in 1791. He had spent the years 1789–90 and 1791–2 in France, where he associated with Girondins and fathered an illegitimate child by Annette Vallon. Since his return he had lived with his sister Dorothy in Keswick and Racedown in Dorset. In March 1797 he visited Coleridge at Nether Stowey. This was the fateful meeting that led to their collaboration in the epoch-making *Lyrical Ballads*. Some date from it the beginning of the English ROMANTIC MOVEMENT. Wordsworth himself claimed in the preface to the edition of 1800 that 'it was published as an experiment', which was 'to ascertain how far, by fitting to metrical arrangement a selection of the real language of men in a state of vivid sensation, that sort of pleasure and that quantity of pleasure may be imparted, which a poet may rationally endeavour to impart'. Wordsworth contributed the lion's share of poems to the volume, including one of his most renowned, 'Lines written a few miles above Tintern Abbey'. Coleridge contributed 'The Rime of the Ancient Mariner' and 'The Nightingale'. Three other poems he wrote about this time were also to be among his best, 'Christabel', 'Frost at Midnight' and 'Kubla Khan'. The visionary 'Kubla Khan' already exhibited signs of the opium habit to which he became addicted in later years.

Coleridge and Wordsworth went to Germany together in 1798. Wordsworth was unhappy with the experience, which he used to write parts of his great autobiographical poem, *The Prelude*, an early version of which was completed by 1799. Coleridge, who thoroughly enjoyed the trip, developed his interest in German Romanticism, and his awareness of continental cultural trends informed much of his own philosophical lectures and writings. His political journalism, however, shows a marked reaction against the progress of the French Revolution. In 1800 he began to contribute to the *Morning Post* articles that he later admitted were 'in defence or furtherance of the measures of government'.

Coleridge quarrelled with Southey over the

collapse of their colonizing scheme and over problems with his marriage, which he blamed on his colleague. Southey continued to write, contributing poems to the *Morning Post* and reviews to the *Critical Review*, including one on the *Lyrical Ballads* in which he dismissed Coleridge's 'Ancient Mariner' as 'a poem of little merit'. He went to Lisbon in 1800. There he completed another epic, *Thalaba the Destroyer*. This was 'an Arabian tale', Southey's contribution to the orientalism that intrigued many Romantic poets. While in Lisbon he also began work on histories of Portugal and Brazil before returning to England. There he saw through the press another poem of epic proportions, *Madoc*. Although not published until 1805 it had long gestated in his mind. The hero is a Welsh warrior who decides to leave Wales after its conquest by Saxons, to take refuge in the wilds of America. This theme has echoes of Southey's pantisocracy – he had even toyed with the idea of settling his utopian community in Wales after deciding he could not afford to go to the Susquehannah.

Meanwhile Coleridge had moved with Wordsworth to the Lake District, settling his family in Greta Hall in Keswick, where Southey's joined them shortly after. There Coleridge met Mary Hutchinson, whom Wordsworth married in 1802, and her sister Sara, to whom he wrote his 'Dejection: an Ode'. He left the Lakes for London and Malta, where he stayed from 1806 to 1808. Back in England he contrived to be a journalist and a lecturer, but largely failed at both since his temperament made him irregular in delivering both copy and lectures. He had a brilliant mind, fertile with ideas, but was too indolent to apply himself to developing them. His opium addiction aggravated his lack of application, and also led to his estrangement from Wordsworth in 1810. In 1816, however, he tried to control his habit, moving in with an apothecary-surgeon in Highgate, who undertook to help him. He stayed there for the rest of his life, becoming known as 'the sage of Highgate'. Coleridge got enough of a grip on his addiction to bring out his *Biographia Literaria*

and *Sibylline Leaves* in 1817, his first major works since leaving Keswick. In his last decade his reputation was probably higher than at any other time in his life. He consolidated the image of the sage with such publications as *Aids to Reflection* in 1825 and *On the Constitution in Church and State* in 1830. Religion had always played a major part in his thinking. In his radical phase he had even preached in Unitarian chapels. Later he became a staunch Anglican. Christianity pervades his poetry from 'Religious Musings' to his own epitaph of 9 November 1833.

Southey too became deeply religious, seeing the Church of England as a bulwark against disturbing social trends. The aspects of English society that Southey disliked so much that they led him to contemplate emigrating to Portugal were the subject of his first major prose work, *Letters from England by Don Manuel Alvarez Espriella*, which appeared in 1807. Thereafter his prose works began to vie with his poetry. While he still published long poems like *The Curse of Kehama* (1810) and *Roderick last of the Goths* (1814), he also wrote biographies, the most famous of which was his celebrated *Life of Nelson* (1813), and histories such as the *History of Brazil* (3 volumes, 1810–19). He also began in 1808 to publish essays and reviews in the *Quarterly Review*, to which he contributed regularly until 1839. Although much of his poetry is now unread – and by many is regarded as unreadable, so that he is remembered largely for his prose works – at the time he was held to be more of a poet than a prose writer. Thus in 1813 he became poet laureate.

Southey's acceptance into the establishment was regarded as the ultimate political betrayal by those who recalled his radical youth. He himself was reminded of it embarrassingly by the pirate publication in 1817 of his youthful poem *Wat Tyler*, a defence of the leader of the peasant revolt against a poll tax in 1381. This piece had languished in a publisher's drawer since 1794. Southey tried to dismiss it as being 'among the follies of my youth', but much damage was done to his reputation. The ridicule he endured then, however, was nothing compared with that poured on him by BYRON in 1821. On the death of George III the poet laureate wrote 'A Vision of Judgement' in which he imagined the late king gaining admission to heaven in defiance of his political enemies, and finding it inhabited by his supporters. In the preface he attacked the younger Romantics for their atheism, calling them the Satanic school of poets. Although he did not name any it was obvious that his main target was Byron. Byron could not resist the challenge and riposted with 'The Vision of Judgement', which mocked not only the conceit of Southey's poem but also the poet himself.

Wordsworth's religion remains problematic. In his later years he revised many of his earlier poems to give them a Christian message. But in his youth he was more of a pantheist than a Christian. His reconciliation with the establishment, however, was complete by 1813 when he was appointed distributor of stamps for Westmoreland. This was the ultimate apostasy to younger Romantics, who criticized him as 'the lost leader'. He succeeded Southey as poet laureate in 1843.
FURTHER READING R. Ashton, *The Life of Samuel Taylor Coleridge* (1996); J. Barker, *William Wordsworth* (2000); S. Gill, *William Wordsworth, A Life* (1989); R. Holmes, *Coleridge: Early Visions* (1989); R. Holmes, *Coleridge: Darker Reflections* (1998); M. Storey, *Robert Southey, A Life* (1997).

landscape gardening. The landscape of the 18th-century country estate was transformed almost beyond recognition by the activities of garden designers. Formal gardens, with their paved parterres and box and privet clipped into topiary shapes – exemplified at Versailles, Het Loo and Hampton Court – were replaced by the informal *jardin anglais.*

Landowners leapt at the opportunity to improve the appearance of their estates. 'Every man now, be his fortune what it will, is doing something at his Place, as the fashionable phrase is,' observed the newspaper *Common Sense* in 1739, 'and you hardly meet with anybody who, after the first compliments, does not inform you that he is in Mortar and moving of earth, the modest terms for building and gardening.' Building and gardening indeed went together, and the country house was the jewel set in the new landscapes. Improving 'the genius of the place'– as POPE phrased it – also symbolized the proprietor's culture, for instance his awareness of classical antiquity and of contemporary political ideologies. Many of the changes were devised by landlords themselves, who knew much about forestry and planting. But the greater landowners who set the pace employed professional gardeners.

These professionals included men such as Charles Bridgeman and William Kent, who led the reaction against the formal garden designs of the 17th-century French gardener Le Nôtre and his followers. Charles Bridgeman (d. 1738) was credited with inventing the ha-ha, the indispensable ditch that protected the house from such livestock as deer, horses and even cattle and sheep that grazed picturesquely in the park. William Kent (1685–1748) – who was also a noted architect and furniture designer – broke with the straight lines of the formal garden to create serpentine alleys and pools. His most famous work was at Rousham House in Oxfordshire, though he also worked for the Pelhams at Claremont and Esher, and even for the king at Richmond.

But the man who above all transformed the estates of 18th-century England was Lancelot 'Capability' Brown (1716–83). He was dubbed Capability Brown because he was known for persuading landowners that their estates had great capabilities for improvement. He was born at Kirkharle in Northumberland and was taken on as gardener by a local country gentleman, Sir William Loraine. Brown's first exercise in landscape improvement seems to have been on Sir William's estate. In 1739 he went to Oxfordshire to work on Kiddington Hall and was introduced to Lord

Cobham, who was engaged on landscaping STOWE. Brown worked as a gardener at Stowe from 1741 to 1751. He learned much from William Kent, who had been employed there since 1733. Kent probably had the idea of the Grecian Valley, which Brown completed. The classical temples, follies and other features at Stowe were widely imitated. While employed as gardener at Stowe, Brown was lent out by Cobham to other landowners such as Richard Grenville, his son-in-law and heir.

After leaving Stowe in 1751 Brown became a freelance. One of his first commissions was to landscape Croome, the Warwickshire home of the earl of Coventry. He so pleased the owner that after his death a memorial was erected at Croome celebrating the gardener 'who by the powers of his inimitable and creative genius formed this garden scene out of a morass'. The garden scenes that Brown created continued the trend, begun by Bridgeman and Kent, away from the formal garden. In place of geometrical and topiary designs he planted woods of beech and oak, chestnut and elm in copses or 'clumps' set in a 'natural' landscape of sweeping meadows. Drawing on Hogarth's 'line of beauty' and BURKE's notions of the sublime and the beautiful, he dammed and diverted streams and rivers to form serpentine lakes. Commissions from wealthy landowners prepared to pay him several thousand pounds poured in, and some two hundred estates, including Alnwick in his native Northumberland, BLENHEIM and Kirtlington in Oxfordshire, and Burton Constable, Harewood and Temple Newsam in Yorkshire, were transformed. At Longleat in Wiltshire the transformation was described as modernization by one visitor in 1760, who observed that 'the gardens are no more. They are succeeded by a fine lawn, a serpentine river, wooded hills, gravel paths meandering around shubbery, all modernized by the ingenious and much sought-after Mr Brown.' Brown, who had spent much of his life in Hammersmith after moving south, became royal gardener at Hampton Court in 1765 with a salary of £2000 a year and a grace-and-favour house in the

grounds. He acquired an estate of his own at Fenstanton, Cambridgeshire, in 1767, where he was buried after his death in 1783.

By the time of his death Brown had gone out of fashion. At Kew Sir William CHAMBERS reacted against Brown's example, saying that his landscapes 'differ very little from common fields'. Instead Chambers drew on his experiences of China to create the pagoda, and he later published a *Dissertation on Oriental Gardening*. This was criticized in its turn: Horace Walpole claimed that it was 'written in wild revenge against Brown' and was 'more extravagant than the worst Chinese paper'.

Humphry Repton (1752–1818) was much inspired by Brown at first and defended him against his critics. But eventually he too departed from the archetypal Brown landscape, preferring even more informal scenes such as he executed at Cobham, his first commission, in 1790. At Kenwood he grew a screen of trees to hide Kentish Town and removed an oak to open up a view of St Paul's Cathedral. Repton sold his ideas to patrons by making sketches, in what were called his 'red books', of how their estates would appear before and after his improvements. In turn he too was criticized: for example, Jane AUSTEN satirized his style in *Mansfield Park*. Such comment notwithstanding, Britain's 18th-century 'revolution' in landscape gardening exerted a considerable influence on continental tastes.

FURTHER READING M. Laird, *The Flowering of the Landscape Garden: English Pleasure Grounds 1720–1800* (1999).

Last Determinations Act (1729). *See* CONTROVERTED ELECTIONS.

Latitudinarianism. *See* HIGH CHURCH.

Law, William (1686–1761), cleric and religious writer. Law was educated at Cambridge, where he was ordained and became a fellow of Emmanuel College in 1711. He lost his fellowship soon after the accession of the house of Hanover when he refused to swear the oaths of allegiance and became a NONJUROR. He championed the cause of non-jurors against Benjamin HOADLY in the BANGORIAN CONTROVERSY and against deists such as Matthew Tindal (*see* DEISM). Bernard MANDEVILLE's *Fable of the Bees* so incensed him with its divorce of economics from morality that he published *Remarks* on it in 1724.

Law's *Serious Call to a Devout and Holy Life* (1729) was his most influential work. It was directed primarily against those who were 'strict as to some times and places of devotion, but when the service of the church is over, they are but like those that seldom or never come there'. The arguments, clearly and cogently expressed, influenced Dr JOHNSON and Edward GIBBON, whose father employed Law as his chaplain. Gibbon's aunt Hester and Mrs Elizabeth Hutchcson lived with Law first in Thrapston, Northamptonshire, then after 1743 at his house in King's Cliffe, and resolved to put in practice the precepts of his *Serious Call*. Above all Law's work had a profound impact on the early METHODISTS. 'This considerable writer', claimed Thomas Coke, one of their number, 'was the great forerunner of the revival which followed, and did more to promote it than any other individual whatsoever.' In 1760 John WESLEY wrote in his journal that 'Mr Law, whom I love and reverence now, was once a kind of oracle'. The following year Law died.

Leeds, town in Yorkshire, which expanded during the 18th century to become the West Riding's leading textile centre. At its incorporation in 1626 it already possessed a merchant elite whose business was increasingly dominated by the manufacture, dyeing and finishing of cloth made from local wool. Leeds specialized in the merchandising of woollens, and by 1707 boasted the largest cloth market in England. In 1698 Celia FIENNES noted that Leeds was 'esteemed an excellent town' which thrived upon 'its manufactures in the woollen cloth'. Thirty years later Daniel DEFOE likewise found the town to be 'large, wealthy and prosper-

ous', and in 1757 John Dyer, in his poem 'The Fleece', also admired the growth of 'busy Leeds'.

Although Leeds's first markets were in the open air, in 1755 the White Cloth Hall was built, to be followed three years late by the Coloured Cloth Hall. Towards the end of the 18th century the town centre itself increasingly assumed commercial and warehousing functions, with manufacturing proper relocated to mills sited in outlying areas. Leeds' dominance of the West Riding textile industry was reinforced by the improved communications that resulted from the phased opening of the Leeds and Liverpool canal after 1770.

From a population of around 6000 in 1700 Leeds experienced rapid growth: by 1775 the number of inhabitants had risen to 30,000, and at the dawn of the 19th century had topped 50,000, ranking as the fifth largest provincial town in England. Before the 1760s much of this population increase was absorbed by infilling vacant lots within the old town centre; the development of 'back-to-back' housing that marked the town's subsequent expansion thereby built upon an established pattern.

Although it had been briefly enfranchised under Cromwell, Leeds lost its representation in Parliament at the Restoration, and only regained it with the Great Reform Act of 1832.

Legge, William, 2nd earl of Dartmouth. *See* DARTMOUTH, WILLIAM LEGGE, 2ND EARL OF.

Leicester House, the town house of the princes of Wales, in Leicester Square, London. When the future GEORGE II quarrelled with his father in 1717 he withdrew there and used it as a base to foment opposition to the government, until he was reconciled with the king in 1720. Similarly his own son FREDERICK PRINCE OF WALES went into opposition in 1737 and built up a clientele of Tories and patriot Whigs. This became a formidable 'shadow government' in the 1740s, since Frederick was never reconciled with George II before his own death in 1751.

Lennox, Charlotte (*née* Ramsay) (1720–1804), woman of letters. She was brought up in New York where her father was governor. After his death she went to England where she married Alexander Lennox. Her talent as a poet attracted the patronage of the Marchioness of Rockingham and Lady Isabella Finch, to whom she dedicated her first publication, *Poems on several occasions*, in 1747. Her novel *The Life of Harriet Stuart* led Dr Johnson to invite her to dinner, where he praised her genius. He was later to flatter her in his entry on 'talent' in his *Dictionary*. She demonstrated this quality in her second novel *The Female Quixote: or the adventures of Arabella* (1752). From 1760 to 1761 she edited a magazine entitled *The Ladies' Museum*.

In 1769 her play *The Sister* – which she dramatized from her novel *Henrietta* – was barracked on the opening night and never recovered. However, *Old City Manners*, a comedy produced at Drury Lane in 1775, was well received. Her last novel, *Euphemia,* appeared in 1790. Thereafter she experienced poverty until she received a pension from the Royal Literary Fund in the last year of her life.

Leslie, Charles (1650–1722), Anglo-Irish cleric, one of the most prominent NONJURORS. Leslie was born in Ireland and educated at Trinity College, Dublin. After practising law he became a minister in the Church of Ireland, which he defended against the Catholic policies of James II. This was used against him after the GLORIOUS REVOLUTION of 1688, when he denounced those who took the oaths to William and Mary. He himself refused, and justified his refusal in a series of controversial writings beginning in 1692. On the death of Queen Mary in 1694 he published *Querula Temporum* in which he argued that by it 'King William's title being now become ... merely elective, and all matrimonial right ceasing with her, we that are of the church of England, and have ever declared our constitution to be hereditary monarchy' no longer owed him any allegiance. At one time in the 1690s his arrest was sought for sedition, and he took refuge at the Pretender's court at St Germain. After his return he involved himself with controversies with the Quakers as well as with those who took the oaths to William.

In Anne's reign Leslie began a nonjuring paper, *The Rehearsal*, which hit out at Whig defences of resistance to tyrannical government in such journals as Defoe's *Review* and George Ridpath's *Observator* – the full title of his own organ being the *Rehearsal of Observator*. When Defoe defended his ironic *Shortest Way with the Dissenters* he claimed that his parody went no further than what was implied in some high-church, nonjuring and Jacobite publications, including Leslie's *The New Association of those called moderate Church men with the modern Whigs and fanatics to undermine and blow up the present church and government.*

Leslie's controversial defence of the hereditary succession led again to a warrant for his apprehension, which he avoided by fleeing to St Germain in 1711. He remained at the Pretender's court for most of the time between his flight and 1719. Then he fell ill and wished to return home. Permission was not given until 1721, by which time he was at death's door, and he died soon after his return to Ireland.

Libel Act (1792), reform of the law on seditious libel. The statute is generally called Fox's Libel Act since it was sponsored by Charles James FOX. It allowed the jury in libel cases to decide not merely whether the author or printer of an alleged seditious libel had been properly identified by the prosecution, but whether the published material was in fact libellous. Previously the judges had decided whether a publication was libellous in law, and juries had only to find whether or not those responsible for its appearing in print were the accused. By making juries the judges of the contents as well as the contrivers of a publication, the act did much to advance the freedom of the press and reduce the power of the state over it.

Ligonier, Sir John (1680–1770), soldier and commander in chief of the British army during the SEVEN YEARS WAR. Of French Huguenot stock, Jean-Louis Ligonier chose exile rather than endure the religious persecution of Louis XIV. At the age of 17 Ligonier joined a soldier uncle who was serving WILLIAM III in Ireland. France's loss was Britain's gain, for in the course of a lengthy and distinguished military career, Ligonier was destined to earn the highest honours from his adopted country.

During the War of the SPANISH SUCCESSION Ligonier volunteered for service in Flanders. His courage at the storming of Liège gained him a captain's commission in the infantry. Ligonier saw extensive service under John CHURCHILL duke of Marlborough, surviving the major encounters at BLENHEIM, RAMILLIES and MALPLAQUET. In 1711 he transferred to the allied army in the Iberian peninsula, subsequently participating in the successful expedition against Vigo in 1719. Despite his unorthodox background, Ligonier's exceptional qualities gained him royal favour and steady advancement. In 1739 he was promoted to major general. The War of the AUSTRIAN SUCCESSION once again saw Ligonier in action at DETTINGEN and FONTENOY. As general of Horse, Ligonier commanded the cavalry at the battle of Laffeldt in 1747: he was captured leading a crucial charge, but was received courteously by Louis XV and released on parole.

In the autumn of 1757, following the duke of CUMBERLAND's resignation as captain general, Ligonier was made commander in chief in England and soon after promoted to the rank of field marshal. During the Seven Years War, Ligonier played a vital role that went far beyond military administration – he not only recommended promising officers for key commands, but participated in formulating the strategy by which the ministry of William PITT THE ELDER achieved a stunning global victory over Britain's Bourbon rivals. Fresh honours followed: he became a baron in 1763 and was raised to an earldom three years later. To the scandal of society, Ligonier conducted his personal life with a vigour equalling that displayed throughout his professional career. A bachelor, the ageing Ligonier continued to enjoy the company of youthful actresses and singers; at one point he simultaneously kept four mistresses with a combined age of just 58 years. He died, aged 89, on his estate at Ripley, Surrey, and is commemorated by a monument in Westminster Abbey.

FURTHER READING R. Whitworth, *Field Marshal Lord Ligonier: A Story of the British Army, 1702–1770* (1958).

literacy. It is difficult to ascertain the degree of literacy at any time, partly because the term is hard to define. Strictly speaking, in the 18th century illiteracy meant an inability to read Greek, or at least Latin. Today it means not being able to read at all, though its opposite, literacy, can span a wide spectrum from an ability to read a tabloid newspaper to comprehending abstruse articles in learned journals. Whereas such skills can today be tested and their distribution through society rendered statistically, this is impossible for the 18th century.

The only literacy test available from that period is the ability to write one's signature. This in itself begs many methodological questions. Did people learn to sign their names to avoid the stigma of marking a sign? Apparently not, since there appears to have been no prejudice against those who could not sign their names. On the other hand to sign a name does not in itself indicate an ability to read. However, it seems that people were taught to read before they were taught to write, so that most historians accept signatures as an underestimate of literacy levels at the time.

The most widespread use of signatures was brought about by the registration of marriages made compulsory by HARDWICKE's MARRIAGE ACT of 1753. It is assumed for the purposes of measuring literacy that those who could sign the registers were literate while those who could only make a mark were not. Around 1760 about 60% of women were unable to sign marriage registers compared with about 40% of men, indicating that more men than women were literate. By this test the gentry, business and professional men at the apex of society were almost all literate. Most tradesmen and craftsmen could apparently read, while the majority of labourers and servants could not. Even at the lowest levels of society, however, there was a substantial minority, around 41%, which was literate.

Geographical distributions of literacy varied enormously from region to region, and even from parish to parish within a region. By and large, urban areas were more literate than rural, while in London possibly a majority of the population could read. London was then the most literate centre in the kingdom: for example, in the late 18th century three-quarters of the children in the parish school of Islington were recorded as being able to read, with little difference between the sexes. By then it is a moot point how far levels of literacy had been sustained, especially in provincial towns. Some historians contend that they continued to rise, especially as an increasingly complex economy came to demand a more literate workforce. Others maintain that it was precisely the industrializing towns that bore the brunt of the population increase of the decades after 1780, and that the provision of education proved inadequate to cope, so that urban literacy levels were actually falling at the end of the century.

SEE ALSO EDUCATION.

Liverpool, port of northwest England. A growing share of Britain's Atlantic trade and close proximity to Lancashire's textile industry underpinned the dramatic growth of 18th-century Liverpool. The port's transformation from a modest harbour to booming international entrepôt was facilitated by an ambitious programme of dock construction: in 1710 the conversion of the original 'Pool' into the Old Dock was followed by a swathe of dockland developments along the north bank of the river Mersey. By mid-century Liverpool had already begun to eclipse BRISTOL, its great rival in the Atlantic SLAVE TRADE. In 1773 Liverpool was described as the 'emporium of the Western World'. Liverpool's eventual triumph over Bristol owed much to the diversity of its trade: the commercial development of Cheshire rock salt from the late 17th century provided Liverpool with a primary product for export alongside manufactured goods from its industrial hinterland.

In a century when urban expansion was most obvious in new manufacturing centres, Georgian Liverpool provides an example of an incorporated 'old' town that nonetheless experienced dramatic growth. In 1700 the population numbered at most 7000; by 1750 it had reached 22,000. During the closing decades of the century the pace of population growth rocketed, so that by the 1801 census it had soared to 83,000, making Liverpool England's second largest provincial town. Despite this rapid increase 18th-century Liverpool remained a compact and overcrowded town. As Dr Currie noted in his *Medical Reports* of 1797, its teeming tenements, cellars and 'back houses' provided a breeding ground for typhus. Like any thriving seaport Liverpool acquired a lively atmosphere and seedy flavour. In 1800 one guide complained about the numerous prostitutes strolling its streets; such women also filled 'infamous brothels' that provided 'a height of wantonness, unknown to any period'. Liverpool's Anglican, pro-slavery elite was Tory in sympathy; it delighted in returning CANNING to Parliament in 1812.

Liverpool, Robert Banks Jenkinson, 2nd earl of (1770–1828), politician; prime minister (1812–27). Jenkinson was educated at Charterhouse and Christ Church, Oxford. He then went on the GRAND TOUR, witnessing the fall of the Bastille on 14 July 1789. The following year, before he returned to England, he was found a seat in Parliament even though he was still under 21. His father, who was first president of the newly reconstituted Board of Trade in 1786, had sufficient influence with Sir John Lowther to persuade that borough-monger to nominate him for Appleby.

Jenkinson impressed PITT THE YOUNGER so much with his speeches, especially on foreign affairs, that the prime minister put him on the BOARD OF CONTROL for India in 1793.

In 1801 Jenkinson did not leave office with Pitt, but instead accepted the foreign secretaryship from ADDINGTON. He was promoted to the peerage in 1803 as Baron Hawkesbury. Pitt bore him no grudge, making him home secretary when he formed a ministry again in 1804. On Pitt's death he did not hold office in the MINISTRY OF ALL THE TALENTS, the only break in his ministerial career between 1793 and his resignation as prime minister in 1827 following a stroke. Thus he became home secretary again in PORTLAND's ministry, a post that he held with the leadership of the House of Lords. On the death of his father in 1808 he inherited the title of earl of Liverpool. The following year he became secretary for war in PERCEVAL's administration. On the assassination of Perceval in 1812 he became prime minister, a position he held for the next 15 years.

FURTHER READING N. Gash, *Lord Liverpool* (1984).

Locke, John (1632–1704), philosopher and political theorist. Locke was educated at Oxford, where he became a student (fellow) of Christ Church. In the early 1660s he taught Greek, rhetoric and moral philosophy. Later he studied medicine, and in 1667 he entered the household of the 1st earl of Shaftesbury as his physician. He then became Shaftesbury's private secretary, and in 1669 helped to draft the constitution of Carolina, of which his patron was a proprietor. When Shaftesbury became lord chancellor in 1672 Locke was appointed secretary to the Lords of Trade. His term of office lasted little longer than Shaftesbury's tenure of the chancellorship, which ended in 1673. Locke visited France from 1676 to 1679, largely for his health.

Locke was closely associated with Shaftesbury during the Exclusion crisis. The first version of his famous *Treatises of Government*, though they were not published until 1690, circulated in manuscript

as an Exclusionist tract. Consequently he was exposed along with Shaftesbury to the backlash of the Tory reaction, and when his patron fled to Holland in 1682 Locke followed shortly afterwards. While he was in the Netherlands he was deprived of his studentship at Christ Church. During his stay he wrote two of his most famous works, the *Letter on Toleration* and the *Essay on Human Understanding*, though they too were not published until 1690 after his return to England. He returned in 1689, and took an active part in affairs of state. Thus he was made commissioner of appeals in 1689, influenced the RECOINAGE OF 1696, and became a member of the newly constituted BOARD OF TRADE in 1696. In the 1690s he published *Some Thoughts concerning Education* (1693) and *The Reasonableness of Christianity* (1695). He died in 1704 at Otes in Essex, the house of Sir Francis Masham, where he had lived since 1691.

The nature and influence of Locke's political thought has been much disputed. At one time his *Two Treatises of Government* were held to have 'supplied the Whigs with their political philosophy for the next century'. More recently they have been dismissed as having been too radical for mainstream Whiggery, and not to have been absorbed into it until well into the 18th century. The dispute involves a close reading of the *Treatises*. They start out with very radical premises, such as the labour theory of value and the right not to obey laws to which one has not consented. But they reach relatively conservative conclusions. Thus agreement to use money implies acceptance of an uneven distribution of wealth, while residence in a country implies consent to its laws. The radical premises were certainly at odds with most Whig political theory at the time, which rather stressed the historical argument that the English constitution was one of limited or mixed monarchy, and that the Stuarts had arrogated to the crown unconstitutional prerogatives. Locke leapt out of history to argue that men set up government as a trust to protect them from the inconveniences of a state of nature. Government was intended to secure the 'natural rights' of life, liberty and property. If the ruler violated the trust he forfeited the government, and men were free to choose another to rule in his stead. It was this argument that Locke employed – against the divine-right theories of Sir Robert Filmer (set out in *Patriarcha*, 1680) and the absolutist conclusions of Thomas Hobbes (set out in *Leviathan*, 1651) – to justify the exclusion of James from the throne. Hobbes maintained that government came about as a result of a contract between subjects to obey their ruler, who was not a party to the contract. In Locke's view the contract was a 'fiduciary' trust, to which the ruler was also a party. Locke argued that ultimately men had the right to resist their ruler. It has been claimed that this was a revolutionary doctrine from which the Whigs shrank at the time of the GLORIOUS REVOLUTION. But it was certainly not too radical a notion for the Whigs who used it at the trial of Dr SACHEVERELL in 1710 to justify resistance during the Revolution. The notion that government existed to uphold liberty and property became a commonplace of 18th-century Whiggism, even if the Whigs under Walpole were more inclined to stress property than liberty.

Locke's religious ideas were rather more radical. In developing them he moved from the strict ERASTIANISM he upheld as a young Oxford don to a more liberal view expressed in his *Letter on Toleration*, and the even more liberal position found in *The Reasonableness of Christianity*, which – despite its title – was taken as a defence of DEISM.

Perhaps Locke's most enduring contribution was his *Essay on Human Understanding*. In it he argued that at birth the mind is a blank sheet lacking any innate ideas. Rather like a computer it was programmed to use reason to process data input from experience by the five senses. This processing, or ratiocination, results in understanding. Although the theory was much criticized – especially by churchmen who defended the concept of innate ideas – it was widely adopted.

SEE ALSO EDUCATION.

FURTHER READING M. Cranston, *John Locke: A Biography* (1957); J. Yolton, *John Locke: An Introduction* (1985).

London. The London that rose again from the ashes of the Great Fire of 1666 was poised upon the brink of dramatic expansion. A population of some 500,000 in 1700 had already topped the million mark by 1810, becoming the biggest city in the world. At the end of the 18th century the built-up zone extended over twice the area covered at the accession of Queen Anne, ranging far beyond the old cities of London and Westminster. London's phenomenal growth was fuelled by steady immigration from the countryside, and this increase continued despite a heavy mortality stemming from poor sanitation, cheap gin and such epidemic diseases as smallpox and typhus.

Some observers were disturbed by the remorseless growth of the metropolis. To Daniel DEFOE, London was 'the monstrous city'; writing a century later, William COBBETT compared London to a 'great wen' disfiguring the face of the land. Yet the same dynamism that so disturbed London's critics represented the very essence of its attraction for others. Foreigners marvelled at the frantic bustle of the capital's crowded streets. For a man with money, and the leisure to enjoy it, London did indeed provide a playground unrivalled in Europe: COFFEE HOUSES, taverns, inns, brothels (*see* PROSTITUTION), THEATRES, and pleasure gardens such as VAUXHALL GARDENS and RANELAGH GARDENS guaranteed an endless variety of stimulation for mind and body alike. As Dr JOHNSON famously observed: 'He who is tired of London is tired of life.'

The decades after the Great Fire saw a major church-building programme. Architects like Nicholas HAWKSMOOR received commissions from Parliament in 1711, instigating a wave of building that lasted into the 1730s. In the course of the century dissenting congregations also built many chapels of their own.

The burgeoning capital functioned as both major consumer and central distribution point for domestic and foreign goods. London was the prime marketplace for British agriculture: livestock from as far afield as the uplands of Scotland and Wales were driven to Smithfield, while fruit and vegetables converged upon Covent Garden. As Britain's leading port, London handled the trade of an expanding empire. By 1800 London had eclipsed Amsterdam as the world's foremost financial centre, while the City's merchants and bankers acquired wealth and political influence. Throughout the century London's maritime trade grew steadily, necessitating the development of purpose-built docks downstream from the Tower. With the Atlantic trade dominated by west-coast ports such as BRISTOL and LIVERPOOL, London concentrated upon the import of goods from Europe and the east, supplemented by a booming domestic coastal traffic in coal.

The emergence of coal as the chief fuel obliged Georgian Londoners to live under a pall of smoke that anticipated the smog of Dickens's day. Such environmental factors prompted an exodus of many wealthier citizens from London's medieval heart. In 1700 each parish had numbered inhabitants of all classes, but a century later the process of social segregation was well advanced. In 1763 James BOSWELL could already observe that 'One end of London is like a different country from the other in look and manners.' While the rich relocated among the fashionable new squares and terraces of the West End, and the 'middling' classes built homes in outlying areas such as Blackheath, Putney and Kew, the poor crammed into the vacated districts on the fringes of the old City. The teeming East End 'rookeries' provided a haven for London's criminal underworld and hosted scenes of squalor and hopelessness typified by HOGARTH's grim engraving of *Gin Lane* in St Giles. Although, by 1815, measures had been taken to improve policing, street lighting and sanitation, the housing of the capital's poor remained appalling: in the mid-Victorian era, the etchings of Gustave Doré portrayed slums as bleak as those of Hogarth's day.

FURTHER READING M.D. George, *London Life in the Eighteenth Century* (1966); G. Rudé, *Hanoverian London* (1971).

longitude, the measurement of position on the earth's surface east or west of the Greenwich meridian. The rapidly increasing volume of British shipping in the early 18th century heightened the demand for an accurate method of ascertaining a vessel's longitude at sea.

In 1713 an act of Parliament established a Board of Longitude, and also offered a reward of £20,000 for the inventor of a method of determining longitude to within 30 nautical miles. Navigators had long appreciated that longitude could be gauged from a clock that was sufficiently accurate to keep the time of the port of departure throughout a lengthy voyage. It required the remarkable talents of the humble Yorkshire carpenter John Harrison (1693–1776) to create such a timepiece.

Although poorly educated, Harrison had a genius for machinery. In 1715 he produced a clock constructed entirely from wood, and subsequently developed a system capable of compensating for the effect of temperature changes upon timekeeping devices. Hearing of the longitude prize, in 1728 Harrison journeyed to London and showed the instrument maker George Graham the design of his proposed chronometer. 'Longitude Harrison' completed this prototype in 1735. In the following year he was permitted to test the device on a voyage to Lisbon, and used it to correct a serious error in the ship's navigation. Interested but unconvinced, the Board granted Harrison an advance of £500 towards his continuing researches. Over the coming three decades Harrison waged a determined struggle to perfect his chronometer and to persuade a sceptical Board of its merits. Harrison's task was hampered by the prejudices of those influential men who believed that longitude could be best established from the consultation of lunar tables; such opponents included the future astronomer royal Nevil Maskelyne.

Between 1739 and 1759 Harrison constructed three further chronometers, each more accurate and compact that the last. The third of these won him the Royal Society's Copley Medal, and the fourth lost less than two minutes when it was tested by Harrison's son William on a return voyage from Portsmouth to Jamaica. Although this amounted to a discrepancy of just 18 nautical miles, the Board of Longitude refused to award Harrison his prize. The frustrated Harrison petitioned Parliament for redress, but the Board continued to demand further proofs of his design's practicability: this was amply demonstrated when a copy of Harrison's latest watch accompanied Captain James COOK on his epic three-year circumnavigation.

It was only in 1773, after lengthy tests upon a fifth watch secured the personal intervention of GEORGE III, that Harrison was finally granted the remaining balance of the award he had worked so long to obtain. Harrison's chronometers represented a remarkable advance upon previous methods of establishing longitude and offered a far more practical solution than the complex mathematical calculations championed by his rival Maskelyne. However, his chronometers remained costly to produce, and it was many years before improvements in manufacturing techniques permitted their general issue.

FURTHER READING D. Sobel, *Longitude* (1995).

Lords, House of, the upper house of Parliament. The House of Lords played a vital role in Parliament throughout the 'long' 18th century, from debates in the CONVENTION PARLIAMENT in 1689 to the passage of the first Reform Bill in 1832. Adverse votes in the upper house brought down the Fox–North coalition in 1783 even though it had a majority in the lower house. Some historians have been led to argue that it was more important than the lower house, the House of COMMONS, during those years, but this claim goes too far. Both in the Convention and in the Reform parliaments the will of the Commons prevailed in the end. After the REVOLUTION SETTLEMENT,

'supply', i.e. taxation, became the most important reason why the executive had to convene the legislature every year, and the convention had already been established that money bills could only be initiated in the lower house. The peers could not alter or amend them, merely pass or reject them. Hence the resort to 'tacking' on to money bills such measures as the resumption of crown grants in Ireland in 1699 and the bill against occasional conformity in 1704 (*see* OCCASIONAL CONFORMITY ACT). The Lords were so incensed by such tactics that they resolved in 1701 not to pass supply bills in which irrelevant clauses had been inserted with the intention of exploiting the inability of the Lords to amend them.

Nevertheless the prestige of a peerage meant that many commoners sought promotion to the upper house. Most ministers throughout the period were noblemen either through inheritance of a title or through ennoblement. Sir Robert WALPOLE broke with tradition by remaining in the Commons throughout his premiership, and he was not promoted to the peerage as earl of Orford until his fall in 1742. His precedent was followed by Henry PELHAM, the elder PITT, Lord NORTH and PITT THE YOUNGER. But other prime ministers of the 18th and 19th centuries sat in the Lords. The 3rd earl of SUNDERLAND was apparently the first leader of the House of Lords in the reign of George I. Thereafter the task of managing the government's business in the upper house was undertaken by a recognized leader. By the late 18th century the position of leader of the Lords usually went to the home secretary whenever that post was held by a peer or to the prime minister if the home secretary was an MP.

Court control of the Lords was relatively easier than of the Commons. For one thing it was a smaller chamber, there being only 200 hereditary peers on average summoned to it, compared with over 500 MPs, until the ministry of the younger Pitt when the number of ennoblements increased quite markedly. Even then the addition of 100 Irish MPs after the UNION OF BRITAIN AND IRELAND kept the Commons twice the size of the Lords. Another reason why the upper house was vulnerable to the court was that new creations could always be made, or threatened, whenever it challenged the ministry. Queen Anne made twelve Tories peers in 1712 to offset a Whig majority that had rejected the ministry's peace proposals.

Under George I there was an attempt to fix a ceiling on the number of peers to prevent the monarch using the same tactic again. Earl STAN-HOPE introduced a Peerage Bill into Parliament in 1719 designed to prevent any addition to the number of Lords once the king had created six new English peers, and the terms of the Act of Union had been altered so that the Scottish nobility, instead of choosing 16 of their number, were to be represented by 25 hereditary nobles (*see* UNION OF ENGLAND AND SCOTLAND). Thereafter the monarch's prerogative of making peers was to be restricted to filling vacancies created by lines becoming extinct. Stanhope's motive was to preserve a permanent majority for his ministry in the Lords even when the prince of Wales, who was then in opposition to it, became king. The bill caused an uproar. The opposition in the Commons, led by Walpole, who was temporarily out of office, appealed to the dreams of country gentlemen who entertained hopes of their families being raised to the peerage. Since the bill blasted all such hopes, the backbenchers in the lower house were roused to oppose it, and it was defeated by the decisive majority of 269 to 177.

Nevertheless until the late 18th century the Hanoverians by and large used their prerogative of ennoblement sparingly, confining it largely to the replacement of extinctions, as the bill had proposed. This helped to preserve the nobility as a separate estate of the realm, and even strengthened its prestige almost as a caste in Hanoverian Britain.

SEE ALSO ARISTOCRACY.

FURTHER READING C. Jones (ed.), *A Pillar of the Constitution: The House of Lords in British Politics, 1640–1784* (1989).

low church, term that came into popular usage at the time of the CONVOCATION CONTROVERSY to distinguish the minority of inferior clergymen and majority of bishops in the CHURCH OF ENGLAND who opposed the HIGH CHURCH party's policy of suppressing dissent. For their pains they were described by Dr SACHEVERELL as 'false brethren' who sought to undermine the Church of England by rapprochement with DISSENTERS. But while they sympathized with dissent they remained staunch Anglicans. They maintained that the best way to deal with the threat of nonconformity was not to persecute those who would not conform to the established church, but to set them an example of tolerance and piety. Although in the short term dissent seemed to thrive, in fact the low-church approach was vindicated. For after the accession of the house of Hanover removed the high-church party from its dominant position, and the low-church approach was officially sanctioned, old dissent did go into decline. In the later 18th and 19th centuries the term was applied to those Anglicans who were sympathetic to the EVANGELICAL REVIVAL.

Luddites, machine-breaking rioters active in the Midlands and the North of England between 1811 and 1816. Their activities reflected the resistance of different groups of textile workers to changes within their industries. Although the term 'Luddite' has frequently been employed to indicate a blinkered opposition to industrial progress, such men were not concerned with the indiscriminate destruction of new machinery. In an era in which trade unions were illegal under the COMBINATION ACTS, the deliberate wrecking of machines was instead employed in an effort to coerce employers who refused to heed the arguments of their workers. Named after 'General Ned Ludd' – the mythical leader of the disgruntled Nottingham framework knitters – the Luddites took action against a background of economic hardship resulting from a succession of poor harvests and a breakdown of international trade during the long REVOLUTIONARY AND NAPOLEONIC WARS.

Luddism was centred upon three regions and industries: it originated in the east Midlands, where discontent drew upon long-standing concerns over conditions in the hosiery trade. It subsequently spread to the south Lancashire cotton region, where anger was directed at steam-powered looms, and to West Yorkshire's woollen industry, whose artisans objected to the 'de-skilling' embodied by shearing frames and gig mills. Luddite 'direct action' was often implemented by groups of men wielding hammers and disguised under blackened faces, masks and women's clothing. Recourse to such methods only followed lengthy campaigns to secure objectives through more peaceful means.

Such 'collective bargaining by riot' sought to maintain the status quo. In this respect the activities of the Luddites conformed to patterns of behaviour typically associated with 18th-century crowds (*see* MOB). More controversial is the extent to which the objectives of Luddism went beyond the settlement of industrial disputes to embrace an underground movement with a truly 'revolutionary' agenda. The government's efforts to tackle Luddism were hampered by the secrecy shrouding the activities of the machine-breakers. That same factor has complicated the task of historians who have attempted to establish the motivation of its adherents. Luddism was never a uniform 'movement', and no concerted uprising against the state took place; in addition, evidence of revolutionary conspiracy rests largely upon the testimony of paid informers who often provided exaggerated reports to justify their continued employment.

However, Luddism prompted a stern reaction from the wartime government of Spencer PERCEVAL. In February 1812 legislation was passed that made frame-breaking a hanging crime, whilst government spies and informers sought to infiltrate the Luddite ranks. Most dramatically, no fewer than 12,000 troops were sent to bring the affected regions to heel: this force was *not*, as is often stated, larger than that at Wellington's disposal in Spain, but its deployment on internal security duties at a crucial phase of the PENINSULAR WAR nonetheless indicates the seriousness with which the authorities viewed the Luddite upheavals. Despite the resources devoted to their eradication, the government experienced considerable difficulty in countering the Luddites: groups targeted mills under cover of darkness, then melted back into their own communities. Luddism took a particularly violent turn in Yorkshire: a 200-strong mob attacked William Cartwright's mill at Rawfolds, and was eventually repulsed by musketry that left two of its members mortally wounded. In April 1812 the assassination of the mill owner William Horsfall – who had allegedly bragged that he would ride 'up to his saddle girths in Luddite blood' – led to an intensification of government activity that eventually secured the arrest of Luddite ringleaders. In January 1813, following special assizes at York that tried 64 people, 17 men were executed and others sentenced to TRANSPORTATION. The Luddite 'crisis' was over, although associated disturbances continued into 1816.

FURTHER READING J. Stevenson, *Popular Disturbances in England, 1700–1800* (1979); M.I. Thomis, *The Luddites* (1970).

Lunar Society, informal organization for the promotion of science and its application to industry. The society was established in Birmingham in 1775, and was so called because it held its meetings monthly at the time of the full moon. Among its distinguished members were the engineers Matthew BOULTON and James WATT, the physician Erasmus DARWIN, the chemist James Keir, the polymath Joseph PRIESTLEY and the pottery manufacturer Josiah WEDGWOOD.

luxury. A central theme in the political discourse of the first half of the 18th century was the notion that a rising standard of living was undermining the country's morals and capacity to wage effective war. It was a major thrust in the propaganda of the societies for the reformation of manners after the Glorious Revolution of 1688. Bernard

MANDEVILLE refuted it in his *Fable of the Bees*, arguing that on the contrary an expanding economy strengthened the sinews of war. But his was a lone voice, most commentators bewailing the demands by consumers of all ranks, especially women, for luxury goods. The idea informed much literature, particularly the novels of SMOLLETT, above all *Humphrey Clinker*. It was linked to the notion that consumer demand led to excessive imports from such countries as France and Italy. This got caught up in patriotic appeals to renounce French goods raised by, for example, HOGARTH.

The climax of the campaign against luxury came in 1757 with the publication of John Brown's *Estimate of the Manners and Principles of the Times*. Brown asserted that England had become so effeminate through the pursuit of luxury that it was incapable of resisting French aggression. The early stages of the SEVEN YEARS WAR seemed to bear out this view, but the ultimate triumph of Britain over France in the conflict made it seem absurd. Thereafter, though denunciation of luxury never disappeared, the idea became peripheral to the economic debate, which took another turn after the publication of Adam SMITH's *Wealth of Nations* in 1776.

FURTHER READING J. Sekora, *Luxury* (1980).

Lyttelton, George (1709–73), Whig 'patriot' politician, writer and patron. Lyttelton entered Parliament in 1735, becoming one of COBHAM's CUBS. When FREDERICK PRINCE OF WALES went into opposition to the ministry of Sir Robert WAL-POLE in 1737 Lyttelton became his secretary and one of the leaders of the 'patriots' associated with the prince. He was made a lord of the Treasury in PELHAM'S BROAD-BOTTOM ADMINISTRATION in 1744, for which he was dismissed by Frederick. After Pelham's death, Lyttelton became chancellor of the exchequer under NEWCASTLE. His ineptitude with figures made this an uncongenial post and he resigned it in 1756 when he was raised to the peerage as first Baron Lyttelton. He never held office again.

Horace WALPOLE caustically observed of Lyttelton's appointment as chancellor that 'they turned an absent poet to the management of the revenue'. For though he made trenchant contributions to debates in both Houses of Parliament, his forte was writing for the press. His first known journalism was for the opposition paper *Common Sense*, though he may have contributed to the *Craftsman* too. His own most celebrated work was *Letters from a Persian in England to his friend at Ispahan*, which appeared in 1735. He was the patron of a coterie of 'patriot poets' including Richard Glover and James THOMSON. He also attracted encomiums from POPE and from Henry FIELDING, who dedicated his novel *Tom Jones* to Lyttelton. His country seat at Hagley in Worcestershire underwent considerable change during his lifetime, with many improvements in building and LANDSCAPE GARDENING, including the first Doric temple to be constructed on an English estate. This set an example which was followed by many other landowners in the 18th century.

M

Macaulay, Catharine (1731–91), historian. She was the daughter of John Sawbridge, a radical who had her privately educated. In 1760 she married George Macaulay, a Scottish physician who died in 1766. The first volume of eight on *The History of England from the Accession of James I to that of the Brunswick line* appeared in 1763. Volumes two to five followed at steady intervals between 1766 and 1771. There was then a hiatus for a decade, when she brought out the remaining three volumes between 1781 and 1783.

Although biased against the Stuarts, Macaulay's *History* was not a Whig history, for she was also critical of the opponents of the Stuarts. Thus she condemned the Revolution of 1688 as not being particularly 'Glorious', since a golden opportunity to extend the franchise and to give dissenters full citizenship had been missed. This attack on the conventional wisdom made her many opponents. Much of the hostile comment was openly sexist in nature. She also had her admirers, including Thomas Wilson, rector of St Stephen's, Walbrook, who in 1777 gave her free residence of a house at Bath. There she completed her *History of England from the Revolution to the Present* (1778), which again was highly critical of William III and the Whigs. Wilson also had a statue of her placed within the altar rails of his church, with her arm leaning on volumes of her *History*. It was removed in 1778, however, when she married William Graham, a man who was her junior by 26 years. In 1784 she showed her sympathy for the American cause by visiting the United States, where she met George Washington. Her last work was a reply to BURKE's *Reflections on the Revolution in France*. Mary WOLLSTONECRAFT observed of her that she was 'the woman of the greatest abilities that this country has ever produced'.

FURTHER READING B. Hill, *The Republican Virago: The Life and Times of Catharine Macaulay, Historian* (1992).

Macaulay, Zachary (1768–1838), colonial administrator and campaigner against the SLAVE TRADE. Macaulay was governor of Sierra Leone from 1791 to 1799 and then secretary of the Sierra Leone Company until 1808, when the African territory became a crown colony. After his return to England he settled down in Clapham and became prominent among the so-called CLAPHAM SECT of evangelicals. Thus from 1802 to 1816 he edited the *Christian Observer*, which promulgated their views. Besides being active in the campaign to abolish the slave trade and slavery, the Clapham sect were also involved in the SUNDAY SCHOOL movement, educational projects generally and the Society for the Suppression of Vice. In 1807, following the suppression of the slave trade, Macaulay became secretary of the African Institute, and sat on its committee until its dissolution in 1834 after the abolition of slavery in the British empire.

MacDonald, Flora (1722–90), rescuer of the Young Pretender, Charles Edward STUART, in the aftermath of the failed '45 JACOBITE RISING. The resourceful heroine of JACOBITE legend was born on the island of South Uist. Her father died when she was a child, and she was raised by her stepfather and the clan chief Clanranald, who gave her a sound education in Edinburgh. During the early summer of 1746, when the hunt for the fugitive Prince Charles was at its height, Flora was visiting her birthplace. Charles was then hiding on the island, and his guide, Neil MacEachain, appealed for help from Flora's stepfather Captain Hugh MacDonald. Despite his official position as commander of the government militia on South Uist, MacDonald was an ardent Jacobite who had no intention of surrendering his prince. Impressed by the captain's intelligent and resourceful stepdaughter, MacEachain lost no time in proposing a plan whereby she would smuggle the prince to Skye, disguised as her maid.

Flora at first refused any involvement with the risky scheme. However, she was persuaded to meet the prince, and, moved by Charles's fortitude in adversity, she rapidly changed her mind. Flora obtained a passport from her stepfather, covering herself, her 'manservant' MacEachain and an Irish maid, 'Betty Burke'; the latter role was assumed by the prince, who laughingly concealed his gangling frame and red hair beneath a print dress, apron and frilled cap. On the evening of 28 June they were rowed across to Skye; although fired upon by government troops they eventually landed safely. With the aid of Lady Margaret MacDonald the prince was concealed, and, after seeing him embark for Raasay, Flora quietly returned home.

Within weeks Flora was arrested and sent to London to share the confinement of other Jacobites who had connived in the dramatic escape of 'Bonnie Prince Charlie'. Flora was already a celebrity: her portrait, suitably bedecked in a tartan dress flaunting white Stuart cockades, was painted by Richard WILSON. She was released at the general amnesty of 1747. A modest and dignified woman, Flora impressed Dr JOHNSON when he met her on his famous tour of the Western Isles in 1773. In the following year Flora and her husband Allan MacDonald emigrated to North Carolina. During the AMERICAN WAR OF INDEPENDENCE both proved loyal to King George III. They later returned to Skye, where Flora died in 1790, having lived long enough to witness the romanticization of the Jacobite cause.

Mackenzie, Henry (1745–1831), essayist, playwright and sentimental novelist. He was born in Edinburgh and attended the university there. He was articled to a lawyer and started a legal practice, becoming a crown attorney. In 1771 he published, anonymously, his first and greatest novel, *The Man of Feeling*. Its hero, Harley, reacts to a series of affecting incidents with excessive SENSIBILITY. He wrote two more novels, neither of them creating as great a stir as the first, and four plays, none of which was successful. Mackenzie was a member of a club of Edinburgh advocates which launched a periodical, *The Mirror*, based on the *SPECTATOR* (Sir Walter Scott was to call him 'the Northern Addison'). It appeared between January 1779 and May 1780, 42 of its 110 papers being written by Mackenzie. Another periodical – *The Lounger* – was published between 1785 and 1787, to which he contributed over half the numbers. He was a founding member of the Royal Society of Scotland, to which he read a paper on the German theatre in April 1788. Mackenzie also wrote tracts defending the ministry of the younger PITT for which he obtained the Comptrollership of Taxes in Scotland in 1804, thanks to the patronage of his friend Henry DUNDAS. He convened and chaired a committee to investigate the authenticity of James MACPHERSON's *Ossian*, which concluded in 1805 that Macpherson had embroidered what was originally genuine Gaelic verse.

Macpherson, James (1736–96), Scottish poet and historian. Macpherson attended both Aberdeen and Edinburgh universities, although he took no degree at either. His early efforts at poetry were unsuccessful, but in 1760 he published *Fragments of Ancient Poetry collected in the Highlands of Scotland, and translated from the Gaelic or Erse language*. These had impressed Hugh Blair of Edinburgh University so much in manuscript that he contributed a preface to the collection. Blair also raised money for Macpherson to visit the Highlands to collect more Gaelic verse. This resulted in *Fingal*, which purported to be an epic by a 3rd-century poet, Ossian. It recounted how Fingal, 'king of those Caledonians who inhabited the west coast of Scotland', went to help the king of Ireland resist an invasion by Swaran from Scandinavia.

Fingal was greeted with enthusiasm at the time, only a few expressing scepticism about its authenticity. However, the appearance in 1763 of a volume including *Temora* and other poems did arouse suspicion. This was partly due to the dedication to 'the earl of Bute, in obedience to whose commands they were translated from the original Gaelic of Ossian the son of Fingal'. Macpherson began to be widely suspected, at least in England, of counterfeiting Gaelic poetry. In Scotland he was stoutly defended as the rediscoverer of ancient verses recording the mythical origins of the nation. Among the English sceptics was Dr JOHNSON, who made no bones about calling Macpherson a liar. Among Macpherson's Scottish defenders Blair continued to be his most ardent supporter. The debate really concerned the authenticity of Macpherson's sources. By and large the English insisted that these should be documentary, with original manuscript materials. Although Macpherson insisted that they existed, he did not help his case by not producing them, so that even David HUME was sceptical about their provenance. Blair and other Scottish men of letters, however, insisted that the poems had mainly descended by oral tradition from the bards of the ancient clans. It is now fairly well established that Macpherson collected some manuscripts for his fragments and for *Fingal*, if not for *Temora*. At the same time it is generally agreed that he embellished fragmentary survivals to produce whole epics.

Macpherson's Ossianic epics had a considerable impact in continental Europe, where their 'wild', pseudo-Gaelic qualities exercised a significant influence on the development of German and French Romanticism. German admirers of Ossian included writers of the stature of Herder, Schiller and Goethe, the last-named incorporating Ossianic passages translated into German into his proto-Romantic novella *The Sorrows of Young Werther* (1774).

The Ossian affair was not the only controversy associated with Macpherson. In 1775 he published a *History of Great Britain from the Restoration to the accession of the house of Hanover*, accompanied by *Original Papers concerning the History of Great Britain*. The *Original Papers* documented his claim in the *History* that many of the Whig statesmen of the reigns of William and Anne were corresponding with the exiled JACOBITE court at St Germain. They shocked readers, who had been brought up on the idea that the GLORIOUS REVOLUTION was the work of patriots, concerned only for the protection of English liberties against Stuart absolutism. Macpherson defended the NORTH ministry's American policies in print. Then around 1780 he became the London agent of the nabob of Arcot, as a result of which he ended his days a rich man.

FURTHER READING F.J. Stafford, *The Sublime Savage: A Study of James Macpheson and the Poems of Ossian* (1988).

Madras. *See* INDIA.

Malplaquet, battle of (11 September 1709), engagement near Mons in modern Belgium, the fourth and costliest of MARLBOROUGH's famous quartet of victories during the War of the SPANISH SUCCESSION.

The battle followed the breakdown of negotiations aimed at bringing the gruelling conflict to a close. In the late summer of 1709, Dutch, English and imperial forces under Marlborough and the Austrian Prince Eugène besieged Mons while a French army under Marshal the duc de Villars approached from the south. The allies proved reluctant to seek battle until reinforcements had arrived. Villars put the delay to good use, choosing a strong position flanked by woods and fortifying it with entrenchments.

Rather than manoeuvre around these formidable defences, the allies mounted a frontal assault. The French were eventually dislodged, but at an appalling cost: some 17,000 allies fell, compared with 11,000 French casualties. The Dutch contingent bore the brunt of the allied losses. Reporting the outcome to his wife Sarah, Marlborough conceded that the clash had proved 'a very bloody battle'. Another of the British commanders, General Lord Orkney, wrote to a friend that the corpses lay 'as thick as ever did a flock of sheep'. He added, 'I hope in God it may be the last battle I may ever see. God send us a good peace.' Although forced from their position, the French had retreated in good order, so denting Marlborough's reputation as the contemporary master of the battlefield. Villars became a national hero, and his stubborn defence restored the flagging morale of his countrymen. In England and the Netherlands by contrast, the heavy losses sustained for little apparent gain bolstered the cause of those who sought a compromise peace, and the English Whig politicians who still hoped for a decisive victory over the Bourbons now faced increasing opposition. Even Queen Anne asked, 'When will all this dreadful bloodshed cease?'

Malthus, Thomas (Robert) (1766–1834), clergyman and economist, noted for his theories on population growth. Malthus was educated at the Warrington Dissenting Academy and Jesus College, Cambridge, of which he became a fellow. In 1798 he published his *Essay on the Principle of Population as it affects the future improvement of society*. In it he argued that population was increasing geometrically while resources were only expanding arithmetically. It followed that its increase would be checked by famine and epidemics unless restraint on reproduction could be practised. This seemed to fly in the face of the biblical injunction to increase and multiply, and many critics condemned Malthus as being un-Christian, despite the fact that he was ordained. The criticisms, and further information received from travelling on the continent, led him to modify his views in a second edition of the *Essay* in 1803. In 1805 he was appointed by the East India Company to be professor of history and political economy at its newly established college in Haileybury. There he turned his attention to the less controversial problems of rent, publishing *The Nature and Progress of Rent* in 1815. He became a fellow of the Royal Society in 1819 and a founder member of the Statistical Society in 1834. His principles of population were applied in the Poor Law Amendment Act passed in 1834.

Manchester, city of northwest England. In the course of the 18th century Manchester emerged as Britain's largest provincial town. Its prominence stemmed from its location at the very hub of Lancashire's textile industry, for which it became both the commercial and manufacturing centre. By the end of the century the concentration of weavers and spinners there had established its role as 'the metropolis of manufactures'. As Dean Tucker observed in 1774, the efforts of such workers had made Manchester 'among the richest and most flourishing towns in the kingdom'. This wealth was not shared by all its inhabitants. In 1755 a magistrate reported that the streets swarmed with 'distressed objects of every kind'. Manchester's high birth rate was countered by heavy infant mortality, so that by 1773 half of all children born there died before their fifth birthday. In the face of such attrition, growth was sustained by immigration from Ireland. By 1801 the Manchester–Salford sprawl embraced a population of 89,000.

Despite its size Manchester remained without any members of Parliament until 1832. After the HANOVERIAN SUCCESSION the town had earned a reputation for disaffection towards the new regime. Alone of English towns it provided substantial support for Charles Edward STUART on his march south during the '45 JACOBITE RISING, and the men of the ill-fated Manchester Regiment subsequently faced the government's retribution after they were captured at Carlisle. As a major manufacturing centre Manchester was hard hit by the economic fluctuations resulting from wartime disruption of cotton supplies during the late 18th and early 19th centuries. The fastest-growing industrial town in the country, Manchester became a hotbed of radicalism. Manchester's involvement in radical protest reached a tragic climax in 1819 when overzealous yeomanry used their sabres to perpetrate the 'Peterloo massacre' upon a crowd of demonstrators.

Mandeville, Bernard (1670–1733), social commentator. Mandeville was a Dutch physician who settled in London. In 1705 he published a doggerel poem, 'The Grumbling Hive, or Knaves turned honest'. This he expanded with 'Remarks' into *The Fable of the Bees*, which first appeared in 1714. A third edition, enlarged with further materials including an 'Essay on Charity Schools', was presented in 1723 to the grand jury of Middlesex, who condemned it. The 'Essay' was regarded as particularly offensive because it attributed the motive of those who subscribed to charity schools not to their benevolence but to their pride and vanity. They were not motivated by the wish to educate poor children to pursue a life of virtue rather than of vice – which Mandeville denied the schools achieved anyway. They rather wished to see their names in the list of subscribers.

What provoked the animosity against Mandeville was his divorce of economics from ethics, summed up in his infamous subtitle 'private vices … public benefits'. Mandeville was more impressed by Thomas Hobbes's view of man as being driven by egoistic hedonism than by the 3rd earl of SHAFTESBURY's view of men as altruistic hedonists. The hedonistic pursuit of immediate self-advantage might be morally reprehensible, but it generated the wealth that had made Britain a great power. This offended upholders of traditional morality such as John WESLEY, who thought that the author had been rightly named 'Man-devil'. In fact these critics misread Mandeville's message. He filled in the dots between 'vices' and 'public' in his subtitle with the claim that vices such as pride could be turned into public benefits by the dexterous management of skilful politicians.

Mandeville went on to shock conventional moralists further with his *Modest Defence of Public Stews*, which he dedicated to the more zealous in their ranks, the societies for the reformation of manners. In it he claimed that brothels prevented the seduction or rape of virtuous ladies. But he drew a sharp distinction between vice and crime. Vice could be condoned, whereas crime was destructive of society. In his *Enquiry into the causes of the frequent executions at Tyburn* (1725) he therefore advocated that hanging should be made more of a deterrent than it was. The fact that they took place at Tyburn in a carnival atmosphere, with the felons frequently drunk, diminished their impact. If they were carried out in the privacy of the prison, with the convict allowed no alcohol, then they might truly deter.

FURTHER READING R. Cook, *Bernard Mandeville* (1974).

Manley, Dela (Mary Delariviere Manley) (1663–1724), author. Manley was the daughter of Sir Roger Manley, lieutenant governor of Jersey. He died in 1688 leaving her £200. About the same time she contracted a bigamous marriage to her cousin John Manley. After he deserted her she had a series of lovers, and made her living by writing. In the 1690s she wrote plays, and in the next decade turned to political satire. Her most notorious work was *Secret Memoirs and Manners of Several Persons of Quality, of both Sexes, from the New Atalantis*.

First published in 1709, it went through seven editions and a French translation. It was a thinly disguised exposé of prominent politicians, mostly Whigs, but including a vicious attack on the duke of MARLBOROUGH. Mrs Manley was tried before the court of Queen's Bench for seditious libel but discharged in 1710. When the Tories came to power that year she benefited from the change in government, and succeeded SWIFT as editor of *The Examiner* in 1711. She published several sequels to *The New Atalantis*, including *The Adventures of Rivella* in 1714.

Manners, John, marquess of Granby. *See* GRANBY, JOHN MANNERS, MARQUESS OF.

Mansfield, William Murray, 1st earl of
(1705–93), judge. Regarded by many as the greatest judge of the 18th century, Mansfield prosecuted on behalf of successive governments in some of the most celebrated trials of the era. A younger son of Lord Stormont, Murray was among those Scotsmen who thrived in London during the reign of George II. When Murray entered the House of Commons as member for Boroughbridge in 1742 he already enjoyed a formidable reputation as a lawyer, and was appointed solicitor general. In the wake of the failed '45 JACOBITE RISING, it was Murray who led the crown's case against his Jacobite countrymen charged with treason. A staunch allegiance to the government of the day was to prove characteristic of the remainder of Mansfield's lengthy legal career. Indeed, the anonymous scribe 'JUNIUS' dubbed Murray a 'political judge'; his tendentious judgments against John WILKES during the 1760s certainly cast him in the role of government enforcer rather than impartial judge.

Murray became attorney general in 1754. He was a skilled Parliamentarian; NEWCASTLE valued Murray's support in the Commons, and regretted his decision to become chief justice two years later. Murray was to sit on the King's Bench for more than three decades, and only resigned in 1788. During his career he was twice offered the office

of lord chancellor but refused on both occasions. He became an earl in 1776.

Although notoriously cautious, Murray remained ready to overturn precedent on a matter of principle: in 1772, during the SOMERSET CASE, he made the momentous ruling that slavery could not exist in Britain, as it was unrecognized in law. He was tolerant in religious affairs, and this stance led the anti-Catholic GORDON RIOTERS to burn down his London home in 1780. Under these circumstances, it was perhaps surprising that Lord Mansfield – as he now was – should be appointed to preside over the subsequent trial of the man believed to have instigated the destruction, Lord George Gordon. In terms of legal procedure, Mansfield's most important contribution was his reform of commercial law; expert juries were enlisted, and the speedier decisions that resulted drew increased business from the City. Despite his litigious calling, Mansfield was noted for his courteous and approachable manner.

FURTHER READING E. Heward, *Lord Mansfield* (1979).

Mar, John Erskine, 11th earl of (1675–1732),
leader of the 1715 JACOBITE RISING in Scotland. Although he had supported the UNION OF ENGLAND AND SCOTLAND in 1707 he was conspicuous among those Scottish peers in the House of Lords who in 1713 voted to hold a debate to consider its repeal. At the accession of George I he declared his allegiance to the house of Hanover, but then prepared to rise up in favour of the Old Pretender, James Francis Edward STUART. For these shifts in loyalty he became known as 'Bobbing John'.

Mar's leadership of the rebels in the '15 was marred by his lack of resolution. Although at Sheriffmuir he was not defeated by the government forces under the duke of ARGYLL, neither did he defeat them. The lack of a decisive victory decided his fate. Although the Pretender – 'James VIII' – landed in Scotland and made Mar a duke, their forces were compelled to retreat before Argyll's, which had been reinforced by Dutch troops. In

February 1716 James and Mar embarked for France. Mar spent the rest of his life on the continent, scheming to betray the Pretender to the British government.

Marlborough, John Churchill, 1st duke of

(1650–1722), British army commander, the victor of several notable battles in the War of the SPANISH SUCCESSION. Churchill entered the court of James duke of York as page of honour, and in 1667 received his first commission as an ensign in the Foot Guards. He was active both at court, where he had an affair with the duchess of Cleveland, and in the field, seeing action in Flanders and Tangiers. In 1678 his court gallantry ended when he fell in love with and married Sarah Jennings (the future duchess of MARLBOROUGH). Churchill accompanied the duke of York in his exiles on the continent and in Scotland during the Exclusion crisis, and was rewarded with a Scottish peerage. When James became king in 1685 he raised Churchill to the English peerage and made him a lord of the bedchamber. Lord Churchill took a leading part in the suppression of Monmouth's rebellion. Thereafter, however, he had scruples about James II's Catholic policies, and as a defender of Protestantism went over to the prince of Orange following his invasion.

After the Glorious Revolution WILLIAM III rewarded Churchill with the earldom of Marlborough. He took part in the conquest of Ireland, taking Cork and Kinsale from James's supporters. However, he became suspected of Jacobitism himself in 1692, and was dismissed from royal service. Through his wife he remained an intimate of Princess ANNE, who became next in line to the throne when her sister MARY died childless in 1694. Anne was reconciled with William and in 1698 brought about a reconciliation between the king and Marlborough. In 1701 William appointed Marlborough to be commander in chief of British forces in the Netherlands.

The following year when Anne succeeded to the throne she made Marlborough captain general of the armed forces, and elevated him to a dukedom. In this capacity he played a leading role in the Grand Alliance that fought Louis XIV in the War of the Spanish Succession. His spectacular victories at BLENHEIM in 1704, RAMILLIES in 1706, OUDENARDE in 1708 and MALPLAQUET in 1709 gave him the reputation of one of the greatest – if not the greatest – of all British generals. The first of these victories, which saved the Austrian Habsburgs from invasion by French and Bavarian troops, led to his being granted BLENHEIM PALACE by Parliament. The second secured the Spanish Netherlands for the Austrians.

Unfortunately for Marlborough he was unable to bring France to its knees, and in 1709 the peace terms that the allies tried to dictate to France seemed to confirm growing suspicions in England that he was prolonging the war for his own ends. The clause that required Louis XIV to help the allies prise his own grandson off the throne of Spain so that the Austrian claimant could replace him seemed particularly unreasonable. Marlborough's opponents used this to discredit him. His reaction, to try to get Anne to grant him the captain generalship for life, was even more counterproductive, apparently confirming his overweening ambition. His unpopularity swelled the war weariness that helped to overthrow the Whig government in 1710 and bring in a Tory ministry pledged to negotiate peace. Marlborough continued as captain general while the negotiations continued. But when the peace preliminaries were placed before Parliament in December 1711 he voted against them, and was consequently dismissed and disgraced by being accused of corruption.

In 1712 Marlborough went into exile on the continent, visiting the principality of Mindelheim that had been conferred upon him by the Holy Roman emperor. To add to his humiliation the territory was taken from him, although he kept the title. He also kept in close touch with the elector of Hanover, and when Anne died in 1714 he returned to England where the elector, now king GEORGE I, restored him to the captain generalship.

His public life was seriously affected by two strokes in 1716, and in his latter years he was virtually confined to Blenheim. Dr JOHNSON observed that 'from Marlborough's eyes the streams of dotage flow', and used this image as an illustration of 'the vanity of human wishes'. After a further stroke in 1722 he died and was buried in Westminster Abbey.

FURTHER READING C. Barnett, *Marlborough* (1974); W. Churchill, *Marlborough, his Life and Times* (2 vols., 1947).

Marlborough, Sarah Churchill, 1st duchess of (*née* Jennings) (1660–1744), wife of the 1st duke of MARLBOROUGH, and one of the most formidable women of the 18th century. According to SWIFT 'five furies reigned in her breast', and others likened her to an elemental force such as a volcano. Certainly she had a volcanic temperament, which could make strong men flinch and women quail.

Unlike her husband Sarah was a staunch Whig, and encouraged James II's daughter Princess ANNE – in whose service she was employed – to escape London and flee to Nottingham during the GLORIOUS REVOLUTION. She remained a confidante of the princess in the new reign, and when Anne quarrelled with her sister MARY she took the former's side. They corresponded in letters wherein they referred to each other by nicknames. Thus Marlborough and his wife were 'Mr and Mrs Freeman', while Anne's husband GEORGE PRINCE OF DENMARK and the princess herself were known as 'Mr and Mrs Morley'. Significantly WILLIAM III was called 'Caliban'.

When William died in 1702 Sarah came into her own at court, becoming mistress of the robes and keeper of the privy purse to the new queen. She used her privileged position to try to persuade Anne not to rely upon Tories but to appoint Whigs to office. This caused a strain between them, with the duke being caught between the two. Ultimately it led to Sarah being dismissed after a ferocious scene in 1710. But relations had broken down long

before that. It seems probable that they cooled as early as 1704, when the death of her only son led Sarah to withdraw from court for some time. The bereavement seems to have unbalanced her mind, and she never behaved civilly towards Anne thereafter. But it was the appointment of Abigail MASHAM – ironically at Sarah's suggestion – as bedchamber woman to the queen that caused an unbridgeable breach between them. For Abigail was a Tory, and she reinforced Anne's political prejudices in favour of that party. This led to a showdown in 1709 when Sarah connived at a scheme by some Whigs to pass an address in Parliament demanding Abigail's dismissal from the queen's service. Although wiser counsels prevailed, and the address was not moved, Anne never forgave Sarah and instead dismissed her at the earliest opportunity.

The duchess never exerted political influence again during Anne's reign. When her husband was dismissed she went with him into exile, and they did not return until after Anne's death. After the duke himself died in 1722 the rest of Sarah's life was spent in a series of bitter quarrels, in which she alienated almost her entire family, and in writing and rewriting justifications of her own conduct.

FURTHER READING F. Harris, *A Passion for Government: The Life of Sarah Duchess of Marlborough* (1991).

Marriage Act (1753). *See* HARDWICKE'S MARRIAGE ACT.

Mary II (1662–94), queen of England, Scotland and Ireland (1689–94), ruling jointly with her husband WILLIAM III. Mary was the eldest child of James duke of York, the future James II, by his first wife Anne Hyde. The question of her marriage partner was already being openly discussed when she was only eight years old. The death of her brother Edgar in 1671 made her second in the line of succession to the throne: in the absence of any legitimate children of her uncle Charles II,

Mary became heiress to the crown after her father James. The disposal of her hand thus became a crucial issue in British politics and European diplomacy.

From the start, the claims of William of Orange were pressed by Protestants. William visited England in the autumn of 1677, where his marriage to Mary was arranged between himself and her father and uncle. She was then informed of the outcome and was married on 4 November. The couple then went to live in Holland. Mary miscarried in spring 1678 and again a year later. These miscarriages were bitter disappointments to her maternal aspirations and dynastic ambitions in the Netherlands and in Britain. She apparently never conceived again.

At the time of Charles II's death Mary and her husband were entertaining his illegitimate son, the duke of Monmouth, at the Hague. The duke went off to raise his fatal rebellion in England against James II. Mary took an interest in English affairs during her father's reign. Thus she intervened in favour of Bishop Compton of London when James II used the commission for ecclesiastical causes to suspend him from his spiritual duties. She also gave £200 to the ejected fellows of Magdalen College, Oxford. When James issued the Declaration of Indulgence in July 1687 she endorsed her husband's objections to it. In view of these gestures in support of the Church of England it is surprising that James sought to convert his daughter to Catholicism. Mary expressed her shock at the trial of the seven bishops, and scepticism about the birth of a male heir to James II (*see* STUART, JAMES FRANCIS EDWARD) in June 1688. In October she went to the Hague to be present at her husband's departure as he set sail to invade England. That was the last time she saw William before she herself followed him to England the following February.

Mary took careful note of the proceedings in the CONVENTION PARLIAMENT when it was discussing the arrangements for the disposal of the crown. There was a strong party led by the earl of Danby that wanted her to be queen regnant.

Danby wrote to urge her to insist on her hereditary right, claiming that her insistence would sway the Convention to declare her queen. Mary replied 'that she was the prince's wife, and never meant to be other than in subjection to him, and that she did not thank anyone for setting up for her an interest divided from that of her husband'. The Declaration of Rights (*see* BILL OF RIGHTS) consequently declared William and Mary both sovereigns, though giving him the sole executive power. Mary was quite happy with this solution. She finally arrived in England on 12 February 1689. The very next day she went with William to the Banqueting House in Whitehall to assent to the Declaration of Rights and to accept the crown.

The coronation of William and Mary took place in Westminster Abbey on 11 April. Her father condemned Mary for usurping his throne, a charge kept up by the JACOBITES. To most of her subjects, however, Mary was more acceptable than her father or for that matter her husband, who was hated as a Dutchman and despised as an alleged homosexual. Soon after the coronation in Westminster Abbey, commissioners arrived from the Convention of Estates that had met in Edinburgh to offer the crown of Scotland to William and Mary. The formal ceremony was held in the Banqueting House where the king and queen accepted the CLAIM OF RIGHT, the Scottish equivalent of the Declaration of Rights, and took the coronation oath. They thereby became king and queen of Scotland as well as England.

William's decision to go to Ireland in June 1690 posed for the first time the problem of what arrangements should be made for the governing of the country in his absence. The Regency Act stated that, notwithstanding the limits agreed in the Bill of Rights, 'whensoever and so often as it shall happen that his Majesty shall be absent out of this realm of England it shall and may be lawful for the Queen's Majesty to exercise and administer the regal power and government of the kingdom'. Mary came out of virtual retirement to take on her new responsibilities.

The major disturbance to Mary's domestic peace up to this point had been a disagreement with her sister ANNE over the latter's intrigues with members of Parliament to get a financial settlement for herself. This was the first round in a quarrel that was to estrange Mary from Anne completely. Mary thought that her sister should be content to depend on herself and her husband for her finances. But Anne, who had agreed to set aside her hereditary claim to the throne in William's favour, thought that an adequate parliamentary grant was a fair compensation, especially since she was in financial difficulties. The matter came to a head in the House of Commons in December, when Anne's supporters voted her an annual allowance of £50,000, much to Mary's chagrin. Apart from this foray into public affairs, however, Mary had been very much left at leisure to pursue her hobbies of gardening and needlework. Now she had to take over the government of the country.

Anne was not left alone to govern, for – although the Regency Act made no mention of such a thing – William appointed a council to advise her. It consisted of nine of the principal ministers of state. Experience did not endear them to Mary, her own comments on each of them being negative, and she proved quite able to divide and rule the nine. Mary's deference to William actually resolved a problem that had agitated debates on the Regency Bill as to the division of the executive power between them. There had been some concern about the consequences of the king and queen not seeing eye to eye. In fact the situation never arose because Mary was anxious to prevent it.

A crisis occurred during Mary's first experience of government, however, that demanded decisions that could not be referred to the king. The defeat inflicted on the English fleet by the French at Beachy Head in June 1690 called for urgent action by the regency council. Mary rose to the occasion. 'Heaven seems to have sent us one of the most threatening junctures that England ever saw,' a newspaper claimed, 'merely to set off with the greater lustre the wisdom, magnanimity and justice of a princess who has made good some people's fears and others' hopes in deserving the character of another Queen Elizabeth.' Fortunately the immediate crisis was offset by William's victory at the battle of the BOYNE. Mary was relieved to learn that her husband had won and – despite Jacobite calumnies to the contrary – that her father had managed to escape unscathed.

By the time William left England again in January 1691, this time for Holland, the previous year's experience had established a routine for the running of the country in his absence abroad. During his stay on the continent – which, apart from a brief return in mid-April, lasted until October – the regency council dealt with routine business while Mary coped with any crises.

Relations with Anne continued to deteriorate over the summer of 1691. Mary and her sister were to quarrel even more fiercely when William returned from the campaign in October 1691 complaining about the conduct of the earl of MARLBOROUGH, Anne's favourite. The king accused Marlborough of corresponding with the exiled James II and of conniving with his wife Sarah to alienate Anne from her sister and himself. Mary ordered her sister to dispense with Sarah's services. When Anne refused, Mary evicted her from her apartment at the Cockpit. Mary attempted a reconciliation with her sister by visiting her after she had given birth to a stillborn child on 17 April 1692. But her insistence on the dismissal of Sarah made the attempt abortive. It was the last time that the sisters met.

Mary was again queen regnant under the terms of the Regency Act when William was out of the country from 5 March to 18 October 1692. She appears to have been more reluctant than before to take decisions without reference to William.

There was unease among officers of the armed forces at the disgrace of Marlborough, who spent some weeks in the Tower in 1692; there was a fear that this treatment of Marlborough was the prelude to a general purge. So seriously was this alarm taken that Mary was moved to reassure naval officers of her faith in their loyalty. This inspired 64 naval officers to sign an address of loyalty, pledging to venture their lives in defence of her rights and the liberty and religion of England. They went on to win the battle of La Hogue, and with it the command of the sea. The queen was as good as her word: she rewarded the seamen with a substantial sum of money, and pledged herself to establish a hospital at Greenwich for those who were disabled. Her feelings for her father hardened during the course of this year. When James issued a declaration on the eve of La Hogue offering vague concessions to English Protestants, Mary allowed it to be published in England in order to discredit him. And when she discovered that he was involved in a plot to assassinate her husband it removed the last vestiges of respect for the former king.

The following year, however, produced friction between Mary and William. She noted in her memoirs that her administration during his absence from 24 March to 29 October 1693 'was all along unfortunate, and whereas other years the King had almost ever approved all [that] was done, this year he disapproved almost everything'. The main reason was that Mary's attachment to the Tories was stronger than ever, while William began to move decisively towards the Whigs. 'When I begin to reflect on this year,' Mary noted at the end of 1693, 'I am almost frightened and dare hardly go on; for tis the year I have met with more troubles as to public matters than any other.' It seems that Mary played less of a role as regent than usual while William was absent from 6 May to 9 November 1694. She continued to preside at meetings of the Privy Council, which met almost twice a week. But she rarely attended cabinet meetings. She was thus less involved in the government of the country in 1694 than she had been in 1690.

Mary died on 28 December 1694. The first signs of her fatal illness appeared on 19 December, and by the end of Christmas Day it became clear that she was suffering from the most virulent smallpox. Archbishop Tenison felt duty bound to inform her that she was dying, for which she thanked him, since 'she had nothing then to do, but to look up to God and submit to his will'. Her death occurred at about one o'clock in the morning of the 28th. Her funeral revealed the great love and respect in which most people held her, and was marked by the solemn music of PURCELL.

FURTHER READING H. Chapman, *Mary II* (1972).

Masham, Abigail (*née* Hill) (d. 1734), courtier. She was a relative of Sarah duchess of MARLBOROUGH, who obtained for her the post of bedchamber woman to Queen ANNE. Sarah later alleged that Abigail had used this position treacherously to undermine her own influence with the queen. There was even a hint of sexual jealousy on the part of the dazzling duchess against her distant cousin, who was so plain that she was nicknamed 'Carbuncunella'. Whether or not there was any lesbian involvement between Anne and her favourites – as Grub Street pamphleteers claimed explicitly, and Sarah merely hinted at – is unclear. What is clear is that Sarah exaggerated Abigail's influence. Anne was quite a snob and looked down on Abigail as the 'dirty chambermaid', preferring the company of the duchess of Somerset after Sarah's hold over her had gone. Abigail was useful as a conduit through which Robert HARLEY could communicate with the queen after his resignation in 1708, though he did not begin to exploit this link until late in 1709. Thereafter Abigail's influence was limited to obtaining a command for her brother Jack in the Quebec expedition of 1711, and to having her husband Samuel Masham, whom she had married in 1707, included among the dozen peers Anne made at a stroke in 1712.

medicine. The 18th is usually regarded as a stagnant century between advances such as the discovery of the circulation of the blood in the 17th and the reforms of the 19th. Certainly such institutions as the Royal College of Physicians and the Company of Surgeons changed little. The College lost its monopoly of prescribing medicines in

London in 1704 when the apothecaries won the right to do so, although they were not permitted to diagnose illnesses. The Company of Surgeons finally separated from the Barbers in 1745; this split formalized the distinction first made in 1540, when the Royal Charter granted to the Company of Barber-Surgeons restricted 'barbers' to teeth-pulling. The subsequent separation permitted the development of both general and dental surgery. Otherwise there was little sign of improvement. The College still required full fellows to be communicants of the Church of England with degrees from Oxford or Cambridge, which kept out the growing numbers of DISSENTERS trained at Edinburgh and Leiden. Dissenters went to Scottish and Dutch medical schools not just because they were excluded from English universities on religious grounds, but also because these schools were more progressive. The medical faculties at Edinburgh and Glasgow were more advanced than those of Oxford and Cambridge.

Yet there were developments in the provision of medical care in England during the century. Most striking was the number of HOSPITALS founded, often by voluntary subscription. There were specialist hospitals in the capital, such as the Lock for venereal diseases (1746) and St Luke's for mental patients (1751). Unlike the older Bethlehem or Bedlam hospital, St Luke's did not put inmates on exhibition, but treated them as patients. There were also private institutions for the treatment of the insane. These became especially appealing to the upper classes after the apparently successful cure of GEORGE III by Francis Willis in 1789, for which a grateful Parliament voted him £1000 a year.

Surgeons like William Cheselden who specialized in such operations as the removal of bladder stones made fortunes from their wealthy patients. Specialists in midwifery, or 'man midwives', also became fashionable for the well-to-do. For the poor there were dispensaries, some 16 being established in London alone in the last quarter of the century. And there were always quacks selling panaceas such as Joshua Ward's pills, and alleged cures for the pox, which took up much of the advertising space in the newspapers. No new drugs were actually discovered in the period (indeed, no particularly effective disease-specific drugs were discovered at all until the 20th century), Jesuit's bark or quinine being employed to treat fever and laudanum to relieve pain as in the past. But the discovery and application of inoculation for small-pox was a breakthrough that has been regarded as the biggest single cause of any fall in mortality rates that can be observed in the century (*see* Edward JENNER).

FURTHER READING R. Porter, *Disease, Medicine and Society in England 1550–1860* (2nd edn, 1993).

Melville, Henry Dundas, 1st Viscount. *See* DUNDAS, HENRY.

mercantilism, a system of economic thought attributed by Adam SMITH to his predecessors. They were held to believe that a country's wealth was represented by its stock of silver and gold bullion. Consequently they advocated a favourable balance of trade, whereby a nation's exports were more valuable than its imports, the difference being made up in shipments of precious metals from its trading partners. To establish a favourable balance, it was believed that the state should encourage the importation of raw materials and the exportation of manufactured articles and discourage the importation of manufactured articles and the exportation of raw materials. These goals could be achieved by a complete ban on the movement of certain commodities, such as the prohibition of raw wool exports, or by financial penalties and inducements. Tariffs on foreign manufactures, for example, or bounties on the export of certain English products were advocated as a means whereby the government could regulate trade to produce a favourable balance. Mercantilism was also seen as a system of economic nationalism. The state was expected to intervene in international trade to protect and enlarge its own country's share. Since it was assumed that the volume of trade was more or less static, this could be achieved only by restricting the share of their trading rivals by economic regulations and, ultimately, by war.

Smith attacked the mercantilist system because it placed restrictions on free trade through favouring the distributors rather than the consumers of goods. Modern studies of economic theory, however, have raised serious objections to his view that there was a coherent body of economic thought which could be classed as mercantilism. Not all theorists were bullionists, nor did they agree on prohibiting the importation of foreign manufactures. Indeed some influential economic theorists justified the export of bullion to India to pay for cotton goods since trade with the subcontinent had a permanent balance of payments deficit.

Metcalf, John. *See* ROADS.

Methodism, revivalist movement that started off within the Church of England, but had become separated from it by the end of the 18th century. The term 'Methodists' seems to have been first applied to the members of the Holy Club, a gathering of HIGH-CHURCH Anglicans that John WESLEY organized at Oxford University in the 1720s when he was a fellow of Lincoln College. He himself did not become a Methodist in the strict sense until 1738, when he was convinced in an instant that he was saved. At that time he was associated with George WHITEFIELD, who had also been a member of the Holy Club. But they parted the following year over the issue of predestination. Whitefield was a strict Calvinist, believing that only the elect would be saved, whereas Wesley held that Christ died for all men, which led him to be regarded as an Arminian.

Whitefield became a chaplain of Selina countess of Huntingdon (*see* HASTINGS, SELINA). Another of her chaplains, William Romaine, preached at the fashionable church of St James's, Hanover Square, in London. She appointed others to chapels in Sussex, the main one being in Brighton. 'The countess of Huntingdon's Connexion', as it became known, was very much an aristocratic association. In 1769 a seminary for training ministers was opened at Trevecca in Wales. Many of its graduates became Lady Huntingdon's chaplains. She exercised her right as an aristocrat to appoint as many chaplains as she wished, thinking that this would protect clergymen from criticism by Anglicans. However, a test case in 1779 established that they were not regarded as regular ministers of the established church, and she had to register her chapels as dissenting conventicles under the terms of the Toleration Act.

Wesley's following became the more numerous and was organized into societies that sent delegates to annual meetings, the first being held in 1744. Methodism, however, was much more than a one- or two-man band. Itinerant preaching, for instance, which was a characteristic of Methodist evangelism, was started by three Welsh ministers, Howell Davies, Griffith Jones and Daniel Rowlands, and a schoolmaster, Howell Harris. In the West Riding of Yorkshire William Grimshaw and John Nelson developed societies on similar lines to the Methodist societies, and these were absorbed into Wesley's organization. Grimshaw was vicar of Todmorden from 1731 to 1742. There he experienced a spiritual awakening similar to that which Wesley and the early Methodists were undergoing at the same time. He became acquainted with them, and when he moved to the perpetual curacy of Haworth in 1742 he made his pulpit available to them. His ministry at Haworth was marked by a substantial increase in communicants, from 12 to 1200, who required 35 bottles of communion wine. He also became an itinerant preacher and kept contact with other parishes, where he established Methodist societies. These sent delegates to conferences that he organized.

Wesley became prominent by dint of a determination to keep control of the movement. This involved an amazing amount of travelling. It has been estimated that he travelled a quarter of a million miles in the course of his ministry. He also kept strict control of his flock. Indeed, he was so autocratic that critics called him 'Pope John'. Wesley was a prolific writer, producing a mass of literature for fellow Methodists. The most enduring literature of the movement, however, was not John's tracts but the hymns written by his brother Charles WESLEY. Charles and John remained members of the Church of England, although there was friction between them and fellow Anglicans from the start, particularly over their employment of itinerant preachers. When some lay preachers requested ordination from Wesley, William Grimshaw resisted a move that in his view threatened 'a manifest rupture with the established church. We must then be declared dissenters.' The question of separation from the established church was debated at the annual conference held in Leeds in 1755. Five years later at Bristol Wesley disavowed the notion of a separate ministry. In 1784, however, he reluctantly made his first ordinations to establish a ministry in the United States of America. Until Wesley's death in 1791 the movement held together. Indeed, for several years it continued to grow: in 1796 membership numbered 77,000 compared with 24,000 in 1767. Within a decade, however, the movement began to fragment. The Methodist New Connexion, led by Alexander Kilham, seceded in 1797; and the Primitive Methodists were formed in 1812 by members expelled from membership by the annual conference of 1810.

FURTHER READING A. Armstrong, *The Church of England, the Methodists and Society 1700–1850* (1973); D. Hempton, *The Religion of the People: Methodism and Popular Religion, c.1750–1900* (1996); B.S. Schleuther, *Queen of the Methodists: The countess of Huntingdon and the 18th-century crisis of Faith and Society* (1997).

Methuen treaty (1703), commercial treaty between England and her 'oldest ally' Portugal, negotiated by John Methuen. The Methuen treaty strengthened ties that dated back to the late 14th century; England and Portugal had been brought still closer together in 1662 when Charles II married Catherine of Braganza. Both nations shared an antipathy towards Spain, and at the onset of the War of the SPANISH SUCCESSION in 1702 England sought an alliance with Portugal to contest Bourbon ambitions in the Iberian peninsula. Under the terms of the subsequent Methuen treaty of December 1703, the Portuguese permitted the importation of English manufactures, while England reciprocated by granting a favourable duty on Portuguese wine, so helping to stimulate Georgian Britain's thirst for port. As a result of these strong commercial ties, Lisbon acquired a community of British merchants.

The Anglo-Portuguese connection remained firm throughout the 18th century: British troops helped to defend Portugal from Spanish invasion during the SEVEN YEARS WAR, and half a century later they fought alongside the Portuguese in their war of liberation against Napoleon's armies. The Methuen treaty remained in force until the eve of the Victorian era.

militia. A citizens' militia of armed amateurs possessed a strong appeal for many members of the mid-Georgian governing classes. Supporters of the 'Country' interest cherished a long-standing suspicion of standing armies composed of professional soldiers (see STANDING ARMY CONTROVERSY), and looked to the Royal Navy for Britain's first line of defence. In their opinion, proposals to revive the militia in 1757 during the opening phase of the SEVEN YEARS WAR offered an acceptable solution to a crisis situation: a militia would not only protect Britain from foreign enemies but could also serve to safeguard hallowed British liberties from the machinations of authoritarian governments. However, those ordinary Englishmen who would be obliged to serve in the ranks of the new militia viewed things very differently; in consequence, a measure intended to bolster Britain's security was itself destined to foment widespread disorder.

England's militia had its origins in the obligations of the Anglo-Saxons to perform military service during national emergencies, and from Elizabethan times until 1735 the institution had existed under law. The impetus to revive the militia in 1756 was prompted by Britain's dismal situation during the opening phase of the Seven Years War. With the regular ARMY desperately attempting to expand from a peacetime establishment to a war footing, it was decided to raise a home-defence force, which would release trained troops for service elsewhere and end the unpopular practice of employing foreign mercenaries on English soil. The measure originated with Charles TOWNSHEND and George Townshend but enjoyed the backing of the elder PITT.

The Militia Act that emerged in England and Wales in 1757 was different from the legislation that had gone before it in that it represented a tax upon manpower rather than property. Most significantly, it introduced a compulsory ballot; each county was required to submit an annual return of eligible men aged 18–50, with the aim of raising a home-defence force of 32,000 men to serve for three years. Certain professions and men with large families were exempt from the ballot. Although recruits were chosen by lot, those selected could escape by paying a £10 fine or hiring a substitute to serve in their place. In consequence, the burden of service fell overwhelmingly upon those members of the 'lower orders' who could not afford the alternatives. While falling short of universal conscription, the act nonetheless involved a degree of compulsion that was perceived as an unacceptable assault upon traditional liberties.

Not surprisingly, efforts to impose the new legislation in August and September 1757 sparked serious rioting. Opposition was increased by fears that the ballot might be 'rigged', and that militiamen would be forced to serve overseas. In Bedfordshire and Yorkshire, large mobs achieved their objective of destroying the ballot lists. Thousands of regular troops were deployed to quell the anti-militia disturbances. Ironically, a measure intended to relieve the pressure on the British army had in fact stretched its resources still further.

It required the invasion scare of 1759 to generate support for the new militia. Nearly every county raised its specified quota of troops, although it was perhaps fortunate that these raw levies were never put to the test of actual combat. Once the emergency of 1759 had receded, the militia continued to face sporadic opposition. The worst rioting occurred at Hexham in 1761, when the notoriously belligerent Newcastle colliers were in the forefront of a confrontation with militiamen from Yorkshire. During the ensuing 'battle of Hexham' three militiamen were killed, along with more than twenty rioters.

Although the revived militia ultimately gained grudging acceptance, attempts to extend it later in the century met with determined resistance. In 1796 legislation to raise a 'supplementary militia' of 60,000 men by ballot sparked serious rioting, while the extension of the ballot to Scotsmen aged between 19 and 23 provoked yet more violent disturbances. Indeed, the flood of recruits to the self-sufficient 'volunteer' formations raised during the early years of the French Revolutionary War can be partially explained by the fact that service in such units gained exemption from the militia – an institution that continued to provoke resentment.
FURTHER READING J.R. Western, *The English Militia in the Eighteenth Century: The Story of a Political Issue, 1660–1802* (1965).

Minden, battle of (1 August 1759), allied victory in Germany over the French, a notable contribution to the so-called *annus mirabilis* of the SEVEN YEARS WAR.

The battle took place when an allied army of British, Hanoverian and Prussian troops under Ferdinand of Brunswick encountered the numerically superior army of the marquis de Contades. Owing to misinterpreted orders, a force of six British and three Hanoverian battalions marched forward alone in an assault upon the centre of the French army. Advancing under heavy cannon fire, these units calmly rebuffed repeated charges by massed cavalry. The horrified Contades observed: 'I never thought to see a single line of infantry break through three lines of cavalry ranked in order of battle, and tumble them to ruin.' Aided by well-directed allied artillery the battered redcoats stood their ground against a counterattack by French infantry. The British infantry regiments lost one-third of their men killed and wounded but earned a glorious reputation.

By contrast the British cavalry was denied its share of the victory. Seeking to exploit the unexpected success of the infantry attack, Ferdinand had ordered Major General Lord George SACK-VILLE, the commander of the British contingent, to bring forward his troopers. Despite repeated requests, Sackville refused to advance until the opportunity to transform the French defeat into a rout had been lost. In consequence, Contades was able to withdraw his shattered units with relatively little interference.

Sackville's inexplicable conduct brought him to a court martial. In a brutal sentence read out at the head of every regiment in the British army he was pronounced unfit to serve the king in any capacity. Thereafter he became notorious as 'the coward of Minden'. His place as commander of the British contingent was taken by the popular and effective John Manners marquess of GRANBY.

Ministry of All the Talents (1806–7), short-lived ministry under Lord William GRENVILLE. Following the death of the younger Pitt in 1806 George III made Lord Grenville prime minister. Although he had resisted appointing Charles James FOX to office ever since the fall of the Fox–NORTH coalition, he accepted Grenville's nomination of Fox as foreign secretary. Henry ADDINGTON (Lord Sidmouth) became lord privy seal and later lord president of the council. The combination of former Pittites and Foxites in the ministry led to its title. It did not last long, though long enough to pass an act abolishing the SLAVE TRADE in the British empire in 1807. When Grenville asked the king for a measure of CATHOLIC EMANCIPATION it was refused and he resigned.

Minorca. The Mediterranean island of Minorca was a strategic objective coveted by Britain and its Bourbon rivals alike: in consequence it was a frequent focus for strife during the conflicts of the 18th century. Minorca first fell under British control during the War of the SPANISH SUCCESSION. In 1708 an expedition from Barcelona commanded by General James STANHOPE forced the surrender of Fort St Philip, the strong point guarding the harbour of Port Mahon, at which the entire island capitulated.

Minorca was retained by Britain at the treaty of UTRECHT, to become a valuable naval base. Whilst the worth of GIBRALTAR to Britain was the subject of considerable debate, the strategic value of Minorca was never in doubt: it provided the perfect base from which to watch over France's Toulon-based Mediterranean fleet and to protect trade with the Levant. Minorca's importance was underlined by the outcry that accompanied its loss to France at the onset of the SEVEN YEARS WAR in 1756. The disaster was regarded as a national humiliation for which Admiral BYNG was obliged to face a firing squad. At the treaty of PARIS in 1763 Britain regained Minorca in exchange for Belle Isle; indeed, this island off the Breton coast had been captured in 1761 with just such a transaction in mind.

Minorca was recaptured by the French in 1781, and restored to Spain two years later under the terms of the treaty of VERSAILLES. Yet the much-contested island was destined to change hands once more before the century was out. In 1798 General Charles Stuart landed with a small force from Gibraltar and bluffed the Spanish garrison into evacuating the island. Minorca's return to British domination was all too brief, and the island was relinquished to Spain at the treaty of AMIENS in 1802.

mob, the. Whether brawling across one of HO-GARTH's canvases or rampaging through the pages of *The GENTLEMAN'S MAGAZINE*, 'the mob' provides a violent counterpoint to the tranquil facade of the

Georgian 'age of elegance'. To contemporary men of property, the term 'mob' usually implied any unlawful gathering of the 'lower orders'. By contrast, modern social historians have regarded such 'crowd' action as striking evidence of the way in which ordinary men and women, who were excluded from the conventional processes of government, expressed a powerful voice of their own. Indeed, when the magistrate and novelist Henry FIELDING ironically described the mob as 'the fourth estate', he was not far from the truth.

For the 'patrician' elites, periodic 'plebeian' rioting was seen as an inevitable manifestation of the 'fevers' of the people: the riot acted as an outlet for discontents that might otherwise accumulate with more dangerous results. Some foreign political thinkers admired the activities of British rioters, and believed such vigorous demonstrations of popular opinion were actually necessary for good government. For example, in 1734 Montesquieu considered that this 'spirit of the people' helped to control abuses of power; later in the century the Virginian Thomas Jefferson maintained that a people's very liberty depended upon a readiness to register disapproval at their rulers' policies.

Rioting was endemic in 18th-century Britain. Benjamin Franklin observed how a single year, 1769, had produced a comprehensive spectrum of disorder embracing a wide variety of causes and protagonists. Franklin had noted: 'riots in the country about corn; riots about elections; riots about workhouses; riots of colliers; riots of weavers; riots of coal-heavers; riots of sawyers; riots of Wilkesites; riots of government chairmen; riots of smugglers, in which custom-house officers and excisemen have been murdered [and] the King's armed vessels and troops fired at'.

Unlike those composed of Franklin and Jefferson's own countrymen in the 1760s and 1770s, most British mobs were essentially 'defensive' or conservative. Rather than aiming to overturn the state itself, such crowds sought limited short-term objectives – the preservation of their established interests, rights or 'liberties', and the maintenance of accepted codes of behaviour. A good example of the self-imposed limitations upon Georgian crowd action is provided by the tussles that periodically erupted at Tyburn between the spectators of hangings and those employees of the surgeons who attempted to secure the bodies of executed felons for dissection. Such crowds were not concerned with rescuing the condemned, but rather with preventing their corpses from undergoing the unacceptable indignity of anatomization.

Despite the connotations of the term, the typical mob was not bent upon mindless violence. While it was possible for men of wealth and influence to hire a mob of bruisers and bullyboys to intimidate political opponents and their supporters at the hustings, such gangs were of limited value. The 'typical' mob possessed its own agenda and leadership. For example, the London mob was usually composed not of the dregs of the capital's slums but chiefly of labourers, shopkeepers, journeymen and small tradesmen, with a sprinkling of 'well-dressed persons'. Indeed, demonstrators often possessed a high level of organization and discipline that were more alarming to the authorities than any rampaging 'mob'; such fears underlay the over-reaction that resulted in Manchester's notorious 'Peterloo massacre' in 1819.

When the mob had achieved its specific objective it usually dispersed with a minimum of bloodshed. Although frequently destructive towards property, rioters only rarely posed a danger to life and limb. As Britain's 'lower orders' had little access to firearms, the most common casualties of popular disorder were those rioters who fell victim to the state's heavy-handed efforts to control it through the 'BLOODY CODE' and use of the military. For example, although the GORDON RIOTS of 1780 wrecked large areas of London, the only fatalities were inflicted by the government: some 25 rioters were hanged, while almost 300 others died of wounds administered by the army and militia.

Such heavy casualties at the hands of the authorities were themselves exceptional. Indeed, the prevalence of mob action throughout the 18th century was encouraged by the customary absence of government agencies capable of containing disturbances at local level. During the 18th century neither London nor the provinces possessed a police force: in consequence, any large-scale demonstration or riot could only be countered through the deployment of the ARMY. The use of troops for riot control posed awkward problems. Firstly, Britain's army was too small and scattered to cope with serious disorder: in periods when rioting was widespread, as in the hunger years of 1757 and 1766, the secretary at war was unable to assist more than a fraction of those magistrates who sought military aid. Secondly, when faced by a mob the troops could inflame the situation if rioters were killed by their actions; in an era when Britain's STANDING ARMY was widely regarded as a threat to the constitution, soldiers sent to tackle rioters were often placed in an impossible situation. The redcoat who refused his officer's command to open fire might suffer a severe flogging if convicted of disobedience at court martial; on the other hand, the soldier who obeyed orders with lethal consequences could be tried in the civil courts on a count of murder. Demonstrators were not ignorant of the difficulties under which the army laboured. They frequently confronted the troops and dared them to fire, especially when they believed that popular sympathy was on their side. For their part, soldiers who were willing enough to fight such external enemies as the French, Spaniards or rebellious American colonists detested domestic riot-control duty. For officers the risks had been all too apparent in the grisly fate of the unfortunate Captain PORTEOUS, who was lynched by a determined Edinburgh crowd in 1736 after firing on a mob.

As Franklin observed, Georgian rioting might be triggered by a bewildering variety of factors. Sometimes a specific issue provided the spark. In 1749 sailors ransacked a brothel in the Strand after it was reported that the proprietor had fleeced customers. Twelve years later an 8000-strong mob of miners marched upon Hexham in protest at the inequality of balloting arrangements for the new

MILITIA. Drury Lane Theatre was repeatedly wrecked by irate audiences who objected to some aspect of the performance. In times of war the draconian recruiting methods employed by the army and NAVY alike resulted in attacks upon 'crimping houses' and press gangs. Along swathes of the coast, spontaneous riots could erupt when troops attempted to keep 'wreckers' from plundering their stricken prey. Other mobs were motivated by 'political' issues, and could be whipped up by Whigs and Tories alike. The crisis posed by the FRENCH REVOLUTION provided the backdrop for the 'Church and King' riots that expressed solidarity with the governing regime. Mobs also targeted religious or ethnic minorities: there were riots against dissenters, Jews and Methodists, while the destructive Gordon Riots tapped into the long-standing suspicion of Catholics. Riot was likewise a bargaining tool in industrial disputes: workers staged strikes for higher wages, and wrecked the new machines that threatened their livelihoods (*see* LUDDITES).

Despite this diversity of discord, by far the most common of all disturbances in 18th-century Britain was the food riot. Scarcely a decade of the century escaped without large-scale outbreaks prompted by the spectre of starvation. In an era in which much of most families' budgets went to buy food, sudden price rises could signal catastrophe. Unlike many of the disturbances mentioned above, food riots were often marked by the conspicuous involvement of women and boys. The lead in rural disturbances was frequently taken by those industrial workers who lived in the countryside: hard-living colliers were notoriously ready to spearhead a riot, although independent-minded artisans such as weavers or nailers might also be noticeable. By contrast, the bulk of rural workers – the agricultural labourers and farmers' servants – were rarely prominent. Not only were such workers directly dependent upon the farmers who might be the rioters' targets, but they were also more likely to be better fed. Urban food riots might involve the townsfolk themselves, an influx of workers from the surrounding countryside, or an alliance of both groups. Such crowds acted upon principles of what E.P. Thompson famously described as 'moral economy': they prevented food from being exported, exposed and punished hoarders, and attempted to impose a 'fair' market price upon the sale of flour and other staples. Where feelings ran particularly high, rioters destroyed the over-priced goods, along with the homes and mills of those who produced them.

As with other Georgian mobs, the violence of food rioters was far from indiscriminate. Crowd action embraced ritualistic aspects that sought to advertise the rioters' fundamental legitimacy. Mobs sometimes styled themselves 'regulators', and they employed banners, slogans and songs to reinforce solidarity and enlist support. Rioters sought to convince traditional figures of authority – the JUSTICES OF THE PEACE in rural areas and the mayor and aldermen in the towns – of both the justification for their actions and the justice of their cause.

The results of Georgian rioting were mixed. For all the panic they inspired, the Gordon rioters failed to secure the repeal of the Catholic Relief Act. By contrast, the protracted metropolitan riots in support of 'WILKES and Liberty' served not only to bolster the position of Wilkes himself but also developed the concept of mass protest that spawned the English radical movement. In the countryside, those crowds of artisans and labourers who vented their anger at change by destroying enclosures (*see* AGRICULTURE), or new machinery, or who secured a brief reduction in the price of essential foodstuffs, were often forced to witness the return of the status quo through the selective retribution that followed the rapid restoration of order. Although their successes were frequently short-lived, the willingness of British 'mobs' and 'crowds' to articulate resentments through direct action served notice that the voice of the 'lower orders' could not be ignored. *See also* RIOT ACT.

FURTHER READING I. Gilmour, *Riot, Risings and Revolution: Governance and Violence in 18th-Century England* (1992); N. Rogers,

Crowds, Culture and Politics in Georgian Britain (1998); G. Rudé, *The Crowd in History* (1964).

monied interest, term used to refer to the state's creditors following the founding of the NATIONAL DEBT.

The FISCAL-MILITARY STATE created huge vested interests that depended on the success of the novel experiment in public credit. The members of the financial corporations and those who serviced them in the stock exchange, together with the bureaucrats employed in the revenue system – not to mention the armed forces – all had a stake in the FINANCIAL REVOLUTION. Among those who welcomed the creation of the system of public credit were the subscribers to the stock of the three great companies, the BANK OF ENGLAND, the EAST INDIA COMPANY and the South Sea Company. These numbered around 10,000 individuals, about a third of whom were proprietors of Bank and East India stock. They were overwhelmingly based in London and the Home Counties, and derived their incomes largely from non-landed sources.

Relatively few landowners had surplus capital to invest in Bank, East India or South Sea stock. Spokesmen for these landowners were very critical of the 'monied interest', as the investors in government loans were called. Thus J. Briscoe wrote *A Discourse on the late Funds of the Million Act, Lottery Bank and Bank of England showing that they are injurious to the nobility and gentry and ruinous to the trade of the nation*, in which he argued that the 'monied men' were 'like a canker, which will eat up the gentlemen's estates in land and beggar the trading part of the nation and bring all the subjects in England to be the monied men's vassals'. In 1709 Henry St John – later Lord BOLINGBROKE – observed that 'we have been twenty years engaged in the two most expensive wars that Europe ever saw. The whole burden of this charge has lain upon the landed interest during the whole time. The men of estates have, generally speaking, neither served in the fleets nor armies, nor meddled in the public funds and management of the treasure. A new interest has been created out of their fortunes and a sort of property which was not known twenty years ago is now increased to be almost equal to the terra firma of our island.'

Jonathan SWIFT also inveighed against this new monied interest the following year in *The Examiner*, observing that 'through the contrivance and cunning of stock jobbers there hath been brought in such a complication of knavery and cozenage, such a mystery of iniquity, and such an unintelligible jargon of terms to involve it in, as were never known in any other age or country in the world.' He pursued the same theme vigorously in *The Conduct of the Allies* (1711). In it he claimed that in William's reign 'a set of upstarts ... fell upon these new Schemes of raising Mony, in order to create a Mony'd Interest that might in time vie with the Landed.' The threat was never realized. This was largely due to a loss of confidence in the stock market following the SOUTH SEA BUBBLE, when there was a panic flight from investments in the City to the security of land.

Montagu, Charles. *See* HALIFAX, CHARLES MONTAGU, 1ST EARL OF.

Montagu, Elizabeth (1720–1800), society hostess who ran a famous literary salon. She was the daughter of Matthew Robinson, a Yorkshireman, and Elizabeth *née* Drake of Cambridgeshire, and the sister of the novelist Sarah Robinson SCOTT. She was brought up on her mother's estate near Cambridge, where she frequently visited Conyers Middleton, her grandmother's second husband, who encouraged her precocious literary talent. This mainly found expression as a prolific correspondent with such friends as Lady Margaret Cavendish Harley, who became the duchess of Portland. In 1742 she herself married Edward Montagu, who owned lucrative estates in the north of England.

The Montagus moved into a house in Hill Street, Mayfair, London, in 1750, which became a leading social centre under her direction. She presided over breakfasts and soirées to which the literati of London were invited. These included not only male authors such as BURKE, GARRICK, JOHNSON and Horace WALPOLE, but also female writers such as Fanny BURNEY and Hannah MORE. After the death of her husband in 1775 left her a very wealthy woman she built Montagu House in Portman Square. This became an even more glittering centre of society, capable of entertaining 700 people.

Montagu, John, 4th earl of Sandwich. *See* SANDWICH, JOHN MONTAGU, 4TH EARL OF.

Montagu, Lady Mary Wortley (1689–1762), traveller and writer. She was the daughter of the duke of Kingston, who planned an advantageous marriage for her in 1712. Instead she eloped with Edward Wortley Montagu, a wealthy Yorkshire landowner and Whig politician. In 1716 he was sent as ambassador to Constantinople, accompanied by Mary. Her letters reveal an intelligent woman fascinated by her exotic location. She helped to popularize the Turkish practice of inoculating against smallpox (*see also* JENNER, EDWARD). She returned to England with her husband after his tour of duty ended in 1718. Back home she moved in literary circles and struck up a friendship with Alexander POPE that turned sour, ending in mutual recriminations. She left her husband in 1739 and spent time in Italy until his death in 1761. Her letters from Italy were as interesting as those from Turkey. She died shortly after returning to England.

FURTHER READING I. Grundy, *Lady Mary Wortley Montagu: Comet of the Enlightenment* (1999).

Moore, Sir John (1761–1809), Scottish general, one of the most distinguished soldiers of his generation. Moore played an important role in forging the British army that was to emerge victorious during the protracted PENINSULAR WAR.

Born in Glasgow's Trongate, Moore was the

son of a doctor and author. When the cultivated Dr Moore was selected to accompany the young duke of Hamilton upon an extensive GRAND TOUR of Europe, the teenage John was taken along. Visits to Paris, Rome, Geneva, Venice and Vienna bequeathed a fluency in French and German, and gave Moore a glimpse of such legendary figures as Frederick the Great and Charles Edward STUART, the Young Pretender.

In 1776, when Moore was just 15 years old, the influence of the duke of Argyll gained him an ensign's commission in the 51st Foot. His first experience of action came in 1779, when he helped to rebuff the American rebels' invasion of Penobscot Bay, Massachusetts. He returned from America to a life on half-pay and a seat in Parliament. At the renewal of hostilities with France in 1793, Moore ranked as a lieutenant colonel. Despatched to the Mediterranean, Moore's leadership qualities were revealed during the campaign on Corsica; on 10 August 1794 he led the successful assault at the siege of Calvi. In 1796 Moore was sent to the West Indies, where he distinguished himself under the command of his fellow Scot, Sir Ralph ABERCROMBY. When Abercromby was subsequently ordered to quell the IRISH REBELLION OF 1798, Moore went with him. The outspoken Abercromby was swiftly recalled, but Moore served through the bloody and vindictive campaign that followed, maintaining a reputation for efficiency and humanity.

In the following year Moore was reunited with his old chief, Abercromby, during the ill-fated expedition to Holland, and was severely wounded. Although resulting in withdrawal, the campaign provided valuable experience that would soon be put to good use in a very different theatre. Moore and Abercromby served together once more during the victorious Egyptian campaign of 1801, in which Moore played a prominent role in the amphibious landing at Aboukir on 8 March and at the confused battle of ALEXANDRIA two weeks later. Abercromby was killed and Moore wounded again, but the campaign inflicted a decisive defeat upon the French Republic's hitherto invincible Army of Italy.

Upon his return from Egypt, Moore was placed in command of a brigade of troops based at Shorncliffe Camp in Kent. These units were intended to meet the shock of French invasion, and included an experimental corps of riflemen. He welded his Light Division into a distinctive organization in which high levels of training were matched by outstanding morale. Moore's methods emphasized the importance of the individual, and were instilled without recourse to the lash. The efficacy of the skirmishing tactics developed at Shorncliffe was soon to be demonstrated during the gruelling Peninsular War.

For Moore, service in Sicily and Sweden was followed in 1808 by appointment to command of Britain's forces in Portugal. In October he moved into northern Spain to relieve pressure on the hard-pressed Spanish forces, where he soon found himself heavily outnumbered and at risk of annihilation. With the canny Marshal Soult dogging his heels, Moore retreated for more than 400 km (250 miles) through the bleak and rugged mountains of Galicia. On 16 January 1809, he finally confronted Soult at CORUNNA. Moore, who had suffered mounting criticism for failing to fight the French sooner, now administered a check that permitted the evacuation of his exhausted troops. He did not accompany them. Fatally wounded by a cannon ball, he died that night and was buried amidst the port's battered defences by his grieving staff.

FURTHER READING C. Oman, *Sir John Moore* (1953).

Moravians, members of the Moravian Church, or Unity of the Brethren as they called themselves, who claimed descent from John Hus, the 14th-century Bohemian heretic or 'reformer'. Their theology stressed the atonement of Christ. Salvation came from a new birth in Jesus, which was a sudden miraculous revelation: 'one moment is sufficient to make us free, to be transformed into the image of the little lamb'. They worshipped Christ in their 'agapes' or love feasts, and sang hymns, many of which had a morbid obsession with the saviour's wounds. Some of them were written by Count Zinzendorf, leader of the Brethren, whose estate at Herrnhut near Dresden was the Moravian base. From it radiated Moravian congregations throughout Europe and North America. The first English congregation was established at Fetter Lane in London in 1738. Zinzendorf himself settled in London from 1753 to 1755. From the capital missionaries went out and founded other communities of Brethren in the provinces, including Fulneck in the West Riding of Yorkshire in 1744 and Ockbrook in Derbyshire in 1750. The acquisition of Fulneck followed the takeover by the Brethren of the Inghamite connexion.

Benjamin Ingham (1712–72) had fallen under the influence of John WESLEY while a student at Queen's College, Oxford, and accompanied him to Georgia in 1735, where he encountered Moravians. He had returned to his native Yorkshire in 1738 where he inspired a religious revival. That summer he visited Herrnhut and then began field preaching in the West Riding. In 1742 Ingham married Margaret Hastings, daughter of the earl of Huntingdon, and used her wealth to acquire property in Halifax and Pudsey (*see* METHODISM). He also accepted help from the Moravians, who formed a Yorkshire Pilgrim Congregation. They insisted, however, that he turn over his own societies – with about 1200 members – to the Brethren. Ingham consented. Although he kept in touch with the Brethren, and was even admitted into their ranks by Zinzendorf himself, he went on to create other societies in Lancashire, which retained a separate identity as his 'connexion' until its demise in 1761. The Brethren made Smith House near Halifax their headquarters in 1742, and then – inspired by Zinzendorf, who visited the site in 1743 – they moved it in 1744 to Lamb's Hill near Pudsey, which they subsequently renamed Fulneck. Like all Moravian centres outside Germany it remained a satellite of Herrnhut even after Zinzendorf's death in 1760.

More, Hannah (1745–1833), moralist and religious writer. More was the daughter of a Norfolk gentleman whose financial hardships obliged him to earn a living as a schoolmaster. His children were inculcated with a spirit of independence and the young Hannah soon joined her elder sister in running a school in Bristol. During the 1770s More enjoyed considerable success on the London literary scene, where her lively intelligence gained the admiration and friendship of influential figures such as Samuel JOHNSON and David GARRICK. More's poem *Sir Eldred* was widely praised, and her play *Earl Percy* enjoyed a lengthy run when it was staged at Covent Garden in 1777. More's interest in the reformation of manners and morals was already apparent: the tragic drama of *Percy* sought to impart an 'improving' message, while in the same year she wrote *Essays Addressed to Young Ladies,* which preached that the very freedoms enjoyed by British women demanded higher standards of 'general conduct'.

Hannah More left London in 1784 to settle in a cottage at Cowslip Green, south of Bristol. Under the influence of the EVANGELICAL REVIVAL, she embarked upon a religious crusade to improve the morals of the Somerset poor. In the 1790s she established SUNDAY SCHOOLS in Mendip villages, whose unruly inhabitants struck her as morally debased and barely human. More sought to impart a spirit of Christian piety and deference to authority using terms that today appear sanctimonious and pontificating. During the troubled era of the FRENCH REVOLUTION More's output of mass-circulation tracts amounted to a systematic campaign to reinforce this simple message, instructing the 'lower orders' to remain content with their lot and respectful of authority.

More never married. She had received a proposal from a middle-aged Bristol merchant in 1767, but the engagement was broken off and she thereafter remained indifferent to matrimony. At her death More bequeathed substantial sums to charities and religious organizations.

FURTHER READING M.G. Jones, *Hannah More* (1952).

Moser, Mary (1744–1819), artist, best known as a painter of flowers. She was a founder member of the ROYAL ACADEMY. Moser was the daughter of the Academy's first keeper, the medal designer George Michael Moser. By her mid-teens Mary had already demonstrated her talents: she won prizes from the Society of Arts in 1758 and 1759, and subsequently exhibited her watercolours with the Society of Artists.

A correspondent of the Romantic painter Fuseli, Moser became a frequent exhibitor at the Royal Academy, producing the occasional 'history' painting or portrait alongside her exquisite floral compositions. She was a favoured artist of Queen CHARLOTTE, and in 1795, as Mrs Mary Lloyd, she produced a room full of flower pictures at the queen's house at Frogmore. With the exception of her contemporary Angelica KAUFFMANN, Moser was the only woman to be elected as a Royal Academician before the 20th century.

Murray, Lord George (1694–1760), JACOBITE general. Murray was a younger son of the 1st duke of Atholl. Despite Whig credentials, the young Murray remained fiercely opposed to the 1707 UNION OF ENGLAND AND SCOTLAND. Following service in the British army, Lord George switched his allegiance to the Old Pretender, James Francis Edward STUART. During the 1715 JACOBITE RISING he fought for the Jacobites under his brother, William Murray marquess of Tullibardine (1689–1746). In its dismal aftermath he escaped to France, returning again with the Jacobite invasion of 1719. When that venture foundered Murray was exiled once more. After service with the Sardinian army, he finally obtained a pardon and returned home to Scotland. In 1739, with the Jacobite cause apparently moribund, he pledged allegiance to George II and settled down to life at Tullibardine Castle.

Murray's peaceful existence was shattered in 1745 when Prince Charles Edward STUART raised his standard in the Highlands. It was Murray's brother the marquess who actually unfurled Charles's standard at Glenfinnan. Military ambition and a deep-rooted loyalty to the Stuarts left Murray little choice: he joined the prince in August and was given the rank of lieutenant general. Murray's formidable reputation among the clansmen, and his extensive military experience, effectively made him the field commander of the Jacobite forces. However, his plain speaking and lack of deference soon alienated the touchy prince, and they frequently clashed over strategy during the coming campaign. It was Lord George who insisted on retreating from Derby, frustrating Charles's wish to advance on London. Murray's generalship was evident throughout the retreat, when he evaded superior government armies and fought a skilful rearguard action at Clifton. He subsequently inflicted a sharp reverse on the royal Hanoverian troops at Falkirk. While vehemently opposed to Charles's decision to fight at CULLODEN, Murray nonetheless charged bravely with his Highlanders, and was among the last to leave the field. Murray later penned a bitter letter blaming Charles for the disastrous outcome of the rebellion, an act that the prince never forgave. Lord George spent the remainder of his life in exile in the Netherlands. His brother, who surrendered after Culloden, died in the Tower of London. Had he pursued his original career in the service of the Hanoverians, Murray's undoubted talents might have earned him a reputation as one of the British army's finest generals.

FURTHER READING K. Tomasson, *The Jacobite General* (1958).

Murray, William, 1st earl of Mansfield. *See* MANSFIELD, WILLIAM MURRAY, 1ST EARL OF.

music. Long viewed as an arid era for British music, the 18th century is now gaining increasing recognition for the vigorous development and dissemination of genres ranging from chamber music to opera. While no English composer emerged to match the genius of PURCELL, or to rival that of the German-born HANDEL, native talent was not lacking, with composers such as Thomas Arne and William Boyce earning widespread praise. The century's outstanding professionals also fostered a lively amateur interest in music, and this generated a steady demand from clubs and individuals for printed scores and song sheets.

The popularity of music at all social levels was most evident in its rapid geographical spread during the course of the century. In 1700 Britain's musical world was dominated by London; indeed, it was the capital's importance as an internationally recognized musical centre that lured the young Handel in 1710. Other leading foreigners to take up residence in London included Johann Christian Bach, Giovanni Bononcini and C.F. Abel. This trend continued in the early 1790s when Joseph Haydn delighted the capital's music-lovers by accepting the promoter Johann Peter Salomon's invitations to perform a series of London concerts; indeed, Haydn's visits produced his dozen 'London' Symphonies.

THEATRES, pleasure gardens, concert rooms, ASSEMBLY ROOMS, taverns, COFFEE HOUSES and the private homes of wealthy enthusiasts all offered showcases for musical events. By 1800 most sizeable provincial towns possessed a theatre and assembly rooms capable of hosting regular concerts and dances, for which the middle classes provided a ready audience. Similarly, while the musical elite of late Stuart England had centred its activities upon the Chapel Royal, succeeding years saw the spread of such talent far beyond the metropolis. In consequence, even distant Newcastle upon Tyne could enjoy the services of a first-rank musician such as Charles Avison (1709–70). A pupil of Francesco Geminiani, Avison was an energetic promoter of public concerts and the author of *An Essay on Musical Expression* (1752). The prolific Avison published no fewer than 50 concertos, which included arrangements of harpsichord sonatas by the illustrious Italian composer Domenico Scarlatti.

The thriving provincial music scene was further stimulated by the growth of an established musical calendar. For example, the Three Choirs Festival drew upon the musical resources of Hereford, Worcester and Gloucester cathedrals; from 1737 the concerts were conducted by Boyce. Like Avison, William Boyce (1711–79) was a musician of great versatility who proved capable of fusing foreign influences with the native musical tradition. His chamber music was widely performed and enjoyed lasting popularity. Alongside the established musical calendar, military victories and royal births provided the excuse for more spontaneous concerts.

A striking aspect of the English musical scene was the appearance of Italian opera – and the response that this exotic invasion stimulated. The century's English audiences had their first taste of what was to come with Thomas Clayton's *Arsinoe, Queen of Cyprus* in 1705, although it required the appearance of Handel to demonstrate the dramatic appeal of the full-blown Italian opera. Audiences were drawn by spectacular stage sets and the vocal powers of the celebrated sopranos and castrati. The latter fuelled xenophobic jibes and were mercilessly lampooned in such paintings as *The Countess's Levée* from Hogarth's *Marriage à la Mode* series. Italian-language opera was propagated by the aristocratic and exclusive Royal Academy of Music. Between 1719 and its closure in 1728, this sponsored more than 30 major works – nearly half of them composed by Handel.

A reaction against the vogue for all things Italian underlay the greatest musical and theatrical success of the century, John GAY's *The Beggar's Opera* (1728). This combined pointed political satire with a lively score by Johann Christoph Pepusch, drawing inspiration from British folk songs. The unique popularity of Gay's creation encouraged further ballad-operas that drew upon the native musical tradition, and Handel embraced this trend through an increasing interest in oratorios featuring English texts and singers. A growing appreciation of traditional English music – particularly the output of the Elizabethan era – led to the foundation of the Academy of Ancient

Music in 1710. This was followed in 1726 by the Academy of Vocal Music, which aimed to rekindle interest in the church music of the Tudor and Stuart eras.

The theatre provided an important arena for musicians. Comedies and dramas alike often employed musical numbers that often obliged the actors to break into song, while the interludes regularly involved musical performances. Masques – a dramatic form dating back to the Jacobean court – depicted the deities of the classical world, while 'pastorals' presented rural scenes inhabited by idealized shepherds and shepherdesses. Pantomimes were frequently performed as an 'afterpiece' following the main play, serving to popularize the Italian comic characters of Pantaloon, Harlequin and Columbine.

FURTHER READING N. Anderson, 'Music' in B. Ford (ed.), *The Cambridge Cultural History of Britain, Vol. 5: The Eighteenth Century* (1993); D. Wyn Jones (ed.), *Music in Eighteenth-Century Britain* (2000).

mutinies, naval. *See* NAVAL MUTINIES OF 1797.

Mutiny Act, annual act that sanctioned the implementation of military discipline in the ARMY. The despotic tendencies of Cromwell and James II had left many Englishmen with an ingrained suspicion of standing armies. Accordingly, the 1689 BILL OF RIGHTS required parliamentary consent for a peacetime army, and this was demonstrated through the passage of the annual Mutiny Act.

SEE ALSO STANDING ARMY CONTROVERSY.

N

Napoleonic Wars. *See* REVOLUTIONARY AND NAP-
OLEONIC WARS.

Nash, John (1752–1835), architect. He began
building in his native Wales, where he designed
Cardigan county gaol and the west front of St
David's Cathedral. But he is most famous for his
impact on London as the prince regent's favourite
architect. His terraces around Regent's Park, and
his dramatic concept of Regent's Street, are among
the most striking examples of urban architecture
in the world. The poet Robert SOUTHEY, when he
visited the capital in 1824 for the first time since
1820, noted that 'even since that time London has
been so altered as to have almost the appearance
of a new city'. John Nash's most remarkable structure, however, is not in London but the Pavilion
in Brighton.

national debt. Governments had borrowed on
the security of revenues to be raised through taxation from time immemorial. Their creditors, however, took a high risk and charged an appropriately
high rate of interest, since the loans incurred were
the personal debts of the monarchs and not the
impersonal debts of the state. The degree to which
the king's private and public finances were inex-
tricable was vividly illustrated in the Stop of the
Exchequer in 1672, when Charles II stopped
paying interest on loans to the crown. The effect
on the City was profound.

After the GLORIOUS REVOLUTION, however,
the relatively massive financial requirements of the
FISCAL-MILITARY STATE brought into being a system
of public credit which was dissociated from the
private finances of the crown, those being provided
for by the CIVIL LIST. The consequent security of
lending to the government brought down the official rate of interest as low as 1% in the first half of
the 18th century, and Henry PELHAM reduced it
further to 3%.

The growth of the national debt, from £3.1
million in 1691 to £54 million by 1720, alarmed
contemporaries, many of whom shared SWIFT's
view that the new phenomenon of public credit
was a 'mystery of iniquity'. The attempt to reduce
it in 1720, which led to the SOUTH SEA BUBBLE,
alarmed them even more. Robert WALPOLE tried
to reduce the alarm as well as the debt by setting
aside a SINKING FUND for the purpose. But the
impact was negligible, and the upward trend continued, especially during wartime. Thus by the
time of the treaty of AIX-LA-CHAPELLE in 1748 it
stood at £76.1 million, by the treaty of PARIS in
1763 it was £132.6 million, by the treaty of VER-
SAILLES in 1783 it was £231.8 million, and by the
end of the REVOLUTIONARY AND NAPOLEONIC WARS
in 1815 it had reached £744.9 million.

naval mutinies of 1797, serious mutinies at the Royal Naval base at Spithead and the station at the Nore that threatened to cripple Britain's fleet in the spring of that year. They marked a crisis in the war with revolutionary France. Confidence in the Royal Navy's ability to confront its combined enemies was badly shaken, but the mutinies nonetheless secured improved conditions for the ordinary sailors, who were soon destined to win its most famous victories.

The outbreaks at Spithead and the Nore were rooted in long-standing objections to the harshness of shipboard life. Sailors' pay had failed to keep pace with inflation; indeed, it remained fixed at the rate laid down in Cromwell's day, while even this meagre remuneration was often months in arrears. Poor food, hard labour, harsh discipline and the widespread use of the press gang in time of war all fostered discontent below decks. Traditional grievances were exacerbated by the dramatic wartime expansion of the Royal Navy. The continuing manpower shortage led to the imposition of a quota system, under which localities were required to provide a specified contingent of men for the fleet. Bounties were offered for volunteers, so attracting debtors and other men who were better educated – and more susceptible to radical ideas – than those who had traditionally crewed the fleet.

By 1797 there was ample evidence of impending trouble. Four years of warfare had generated repeated complaints to the Admiralty from irate seamen. Many captains warned that unless official action was taken soon to redress such grievances their men would act themselves. In March 1797 the crews of the Spithead fleet petitioned the popular Admiral Richard HOWE, emphasizing that their paltry pay was inadequate to support their families ashore. Howe presented the petitions to the Admiralty, which failed to respond – and the seamen's patience finally ran out. When the fleet was ordered to sea on 16 April a concerted mutiny resulted. The ships' officers were replaced by the men's own elected 'delegates', although careful

organization and strong leadership minimized violence and guaranteed the maintenance of discipline. The mutineers' demands were as moderate as their behaviour; they stressed their loyalty and continued willingness to fight Britain's enemies.

After contemplating the use of force to crush the mutiny, the Admiralty wisely decided to negotiate instead. The delegates secured a pay rise, coupled with the king's pardon for the entire fleet to prevent reprisals against individuals. The situation appeared to be returning to normal when Admiral Colpoy's refusal to allow delegates aboard his ship sparked a bloody confrontation and rekindled the mutiny. Luckily, the delicate final negotiations were handled by Lord Howe, who enjoyed the trust of the delegates and dealt with them directly. There was widespread recognition that the mutineers' complaints were just, and this resulted in further concessions, including the removal of more than 50 notoriously unpopular officers. The Spithead mutiny ended on 15 May with a clear victory for the ordinary seamen. The fleet put to sea two days later.

A belated mutiny in support of the Spithead men, by crews anchored at the Nore off Sheerness, was resolved less happily. Rather than returning to duty on the basis of the Spithead gains, the Nore men pushed for more. Their complaints were no less just, but the government's stance had now hardened. In addition, while the Spithead mutiny had enjoyed the unanimous backing of the crews, the Nore outbreak led to divisions within the ships' companies, with many men considering that their objectives had already been met. The Nore mutineers were led by Richard Parker, an educated 'quota man' who adopted the title of 'president' and assumed airs that irritated the Admiralty and mutineers alike. Although more violent than the Spithead men, the Nore mutineers likewise affirmed their loyalty, and characterized their action as a 'strike' for improved conditions. In no mood to bargain and convinced that sedition was at work, the Admiralty responded by denying them food and water. The Nore mutineers soon began to defy their own delegates. Government retribution was harsh: Parker and 29 others were hanged from the yardarm.

FURTHER READING C. Gill, *The Naval Mutinies of 1797* (1913); R. Wells, *Insurrection: The British Experience 1795–1803* (1983).

Navigation Acts, series of measures intended to protect English (and subsequently British) trade. The trading network that linked 18th-century Britain with its American, Indian and African colonies was founded upon 'mercantilist' principles (*see* MERCANTILISM): from this perspective, the world was a collection of states, each of which competed for a limited amount of available wealth; it followed that one state's gain in trade was another's loss.

England sought to apply these principles through a succession of Navigation Acts passed in the second half of the 17th century. Under these laws, only English or colonial merchants and ships could engage in trade with English colonies. In addition, certain 'enumerated' goods – such as sugar or tobacco – could only be sold in home markets. Foreign goods destined for sale in the colonies had to be exported via England and remained subject to English import duties. The first of the acts was passed in 1651. The Dutch regarded it as a deliberate attack upon their trade, and protracted warfare between the rival marine powers followed. The Act of UNION OF ENGLAND AND SCOTLAND extended these trading rights to Scots.

During the 18th century, new laws were added aimed at preventing the colonies from manufacturing and exporting goods that competed directly with items produced in Britain. From Britain's point of view, the thriving carrying trade had the added advantage that it helped to maintain a large pool of trained seamen who were crucial for the maintenance of sea power.

Although such legislation appeared oppressive, it was less onerous than that imposed by Spain on trade with its colonies. The impact of the Navigation Acts upon Britain's booming American colonies has been the subject of considerable debate. Although earlier historians argued that the system stifled the economic development of the colonies, others have since emphasized the benefits resulting from protected markets for American goods and easy access to cheap British manufactures. The importance of these links was clear after the American colonies broke away from Britain. Despite Congress's decision to open their ports to all except British ships, trade failed to match its old prewar levels: free access to previously restricted European markets was insufficient to compensate American traders for the loss of British bounties on crops such as indigo, which would not otherwise have been viable. In addition, participation within Britain's trading system had guaranteed imperial protection. For example, during the opening decades of the century, the Royal Navy's ships eradicated the threat to colonial trade posed by pirates such as Blackbeard (*see* PIRACY). The Navigation Acts were finally repealed in 1849 as Britain moved towards an era of free trade.

navy. The Georgian era has long enjoyed a reputation as the 'golden age' of British sea power. Indeed, the century culminating in NELSON's spectacular victory at TRAFALGAR in 1805 saw the Royal Navy establish an ascendancy over its European rivals that was destined to endure until the eve of World War I. However, though 'Rule Britannia' received its first public performance in 1740, the Royal Navy's dominance of the waves in the 18th century was frequently more precarious than such patriotic sentiments suggested and Edwardian strategists believed.

In marked contrast to the ARMY, Britain's navy enjoyed the approval of public and Parliament alike. While soldiers could be used to oppress their fellow countrymen, sailors manned the 'wooden walls' that defended Britain's shores and conducted the trade upon which its wealth increasingly depended. The spectacular successes of the SEVEN YEARS WAR – under admirals such as HAWKE, RODNEY and

BOSCAWEN – only reinforced widespread faith in Britain's 'BLUE-WATER POLICY' of colonial conquest through sea power. In consequence, British seamen were accorded popular acclaim as bluff Jack Tars, who came ashore with their pockets full of prize money, while some further endeared themselves to the public by such open-handed antics as scattering coins from the windows of coaches or playing conkers with their watches. Yet there was a downside to this relationship. With civilian expectations running so high, naval officers who failed to meet them risked opprobrium or worse: when Admiral BYNG neglected to save MINORCA in 1756 he paid with his life.

Britain's naval expansion gathered momentum after 1690, when defeat off Beachy Head sparked the first of many succeeding invasion scares. By the end of the Napoleonic Wars the size of the fleet, as reckoned in tonnage displaced, had increased fourfold. The ships for the fleet were built and maintained by extensive royal and private dockyards; these were concentrated in the southwest to counter the Bourbon enemy. The Royal Navy's growth outpaced that of the old French adversary across the Channel. Yet for much of the 18th century Britain faced, and sought to match, the combined fleets of France and Spain. Although this 'two power standard' was exceeded during the Seven Years War, the balance swung against Britain in the years of peace that followed. When the ensuing AMERICAN WAR OF INDEPENDENCE escalated into global war, the Royal Navy proved unable to maintain superiority in both home and foreign waters. Such shortcomings permitted the unopposed appearance of a large Franco-Spanish fleet in the Channel in 1779, and led to the isolation and capture of a British army at YORKTOWN in 1781.

Within a year Britain exacted vengeance when Sir George Rodney defeated the French fleet in the West Indies at the battle of the Saints. Rodney's belated victory serves as a reminder of the underlying strengths of British sea power in relation to that of its enemies; these stemmed from sound administration centred upon the Admiralty, efficient dockyards and victualling procedures, and the combat and seamanship skills of officers and men imbued with a strong service tradition.

Trained at sea from their early teens as midshipmen, Britain's naval officers were obliged to pass an examination before promotion to lieutenant. Subsequent advancement depended upon luck, merit and the interest of influential patrons. Given the complexities involved in commanding a ship of the line during the age of sail, incompetents were unlikely to prosper: regardless of connections, high command required extensive practical experience. For example, the first lord of the Admiralty from 1801 to 1805, John Jervis earl of St Vincent, boasted a service record dating back to the Quebec campaign of 1759.

Manning the fleet proved problematic throughout the century. Navy wages compared poorly with those of the merchant service, and it required the great Spithead mutiny of 1797 to gain Britain's seamen their first pay rise for more than a century (*see* NAVAL MUTINIES OF 1797). In addition, shipboard life was notoriously harsh. Discipline depended partly upon the whim of the captain; some were sadists who flogged for trifling errors, others humanitarians capable of commanding respect and devotion without resort to the lash. Low pay and hard labour necessitated the extension of impressment over the seafaring population. Yet the press gangs that trawled the waterfronts were not the sole source of recruits. Despite the rigours of navy life other men volunteered in wartime, tempted by generous bounties and the prospect of prize money from captured vessels. Whatever their origins, Britain's sailors demonstrated a proficiency in seamanship and gunnery that their enemies proved unable to match.

Other developments also gave the Royal Navy an edge over its rivals. The use of citrus fruits in combating scurvy had been recognized by James Lind as early as 1747; although it took half a century for the message to spread, the traditional scourge of the mariner was conquered in time to permit the prolonged blockades that bottled up the battle fleets of revolutionary and Napoleonic France. Technical improvements were equally significant. During the American War of Independence the copper sheathing of hulls increased speed and reduced laborious cleaning. The 1780s witnessed the introduction of the carronade, the so-called 'smasher' that represented a potent addition to firepower in ship-to-ship duels.

British naval tactics were supposed to conform to strict 'Fighting Instructions'. Convention dictated a line-of-battle formation, whereby each ship presented its broadside armament to a parallel array of opponents. Officers who flouted the regulations risked displeasure or worse: in 1744 Admiral Mathews was dismissed after the battle of Toulon on the grounds that he engaged before forming such a line. As the century progressed a new breed of aggressive officers breached the code in quest of decisive victory. For example, in 1759 Hawke braved a gale to harry the French fleet to destruction at QUIBERON BAY, while Nelson's great victories at the NILE in 1798 and Trafalgar seven years later were won by headlong assaults calculated to rupture the enemy's line. As far as the vain and valiant Nelson was concerned, the task of his subordinate 'band of brothers' was to sail to close quarters, so permitting the peerless British gunners to pound their opponents into submission. The legendary 'Nelson touch' influenced the Royal Navy's self-image into an era when steam power and explosive shells rendered such daring obsolete.

FURTHER READING J. Black and P. Woodfine (eds.), *The British Navy and the Use of Naval Power in the Eighteenth Century* (1988); G.J. Marcus, *Heart of Oak: A Survey of British Seapower in the Georgian Era* (1975); N.A.M. Rodger, *The Wooden World: An Anatomy of the Georgian Navy* (1986).

Nelson, Horatio (1758–1805), naval commander who became England's greatest hero following his death at the moment of victory in the battle of TRAFALGAR. On 9 January 1806 the body of Admiral Horatio Nelson was buried in St Paul's Cathedral. Four dozen sailors from Nelson's flagship the *Victory* had walked ahead of the admiral's funeral carriage as it progressed from Whitehall, displaying the great shot-torn ensign that their ship had flown four months before in the decisive battle off Cape Trafalgar. Inside the cathedral, as Nelson's coffin was prepared for lowering into the crypt, the veteran tars gave way to a remarkable breach of discipline. Instead of folding the flag upon the coffin, they tore off a large section and divided it among themselves so that each man received a small memento of their late commander: it was an apt tribute to a leader who had never failed to seize the initiative.

Undoubtedly Britain's most famous sailor, Nelson guaranteed his immortality by dying at the climax of the encounter that shattered the combined Franco-Spanish fleet and removed any lingering fear of invasion by Napoleon's Grande Armée. At the time of his death, Nelson already enjoyed a hero's reputation. Prematurely grey-haired, with an empty sleeve and a sightless eye, the admiral's battered body offered poignant proof of the personal price of glory. Nelson's obvious willingness to share the risks of his men was one explanation for his immense popularity. Equally endearing were Nelson's all too human failings – the vanity that led him to sport a lavish display of decorations, and the craving for approval that underlay his notorious affair with the buxom and motherly Emma Hamilton.

The son of a Norfolk rector, Horatio Nelson was born in 1758 – the year before his own role model, General James WOLFE, was killed in the hour of victory at Quebec. Although slightly built, Nelson possessed a robust constitution; in the coming years he was to need all his strength as weather, disease and wounds exacted their toll. Nelson was the nephew of the successful naval captain Maurice Suckling, whose patronage was crucial in securing Nelson's first posting to sea in 1771. Suckling's growing influence continued to smooth Nelson's early career. By April 1777, when he passed his lieutenant's examination, Nelson was already familiar with seafaring from the Arctic to the Caribbean. During this roving apprenticeship he had survived hazards ranging from a charging polar bear to tropical illness. It was while stricken with malaria on the return leg of a voyage to the East Indies that the 17-year-old Nelson apparently experienced a semi-religious vision, in consequence of which he acquired a heroic sense of mission and vowed to dedicate himself wholeheartedly to the service of his country.

In 1780, at the age of 21, Nelson participated in an expedition sent from Jamaica against Spain's South American possessions. Although the command reached its objective up the San Juan river, Nelson was soon sent back suffering from dysentery. Nelson was lucky: most of the men who remained swiftly succumbed to disease. During the decade of peace that followed the loss of Britain's American colonies, Nelson lacked opportunity to distinguish himself. His chance came in 1793, when war erupted with revolutionary France. As captain of the *Agamemnon*, Nelson joined the Mediterranean fleet under the command of Lord Hood. In July 1794, during the siege of Calvi on Corsica, Nelson was wounded in the face, losing the effective use of his right eye. Succeeding years of unglamorous blockading and convoy duty failed to douse his burning ambition. Promoted to commodore by Sir John Jervis, Nelson finally demonstrated his true potential on Valentine's Day 1797. A Spanish fleet bound for Cadiz was intercepted by the British off CAPE ST VINCENT. On his own initiative, Nelson took his ship out of the line of battle to head off the enemy; others followed his decisive lead. When two Spanish warships collided in the confusion, Nelson led the boarders that subdued the first, then used that vessel as a platform from which to capture the second. This exploit entered Royal Navy lore as 'Nelson's patent bridge for boarding first rates', and it gained Nelson a knighthood and popular acclaim.

The impetuous courage that made Nelson's name at Cape St Vincent soon after led to bloody defeat. In July 1797 Rear Admiral Nelson led a landing party of seamen and marines against the heavily fortified harbour of Santa Cruz on Tenerife. Although gaining a foothold, the British were themselves surrounded by a superior Spanish force and obliged to withdraw with the loss of almost 250 men killed and wounded; the latter included Nelson himself, whose right arm was amputated after being smashed by a musket ball in the opening minutes of the assault. The following spring saw Nelson once again fit for action and ready to embark upon the most important campaign of his career. A prolonged pursuit of Bonaparte's Mediterranean fleet ended at Aboukir Bay on 1 August 1798. Caught unprepared for action, the anchored French fleet was savaged in one of the most decisive encounters in naval history. The battle of the NILE ended the French menace to British India. Nelson, who suffered a troubling head wound during the action, acquired a pension and a peerage from a grateful nation.

In the following summer Nelson became embroiled in an episode destined to cast a shadow across his reputation for humanity. The French conquest of Naples in January 1799 led to the establishment of a republic backed by local Jacobins. Nelson's subsequent action in repudiating the truce – which permitted these rebels to leave with the French garrison – sacrificed hundreds of men and women to the bloodthirsty vengeance of returning royalists. The resulting mass executions remain controversial to this day.

Nelson's next major sea battle, at COPENHAGEN on 2 April 1801, produced one of the most famous anecdotes of his career. The attack upon the anchored Danish fleet resulted in fierce fighting. When Admiral Sir Hyde Parker hoisted the signal to disengage, Nelson responded by putting his telescope to his blind eye and declaring that he simply could not see the signal. That summer, as Napoleon's troops gathered for the projected invasion of England, Nelson was appointed to command the crucial Channel squadron. On the night of 15 August a misguided attempt to attack the French at Boulogne ended in a disaster that recalled memories of Tenerife; once again, the attackers sustained heavy casualties with nothing to show for their losses.

In the spring of 1803, when the war with France resumed following the breathing space created by the treaty of AMIENS, Nelson secured command of the Mediterranean fleet. His final command was dominated by the need to seek and destroy the Toulon-based fleet of Admiral Villeneuve. Just as the great hunt of 1798 had ended with the confrontation at the Nile, so the hounding of Villeneuve culminated in the epic encounter off Cape Trafalgar. There, on 21 October 1805, Nelson's seasoned crews overcame the numerically superior Franco-Spanish fleet. It was a great victory, although Nelson did not live to reap the laurels. Shot through the spine by a marksman aboard the *Redoutable*, he expired in the *Victory*'s cockpit.

Despite his flaws, Nelson had come to epitomize the national spirit of resistance to Napoleon. Nelson's death generated a genuine tide of mourning, and the fighting spirit he had inculcated into the Royal Navy ensured that Britannia would continue to rule the waves for another century.

FURTHER READING T. Pocock, *Horatio Nelson* (1987).

neoclassicism, artistic and architectural movement that emerged in the mid-18th century, inspired by a growing interest in the cultural heritage of the ancient Greek and Roman worlds.

The excavations at Herculaneum, Paestum and Pompeii between 1738 and 1756 had attracted tourists and artists alike, and the buildings revealed by the spade gave an insight into the domestic architecture of the Roman world, in contrast to the public and religious buildings that had previously dominated the classical revival. Heavily illustrated descriptions of the finds helped to bring them to the attention of a wider audience. In addi-

tion, artists and architects who had strayed beyond the traditional limits of the GRAND TOUR were broadening the available knowledge of classical architecture. For example, Robert ADAM surveyed Diocletian's palace at Split in Dalmatia, while James 'Athenian' Stuart (1713–88) and Nicholas Revett (1725–1804) embarked upon an extensive tour of Greece that yielded the first accurate account of the ancient buildings of Athens. From the 1760s onwards the fruits of such meticulous labours were apparent in both exteriors and interior decoration in Britain, initiating the so-called 'Greek Revival'. Adam proved especially prolific: fine examples of his work may be seen at Kedleston Hall, Derbyshire, and in the decorative Pompeian rooms at Heveningham.

As a decorative style the neoclassical was characterized by linear and symmetrical designs that provided a marked contrast to the curves and scrolls of the ROCOCO. In terms of British ARCHITECTURE, neoclassicism can be seen as a logical progression from the careful observation of Roman buildings that had characterized the earlier PALLADIAN movement.

Neoclassicism's influence upon the later Georgian era is exemplified by the career of the sculptor John FLAXMAN (1755–1826). After working for the potter Josiah WEDGWOOD, Flaxman travelled to Rome in 1787, where he remained for seven years while studying both ancient and medieval art. During that period Flaxman drew illustrations for Homer's *Iliad* and *Odyssey* that were heavily influenced by Greek vase paintings. Flaxman's meticulous study of classical art later surfaced in his best sculpture, which often employed a linear design and was executed in low relief.

Newcastle, Thomas Pelham-Holles, 1st duke of (1693–1768), Whig politician; prime minister (1754–56 and 1757–62). He was the elder brother of another Whig prime minister, Henry PELHAM. Newcastle – who was made a duke in 1715 – held high office from 1717, when he became lord chamberlain, to 1762, when he resigned as first

lord of the Treasury, with only a short break from November 1756 to June 1757.

Although Newcastle was often dismissed as mediocre by observers such as GEORGE II, Lord HERVEY and Horace WALPOLE, a mere mediocrity could not have achieved such longevity at the top of the political ladder, even in the 18th century. His personal foibles, his extreme timidity, his absurd anxieties about such matters as unaired beds – which led him to get a footman to lie between fresh sheets before he himself would use them – made him a prime subject for gossip and tittle tattle. It is sometimes suggested that he owed his favour in high places to his electoral patronage, which was vast, extending to Nottingham, Sussex and Yorkshire. Certainly he spent a fortune maintaining his interest in so many constituencies, though his parlous financial state was due more to upholding a ducal lifestyle than to electioneering.

But to ascribe Newcastle's political career to his power as the biggest electoral magnate of the period undervalues his usefulness to the government in other spheres. The very fact that he left behind him the largest collection of papers of any politician of the age in itself documents the astonishing degree to which he was prepared to do the essential donkey work of a system that depended on patronage. His political rival, Lord Waldegrave (1715–1763), acknowledged this when he observed that 'upon the whole, he seems tolerably well qualified to act a second part, but wants both spirit and capacity to be first in command'. There was a lot of truth in this observation. When Newcastle played second fiddle to WALPOLE, or to his own brother Henry Pelham, or to the elder PITT, his performance was accomplished. But when he tried to play the lead after his brother's death in 1754 he was no virtuoso.

Throughout his career Newcastle was a staunch Whig, upholding the Protestant succession in the house of Hanover. He even boasted that he had taken part in a mob in support of Whig candidates at the polls. During Walpole's administration he was a loyal supporter of the prime minister, and dispensed government patronage to build up a COURT PARTY in the Commons, a grouping that became known as the 'Old Corps'. Walpole rewarded him with the post of secretary of state in 1724. Newcastle reciprocated the favour by backing Walpole's foreign policy against his fellow secretary, 2nd Viscount TOWNSHEND, and took over as principal secretary on Townshend's fall in 1730. Only towards the end of the ministry, when Walpole stubbornly resisted the clamour for war against Spain, did Newcastle waver in his support, so earning the prime minister's rebuke, 'It is your war and I wish you well of it', when the War of JENKINS'S EAR broke out.

In the infighting that took place among the Whigs after Walpole's fall, Newcastle and his brother Henry Pelham emerged victorious over their rivals CARTERET and PULTENEY. George II preferred the rival ministers, as he demonstrated in 1744 and 1746. On both occasions the Pelham brothers had to show their control of Parliament in order to get the king to back down, which he did with an ill grace. There was friction between the Pelhams, however, as Newcastle became more involved with foreign policy, and tried to commit Britain to grandiose schemes that Henry as first lord of the Treasury had to finance. Eventually Newcastle was persuaded to accept the peace terms of AIX-LA-CHAPELLE that ended the War of the AUSTRIAN SUCCESSION in 1748. The strain between them survived into the peace, however, as Henry objected to Newcastle's penchant for expensive and in the end pointless subsidy treaties. They were rendered redundant by the DIPLOMATIC REVOLUTION of 1755–6, which was brought about partly through Newcastle's search for the security of HANOVER.

Where Britain had been allied with Austria against France and Prussia in the War of the Austrian Succession, in the SEVEN YEARS WAR Britain and Prussia fought France and Austria. By then Newcastle was prime minister, having succeeded his brother on Henry's death in 1754. He found controlling the Commons from the upper house difficult, even though the general election of 1754 had produced a government majority of over 200, the largest of the century. The duke himself had much to do with bringing about this result, presiding for the first time over the government's electoral management as well as his own constituencies, and spending £27,000 in the process, which helped to return some 70 members. He was delighted at this outcome, claiming, 'The Parliament is good beyond my expectations, and I believe there are more Whigs in it, and generally well disposed Whigs than in any Parliament since the Revolution.' They were not well disposed enough to accept the loss of MINORCA, however, which led Newcastle's chief manager in the Commons, Henry FOX, to resign. As a result the ministry lost control of the lower house. This was not just because Newcastle was in the upper house, for his whole style of leadership proved unequal to the task, and he resigned in November 1756.

Yet, if he could not lead himself, Newcastle had enough support to prevent others leading too. The Pitt–DEVONSHIRE ministry that replaced him was short-lived, and ministerial instability ensued until the duke came to terms with Pitt. Together they formed one of the strongest and most effective administrations of the century. The Pitt–Newcastle ministry presided over the great triumphs of the Seven Years War. After the accession of GEORGE III, however, it disintegrated under pressure from the new king to replace it with his own choice. Pitt resigned in 1761 to be followed by Newcastle in 1762. He was out of office until 1765, when he became Lord Privy Seal. One of his last public acts was to vote for the repeal of the STAMP ACT in 1766.

FURTHER READING R. Browning, *The Duke of Newcastle* (1975).

Newcomen, Thomas (1664–1729), pioneer of steam power. Born in Dartmouth, Devon, Newcomen served an apprenticeship in engineering before seeking to develop an engine employing steam to pump water from flooded mine workings. Newcomen's atmospheric engine improved upon the steam pump evolved by another Devonian, Thomas Savery (1650–1715), in 1698. Erected at Dudley in 1712, the Newcomen engine featured an important innovation by injecting cold water directly into the cylinder. Savery had protected his own invention under an extremely broad patent embracing 'vessels or engines for raising water or occasioning motion to any sort of millworks by the impellent force of fire'; this prevented Newcomen from patenting his own very different engine, and obliged him to build machines under licence from Savery.

Newcomen's engines, which employed a long beam to transmit power from piston to pumps, remained cumbersome, slow and strictly limited in their uses; they nonetheless spread to the colliery regions of Wales, Newcastle and the Midlands where their heavy consumption of fuel was offset by ample supplies of local coal. As many as 60 may have been operating by the time Savery's patent finally expired in 1733. With John SMEATON's refinements, Newcomen's engines remained popular throughout the 18th century. For all their inefficiency, such machines were robust and relatively cheap; even after WATT improved the performance of steam engines through his invention of the separate condenser in 1765, many mine owners preferred to retain their existing Newcomen engines rather than invest in the costly new technology.

newspapers. *See* PRESS, THE.

Newton, Sir Isaac (1642–1727), physicist, astronomer and mathematician. Newton was educated at Grantham Grammar School and Trinity College, Cambridge, of which he became a fellow in 1667. In the previous two years he had been absent from Cambridge because of the plague, and in that time, while still in his early 20s, he had worked out the first rough ideas of some of the mathematical theories that were to revolutionize physics. As he himself put it, 'I was in the prime of my age for invention and minded Mathematics and Philosophy more than at any time since.' The story that while absent from Cambridge he deduced the theory of gravity from a falling apple was apparently a family anecdote popularized by Voltaire. Newton acknowledged that he then hit on the idea of gravity extending to the moon, and that all matter was affected by its attraction.

In 1669 Newton was appointed to the Lucasian chair of mathematics at Cambridge. In 1672 he was elected a fellow of the Royal Society and presented his first paper to it. This was the initial exploration of the qualities of light that ultimately found expression in his *Optics* published in 1704. It also brought about a quarrel with Robert Hooke, who was himself investigating the properties of light and accused Newton of appropriating some of his findings. Their disagreement was to lead to Newton's famous statement that if he had seen further it was by standing on the shoulders of giants; this was not the compliment it appears to have been, but a barbed reference to the diminutive Hooke. Certainly Hooke did not take it as a compliment and he continued to belittle Newton's achievements bitterly. These achievements were most notable in his work on motion, which informed his lectures at Cambridge and a paper presented to the Royal Society in 1684: *De motu corporum in gyrum* ('the motion of bodies in orbits'). This was the germ of his greatest achievement, *Philosophiae Naturalis Principia Mathematica* ('The mathematical principles of natural philosophy', usually known as Newton's *Principia*). This was first submitted to the Royal Society in 1686 and published in 1687.

The *Principia* formulated three laws of motion. Firstly, 'Every body continues in its state of rest, or of uniform motion in a straight line, unless it is compelled to change that state by forces impressed upon it.' Secondly, 'The change of motion is proportional to the motive force impressed; and is made in the direction of the right line in which that force is impressed.' Thirdly, 'To every action there is always opposed an equal reaction.' By calling them laws Newton implied that they were eternally valid. But in the 20th century the basis on which they rested, that time and space are absolute, was questioned by Einstein's theory of relativity, while his notion that all matter obeys the same laws was undermined by quantum physics.

Newton's laws also implied a lawgiver, which he found in God. Clearly he saw no conflict between science and religion, but on the contrary felt that mathematics explained God's creation. He left behind copious theological writings. Whether he was a Christian rather than a DEIST is another matter. His discoveries seemed to justify the deists' belief in their argument, from the design of the universe, that God existed, and that his existence did not require revelation. However, Newton was an Anglican, and defended the established church at Cambridge against James II's attempts to promote Catholicism there. Newton was elected to the CONVENTION PARLIAMENT in 1689 as a Whig member for the university. In 1696, through the influence of his friend Lord HALIFAX, a member of the JUNTO, he was made master of the mint, and implemented their policy of RECOINAGE. He represented the university again from 1698 to 1702. In 1703 he was elected president of the Royal Society, to which he was chosen annually for the next 25 years. In 1705 he stood again as a Whig candidate for the university, but was defeated despite being knighted by Queen Anne, who visited Cambridge during the election campaign. He spent his last years engaged in controversy with Flamsteed and Leibniz.

Newton's work demonstrated that scientific principles derived from observation and experiment are of universal application.

FURTHER READING F.E. Manuel, *A Portrait of Isaac Newton* (1968); B.J. Tecter Dobbs and M.C. Jacob, *Newton and the Culture of Newtonianism* (1995).

Newton, John (1725–1807), Evangelical minister. From the age of 11 to the age of 30 Newton was a seaman, latterly sailing on and commanding slave ships. He was converted to Christianity while navigating through a storm in 1748. From 1755 to 1760 he was surveyor of tides at Liverpool. There he encountered both George WHITEFIELD and John WESLEY and became a METHODIST. After applying unsuccessfully to be ordained in the Church of England he became an independent minister. This brought him to the notice of the earl of DARTMOUTH, who, after Newton's ordination as a deacon in 1764, presented him to the living at Olney. The stipend was a mere £60 a year, but John Thornton, a prominent evangelical merchant in London, augmented it by £200. Newton built up such a following that the church at Olney had to be enlarged. He also befriended the poet William COWPER when he moved into the town, and together they wrote the *Olney Hymns*. Newton antagonized some of the inhabitants, who threatened him with violence. He was rescued from them by Thornton, who procured for him the living of St Mary Woolnoth in 1780. In London he made the acquaintance of WILBERFORCE, and drew on his own experiences of the SLAVE TRADE to help in the campaign to abolish it, which he lived just long enough to see accomplished.

Nile, battle of the (1–2 August 1798), naval engagement within the confines of Aboukir Bay, Egypt, during the REVOLUTIONARY AND NAPOLEONIC WARS, in which NELSON's fleet defeated the French.

The battle of the Nile afforded a dramatic climax to Nelson's dogged pursuit of the French Mediterranean fleet throughout that summer. The French fleet, consisting of 13 ships of the line and 4 frigates under the command of Admiral Bueys, was caught unprepared; its guns were only ready on the seaward side, and many crew members were ashore. Nelson, whose own squadron mustered 13 men-of-war, resolved to attack immediately. Heading the British assault, Captain Foley of the *Goliath* discovered that there was sufficient room to sail between the French line and the Egyptian

shore. Several vessels followed his lead, while the others continued the attack to seaward, so subjecting the enemy to a devastating crossfire.

As the fighting intensified in the growing darkness, Bruey's flagship *L'Orient* exploded with appalling loss of life. The shock of the blast stunned both sides into silence for several minutes. When the fighting resumed Nelson's captains completed their destruction of the enemy fleet. The French fought bravely: despite losing both arms and a leg the gallant captain of the *Tonnant* continued to command his ship propped up in a bran tub.

Just four French vessels escaped the carnage, so making the encounter one of the most decisive in the history of war at sea. The battle left Napoleon's army stranded in Alexandria. Nelson, who received a head wound in the engagement, was rewarded with a peerage. The victory at the Nile was one of Nelson's greatest achievements; he was buried in a coffin constructed from the remains of *L'Orient*'s mainmast.

Nine Years War (1688–97), conflict between France and a 'Grand Alliance' that included Britain, the Dutch Republic and the Holy Roman Empire. It is so called because it lasted from William of Orange's invasion of England in 1688 to the treaty of Ryswick in 1697; it is also known as King William's War and the War of the League of Augsburg. (More detail on the fighting in Ireland and Scotland in the earlier part of the war will be found under the WILLIAMITE WARS OF SUCCESSION.)

The League of Augsburg had been established to resist the perceived French threat to its neighbours under Louis XIV. His siege of Philipburg in September 1688 precipitated hostilities on the continent. William's invasion, followed by James II's flight and the GLORIOUS REVOLUTION, brought Britain into the conflict. For the British it became a 'war of the succession' since James landed in Ireland in an attempt to reclaim his kingdoms early in 1689. Initially he had considerable success, holding a Parliament in Dublin and laying siege to the northern stronghold of Londonderry. The naval action off Beachy Head in 1690 seemed to presage an invasion of England by James's French allies. But William's defeat of James at the battle of the BOYNE in 1690 destroyed the former king's hopes of restoration, while the naval victory in the battle of La Hogue in 1692 ended the serious threat of invasion.

The war in Europe took the form of a series of sieges, with few pitched battles, those of STEENKIRK in 1692 and Landen in 1693 going badly for William. His greatest success came at the siege of Namur in 1695. Thereafter the war became bogged down and the exhausted combatants agreed to peace at Ryswick on the basis of the restoration of conquests. Louis XIV recognized William as king 'by the grace of God', a recognition repudiated in 1701 when he accepted James II's son – James Francis Edward STUART, the Old Pretender – as James III.

FURTHER READING J. Childs, *The Nine Years' War and the British Army, 1688–1697: The Operations in the Low Countries* (1991).

nobility. *See* ARISTOCRACY.

Nollekens, Joseph (1737–1823), sculptor. The son of an Antwerp artist, Nollekens vied with John FLAXMAN as the leading practitioner of his craft in late Georgian Britain. Whilst a teenager, Nollekens was apprenticed to the Antwerp-born monumental sculptor Peter Scheemakers. He spent the 1760s studying in Italy, imbibing the sculptural heritage of antiquity. Nollekens helped to fund his sojourn in Rome through a somewhat shady trade that sought to satisfy the insatiable demand for classical statuary amongst connoisseurs undertaking the GRAND TOUR.

Upon returning to London, Nollekens established a fashionable and lucrative practice. His studio in Mortimer Street drew patrons including royalty, leading politicians and literary figures. Like RYSBRACK and ROUBILIAC before him, Nollekens demonstrated a mastery of the portrait bust. He produced memorable likenesses of the great political protagonists of the era, notably Charles James FOX and William PITT THE YOUNGER. Although Pitt had resolutely refused to sit for him, Nollekens nonetheless achieved his ambition by making a bust from his death mask. The resulting likeness was so popular that Nollekens was kept busy meeting requests for copies. Besides his popular busts, Nollekens also executed large-scale funeral monuments for Westminster Abbey and St Paul's Cathedral.

nonjurors, collective term for those clerics – numbering nine bishops and some four hundred clergymen – who were deprived of their livings in 1689 for refusing to take the oaths of allegiance to WILLIAM III and MARY, on the grounds that they had taken oaths to James II that they could not break.

Bishop Ken of Bath and Wells, one of the more prominent of the nonjurors, tried to persuade his fellow nonjuring bishops not to ordain any more clergy, so that the schism would die out with the deaths of the original nonjurors. Archbishop Sancroft, their leader, refused such a self-denying ordinance, and so the division in the Church of England was prolonged. The first generation tolerated communion with the established church, but the second threatened to excommunicate from their own body, which they claimed was the one true church, those of their number who continued to attend the state church.

In 1716 the BANGORIAN CONTROVERSY began when Bishop HOADLY justified the deprivation of the original nonjurors. By 1721 the nonjurors were divided into three bodies, none of whom would communicate with the others. Although the division lasted throughout the 18th century, it ceased to be central to church history following these schisms.

Nootka Sound. A harbour on America's northwest Pacific coast, Nootka Sound provided the unlikely flash-point for an international incident that brought Britain and Spain to the brink of war in 1790. Although both nations had already explored the region, it was only in 1778, following the landfall of Captain James COOK, that trading contacts were established with the local peoples. Spain claimed the entire Pacific coast under the terms of the 1493 treaty of Tordesillas and, alarmed by the activities of British fur traders and by growing Russian interest in Alaska, sent an expedition to Nootka Sound to reassert its ancient rights.

The Spaniards impounded ships and goods belonging to the British trader John Meares. His complaints at this treatment lost nothing in the telling, and whipped up traditional British animosities against the old Bourbon enemy. Like the events leading to the War of JENKINS'S EAR half a century before, the incident also raised the issue of Spanish interference with British trade. The ministry led by the younger PITT responded by placing the Royal Navy on a war footing and launching a diplomatic drive to secure promises of aid from Britain's Triple Alliance partners – Prussia and the Dutch United Provinces. Both agreed to back Britain in event of war. Faced with Britain's stance, Spain was obliged to back down. At the Nootka Sound Convention of October 1790, Meares received compensation for his losses, whilst Spain relinquished its exclusive rights to the region, thereby opening up a large swathe of America's Pacific coastline to British shipping. The decisive outcome of the incident provided proof of Britain's recovery upon the international stage since the humiliating loss of its American colonies.

North, Frederick, Lord (1732–92), politician; prime minister (1770–82). Despite being an outstanding parliamentarian, North is nonetheless remembered as an ineffective prime minister who presided over the loss of Britain's North American colonies.

The eldest son of Francis 1st earl of Guilford, North's aristocratic background failed to convey the advantages it might have. His father was far from generous and North, who did not inherit the title until two years before his death, was often

short of funds. After education at Eton and Oxford, North entered the House of Commons in 1754 as MP for the safe family seat of Banbury. Plump and affable, he rapidly established himself as an ambitious and hard-working parliamentarian. He possessed a flair for financial affairs: in 1759 he was recruited to the Treasury Board by the duke of NEWCASTLE, and remained in office when Newcastle was ousted in 1762. Upon the fall of George GRENVILLE in 1765 North refused to serve with the ROCKINGHAMITES but regained office in GRAFTON's 1766 administration.

North's opportunity to prove himself came in 1767 when the sudden death of Charles TOWNSHEND gained him appointment as chancellor of the exchequer; in the following year he became leader of the House of Commons. As the Grafton government's key spokesman in the Commons, it was North who handled the complex debates surrounding John WILKES and the Middlesex elections of 1768–9. On Grafton's resignation in January 1770, North succeeded him as first lord of the Treasury. North had accepted the post at the urging of GEORGE III. Monarch and prime minister enjoyed a close relationship; the king's approval was demonstrated in 1772 when North received the order of the Garter, and in 1777 it was the king who cleared his first minister's substantial debts, an act of generosity that left North under a deep sense of obligation.

During his first few years in office North established a strong position as he worked to restore government majorities in the wake of the Wilkesite disturbances. North's financial expertise helped to reduce the NATIONAL DEBT and ensured that his budgets proceeded smoothly. The first international crisis of North's ministry, the 1770 dispute with Spain over the Falkland Islands, was handled with confidence. North also sought to overhaul the ramshackle administration of Britain's growing Indian empire through the 1773 East India Company Regulation Act; in order to improve control, North's ministry appointed a governor-general, officials and judges. His handling of Indian affairs won the support of Horace WALPOLE, who considered him 'an honest and moderate man'. This moderation was epitomized by the Quebec Act (*see* QUEBEC) of 1774: by conciliating Canada's Catholic majority North faced accusations of pandering to 'popery'; however, his judgment was soon vindicated when Canada remained loyal after Britain's American colonies rose in revolt.

Although the policies that provoked the crisis were not of his making, it was the AMERICAN WAR OF INDEPENDENCE that ruined North's political reputation. By the time North took office in 1770 the battle lines were already firmly set (*see* AMERICAN COLONIES 1763–1776). Characteristically enough, North's first action towards America was conciliatory – he removed all of the Townshend duties save for that on tea. By doing so he hoped to appease colonial opinion while maintaining a symbol of parliamentary authority. However, events had already developed a momentum of their own. Ironically, on the very day that North outlined his proposals, the 'Boston Massacre' served to deepen the rift between crown and colonies. The 'Boston Tea Party' of 1773 – a reaction against North's decision to permit the East India Company to export tea directly to the American colonies – prompted widespread support for the government's subsequent 'Intolerable Acts' against Massachusetts in 1774. With the drift into war, North's attempts to negotiate a settlement through concessions were overtaken by the escalating conflict. As late as 1778 North worked feverishly to achieve a compromise peace with Congress. However, his initiatives foundered when the Franco-American alliance transformed the rebellion into a global conflict.

North loathed his role as the head of a ministry waging a war that he did not believe could be won. He repeatedly begged the king to allow him to retire; George, who valued North's well-honed parliamentary skills, just as consistently refused his pleas. Following the crippling defeat at YORKTOWN in 1781, North's majority was cut to nine, and he was finally permitted to resign in March 1782. In 1783 North returned to office as home secretary in the notorious coalition with Charles James FOX, although poor health led him to take a back seat. After dismissal in December 1783 he assumed the role of elder statesman and staunch defender of the established constitution against what he described as 'the reforming notions of this age'. In his final years North became blind, and had to be guided to his seat in the House. Despite his failings as a wartime political leader North remained personally popular. Edward GIBBON, who admired North's mastery of parliamentary debate, dedicated *The Decline and Fall of the Roman Empire* to him.

FURTHER READING J. Cannon, *Lord North. The Noble Lord in the Blue Ribbon* (1970); P.D.G. Thomas, *Lord North* (1976).

North Briton, The. *See* WILKES, JOHN.

Nottingham, Daniel Finch, 2nd earl of (1647–1730), Tory politician. 'Dismal Daniel', as Nottingham was called – partly from his morose countenance and partly from his prolix speeches in Parliament – emerged as the leader of the HIGH-CHURCH Tories in the aftermath of the GLORIOUS REVOLUTION.

Before that Nottingham had been a supporter of the earl of Danby in the Cavalier Parliament and an opponent of the Whigs during the Exclusion crisis. He was rewarded by being appointed a commissioner of the Admiralty from 1679 to 1684. During James II's reign he allied with the marquess of Halifax to oppose the king's recruitment of Catholic officers for the army. Although he was invited to join with those who sent an invitation to William of Orange to come over from Holland he declined. In the CONVENTION PARLIAMENT he opposed the offer of the crown to WILLIAM or MARY, leading those who would have preferred a regency. Whereas most of these can be suspected of keeping the option of James's return open, Nottingham was never a JACOBITE. On the contrary he reconciled Tories to the post-Revolution regime by his advocacy of a new oath recognizing William and Mary as de facto monarchs. He even tried to reconcile DISSENTERS with Anglicans by advocating COMPREHENSION. Although this failed, he was instrumental in guiding the Church of England through the crisis of the nonjuring schism (*see* NON-JURORS), advising Queen Mary on the appointment of bishops to replace those whose refusal to take the oaths to her and William led to their being deprived of their sees.

Nottingham held the post of secretary of state from 1689 to 1693, when he was obliged to resign under pressure from the Whigs, to whom the king increasingly turned because they were more supportive of his war strategy in the NINE YEARS WAR than were the Tories. For the rest of William's reign he was in opposition, but on ANNE's accession he became secretary of state again. There was almost an action replay of the pattern of his previous tenure of the post, this time with the duke of MARLBOROUGH playing the role of William. Once again Tory strategy was held to be less supportive of the war effort in the War of the SPANISH SUCCESSION than that of the Whigs, and once again the ministry was changed accordingly, with Nottingham leaving office in 1704. This time he added to his sins the championship of bills to outlaw the practice of OCCASIONAL CONFORMITY, which led him to countenance the attempt to 'tack' it to the land tax bill in 1704 after he had left office.

Nottingham was never to hold office again under Anne, for she was outraged at his suggestion in 1705 that the electress of Hanover should reside in England to prevent a Jacobite coup when the queen died (*see* HANOVERIAN SUCCESSION). Consequently he was overlooked in the ministerial revolution of 1710 that brought a Tory ministry to power. He took out his frustration by allying with the Whig JUNTO to oppose the peace preliminaries presented to Parliament in 1711, in return for their help in promoting an occasional conformity bill, which finally reached the statute book that year.

When GEORGE I succeeded Anne, Nottingham was appointed lord president of the council. He was, however, one of a very few Tories to be promoted at the accession of the house of Hanover. When he was dismissed in 1716 for objecting to severity in the treatment of those implicated in the JACOBITE RISING of the previous year, the ministry became entirely Whig. By then Nottingham was nearly 70 years old, and although he did attend key debates in the Lords, he no longer took a leading part in them. He died on New Year's Day 1730.

FURTHER READING H. Horwitz, *Revolution Politics: The Political Career of Daniel Finch second earl of Nottingham* (1968).

novels. The novel in English is generally agreed to have emerged in the 18th century. Although the word 'novel' was used earlier, previous writings so described were for the most part set either in fabulous or exotic locations, or in rather sketchy parts of France, Italy, Spain or other European countries. *Oroonoko* (1688), for example, a novel by Aphra Behn (1640–89), was set in the then English colony of Surinam and had as its hero an African prince who displays prototypical features of the 'noble savage'. It reaches beyond the conventions of the European prose romances that influenced it, however, in its vigorous protest against the slave trade. The exotic is also to the fore in Daniel DEFOE's hugely influential *Robinson Crusoe* (1719), which has a desert-island setting. Its shipwrecked hero, however, proves to be a resolute defender of bourgeois values, recreating in the wilderness the ordered world of 18th-century mercantile society.

Relatively few early novels were located in England, and even these tended to be vague about their actual settings. The modern novel, characterized by social realism, arrived with DEFOE's *Moll Flanders* (1722), whose eponymous heroine threads her way through the alleys of contemporary London, and with FIELDING's *Tom Jones* (1749), whose hero chases across the countryside from Somerset to the capital.

London features in a number of early novels. Defoe's *Journal of the Plague Year* (1722) is located in the city, as is Fielding's *Jonathan Wild the Great* (1743) and much of *Amelia* (1751). SMOLLETT's *Roderick Random* (1748) and *Humphrey Clinker* (1771) both pay visits to London, as does Fanny Burney's *Evelina* (1778). It was in London, more than in provincial towns and cities, that there existed a large middle-class audience for novels.

'Formal realism' has been cited as an aspect of the novel that satisfied an emergent bourgeois readership, which sought not diversions from the real world but explorations of it. The autobiographical or biographical form of many early novels – from 'memoir-novels' such as Defoe's *Robinson Crusoe* and *Moll Flanders* to Fielding's *Joseph Andrews* (1742) and his sister Sarah's *David Simple* (1744) – particularly appealed to them. The predilection of many early English novelists for these forms also reflects their concern with verisimilitude – with appearing to present events that are genuine rather than fictitious. This concern also lay behind the use by some novelists of the epistolary technique, in which events were recounted via the medium of a series of letters. Examples of epistlary novels are Samuel RICHARDSON's *Pamela* (1740) and Tobias SMOLLETT's *Humphry Clinker* (1771).

The fact that many novels were written by women, prominent among whom were Eliza Haywood, Charlotte LENNOX and Sarah SCOTT, and that their protagonists included heroines as well as heroes – Richardson's *Pamela* and *Clarissa* (1748), for instance – was significant since the new reading public comprised especially bourgeois women, who had the leisure to read novels. They could also afford them. Defoe's *Robinson Crusoe* (1719) sold for five shillings a copy, and Fielding's *Joseph Andrews* for six. This was beyond the means of labourers, even if they could read. It would stretch the resources of journeymen, who earned between nine shillings and two pounds a week in London. But it was affordable by the business and professional classes of the capital. Novelists could make money from sales of their works. JOHNSON paid for his mother's funeral with the proceeds of *Rasselas* (1759), and Fanny BURNEY was rescued from penury by royalties of £3000 on her *Camilla* (1796). Novels were thus new commodities in the growing market for the products of the press.

Novels were much criticized for encouraging idleness and even for inculcating lax morals. Laurence STERNE's *Tristram Shandy* (1759–67), despite its popularity and its innovative techniques, provoked outcries against its prurience. The sentimental novel, which Sterne pioneered in *Tristram* and *A Sentimental Journey* (1768), reached its apogee with Henry MACKENZIE's *The Man of Feeling* (1771), though even this was censured for its lachrymose indulgence (*see* SENSIBILITY). If anything the criticisms increased towards the end of the century, with the appearance of lurid GOTHIC tales and even more alarming JACOBIN NOVELS. The sexual suggestiveness of Ann Radcliffe's *Mysteries of Udolpho* (1794) and of Matthew Lewis's *The Monk* (1796) attracted censure. But the political message of 'Jacobin' novels was regarded as subversive. They were attacked in many anti-Jacobin novels that sought to uphold traditional moral and political values.

In the opening decades of the 19th century the novel's continuing appeal was underlined by the success of two very different British authors. Whilst Jane AUSTEN satirized the social world of her genteel contemporaries, Walter Scott (1771–1832) drew inspiration from the turbulent past in such historical novels as *Waverley* (1814) and *The Heart of Midlothian* (1818).

FURTHER READING M. Grenby, 'The anti-Jacobin Novel: British Fiction, British Conservatism and the Revolution in France' in *History* LXXXIII (1998), 445–471; M. McKeon, *The Origins of the English Novel, 1600–1740* (1987); C.T. Probyn, *English Fiction of the Eighteenth Century, 1700–1789* (1987).

O

Occasional Conformity Act (1711), act that closed certain loopholes in previous legislative measures against DISSENTERS. The Corporation Act of 1661 required members of borough corporations to take communion in the Church of England within one year of their election. Some dissenters, who were prepared to communicate with the Church of England, did so to qualify as mayors, aldermen and so on, but the rest of the time frequented their own places of worship. The most sensational example of such 'occasional conformity' occurred in 1697 when the mayor of London, Sir Humphrey Edwin, attended a conventicle preceded by the mayoral sword bearer.

The Tories were outraged at this practice and determined to suppress it by fining those who indulged in it. Bills to this effect were introduced into Parliament by Tories three times between 1702 and 1704, but were defeated by Whigs in the House of Lords. One leading Tory denounced Occasional Conformity as being 'abominable hypocrisy' and 'inexcusable immorality'. Even the dissenter Daniel DEFOE criticized it as 'playing Bopeep with God Almighty'. But the real aim of the Bill was revealed when some Tories admitted they were prepared to replace it with one that would disenfranchise dissenters. Tory frustration with the rejection of the second bill by the Lords led a large number of Tories to attempt to force the third through the Upper House by tacking it to a supply bill, for which they were dubbed 'Tackers'. The 'tack' was unsuccessful. In 1711, however, the Whigs were prepared to support a bill sponsored by Tories since they were anxious to get Tory backing for a resolution attacking the preliminary terms of the treaty of UTRECHT. The result was that an act was put on the statute book until the Whigs repealed it in 1719. It does not appear to have had much impact on borough corporations.

October Club, association of backbench Tory members of the Parliament elected in 1710. The elections had been fought round the issues of 'the church in danger', raised by the trial of Dr SACHEVERELL earlier in the year, and also on the claim that the Whigs were deliberately prolonging the War of the SPANISH SUCCESSION. HIGH-CHURCH Tories and Tory gentry weary of paying taxes to finance the protracted war hoped for speedy relief for the church and for taxpayers. But the 'prime minister' Robert HARLEY was reluctant to disturb DISSENTERS or to conclude a hasty peace at any price. Consequently little was done in the first session of the Parliament to appease the prejudices of the high-church Tories.

A number of these Tories took out their frustration by forming a club called October because they drank October ale, taking as their motto 'We shall not be harl'd', apparently a Scotticism for 'we shall not be messed about'. Harley threw sops to them, such as a bill to build 50 new churches in London and an allegation that the accounts of the outgoing lord treasurer, GODOLPHIN, were short by £35million. He also ensured that the club was infiltrated by his own supporters. The result of these tactics was that the guns of the Octobrists were spiked, and by the second session, 1711–12, little more was heard of the club.

Oglethorpe, James Edward (1696–1785), army officer turned philanthropist, who played a pivotal role in establishing the American colony of GEOR- GIA. Following varied military service during the Iberian campaigns of the War of the SPANISH SUC- CESSION, and with Prince Eugène against the Turks, Oglethorpe entered the House of Commons. He became notorious for his unabashed Toryism, and was suspected of Jacobite sympathies.

Oglethorpe was an early advocate of prison reform. Shocked by the death of a friend in the Fleet debtors' prison, in 1729 Oglethorpe insti- gated a parliamentary inquiry that revealed the horrific conditions endured by inmates. However, as John HOWARD was to discover later in the cen- tury, it was easier to expose such abuses than to end them.

Oglethorpe's continuing interest in the plight of debtors underlay his initiative to establish a new settlement on the eastern seaboard of America. He aimed to found his colony upon the labours of London's poor, who would receive free passage across the Atlantic and sufficient livestock and land to establish themselves as yeoman farmers. The charitable venture had the strategic bonus of pro- viding a buffer between vulnerable South Carolina and Spanish Florida. It attracted substantial finan- cial backing, and in 1732 Oglethorpe sailed with the first wave of settlers.

In 1740, during the War of JENKINS'S EAR, Oglethorpe launched a controversial attack upon the Spanish stronghold of St Augustine. Although obliged to retreat, he defeated a subsequent Bour- bon counterattack on Georgia at the battle of the Bloody Swamp. Oglethorpe had hoped to found a model colony where hard liquor and the slavery so dominant in the Carolinas and Virginia would have no place. Unfortunately, the settlers had their own ideas. In the years after the Spanish war, rum flowed freely and Georgia rapidly adopted the plan- tation culture of its northern neighbours.

Back in England, Oglethorpe served against the Jacobites during the '45 rebellion. Old stories of suspected Jacobitism continued to arouse doubts about his loyalty to the Hanoverians, and he faced a court martial after failing to engage the High- land army as it retreated through Westmorland on its way back to Scotland, but was acquitted. Oglethorpe never returned to Georgia. A close friend of Samuel Johnson, he lived long enough to see his cherished colony become one of the United States of America.

Old Corps, name given to those Court Whigs who supported Sir Robert WALPOLE and the PELHAMS. It consisted primarily of the PLACEMEN who formed the Court and Treasury party and the personal fol- lowers of the Pelhams, particularly those MPs returned to Parliament through the influence of the duke of NEWCASTLE. When the duke resigned from the ministry in 1762 there was an expecta- tion in some quarters that many of the Old Corps would go into opposition with him. But most showed that their primary allegiance was to the court and continued to support the government. The few who did show loyalty to the duke were dismissed from office in the so-called 'massacre of the Pelhamite innocents'.
SEE ALSO COURT PARTY.

opera. *See* MUSIC.

Orford, Edward Russell, 1st earl of (1653– 1727), admiral and member of the Whig JUNTO. Russell saw active service at the naval battle of Solebay when he was only 19 years of age. He continued his career in the navy until 1683, when he left apparently in consequence of his brother Lord William Russell's execution for complicity in the Rye House plot. He then became actively involved with WILLIAM of Orange, whom he joined in Holland during James II's reign and accompanied to England in 1688. The following year he was made treasurer of the navy.

In 1691 Russell replaced Torrington as admiral and beat the French at the battle of La Hogue in 1692. He then ran foul of political intrigues, which led to his dismissal in 1693, only to be reinstated in his command and subsequently appointed first lord of the Admiralty in 1694. Russell wintered the fleet in the Mediterranean in the winter of 1694–5, the first time this was done, showing the advantages of a naval base there. (This was to inspire the capture of Gibraltar in 1704.) In 1697 he was made earl of Orford. Along with his Junto colleagues he left office in 1699.

It took a decade for Orford to regain the post of first lord of the Admiralty, despite the fact that he was a commissioner of the union with Scotland in 1706. Queen ANNE was adamant that her husband GEORGE PRINCE OF DENMARK should remain in the post. The Whigs kept up the pressure on the prince, but he remained as lord admiral until his death in 1708. Even then Anne held off promoting Orford until November 1709. He held the office of first lord for just under a year, when the advent of a Tory government led to his resignation. Following the death of Queen Anne he was again appointed first lord, holding the post until 1717, when he retired from public life to his home at Chippenham in Cambridgeshire.

Orford, Horace Walpole, 4th earl of. *See* WALPOLE, HORACE.

Orford, Robert Walpole, 1st earl of. *See* WALPOLE, SIR ROBERT.

orientalism. Term used to describe the impact of 'Eastern' culture upon the arts in Europe during the 18th century. Not long before the period began, the concept of Christendom was still viable, and the East was the non-Christian 'other' extending from the Moslem Ottoman empire to the Hindu Indian subcontinent and beyond to China and Japan. There had been trading contacts with the East for centuries, and these had been strengthened by the formation of the Levant and EAST INDIA companies. Hostilities between Europeans and the Ottoman Turks in the 17th century, culminating in the siege of Vienna in 1683 and the subsequent conquest of Hungary, had led to a very negative image of their nearest eastern neighbours. The Turkish empire was regarded as the very model of despotism. The *modus vivendi* achieved in the 18th century between the Turks and the Europeans aroused curiosity about the Moslem domains in European minds, which was catered to by such anonymous publications as *Turkish Tales* (1708), *Persian Tales* (1714) and *The Arabian Nights* (1704–17). Lady Mary Wortley MONTAGU's sojourn in Constantinople when her husband was ambassador to the Grand Porte between 1717 and 1718 led to her introducing Turkish culture into Britain, long before her experiences were posthumously published in *Embassy Letters* in 1763.

Curiosity about remoter regions was fed by DEFOE's *Robinson Crusoe* (1719) and SWIFT's *Gulliver's Travels* (1726), as well as by genuine travel narratives. In the early years of the 18th century, European cultural knowledge of the Far East was hazy enough for George Psalmanazar to be able to publish an entirely fictitious *Historical and Geographical Description of Formosa* in 1704 which was nevertheless taken seriously. Scholarly interest in the Far East was transformed by Sir William Jones (1746–94), who went to India as a justice in Calcutta's supreme court in 1783. The following year he established the Royal Asiatic Society of Bengal. His study of oriental languages led to his conclusion that Sanskrit and the Latin-based languages of Europe had a common origin. The result of investigations of Eastern philosophies and religions was to challenge the assumption that

Christianity was superior. By the late 18th century interest in Asia extended throughout the educated classes, inculcating a taste for chinoiserie, which manifested itself in collections of porcelain, while whole rooms in the houses of the elite were decorated and furnished in Chinese style. Such interests were encapsulated in the Indian exterior and Chinese interior of the Royal Pavilion at Brighton (1815–23). The Napoleonic invasion of Egypt had perhaps the greatest single impact on western Europe's obsession with the East, with Egyptian influences overtaking those of Japan and China during the Regency, and finding expression at residences such as Goodwood House.

FURTHER READING E. Said, *Orientalism* (1978).

Ormonde, James Butler, 2nd duke of (1665–1745), Anglo-Irish military commander. Ormonde was the head of one of the leading Irish noble families, although he spent most of his life outside Ireland. Thus he was educated in France and Oxford, served with the French army and helped suppress Monmouth's rebellion in 1685. He succeeded his grandfather as duke of Ormonde in July 1688, and was chosen to succeed him also as chancellor of Oxford University. He thus identified with the Tory opposition to James II, and went over to William of Orange when he invaded. Although he voted for a regency in the CONVENTION PARLIAMENT, he accepted the offer of the crown to WILLIAM and MARY, officiating at their coronation. His military career then took him to Ireland in 1690, where he fought at the battle of the BOYNE, and then to the continent, seeing action at STEENKIRK and Landen, where he became a prisoner of war until he was exchanged for the duke of BERWICK.

After ANNE's accession, and with the onset of the War of the SPANISH SUCCESSION, Ormonde was sent to Spain, where in 1702 he commanded an ignominiously unsuccessful siege of Cadiz, offset by the capture of the Spanish treasure fleet in Vigo Bay. The following year he was appointed lord lieutenant of Ireland, a post he held until 1706 and again from 1710 to 1714. In 1712 he was appointed commander in chief of the army in succession to the duke of MARLBOROUGH, but was ordered not to engage the enemy by the 'restraining orders' of the government. In the last years of Anne's reign he was suspected of being implicated in BOLINGBROKE's Jacobite intrigues, and on the accession of GEORGE I he was stripped of his offices. In 1715 he was impeached. He then confirmed Whig suspicions by fleeing to France. There he became involved in plans for a rising in the west of England to coincide with the JACOBITE RISING in Scotland. When this proved abortive he returned to France. He was then attainted by the British Parliament. In 1719 he again became involved in a Spanish plan to assist the Old Pretender, James Francis Edward STUART. Thereafter he remained in exile on the continent, spending much time in Avignon until his death.

Ossian. *See* MACPHERSON, JAMES.

Oudenarde, battle of (11 July 1708), engagement in Spanish Netherlands (modern Belgium) during the War of the SPANISH SUCCESSION in which an army of British, Dutch and Austrian troops under the duke of MARLBOROUGH and Prince Eugène defeated a French force under the duke of Burgundy and Marshal Vendôme. The engagement was not so much a set battle as a chance encounter between the opposing forces. The French generals acknowledged defeat at the end of the day and withdrew from the field, leaving 7000 casualties and 9000 men taken prisoner.

Owen, Robert (1771–1858), radical entrepreneur. Owen was born in Welshpool, the son of a saddler. He left school at the age of nine to work in a draper's shop and left home at the age of ten to join his brother, a saddler, in London. Helped by his brother, he worked in retailing in various towns before settling in Manchester to learn cotton spinning. In 1791 he set up a partnership with John

Jones and then became manager of a cotton mill. He spent the 1790s in Manchester, where he was a member of the town's Board of Health and its Literary and Philosophical Society. At the end of the decade he went to Glasgow where he bought a mill at New Lanark from David Dale for £60,000 and shortly after married Dale's daughter. From 1800 to 1825 he successfully managed the mill, which had 1500 employees. He treated his employees paternalistically, housing them and providing shops and schools. His success reinforced his conviction that environment influenced behaviour, and that cooperation rather than competition between capital and labour could benefit both. His approach, called Owenism at the time, influenced the development of the cooperative, socialist and trade-union movements.

Oxford, Robert Harley, 1st earl of. *See* HARLEY, ROBERT.

P

Paget, Henry William, 1st marquess of Anglesey (1768–1854), military commander who saw extensive service during the REVOLUTIONARY AND NAPOLEONIC WARS before embarking upon a controversial political career. At the outbreak of hostilities in 1793 Paget raised a battalion of volunteers from among his father's Staffordshire tenantry; as the 80th Foot, this unit subsequently joined the duke of YORK's army in Flanders. During the dismal campaign of 1794–5 the young Paget rose to command a brigade. In 1799, when York returned to the Netherlands in command of an Anglo-Russian force, Paget distinguished himself at the head of the cavalry.

It was as a dashing and skilful leader of mounted troops that Paget proved his real worth. During MOORE's Spanish campaign of 1808–9 Paget's troopers inflicted a sharp reverse upon the French at Sahagun, and later covered the rear of the British army during its grim retreat through the mountains to CORUNNA; there, Paget's men faced the heartbreaking task of destroying their surviving horses as there was insufficient space in the transports to evacuate them.

Paget's talents as a leader of cavalry would have proved priceless to WELLINGTON during his protracted Peninsular campaigns. However, they were denied to him after Paget eloped with the wife of Wellington's brother Henry, so provoking a major scandal. By 1815, when the return of Napoleon from exile on Elba prompted fresh fighting, Wellington and Paget were reconciled. As the earl of Uxbridge, Paget was appointed to command all the cavalry and horse artillery in Wellington's motley army. At Waterloo he led the Household Brigade of heavy cavalry against Napoleon's famed cuirassiers; although successful, the charge proved costly. During the closing stages of the battle, while talking to Wellington, Paget was severely wounded by one of the last shots to be fired by the enemy. Turning to Wellington he exclaimed 'By God! I've lost my leg'; to this the duke responded with characteristic coolness, 'Have you, by God?'

In recognition of his services, Paget was created marquess of Anglesey in July 1815. As lord lieutenant of Ireland from 1828, Anglesey favoured CATHOLIC EMANCIPATION, a stance that led to his recall in 1829 by his old commander Wellington – now the prime minister. Although reinstated by Lord Grey, Anglesey was soon mired in bickering with Daniel O'Connell. Promoted to field marshal in 1846, he died in 1854 at the age of 86. The subject of a fine painting by Thomas Lawrence, Anglesey was buried in Lichfield Cathedral.

Paine, Thomas (1737–1809), radical, revolutionary and political theorist. Although usually described as being born into a Quaker family, Paine was in fact baptized in the Church of England; his father was a Quaker but his mother was an Angli- can. He was brought up at Thetford in Norfolk, and went to Thetford Grammar School, an Angli- can establishment, though his father forbade him to be taught Latin. At the age of twelve he was apprenticed to his father's staymaking business. His trade was much satirized later, particularly in GILLRAY's print showing Paine dressed as a French Jacobin pulling on strings tightening a corset round an ample Britannia, who is clinging to an English oak, with the inscription 'a good constitution sac- rificed to a fantastic form'. He did not practise his trade long after serving his time, however, and became an exciseman in 1761. His career in the Excise, which took him to Lincolnshire, was cut short in 1765 when he was dismissed for alleged malpractice.

After spending some time in London as a teacher and Methodist lay preacher, Paine applied to the Board of Excise for reinstatement and again became an exciseman, based in Lewes in Sussex. He was again dismissed in 1772, this time for taking time off his duties in order to present a peti- tion to Parliament urging an increase in the wages of excisemen. He then set up as a shopkeeper, but went bankrupt in 1774, and separated from his second wife, his first having died in childbirth. On the advice of Benjamin Franklin he decided to start a new life in Pennsylvania.

Paine arrived in Philadelphia at a critical moment in the breakdown of the relationship between the mother country and the American colonies (*see* AMERICAN COLONIES 1763–1776). He took the side of those Americans who challenged the claim of the British Parliament to sovereignty over them. Shortly after his arrival he accepted the editorship of *The Pennsylvania Magazine*, in which he contributed to the debate. In 1776 his pam- phlet *Common Sense* articulated the views of those who thought that the only solution to the crisis was independence. Previously colonists had urged Britain to go back to the days of 'salutary neglect', when it did not exercise sovereign claims over

them. But after the bloodshed at Lexington and Concord such an aim was, in Paine's view, point- less. Men could only be encouraged to fight and die for the cause of independence. That was the real common sense of his tract. It also wrapped its argument up in political theory, with an attack on monarchy. By attacking monarchy in general, and George III as a 'sullen tyrant' in particular, it sym- bolically executed the king, and gave Americans the confidence to declare their independence on 4 July.

To declare independence was one thing; to win it another. The outcome of the AMERICAN WAR OF INDEPENDENCE was no foregone conclusion. On the contrary, the second half of 1776 saw the Continental Army, which Paine had joined, driven back across New Jersey and the Delaware into Pennsylvania. Morale slumped. Paine sought to revive it with his pamphlet *The American Crisis*, which urged that 'these are the times that try men's souls. The summer soldier and the sunshine patriot will, in this crisis, shrink from the service of their country; but he that stands it now, deserves the love and thanks of man and woman. Tyranny, like hell, is not easily conquered; yet we have this con- solation with us, that the harder the conflict, the more glorious the triumph.' Paine's pamphlet appeared in mid-December, just in time to rally George Washington's troops before they crossed the Delaware on the 26th to take Trenton.

Paine continued to write in support of the American cause, and after the war was rewarded with a pension that enabled him to live comfort- ably in New Rochelle. There he undertook scien- tific pursuits, devising an iron bridge, a model of which he took to France and England in 1787. He divided his time between the two countries, and was actually in Paris in 1791 when he wrote the first part of *Rights of Man* in reply to BURKE's *Reflections on the Revolution in France*. He was in England when part two was published, which led to his flight back to France to escape prosecution. Both parts circulated widely in various editions, some 200,000 copies of the second part being in circulation. The popularity of *Rights of Man* alarmed the authorities, already apprehensive of the course of the FRENCH REVOLUTION, whose principles Paine seemed to be adopting. Certainly he denounced the much vaunted constitution of England – the limited monarchy set up in the REVOLUTION SETTLEMENT. Thus he called the BILL OF RIGHTS a 'Bill of Wrongs'. 'The defect,' Paine insisted, 'lies in the system.' He asserted the sovereignty of the people against that of Parliament, and attacked the hereditary basis of aristocracy and monarchy. In part two he even advocated a rudimentary welfare state, with provision for old-age pensions.

The reaction to such radical views was strident, and Paine in the late 1790s became as unpopular in Britain as he had been popular in the early years of the decade. He was burned in effigy on at least 25,000 occasions during those years. But Paine was feted when he went back to France, and was returned as a member of the Convention, where he sided with the Girondins. On the fall of that party and the triumph of the Jacobins he was arrested, and spent some time in prison under sentence of death. The fall of Robespierre reprieved him, and he was released. While in prison he began *The Age of Reason*, which was published in two parts in 1794 and 1795. It was a scathing critique of scriptural revelation and organized religion. 'Of all the systems of religion that ever were invented,' he concluded, 'there is none more derogatory to man, more repugnant to reason and more contradictory in itself, than this thing called Christianity.' Paine's position was more that of a DEIST who believed in natural religion than that of an atheist, but his denunciation of cherished Christian beliefs in the name of 'reason' discredited his reputation in Britain even with DISSENTERS, who had previously been among his most ardent disciples.

Paine stayed in France until 1802 when he returned to America, where he died in 1809.

FURTHER READING J. Keane, *Tom Paine: A Political Life* (1995).

painting. From being marginal in European art, British painting entered the European mainstream during the 18th century. William HOGARTH was the first innovative native painter in this process, his 'progresses' inventing a whole new genre. Portraits by, for example, GAINSBOROUGH, REYNOLDS and Thomas Lawrence (1769–1830) captured personality as well as mere likenesses. History painting, exemplified by Benjamin WEST in such scenes as *The Death of Wolfe* and *William Penn's Treaty with the Indians*, documented events in the recent past.

British art also became institutionalized in the 18th century. In 1711 the first Academy of Painting was founded in London. Another was established in St Martin's Lane in 1720, and was revived by Hogarth in 1735. This eventually became the Society of Artists, which received a royal charter in 1765. These anticipated the establishment of the ROYAL ACADEMY in 1768. Although patronized by GEORGE III, the Royal Academy marked a move away from the royal and aristocratic patronage on which artists had hitherto greatly depended. With its funds to assist painters and its exhibitions at which paintings were not only displayed but sold, it crowned a process whereby market forces as well as elite taste stimulated artistic production. The result was to encourage the efforts of British artists.

At the beginning of the century the elite had generally looked to native talent simply to paint family portraits, and had imported other genres from abroad, principally from Italy. There was some institutional patronage. The court commissioned Sir James THORNHILL to decorate Greenwich Naval Hospital with murals depicting historical scenes. The church had employed artists as well as architects and sculptors in the building or renovation of churches. Charities such as the Foundling Hospital, which paid Hogarth for paintings to adorn its walls, also fostered British art. Such commissions continued. George III commissioned Allan RAMSAY and his studio to paint and reproduce his portrait for diplomats and others to exhibit overseas. He appointed Benjamin West to be his history painter in 1772 and got him to paint eight pictures depicting the life of Edward III for St George's Chapel, Windsor. West also painted altar pieces for Trinity College, Cambridge, and several London churches. But his most famous painting, *The Death of Wolfe*, was exhibited at the Royal Academy – of which he was a founder member – and sold in 1771.

The fostering of talent encouraged an expansion of genres. Besides portraits the century produced some of the most celebrated landscapes. Other artists specialized in more esoteric subjects. William STUBBS became the most famous painter of horses in history. In 1790 he accepted £9000 from the *Turf Review* to paint the great racehorses of the century. Mary MOSER, one of the first lady academicians, was noted mainly for her watercolour paintings of flowers. The era's growing industrialization was reflected in the works of Joseph WRIGHT of Derby. Above all, landscapes such as CONSTABLE's *The Haywain*, which won a medal in Paris in 1824, and those by Turner, widely regarded as the greatest artist Britain has ever produced, illustrated the Romantic exploration of nature and the imagination (*see* ROMANTIC MOVEMENT).

SEE ALSO BLAKE, WILLIAM; COPLEY, JOHN SINGLETON; KAUFFMANN, ANGELICA; KNELLER, SIR GODFREY; RAEBURN, HENRY; ROMNEY, GEORGE; ROWLANDSON, THOMAS; WILSON, RICHARD; WRIGHT, JOSEPH; ZOFFANY, JOHANN.

FURTHER READING W. Vaughan, *British Painting: The Golden Age from Hogarth to Turner* (1999).

Paley, William (1743–1805), influential theologian. Paley was the son of the headmaster of Giggleswick School, where he himself was educated, and obtained a scholarship attached to the school at Christ's College, Cambridge. After graduation he was ordained and became a fellow of Christ's. He was sympathetic to the movement to relax subscription to the Thirty-nine Articles, and wrote a pamphlet on the subject, but declined to sign the FEATHERS TAVERN PETITION on the grounds that he 'could not afford to keep a conscience'. In 1780

he became a prebendary of Carlisle, and two years later archdeacon.

Paley had been an effective lecturer at Cambridge and in 1785 he published his lectures as *Principles of Moral and Political Philosophy*. These were regarded as utilitarian in calculating the good or bad moral effects of decisions on their consequences rather than on their motives, and Jeremy BENTHAM was informed that his system of utility had been anticipated by a parson. Paley supported the campaign to abolish the SLAVE TRADE, but was otherwise reactionary. Thus in 1793 he published *Reasons for contentment addressed to the labouring part of the British public*. His most famous work, *A view of the Evidences of Christianity*, appeared the following year. It procured for him a series of advantageous appointments in the church culminating in the rectory of Bishop Wearmouth, worth £1200 a year.

His *Natural Theology* of 1802 was also influential, with its image of the creator as a watchmaker. Darwin's *Origin of Species* is sometimes seen as a response to this work, which also inspired the title for Richard Dawkins's more recent book on evolution, *The Blind Watchmaker*.

Palladian, classical style of ARCHITECTURE that became fashionable in 18th-century Britain. The style was based on the work of the Venetian Renaissance architect Andrea Palladio (1508–80), who was himself a leading disciple of the ancient Roman architectural theorist Vitruvius.

Hanoverian Britain's Whig oligarchy sought to express its ethos in many ways. Conspicuous among them was an adoption of the restrained and classically inspired architecture that has since come to epitomize the Georgian age. This Palladian movement shaped the country homes of the elite between 1720 and 1770 and underpinned the spread of NEOCLASSICISM that was to be harnessed by outstanding architects such as Robert ADAM during the remainder of the century.

In Stuart England the example of Palladio had been followed by the outstanding court architect

Inigo Jones (1573–1652). Under the patronage of James I and Charles I, Jones designed austere and carefully proportioned classical facades: these contrasted with the looser interpretations of ancient architectural forms that characterized the heyday of English BAROQUE architecture between 1670 and 1720.

During the opening decades of the 18th century a growing appreciation of Jones's work – combined with the changing political climate following the accession of George I – encouraged a reaction against the prevailing baroque architecture of WREN, VANBRUGH and HAWKSMOOR. The baroque was increasingly seen as overly fussy and suggestive of such absolutist regimes as Bourbon France; it was therefore deemed inappropriate for independent Protestant Englishmen. By the time Wren finished St Paul's Cathedral in 1709 the backlash against his personal interpretation of classical architecture was already beginning, as a group of Palladio's devotees sought a return to what they considered to be the true purity of classical architecture.

Typical of such devotees was the Whig MP William Benson, who in 1710 built Wilbury House, Wiltshire. Wilbury drew inspiration from the nearby Amesbury House, which was popularly ascribed to Inigo Jones himself. The movement gathered momentum when the Scottish architect Colen Campbell published the three volumes of his *Vitruvius Britannicus* between 1715 and 1725. Campbell's visual guide to contemporary British architecture praised the 'great Palladio' and castigated those modern Italian architects who had abandoned his 'Antique simplicity' in favour of 'capricious ornaments'. It paid scant attention to Wren, Hawksmoor and Vanbrugh, but lauded the legendary Jones for the 'regularity, beauty and majesty of his works'. The close association of Jones with the virtues of Protestant purity was not without its ironies: it was Jones who had designed the Banqueting House in Whitehall, from which his patron, the Stuart 'tyrant' Charles I, had stepped to his execution in December 1649.

The subscribers to *Vitruvius Britannicus* included Richard Boyle, the 3rd earl of BURLINGTON. Burlington was a fervent patron of the arts whose friends numbered Campbell, Handel and the architect, painter and landscape designer William Kent. Having undertaken the customary GRAND TOUR of Italy in 1714–15, Burlington retraced his steps several years later with the specific aim of studying the works of Palladio. Upon returning to England, the amateur Burlington began to produce architectural designs of his own that drew directly from Palladio and Jones. In 1722, Campbell designed Mereworth in Kent, a house that mimicked Palladio's own famous Villa Rotonda near Vicenza; five years later, Burlington began building himself a Palladian villa beside his country house at Chiswick.

Such concrete examples of the enduring merits of Vitruvius and Palladio won growing admiration among the Whig elite; for example, the prime minister Sir Robert WALPOLE commissioned Campbell to build him a vast country house at Houghton in Norfolk. Although Burlington designed a relatively small number of buildings, these nonetheless enhanced his reputation as a leading patron of the arts and the high priest of Palladianism. Burlington's structures include the much-praised Assembly Rooms at York; dating from 1730–2, their massive columns recalled the city's origins as a Roman legionary fortress.

English Palladianism had begun as the distinguishing style of a clique of gentlemen amateurs who possessed the time and money to indulge their personal taste for classical architecture. By Burlington's death in 1753 these notions had spread far beyond such exclusive circles. Indeed, the Palladian creed left its mark upon buildings across Britain. In the provinces local builders and masons sought inspiration from a mass of publications, including budget editions of Palladio's own architectural treatise. Such books provided illustrations of specimen decorations and mouldings, detailed the various classical orders of architecture, and gave guidance on the handling of proportions. Their impact is evident in the many hundreds of country houses that were built or reshaped during the mid-Georgian period. While some provincial architects applied the principles of Palladianism with real flair, the limitations of others produced more pedestrian copies. Despite the resulting fluctuations in quality, the fruits of their efforts frequently maintain standards of design that would have earned the grudging approval of that choosy arbiter of taste, Lord Burlington himself.

FURTHER READING M. Reed, *The Georgian Triumph 1700–1830* (1983); J. Summerson, *Architecture in Britain 1530–1830* (7th edn, 1983).

panopticon, an innovatory type of PRISON envisioned by Jeremy BENTHAM in 1791. The closing decades of the 18th century saw a growing interest in the use of imprisonment as a punishment in its own right. The prison debate attracted many participants; they included utilitarian reformers such as Bentham who believed that punishment could be refined into an exact science. Bentham's model prison had many innovatory features, including solitary confinement for all prisoners. Both the prisoners and their warders would fall under the constant gaze of an inspector housed in a central watchtower, and, in keeping with the emphasis upon surveillance, Bentham suggested that members of the public should be allowed into the tower to monitor the inspectors themselves. Bentham sought to reclaim criminals through the benefits of hard labour, and promoted his all-seeing panopticon as 'a machine for grinding rogues honest'. It was never built.

Paris, treaty of (1763), treaty that ended the SEVEN YEARS WAR. The treaty, signed in February 1763, confirmed many of the gains that Britain had made during the victorious final phase of the war: Britain had halted French imperial ambitions in INDIA, regained MINORCA and retained the conquered territories of Canada, St Vincent, Grenada, Dominica, Tobago in the West Indies and Senegal in Africa.

Yet for all the undoubted decisiveness of Britain's victory, the peace itself was surrounded by controversy. The elder PITT – who had done so much to promote the vigorous prosecution of the war and was now in opposition to the BUTE ministry – felt that the negotiations conducted by the duke of Bedford conceded too much to the vanquished: in the West Indies, the rich islands of Martinique, Guadeloupe and St Lucia had all been restored to France, along with Goree in Africa. There was especial anger that Spain, which had sided with France in 1762, had escaped so lightly: Havana had been returned to it in exchange for the dubious acquisition of Florida, while Manila was restored without any territorial compensation at all. In addition, the preliminaries to the peace had involved what the opposition considered to be a shameful desertion of Britain's staunch ally during the struggle, Frederick the Great of PRUSSIA.

Despite such criticisms, Britain's gains were unquestionable. Indeed, the scale of her victory was so overwhelming that it was unlikely that the Bourbon powers would long allow such supremacy to remain unchallenged. For France in particular, a reversal of the war's verdict became the overriding objective of foreign policy. The years after 1763 therefore saw Britain increasingly isolated: Bourbon vengeance would soon be exacted when the revolt of Britain's own American colonies exposed her vulnerability (*see* AMERICAN WAR OF INDEPENDENCE).

Park, Mungo (1771–1806), Scottish explorer, celebrated for his explorations of the Niger river in Africa. The exploits of men such as James BRUCE promoted an interest in Africa that led to the foundation of the African Association in 1788, dedicated to supporting the exploration of the continent. Sir Joseph BANKS was a member of its committee, and had been impressed by the botanical expedition that Mungo Park had led to the East Indies between 1792 and 1794. Banks recommended that the Association appoint Park to find the source of the Niger river, an expedition sent out by them in 1790 having failed to return.

Park was duly appointed, and set off in 1795. When he started up the Niger he was robbed of almost all his baggage and then imprisoned for several months by a hostile chief. Eventually he was forced to turn back, and on reaching the coast he managed to board a slave ship. He did not get back to England until 1798. His account of his travels was published by the African Association the following year. In 1803 the Colonial Office commissioned him to lead another expedition to find the source of the Niger. He stated his objectives as being 'the extension of British commerce and the enlargement of our geographical knowledge'. This time he was well equipped, being provided with £5000 and a company of 30 soldiers. But by the time they reached the river in August 1805 only eleven members of the expedition were alive – disease took a frightful toll of African explorers in this period. Park nevertheless carried on. 'Though all Europeans who are with me should die,' he wrote on 17 November, 'and though I myself were half dead I would still persevere.' The letter was the last ever heard from him, as he perished in this second attempt.

Parliament. *See* COMMONS, HOUSE OF; LORDS, HOUSE OF.

parliamentary reform. Demands for parliamentary reform took many forms in the 18th century. Some sought to eliminate the influence of the executive over the legislature. In the early 18th century this found expression in campaigns to remove PLACEMEN from the Commons. Later this evolved into a campaign to reduce the influence of the crown by 'economical reform'. Another reforming aspiration – which became a movement towards the end of the century – was for reform of the electoral system.

The term 'placemen' referred to those members of the House of Commons who had positions – 'places' – in the administration. They were regarded by COUNTRY members suspicious of the court as placing their loyalty to the ministry above their duty to their constituents. Attempts were therefore made to make acceptance of a place incompatible with membership of the Commons. Such moves led to the elimination of customs and excise officers from the Commons in 1700 and their disenfranchisement in 1782.

But the most stringent exclusion was made in 1701 when the ACT OF SETTLEMENT made membership of the lower house incompatible with the holding of any post in the administration. Had this clause come into operation it would have nipped CABINET government in the bud, as cabinet government depends on ministers sitting in the Commons as MPs. Fortunately for the government, the act was not to come into force until the accession of George I in 1714, and under Anne the opportunity was taken to repeal this clause. Instead the Regency Act of 1706 added to the list of positions – such as being a government contractor – that members were debarred from holding. The principle that MPs appointed to office should also uphold their responsibilities to their electors was enshrined in the provision that any member appointed to a place should vacate his seat and seek re-election in a by-election.

This provision, although it lasted into the 19th century, did not effectively remove placemen from Parliament. This was because the government had sufficient influence over small boroughs to ensure that members who were promoted to offices under the crown could find a seat in the Commons without great difficulty. There consequently arose a demand for 'economical reform'.

Economical reform was aimed at reducing the influence of the executive by pruning the administration of posts that had ceased to have any other use than that of rewarding members of Parliament. In 1780 John Dunning's famous but often misquoted resolution 'that the influence of the crown has increased, is increasing and ought to be diminished' passed the House of Commons by 233 votes to 215. It was sponsored by the ROCKINGHAM Whigs and, although attempts to follow up the motion with practical measures failed while Lord NORTH was in power, when the marquess of Rockingham succeeded him as prime minister in 1782 the way was clear to implement them. Thus a bill sponsored by Edmund BURKE eliminated 134 household offices, the secretaryship of state for the colonies and the BOARD OF TRADE. It also reduced the civil list to £900,000 per annum. Further measures of economical reform significantly reduced the crown's ability to build up support in Parliament from the exercise of patronage.

The inadequacies of some features of parliamentary representation were well known before the Revolution of 1688. Indeed the most thorough reform of the constituencies before 1832 were made in the Instrument of Government in 1653. The old ELECTORAL SYSTEM had been restored by 1660, however. Two main aims of reformers can be discerned: to reduce the number of seats for small boroughs and increase county representation; and to enlarge the electorate by widening the franchise. The first was an aim of Country politicians who sought to restore the independence of Parliament, which they believed had been achieved in the REVOLUTION SETTLEMENT but which had since been eroded by the growth of venal and rotten boroughs (*see* ELECTORAL SYSTEM). The second emerged from the 1760s as a movement that sought not so much to restore the constitution as to reform it.

John WILKES's supporters were a bridge between the two aims, for while they called their association the SOCIETY OF SUPPORTERS OF THE BILL OF RIGHTS they did seek to widen the franchise too. The Society was a movement intended to bring together advocates of parliamentary reform. It thus sought at the general election of 1780 to coordinate the efforts of such diverse bodies as Christopher WYVILL's Yorkshire Association and Major John CARTWRIGHT's Society for Constitutional Information.

The first – the Yorkshire Association – established at a meeting of the county gentry in December 1779, sought to make MPs independent of the executive, partly by economical reform and partly by abolishing some rotten boroughs and redistributing their seats to the counties. Early in 1780 Wyvill obtained 38 petitions from various constituencies, mostly counties, to present to Parliament in support of his recommendations. He proceeded to summon a convention, or general assembly, representing those constituencies that had petitioned.

Meanwhile Major Cartwright in his *Take your choice* (1776) had advocated much more radical measures of reform, including the secret ballot and universal manhood suffrage. These measures inspired the programme of the Society for Constitutional Information set up in 1780. Like Wyvill, its leaders – who included John Jebb and Brand Hollis as well as Cartwright – urged the convening of a general assembly or 'association'. Jebb suggested that this should be a permanent standing body, elected by universal manhood suffrage. Thus the Society had similar methods to the Yorkshire Association but much more radical aims.

Wyvill's supporters were alarmed at this trend, especially when the GORDON RIOTS erupted in June 1780 and brought home to them the reality of MOB rule. The radicals did not make much headway in the ensuing general election, and when Wyvill summoned a convention in 1781 only eleven constituencies responded. The fall of North's ministry raised hopes of reform, and indeed some measures of economical reform were passed by the incoming Rockingham administration. But parliamentary reform made no progress during the 1780s, despite the support of the younger PITT, and the association movement petered out. Although in the 1790s Charles GREY and Charles James FOX sought to revive interest in electoral reform, through the SOCIETY OF THE FRIENDS OF THE PEOPLE, it was practically a dead letter until after 1815.

FURTHER READING J. Cannon, *Parliamentary Reform 1640–1832* (1982).

parties. The nature of political parties in the 18th century has been a source of much dispute. Certainly contemporaries used the term 'party' to describe associations of members of Parliament. But what they meant by the expression is problematic. Clearly they did not mean organizations akin to modern parties, with party headquarters, membership cards and fees, and discipline in Parliament enforced by whips.

At the beginning of the 18th century the word 'party' was particularly associated with the TORIES and the WHIGS. Then most if not all peers and members of Parliament do seem to have been identified either as Tories or as Whigs, and it is possible to discern that both Whig and Tory parties sustained combined and disciplined campaigns in both Houses of Parliament and even in the constituencies. Indeed in ANNE's reign something like a two-party system emerged, in which the Tories and the Whigs alternated in power.

After Anne's death, however, the Tory party was effectively consigned to permanent opposition, never again enjoying a majority of seats in the Commons. Meanwhile the Whig party disintegrated into COURT PARTY Whigs, COUNTRY PARTY Whigs, and patriots (*see* PATRIOTISM). This disintegration has been seen as marking the emergence of 'connexions' such as the duke of Bedford's, which, though called a 'party', consisted of the personal and electoral adherents of the duke. However, the words 'Tory' and 'Whig' are generally accepted as meaningful descriptions of the primary political polarity at least until the 1740s. By 1760, however, most historians seem to be in agreement with the words of Sir Lewis Namier that 'the words Whig and Tory explain little and require a great deal of explanation', at least in the Commons if not in the constituencies. Yet even Sir Lewis said that his next book, if he ever wrote it – which alas he never got round to – would be on 'the rise of party'. Some historians have supplied the missing volume with studies that stress the re-emergence of party in the reign of GEORGE III, identifying it principally with the rise of the ROCKINGHAMITES.

After ROCKINGHAM's death, the leadership of his party fell to Charles James FOX, whose followers were known as Whigs. Though they tried to fix the label 'Tory' on the government of William PITT THE YOUNGER, he insisted that he was also a Whig. Distinct parties of Tories and Whigs had not fully emerged by 1815.

FURTHER READING L. Colley, *In Defiance of Oligarchy: The Tory Party 1714–1760* (1982); T. Harris, *Politics under the Later Stuarts: Party Conflict in a Divided Society* (1993); F. O'Gorman, *The Emergence of the British Two-Party System* (1982).

patriotism. In 1783 the artist John Singleton COPLEY completed his massive painting of *The Death of Major Pierson*. Copley's action-packed canvas depicted the demise of the young British officer, who had been killed in action while repelling a French assault upon Jersey two years earlier. It was exhibited in the year that Britain formally acknowledged the loss of its prized American colonies. As if to counter this national humiliation Copley offered an intensely patriotic celebration of British valour and sacrifice, with the dying Pierson positioned below billowing regimental colours dominated by the red, white and blue of the Union flag.

It has been argued that artists such as Copley encouraged the leaders of Georgian society to regard themselves as participants in a heroic struggle. That conflict frequently involved Protestant Britons fighting to defend their religion and freedoms against the ambitions of Catholic France. Ironically enough Copley was himself an American, albeit one who had chosen to remain loyal to King George. Copley's success built upon that of his fellow countryman Benjamin WEST, who had earlier created a similar scene of patriotic sacrifice in his *Death of General Wolfe*. Like Pierson, the equally young WOLFE was shown expiring beneath the country's national flag. West's painting was subsequently engraved and enjoyed one of the healthiest print runs of the century. In this form it was no doubt familiar to Horatio NELSON, for whom Wolfe became a hero and role model. In due course several distinguished artists, including the ageing West himself, would reconstruct the poignant scene of Nelson's own death in the cockpit of the *Victory* at the hour of his own great triumph at Trafalgar. In his celebrated signal before that battle Nelson had made it clear what England expected from its sailors, and had himself died in the knowledge that he had 'done his duty' to his country.

The origins of Nelson's intense patriotism are established in his own words: in 1776, while recovering from a bout of tropical illness, he experienced a 'sudden glow of patriotism' that 'presented my King and Country as my patron'. However, the patriotic feelings of those many thousands of humbler Britons who participated in the wars with France are more difficult to establish. Some sort of popular patriotism can be detected throughout the Georgian era: 'Rule Britannia' was composed in 1740, and 'God save the King' received its first public performance in 1745, the year that JACOBITE rebellion threatened the Hanoverian regime. At mid-century the painter HOGARTH demonstrated his vigorous patriotism through such works as *Calais Gate*, while the philanthropist Jonas HANWAY tapped patriotic sentiment in support of the Marine Society, which combined charity with patriotism by plucking young men from a life of poverty to serve their country at sea.

Such manifestations of 'patriotic' sentiment equate with modern definitions of the term. However, when discussing 'patriotism' in the context of 18th-century Britain it is necessary to appreciate that the word possessed other connotations. Indeed, during the reign of GEORGE II the term 'patriot' was appropriated by opposition Whigs, who claimed to be upholding British interests against those of HANOVER allegedly upheld by the administration. 'Patriot' fears of corruption bolstered the 'country' ideology ranged against the Walpolean 'court'. Especially influential in shaping this opposition programme was Henry St John

1st Viscount BOLINGBROKE, whose *The Idea of a Patriot King* argued that civic virtue was best expressed through a patriotic commitment to the public good – the very antithesis of the corruption seeping from cynical and self-serving politicians. Indiscriminate use of the word for political ends led Samuel JOHNSON to make his famous remark that 'patriotism is the last refuge of a scoundrel'. Under GEORGE III, however, patriotism was espoused by the regime. George III himself 'gloried in the name of Briton'. As the long wars against France reached a climax in the gruelling final conflict of the REVOLUTIONARY AND NAPOLEONIC WARS, the threat of foreign invasion generated a wave of volunteer units imbued with a determination to defend their country against 'Boney's' veterans. Such amateur soldiers were never put to the test; indeed the development of an increasingly chauvinist sense of Britishness may have been kindled by the fact that Georgian Britons never had to endure invasion and occupation by a foreign power. Although influential, arguments that the wars of 1793–1815 'forged' a British identity remain controversial. In particular, the extent to which Irish, Scots and Welsh subscribed to a common and all-embracing notion of 'Britishness' during this period continues to generate debate. **SEE ALSO** BRITAIN.

FURTHER READING L. Colley, *Britons: Forging the Nation 1707–1837* (1992); A. Murdoch, *British History 1660–1832: National Identity and Local Culture* (1998); G. Newman, *The Rise of English Nationalism: A Cultural History, 1740–1830* (1987).

peerage. *See* ARISTOCRACY; LORDS, HOUSE OF.

Peerage Bill. *See* LORDS, HOUSE OF.

Pelham, Henry (1695–1754), Whig politician; prime minister (1743–54). He was the younger brother of Thomas Pelham-Holles 1st duke of NEWCASTLE, who also became prime minister. Pelham entered Parliament in 1717 and supported the Whigs led by 2nd Viscount TOWNSHEND and WALPOLE. This ensured his rapid promotion when they came to power. Pelham was made a lord of the Treasury in 1721, secretary at war in 1724 and paymaster general of the forces in 1730. He defended Walpole against his detractors to the end, and after his fall refused to serve under his rival Spencer COMPTON, the earl of Wilmington.

On Wilmington's death in 1743 Pelham became first lord of the Treasury and chancellor of the exchequer. This brought the Pelham brothers, Henry and the duke of Newcastle, to power, with the former effectively prime minister. Though they could manage Parliament, they still had to deal with the influence of CARTERET on the king. Carteret's arrogance stung Pelham, for the former once said of the prime minister that he was 'only a chief clerk to Sir Robert Walpole', adding, 'and why he should expect to be more under me I can't imagine: he did his drudgery and he shall do mine'. Matters came to a head in November 1744 when the Pelhams gave the king an ultimatum that either Carteret should go or they would resign. George was forced to drop Carteret, but resented it bitterly.

The reconstruction following Carteret's departure from the ministry brought about the so-called BROAD-BOTTOM ADMINISTRATION. This had the support of the Commons but not that of the king, who continued to seek Carteret's advice. The Pelhams therefore staged another showdown in February 1746, while the JACOBITE RISING was still raging. This time they did resign. George II tried to form another ministry around Carteret, but it proved impossible. Within two days the Pelhams were reinstated, this time on their own terms. The most important of these was that the king should show his entire confidence in them. George did this, at first reluctantly but increasingly with conviction as he came to admire Henry Pelham; and when Pelham died in 1754 the king lamented, 'Now I shall have no more peace.'

The one threat Pelham faced after 1746 was from the opposition of FREDERICK PRINCE OF WALES. Frederick's Leicester House party hoped to make gains in the next election, which was expected in 1748. Pelham got the king to dissolve Parliament in 1747, catching Frederick on the hop and reinforcing the ministerial majority in the ensuing election. Pelham then managed the national finances with considerable ability. Once peace had been signed in 1748 at the conclusion of the War of the AUSTRIAN SUCCESSION he demobilized the armed forces and reduced government expenditure from £12 million to £7 million a year. In 1749 he introduced a measure to consolidate the NATIONAL DEBT and to reduce the rate of interest from 4% to 3% by 1757. In 1752 he was able to reduce the land tax from four to two shillings in the pound (20–10%). The Pelham ministry also passed measures to reform the CALENDAR in 1751, to drastically reduce the consumption of gin (*see* GIN ACTS) and to tighten up the law on clandestine marriages with HARDWICKE'S MARRIAGE ACT.

Although Pelham seems a pallid prime minister between the robust Walpole and the manic PITT, his more subdued manner concealed a shrewd and calculating politician. He was reserved and cautious, but behind the reserve was steel. All agreed on his integrity, which was remarkable in a venal age; unlike Walpole he died relatively poor.
FURTHER READING J. Wilkes, *A Whig in Power: The Political Career of Henry Pelham* (1964).

Pelham-Holles, Thomas, 1st duke of Newcastle. *See* NEWCASTLE, THOMAS PELHAM-HOLLES, 1ST DUKE OF.

Peninsular War (1808–14), conflict in the Iberian peninsula in which British forces ousted the French from Spain and Portugal. It was the most sustained campaign by British land forces in the REVOLUTIONARY AND NAPOLEONIC WARS.

For Britons, the bloody and protracted conflict that Napoleon Bonaparte dubbed his 'Spanish ulcer' has traditionally been viewed in terms of the exploits of the British army. More recently, revisionist historians have emphasized the contribution of Spanish and Portuguese peoples in securing their own liberties. While WELLINGTON's highly trained army remained crucial for the maintenance of resistance against the French, local guerrilla bands undoubtedly injected a spirit of popular struggle into the years immortalized by Goya's stark etchings of the *Disasters of War*.

Britain's return to the Iberian peninsula after a century's absence was prompted by the French invasion of Portugal in the autumn of 1807. Portugal was Britain's oldest continental ally, and by offering it assistance Britain could open a fresh front in the war against Napoleon. In the following summer, when Napoleon's attempt to reform Bourbon Spain as a satellite kingdom under his brother Joseph sparked widespread popular resistance in support of the ousted Prince Ferdinand, British politicians proved ready to help the rebels. Although Spain represented a traditional foe, and had been allied to France since 1795, *any* opponent of Bonaparte was deemed worthy of British backing. The Spanish revolt had important ramifications for British strategy, in that it minimized the threat of attack upon Britain's overseas possessions and permitted significant inroads upon French colonies. War in the peninsula also drained French resources and provided an encouraging example of resistance for Prussia, Russia and Austria.

While willing enough to accept British gold, gunpowder and naval assistance, the Spanish provincial juntas remained suspicious of direct military intervention by their old and heretical enemy. In consequence, the British initially concentrated their efforts upon Portugal, where an army under Sir Arthur Wellesley (the future duke of Wellington) was landed in August 1808. Within days, the British defeated a French division at Rolica, so stiffening Portuguese resistance. Exploiting the careful defensive tactics that were to become his trademark, Wellesley soon after inflicted a heavier reverse upon the impetuous French commander Junot at Vimeiro. Before he could exploit his success Wellesley was replaced by more cautious officers sent from Britain; these preferred negotiation to fighting. By the notorious Cintra convention of 30 August Junot's remaining troops, along with their loot, were repatriated by the Royal Navy.

Although the French position in the peninsula had been dangerously weakened following the capture of 20,000 men by a Spanish army at Bailen in Andalusia, news of Cintra dampened British enthusiasm for the conflict. However, a fresh expeditionary force under Sir John MOORE had already been authorized to cooperate with Spanish forces in the hope of ejecting the French. In the wake of the Bailen debacle, Napoleon took personal command in the peninsula, and his veterans swiftly inflicted a series of defeats upon the overconfident Spaniards. Napoleon subsequently sought to isolate and destroy Moore's vulnerable army. To escape the snare, Moore conducted a nightmarish retreat to the northern coast across the snow-bound mountains. On 16 January 1809 Moore's army turned at bay at the port of CORUNNA and rebuffed its pursuers. The British expeditionary force was evacuated successfully by the Royal Navy, yet the campaign had cost some 8000 men, including Moore himself. Moore's withdrawal, and the appalling condition of the troops who returned home, increased doubts about future British involvement in the peninsula.

Moore's fighting retreat had nonetheless distracted Napoleon from the reconquest of Portugal, thereby leaving Britain with a toehold upon the continent from which Wellesley and his allies would ultimately eject the French armies from the peninsula. The forces of Marshal Soult were pushed out of Portugal in May 1809, and Wellesley thereafter advanced into Spain. Although cooperating with Spanish forces, it was British redcoats who repulsed Soult at Talavera in July. Despite this hard-fought victory, the allies retreated in the face of heavy odds, causing an exasperated Wellesley (now Viscount Wellington) to lose faith in the unreliable Spanish generals and to question the motives of their central government, the Suprema.

Spanish armies subsequently suffered a spate of disastrous defeats at French hands, triggering the fall of the discredited Suprema.

In consequence, from 1810 Britain bore an even greater share in bolstering anti-French resistance. When French forces under Masséna invaded Portugal, Wellington's army – including a contingent of new-modelled Portuguese troops – repulsed them at Bussaco before retreating towards Lisbon. Masséna followed, only to find the capital defended by the fortified lines of Torres Vedras. The spring of 1811 saw Wellington fighting on the Portuguese-Spanish border, and by early 1812 he had stormed the strongholds of Ciudad Rodrigo and Badajoz, so providing the springboard for a major offensive into Spain itself. With Napoleon's Russian campaign precluding further reinforcements for the Iberian sideshow, Wellington took the initiative and routed Marmont's army at SALAMANCA in July. Although pushed back again that winter, Wellington advanced once more in the spring of 1813, capturing Burgos and defeating King Joseph at Vitoria on 21 June. Thereafter the war consisted of methodical campaigns to drive the remaining French armies back across the Pyrenees. In October 1813, Wellington's veterans crossed the Bidassoa river to carry the war onto French soil, so helping to close the allies' net on the beleaguered Napoleon.

Wellington's chain of triumphs in the Peninsular War established his own reputation and enhanced the prestige of the British army. The Spain that British efforts had helped to liberate from French rule witnessed an orgy of vengeance against those who had collaborated with the invaders. Whereas a famously liberal constitution had been enacted in Spain in 1812, after the war the country rapidly reverted to a reactionary regime based upon a restoration of the old absolutism.

FURTHER READING D. Gates, *The Spanish Ulcer: A History of the Peninsular War* (1986).

Penn, William (1644–1718), Quaker leader who founded Pennylvania as colony for Quakers and other settlers. Penn was the son of Sir William Penn, a prominent admiral and Presbyterian under Cromwell who retained his naval command and conformed to the Church of England under Charles II. Penn went to Oxford after the Restoration, but left the university refusing to conform to the Anglican requirements for vestments. After a brief spell on the continent he returned to start a military career in Ireland, where he suppressed a mutiny at Carrickfergus.

About 1667, however, Penn became a Quaker after attending a meeting of Friends in Cork, and thereafter a career in the army was ruled out because of the pacifism of his sect. He published several tracts defending the principles of the Quakers. His prominent position in a dissenting sect brought him into collision with the authorities on several occasions, notably in the Penn–Mead trial of 1670, which established the independence of juries. In the 1670s he became involved in the proprietorship of the colony of New Jersey, which was in the hands of Quakers, and about 1674 began to solicit the crown for a colony of his own in lieu of debts owed by the crown to his father, who had died in 1670. It took the king until 1679 to respond, indicating that a petition for a colony would be favourably received. Penn consequently petitioned in 1680 and obtained a charter for a colony, which was named Pennsylvania in 1681. Although many Quakers were persuaded to go there it was not intended to be a haven for them alone, and Penn recruited colonists from all over the British isles and northern Europe.

Penn drew up a constitution for Pennsylvania that gave him, as proprietor, executive authority, assisted by a council that also served as the upper house of a general assembly. The lower house was merely intended to accept or reject laws submitted to it but not to initiate legislation. When he went to Pennsylvania in 1682 to get this constitution ratified by a general assembly, however, he met immediate opposition. Assemblymen were not prepared to accept the sweeping powers he had retained for himself and the council nor the passive role he envisaged for them. Over the 1690s he had to concede changes to the constitution, culminating in the Charter of Liberties of 1701. This abolished the legislative functions of the council, making Pennsylvania's assembly unicameral, a unique arrangement in the British colonies in North America. The assembly also obtained the right to initiate legislation.

Penn acted as a sovereign in his colony, most famously negotiating a treaty with the Native North Americans at Shackomaxon, near Philadelphia, in 1682. This is best known from the history painting of the scene by Benjamin WEST. Penn might have been able to retain more authority over his colony if he had not felt obliged to return to England in 1684 to defend his territories from claims made upon them by Lord Baltimore, proprietor of neighbouring Maryland. The boundaries between the lands of the two proprietors were ill defined in their respective charters, and were to be a bone of contention until the delineation of the Mason–Dixon line in the 1760s. The immediate dispute with Baltimore, however, was resolved to Penn's satisfaction. Baltimore claimed that the area that later became the state of Delaware – which had been added to Charles II's grant of Pennsylvania to Penn – was within the territories granted to Maryland by Charles I. This plea was rejected on the grounds that it had been inhabited by Dutch and Finns when the charter had been issued to Maryland in 1633, and therefore fell outside the colony. Delaware had subsequently been conquered from the Dutch in the second and third Anglo-Dutch wars. There was friction between Delaware, which was largely Anglican, and the Quaker-dominated colony of Pennsylvania, which resulted in Penn allowing a separate assembly for Delaware in the final Charter of Liberties in 1701.

Shortly after Penn's return to England, and his successful defence of his claim to Delaware against Baltimore, Charles II died and James II succeeded. Penn was to become very influential in the counsels of the new king. For James sought to remove the disabilities on fellow Catholics, and turned for allies to the DISSENTERS, who were also adversely affected by the penal laws. Outstanding among these collaborators was Penn, who helped to draft the Declaration of Indulgence, or Edict of Toleration, which James issued in 1687. He reissued it in 1688 as a prelude to the calling of a packed Parliament that would enact it onto the statute book. Penn had taken part in the campaign to pack Parliament. Consequently when the GLORIOUS REVOLUTION occurred and James fled to France he was a marked man.

Between 1689 and 1691 Penn was arrested four times on suspicion of being an active JACOBITE, as supporters of the exiled James II were known. Historians hotly debate whether or not Penn was guilty as charged. That the charges were dropped and he was never brought to trial persuades some that he was innocent of actual plotting. But that he was deeply involved in conspiracy is hard to explain away. At all events he was deprived of the government of Pennsylvania in 1692, and did not have it restored to him until 1694. It was not until 1696, when he organized a Quaker Association in response to the assassination attempt against WILLIAM III, that he was fully reconciled to the Williamite regime. In return, his efforts to obtain an act to allow Quakers to make an affirmation in lieu of taking an oath were rewarded by the passing of a statute granting that concession in 1696.

Just when Penn might have thought that he had finally come out of the cold, another threat to his colony emerged. This was the establishment of the BOARD OF TRADE, again in 1696. The Board began a campaign to take all proprietary colonies back under the control of the crown. This policy achieved success with the surrender of New Jersey by its proprietors in 1702. The previous year a bill was introduced into the House of Lords to resume all such colonies. Penn, who was then in Pennsylvania – having gone for the second and last time in 1699 – felt threatened, and pulled every string he could to obviate the threat. By then there were many such strings, for Penn had cultivated friends at court over the years, and could draw on a wide range of influential politicians to help draw the sting of the Board of Trade's attack. In the event the bill made little progress before the session of Parliament ended in 1701, but Penn feared that another would be introduced in the next, and hurried back to England to take care of his colony there. Although no further bill was ever forthcoming, the Board kept up its campaign into ANNE's reign. By then, however, Penn's friends at court included Lord Treasurer GODOLPHIN, the duke of MARLBOROUGH and Robert HARLEY. This formidable triumvirate was unassailable by Penn's enemies at court. Consequently, even though he was in prison for debt from 1707 to 1708, he kept his colony.

Penn's indebtedness, however, led him to consider selling the government of Pennsylvania in 1703, and he negotiated for its conveyance to the crown for £30,000. The negotiations dragged on for years, and Penn's price fell to £20,000 and then to £12,000, a figure that seems to have been agreed by 1712, as the crown then paid him an advance of £1000 on it. But the deal was never finalized. He suffered a severe stroke in October that year which incapacitated him. Although he survived until 1718 his wife had to manage all his affairs for him. On his death he still had both the government and the territory of Pennsylvania, and although quarrels in his family about the proprietorship kept it in jeopardy for a decade, it remained in their hands until 1776.

FURTHER READING M.K. Geiter, *William Penn* (2000).

Perceval, Spencer (1762–1812), politician; prime minister (1809–12). He is notable as the only British prime minister to have been assassinated. Perceval was a barrister who came to the notice of the younger PITT by publishing a tract on the Warren HASTINGS affair in 1790. Thereafter he pleaded for the crown in such leading cases as those against Thomas PAINE in 1792 and Thomas Hardy

in 1794. As a result of his advocacy he was made king's counsel in 1796. That summer he entered Parliament as member for Northampton.

Perceval was a firm supporter of Pitt, although when the latter was replaced in 1801 by ADDINGTON, Perceval served in the new administration as solicitor general and then attorney general. In the latter capacity he successfully prosecuted DESPARD and COBBETT. Pitt retained him as attorney general on his return to power in 1804, but after Pitt's death in 1806 Perceval declined to serve in the MINISTRY OF ALL THE TALENTS. On the appointment of the duke of PORTLAND as prime minister in 1807 Perceval was made chancellor of the exchequer. His income from the law had been so great, however, that he was also given the chancellorship of the duchy of Lancaster to offset financial loss. In 1809 he succeeded the ailing Portland as prime minister.

Perceval showed his support of the EVANGELICALS by banning Monday sessions of Parliament so that members would not have to travel on the Sabbath. His ministry presided over most of the successes of the PENINSULAR WAR. On 11 May 1812 as he entered the lobby of the house, one John Bellingham – a deranged merchant with a personal grievance against the government – went up to him and shot him at point-blank range. His assassination sent shock waves through the political system, and helped to rally the forces of reaction that were to prove so strong in the first years of the ministry of Lord LIVERPOOL, Perceval's successor.

FURTHER READING D. Gray, *Spencer Percival: The Evangelical Prime Minister, 1762–1812* (1963).

Percy, Thomas (1729–1812), scholar and antiquarian who played a key role in preserving Britain's rich heritage of medieval BALLADS. The son of a Shropshire grocer, Percy was educated at Oxford and entered the church. He held the living at Easton Maudit, Northamptonshire, and later rose to become the bishop of Dromore in

County Down. Percy's passion for ballads was appropriate for a man whose own surname recalled the legendary hero of 'Chevy Chase'. This passion was kindled by chance after he rescued an early 17th-century manuscript collection of verse that maids had been using to light a fire. Samuel JOHNSON supported Percy's researches, and wrote the preface to his important collection of ballads, *The Reliques of Ancient English Poetry,* which was published in 1765. At a period when interest in Britain's 'Gothic' past was becoming increasingly fashionable, Percy's *Reliques* proved highly influential. His readers included Walter Scott, whose own interest in collecting and rewriting ballads bore fruit in the *Minstrelsy of the Scottish Border* of 1802.

Petty, William, 2nd earl of Shelburne. *See* SHELBURNE, WILLIAM PETTY, 2ND EARL OF, AND 1ST MARQUESS OF LANSDOWNE.

philanthropy. *See* CHARITY.

piracy. When Lieutenant Robert Maynard of the Royal Navy made sail for the coast of Virginia in November 1718 the bowsprit of his sloop sported a grisly trophy – the severed head of Edward Teach, alias 'Blackbeard'. Along with ten of his crew, Teach had been slain in a brief but bloody encounter after his vessel, the *Adventure,* was trapped by Maynard's command within the confines of North Carolina's Ocracoke Inlet. Although suffering from the consequences of a heavy drinking bout, Teach had put up an impressive fight; no less than 25 wounds were later counted on his body. Blackbeard's fate had been sealed by the royal governor of Virginia, Alexander Spotswood, an official with a crusading mission to exterminate the pirates who increasingly disrupted his colony's economy.

Along with men like William Kidd, 'Long Ben' Every, Stede Bonnet, Bartholomew Roberts and 'Calico Jack' Rackham – not forgetting their female counterparts Mary Read and Anne Bonny – the infamous Blackbeard was a product of what has since been dubbed the 'golden age' of piracy. In

1724, as that era was coming to a violent finale, the short and savage careers of such malefactors provided ready raw material for Daniel DEFOE's best seller, *A General History of the Robberies and Murders of the Most Notorious Pirates,* which was written under the suitably nautical pseudonym of 'Captain Charles Johnson'. For some thirty years prior to the volume's appearance, thousands of pirates – most of them drawn from the Anglo-American seafaring community – had preyed upon shipping from the Caribbean to the Indian Ocean. The dislocation of trade caused by these predators, allied with their open defiance of royal authority, eventually proved so troubling that the Royal Navy was instructed to devote unprecedented resources to rooting them out. The resulting mass trials and executions ended the pirate scourge, but not before the colourful lives and spectacular exploits of men such as Blackbeard had taken a grip upon the popular imagination that has yet to be released. Thanks to the efforts of journalists like Defoe, some pirates became legends in their own lifetimes. A merging of fact with fiction has characterized the depiction of pirates ever since. For example, the Israel Hands immortalized in Robert Louis Stevenson's classic *Treasure Island* took his name from a real pirate who had served as Blackbeard's navigator and only survived his notorious captain owing to crippling wounds.

Men like Blackbeard – a Bristol-born psychopath who reputedly drank his rum spiked with gunpowder – inherited and developed a tradition established by the Caribbean-based 'buccaneers' who had assaulted the 'Spanish Main' during much of the 17th century. Buccaneering had peaked in 1671, when Sir Henry Morgan sacked Panama, the jewel in Spain's colonial crown, but its justification vanished at the onset of peace with the old enemy. The English, Dutch and French buccaneers had all focused their attentions upon a common foe; by contrast, the new breed of pirates who succeeded them from the 1690s onwards attacked vessels irrespective of nationality. Swift-sailing and heavily armed pirate craft hunted Spanish treasure ships, Bristol slavers and Moghul merchantmen alike. Sailing under black or red ensigns featuring such ghoulish images as skeletons bearing hourglasses and bleeding hearts, or the infamous skull and crossed bones, pirates sought to intimidate their prey into striking their colours without a fight. Merchant captains who persisted in resistance might expect a far more painful and protracted fate than the mythical doom of 'walking the plank'.

By the early 18th century some islands, such as Madagascar in the Indian Ocean and New Providence in the Bahamas, hosted established pirate settlements. Although living beyond the reaches of the official law, pirates were far from lawless; indeed, pirate crews were governed by self-imposed codes of conduct, resulting in egalitarian communities where captains were elected upon merit alone, and could be deposed, or even executed, for abusing their position. With the exception of captains and quartermasters, who received twice the usual share in recognition of their responsibilities, pirate crews divided their spoils equally among those men who had fought to gain it.

Pirates regarded themselves as an elite fraternity, despising landlubbers and those merchant or Royal Navy seamen who lacked the spirit to join them in their risky but potentially lucrative calling. Like other violent criminals of the era, pirates aimed to die 'game', often toasting their comrades and damning their judges as they faced the gallows. The pirate creed was memorably encapsulated by one of its most prolific practitioners, Bartholomew Roberts. 'Black Bart', who sailed under an ensign depicting himself and a grinning skeleton drinking a toast to death, observed: 'In an honest service there is thin rations, low wages and hard labour; in this, plenty and satiety, pleasure and ease, liberty and power; and who would not balance creditor on this side, when all the hazard that is run for it, at worst, is only a sour look or two at choking. No, a merry life and a short one shall be my motto.' Roberts's own career matched his words: in less than four years of roving

the Atlantic he bagged more than 400 vessels before being killed in 1722 during an encounter with the Royal Navy in the Gulf of Guinea. In keeping with his wishes Roberts's body was pitched overboard by his grieving crew, still resplendent in all its finery.

Already encouraged by the increasing tempo of international trade, piracy gained further impetus after 1713 when the ending of the War of the SPANISH SUCCESSION led to the demobilization of thousands of seafarers. Many of these veteran mariners were practised in the art of privateering, the wartime arrangement by which the shipping of an enemy power was deemed a legitimate target to any officially licensed vessel. The line between pirate and freelance privateer was always a fine one; it was crossed by William Kidd, whose pirate-hunting voyage to the Red Sea in the closing years of the 17th century took on a very different character after a surly crew persuaded him to plunder at will. Kidd had received his commission from King WILLIAM III himself, but the syndicate of Whig politicians who had backed the cruise in the hope of profit left Kidd to his fate when the legality of his actions was questioned. Like many other pirates, the unlucky Kidd ended his days at Wapping's 'Execution Dock'; his tarred corpse subsequently dangled in irons at Tilbury as a grim warning to passing seamen tempted by a life of robbery with violence on the high seas.

FURTHER READING D. Cordingly, *Life Among the Pirates. The Romance and the Reality* (1995); M. Rediker, *Between the Devil and the Deep Blue Sea: Merchant Seamen, Pirates, and the Anglo-American Maritime World, 1700–1750* (1987).

Pitt, William, the Elder, 1st earl of Chatham

(1708–78), statesman who directed Britain's foreign policy and global strategy during the SEVEN YEARS WAR and who subsequently became prime minister (1766–8). Pitt has long enjoyed a reputation as the charismatic architect of Britain's stunning triumph during the Seven Years War. However, while Pitt's role as single-minded war leader was undoubtedly significant, historians have recently offered more cautious assessments of the degree to which 'the Great Commoner' was personally responsible for victory in the 'great war for the empire'.

Following education at Eton and Oxford, Pitt was commissioned into a cavalry regiment in 1731 and entered Parliament four years later. Pitt's talents as an orator were soon apparent in his vehement criticisms of Sir Robert WALPOLE, but his path to office was hampered by a dismal relationship with GEORGE II. The king's dislike of the domineering young member for Old Sarum was sustained by Pitt's consistent opposition to the policy of support for the monarchy's cherished electorate of HANOVER and advocacy of a BLUE-WATER POLICY. In 1746 Pitt eventually secured the position of paymaster general. This potentially lucrative post provided Pitt with an opportunity to enhance his reputation for honesty, but denied him cabinet office and any real share of political power.

Pitt's chance came in 1754, with the death of the prime minister, Henry PELHAM. When Pelham's successor the duke of NEWCASTLE proved wary of offering encouragement to such an ambitious and aggressive rival, Pitt allied himself with Henry FOX to mount devastating attacks upon the administration in the House of Commons. Fox subsequently joined the cabinet, leaving Pitt bewildered and frustrated at his exclusion from office. However, as the opening phase of the Seven Years War brought dispiriting news of embarrassing defeats in North America and the Mediterranean, the uneasy alliance between Fox and Newcastle foundered, and the popular clamour for Pitt soon became irresistible. In December 1756 George II finally swallowed his pride and invited Pitt to form a government fronted by the duke of DEVONSHIRE. The ministry proved short-lived and Pitt was dismissed in April 1757. That summer, the continuing reports of disasters around the globe left little alternative but to form a coalition government that pooled the diverse talents of Pitt and Newcastle.

Although Newcastle was appointed first lord, it was Pitt, as secretary of state for the Southern Department, who dominated the conduct of the war. Pitt's earlier antipathy towards British intervention in Europe was now reversed, and his continuing emphasis upon a 'blue-water policy' of colonial conquest was counterbalanced by the despatch of British troops to Germany and massive financial support for Britain's continental ally, Frederick the Great of PRUSSIA. The strategy ultimately paid dividends: with the bulk of French forces concentrated within the European theatre, Britain used her amphibious capacity to harvest France's vulnerable colonies. As Pitt later claimed, America had indeed been won on the plains of Germany.

Pitt took a keen interest in the minutiae of the conflict, sending detailed directives to Britain's commanders. Such interventions from a politician so distant from the scene of action were not always helpful, and sometimes upset the careful plans of the men actually on the spot. In addition, recent research indicates that the policies responsible for victory did not stem from Pitt alone, but were rather the product of an experienced team of strategists and planners that included the commander in chief, Sir John LIGONIER, the first lord of the Admiralty, Admiral George ANSON, and the much maligned Newcastle himself.

From 1758 onwards, the ministry's advocacy of a vigorous war of empire began to yield spectacular results, with key territorial gains in the Americas, India and Africa. However, by the accession of GEORGE III in October 1760 the national mood was turning against the continuation of a victorious but increasingly costly conflict. Under the influence of his tutor Lord BUTE, the young king craved peace. Pitt remained determined to prosecute the war to the bitter end. He resigned in October 1761 when the cabinet refused to approve a pre-emptive strike against Britain's old enemy Spain. In fresh fighting that erupted soon after, Spain allied herself with France, and Britain again enjoyed overwhelming success. During the negotiations that led to the treaty of PARIS in 1763 Pitt railed against the leniency displayed towards the defeated Bourbons and the ministry's cynical abandonment of Prussia.

During the 1760s Pitt's vacillating position contributed to the decade's political instability. Having toiled to free British North America from the menace of Canada, Pitt remained a supporter of the colonists when tension mounted with the mother country over the issue of taxation (*see* AMERICAN COLONIES 1763–1776). He opposed his brother-in-law George GRENVILLE's Stamp Act and later attacked the American policies of Lord NORTH's administration. In July 1766 Pitt had been persuaded by the king to form a ministry with GRAFTON as first lord. Pitt, who had now been ennobled as the earl of Chatham, soon suffered a bout of madness. Denied Pitt's prestigious leadership, the ministry's mediocre members drifted rudderless into disarray. Pitt resigned in the autumn of 1768; it was more than a year before he recovered. When his illness permitted, Pitt continued to make memorable appearances in the House of Lords. Although opposed to American independence, he never lost hope of a settlement that would maintain the integrity of Britain's Atlantic empire. In April 1778 Pitt collapsed during a debate in the House; he died in the following month and was buried in Westminster Abbey.

Pitt possessed a complex character. Despite his immense popular appeal, he remained an intensely private man: like his equally famous son, he was notoriously aloof and demonstrated little interest in cultivating friendships among his colleagues. Yet Pitt was devoted to his wife Hester and their five children. Tall and hawk-like, Pitt intimidated opponents through the sheer power of his personality; indeed, Pitt's dignity of appearance and speech led to comparisons with the great statesmen of ancient Rome. Throughout his political career Pitt was dogged by mental and physical illness: besides the deep depressions that underlay his occasional lapses into insanity, Pitt was a lifelong sufferer from gout and often appeared in Parliament hobbling on crutches and swathed in flannel bandages. For all his contradictions, Pitt remained fiercely independent and unswerving in his patriotic devotion to what he perceived to be Britain's interests. While the finer details of Pitt's role in transforming his country into the era's leading prime imperial power are open to debate, his position as a leading British politician of the 18th century remains undisputed.

FURTHER READING J. Black, *Pitt the Elder* (1992); R. Middleton, *The Bells of Victory: The Pitt–Newcastle Ministry and the Conduct of the Seven Years' War 1757–62* (1985); M. Peters, *The Elder Pitt* (1998).

Pitt, William, the Younger (1759–1806), politician; prime minister (1783–1801, 1804–6), who led the country through much of the REVOLUTIONARY AND NAPOLEONIC WARS. The son of William PITT earl of Chatham, the younger Pitt entered Parliament in 1781. He rapidly rose to power, becoming chancellor of the exchequer in the SHELBURNE ministry in 1782 and, after the fall of the FOX–NORTH coalition, prime minister in 1783, at the age of 24 the youngest in British history. At first it was a minority government and he was defeated on division after division in the Commons, including one on a vote of confidence. To give him a majority GEORGE III dissolved Parliament in 1784, and Pittites were elected in sufficient numbers at the polls to ensure control of the House. They were returned not only for boroughs where the government had influence, but from counties and other large constituencies where public opinion was also influential.

Pitt was popular. He had expressed support for PARLIAMENTARY REFORM before the election, and in 1785 introduced a bill to effect it. However, he was only allowed to do so as a private and not as a ministerial measure, and it was defeated. He did, however, continue the process of 'economical reform' by eliminating sinecures, which diminished the patronage of the crown. He also persuaded George III to expand the peerage, significantly increasing the size of the House of LORDS. Pitt adroitly handled the REGENCY CRISIS of 1788–9, which consolidated his strong relationship with the king.

Pitt's prudent handling of the public finances was put severely to the test by the outbreak of war with revolutionary France in 1793. Yet even in wartime Pitt continued to pursue sound financial policies. Where earlier wars had been largely financed by loans advanced on the security of future taxes, Pitt took steps to ensure that this war was paid for largely from current taxation. This involved increasing the rates of existing taxes and introducing new ones, most notably the first income tax, raised in 1799.

The war also led Pitt to clamp down on radicalism, which seemed to threaten revolution in Britain too. The suspension of habeas corpus, the passing of the Seditious Meetings Act and the Treasonable Practices Act, and the trials of members of the London Corresponding Society for treason have been called 'Pitt's Reign of Terror'. Though this is a grotesque exaggeration, the attempt to suppress radical agitation did betray a determination to eradicate criticism of the constitution. The ruling classes were not prepared to succumb to demands for constitutional change from below, as the duke of PORTLAND, leader of the Whigs, showed in 1794 when he went over to Pitt's side.

The impact of the FRENCH REVOLUTION on Ireland was more of a threat to Pitt's government than it was in Britain. The Society of United Irishmen formed in 1791 agitated for reforms that Pitt perceived as threatening independence, and he dissolved the Society in 1794. The more determined members founded the United Irish Society the following year. The French tried to exploit Irish aspirations in their own struggle with Britain. They attempted a landing in Bantry Bay in 1797, while expectations of another invasion inspired the IRISH REBELLION OF 1798. Pitt was converted to the view that the only safe solution was to incorporate Ireland into the United Kingdom, and passed the Act

of Union in 1800 (*see* UNION OF BRITAIN AND IRELAND). When he insisted that CATHOLIC EMANCIPATION was a necessary corollary of union George III refused to concede it, and Pitt resigned in 1801. The ministry of Henry ADDINGTON that replaced him really only lasted as long as Pitt refused to oppose it. When he did go into opposition in 1804 Addington fell and Pitt again became prime minister. His second ministry came to an unexpected end in 1806 with his death at the age of 45. The war with France had almost a decade to go. But Pitt had proved a capable and resourceful wartime prime minister who provided the ways and means by which Britain was ultimately to prevail.

FURTHER READING J. Ehrman, *The Younger Pitt*, Vols. 1–3 (1969; 1983; 1996).

placemen, those members of Parliament who had 'places' or offices of profit under the crown. These ranged from the key offices of state – first lord of the Treasury, SECRETARY OF STATE and chancellor of the exchequer, for instance – to sinecures like the Clerks Comptrollers of the Green Cloth. Numbers of placemen grew in the course of the 18th century from about 120 in Anne's reign to 150 in the reign of George II and 180 by George III. Their presence and growth aroused suspicion that the ministers were attempting to create a majority in the House of Commons by appointing MPs to such offices. This led to attempts to curb the power of the crown to make such appointments. In 1700 excisemen and customs officers were debarred from sitting in the Commons, and both categories were deprived of the vote in elections in 1782. In 1701 the Act of Settlement actually carried a clause making the possession of an office under the crown incompatible with holding a seat in Parliament. Had this come into effect it would have stifled CABINET government at birth. The Act was not to be implemented, however, until the death of Anne in 1714, by which time the clause itself had already been repealed in the Regency Act of 1706. In its place a complicated measure was enacted which made the possession of certain offices incompatible with a parliamentary seat, including all posts which might be created after the Regency Act was passed. Offices which were not barred from being held by an MP were dealt with by making those appointed to them resign their seats and face a by-election. These measures, however, did little to prevent the increase in the number of placemen in the Commons during the century, until John DUNNING'S MOTION was passed in 1780. Although this had no immediate practical effect, when ROCKINGHAM led his second administration in 1782, measures to reduce the crown's influence through economic reform were enacted. Thus an act sponsored by Edmund BURKE eliminated 134 household offices, the secretaryship of state for the colonies and the Board of Trade. It also reduced the civil list to £900,000 per annum. Further measures of economical reform (*see* PARLIAMENTARY REFORM) significantly reduced the crown's ability to build up support in Parliament from the exercise of patronage.

FURTHER READING W.D. Rubinstein, 'The end of "Old Corruption" in Britain, 1780–1860' in *Past and Present* C1 (1983), 55–86

Plassey, battle of (3 June 1757), British victory over the forces of the nawab of Bengal, and a milestone in the spread of Britain's power in INDIA. Following his recapture of Calcutta in February 1757, Colonel Robert CLIVE anticipated further resistance from Siraj-ud-Daula, the French-backed nawab, or ruler, of Bengal. Siraj was indeed determined to oppose the continuing expansion of Britain's East India Company, and Clive sought to counter him by enlisting the support of his local opponents; these included the nawab's own general, Mir Jaffir.

When Clive marched upon Siraj's capital of Murshidabad he found his path blocked by a vast native force near Plassey on the river Bhagirathi. The nawab's undisciplined army numbered 50,000 men, whilst Clive commanded some 2000 trained native troops and about 800 Europeans. A rain storm soaked the powder of the nawab's French-manned cannon and put them out of action. Clive's own guns had remained dry under tarpaulins and now resumed fire with devastating effect. The nawab's host suffered mounting casualties, whilst Clive's intrigues also helped to turn the odds in his favour: Mir Jaffir's men took no part in the battle, and at a cost of just 60 men killed and wounded, Clive achieved a decisive victory. In the wake of the encounter the nawab was murdered and replaced by Mir Jaffir. The outcome of Plassey earned Clive both fame and fortune and represented a significant step towards British domination of Bengal.

poaching. *See* GAME LAWS.

poetry. The traditional literary canon of poetry from John Dryden (1631–1700) to William Wordsworth (1770–1850) concentrates upon the verse of a select group of poets led by POPE, THOMSON, GRAY, BURNS, BLAKE, COWPER, and the LAKE POETS. Literary critics tend to arrange them into chronological categories such as AUGUSTAN, pre-Romantic and Romantic. Thus Dryden and Pope are regarded as neoclassical poets, producing mock epics like 'Mac Flecknoe' and 'The Dunciad', creating poems based on the works of the Romans Horace and Juvenal and employing 'heroic' couplets, each formed of two lines of rhyming iambic pentameters. These classical models are then held to have inspired verse which became atrophied and stilted into 'poetic diction', until there was a reaction against it brought about by the ROMANTIC MOVEMENT. Romantic poets, responding to Wordsworth's manifesto in the *Lyrical Ballads*, employed 'the real language of men'. Their poems were reflective of private rather than public experiences, capturing 'emotion recollected in tranquillity'.

This view of 18th-century verse has been much criticized of late. The canonical approach overlooks too much that was published at the time. It was always contemptuous of the output of the poets laureate who followed Dryden, starting with Nahum Tate and ending with Robert Southey. Feminist critics rightly pointed out that it neglected the output of women poets, such as Jane Barker, Mary Collier, Mary Leapor, Anna Seward and Anna Laetitia BARBAULD. Above all it ignored a host of little-known and anonymous poets whose verses have only recently been rescued from oblivion.

When attention is drawn from the canon to the poets previously dismissed as 'minor', the alleged sequence of poetry from neoclassical to Romantic is also called into question. A popular genre at the beginning of the period, for instance, was 'Poems on Affairs of State'. Many were indeed written in mock epic form based on classical models. Some were even the work of canonical poets such as PRIOR and SWIFT. But they also inspired a variety of poems from hacks like DEFOE and obscure, even anonymous, versifiers, some based on ballads like 'Chevy Chase' which, according to many canonical accounts, were to be discovered by the Romantics.

The subject matter and verse forms of the mass of poetry which appeared in the Georgian age defy categorization. For example, while George CRABBE (1754–1832) employed couplets to a degree that earned him the nickname 'the Last Augustan', his verse nonetheless exposed the harsh realities of rural life in a fashion that contrasted with the idealized picture contained within GOLDSMITH's *The Deserted Village* (1770), which laments a 'lost age' of village life despoiled by the effects of enclosure (*see* AGRICULTURE). While such diversities challenge the canonical periodization of the century's poetry, a new chronological pattern has yet to be established.

SEE ALSO BALLADS.

FURTHER READING G. de Forest Lord (ed.), *Anthology of Poems on Affairs of State* (1975); R. Lonsdale (ed.), *The New Oxford Book of Eighteenth-Century Verse* (1984).

police. *See* BOW STREET RUNNERS.

Poor Law, legislation dating from the Elizabethan period under which relief for the poor was organized. During the Georgian era the time-honoured system by which local authorities in England and Wales provided relief came under increasing strain. As the number of those seeking assistance rose steadily, drastic new solutions to the problem of poverty were implemented.

Under the terms of the Poor Law Act of 1601, every parish was obliged to assume responsibility for its own poor. Relief was organized and administered by a panel of local worthies headed by the JUSTICES OF THE PEACE; the JPs operated in conjunction with churchmen and those solid householders who composed the parish meeting or 'vestry'. Assistance to the poor was provided from a rate fixed and levied by the vestry; its verdicts were enforced by parish constables and paid overseers of the poor.

The parochial nature of poor relief had been confirmed by the 1662 Act of Settlement. In an effort to control the movement of population following the upheavals of the civil wars, this legislation limited aid to those possessing strong roots in the parish, including illegitimate children born there. All others seeking assistance – regardless of their age or state of health – were obliged to return to their own parish of origin for help.

Such a system was designed to cater for close-knit agrarian societies where outsiders were a rarity. Those powerful men who administered the poor law enjoyed a significant degree of control over their communities; while providing the overseers with an opportunity to demonstrate their paternalism towards the deserving poor, the system also allowed them to register their disapproval of vagrants and other undesirables. The fundamental link between relief and 'settlement' led to drastic action against 'aliens' who threatened to become an unwanted burden upon the local rates. In addition, because bastard children born in the parish gained a settlement and therefore the right to relief, unmarried pregnant women frequently faced heavy pressure to move on.

During the course of the 18th century, increasing hardship among those workers who had migrated to the growing urban centres of industry, as well as amongst a rapidly expanding workforce of agricultural labourers, underpinned a dramatic escalation in total poor rates: an annual expenditure of some £700,000 at the accession of Anne had topped £4 million by the outbreak of the Napoleonic Wars. The growing cost of relief prompted new approaches to the perennial problem of the poor. Men such as Joseph Townsend pushed for the total abolition of relief. According to this harsh argument, when the poor were denied their customary support they would be obliged to work or starve. Such schemes were not adopted, although others that found favour were not much more humane. Some parishes joined forces in a union, building a central workhouse where the poor were fed and housed in return for their forced labour; such bleak institutions acquired an unsavoury reputation that alarmed genuine philanthropists such as Jonas HANWAY and John HOWARD.

In the final years of the century, continuing rural poverty led to the widespread adoption of a new system of aid for the poor. Evolved at SPEENHAMLAND in Berkshire, it used poor relief to augment the paltry wages of farm labourers. All politicians and economists recognized that the existing system was too expensive and was not working well, but dispute about what should be done continued until the passing of the Poor Law Amendment Act in 1834.

FURTHER READING J.D. Marshall, *The Old Poor Law, 1795–1834* (2nd edn, 1985).

Pope, Alexander (1688–1744), the leading poet of the early 18th century. Pope was a Roman Catholic and therefore obliged by the penal laws to live ten miles (16 km) out of London. His family home was in Windsor Forest, from which he moved at first to Chiswick, and then in 1717 to Twickenham, where he settled. Although barred by his religion from the universities he acquired sufficient understanding of Greek to translate Homer, the *Iliad* appearing in the years 1715 to 1720 and the *Odyssey* in 1725–6. Despite the dismissive comments of the classical scholar Richard BENTLEY, they sold well, especially in superb subscription editions, and earned Pope some £10,000, making him financially independent. He also edited Shakespeare's works in 1725, but that was less successful.

Pope's own major poems appeared before and after the translations of Homer. The best known of his early poems, *The Rape of the Lock*, is usually read as a *jeu d'esprit*, lightly mocking the dishonour done to Belinda by the Baron's snipping a lock of her hair while playing cards at court. However, a political message has been read into it by those who see the image of rape, and of the Baron as a ravisher, as a condemnation of the GLORIOUS REVOLUTION. Yet it is good-natured in its attitude to Queen ANNE, 'who sometimes counsel takes and sometimes tea'.

Anne is given more reverential treatment in Pope's *Windsor Forest*, written to celebrate the treaty of UTRECHT in 1713:

> At length great ANNA said – Let Discord cease!
> She said, the World obey'd, and all was Peace!

The passage that concludes 'And peace and plenty tell, a Stuart reigns' has been read as expressing JACOBITE sympathy. Yet Pope had no great regard for the Stuarts, dismissing James I's reign as 'absolutely the worst reign we ever had – except perhaps that of James the Second'. He did, however, criticize WILLIAM III in *Windsor Forest*, comparing him with William the Conqueror. Under them, so far from there being peace and plenty in the forest, it appeared 'a dreary desert and a gloomy waste' because both kings 'dispeopled air and floods'. 'Oh may no more a foreign master's rage', he wished, 'with wrongs yet legal curse a future age.'

Pope's notion that the forest suffered under 'foreign' kings, William the Conqueror, William III and, by implication, GEORGE I, has been cited to support the view that he would have been appalled at the suppression by the Hanoverians of the traditional rights of those who lived there. He would therefore have sympathized with the 'Waltham Blacks' – among whom were two of his kinsmen – who with blackened faces defied the new rulers of the forest. There is some evidence that the Blacks were Jacobites which, if Pope had been inclined towards that lost cause, would have further endeared them to him. It has even been alleged that WALPOLE suspended proceedings against Pope's relatives in order to have a hold over the poet, and that this succeeded, since for several years his poetry was not overtly political.

Yet this is all deduction, for no documentary evidence can be cited to establish Pope's attitude to his criminal kinsmen. It is just as likely that he was ashamed of their deer stealing, especially since he was on good terms with such figures as Lord Cobham, the governor of Windsor castle who had to deal with their depredations. His failure to produce political verse in the early 1720s was probably more the result of his being absorbed, as we have seen, in the translations of Homer and his edition of Shakespeare, than of Walpole's blackmailing him to keep silent. Certainly by the late 1720s Pope was treated cordially by the prime minister, and frequently dined with him.

By the 1730s, however, Pope became identified with the opposition. The turning point was marked by the publication of the *Dunciad Variorum* in 1729. Although it teems with the names of hack writers and scribblers in the government's cause, the *Dunciad*'s prime target is not the dunces themselves but those 'great Patricians' who 'inspire these wond'rous works'. Among the patricians are the kings themselves – 'still Dunce the second reigns like Dunce the first' – and the Whig oligarchs presided over by Walpole. When Pope came to rewrite the poem in the *Dunciad in four books* (published in 1743) the political content became more explicit, with Walpole appearing as a 'wizard old' and 'tyrant supreme'. Between the two *Dun-*

ciads Pope wrote the *Epistles*, which are generally called *Moral Essays*. Those to Lord BATHURST and Lord BURLINGTON on 'the use of riches' further attack the Whig oligarchy by developing the notion that they had encouraged the rise of a corrupt MONIED INTEREST that undermined the values of the traditional landed elite. The political message of these poems is profoundly pessimistic, culminating in the despairing vision of society's future in the closing lines of the *Dunciad*:

> Lo! thy dread Empire, CHAOS! is restor'd;
> Light dies before thy uncreating word:
> Thy hand, great Anarch! lets the curtain fall;
> And Universal Darkness buries all.

By contrast Pope's *Essay on Man* (1733–4) is usually considered to be an optimistic poem. So it is, in the sense that Pope considered the pursuit of happiness to be a worthy human goal and even held that it was possible attain it. However, the vast majority of mankind who sought it in wealth, greatness and fame, were doomed to disappointment:

> If all, united, thy ambition call,
> From ancient story learn to scorn them all.
> There, in the rich, the honour'd, fam'd and
> great,
> See the false scale of Happiness complete!

True happiness was to be found in 'health, peace and competence'.

How far Pope himself found true happiness is difficult to determine. His satiric wit made him many enemies who gave him back their spleen in good measure. At the same time he made lasting friendships with men such as ARBUTHNOT, BOLINGBROKE and SWIFT, friendships that clearly sustained him. He suffered from a childhood illness that stunted his growth, so that he was less than five feet in height, and led him to complain of 'this long disease, my life'. It ended on 30 May 1744.

SEE ALSO AUGUSTAN AGE, CRIME.

FURTHER READING M. Mack, *Alexander Pope: A Life* (1985); P. Rogers, *Essays on Pope* (1993).

population. Until the findings of the Cambridge Group for the History of Population and Social Structure were made public in 1981, estimates of the numbers of people in Britain in the 18th century were based on those of John Rickman, the first registrar general for the census, in the early 19th century. It was on the basis of his calculations, and the intelligent guesses of Gregory KING in the 1690s, that the historian Thomas Babington, 1st baron Macaulay (1800–1859) reached the conclusion that there were between 5 million and 5.5 million people in England and Wales at the accession of James II in 1685. From computerized analyses of parish records the Group concluded that the total numbers in 1686 were 4,864,762. They also calculated that they had actually *fallen* from 5,281,347 in 1656. After the 1680s there was a slow recovery, though numbers did not reach 5 million until 1701. There was a slow rise in the early 18th century, to 5.3 million in 1721. The late 1720s witnessed a fall, however, so that that the estimate for 1731 is 5.2 million. Thereafter there was a steady increase, to 6.1 million at the accession of GEORGE III in 1760. His reign saw a population boom, with the first CENSUS in 1801 recording 8.8 million inhabitants in England and Wales. The 1821 census registered 12 million. Figures for Scotland before the census of 1801, which recorded 1.6 million, are more conjectural. There may have been a million in 1701, perhaps 200,000 less than in 1690. By 1821 there were 2 million. The population of Great Britain therefore more than doubled between 1680 and 1820. In Ireland, population growth during the 18th century was more rapid than anywhere else in Europe. An estimated population of 3 million at midcentury had risen to 5.5 million by 1800. The upward trend continued unchecked, and by 1845, on the eve of the Great Famine, Ireland held more than 8 million people.

It has long been known that the population increased over the 'long' 18th century, though the rate and scale of the increase have only recently been appreciated. However, the cause of the rise has been a matter of much dispute. It used to be attributed to a drop in the death rate. Certainly mortality from disease and famine is still regarded as the cause of the apparent falls in the population of England and Wales in the decades between the 1650s and the 1680s, and of Scotland in the 1690s. But where successful inoculation against smallpox used to be cited as the main cause of the population expansion of the late 18th century, now a rise in the birth rate is accepted as the more significant cause. Childbearing increased as a greater proportion of the population married, rising from 84% to 93% over the century. Probably more significant was a fall in the mean age of marriage for women, from 26.5 in the late 17th century to 23.4 in the early 19th century. This gave rise to more births, while younger mothers ensured that there would be more surviving children. These mean averages conceal different trends in different regions. In largely agricultural communities there was little appreciable fall in the mean age of marriage for brides. It was in the growing commercial and manufacturing districts that women tended to marry earlier. This was because marriage was generally postponed in early modern Britain until the couple could be economically independent of their parents. Opportunities for earning higher wages in manufacturing than in agriculture assisted the trend to early marriage and thereby an increase in the population.

FURTHER READING E.A. Wrigley and R.S. Schofield, *The Population History of England and Wales 1541–1871: A Reconstruction* (2nd edn., 1989).

Porteous riots (1736), one of the 18th century's most notorious incidents of direct 'crowd action'. The riots were sparked by the execution of a popular smuggler in Edinburgh in 1736. Despite widespread sympathy for the condemned man, no attempt was made to interfere with the hanging on 14 April. However, the insensitive attitude of Captain John Porteous, who commanded the prisoner's escort, led to disturbances when the body was cut down. Stones were thrown at the soldiers; instead of withdrawing, Porteous allegedly grabbed a musket, shot one of the rioters and ordered his men to open fire. Several fatalities resulted. Pursued by an outraged mob, the soldiers turned and opened fire without orders, bringing the death toll to six. Porteous was prosecuted by the lord advocate, convicted of murder and sentenced to death.

The verdict met with an enthusiastic local response; the subsequent decision of Queen CAROLINE to reprieve the captain for six weeks provoked equally widespread anger. Those killed by Porteous's men had included a cross-section of Edinburgh society; the captain's enemies therefore included men of influence. Instead of being housed within the secure walls of the Castle, Porteous was placed in the feeble Tolbooth prison. On 7 September a large but orderly crowd broke into the jail, removed Porteous to the Grassmarket, and lynched him. Having achieved its objective, the mob dispersed without causing any further disturbance. Troops were available to rescue Porteous, but their commander, General Moyle, was unwilling to act without the protection offered by written orders from the city magistrates.

The captain's killers were never punished. Instead, in a desperate face-saving measure the government decided to take punitive action against the city of Edinburgh itself. An original proposal to abolish the city's charter and impose other humiliating penalties met fierce opposition in Scotland; it was eventually replaced by the milder punishment of a £2000 communal fine – to provide a pension for Porteous's widow – and the dismissal of the provost. WALPOLE's handling of the incident cost him the support of the powerful duke of ARGYLL, and thereby contributed to his downfall in 1742. The Porteous riots feature vividly in the early part of Walter Scott's *Heart of Midlothian*.

Portland, William Bentinck, 1st earl of (1649– 1709), close friend of WILLIAM III, who made him earl of Portland for his support in the GLORIOUS REVOLUTION. As a Dutchman he was the chief object of xenophobic sentiment expressed by the English. Grants made to him in Ireland by the king were revoked by Parliament. His involvement in foreign affairs, especially in the partition treaty of 1699, led to an abortive attempt to impeach him in 1701.

Portland, William Henry Cavendish Bentinck, 3rd duke of (1738–1809), politician; prime minister (1783, 1807–9). He succeeded to his title in 1762. He attached himself to Lord ROCKINGHAM's party in the House of Lords, becoming lord chamberlain in his first brief ministry from 1765 to 1766. He went into opposition with the ROCKINGHAMITES and became a leading member of the Whig party that developed from that group. When Rockingham formed his second administration in 1782 Portland became lord lieutenant of Ireland. In the struggle between Charles James FOX and Lord SHELBURNE that broke out on Rockingham's death, Portland sided with Fox, and when the Fox–NORTH coalition was formed in 1783 Portland was nominally prime minister.

Portland went into opposition against the younger PITT but following the outbreak of the French Revolution closed ranks with the government, formally going over to it in 1792. He became home secretary in 1794, a post he held until 1801, acquiring a reputation for sensitive handling of the controversial policies of repression. Thereafter he served under ADDINGTON and in Pitt's last ministry. On Pitt's death he retired from politics but was called back on the collapse of the MINISTRY OF ALL THE TALENTS to become prime minister again from 1807 until his death. His term of office was made difficult by lack of success in war and by the rivalry of his two most prominent ministers, CASTLEREAGH and CANNING.

Pratt, Charles, 1st Earl Camden. *See* CAMDEN, CHARLES PRATT, 1ST EARL.

press, the. Britain's newspaper press came of age during the 18th century. Not only did an ever-expanding range of daily and weekly publications offer detailed coverage of domestic and foreign affairs, but they increasingly moulded and vocalized public opinion. In doing so, newspapers played a key role in spreading a culture of popular political participation.

The rise of the 18th-century press was all the more impressive because it built upon modest precedents. Broadsheets recording the continental upheavals of the Thirty Years War had appeared sporadically in London during the first half of the 17th century. However, it was Britain's own ideologically charged Civil Wars of the 1640s that first provided the impetus for regular newspapers. During the conflict, rival royalist and parliamentarian newsheets – printed in Oxford and London respectively – each propagated their own version of events. In 1665 a proliferation of unauthorized publications prompted the foundation of the *London Gazette*, which offered officially approved bulletins. Those seeking to compete with such bland fare came under the scrutiny of a surveyor of the press armed with extensive licensing powers. Despite these sanctions, during the 1670s the furore surrounding the Popish Plot tempted some printers to risk prosecution by publishing unlicensed papers.

The birth of a recognizably 'modern' newspaper press dates from the failure to renew the Licensing Act in 1695; this effectively ended state censorship, thereby opening the floodgates to a newspaper and pamphlet press capable of expressing independent views. Printers were quick to exploit an opportunity denied to most of their continental counterparts: tri-weekly titles soon emerged, and the first daily newspaper, the *Daily Courant*, appeared in 1702. By 1710 provincial newspapers had surfaced in Norwich, Bristol, Exeter and Worcester. Although titles were founded and folded with alarming frequency, the trend towards growth remained startling: during the era of the French Revolution, London boasted no fewer than 14 daily newspapers. The evolution of the provincial press was yet more impressive: in the reign of George III the number of titles rose from 35 to 150. The expansion of the newspaper press was not limited to England: by 1820, even the remote reaches of north Wales and the Scottish Highlands were served by their own titles; at the death of George III, Great Britain possessed more than 300 newspapers.

The early emergence of metropolitan tri-weekly and daily newspapers was especially significant. These permitted a far more rapid response to political events than was possible through the medium of the pamphlet or weekly publication. The growing role of the London and provincial press in orchestrating extraparliamentary opposition to unpopular government policies became clear during the long ascendancy of Sir Robert WALPOLE. The prime minister faced repeated attacks in the pages of *The Craftsman*, whose editorials were themselves regularly reproduced in the *York Courant*. Printed assaults upon Walpole reached their peak in 1740, leading the bishop of Chester to complain to the duke of NEWCASTLE that the 'common people' were being roused against the administration by the biased coverage of cut-price newspapers that highlighted the most hostile observations of the London press. Walpole's attempts to retaliate by subsidizing a pro-government press proved ineffective, and his efforts to gag offending publications could likewise backfire: in 1737 the government halted publication of *The Craftsman* and jailed its printer for libel following a broadside against the Licensing Bill that authorized the Lord Chamberlain to act as censor; when publication recommenced, the unrepentant paper proceeded to cite such treatment as an example of tyrannical behaviour. Alongside its attacks upon specific policies of the Walpole ministry, the opposition press voiced broader concerns focusing upon the themes of governmental corruption and the overriding need to protect the liberty and freedoms of the individual.

Through its efforts to reflect and shape public

opinion, the Georgian press played a significant part in the spasmodic Wilkesite agitation (*see* WILKES, JOHN); its influence increased during the 1770s when efforts to prevent the reporting of parliamentary debates were defeated. The continuing importance of the press was recognized during the crisis posed by the FRENCH REVOLUTION, when the government sought to encourage loyal sentiment through the foundation of such patriotic titles as the *True Briton*. Attempts to enlist the press in the anti-revolutionary cause included punitive action against opposition publications. The traditional charge of seditious libel was levelled against the printer and editor of the *Morning Chronicle* in 1793; both were acquitted, although the same year witnessed the closure of the *Leicester Chronicle* and *Manchester Herald* through government pressure. Despite such attempts to muzzle the media, radical views and opposition sentiment continued to surface in both metropolitan and provincial newspapers. Although legislation was passed in 1798 to control aspects of newspaper production, in the following year the PITT ministry proved reluctant to adopt the more systematic regulation of the press proposed by the lawyer and historian John Adolphus (1768–1845).

While hefty stamp duties rendered 18th-century newspapers expensive by modern standards and thereby restricted sales, actual readership was increased by the widespread availability of printed matter in COFFEE HOUSES and taverns throughout Britain (*see also* LITERACY). Newspaper circulation was enhanced further by improvements to roads and the evolution of a swift mail-coach service. In consequence, influential London newspapers were disseminated throughout the country with increasing speed. Provincial titles blatantly 'lifted' large sections of their copy from the metropolitan press, but also sought to provide detailed coverage of local events. London and provincial newspapers alike attempted to boost circulation by devoting numerous column inches to sensational stories – lurid crimes, messy divorce cases, and weird phenomena – that would not be incongruous in the pages of today's tabloid press. The 'special correspondent' was a feature of the Victorian rather than Georgian press; sadly, there was no 'Russell of *The Times*' with Wolfe at Quebec or Burgoyne at Saratoga. Nonetheless, 18th-century newspapers kept their readers informed of foreign affairs by printing despatches from generals, admirals and ambassadors, often supplementing these 'official' accounts with particularly interesting personal letters.

It was only during the 19th century, when advances in printing technology permitted the production of mass-circulation 'penny dailies', that the British newspaper press realized its true potential as a shaper of public opinion. However, the vigour and influence of the Victorian press owed much to journalistic techniques pioneered in response to the volatile politics of an earlier age.
FURTHER READING J. Black, *The English Press in the 18th Century* (1987).

Pretender, Old. *See* STUART, JAMES FRANCIS EDWARD.

Pretender, Young. *See* STUART, CHARLES EDWARD.

Price, Richard (1723–91), dissenting minister, demographer, economist and supporter of the American and French revolutions. Price was the son of a Welsh dissenter who was educated in a dissenting academy and became minister at Stoke Newington. He wrote on moral and religious issues in the 1760s, which brought him to the attention of Lord SHELBURNE, who became his patron. When Shelburne became prime minister in 1782 he offered Price the position of his private secretary, but he declined.

In the 1770s Price published essays on political economy, which brought him to the notice of the ROYAL SOCIETY. His advocacy of the reduction of the NATIONAL DEBT by the re-establishment of a SINKING FUND attracted considerable notice at the time, and resulted in the younger PITT promoting it in 1786.

Price's contemporary reputation as a demographer is now discounted on account of his calculations of the number of inhabitants in his *Essay on the Population of England from the Revolution to the present time* (1780), which have been shown to be serious underestimates (*see* POPULATION).

When the dispute with the American colonies escalated to hostilities Price took their side. In 1776 he published *Observations on Civil Liberty and the Justice and Policy of the War with America*. He was considered to be so great a 'friend of America' that Congress invited him to emigrate there in 1778. After American independence had been recognized Price published *Observations on the importance of the American Revolution and the means of making it a benefit to the world* in 1785. In it he claimed that, next to Christianity, 'the American revolution may prove the most important step in the progressive cause of human improvement'.

After 1789 this accolade was transferred by Price to the FRENCH REVOLUTION. In his *Discourse on the Love of our Country*, delivered to his congregation at Newington Green on 4 November 1789, he applauded the French for carrying out a much more thorough revolution than the English had done in 1688, which in his view had not secured civil liberties for DISSENTERS. It provoked BURKE to riposte with his *Reflections on the Revolution in France*, which accused Price of condoning bloodshed. Price insisted that he was not in favour of violence but approved of the measures taken to launch a liberal constitution in France. He did not live to see the worst excesses of the French Revolution, dying on 19 April 1791.

FURTHER READING D.O. Thomas, *The Honest Mind: The Thought and Work of Richard Price* (1977).

Priestley, Joseph (1733–1804), scientist, Unitarian minister and radical. Priestley was born into a dissenting family in the West Riding of Yorkshire

and was educated in dissenting schools and at Daventry Academy. From 1761 to 1767 he was a tutor at Warrington Academy where he taught classics and history. He also pursued scientific inquiries, which obtained for him a fellowship of the ROYAL SOCIETY in 1766. His application was sponsored by Benjamin Franklin, whom he had met the previous year, when he was introduced to him in the 'club of honest Whigs' at the London Coffee House. This group were also known as 'friends of science and liberty', acknowledging the two interests that drew them together.

Priestley sympathized with the complaints of the Americans against British attempts to tax them. He expressed his views in *The Present State of Liberty in Great Britain and Her Colonies*, published in 1769. In 1767 he was appointed minister at Mill Hill Unitarian chapel in Leeds. There he established the Leeds Library, which is still in existence. His prodigious publications in defence of Unitarianism began to appear while he was librarian at Leeds. Lord SHELBURNE also employed him as his librarian at Bowood House near Calne from 1773 to 1780.

It was at Bowood that Priestley discovered oxygen, his most famous scientific achievement. Priestley's other scientific achievements include the discovery and production of gases such as nitric oxide, nitrous oxide, sulphur dioxide and ammonia. His experiments with dissolving carbon dioxide in water led to the fashion for soda water.

Priestley continued to defend the cause of the colonists, publishing in 1774 an anonymous *Address to Protestant Dissenters of all denominations on the approaching election of members of Parliament with respect to the state of public liberty in general and American affairs in particular*. It began startlingly with the words 'my fellow citizens', not 'my fellow subjects', which implied an anti-monarchical if not a republican stance on the part of the author. He pursued the anti-monarchical theme by asserting that there was a conspiracy by GEORGE III to undermine the liberties of Englishmen on both sides of the Atlantic. Thus he warned DISSENTERS that ministerial measures were aimed at them as much as against the colonists. Indeed they were seen as the same targets, since in Priestley's view the colonists were perceived as dissenters like the nonconformists of England. He urged the English dissenters to resist passively, not wishing them to take arms in defence of their liberties. But he ominously predicted that their 'brethren in America will probably be compelled to do [so]'. This was an early anticipation of the hostilities that were to break out at Lexington and Concord in 1775.

Priestley did not publish views on the colonies after 1774. This was possibly because when the AMERICAN WAR OF INDEPENDENCE broke out it was regarded as comforting the king's enemies to show sympathy for their cause. However, while Priestley was in Shelburne's employment he spent the winters in his employer's town house in London, where he continued to see Franklin. Priestley was later to claim that 'from the commencement of the American war I wished for the independence of this country'. That Priestley continued to be regarded as a 'friend of America' after the States became independent is indicated by his election to a fellowship of the American Philosophical Society in 1786.

After the outbreak of the FRENCH REVOLUTION Priestley was considered more as a friend of France than of America. It was his support of the revolutionary movement across the Channel that made him notorious enough for a 'Church and King' MOB to destroy his house and laboratory in Birmingham, where he had moved after leaving Shelburne's employ, in 1791. This caused him to seek refuge at first in London, and then in America, where he went in 1794.

He arrived in New York City on 4 June to be greeted by the principal inhabitants who 'came to pay their respects and congratulations'. Among those who received Priestley as a welcome refugee from tyranny were the Democratic Society and the Republican Natives of Great Britain and Ireland. In their address to him the Democratic Society

accusing the British government of plotting with others 'to prevent the establishment of liberty in France and to effect the total destruction of the rights of man', while the Republican Natives welcomed his escape 'from the immediate tyranny of the British government'. Priestley replied to these addresses by praising republican forms of government such as existed in America and denouncing 'the evils arising from hereditary monarchical ones'

An even more distinguished reception awaited Priestley in Philadelphia, including none other than President George Washington. He was also received by David Rittenhouse, president of the American Philosophical Society. Although Priestley was pressed to take a house and reside in what was still the capital city of the United States, he declined. After a month's stay in Philadelphia he moved to Northumberland on the Susquehanna river, which to him was so remote as to be 'seemingly out of the world'. His initial sense of isolation made him regret not making his principal residence in Philadelphia. It was apparently his wife who determined that they would settle down there. On 24 August 1794 he wrote to a friend in England that 'she is so fond of this place that nothing can draw her from it, and therefore I have agreed to buy ground, on which to build a house, which will be begun very soon'.

In the same letter he observed that 'the most virulent pamphlet that I have yet seen is just published here against me'. Unfortunately for Priestley the addresses and his replies to them in New York were published in the newspapers and widely distributed. They circulated to Philadelphia and stung the journalist William COBBETT to publish the pamphlet entitled *Observations on the Emigration of Dr Joseph Priestley*. Cobbett became celebrated later as a radical. But that was after his return to England. In 1794 he was still very much a conservative, and a staunch defender of the British constitution in church and state. Writing under his pseudonym of Peter Porcupine he delivered a scathing rebuttal of Priestley's politics:

When the arrival of Doctor Priestley in the United States was first announced I looked upon his emigration ... as no more than the effect of that weakness, that delusive caprice, that too often accompanies the decline of life; and which is apt, by a change of place, to flatter age with a renovation of faculties and with the return of departed genius. Viewing him as a man that sought repose, my heart wished him what he certainly ought to have wished himself, a quiet obscurity. But his Answers to the Addresses of the Democratic and other societies at New York place him in quite a different light.

Cobbett challenged Priestley's claim to be a refugee seeking asylum. So far from being a persecuted martyr he had been protected by the law from the depredations of the mob. Two of those charged with the riot had been subsequently hanged for the offence. Priestley had himself been compensated with £2502 18s 0d damages for the losses he had incurred.

Priestley found himself sucked into the vortex of party warfare in the infant republic. He was aware of the existence of parties, and explained them succinctly to a friend thus as 'the Federalists and the anti-Federalists; the former meaning the friends of the present system, with a leaning to that of England and friendship with England; the latter wishing for some improvements, leaning to the French system and rather wishing for war'. He himself expressed no desire to enter the fray on either side. 'I shall carefully avoid all the party politics of the country,' he declared in a letter of 15 June 1794 shortly after his arrival in the United States. But he was too much of a political animal not to become involved. As a contemporary caustically observed, 'This eldest son of disorder will never obtain his sought for "Reform" on this side of the Grave, and I believe the Government of Heaven itself, should he ever get there, will, in his opinion, want Reformation.'

The writer satirized an aspect of Priestley's politics that might be described as political paranoia. As has been mentioned, he shared the view that there was a conspiracy in England to deprive the American colonists and the English dissenters of their liberties. He took his conspiracy theory with him to America, seeing in the government of President Adams parallels with that of George III. 'There is the true spirit of Church and King here,' he wrote in 1799, 'though under other names.' Priestley's conviction that all governments were conspiring to rob people of their liberty led him to gravitate naturally into the anti-Federalist camp led by Thomas Jefferson.

Priestley and Jefferson also had a natural affinity because of their scientific pursuits. Their houses at Monticello and Northumberland, though different in almost every other way, share the obsession with science. Both thought that scientific investigations were linked with political liberty, free enquiry demanding free institutions. They also shared a preference for France over Britain. Jefferson had been ambassador in Paris, and Priestley even seems to have thought seriously about going to France in the late 1790s, especially when he feared that the strife of parties in America might end in civil war. By 1797 Priestley was really a partisan on the side of the Jeffersonians. The following year Priestley wrote *Maxims of Political Arithmetic*, which were published in an anti-Federalist paper, the *Aurora*.

Known Francophiles were not popular in the United States in 1798. The Adams administration passed Alien and Sedition Acts that severely circumscribed the ability of foreigners like Priestley to criticize the government. 'It does not become an alien to say much about Politicks,' Priestley observed, 'especially in these dangerous times.' Yet he indiscreetly said a great deal about politics. In 1800 he published *Letters to the Inhabitants of Northumberland* as a contribution to the election campaign that Jefferson fought against Adams in 1800. He sent copies of them to Jefferson, who arranged for sets of them to be distributed among his supporters in Virginia. In a second edition of the *Letters* Priestley stated in the new preface that 'as far as circulation extended' they had 'contributed something' to Jefferson's successful bid for the presidency. This marked the victory of the Jeffersonian party over the Federalists. Priestley's political stance had been vindicated. 'I rejoice more than I can express in the glorious reverse that has taken place and which has secured your election,' he wrote to Jefferson. 'This I flatter myself will be the permanent establishment of truly republican principles in this country, and also contribute to the same desirable result in more distant ones.' He wrote to George Logan after Jefferson's inauguration in 1801:

> what a contrast does this country under the administration of Mr Jefferson make with England under George III ... To me the administration of Mr Jefferson is the cause of peculiar satisfaction, as I now, for the first time in my life (and I shall soon enter my 70th year) find myself in any degree of favour with the governor of the country in which I have lived, and I hope I shall die in the same pleasing situation.

He was indeed to do so, spending his last four years in America and abandoning all thought of returning to Europe.

FURTHER READING J. Graham, 'Revolutionary Philosopher: The Political Ideas of Joseph Priestley' in *Enlightenment and Dissent* VIII (1989), IX (1990); J. Graham, 'Revolutionary in Exile: The Emigration of Joseph Priestley to America 1794–1804' in *Transactions of the American Philosophical Society* (1995).

prints. One of the most characteristic genres of 18th-century publication was the print. Ranging in quality from crude woodcuts to copperplate engravings and mezzotints, prints embellished newspaper titles, illustrated periodicals and adorned the windows of print shops, where they were sold as individual items. Individual prints cost anything from one penny for a woodcut to one shilling and sixpence or even more for an engraving, especially if it was hand-coloured. This and the fact that a print run from a copperplate was restricted to around 1000 – unless it was recut – confined the more elaborate prints to a restricted audience. They did not represent the opinions of the masses as is often claimed. Certainly it would be hazardous to document 'public opinion' from those prints that have survived, since so many more were printed ephemera.

At the outset of the century many prints sold in England were actually produced abroad, particularly in France, Holland and Italy. But from the 1720s on there developed a lively domestic output based on London and spearheaded by HOGARTH. By the late 18th century British prints dominated the European market, illustrating almost every aspect of contemporary life, from sublime views of rural and urban landscapes to the most bawdy and vulgar representations of politics and politicians. Perhaps above all, prints produced throughout the century reproduced works of art, both foreign and domestic, making the subject matter of great paintings available to a wider public.

SEE ALSO CARICATURE.

FURTHER READING T. Clayton, *The English Print 1688–1802* (1997).

Prior, Matthew (1664–1721), poet and diplomat. Prior was educated at Westminster School and St John's College, Cambridge. At Cambridge he got to know Charles Montagu earl of HALIFAX, with whom he collaborated in writing a burlesque of Dryden's 'The Hind and the Panther', which they 'transversed to the story of the Country Mouse and the City Mouse' (1686). Prior's Whig connections led to his being employed as a diplomat in the reign of WILLIAM III, to whom he became a gentleman of the bedchamber, being secretary at the treaty of Ryswick in 1697.

By the end of the reign, however, Prior had gravitated to the Tories, being undersecretary to the earl of Jersey. Thus he joined with Jersey in attacking the JUNTO when they were impeached for their part in the partition treaties, even though Jersey, as secretary of state, was equally involved in their negotiation. Prior became a member of the BOARD OF TRADE, a post he held until 1707 when the Whig ministers got him dismissed. When Robert HARLEY became prime minister Prior was again employed, this time as a commissioner of customs. He was also sent on a clandestine mission to Paris in connection with the peace negotiations of the Tory ministry. When he was discovered returning through Dover the Whigs exposed his trip in a poem entitled 'Mat's Peace'. Prior had himself continued to write poems on affairs of state throughout the reigns of William and Anne. In 1712 he again went to Paris, where he became plenipotentiary. Following the death of ANNE the Whigs attempted to impeach him for his part in the making of the treaty of UTRECHT, and he was in gaol from 1715 to 1717.

Thereafter Prior retired from public life to Down Hall in Essex, purchased by the proceeds of a subscription volume of his poems and a gift of £4000 from Lord Harley. In retirement he wrote his most celebrated poem 'Alma' (1718). He was best known in his lifetime for his couplet 'Life's a jest and all things show it / I thought so once and now I know it.' He died of cholera in 1721.

prisons. The modern concept of prison remained alien to most Georgian Britons. Execution or TRANSPORTATION dominated the penal code, and it was only during the era's closing decades that calls for prison reform coincided with changing attitudes towards crime to promote 'penitentiaries' as a means of punishing and reforming offenders.

During the 18th century few prisons were interested in either punishment or rehabilitation. Although 'bridewells' had been established in an effort to 'correct' the habits of prostitutes and other petty criminals, the average 18th-century gaol instead concerned itself with the confinement of debtors or prisoners awaiting trial and sentence. Such establishments were run as profit-making enterprises. Inmates were exploited through a wide range of levies. Custom decreed that new arrivals furnish 'garnish' to provide drinks for all or suffer ill-treatment as a consequence. Fees were payable to the gaol's proprietor on entry and discharge; extra cash could secure superior food and accommodation. It followed that a prisoner's health was often dependent upon the size of his or her purse. Notorious highwaymen with wealthy admirers could entertain lavishly while awaiting trial or execution; by contrast, penniless inmates who had been found not guilty were denied release through lack of the discharge fee.

Although gaols were often well fortified and manned by heavily armed warders to baffle escape attempts, discipline within was usually imposed by the inmates themselves. Except in the capital, where debtors were accommodated in the Fleet, King's Bench and Marchalsea prisons, those committed to gaol for minor debts were incarcerated alongside professional criminals. As a result, gaols habitually served to spread rather than curtail crime. In addition, lack of segregation between the sexes encouraged promiscuity and casual prostitution; such mingling aided those female prisoners who hoped to gain a pardon by 'pleading their bellies' and demonstrating pregnancy. The crowded and filthy conditions and lack of ventilation meant that prisons acted as incubators for the virulent form of typhus dubbed 'gaol fever'. Prisoners on remand frequently succumbed. They were not the only casualties of the disease. In April 1750, the infamous 'Black Assize' at the Old Bailey saw two infected prisoners spread the disease throughout the court: the resulting death toll of 50 included the judge, lawyers and all twelve jurymen.

From 1718 to 1775, in the period between the Transportation Act and outbreak of the American War of Independence, forcible exile rather than imprisonment was Britain's dominant means of 'secondary' punishment. Although the 1744 Vagrancy Act permitted magistrates to confine local troublemakers, it was only after 1780 that imprisonment emerged as a common punishment in its own right. Earlier proponents of the prison had emphasized the punishment role of such a regime: a contributor to *Fog's Weekly Journal* in 1737 proposed that those convicted of capital offences should undergo hard labour for life on the grounds that simple death, which came naturally to all citizens good or bad, was insufficient retribution for heinous offences. The combination of prison and hard toil was also proposed in 1751 when a Commons committee chaired by Sir Richard Lloyd suggested the employment of convict labour in royal dockyards. Such initiatives to harness convict labour drew inspiration from the 'correction' espoused by the old bridewells.

Given the state of Britain's existing prisons, it was only wide-reaching reform that would allow the expansion of imprisonment as a mode of punishment. The immediate success of prison reform was limited. Legislation in 1774 associated with Alexander Popham aimed to regulate fees payable by acquitted prisoners and to reduce the incidence of fever. The continuing defects of England's prisons were exposed by the philanthropist John HOWARD. According to Howard's meticulous investigations, which were published in his *The State of the Prisons* (1777), diet, sanitation and exercise facilities all remained grossly inadequate. Even in London, Popham's Acts made little impact: the rebuilt Newgate Prison was scarcely an improvement upon its notorious predecessors. In 1779 the Penitentiary Act proposed the construction of two 'houses of correction' within which hard labour and solitary confinement would be combined with the ultimate aim of rehabilitation. The scheme foundered when Howard and the other commissioners appointed to supervise the project failed to agree upon a site for the first penitentiary.

Although still-born, the 1779 act represented a significant step on the path towards prison reform. Interest in imprisonment as a major secondary punishment was further stimulated after the loss of Britain's American colonies eliminated the established destination for transported convicts. Although the new penal colony established in AUSTRALIA during the late 1780s went some way to compensate, Britain's expanding population, and the corresponding rise in the number of offenders, made it clear that alternative methods of punishment would have to be employed. In the closing decades of the 18th century traditional corporal punishments such as branding, whipping and the pillory gradually fell into abeyance in line with 'Enlightened' attitudes towards violence. By the onset of the 19th century imprisonment was rivalling transportation as the likely consequence of conviction for a non-capital property offence: criminals who would once have been set free after a painful but perfunctory whipping now faced the even grimmer prospect of years behind bars.

SEE ALSO CRIME AND PUNISHMENT.

FURTHER READING M. Ignatieff, *A Just Measure of Pain: The Penitentiary in the Industrial Revolution, 1750–1850* (1978).

prostitution. In 1732 William HOGARTH published the first of a series of engravings that told an all too familiar story: a young girl, fresh from the countryside, has barely stepped down from the carrier's wagon before she is recruited into a life of vice by a sharp-eyed procuress. Subsequent images in *The Harlot's Progress* chart the speedy corruption and dismal fate of the innocent lass following her initiation into the ranks of London's professional prostitutes.

Hogarth's morality tale reflected grim reality. Prostitution formed a conspicuous and continuing feature of the Georgian social scene; in 1780, a further series of prints featuring the fate of 'Harriet Heedless' was published under the title *A Modern Harlot's Progress*. At the end of the century, the Westminster magistrate Patrick Colquhoun estimated that some 100,000 prostitutes were operating in England: of this total, he believed that no fewer than half were concentrated within London. While there is no way of testing the accuracy of Colquhoun's suspiciously rounded figures, their size does at least reflect contemporary perceptions of the scale of a genuine social problem.

Visitors to 18th-century London were quick to remark upon the number and brazenness of the city's prostitutes. During the 1650s the Cromwellian regime had enforced a strict morality that rendered brothel-keeping a capital offence. Such draconian legislation had been repealed at the Restoration. Despite the formation of 'societies for promoting a reformation of manners', the rise of METHODISM and the determined efforts of crusading moralists such as Henry FIELDING, prostitution continued to flourish. Prostitution was rated as a misdemeanour rather than a crime; in 1752 attempts to regulate the activities of brothels proved ineffective.

Although prostitution frequently faced opposition on moral grounds, other critics were more concerned with its clear role in fostering serious crime. Both brothel-based prostitutes and street walkers were regularly accused of robbing, assaulting or murdering clients. As the famous 'Tavern Scene' from Hogarth's *A Rake's Progress* of 1732 illustrates, drunken beaux offered tempting prey for prostitutes. Particularly prevalent was the so-called 'buttock and file' ploy, where a customer was enticed into an alleyway by the prospect of sex; while his attentions were directed elsewhere, the hapless victim would be stunned and robbed by the woman's male accomplice.

Despite such undoubted connections with wider criminal activity, prostitution was tolerated by the authorities because it was perceived to serve a genuine need. In an age when labouring men were often obliged to delay marriage for economic reasons, 'common' prostitutes were viewed as a necessary outlet for lusts that might otherwise be directed at respectable wives and daughters. In consequence, well-run brothels aimed at wealthier clients were likewise left in peace by the authorities and even advertised their services in such publications as *Henry's List of Covent Garden Ladies*. Such 'bawdy houses' and 'bagnios' catered for a variety of tastes. Although proven 'sodomitical acts' carried the death penalty, London offered homosexual brothels or 'Molly Houses', while other establishments specialized in lesbianism and flagellation. Less exotic and more conspicuous were the numerous street walkers who openly plied their trade from Hyde Park to Vauxhall Gardens. James BOSWELL, who provided such women with a regular source of custom, commented upon the variety to be found within the prostitutes' ranks. In his wanderings Boswell encountered what he described as 'free-hearted ladies of all kinds'; they ranged 'from the splendid Madam at fifty guineas a night down to the civil nymph with white-thread stockings who tramps along the Strand and will resign her engaging person to your honour for a pint of wine and a shilling'. Boswell's *London Journal* records encounters in a bewildering variety of locations; his sexual partners included the 'strong jolly young damsel' whom he 'engaged' on Whitehall Bridge with the Thames thundering below them. While Boswell's sexual satisfaction was sometimes obtained free of charge, he frequently paid a painful price for his pleasures. Despite employing the era's primitive sheep-gut condoms, Boswell regularly fell victim to venereal diseases; indeed, he once lost a wager that he could avoid such illness for the space of three years.

Like other aspects of Georgian society, prostitution was expected to operate within popularly recognized codes of behaviour. Upon occasion, those organizers of the sex trade who flouted such conventions could attract the wrath of the mob. Mother Needham, the real-life prototype of the procuress in Hogarth's *Harlot* series, died from the savage pelting she sustained when placed in the pillory for her crimes. In 1749, a bawdyhouse in the Strand was wrecked after its keeper refused to return money stolen from sailor patrons. An indignant mob swiftly gathered and announced its intention of destroying all the brothels, and a worried Henry Fielding – the chief magistrate for Westminster – was obliged to summon the military to quell the riot.

As Boswell appreciated, Georgian prostitution embodied a hierarchy of extremes. At the very top were those celebrated courtesans whose charms had proved capable of securing the patronage of a single wealthy client. Upon occasion, such lovers might actually wed their mistresses. For example, Charles James FOX married Elizabeth Armistead in 1796 after living with her for a decade. Similarly, Emma Lyon began a liaison with Sir William Hamilton in 1785; Emma subsequently became Lady Hamilton and mingled fame with notoriety as the devoted mistress of England's great naval hero, Horatio NELSON. More typical were those women who sold themselves on the streets for sixpence or a shilling. Efforts to protect homeless girls from such a fate included the Asylum for Female Orphans and the Magdalen Hospital for Penitent Prostitutes, both founded in 1758. Many women probably turned to casual part-time prostitution to supplement their incomes during spells of economic hardship; for others, it was the notorious vulnerability of female domestic servants at the hands of predatory masters that led to pregnancy, dismissal and life on the streets. Classifying London's '50,000' prostitutes in 1800, Colquhoun reckoned that 20,000 of these women were 'Of the class who may have been employed as menial servants, or seduced early in life'. As court records indicate, the drift from destitution to prostitution and theft could often lead swiftly to transportation or the gallows.

FURTHER READING T. Henderson, *Disorderly Women in 18th-Century London* (1999).

Prussia, state of northeastern Germany, which during the course of the 18th century became one of the leading military powers of Europe.

On the evening of 18 June 1815 Marshal Blücher's Prussian troops flooded onto the field of WATERLOO to clinch the verdict in Wellington's gruelling encounter with Napoleon. The shared victory provided a dramatic climax to an era in which Anglo-Prussian relations had not always reflected such harmony.

Backed by a highly disciplined standing army, Prussia had emerged as a major European political power during the first half of the 18th century.

During the opening campaigns of the War of the AUSTRIAN SUCCESSION, Prussia acted with France against Britain's traditional ally Austria: a prime concern of CARTERET's diplomacy during 1742–3 was to engineer Prussia's withdrawal from the conflict. This objective was gained after Maria Theresa of Austria was persuaded to recognize Prussia's annexation of Silesia, only to be lost again when a resurgence of Habsburg fortunes prompted Frederick the Great of Prussia to establish the League of Frankfurt and invade Bohemia.

By the DIPLOMATIC REVOLUTION that preceded the eruption of the SEVEN YEARS WAR in 1756, the established system of alliances was overthrown. Austria now sought French assistance against its archrival Prussia, while GEORGE II established a defensive alliance with Frederick II to protect his vulnerable electorate of HANOVER. During the course of the war, hefty British subsidies helped to sustain a beleaguered Prussia against the French, Austrian and Russian armies ranged against it. The exploits of Frederick's formidable blue-coats were afforded extensive coverage in British newspapers, while 'Old Fritz' himself emerged in the rather improbable role of Protestant hero.

The diversion of Bourbon troops to Germany allowed Britain to make substantial inroads upon France's poorly defended colonies. In 1762 the BUTE ministry's decision to terminate the Prussian subsidies before Frederick had himself secured a peace settlement was therefore seen by many as a shameful betrayal of a faithful ally. Although the wily Frederick would have had few qualms about adopting such a self-seeking policy himself, Bute's stance towards Prussia heightened the diplomatic isolation that left Britain dangerously exposed upon the outbreak of the American rebellion in 1775. In 1781 Prussia demonstrated her hostility towards Britain by joining the ARMED NEUTRALITY declared by Russia in the previous year; this pact advertised a willingness to deploy force in the protection of neutral vessels carrying naval stores to Britain's enemies.

A gradual thawing of Anglo-Prussian relations

in the late 1780s was quickened by the onset of war with revolutionary France (*see* REVOLUTIONARY AND NAPOLEONIC WARS). The old allies joined ranks in the First Coalition, although the French republican armies inflicted reverses that obliged Prussia to seek peace in 1795. While Prussia was absent from the Second and Third Coalitions that were ranged against Napoleon with British financial backing, Napoleon's disastrous Russian campaign of 1812 encouraged Prussia to resume the struggle with crusading zeal: in 1813 Prussian troops played a major role in the Fourth Coalition's defeat of Napoleon at Leipzig. During the lengthy peace negotiations that straddled the dramatic Waterloo campaign, British diplomats were opposed to Prussia's efforts to impose a punitive settlement upon France, and at the Congress of Vienna CASTLEREAGH worked to limit the extent of Prussian encroachments upon Saxony.

public sphere, concept formulated by Jürgen Habermas in *The Structural Transformation of the Public Sphere: An Inquiry into a Category of Bourgeois Society*. When this work first appeared in German in 1962 it had little influence outside Germany. After an English translation became available in 1989, however, it had considerable impact among historians in Britain and the United States. This was despite the fact that it was placed in the context of an outmoded Marxist historiography.

Habermas's account, based on continental rather than British experience, depicted a traditional culture at the beginning of the 18th century almost completely dependent on the church, the courts and the aristocracy, which was soon to be challenged by a more or less independent public sphere exemplified in the growth of COFFEE HOUSES and the PRESS. While this has been generally accepted, Habermas's dating of it to after 1688 has been challenged, with scholars identifying bursts of 'public sphere' activity earlier in the 17th century. He cited developments in capitalism in England towards the end of the 17th century as a major cause of this change. These included 'a con-

flict of interests between the restrictive interests of commercial and finance capital on one side and the expansive interests of manufacturing and industrial capital on the other.' Such statements would no longer find support among many economic historians. Stripped of its Marxist trappings, however, the idea of the public sphere has been found useful to describe developments in Britain and Ireland as well as on the continent. Even in Britain, where absolutism had been defeated, down to about 1720 the major architectural and musical projects were promoted by the court, the church and the aristocracy – for example, the enlargement of Kensington and Hampton Court palaces, the building of St Paul's Cathedral and of the numerous Wren churches in London, the construction of great country houses like CHATSWORTH, BLENHEIM and CASTLE HOWARD, the operas and anthems of PURCELL and HANDEL. The success of the *Spectator*, Defoe's novels, *The Beggar's Opera* and Handel's oratorios, and the building and marketing of BATH as a commercial enterprise, all illustrate that major cultural initiatives were now being taken in the public sphere. MUSIC provides one of the best examples: musical church services, open to all, and operas that were virtually confined to the court were now supplemented by advertised public concerts for which anyone who could afford to pay could obtain a ticket.

Pulteney, William, 1st earl of Bath (1684–1764), politician who emerged as one of the leading Whigs in the House of Commons during the reign of George I. A supporter of 2nd Viscount TOWNSHEND and WALPOLE, Pulteney resigned the post of secretary at war when they left office in 1717. He felt slighted at being overlooked when they returned to power, obtaining only the office of cofferer of the household. On the removal of CARTERET from the secretaryship of state in 1724 Pulteney hoped to replace him, but was mortified when the duke of NEWCASTLE was appointed instead. In 1725 he resigned as cofferer and went into opposition.

The following year Pulteney allied with BOLINGBROKE to launch the *Craftsman*, the principal adversary of the government in the press for the next decade. This hammered home in its weekly essays the message that Walpole was kept in power by corruption and by the division of his opponents into Whigs and Tories. To eliminate corruption the opposition must unite into a COUNTRY PARTY against the court. Then they would remove PLACEMEN from Parliament, reduce the standing ARMY, and restore triennial if not annual elections.

Pulteney also lambasted the prime minister in the Commons, where he was generally regarded as one of the finest orators of the day. Walpole allegedly said he feared Pulteney's tongue more than another man's sword. When FREDERICK PRINCE OF WALES joined the opposition in 1737 Pulteney attached himself to the prince's Leicester House faction and promoted the idea of a patriot king.

The outbreak of the War of JENKINS'S EAR with Spain at last gave Walpole's critics an issue that did eventually prove to be his undoing. Pulteney led the attack on the prime minister. On Walpole's fall in 1742, however, Pulteney disappointed those who hoped for a 'patriot' administration (*see* PATRIOTISM). He became a privy councillor and a peer in 1742, but failed to persuade the king to appoint Tories to the ministry. It was generally held that he had been bought off. He was outmanoeuvred by the PELHAMS, who twice – in 1744 and 1746 – successfully challenged his influence with the king. On the second occasion they resigned and George tried to persuade Lord Bath, as Pulteney had become, together with Carteret to form a ministry. Though they tried for two days they failed to construct a cabinet that could hold its own against the Pelhams in the Commons. Thereafter Pulteney largely withdrew from public life.

punishment. *See* CRIME AND PUNISHMENT; PRISONS; TRANSPORTATION.

Purcell, Henry (1659–95), composer who established a reputation as England's foremost baroque musician. His varied and prolific output has stood the test of time, and he is today ranked among the finest of Britain's composers.

Born during the twilight of the Interregnum, Purcell made his name in the service of successive monarchs. In keeping with the expectations of his age, Purcell exhibited a varied musical repertoire; he composed and performed both sacred and secular music, and proved equally skilled at providing settings for psalms and theatrical verse. Although drawing upon both French and Italian influences, Purcell's output was characterized by a strong personal streak.

The son of a court musician and composer, Purcell began his musical career as a chorister of the Chapel Royal; he was a pupil of John Blow, a composer whose example influenced the young Purcell. By his mid-teens Purcell was assistant keeper of the king's instruments, and in 1679 he became organist at Westminster Abbey. Purcell subsequently composed royal welcome odes for Charles II, and provided the music for the coronation of James II in 1685. These prestigious commissions, performed on state occasions, ensured that Purcell's efforts received maximum publicity. Such talents gained Purcell appointment to the king's private music and enabled him to weather the political upheavals of the GLORIOUS REVOLUTION. Indeed, Purcell composed the music for William and Mary's coronation in 1689, and he subsequently produced no fewer than six birthday odes for Mary.

Although the new monarchy signalled some contraction of the royal music, Purcell found ready outlets for his abilities through the provision of incidental music for the London theatre. Purcell's atmospheric settings lent dignity to such poor fare as Richard Norton's play *Pausanius, the Betrayer of his Country*. When the poet John Dryden presented him with his patriotic libretto *King Arthur* in 1691, Purcell provided a memorable climax with the moving final-act song 'Fairest

Isle'. In the following year Purcell again collaborated with Dryden, providing a score for *Oedipus* that included the haunting and innovative 'Music for a While'. Indeed, this gift for vocal composition earned Purcell the title of 'the British Orpheus'. Purcell's only true opera was the short but remarkably diverse *Dido and Aeneas*, now widely regarded as his masterpiece; the work was originally composed for a girls' boarding school in Chelsea. Another memorable work, *The Fairy Queen* (1692), once again demonstrated Purcell's flair for interpreting texts, in this case a heavily doctored version of Shakespeare's *Midsummer Night's Dream*.

One of Purcell's most powerful works was his music for Queen Mary's funeral in March 1695; within months, the young composer was himself laid to rest to the same sombre strains after succumbing to consumption at the age of 36. The final year of Purcell's life had proved one of his busiest, adding to an impressive legacy of church, stage and chamber music that swiftly secured his posthumous reputation.

FURTHER READING F.B. Zimmerman, *Henry Purcell (1659–95): His Life and Times* (1983).

Q

quarter sessions, court sessions for serious offences held in each county four times a year.

During the 18th century the responsibility for maintaining law and order at local level rested largely with JUSTICES OF THE PEACE recruited from the gentry. Such men were accustomed to handling a wide range of business on their own, and in conjunction with another justice could hold 'petty sessions' capable of dealing with a much more; their judicial powers included the punishment of relatively minor offenders.

Since the reign of Edward III the justices of each country were obliged to meet four times a year; along with the travelling assize courts attended by circuit judges, these so-called 'quarter sessions' dealt with all cases of serious crime. However, over the course of the 18th century capital cases were increasingly reserved for the assizes, and in the early Victorian era the restricted jurisdiction of the quarter sessions was confirmed by law.

As the quarter sessions involved a major gathering of county dignitaries they also provided an opportunity for non-judicial business, including the discussion of political issues and the selection of parliamentary candidates. It became customary for one of the quarter sessions to gain precedence over the others and serve as an annual meeting of the most influential figures in the county.

Quebec, province of Canada, originally established as a French colony. Founded by Samuel de Champlain in 1608, the settlement of Quebec was destined to become a focus of imperial strife in North America. Built high above the St Lawrence river, the site dominated the northern route into the future Bourbon colony of New France. It first came under English rule in 1628 when the fledgling community was captured by a small fleet of privateers, but was returned to France in 1632.

In 1690 the onset of the NINE YEARS WAR in Europe was reflected in colonial bickering between French Canada and the English colonies to the south. A major expedition under the command of Sir William Phips was assembled in Massachusetts and sent against Quebec. Although Phips managed to land part of his force below Quebec, the ill-equipped New Englanders were unequal to the task of subduing the city and the expedition withdrew in confusion.

In 1711, as the War of the SPANISH SUCCESSION drew to a close in Europe, Quebec was the target of attack from both land and sea: a formidable armada under Admiral Sir Hovenden Walker ferried British regular soldiers from Boston, while another force advanced overland via Lake Champlain. Despite the resources allocated to the expedition, it was abandoned after nine ships were wrecked at the mouth of the St Lawrence.

During the SEVEN YEARS WAR Quebec remained a prime objective of British strategists. In the summer of 1759 an expedition under Major General James WOLFE advanced to the city. Wolfe's lengthy siege culminated in dramatic fashion on 13 September when cooperation between the army and the navy permitted the landing of British troops in a cove above Quebec. During the short, sharp battle that ensued on the Plains of Abraham, Wolfe's veteran redcoats shattered the army of the Marquis de Montcalm. Wolfe was killed in the hour of victory, but Quebec surrendered five days later.

It was one thing to capture Quebec, quite another to keep it. In the spring of 1760 the French forces in Canada launched a determined effort to retake the city. This came close to success after the British commander, Brigadier General James Murray, rashly ventured forth with his sickly and outnumbered garrison to confront the forces of the duc de Levi. In the fierce combat that followed at Sainte-Foy, Murray's mauled command was obliged to retreat back into the city, and it was only in the following month, with the timely arrival of a Royal Navy squadron in the St Lawrence, that the French lifted their siege.

Following the treaty of PARIS of 1763 when Canada was absorbed into the British empire, attempts were made to conciliate the French-speaking Catholic population of the St Lawrence valley. This policy reached a controversial climax with Lord NORTH's Quebec Act of 1774. North's legislation not only extended the province to include the Ohio river valley to the south but guaranteed the religious freedom and legal customs of its Catholic inhabitants. It was therefore viewed in a sinister light by Britain's increasingly defiant American colonists, who included it among the so-called Intolerable Acts (*see* AMERICAN COLONIES 1763–1776). When the AMERICAN WAR OF INDEPENDENCE erupted in 1775 the French populace perceived the British regime as the lesser of two evils and remained loyal to it. On 31 December 1775 an American attempt to storm Quebec was repulsed following the death of its leader, Brigadier

General Richard Montgomery. After the peace of 1783 Quebec remained the major garrison and administrative centre of Britain's surviving possessions in North America.

FURTHER READING H.B. Neatby, *Quebec: The Revolutionary Age 1760–91* (1966); C. P. Stacey, *Quebec 1759: The Siege and the Battle* (1959).

Queen Anne's bounty, fund set up by Queen ANNE to relieve the plight of poor clergymen. The discrepancies in clerical incomes from the richest to the poorest livings had been notorious at least since the Reformation. A few below the bishops lived comfortably on incomes of many hundred pounds, but most had to survive on considerably less than this, many receiving under £50 a year and some no more than £20. Moreover they were dependent still upon tithes paid by their parishioners. Although the TOLERATION ACT of 1689 upheld the compulsory payment of tithes, in many parishes there was a reluctance by some dissenters, especially Quakers, to pay.

On her 39th birthday, 6 February 1704, Anne sent a message to the House of Commons informing them that she proposed to devote the revenue raised from clerical first fruits and tenths to the augmentation of low stipends. The sums involved, between £16,000 and £17,000 a year, were insignificant to the crown, but could lift a living worth less than £50 a year above the poverty line when administered by a trust set up specially for the purpose. Queen Anne's bounty, as it was known, did much to alleviate clerical poverty.

FURTHER READING G. Best, *Temporal Pillars: Queen Anne's Bounty, the Ecclesiastical Commissioners and the Church of England* (1964).

Quiberon Bay, battle of (20 November 1759), British naval victory during the SEVEN YEARS WAR, in which Admiral Sir Edward HAWKE (1705–81) hounded a French fleet to destruction amidst the treacherous shoals of Quiberon Bay on the Biscay coast of France.

The battle crowned Britain's spectacular 'year of victories', and provided a dramatic finale to a gruelling phase of the war in which Hawke's Western Squadron had blockaded Brest in an effort to baffle a French plan to invade Britain. As the winter weather worsened, Hawke was blown off station, so allowing the French under Conflans to emerge and make sail for Scotland. Although Conflans enjoyed the advantage of a two-day start, Hawke gave chase through the Bay of Biscay. On 20 November he learned that the French fleet of 24 ships had sought refuge within the confines of Quiberon Bay.

Despite a full gale and fading daylight, Hawke took the bold decision to seek an engagement in the bay's uncharted waters. Hawke lost two ships to the appalling weather but scattered the opposition: six French vessels were destroyed, and many others suffered extensive damage as they fled from the encounter. The survivors sought shelter in the river Vilaire, and Hawke's display of aggression at Quiberon did much to ensure that they remained there for the remainder of the war.

The dramatic circumstances of the victory, which was described by NEWCASTLE as 'the most glorious event at sea this century', captured the public imagination. Quiberon Bay inspired the patriotic song 'Heart of Oak'; written by the great actor David GARRICK and with music composed by William Boyce, it was first performed that Christmas during the pantomime *The Harlequin's Invasion* staged at Drury Lane. As the stirring words proclaimed, Hawke's glorious victory had indeed added something more to the 'wonderful year'.

R

radicalism. The words 'radical' and 'radicalism' date from the 1790s, and were derived from the Latin *radix*, meaning 'root', indicating that those to whom the terms were held to be appropriate wished to uproot existing institutions. Although historians have applied the expressions to reformers like John WILKES and Christopher WYVILL before the 1790s, few of them wished to undo the REVOLUTION SETTLEMENT. On the contrary most praised the GLORIOUS REVOLUTION and wished to restore its principles. To them the CONSTITUTION was the finest that could be devised, but it had been undermined by corrupt ministers. They therefore sought to eliminate corruption and to remove opportunities for its operation. Genuine radicalism came when people like Thomas PAINE, Joseph PRIESTLEY and Richard PRICE attacked the constitution itself and sought to make it more democratic. Priestley and Price were leaders of rational dissent, which campaigned to remove the legal barriers to full citizenship from dissenters through PARLIAMENTARY REFORM. Though the cause made much progress in the 1780s, it received a setback in the 1790s from the conservative backlash to the French Revolution.

Raeburn, Henry (1756–1823), the leading artist of the SCOTTISH ENLIGHTENMENT. Raeburn lived and worked at its very hub, the city of Edinburgh. He was largely self-taught, although his natural talent was recognized and encouraged by REYNOLDS. A wealthy wife permitted Raeburn to undertake a two-year sojourn in Rome between 1784 and 1786, after which he returned to Scotland. By the late 1790s Raeburn had established himself as Edinburgh's outstanding portrait painter; continuing success allowed him to construct his own studio. Although he contemplated a move to London in 1810, Raeburn rapidly concluded that his native city offered more promising prospects for his restrained style.

Raeburn was the first Scottish painter to earn international acclaim while remaining based in his homeland. He became president of the Society of Scottish Painters in 1812, and gained a knighthood in 1822. Raeburn's contribution to Scottish art was further recognized shortly before his death, when he was made king's limner and painter for Scotland. Despite his role as the doyen of Scottish painters, Raeburn proved reluctant to provide visual counterparts to the literary glamorization of his country's past propagated through the novels of Sir Walter Scott. In consequence, although such works as *Sir John Sinclair* (1794) capture the dramatic character of the Highlands, his portraits lack the dashing Romanticism of his contemporary Sir Thomas Lawrence (1769–1830). Raeburn is usually credited with the striking portrait of *The*

Reverend Robert Walker Skating on Duddingston Loch (*c*.1790), although doubt has recently been cast upon this attribution.

FURTHER READING D. Macmillan, *Painting in Scotland: The Golden Age* (1986).

Ramillies, battle of (21 May 1706), engagement during the War of the SPANISH SUCCESSION fought between Louvain and Namur, where forces led by the duke of MARLBOROUGH inflicted a major defeat on the French army and as a result annexed almost the whole of the Spanish Netherlands for the Grand Alliance.

Ramsay, Allan (1713–84), Scottish painter who, until the emergence of Sir Joshua REYNOLDS, was the outstanding fashionable portrait painter of the age. Indeed, even after the dramatic appearance of Reynolds on the London art scene Ramsay did not lack champions: Horace WALPOLE considered his female portraits to be second to none, while George III, who had become friendly with Ramsay when prince of Wales, made him king's painter upon his accession in 1760.

The son of an Edinburgh poet, Ramsay studied in London and Italy. Upon returning to Britain in 1738 he settled in London where his elegant style soon attracted the custom of aristocratic patrons. Unlike HOGARTH, Ramsay was prepared to deploy a knowledge of the old masters and an admiration for foreign artists. Between 1754 and 1757, while Reynolds was establishing his reputation in London, Ramsay embarked upon a further tour of Italy. He returned with a refined technique that is readily apparent in his portrait of his second wife Margaret Lindsay. After becoming king's painter, Ramsay and his assistants concentrated upon multiple copies of official royal portraits for distribution to Britain's burgeoning colonies. Ramsay's output was already slackening in 1773 when a fall from a ladder injured his right hand and rendered painting difficult.

Ramsay exploited his Scottish roots: for some time he maintained a studio in Edinburgh, and

his dominance at court was strengthened by close contacts with his influential countryman Lord BUTE. Ramsey was a man of considerable intellectual ability, whose circle included Dr JOHNSON, HUME, Diderot, Rousseau and Voltaire, and his best work embodies the enquiring approach of the SCOTTISH ENLIGHTENMENT.

FURTHER READING A. Smart, *Allan Ramsay: Painter, Essayist and Man of the Enlightenment* (1992).

Ranelagh Gardens, pleasure gardens in Chelsea, London. Opened in 1742, Ranelagh Gardens vied with VAUXHALL GARDENS as the leading leisure facility for well-heeled visitors to London. Situated alongside the Royal Hospital in the grounds of a residence built for Lord Ranelagh during the reign of William III, the gardens were laid out at a reputed cost of £16,000.

Although smaller than Vauxhall, Ranelagh sought to compensate by catering for a more sophisticated clientele than its archrival; the entry price of half a crown was more than double that of Vauxhall, although aficionados considered the difference to be worth it. Horace WALPOLE, who was a regular visitor to both Ranelagh and Vauxhall, observed in 1744: 'Every night I constantly go to Ranelagh, which has totally beat Vauxhall. Nobody goes anywhere else – everybody goes there.' Indeed, the gardens reminded Tobias SMOLLETT of 'the enchanted palace of a genie ... crowded with the great, the rich, the gay, the happy, and the fair'.

Ranelagh was dominated by a vast rotunda, which housed an orchestra surrounded by tiers of private boxes; its glory days included a performance by the child prodigy Mozart. In 1775 Ranelagh hosted an exclusive fancy-dress supper ball following a Thames regatta staged by the leading clubs of St James's – the lavish boat race ended in chaos after the contestants became entangled with the busy river traffic. The original Ranelagh closed in 1803, although the site is now occupied by gardens constructed in the 1860s.

recoinage of 1696, recall of debased coins and issue of a new coinage. By the 1690s the silver coins issued by earlier regimes had become much debased by clipping. Coin clippers sheared the edges off and sold the shavings to silversmiths. The practice had begun much earlier, but increased during the NINE YEARS WAR, stimulated by demand for silver bullion to sustain England's commitments on the continent. The result was to undermine confidence in the coinage as it decreased in size – sometimes by as much as half. In 1696 an act was passed to call in the clipped coins and to replace them with new ones. The process was overseen by Isaac NEWTON, who was then master of the mint. The recoinage led to a shortage of specie and much hardship, but the new coinage eventually restored confidence, having milled edges to discourage clipping.

FURTHER READING Ming-Hsun Li, *The Great Recoinage of 1696 to 1699* (1963).

Reeves, John (*c.*1752–1829), prominent disseminator of loyalist literature in reaction against the excesses of the FRENCH REVOLUTION. After serving as chief justice for Newfoundland, Reeves had returned to England in 1792. To counter the activities of the British 'JACOBINS', Reeves founded the Association for the Preservation of Liberty and Property Against Republicans and Levellers (APLP). The first APLP meeting was chaired by Reeves at the Crown and Anchor tavern in London in November 1792. With government backing, Reeves's initiative spread until similar associations had been established throughout the country. Reeves himself reckoned that 2000 APLP branches were formed; while this may be an exaggeration, the APLP represented England's largest political organization.

The loyalist associations played a crucial role in spreading conservative literature. In London, Reeves's Association printed its own pamphlets and also served as a distribution point for the writings of other authors such as Hannah MORE who sought to contrast the stability of England's gov-

ernment with the anarchic conditions across the Channel. Reeves's publications included the 1795 pamphlet *Thoughts on the English Government*, which was condemned by the House of Commons for its overly monarchical view of the CONSTITUTION. Between 1783 and his death he published his multivolume *History of the English Law*, covering the period from the Anglo-Saxons to the reign of Elizabeth.

Reeves enjoyed the confidence of the younger PITT, and in 1800 he was appointed to the office of king's printer. A fellow of the Society of Antiquaries and the Royal Society, Reeves was also a noted scholar of Greek and Hebrew.

reform, parliamentary. *See* PARLIAMENTARY REFORM.

reformation of manners. There were two movements aimed at reforming the morals of the country. The first emerged in the 1690s and petered out in the 1730s. The second was launched in 1787 with a royal proclamation against vice and immorality.

The crown was associated with the initiative that led to the founding of the original Society for the Reformation of Manners in London. Those who formed it urged Bishop Stillingfleet of Worcester to persuade Queen MARY to write to the magistrates of Westminster in June 1691 requiring them to enforce the laws against vice and immorality. There was a whole raft of legislation from earlier reigns penalizing profane swearing, drunkenness and 'night walking' after prostitutes. That these activities were widespread in the view of the reformers led to fears that divine providence would inflict punishment on the nation for its sins. It was particularly to be feared since God had so recently blessed the country with the GLORIOUS REVOLUTION. Unless there was a general reformation, however, it would not continue to deserve that blessing. Such afflicting providences as the earthquake in Jamaica in 1692, the loss of the Levant Company's fleet to Turkey in 1693 and the death of Queen

Mary in 1694 seemed to justify the jeremiads of the reformers.

Several societies for the reformation of manners sprang up not only in the capital but in the provinces. There was a particularly active society in Bristol. The societies published annual blacklists of those they had successfully prosecuted, with the controversial use of informers, for breaches of the laws against immorality. But, as DEFOE observed in his poem *Reformation of Manners*, 'Your annual lists of criminals appear / But no Sir Harry or Sir Charles is there.' The societies were concerned to suppress public manifestations of vice, which inevitably involved them more with the 'lower orders' than with the gentry. They were also concerned to prosecute Sunday traders, who loomed larger in the annual accounts as the period progressed. This suggests that the societies' members were drawn disproportionately from the ranks of tradesmen who were anxious about unfair competition. Certainly the membership of the societies combined dissenters, many of whom came from that class, with low-church Anglicans. This characteristic led the high-church preacher Dr SACHEVERELL to denounce them as a 'mungril institution'.

The last blacklist was published in 1738, and thereafter there is no overt sign of the formal existence of the societies, though the METHODISTS continued many of their practices.

The royal initiative of 1787 gave rise to a Proclamation Society. The chief instigator of this movement was the evangelical William WILBER-FORCE. Unlike the earlier societies it was aimed at reform from above, so that the elite could set a good example to the rest of society. Hannah MORE urged them to do this in her *Thoughts on the Importance of the Manners of the Great to General Society* (1787). This aim became increasingly conspicuous during the wars with revolutionary France as the aristocracy sought to justify its position at the apex of society, and so ensure that it did not deserve the fate of aristocrats across the Channel. In 1802 the Proclamation Society was relaunched as the Society for the Suppression of Vice, with

aims similar to those of the societies a hundred years before.

regency crisis, controversy surrounding the Regency Bill of 1788. In the autumn of 1788 GEORGE III displayed symptoms of mental instability. Although modern medical historians have identified the complaint as porphyria, which is physical in origin, his physicians diagnosed it as 'entire alienation of mind'.

A bill had to be introduced into Parliament to provide for a regency during the king's incapacity. During the debates on the bill Charles James FOX championed the right of the prince of Wales (the future GEORGE IV) to preside over the regency. This was controversial since the two were boon drinking and gambling companions whose antics were detested by the king. George had particularly objected to bailing his son out financially. Fox's stance was held to be at odds with his previously expressed Whig view of the royal prerogative. The prime minister PITT THE YOUNGER bought time by spinning the debates out, hoping that George would recover. By the middle of February 1789 the king had recovered sufficiently for the bill to be abandoned. Pitt had triumphed and remained in power another twelve years.

Repton, Humphry. *See* LANDSCAPE GARDENING.

reversionary interest. GEORGE I, GEORGE II and GEORGE III all quarrelled with their sons and heirs. This led politicians who were out of favour with the king to look to the heirs for advancement as the king grew older and his death seemed imminent. Those who gathered round George Augustus, the future George II, in the reign of George I, or Frederick, Prince of Wales in that of George II or the future prince regent during that of George III, hoping to take office when their patron succeeded, were known as the reversionary interest, since power was expected to revert to them when the king died or was incapacitated from ruling.

Revolutionary and Napoleonic Wars (1793–
1815), series of conflicts between Britain and its
allies on the one side and France and its allies on
the other. Hostilities initially erupted with the various revolutionary regimes in France, and subse-
quenty involved Napoleon Bonaparte's French
empire. The wars ended with the British and Prussian victory at WATERLOO in 1815.

The battle of Waterloo was the first occasion
in the history of the British ARMY when all ranks
engaged were awarded a commemorative medal.
The innovation serves as an indication of the significance attached to an event that brought a
bloody and conclusive close to more than 20 years
of warfare with revolutionary and Napoleonic
France. For Britons born before World War I, the
long struggle between 1793 and 1815 was *the*
'Great War'.

During those years, as throughout the pre-
ceding century, Britain represented the most
consistent and determined opponent of French
territorial expansion. In the Revolutionary and
Napoleonic wars, not only did the Royal NAVY
remain sovereign of the seas, but it ferried British
soldiers to snap up enemy colonies around the
globe, and blockaded French ports. With the most
advanced industrial base in Europe, Britain's
economic muscle allowed it to provide vast cash
subsidies to bolster the flagging war efforts of
its fluctuating continental allies. Well might a frustrated Napoleon rage against 'perfidious Albion'.

The outbreak of the French Revolution in
1789 had initially caused British politicians little
concern for Europe's balance of power; indeed,
the fall of the Bourbon regime appeared to signal
the fortuitous demise of Britain's traditional trade
and colonial rival. When the revolutionary regime
went to war with Austria and Prussia in 1792,
Britain accordingly remained aloof from the struggle. However, British politicians rapidly grew
alarmed at the new republic's increasing belliger-
ence. The execution of Louis XVI in January 1793
triggered widespread revulsion, while the French
occupation of Belgium registered concern for an

area traditionally viewed as the strategic 'cockpit
of Europe'. Britain declared war in February,
joining ranks with a motley coalition consisting of
Austria, Prussia, Spain, Sardinia and the Dutch
Republic.

From the very beginning of hostilities Britain
adopted the strategy that it was to follow throughout the coming years of warfare. Lacking a substantial army, Britain relied chiefly upon sea power:
the Royal Navy's ascendancy over the republican
fleet was quickly confirmed in 1794 by Admiral
Richard HOWE's great victory of 'the Glorious First
of June'. By contrast, direct military intervention
on the continent was restricted in both scale and
impact: a brief campaign in Flanders under the
duke of YORK and half-hearted support for royalist
revolts in the west of France both failed to check
the republic's sprawling conscript armies. Expeditions against French possessions in the Caribbean
produced some territorial gains, but at a terrible
cost as tropical fevers swept through the troops.
By 1795 French armies had scored victories that
obliged Prussia, Spain and the Dutch Republic to
sue for peace; the latter two powers promptly sided
with France against an increasingly beleaguered
Britain. This isolation was soon exacerbated in
1797 when Bonaparte's dazzling Italian campaign
brought Austria to the peace table and forced it
to recognize the republic's territorial gains.

A growing sense of crisis was heightened in
1797 when determined NAVAL MUTINIES appeared
to jeopardize the 'wooden walls' upon which
Britain's security depended. However, the unrest
was quelled without serious repercussions for the
efficiency of the fleet, which was demonstrated by
victories over Spain at CAPE ST VINCENT and the
Dutch at CAMPERDOWN. In 1798 the outbreak of
the IRISH REBELLION provided the republic's armies
with their best opportunity to gain a foothold
within the British Isles. Bonaparte's ambitions lay
elsewhere, however, and he instead mounted an
expedition to Egypt designed to menace Britain's
lifeline to the East and encourage native resistance
to British rule in India. Once again, Bonaparte's

plans were scuppered by the Royal Navy. NELSON's crushing victory over the French fleet at the NILE left the French army dangerously isolated, and obliged Bonaparte to restore his authority at home; there he seized power and began his dictatorship as first consul. Britain's perilous position in the East was stabilized when Lieutenant General George Harris defeated Tipu Sultan of Mysore in 1799, and Ralph ABERCROMBY routed the remaining French troops in Egypt at ALEXANDRIA in 1801.

Early in 1799 British diplomacy and gold were instrumental in the construction and support of the Second Coalition in alliance with Austria, Russia, Portugal and Naples. This new grouping achieved little: Russia and Austria proved incapable of cooperating in the field, while an Anglo-Russian expedition to Holland offered little encouragement. A disillusioned Russia soon withdrew from the war effort, and by 1801 heavy defeats had forced Austria to accept another humiliating peace. Alone again, Britain's sense of isolation was increased when Russia joined Denmark and Sweden in the so-called League of ARMED NEUTRALITY; this objected to British interference with the shipping of neutral powers, so posing a threat to the Royal Navy's long-running blockade of France. Although the death of Tsar Paul, combined with Nelson's vigorous attack upon the Danish fleet at COPENHAGEN, helped to sink the League, in 1802 Britain had little option but to acquiesce in French domination of western Europe through the treaty of AMIENS.

Amiens represented no more than a brief pause for breath in the continuing conflict between Britain and France, and in May 1803 Britain reopened hostilities. Alongside continued French encroachments in southern Europe, Britain was angered by Bonaparte's encouragement of its enemies in India; the latter danger was scotched when Arthur Wellesley, the future duke of WELLINGTON, finally broke the power of the Mahrattas at Assaye in 1803. The younger PITT engineered a Third Coalition – again in alliance with Austria and Russia

– so obliging Bonaparte (who had crowned himself emperor as Napoleon I in 1804) to divert the Grande Armée that had been menacing England towards fresh campaigns in the east. Soon after, in October 1805, Nelson finally removed any lasting fears of invasion with his spectacular destruction of the Franco-Spanish fleet at TRAFALGAR. French soldiers enjoyed more success than French sailors. Napoleon proceeded to despatch his continental opponents in a brilliant series of campaigns, and by 1807 Austria, Prussia and Russia had all been subdued. The emperor attempted to build upon these victories by striking at the very root of Britain's ability to maintain the war – its economy. Napoleon's 'Continental System' sought to achieve this goal by banning the importation of British goods into France or its dependent territories. Widespread hardship and popular discontent resulted in Britain, although the emergence of fresh markets in South America went some way to offset the trade depression. In response to Napoleon's gambit, Britain waged economic warfare through the 1807 'Orders in Council', which were intended to prevent neutral powers from trading with France. Determined implementation of the Orders led to friction with the United States of America, ultimately leading to the WAR OF 1812; this sparked fighting on fresh fronts as British and American warships duelled in the Atlantic, while land forces clashed from Canada to Louisiana. Peace was signed at the treaty of Ghent in 1814.

Scattered British amphibious expeditions to Buenos Aires in 1806 and the island of Walcheren off the Dutch coast in 1809 both proved costly failures. However, from 1808 onwards Britain adopted a more successful policy of intervention in the Iberian peninsula in support of Spanish and Portuguese nationalist revolts against French invaders. During a succession of hard-fought campaigns, British troops under the inspired leadership of Wellington provided a focus for opposition against the imperial armies. The bloody PENINSULAR WAR drained thousands of veteran French troops from their business of conquest elsewhere.

In 1812, when Napoleon withdrew forces from Spain to bolster his invasion of Russia, Wellington finally turned the tide in the Iberian theatre with the decisive victory at SALAMANCA. Napoleon's Russian campaign foundered during the disastrous retreat from Moscow, and the emperor's discomfiture encouraged the Fourth Coalition, in which British subsidies underpinned an alliance with Russia, Prussia and Austria. In October 1813 the Coalition armies inflicted a crucial defeat upon Napoleon at Leipzig, so seconding Wellington's victorious summer campaign in Spain. With his foes closing in for the kill, the emperor opted to abdicate in April 1814. Napoleon was imprisoned on Elba and the exiled Bourbon Louis XVIII restored to the throne of France. Britain's diplomatic leadership and lavish financial aid had maintained the triumphant Coalition, and British prestige was recognized during the peace negotiations at Vienna in which the foreign secretary Lord CASTLEREAGH took a prominent role. When Napoleon launched his desperate bid to regain power during the 'Hundred Days' of 1815, it was fitting that British troops, under the experienced Wellington, should play a key role in snuffing out his ambitions at Waterloo.

FURTHER READING T.C.W. Blanning, *The French Revolutionary Wars, 1787–1802* (1996); C. Emsley, *British Society and the French Wars* (1979); C.J. Esdaile, *The Wars of Napoleon* (1995); C. Hall, *British Strategy in the Napoleonic Wars* (1992); P.W. Schroeder, *The Transformation of European Politics 1763–1848* (1994).

Revolution settlement, the constitutional and religious settlement that took place after the GLORIOUS REVOLUTION. The CONVENTION PARLIAMENT elected in January 1689 following the Revolution proceeded to enact a BILL OF RIGHTS that censured several actions of James II and declared them to be illegal. Thus his use of the suspending and dispensing powers to immunize Catholics from prosecution under the penal laws and Test Act was condemned. The framers of the bill maintained that they were simply declaring what the law was and not making new law. By and large this was a tenable position, but in asserting that the maintenance of a STANDING ARMY in peace-time without consent of Parliament was illegal they were undoubtedly making new law. WILLIAM III nevertheless gave his assent to it not because this was a condition of his accepting the crown – the throne was filled before he assented to the Bill of Rights – but because he considered that it did not seriously infringe the royal prerogative. Thus the monarch's rights to declare war and make peace, veto legislation passed by both Houses, prorogue and dissolve Parliament and choose and dismiss ministers were all left intact. In the coronation oath, however, William and Mary, unlike James II, swore to observe 'the statutes in parliament agreed on'. Thus the royal prerogatives could no longer be claimed as being superior to statute.

These prerogatives were eroded not by the Bill of Rights, however, but by the necessity to raise unprecedented sums of money to fight the war against Louis XIV – the NINE YEARS WAR – which was the consequence of the accession of William and MARY, whom the Bill recognized as joint sovereigns. Where the parliamentary grants to their predecessors had been of the order of £1.2 million, their war budgets came to an average of £5 million. To raise these sums required the consent of Parliament, which had to meet every year after 1689. Annual sessions enabled the politicians to exert more influence over the crown. A TRIENNIAL ACT in 1694 limited the prerogative of summoning and dissolving Parliament since by it a dissolution had to take place at least every three years. Ministers had to cultivate the support of the Commons as well as of the crown. Even some treaties of alliance were now laid before Parliament for discussion and approval.

Besides making the monarchy more dependent upon Parliament the Revolution settlement also settled the succession and the religious disputes between the established church and

327 Reynolds, Sir Joshua

Protestant nonconformists – at least temporarily. The Bill of Rights provided that children of William and Mary should succeed, failing whom those of Mary's sister ANNE, and in the event of her failure to provide an heir those of William should she die and he marry again. At the time it seemed as if every possibility had been catered for. But in fact Mary died childless in 1694, Anne's only child of several pregnancies to survive babyhood died in 1700 and William never married again. So in 1701 the ACT OF SETTLEMENT had to be passed conferring the succession on the house of Hanover, the nearest Protestant heirs (*see also* HANOVERIAN SUCCESSION).

The religious disputes were taken care of by the TOLERATION ACT of 1689. This allowed Protestant dissenters who believed in the Trinity to worship separately from the Church of England, but did not exempt them from the Corporation and Test Acts nor from the payment of tithes to the established church.

FURTHER READING W.A. Speck, *Reluctant Revolutionaries: Englishmen and the Revolution of 1688* (1988).

Reynolds, Sir Joshua (1732–92), Britain's leading artistic figure during the second half of the 18th century. Reynolds was highly influential both as a painter and as the first president of the ROYAL ACADEMY.

Born near Plymouth, Reynolds was apprenticed to Thomas Hudson before beginning work in London and his native Devon. During the early 1750s Reynolds visited Rome, Florence and Paris – a crucial study trip that brought him into contact with the works of the old masters. Returning to England in 1753, Reynolds set about establishing a reputation in London. Developing the approaches to portraiture pioneered by HOGARTH and RAMSAY, he produced canvases that gave full scope to the dramatic and sensitive exploration of character. Powerful and original life-size portraits, such as that of his naval friend Commodore KEPPEL (1754), ensured that by the time

of his first exhibition in 1760 Reynolds had already emerged as the capital's leading portrait painter.

Although Reynolds lacked the admiration and patronage of George III, his fame was such that when the Royal Academy was established in 1768 he was the clear front runner for the presidency; a knighthood followed in 1769. Presidency of the Academy brought massive prestige, and allowed Reynolds to exact unprecedented fees from his sitters. Like Hogarth before him, Reynolds was keen to disseminate his own theories of art; unlike Hogarth, he proved successful in this ambition. The academy's annual prize-givings provided Reynolds with an opportunity to showcase his ideas in his famous *Discourses*.

In contrast to Hogarth, Reynolds took considerable pains to reflect the traditions of those old masters who continued to attract the admiration of wealthy connoisseurs. Titian, Rembrandt and Rubens all influenced Reynolds's work, a debt that is clear in his *Self-Portrait* (*c.*1773); some of his most striking portraits, of which the dashing *Colonel Banastre Tarleton* (1782) provides a fine example, incorporated unconventional poses that unashamedly mimicked the statues of ancient Greece and Rome. As Reynolds freely admitted, such heroic portraits were designed not merely to reproduce reality, but to enhance it. Goldsmith called him: 'A flattering painter who made it his care / To draw men as they ought to be, not as they are.' (*Retaliation*, 1774). Although he excelled in depictions of soldiers and sailors, Reynolds's versatility was apparent in his portraits of women; Horace WALPOLE considered him inferior to Ramsay in depicting female sitters, yet such works as *Nellie O'Brien* (1763) demonstrate considerable sympathy and reveal a sensitive use of light.

Reynolds possessed a keen awareness of the value of publicity: the key painting of Keppel remained in his studio for 17 years as an advertisement designed to lure future clients. His paintings achieved a wider circulation, and generated further revenue, through sale as engravings. A life-long bachelor, Reynolds enjoyed the friendship of such leading London figures as JOHNSON, BURKE and GARRICK. Reynolds's mastery of both the practical and theoretical aspects of painting, and his tireless efforts to enhance the standing of English artists, gained him widespread respect during his lifetime and enduring recognition as the 'father' of British painting.

FURTHER READING N. Penny (ed.), *Reynolds* (1986).

Richardson, Samuel (1689–1761), novelist. Richardson was apprenticed to a printer at the age of 17, and after serving his time became a master printer in London. He had previously helped people to compose letters, resulting in a commission to write a manual for letter writing. This led him to produce his first novel, *Pamela: or virtue rewarded*, in 1740–1. It told the story in her own letters of a servant who resisted the advances of her master, Mr B., until he married her. Henry FIELDING, who thought virtue should be its own reward, parodied it in *Shamela*. The attack stung Richardson, who never forgave Fielding. More popular and widely read than *Pamela* – despite its 2000 pages – was Richardson's next novel, *Clarissa*, which appeared in 1747–8. Where *Pamela* had just related the heroine's own side of the story, *Clarissa* had letters from various correspondents as well as the heroine, including her nemesis Lovelace. Richardson's final novel, *Sir Charles Grandison* (1753–4), attempted to portray a 'good man' and was consequently not so well received. In the same year Richardson became the master of the Stationers' Company in recognition of his achievements as a writer.

FURTHER READING J. Harris, *Samuel Richardson* (1987).

Riot Act (1715), legislation following riots in Bedford, Birmingham, Chippenham, Norwich, Oxford and Reading on the coronation day of GEORGE I. The act received the royal assent in July. Thereafter those in a crowd of twelve or more could be found guilty of a capital offence if they did not disperse within one hour of being commanded to do so by a magistrate, the so-called 'reading of the Riot Act'. There was some confusion as to whether the procedure had to be followed for a riotous assembly to be subject to the act. This paralysed the authorities in some riots when the reading had not taken place. When this situation arose in the GORDON RIOTS in 1780, however, it was established that the act did not make a new offence – riots being capital offences before 1715 – but merely reinforced the power of the authorities who sought to suppress them.

The Riot Act also contained a clause making it a capital offence to demolish or begin to demolish any church or chapel or any other building for religious worship, or any dwelling house, barn or other outhouse. This was inserted because the coronation-day riots had been characterized by high-church mobs destroying dissenting meeting houses. The act was rarely invoked after 1715, there being only two prosecutions under it before the Penlez riot of 1749, when Bosavern Penlez was found guilty of gutting the Star tavern, a brothel off the Strand. The fact that it was a house of ill repute rather than a chapel provoked a wave of sympathy for him, but calls for his reprieve from the death penalty were unavailing.

SEE ALSO MOB.

roads. From the journeys of Celia FIENNES in the 1690s and those of Daniel DEFOE in the next decade, to those of Arthur YOUNG in the 1760s, travellers complained about the state of the roads. Defoe drew attention to the poor condition, especially in winter, of the roads that crossed the Midland clay. The language of the turnpike acts tells the same story; that for repairing the road from Leeds to Ripon, passed in 1752, describing its existing state as 'so very ruinous and bad, especially in the winter season, that travellers cannot pass without great danger'.

It was hoped that the turnpike system would

greatly improve the situation. Turnpikes relied on tolls levied on road users rather than on the statutory obligations laid on parishes for repairing roads. The first turnpike had been administered by justices of the peace along a stretch of the Great North Road, for which purpose they had obtained a private act of Parliament in 1673. The first turnpike to be run by a trust of private citizens, rather than by Justices of the Peace, was established in 1706. There were objections from road users protesting against the tolls, which occasionally erupted into riots. Nevertheless by 1770 there were 24,000 km (15,000 miles) of turnpikes, which created a network linking London with most English provincial towns. When it was complete it brought down the cost of moving heavy freight around England. As a contemporary observed in 1752, 'carriage in general is now thirty per cent cheaper than before the roads were amended by turnpikes'. Turnpikes also enabled passengers to be conveyed more swiftly by coach, creating an infrastructure of coaching inns. New roads in Scotland were constructed by General WADE, who also built the military road between Newcastle and Carlisle, after the '45 JACOBITE RISING. Wade's roads opened up the Highlands to wheeled vehicles.

New methods of surfacing roads were devised by John Metcalf, otherwise known as 'Blind Jack of Knaresborough', and John McAdam. Metcalf improved the drainage, while Macadam used variegated stones to make a more solid roadway. Although the construction of turnpikes continued into the 19th century, so that by 1830 the system extended for 35,000 km (22,000 miles), they could not compete with canals for the movement of freight or with railways for the conveyance of passengers.

FURTHER READING E. Pawson, *Transport and Economy: The Turnpike Roads of 18th-Century Britain* (1977).

Robertson, William (1721–93), Scottish historian and a leading figure of the SCOTTISH ENLIGHTEN-

MENT. Robertson made less money from his histories of Scotland, Charles V and America than did David HUME from his historical writing. Although he was not as popular as Hume he earned the appreciation of fellow scholars. Even Hume congratulated him on his achievement, writing, 'A plague take you! Here I sat on the historical summit of Parnassus, immediately under Dr Smollett, and you have the impudence to squeeze yourself past me and place yourself under his feet.' In 1762 Robertson was elected principal of Edinburgh University, and the following year became historiographer for Scotland.

Rochester, Laurence Hyde, 1st earl of (1641–1711), Tory policitian. Rochester rose to prominence under Charles II, becoming first lord of the Treasury in 1679. His rise was largely due to his connection with the king's brother, James duke of York. They spearheaded the 'Tory reaction' that set in after the Exclusion crisis. There were signs that Charles was cooling towards them in the last months of his reign, during which Rochester was 'kicked upstairs', first to the post of lord president, then to the lord lieutenancy of Ireland. Shortly before the king died an investigation was being launched into his conduct at the Treasury.

James II, however, made Rochester lord treasurer on his accession in 1685. The latter's refusal to convert to Catholicism led to his dismissal in January 1687, although he was compensated with a pension of £4000. He continued to collaborate with James and tried to rally support to him after the arrival of William of Orange in 1688, heading a provisional government in London that sought to prevent a full-scale revolution. When James's flight to France ended all such hopes of a counterrevolution of loyalists, Rochester supported the proposal in the CONVENTION PARLIAMENT that a regency should be established to govern the kingdom. When this failed, and WILLIAM and MARY were declared king and queen, Rochester took the oaths to them – unlike his elder brother Henry, the 2nd earl of Clarendon.

In 1692 Rochester was readmitted to the privy council. It appears that he was more reconciled to Mary than to William, and that he advised the queen on ecclesiastical affairs. After Mary's death, when the Whigs consolidated their hold on power, Rochester emerged as a leader of the HIGH-CHURCH Tories in opposition to them. When William III decided to reconstruct the ministry in favour of Tories in 1700 Rochester became lord lieutenant of Ireland, a post he retained at the accession of Queen ANNE. His objections to MARL-BOROUGH's continental strategy in favour of a BLUE-WATER POLICY, however, led to his losing favour. In 1703 he was given the alternative of going to Dublin or leaving office; he chose the latter. From then until 1710 he was a leading light in the high-church Tory opposition, and in the ministerial revolution of 1710 returned to office as lord president. He supported Robert HARLEY's Tory ministry until his death in May 1711.

Rockingham, Charles Watson Wentworth, 2nd marquess of (1730–82), Whig politician; prime minister (1765–6, 1782). Watson Wentworth was educated at Westminster School and St John's College, Cambridge. He succeeded his father as marquess of Rockingham in 1750, and with the title also inherited vast estates in York-shire and Ireland. Thus he entered the House of Lords when he attained his majority, and never sat in the Commons. He immediately obtained the office of lord of the bedchamber from the PEL-HAMS, and justified their choice by voting steadily for their government. He was thoroughly Whig in his political principles and practice, becoming one of the OLD CORPS whom GEORGE III wished to disband on his accession. Rockingham resigned from the bedchamber in 1762 and went into oppo-sition to BUTE's ministry.

When the king dismissed GRENVILLE in 1765 he was persuaded by his uncle the duke of CUM-BERLAND to make Rockingham prime minister. The first Rockingham administration lasted long enough to repeal the STAMP ACT in 1766 but, lack-ing the support of Cumberland – who died shortly after it was formed – it fell when the king persuaded PITT to form a ministry. Rockingham then went into a long and largely futile opposition, particularly against the American policies of successive gov-ernments. His followers or 'connexion', the ROCK-INGHAMITES, held together through 16 years, until news of Britain's final humiliating defeat of the American war at YORKTOWN brought about the fall of NORTH's ministry in March 1782. The second Rockingham administration was then formed, which carried measures of 'economical reform' (*see* PARLIAMENTARY REFORM), granted legislative inde-pendence to Ireland and initiated peace negotia-tions with the United States. The ministry was short-lived, however, as Rockingham died sud-denly on 1 July 1782.

FURTHER READING R. Hoffman, *The Marquis: A Study of Lord Rockingham* (1973).

Rockinghamites, the followers of the second mar-quess of ROCKINGHAM, especially between the end of his first ministry (1765–6) and the beginning of his second (1782). Throughout these years they held together in opposition.

The significance of their organization has been much disputed. To some historians they were just another aristocratic 'connexion', such as that of the 4th duke of Bedford. Thus they were mainly composed of the relatives and electoral nominees of Rockingham. To other historians (and to them-selves) they were much more than that, inheriting the remnants of the OLD CORPS Whigs and inde-pendents such as Sir George Savile and William Dowdeswell to form the first recognizable political party since the eclipse of the Tory and Whig parties in the later years of GEORGE II.

The dispute involves an assessment of the role of Edmund BURKE, Rockingham's private secre-tary. Certainly Burke argued in *Thoughts on the cause of the present discontents* (1770) and elsewhere that the Rockinghamites met his definition of a party, 'a body of men united, for promoting by their joint endeavours the national interest, upon some particular principle in which they are all agreed'. While those who associate the Rockinghamites with the 'rise of party' are satisfied that they met these requirements, those who are sceptical maintain that they were an aristocratic connection that just happened to have excellent public relations in Burke's propaganda.

FURTHER READING F. O'Gorman, *The Rise of Party in England: The Rockingham Whigs 1760–82* (1975).

rococo, 18th-century style in painting, architecture and the decorative arts, originating in France, which has been characterized as a lighter and more fragile version of the BAROQUE. The term 'rococo' was first employed during the 19th century, when it initially carried negative connotations based upon the prevailing verdict that the style was trivial and frivolous compared with those that preceded and followed it.

Rococo reached the height of its influence in the 1750s during the reign of Louis XV, and is particularly associated with François Boucher, who employed it in paintings, tapestries, engravings and ornamental designs. Although spreading as far afield as Spain and Russia, the rococo had less impact in England; there its distinctive asymmetrical curves, scrolls and naturalistic motifs were largely restricted to FURNITURE, although rococo influence has been detected in media as diverse as the sculpture of ROUBILIAC and the watercolours of ROWLANDSON.

Rococo was already declining in France when the vogue for NEOCLASSICISM gathered momentum during the 1760s. Under the French Revolutionary regime the rococo was condemned on both moral and artistic grounds. It was associated with the excesses of the Bourbon court at Versailles and the extravagances of Madame de Pompadour and Marie Antoinette; in painting, the carefree pastoral themes associated with Jean-Antoine Watteau and his imitators were replaced by the stern classical compositions of the 'politically correct' David.

Rodney, George Brydges (1719–92), admiral. Despite a difficult temperament and notorious hunger for prize-money, Rodney earned the gratitude of the nation when he inflicted a crucial defeat upon the French at the battle of the Saints during the closing stages of the AMERICAN WAR OF INDEPENDENCE.

A protégé of the wealthy and influential James Brydges duke of Chandos, Rodney was educated at Harrow before entering the navy in 1732. Rodney's powerful connections may have expedited the promotion that gained him a captaincy at the age of 23, but he consolidated his reputation through active service. After Lord ANSON's victory at Cape Finisterre in 1747 he presented Rodney to George II with the hearty wish that the king had 'one hundred such captains, to the terror of your Majesty's enemies'. During the SEVEN YEARS WAR Rodney further distinguished himself in the West Indies; in 1762, as rear admiral, he commanded the naval forces during the successful expedition against Martinique.

Rodney proved less fortunate in his political career. In 1751 he entered Parliament as the Admiralty's nominee for Saltash; he subsequently bankrupted himself by his extravagant spending during the Northampton election of 1768. Combined with heavy gambling losses, these debts obliged Rodney to seek refuge in Paris from his creditors. The outbreak of war with America and then the Bourbons provided Rodney with the opportunity to restore both his reputation and fortune.

In 1780, while en route to his old Caribbean haunts, Rodney orchestrated the first relief of GIBRALTAR. During the following year the belated entry of the Dutch into the war against Britain provided Rodney with the opportunity to capture the wealthy Dutch island of St Eustatius – although the greed with which the victors fell upon the spoils prompted questions in Parliament. Rodney soon silenced his critics by countering Bourbon naval superiority in the western Atlantic. French warships had already forced the surrender of Cornwallis at YORKTOWN, and now menaced Britain's vulnerable West Indian possessions. Early in 1782 Rodney was despatched to the Caribbean, where he encountered the French Admiral de Grasse among the Leeward Isles. During the following 'battle of the Saints' Rodney employed unorthodox tactics, attacking the French line head-on instead of engaging the enemy broadside to broadside in the approved fashion. Rodney's departure from the recognized 'Fighting Instructions' was justified by results: five enemy vessels were accounted for and de Grasse was captured. Despite Rear Admiral Samuel Hood's criticisms that Rodney had failed to exploit his success, the victory went far to restore British prestige at the war's close and strengthened Britain's hand during the coming peace negotiations at VERSAILLES. It also secured Rodney a peerage and an annual pension of £2000, although the reward proved insufficient to restore his ravaged finances.

FURTHER READING D. Spinney, *Rodney* (1969).

Romantic movement, broad cultural movement of the later 18th and earlier 19th centuries, representing a reaction against the rationalism of the ENLIGHTENMENT and against classical restraint, objectivity and balance as aesthetic values. The new emphasis upon individuality, spontaneity, emotion and freedom of expression characterized as 'Romanticism' surfaced most strongly within the arts in England and Germany: there, the prevailing obsession with the classical world was rivalled by an interest in local identities, folklore and the medieval past. Romanticism therefore fostered the growth of liberal nationalism, a trend that was encouraged throughout Europe by the prolonged struggles of the REVOLUTIONARY AND NAPOLEONIC WARS.

The clearest expression of Romantic ideas came from writers and poets, who in turn helped to inspire the output of artists and musicians. In Germany, Romanticism first surfaced in the *Sturm und Drang* literary movement of the 1770s. Although typical Romantic elements had been anticipated in the melodramatic GOTHIC novels of

Horace WALPOLE and his imitators, the movement's appearance in English literature is conventionally dated to 1798, the year of publication of the *Lyrical Ballads* by the LAKE POETS William Wordsworth and Samuel Taylor Coleridge. Through both his verse and personality, Lord BYRON also proved a key figure in the movement. During the opening decades of the 19th century the Romantic novel was perfected through Sir Walter Scott's forays into the Middle Ages and the more recent past of his native Scotland.

In painting and architecture, Romanticism has often been regarded as the very antithesis of the carefully ordered NEOCLASSICISM that exerted such dominance during the second half of the 18th century. Here, Britain's contribution to the Romantic movement was significant. The GOTHIC revival in architecture that gathered momentum during the second half of the 18th century offered a marked contrast to the fashion for building styles derived from the ancient world. By the 1780s, artists such as the London-based American John Singleton COPLEY were already executing dramatic 'history' paintings that anticipated the later efforts of such French Romantic painters as Eugène Delacroix and Théodore Géricault.

Working in watercolour, the visionary painter and poet William BLAKE produced images culled from his own imagination that owed nothing to the classically inspired teachings of the Academy. Blake's contemporaries, the landscape painters Thomas Girtin and Alexander Cozens, likewise abandoned the conventions of the studio to seek inspiration from nature itself. An overwhelmingly emotional response to the natural world influenced the output of the great English landscape painters of the early 19th century, J.M.W. TURNER and John CONSTABLE: their highly individual techniques and emphasis upon a free expression of light and colour won acclaim in France and prefigured the impressionists.

FURTHER READING S. Curran (ed.), *The Cambridge Companion to British Romanticism* (1993).

Romilly, Sir Samuel (1757–1818), prominent law reformer who campaigned for a dilution of the 'BLOODY CODE' that obliged British judges to impose the death sentence for trifling thefts.

Romilly was born in London's Soho to French Huguenot parents. He endured a lonely childhood, but a legacy left by one of his mother's relatives permitted him to follow a legal career. His prowess at the Bar gained him a handsome income, and was underpinned by an encyclopedic knowledge of the criminal law in Britain and Europe. Romilly greeted the outbreak of the FRENCH REVOLUTION with enthusiasm, and in 1797 he defended the Irish radical John Binns on a charge of sedition. Although he remained an admirer of Napoleon, Romilly's loyalty was not in question: he became a king's counsel in Chancery in 1800, and in 1806 served as solicitor general in the MINISTRY OF ALL THE TALENTS.

Following the fall of that short-lived administration Romilly used his seat in the Commons to launch an assault upon Britain's draconian penal code. Romilly's campaign was waged against the backdrop of protracted warfare and domestic disorder and met with only limited success: his bills to repeal the Shop-Lifting Act, which permitted execution for theft from shops, met with repeated rejection in the Commons and Lords. However, Romilly's advocacy did succeed in removing statutes that retained the death sentence for such crimes as theft from bleaching grounds; in that instance the manufacturers themselves had petitioned for repeal on the grounds that the very severity of the act made it virtually unenforceable in the face of widespread reluctance to prosecute or convict.

Romilly supported CATHOLIC EMANCIPATION and the abolition of slavery. In 1818 his depression at the latest rebuttal of his efforts to repeal the Shop-Lifting Act was deepened by the death of his beloved wife, and he committed suicide soon after.

FURTHER READING P. Medd, *Romilly: A Life of Sir Samuel Romilly, Lawyer and Reformer* (1968).

Romney, George (1734–1802), painter, an aspiring rival of REYNOLDS and GAINSBOROUGH. Born in Lancashire, Romney painted portraits in Kendal before arriving on the London art scene in 1762. He made an early impression and won a Society of Arts prize for his painting of *The Death of Wolfe*; by depicting the scene in modern dress, Romney anticipated Benjamin WEST's more celebrated version by a decade. Leaving his wife and children behind him in the north of England, Romney proceeded to establish himself as one of the capital's leading fashionable portrait painters.

From 1773 to 1775 Romney visited Rome, Parma and Venice, encountering the early Romanticism of Fuseli and returning with an ambition to inject a more heroic element into his work. Few of Romney's projected 'history' paintings progressed beyond the sketch stage, although his portraits benefited from a more vigorous handling. Romney's prices undercut both Reynolds and Gainsborough, while his direct yet elegant style accumulated numerous admirers, among the most influential of whom was the duchess of DEVONSHIRE. Romney also painted a series of portraits marking the departure of wealthy young men from Eton; they included such future statesmen as the younger Pitt. In 1781 a meeting with the famous beauty Emma Hart – the future Lady Hamilton and mistress of Nelson – made a deep impression upon Romney. He painted some fifty portraits of Emma, clad in fancy mythological garb or respectable modern dress, and in poses ranging from the provocative to the demure. A prolific artist, Romney remained shy about his work, and Reynolds's undisguised hostility discouraged him from exhibiting at the Royal Academy. In 1798 Romney sold his Hampstead home and returned to his long-forsaken wife; she cared for him in his final years as he lapsed into insanity.

Roubiliac, Louis-François (*c.*1702–62), sculptor, widely regarded as the most gifted sculptor ever to work in 18th century Britain. Roubiliac executed some of the most dramatic monuments in Westminster Abbey.

Born in Lyons of Huguenot stock, he studied under the German master of BAROQUE sculpture, Permoser, and had settled in London by the mid-1730s. According to tradition, Roubiliac's rise to fame began after he found and returned a pocket book full of bank notes belonging to the illegitimate son of Sir Robert WALPOLE. Roubiliac's honesty gained an introduction to the sculptor Sir Henry Cheere, who obtained him his crucial first commission; this was the ground-breaking marble statue of HANDEL, which attracted much attention after Jonathan Tyers placed it amidst his revamped pleasure gardens at VAUXHALL in 1738. The statue is now in the Victoria and Albert Museum.

By 1745 Roubiliac was teaching his inspired blend of European baroque and ROCOCO sculpture at HOGARTH's academy in St Martin's Lane. Roubiliac executed realistic portrait busts that were less strictly classical and more animated than those of his great Flemish predecessor RYSBRACK. In Roubiliac's hands no unflattering detail was suppressed; his busts include a vivid likeness of his friend Hogarth that captures the painter's proverbial pugnacity.

A sense for drama and a naturalistic treatment of figures was also evident in Roubiliac's funeral monuments, of which seven major examples survive in Westminster Abbey. These broke with tradition by abandoning the customary calm repose of the deceased and replacing it with stances of startling action. The most striking monuments are those commemorating General William Hargrave, completed in 1757, and the equally dramatic memorial to Joseph and Lady Elizabeth Nightingale, of 1761. In the Hargrave monument death is banished as the general rises again from the ruins of a collapsing pyramidal tomb at the summons of the last trump; the composition provides a powerful image of the Resurrection. By contrast, in the Nightingale tomb Roubiliac casts death as the victor. Lady Nightingale had died from a miscarriage after being frightened by a bolt of lightning; Roubiliac depicts a shrouded skeleton emerging from a vault to cast his own dart of death at the helpless Elizabeth, while her husband vainly attempts to protect her. The Nightingale tomb is a dramatic statement of the inevitability of death; Roubiliac's own was to follow soon after its completion.

FURTHER READING D. Bindman and M. Baker, *Roubiliac and the Eighteenth-Century Monument. Sculpture as Theatre* (1995).

Rowlandson, Thomas (1756–1827), painter and caricaturist, one of the most popular artists of his day. If HOGARTH reigns supreme as the outstanding visual guide to the society of mid-18th-century Britain, Rowlandson represents a worthy successor for its closing decades.

Born and living mainly in London, Rowlandson viewed his world with a humour that was often bawdy and sometimes pornographic. A student of the Royal Academy, Rowlandson's prolific output was characterized by a mastery of line that is equally apparent in swift sketches or elaborate compositions such as his famous view of VAUXHALL GARDENS in 1784. Unlike his friend GILLRAY, whose work represented a swift and hard-hitting response to politics and personalities, Rowlandson was more concerned with broader social commentary. Both shared a taste for the grotesque. In works such as his *Box Lobby Loungers*, which was exhibited at the Royal Academy in 1786, Rowlandson caricatured both recognizable society figures and amusing 'types'.

Rowlandson depicted the contemporary scene with inimitable gusto and without Hogarth's moralizing agenda. He recorded high life and low, town and country: crowded boxing matches and London theatre audiences are balanced by atmospheric scenes of Cornish wreckers and quaint cottages. Indeed, although he satirized the contemporary search for the 'picturesque' in the character of the long-suffering travelling painter 'Dr Syntax', with verses by William Combe, Rowlandson was himself a gifted landscape artist.

Troubled by failing eyesight in his later years, Rowlandson nonetheless remained capable of such masterpieces as *Smithfield Market* (*c*.1816–20), a work that reveals not only his eye for telling detail but also a bravura depiction of architecture.

FURTHER READING J.T. Hayes, *The Art of Thomas Rowlandson* (1990).

Royal Academy (in full, the Royal Academy of Arts), institution designed to encourage standards of excellence among British painters. GEORGE III gave it his seal of approval in 1768. The king had been approached by the American painter Benjamin WEST and the architect William CHAMBERS, who envisaged a national institution that would establish an artistic training centre based upon continental models, promote the highest standards of taste and provide free exhibition for works of recognized merit.

The foundation of the Academy coincided with an era in which the efforts of native-born artists such as RAMSAY, REYNOLDS and GAINSBOROUGH had gained British painting unprecedented recognition – at home, if not abroad. The Academy's emergence was a key event in the history of painting in Britain; it gave leading artists the backing of a prestigious organization that enjoyed the patronage of the monarch himself. While lacking the official powers of the French Academy founded in the mid-17th century, the Royal Academy nonetheless sought to promote the professional status of artists and sculptors and offer the kind of carefully regulated training in the visual arts that existed elsewhere in Europe. During the century that followed its foundation the Academy became the most influential institution in British artistic life, although the ideals it embodied drew increasing criticism.

The Academy was concerned to elevate visual artists above the level of mere craftsmen; hence, engravers, deemed to be concerned in manual reproduction rather than a true creative process, were excluded before 1857. Long-established elsewhere in Europe, the concept of the artistic academy was not unknown in early-Georgian England. William HOGARTH had propagated his techniques and promoted ideas of artistic fraternity through his school in St Martin's Lane. However, the Royal Academy envisaged a more formalized approach.

The Royal Academy's ideals were personified in its first president, Sir Joshua Reynolds, who believed in the acquisition of knowledge through careful study of – and a profound respect for – the old masters and the timeless classical traditions of ancient Greece and Rome. Reynolds disseminated his creed through his famous *Discourses*, which were delivered at the Academy over two decades. The Academy's annual summer exhibition, which built upon precedents established by the existing Society of Artists, rapidly became a mainstay of the London social calendar. It provided a showcase in which reputations could be established or wrecked; for example, West's own *Death of Wolfe* proved a crowd-pulling sensation when it was put on show in 1771.

Membership of the Academy was by election, and was initially restricted to about 40 artists. ZOFFANY's sprawling group painting of 1772 shows almost all of the original academicians. The Academy amounted to a club, and rapidly established a reputation for exclusivity and conservatism that was to alienate some of the era's more imaginative artists; this was particularly true of those painters who shunned London for the provinces or whose choice of subject matter failed to accord with the Academy's preference for 'history' painting and portraiture. Critics included Joseph WRIGHT of Derby, who believed that the Academy's stilted training techniques – whereby massed ranks of students copied the same subject – instilled method at the expense of imagination.

It is also significant that Zoffany's canvas includes the female academicians Angelica KAUFFMANN and Mary MOSER only as portraits hanging upon the wall; while both were ostensibly excluded on grounds of modesty because of the presence of a nude male model, there were to be no other female academicians before the 20th century. It was not until the late Victorian period that women were even permitted to study in the Academy schools. By then the Academy's failure to keep pace with changing trends in painting had already tarnished the prestige it enjoyed during its 18th-century heyday.

FURTHER READING S.C. Hutchison, *The History of the Royal Academy* (1986).

Royal Navy. *See* NAVY.

royal prerogative. *See* REVOLUTION SETTLEMENT.

Royal Society (in full, the Royal Society of London for Improving Natural Knowledge), institution that received a royal charter in 1662 for 'advancing the knowledge of nature and useful arts by experiment to the glory of God the Creator and application to the good of mankind'.

The early fellows of the Society – many of whom had pursued scientific investigations in Oxford during the Interregnum before associating informally at the Restoration – were a mixture of classes and creeds. They deliberately barred political and religious matters from discussion at their meetings. As Bishop Sprat, the first historian of the Society, observed in 1667, they eschewed 'spiritual frenzies'. The Society published its proceedings in its *Philosophical Transactions* after 1695. In its early years it was distinguished by such luminaries as Robert Boyle, Robert Hooke and Sir Isaac NEWTON, who served as its president from 1703 to 1727.

By the reign of George II, however, the Society had already become a dilettante club, making its fellowships available on social as well as scientific criteria. SWIFT satirized some of their trivial and unscientific experiments in his account of the Academy of Lagado in *Gulliver's Travels* (1726). Martin Folkes, president from 1741 to 1752, was an antiquarian, and its meetings during his presidency were characterized as 'a most elegant and agreeable entertainment for a contemplative person'.

Folkes was succeeded by the earls of Macclesfield and Morton.

In 1772, however, the eminent physician Sir John Pringle became president, and under him the Society flourished as a genuine forum for the exchange of scientific ideas. Pringle took the opportunity at the annual award of the Copley medal to discourse on the subject of the prize-winning paper. These included Captain COOK's report on his measures to prevent scurvy on his voyages, Nevile Maskelyne's account of his measurements of the force of gravity, and Joseph PRIESTLEY's investigations of the properties of various gases. Under Pringle the Society recovered its reputation for encouraging serious research. He was followed in 1778 by Sir Joseph BANKS, who held the presidency for 42 years despite criticism of his autocratic manner. Although Banks appeared to be continuing the tradition of the gentleman amateur, he was a naturalist who had accompanied Cook on the voyage of the *Endeavour* and whose interest in natural history led to Botany Bay being so called.

FURTHER READING M. Hunter, *Establishing the New Science: The Experience of the Early Royal Society* (1989).

Russell, Edward, 1st earl of Orford. *See* ORFORD, EDWARD RUSSELL, 1ST EARL OF.

Rysbrack, John Michael (1694–1770), Flemish-born sculptor. Born in Antwerp, Rysbrack became the outstanding sculptor working in England during the age of Walpole.

The son of a landscape painter who had practised in England during the reign of Charles II, Rysbrack followed his father's lead and arrived in London around 1720. Rysbrack gained a crucial stamp of approval when the leading portrait painter of the day, Sir Godfrey KNELLER, approached him to design his monument; Kneller was pleased with the result, which was erected in Westminster Abbey in 1730. Rysbrack's talents as a tomb sculptor were widely recognized: his monument to Sir Isaac

NEWTON, which was created in collaboration with William Kent and unveiled in 1731, has been described as 'perhaps the finest of all the post-medieval tombs in the Abbey'. The Rysbrack–Kent partnership was likewise responsible for another celebrated memorial – the 1732 tomb of John Churchill 1st duke of MARLBOROUGH in the chapel at BLENHEIM PALACE. The quality of such large-scale commissions was matched by more intimate works, such as Rysbrack's monument to the drama-tist John GAY in Westminster Abbey.

Rysbrack was equally renowned for his busts in marble and terracotta. He introduced a classi-cal style – epitomized in the Caesar-like bust of Daniel Finch 2nd earl of NOTTINGHAM (1723) –

that tailored late BAROQUE sculpture to English tastes. Rysbrack created more than sixty busts, with subjects ranging from GEORGE I and GEORGE II to Sir Robert WALPOLE, Alexander POPE and long-dead 'British worthies' such as Oliver Cromwell and the Black Prince. A debt to the sculpture of the ancient world was equally apparent in Rys-brack's superbly executed equestrian subjects – notably the 1735 statue of WILLIAM III in Queen's Square, Bristol. Although ROUBILIAC ultimately eclipsed him in terms of popularity, Rysbrack's dig-nified and restrained approach made him a worthy rival of the great Frenchman.

Ryswick, treaty of. *See* NINE YEARS WAR.

S

Sacheverell, Henry (1674–1724), HIGH-CHURCH clergyman who was impeached in 1710 for preaching a sermon regarded as subversive by the Whig government.

A fellow of Magdalen College, Oxford, Dr Sacheverell was popular as a preacher of fiery high-church sermons. One he preached at St Mary's, Oxford, in May 1702 was immediately printed as *The Political Union*. In it he urged Anglicans to have no truck with DISSENTERS, but instead to 'hang out the bloody flag and banner of defiance'. In print it circulated far from Oxford and attracted attention in London, not least from Daniel DEFOE, who dubbed Sacheverell 'the bloody flag officer' and based his *Shortest Way with the Dissenters* on the style of the sermon.

In July 1706 Sacheverell gave an assize sermon (*see* JUSTICES OF THE PEACE) at Leicester on *The nature, obligation and measures of conscience*, which inveighed against dissenters. But it was another assize sermon, *The communication of sin*, preached at Derby in 1709, that first led some Whigs to consider taking proceedings against him. A sermon given to the lord mayor, aldermen and council of London in St Paul's Cathedral on 5 November 1709 was considered too subversive to be ignored. Such sermons normally took the opportunity to compare the foiling of the Gunpowder Plot with the landing of William of Orange on 5 November

1688 as 'a double deliverance' from popery. Instead Sacheverell compared the Plot not with the GLORIOUS REVOLUTION but with 30 January 1649, the day of Charles I's execution; both were 'indelible monuments of the interminable rage and blood-thirstiness of both the Popish and Fanatick enemies of our Church and Government. These two days indeed are but one united proof and visible testimonial of the same dangerous and rebellious principles these confederates in iniquity maintain.' He thus turned the anniversary of the Gunpowder Plot into an attack upon dissenters. Above all he denounced the 'false brethren' who abetted them in the undermining of the constitution in church and state.

The publication of Sacheverell's sermon caused a sensation. Whigs were outraged that so far from linking 5 November 1688 with the Gunpowder Plot the sermon had actually denied that there was any such link by denying that there had been resistance to the sovereign in the Glorious Revolution. The Whig government determined to bring him to book. Lord Treasurer GODOLPHIN was particularly incensed against him since Sacheverell had referred to him by his nickname of 'Volpone' as one of the false brethren. It was decided to impeach Sacheverell before the House of Lords, and the Commons drew up four articles of impeachment against him. The first and most important was that

Sacheverell's sermon suggested that there had been no resistance in the Revolution, so that 'the necessary means used to bring about the said happy Revolution were odious and unjustifiable'.

The Whigs fielded their finest talents as managers of the articles. 'The night of fire' on 1 March 1710 witnessed riots in which several dissenting chapels were attacked and gutted; this seemed to confirm the fourth article's claim that Sacheverell stirred people up to arms and violence. On 3 March Simon Harcourt, Sacheverell's defence lawyer, got Sacheverell off the hook of denying that there had been resistance in 1688 by defining the supreme power that could not be resisted as the king, Lords and Commons and not the king alone. On 20 March the Lords found Sacheverell guilty by 69 votes to 52. Next day they had to sentence him. The government had wanted him to be incapacitated from preaching, fined and imprisoned, but the actual sentence was surprisingly lenient. He was only prevented from preaching for three years. Although Parliament was not dissolved until September, electioneering had already begun in earnest. Sacheverell himself indulged in it by making a triumphal progress in June to Selattyn, a Shropshire living given him by an admirer at the time of the trial, visiting eight counties and twelve parliamentary boroughs on his journey to and from his new parish, which took him six weeks to complete. His career after his triumph, however, was something of an anticlimax. Although he obtained the rectory of St Andrew's, Holborn, in 1713 it was not the high preferment he thought he deserved. He enjoyed a brief resurgence of fame in 1713 when the bar on his preaching was lifted. The death of Anne in 1714 and the consequent triumph of the Whigs under George I spelled the end of all hopes of preferment for high-church clergymen.
FURTHER READING G. Holmes, *The Trial of Dr Sacheverell* (1973).

Sackville, Lord George (1716–85), soldier and politician. The third son of the duke of Dorset, Sackville was educated at Westminster School and Trinity College, Dublin, before embarking upon what promised to be a glittering career in the army. During the War of the AUSTRIAN SUCCESSION he was seriously wounded at the battle of FONTENOY, and subsequently campaigned against the JACOBITES in the rebellion of 1745. By the outbreak of the SEVEN YEARS WAR, Sackville's background and abilities had secured him the rank of major general; in 1758 he was appointed second-in-command of the British contingent sent to serve under Ferdinand of Brunswick in Germany. Upon the death of the duke of Marlborough, Sackville became the commander of the British troops. Aloof and haughty in temperament, Sackville proved an awkward colleague for Ferdinand, and their mutual dislike surfaced with dramatic results during the battle of MINDEN in 1759, when Sackville disregarded the prince's orders to lead forward the cavalry immediately. His hesitation permitted the beaten French to retreat unmolested, and led to accusations of cowardice. The stubborn Sackville insisted upon a court martial to clear his name from these aspersions. Instead, the court found him guilty and Sackville was deemed unfit to serve the crown in any capacity, dismissed from the army in disgrace and struck off the list of privy councillors.

It was a tribute to Sackville's abilities and strength of character that he survived this crushing sentence and slowly clawed his way back to favour under the new monarch, GEORGE III. During the 1760s, Sackville became known as a staunch advocate of Parliament's supremacy over the disgruntled and increasingly disorderly American colonists. In 1770 Sackville adopted the title of Lord George Germain; the change coincided with the establishment of Lord NORTH at the head of a ministry that shared Germain's own hardline attitudes. By the first skirmishes of the AMERICAN WAR OF INDEPENDENCE in 1775, Germain had established himself as a valued ministerial spokesman on events across the Atlantic, this expertise bringing about his appointment to the key post of American secretary.

As the man responsible for the American colonies, Germain was destined to play a major role in formulating the strategies intended to coerce them back within the imperial fold. He worked industriously towards this end, but was hampered by the sheer distance separating him from the scene of conflict and by divisions inside North's cabinet. He also maintained a misplaced faith in the strength of loyalism in America, and proved susceptible to the schemes of ambitious officers such as BURGOYNE, whose attempt to invade New England from Canada ended in disaster at SARATOGA. Germain likewise favoured the aggressive CORNWALLIS over his more cautious superior CLINTON. Despite his occasional flaws of judgement, Germain proved a vigorous war leader who never lost his determination to crush the rebellion: even after the news of YORKTOWN in 1781, he urged his cabinet colleagues to continue the fight. He resigned in 1782 and assumed the title of Viscount Sackville. The old Minden slurs, compounded by prejudice against Sackville's rumoured homosexuality, dogged him to the end of his days.

FURTHER READING P. Mackesy, *The War for America, 1775–1783* (1963); P. Mackesy, *The Coward of Minden: The Affair of Lord George Sackville* (1979).

St George's Fields, massacre of (10 May 1768), tragic climax to demonstrations of popular support for the radical demagogue John WILKES. Wilkes had been outlawed in 1764 after he fled to France rather than face trial on charges of seditious and obscene libel. Soon after returning from exile and triumphing in the Middlesex election in March 1768, Wilkes was arrested and prosecuted on the original charges against him. During his lengthy trial Wilkes was housed in the King's Bench Prison, adjoining St George's Fields in London. On the day appointed for the opening of Parliament large crowds began to assemble in front of the prison. Rumours spread that Wilkes would be released to take up his seat in the House, and by the afternoon the throng was estimated at 20,000. Anticipating trouble, the government had already ordered a troop of cavalry and 100 men of the Foot Guards to support the Surrey magistrates at the King's Bench Prison. When a pro-Wilkes paper was removed from the prison wall the angry crowd responded with cries of 'Wilkes and Liberty for ever!' As the mood of the demonstrators turned ugly, Justice Samuel Gillam ordered three soldiers to apprehend a suspected stone-thrower. In executing this task, the over-zealous guardsmen shot dead William Allen, a publican's son who had not even been involved in the riot. After the RIOT ACT had been read twice in an unsuccessful effort to disperse the crowd, other troops opened fire indiscriminately; in all, between ten and twelve 'rioters' were killed and many others wounded. The 'massacre' led to further disturbances in London and gave the cause of Wilkes its first martyrs. The incident caused considerable embarrassment to the government, which appeared tyrannical and militaristic. At a time when anti-Scottish feelings still ran high, it was an unlucky coincidence that the trio of soldiers who had caused Allen's death were all themselves Scots. Although a coroner's inquest found these men to be guilty of murder, at their subsequent trial in Guildford the evidence proved insufficient to secure a conviction. The government's credibility was not enhanced by the mysterious disappearance of the guardsman who was believed to have fired the fatal bullet.

St John, Henry. *See* BOLINGBROKE, HENRY ST JOHN, 1ST VISCOUNT.

Saints, battle of the. *See* RODNEY, GEORGE BRYDGES.

Salamanca, battle of (22 July 1812), major British victory in Spain during the PENINSULAR WAR with France. In the summer of 1812, WELLINGTON mounted an offensive leading to the liberation of Salamanca on 17 June. Within weeks, a French army of 48,000 men under Marshal Marmont advanced to menace Wellington's line of communications. Although Wellington's Anglo-Portuguese force was slightly larger, he cautiously withdrew into terrain where he could tackle Marmont under favourable conditions. For several days the rival armies manoeuvred to gain the advantage, sometimes marching in parallel columns within gunshot range of each other.

Wellington's reaction convinced the aggressive and glory-hungry Marmont that his opponent was incapable of fighting anything other than a defensive action. However, on 22 July, some 10km (6 miles) south of the city, he learned differently. Misreading movements in Wellington's army for a retreat, Marmont sent his leading division hurrying forward to exploit the situation. By extending his line, Marmont made a fatal blunder. Observing the widening gap between the French divisions, Wellington dropped the chicken leg he was munching, raised his telescope and exclaimed, 'That will do!' Unlike Marmont's men, Wellington's concealed troops were concentrated, and their sudden attack broke the French advance. As the enemy fled, Wellington unleashed his heavy cavalry in a devastating charge commanded by Major General Le Marchant. Although the remaining French divisions fought stoutly, they were eventually broken by Wellington's reserves. The French suffered 15,000 casualties to Wellington's 5000; the outcome would have been even more decisive but for the negligence of a Spanish officer who abandoned his post guarding the bridge over the river Tormes by which the defeated survivors escaped.

Salamanca provided proof of Wellington's ability to fight an offensive battle. The destruction of Marmont's army of Portugal opened the way to Madrid, although the presence of further French forces obliged Wellington to retreat that August after failing to capture the fortress of Burgos.

Sandwich, John Montagu, 4th earl of (1718–92), politician and naval administrator. Sandwich remains a controversial figure: while his political career has traditionally been cited as evidence of the harmful influence of patronage in 18th-century politics, he has more recently been given credit for important naval reforms that helped to minimize the scale of Britain's defeat during the AMERICAN WAR OF INDEPENDENCE. A sophisticated patron of the arts and dedicated gambler, Lord Sandwich is today popularly remembered for inventing the snack that bears his name. Sandwich was a major landowner who gained a reputation as a rake that included membership of the infamous HELL-FIRE CLUB. In 1763, when he was prominent in the government's attack upon John WILKES's obscene *Essay on Woman*, Sandwich earned the unflattering nickname of 'Jemmy Twitcher' – a character in John GAY's *Beggar's Opera* – for turning against his old friend. Although Sandwich had served in the army as a young man, his subsequent political career was anchored firmly to the NAVY. From 1748 to 1751 he was first lord of the Admiralty; he held the same post in 1763 and again from 1771 to 1782 during the ministry of Lord NORTH. In his third stint at the Admiralty, Sandwich faced the unenviable task of maintaining the fighting efficiency of the Royal Navy in a climate of peacetime retrenchment. Despite Sandwich's efforts, the intervention of France and her powerful navy on behalf of Britain's rebellious American colonies in 1778 left the Royal Navy unable to maintain its customary supremacy. Faced with the task of guarding against a Bourbon invasion of Britain itself – a priority that Sandwich regarded as paramount – British warships proved incapable of dominating the Atlantic. French naval superiority in American waters subsequently led to Britain's disastrous defeat at YORKTOWN in 1781. Sandwich was also blamed for exacerbating the political faction fighting that divided the Royal Navy during the American war; several senior officers even refused to serve while Sandwich remained at the helm. Sandwich's reputation at the Admiralty was damaged further by his persecution of Lord Augustus KEPPEL following an indecisive encounter with the French off Ushant in 1778; cleared of misconduct, Keppel became a popular hero while Sandwich was vilified. Sandwich had nonetheless played a more creditable role by instigating the reforms that ultimately allowed the Royal Navy to regain the initiative during the closing years of the American war. Ironically, RODNEY's great victory at the Saints in April 1782 came too late to redeem Sandwich's name: the North ministry in which he had served for so long resigned just weeks before, permitting his successor to take credit for the navy's belated triumph. **FURTHER READING** N.A.M. Rodger, *The Insatiable Earl: A Life of John Montagu, Fourth Earl of Sandwich, 1718-1792* (1993).

Saratoga, surrender at (17 October 1777), capitulation of British forces under General John BURGOYNE in New York state. The surrender marked the turning point in the AMERICAN WAR OF INDEPENDENCE, as it encouraged the French to intervene on the side of the colonists, thereby transforming rebellion in America into a war on several fronts. Burgoyne's advance from Canada had initially enjoyed considerable success, capturing the important fortress of TICONDEROGA in early July. However, as he continued his progress southwards Burgoyne encountered increasing problems in negotiating the rugged and wooded terrain: the wilderness also provided perfect cover for militias that would have been reluctant to encounter his highly trained redcoats in open country. On 16 August a major foraging expedition was surrounded and destroyed at Bennington by local patriots. The exasperated Burgoyne observed: 'wherever the King's forces point, militia to the amount of three or four thousand assemble in twenty four hours'. Despite gathering opposition, Burgoyne recklessly continued his advance. He marched straight into a trap as his army filed through a narrow gap in the Hudson river valley to come face to face with American troops under Horatio Gates, who were well entrenched in the commanding defensive position of Bemis Heights. On 19 September Burgoyne sought to dislodge them: bitter fighting centred on the clearing at Freeman's Farm, with the British sustaining the heavier casualties. For more than two weeks Burgoyne hoped for relief as his supplies dwindled and his exhausted men were harassed by rebel riflemen. Further heavy fighting erupted on

7 October, when Gates's fiery subordinate, Benedict Arnold, distinguished himself in an attack on Burgoyne's position. The disheartened Burgoyne gradually withdrew his depleted forces to Saratoga. With his 6000 troops surrounded and outnumbered by more than three to one Burgoyne capitulated on 17 October. The surrender 'convention' permitted his troops to leave for Britain on condition that they did not serve again in America. Fearing that such generous terms would release other British soldiers to take their place, Congress repudiated the agreement and impounded Burgoyne's men until the end of the war.

Schism Act (1714), legislation that sought to eliminate the separate education of DISSENTERS by making illegal any educational establishment that lacked a licence from a bishop. The act was passed by the Tories who then monopolized the cabinet and had the greatest majority in the Commons they ever enjoyed in the 'first age of party'. Fortunately for the dissenters the act was due to come into operation on the very day Queen Anne died, so that, although it was not repealed until 1719, it remained largely a dead letter.

schools. *See* CHARITY; EDUCATION; SUNDAY SCHOOLS.

science. Scientific enquiries in the 18th century were inspired by the discoveries of Sir Isaac NEWTON. Alexander POPE expressed the regard in which he was held by natural philosophers (scientists) when he wrote:

> Nature and Nature's Laws lay hid in night;
> God said 'let Newton be' and all was Light.

Pope exaggerated of course. Science had progressed a great deal in the 17th century, assisted in England by the foundation of the ROYAL SOCIETY. But there was a sense in which men felt that Newtonian mathematics had made a fresh start. His friend John Thomas Desaguliers published a poem, *Newtonian system of the world, the best model of Government,* in 1728 which claimed that Newton's methods could be applied to all human investigations. Astronomy was one branch of science which benefited from the application of his principles. James Bradley (1693–1762), who succeeded Edmond HALLEY as Astronomer Royal, discovered the law of the constant of aberration, which calculated the effect of the earth's rotation on the study of starlight. This was the first scientific proof that the earth moved. Bradley taught Nevil Maskelyne (1732–1811), who published the first issue of the *Nautical Almanac* in 1766 and supervised the publication of the succeeding 45 annual issues. Maskelyne hoped that his observations would solve the problem of LONGITUDE but was unsuccessful. They did, however, enable William Herschel (1738–1822), a German-born musician turned astronomer, to discover Uranus in 1781. Herschel was elected as first president of the Royal Astronomical Society when it was established in 1817.

The precise plotting of longitude was effected not by the application of Newtonian astrophysics but by the manufacture of precision chronometers by John Harrison, an uneducated carpenter. This raises questions about the nature of the connection between scientific theories and their technological implementation in the 18th century. Many of the inventions which led INDUSTRY to make progress, such as Edmund CARTWRIGHT's power loom and Samuel CROMPTON's spinning mule, were made by men with little or no theoretical aptitude. One example of fruitful cooperation between a scientist and an inventor, however, was that between Joseph Black and James WATT. Black was professor of anatomy and chemistry at Glasgow University from 1756 to 1766, when he moved to the chair of medicine and chemistry at Edinburgh. His researches into latent heat assisted Watt's development of the steam engine.

Black's professorships combining chemistry and medicine indicate that the rigorous division of science into specific categories still had a long way to go even in forward-looking Scottish universities in the 18th century. Outside the academy, scientific investigations of all kinds were conducted by enthusiastic amateurs or dilettanti, many of whom even became Fellows of the Royal Society. Scientific research could sometimes be presented in unorthodox ways. For example, Erasmus DARWIN employed the medium of verse to publicize his investigations in biology, botany and chemistry. In 1799 the Royal Institution was set up as a centre in which the application of scientific discovery to industry could be facilitated. In 1801 Sir Humphry DAVY was appointed to it. His researches and lectures on chemistry and its application to agriculture made it a major forum for science and technology.

FURTHER READING J. Golinski, *Science as Public Culture: Chemistry and Enlightenment in Britain, 1760–1820* (1992); P Mathias, *Science and Society, 1600–1900* (1972).

Scott, Sarah Robinson (1723–95), novelist. Scott was the daughter of Matthew Robinson, gentleman of Yorkshire, and sister of the society hostess Elizabeth MONTAGU. In 1751 she married George Lewis Scott, sub-preceptor to Prince George, the future George III. They separated in 1753 and she settled in Bath with Lady Barbara Montagu. Scott published several novels, of which the most celebrated, going through four editions, was *A Description of Millenium Hall and the country adjacent, together with the characters of the inhabitants and such historical anecdotes and reflections as may excite in the reader proper sentiments of humanity and lead the mind to the love of virtue, by a gentleman on his travels* (1762). The 'gentleman' narrates the novel in the form of a long letter to a friend. He is travelling in Cornwall with a young man, Lamont, when their chaise breaks down and they are taken in by the occupants of a country house, which he calls 'Millenium Hall', until their conveyance is repaired. The house is run by twelve ladies who act as guardians to women they have rescued from the 'voluntary slavery' of domestic service, every child above the fifth of married couples in the neighbourhood, and diminutive adults. They also run schools for boys and girls and a manufactory of worsted cloth. The gentleman's account of this undertaking is interrupted by several digressions in the form of biographies of some of the ladies who run it, narrated by one of them, Mrs Maynard. The novel has been taken for a feminist manifesto, especially since some of the ladies were the victims of unscrupulous men bent on assailing their virtue. Certainly the account of ladies successfully managing an enterprise as a 'sisterhood' was a statement of female independence by Sarah Scott. But it was not crude feminism, for Mrs Maynard narrates how some of those who sought an alternative to marriage in Millenium Hall had been thwarted in their lives by scheming women, while the ladies themselves encourage their charges to marry, insisting that 'we consider matrimony as absolutely necessary for the benefit of society'.

FURTHER READING S. Scott, *A Description of Millenium Hall*, ed. G. Kelly (1995).

Scottish Enlightenment, term applied to the flowering of intellectual activity in Scotland during the 18th century. 'At the present time it is from Scotland we receive rules of taste in all the arts,' observed Voltaire, 'from the epic poem to gardening.' He was paying tribute to the astonishing efflorescence of Scottish culture that led to EDINBURGH becoming known as the Athens of the north. It was no accident that Britain's response to the European ENLIGHTENMENT, the *Encyclopaedia Britannica*, was published in Edinburgh between 1768 and 1771. Leading figures of the Scottish Enlightenment – who were the equivalent of the French *philosophes* – included Joseph Black (1728–99), Adam FERGUSON, Francis HUTCHESON, David HUME, James Hutton (1726–96), Thomas Reid (1710–96), Dugald Stewart (1753–1828), William ROBERTSON, James Burnett, Lord Monboddo (1714–1799), Henry Home, Lord Kames (1696–1782) and Adam SMITH. Joseph Black was professor of anatomy and chemistry at Glasgow Univer-

sity from 1756 to 1766, when he moved to Edinburgh. He was noted for his work on latent and specific heat. James Hutton was a geologist who held that the formation of the earth's surface was perpetually evolving. This provoked criticism from fundamentalists who saw it as a critique of the biblical account. Thomas Reid wrote *An Inquiry into the Human Mind and the Principles of Common Sense* (1764), for which he became famous as the philosopher of common sense. Dugald Stewart studied under Reid at Glasgow University and obtained the chair of moral philosophy at Edinburgh in 1798. He developed Reid's commonsense philosophy in *Elements of the Philosophy of the Human Mind* (1792). Lord Monboddo published two six-volume works between 1773 and 1779, *Ancient Metaphysic* and *The Origin and Progress of Language*. He was much ridiculed for his claim in the latter that the orang-utan was a member of the human race. His fellow lawyer Lord Kames was also interested in human evolution, and in *Sketches of the History of Man* (1774) traced the four stages of the progress of society from hunting to commerce via pasture and agriculture.

This spectacular display of intellectual achievement in Scotland invites speculation as to why it occurred there. An answer has been sought in the political vacuum left by the ending of the Scottish Parliament in the UNION OF ENGLAND AND SCOTLAND of 1707 and the removal of the politicians from Scotland to London. Where the church might have filled it, the sorry state of the CHURCH OF SCOTLAND in the 18th century with its fissiparous tendencies left it enervated for such a role. In their place, clubs such as the Easy and the Rankenian emerged to act as centres for discussion of questions that the Edinburgh Parliament might have debated had it still been in existence. Thus members of the Select Society, founded in Edinburgh in 1754 by the artist Allan RAMSAY, which included Adam Ferguson, David Hume, William Robertson and Adam Smith among its members, discussed the issues raised by the confinement of the MILITIA Act of 1757 to England and Wales. They demanded its extension to Scotland. These social gatherings provided a public space for the spread of enlightened ideas. As Nicholas Phillipson has observed, 'Scots seem to have believed that the adaptable, modest principles of Addisonian propriety, undertaken in a patriotic spirit, could be developed into a system of civic morality which was appropriate to the needs of the provincial citizen, preoccupied with preserving the independence of his community.'

SEE ALSO UNIVERSITIES.

FURTHER READING N. Phillipson, 'The Scottish Enlightenment' in R. Porter and M. Teich (eds.), *The Enlightenment in National Context* (1981).

Scriblerus Club, largely literary club, which first met in March 1714 in London. Its membership comprised John ARBUTHNOT, John GAY, Robert HARLEY earl of Oxford, Thomas Parnell, Alexander POPE and Jonathan SWIFT. Apart from Harley, who was prime minister, the members were among the leading authors of their day. They shared a political viewpoint which can be called 'Tory' only with reservations. Harley himself had started his political career as a Whig, and until 1704 had attended Presbyterian services. His premiership over a Tory ministry was viewed with suspicion by some high- church Tories. Gay too came from a dissenting background, while Pope was a Catholic, Arbuthnot a Scottish Episcopalian, and Parnell and Swift ministers in the Church of Ireland. They were all therefore to a significant extent 'outsiders' in the context of English Tory politics, and able to view them with a satirical detachment. This found expression in the *Memoirs of Martinus Scriblerus* (1741), to which they all contributed. The *Memoirs* in turn inspired such later works as Gay's *Beggar's Opera*, Pope's *Dunciad* and perhaps above all Swift's *Gulliver's Travels*.

Although formal meetings of the club were scarcely possible after Anne's death, when Harley was sent to the Tower and Swift went to Ireland, the Scriblerians continued to have a distinct literary identity in the new Hanoverian era.

secretaries of state. There were two secretaries of state for most of the period. In the years 1688 to 1782 these were known as the secretaries for the north and the south. The secretary for the north had responsibility for dealing with the diplomatic affairs of northern Europe: the Dutch Republic, the Holy Roman Empire, Russia and Scandinavia. The secretary for the south dealt with the diplomacy of southern Europe: France, Italy, Portugal, Spain, Switzerland and Turkey. Each was responsible for domestic affairs. In 1782 their responsibilities were reorganized into those of the foreign and home secretaries.

Security Act (1704). *See* UNION OF ENGLAND AND SCOTLAND.

sensibility, the notion of innate sympathy for the suffering of others, which developed from moral philosophy in the 18th century. Such works as the 3rd earl of SHAFTESBURY's *Characteristics* (1711) and Adam SMITH's *Theory of Moral Sentiments* (1759) repudiated the egoistic hedonism of Thomas Hobbes as developed by Bernard MANDEVILLE and replaced it with altruism. This notion was complemented by medical research into the nerves and nervous system which provided a physiological explanation for refined feelings concerning the plight of others. Such ideas were brought together in literature. Samuel RICHARDSON played like a virtuoso on the sympathies of his readers by portraying virtue in distress in his heroines Pamela and Clarissa. The reactions of readers, who could be reduced to tears of sympathy for these damsels, and roused to anger by the actions of their betrayers Mr B. and Lovelace, were measures of their sensibility. Such emotions were exploited to excess by Laurence STERNE in *A Sentimental Journey* (1768) and above all by Henry MACKENZIE in *The Man of Feeling* (1771). In these works the reader's sensibility was manipulated to the point of indulging in sorrow, not just out of sympathy for victims of evil actions, but for its own sake, the shedding of tears becoming an expression of 'the

luxury of grief'. Jane Austen's *Sense and Sensibility* (1811) satirizes the extremes of the cult, which nonetheless prefigured the development of Romanticism (*see* ROMANTIC MOVEMENT).
FURTHER READING J. Todd, *Sensibility: An Introduction* (1986).

Septennial Act (1716), statute that extended the maximum interval between general elections established by the TRIENNIAL ACT from three to seven years. This was justified by the Whigs who introduced it on the grounds that the previous act had caused political instability and generated enormous expenditure on frequent elections. It had also produced more Tory than Whig majorities, which was another motive for delaying a general election due in 1718. In fact the next was held in 1722, and until 1784 most Parliaments were allowed to run the full course allowed by the new act. As a consequence, seats in the House of Commons rose in value, pushing up election expenses and leading to the growth of oligarchy, as saving costs eliminated competition. This is reflected in the drop in the incidence of contests after 1734.

Settlement, Act of (1701). *See* ACT OF SETTLEMENT.

Seven Years War (1756–63), global conflict involving Britain and its allies PRUSSIA and HANOVER on the one side and FRANCE, Austria, Russia and ultimately Spain on the other. Fighting took place not only in Europe, but also in India, North America and the Caribbean. The war secured British domination of INDIA and Canada.

A brief but bloody skirmish in the backwoods of the Ohio valley provided the spark for one of the most successful wars that Britain ever waged. The Seven Years War confirmed Britain's status as the leading European power, yet the stunning victories of the 'wonderful year' of 1759 only followed long years of conflict that had seen its armed forces humiliated across the globe.

Growing friction between the British and French North American colonies in 1754, culmi-

nating in the defeat of an Anglo-American force commanded by George Washington, prompted both powers to reinforce their possessions with regular troops. In the following year a Royal Navy squadron failed to intercept a French convoy bound for Canada, while a British army under the command of Major General Edward Braddock was massacred by the French and their Native American allies in the Pennsylvanian forest. The onset of 1756 brought further disasters at French hands: in America, the key trading post of Oswego was snuffed out by Montcalm; Calcutta fell to the pro-French ruler Siraj-ud-Daula; and worst of all, Britain's prized Mediterranean base of MINORCA was lost. Such setbacks served to discredit the administration of the duke of NEWCASTLE, which was succeeded by the short-lived coalition government of the elder PITT and the duke of DEVONSHIRE.

The official declaration of war between Britain and France occurred against the backdrop of the 'DIPLOMATIC REVOLUTION' that had transformed Europe's political landscape. In an effort to protect George II's electorate of Hanover, Britain constructed a defensive alliance with Prussia; her erstwhile ally Austria courted France to aid its schemes to recover Silesia from Frederick II ('the Great') of Prussia. In the years to come, British subsidies would help a hard-pressed Prussia to endure the onslaught of Habsburg, French and Russian enemies, while the military genius of Frederick the Great made him a popular hero in Britain.

The summer of 1757 saw the formation of the legendary Pitt–Newcastle ministry. With hindsight it is tempting to view this development as the turning point of Britain's fortunes in the war, yet the dark days of defeat were not yet over. In Germany, the army of observation commanded by the duke of CUMBERLAND was soundly defeated and forced to negotiate to save Hanover. Expeditions to the French coast, which were intended to distract Louis XV's attention from Germany, proved expensive failures that Henry FOX memorably likened to 'breaking windows with guineas'.

It was from America, hitherto the source of nothing but gloom, that Pitt and the nation drew badly needed encouragement. In the summer of 1758 an amphibious expedition under the command of AMHERST and BOSCAWEN captured Louisbourg, the strategic key to the St Lawrence valley. By the end of the year, Goree on the West African coast had likewise fallen to British arms. The new year saw the conquest of Guadeloupe – the pride of French Caribbean possessions – followed that summer by WOLFE's spectacular victory at QUEBEC. In Germany a British contingent under the capable command of Ferdinand of Brunswick distinguished itself at MINDEN. To crown this glut of glory, on the high seas both the Brest and Toulon fleets suffered crippling reverses at the hands of the Royal Navy.

George II lived long enough to savour these triumphs, and when his grandson succeeded him as George III in the autumn of 1760 the flood tide of victories showed no sign of abating: Canada finally succumbed, while French power in India was crushed at the battle of Wandewash. Despite such successes, George III and many of his subjects were wearying of a struggle that cost heavily in blood and gold. Fearing the intervention of the Spanish king on the side of his beleaguered Bourbon relatives in France, Pitt urged a pre-emptive strike; he resigned after the cabinet failed to back him, only to be vindicated when Charles III of Spain entered the war in January 1762. The ministry, which was now dominated by the king's favourite Lord BUTE, responded with expeditions to Cuba and Portugal; Havana was stormed, while the remarkable reach of Britain's power was demonstrated by the capture of Manila in the Philippines.

By 1763 the Bourbons had been humbled. Although France regained some of its most prized losses at the subsequent treaty of PARIS (1763), repeated setbacks around the globe had planted a deep-seated desire for vengeance. The perfect chance to satisfy that craving would come 15 years later when a dangerously isolated Britain found herself struggling to curb rebellion in America (see AMERICAN WAR OF INDEPENDENCE).

FURTHER READING F. Anderson, *Crucible of War. The Seven Years' War and the Fate of Empire in British North America, 1754–1766* (2000); R. Middleton, *The Bells of Victory: The Pitt-Newcastle Ministry and the Conduct of the Seven Years' War, 1757–62* (1985).

Shaftesbury, Anthony Ashley Cooper, 3rd earl of (1671–1713), philosopher. Shaftesbury was a pupil of LOCKE, but disputed with him the notion that there were no innate ideas. Shaftesbury believed in an innate 'moral sense', so anticipating the views of Francis HUTCHESON. His *Characteristics of Men, Manners, Opinions, and Times*, published in 1711, was extremely influential in the 'civilizing' process of the 18th century. Whig principles were basic to Shaftesbury's stress on the role of politeness. He sided with the COUNTRY Whigs in Parliament in the 1690s, then gravitated to the JUNTO Whigs during Anne's reign. To him polite Whiggism was an essential alternative to the Tory emphasis on the church in restraining man's antisocial impulses; HIGH-CHURCH restraint did not promote civic virtue whereas Whig politeness was based on liberty.

Sharp, Granville (1735–1813), key figure in the crusade to abolish slavery. He was also the prime mover behind the establishment of Britain's African colony of Sierra Leone.

Sharp hailed from a religious background; his grandfather was John Sharp, archbishop of York. The straitened circumstances of a large family led to Granville's apprenticeship to a London linen draper. It was in 1765, while employed as an Ordnance Department clerk, that Sharp befriended a destitute slave, Jonathan Strong, who had been abandoned by his master James Lisle. When Lisle subsequently secured Strong's imprisonment as a runaway slave, Sharp gained him his liberty. However, when Sharp proceeded to prosecute Lisle for assault he was himself charged with detaining the property of another man. The case led the litigious Sharp to undertake a detailed examination of the law of personal liberty. It was Sharp's determination and expertise that lay behind victory in the Somersett case of 1772; this produced the breakthrough ruling that slavery did not exist under English law.

The growing number of freed blacks in Britain prompted Sharp to propose the foundation of an African home for them in Sierra Leone. The first former slaves sailed in 1787 and established a colony around the settlement of Freetown. Sierra Leone's first years were troubled; in 1808 it was absorbed as a British colony, so providing a base for the continuing naval war against the SLAVE TRADE.

Like that other mainstay of the antislavery campaign, William WILBERFORCE, Sharp was a committed evangelical Christian. Despite the philanthropy that led him to champion the plight of slaves and espouse the cause of the native Caribs of the West Indies, Sharp was not free from prejudice: in 1808 he was instrumental in founding the Society for the Conversion of Jews, and in the year of his death became the first chairman of the Protestant Union against CATHOLIC EMANCIPATION.

Shelburne, William Petty, 2nd earl of, and 1st marquess of Lansdowne (1737–1805),

politician; prime minister (1782–3). After military service in the SEVEN YEARS WAR, Shelburne entered the House of Lords in 1761 on the death of his father. In 1763 he became president of the BOARD OF TRADE in George GRENVILLE's government. After a few months he resigned and attached himself to the elder PITT. Though he declined to serve in ROCKINGHAM's administration, he voted for the repeal of the STAMP ACT. When Pitt – now Lord Chatham – came to power again in 1766, Shelburne, as a leading Chathamite, became secretary of state. He dealt with the American colonies until a separate colonial secretaryship was created in 1768, advocating conciliation until 1769, when, at loggerheads with the cabinet over their firm line against the Americans, he resigned. Throughout the 1770s

he was a prominent 'friend of America'. In this decade too he made his house at Bowood in Wiltshire an intellectual centre. Among those who were invited there were Jeremy BENTHAM, Benjamin Franklin, Joseph PRIESTLEY (who became his secretary), Richard PRICE and Samuel ROMILLY. Towards the end of the decade he drew attention to developments in Ireland, believing that the Irish had stronger grounds for revolt than the Americans.

When Rockingham's second ministry was formed in 1782 Shelburne accepted the newly created post of home secretary. On the prime minister's sudden death he outmanoeuvred Charles James FOX to succeed Rockingham. Shelburne's ministry, which included the younger Pitt and six other Chathamites, recognized the independence of the United States. But it was short-lived, as Fox made his notorious alliance with Lord NORTH to bring it down. Shelburne was not, however, invited to join the younger Pitt's ministry and never held office again.

This was due to a variety of shortcomings on Shelburne's part as far as other politicians were concerned. The king objected to his failure to vote in the House of Lords against Fox's India Bill (*see* BOARD OF CONTROL), and thus help to bring down the Fox–North coalition. Shelburne had isolated himself from other peers by his perceived arrogance and untrustworthiness. However, Pitt did have him created marquess of Lansdowne, and obtained his support in Parliament until the outbreak of war with France in 1793. Lansdowne thereafter opposed the war and the repression of radicalism. This led him to move away from Pitt and towards Charles James Fox. When Lansdowne died he left behind one of the greatest collections of books and manuscripts assembled in the 18th century. The sale of his books took 31 days. The manuscripts were acquired by the British Museum. **FURTHER READING** J. Norris, *Shelburne and Reform* (1963).

Sheridan, Richard Brinsley (1751–1816),

Anglo-Irish playwright and Whig politician.

Sheridan deployed enormous wit and charm to establish a reputation as a leading playwright and parliamentary orator. Since he was the offspring of Irish actors, it was fitting that Sheridan should make his name in the theatre. After education at Harrow, Sheridan lived in Bath where he wooed the famous singer Elizabeth Linley; he defended her honour in two celebrated duels, the second of which was a particularly brutal affair that left Sheridan battered and bloody (see DUELLING). After moving to London, Sheridan produced a clutch of plays that won him acclaim as a master of social comedy: *The Rivals* (1775) was followed by *The School for Scandal* (1777) and *The Critic* (1779). In contrast to the idealized sentimental dramas that dominated the contemporary stage, Sheridan's works included believable characters drawn from his own chequered experiences. Sheridan's abilities impressed the great actor-manager David GARRICK, who invited him to become a partner at the Drury Lane Theatre.

Sheridan entered Parliament in 1780. This change of direction brought Sheridan's career as playwright to a close, although it by no means ended his connection with theatrical performance. Indeed, Sheridan drew upon all his eloquence and oratory to mesmerize the Commons with his polished speeches and keen debating skills. Some members felt that Sheridan should save his talents for the stage; when the younger Pitt voiced this opinion in 1783 Sheridan swiftly turned the tables by labelling him 'the Angry Boy'. Six years later, during the debates surrounding the impeachment of Warren HASTINGS, Sheridan spoke for more than five and a half hours: the speech was regarded as among the most effective ever delivered in the House.

From the beginning of his political career Sheridan proved a staunch adherent of Charles James FOX, later declaring that it had been 'the pride and glory of his life to enjoy the happiness and honour of his friendship'. Sheridan's personal charms also won him the friendship of the prince of Wales (the future GEORGE IV) – an intimacy that was to encourage his taste for reckless gambling and drinking. Despite his abilities as a speaker and debater, Sheridan lacked the clear head for business that might have gained him cabinet rank, although he did hold posts as undersecretary at the Foreign Office in 1782, Treasury secretary in the short-lived FOX–NORTH coalition government, and treasurer of the navy within the MINISTRY OF ALL THE TALENTS in 1806–7. Sheridan's theatrical background continued to undermine his credibility in some quarters, and probably denied him appointment as chancellor of the exchequer. He was frequently at loggerheads with Edmund BURKE, a personality clash that was only exacerbated by Sheridan's enthusiastic response to the outbreak of the FRENCH REVOLUTION. In 1792 Sheridan joined with Charles Grey and others to form the SOCIETY OF THE FRIENDS OF THE PEOPLE, which campaigned for parliamentary reform.

In his later years Sheridan grew apart from Fox, and after his old friend's death he failed to find favour with the Whig leadership. Sheridan fared little better in his personal affairs: Drury Lane Theatre burned down in 1791, and, although it was replaced at enormous cost, it succumbed to fire once more in 1809. By the time of his death Sheridan was heavily in debt. Although his political career palled, Sheridan's classic plays lost nothing of their sparkle and today continue to provide an entertaining insight into the fashionable society of Georgian Britain.

FURTHER READING F. O'Toole, *A Traitor's Kiss: the life of Richard Brinsley Sheridan* (1997).

Shovell, Sir Cloudesley (1650–1707), admiral, one of the most remarkable men ever to sail with the Royal Navy. He rose from cabin boy to admiral by dint of superlative seamanship and bravery in action.

A native of Cockthorpe on the Norfolk coast, Shovell entered the service in 1664 as a captain's servant; under the patronage of his neighbour, Sir John Narbrough, he progressed from midshipman to master's mate. During the 1670s and 1680s

Shovell established a reputation for courage and daring, and while serving in the Mediterranean he won the influential backing of the duke of Grafton, a bastard son of Charles II, who had joined the fleet as a volunteer. In 1682 Captain Shovell was given command of a squadron designated to protect English shipping from the depredations of the Barbary corsairs.

Shovell's talents were prominent during the naval operations of the NINE YEARS WAR. He played a key role in the victories at Beachy Head and Barfleur, and was promoted to admiral in 1695. In the War of the SPANISH SUCCESSION, Shovell returned to the familiar waters of the Mediterranean: he was conspicuous at the capture of GIBRALTAR and the action at Malaga in 1704; in the following year Shovell's energy and determination contributed to Lord Peterborough's capture of Barcelona.

In 1707, while returning from the failed Toulon expedition, Shovell's flagship the *Association* foundered off the Isles of Scilly with heavy loss of life. Shovell was washed ashore in Porthellic Cove. As he lay unconscious on the sands, the admiral was reputedly murdered by a local woman who stole his emerald ring – the story of Shovell's death rests upon the confession of his killer some 30 years after the event. Shovell's body was recovered and buried in Westminster Abbey. ADDISON remained unimpressed by the monument, which represented Shovell as a bewigged beau reclining on velvet cushions rather than 'the brave, rough English Admiral, which was the distinguishing character of that gallant man'. His popularity among the sailors was perpetuated throughout the century by their calling the rum-based beverage of eggnog a 'Sir Cloudesley'.

Shrewsbury, Charles Talbot, 1st duke and 12th earl of (1660–1718), Whig politician who at times veered towards the Tories. Nevertheless, during his brief period as lord treasurer in the summer of 1714, Shrewsbury helped to secure the HANOVERIAN SUCCESSION.

Shrewsbury came from a Catholic family but after suceeding his father at the age of eight, he became an Anglican in 1679. He was one of the gentlemen of the bedchamber to Charles II and served as a cavalry officer under James II. However, he disapproved of the king's policies and began to intrigue with emissaries of WILLIAM of Orange. In June 1688 Shrewsbury put his cipher to the invitation to William to invade England. He went over to Holland where he contributed £12,000 to William's campaign coffers, and landed with him at Brixham in November. In the CONVENTION PARLIAMENT he approved of the offer of the crown to William, and became secretary of state. Shrewsbury's wholehearted support of Whig measures made the king's appointment of a largely Tory ministry in 1690 uncongenial to him, and he resigned the secretaryship in March.

For the next four years Shrewsbury was out of office. In 1693 he sponsored a bill for triennial elections that passed both Houses of Parliament, only to be vetoed by the king. The following year the Whigs included William's acceptance of the bill, and of Shrewsbury's return to the secretary's office, among the conditions they laid down for joining the ministry. Soon after resuming the seals of office Shrewsbury was raised to a dukedom. At the time of the assassination plot against William in 1696 he was named by JACOBITES as being in league with the exiled James II. Shrewsbury was apparently in correspondence with the court of St Germain, and the discovery unnerved him enough to leave London and lie low in the country. But the king seems to have taken a very sanguine view of the matter, and Shrewsbury survived the crisis. In 1699 he exchanged the secretaryship for the post of lord chamberlain.

Shrewsbury's health, never very robust, deteriorated in the 1690s with frequent bouts of bloodspitting. Consequently he resigned from the chamberlain's office and in 1700 he went abroad, where he stayed until 1705. Shortly before his return to England he married the daughter of the marquis Palleoti of Bologna. His wife was to become the subject of much scurrilous gossip after his return, and was said to be the 'constant plague of his life'.

Soon after Shrewsbury's return to England he was inveigled into the intrigues of Robert HARLEY against Lord Treasurer GODOLPHIN. Although these intrigues ended with Harley's resignation in 1708, it was a considerable coup for Harley to include a major figure of previously impeccable Whig credentials in his scheme. He kept the duke in his confidence during the next two years. Shrewsbury showed his change of political inclination by voting in favour of Dr SACHEVERELL during the latter's impeachment in 1710. The virtual acquittal of Sacheverell was the signal for the ministerial revolution engineered by Harley, which began when Queen Anne made Shrewsbury lord chamberlain in March. His wife became a lady of the bedchamber to Queen Anne in 1711. Shrewsbury was involved in the peace negotiations, going to France as ambassador extraordinary from November 1712 to June 1713. On his return he was appointed lord lieutenant of Ireland. In Dublin he was alarmed by the overt Jacobitism of many Irish Tories and leaned rather towards the Whigs.

Shrewsbury was back in England at the final crisis of Anne's reign, when BOLINGBROKE expected to succeed Harley as lord treasurer after the latter's fall. Instead, in July 1714, the queen gave the office to Shrewsbury, an appointment that more than anything else secured the peaceful accession of the house of Hanover. Soon after the accession of George I, Shrewsbury resigned the lord lieutenancy and treasurership (October 1714), becoming lord chamberlain again. Bad health led him to resign from this post in June 1715. He also felt out of place in the new world of Hanoverian Whiggery. Many of the politicians who like him had survived through the reigns of James II, William III and Anne were dead, and Shrewsbury, an aristocratic elder statesman who found holding office uncongenial, was quite ready to leave the field to careerists such as SUNDERLAND and WALPOLE.

Siddons, Sarah (1755–1831), the most celebrated actress to appear upon the late Georgian stage. She was described by the critic Hazlitt as 'tragedy personified'. Sarah was the eldest of the actor-manager Roger Kemble's twelve children, of whom several would follow her into the theatre including Charles Kemble, who was to become one of the most famous actor-managers of the earlier 19th century.

After marriage to the actor William Siddons, Sarah made her first appearance on the London stage in 1775. She played alongside the great David GARRICK but failed to impress audiences; the intense dramatic style that was to make her a stage legend had yet to mature. Returning to the provinces, Sarah succeeded in reinventing herself as a tragic actress, and she consolidated her reputation with performances at the fashionable Mecca of Bath. In 1782, with the backing of the duchess of DEVONSHIRE, she returned in triumph to Drury Lane – the scene of her earlier humiliating failure. Until her official retirement in 1812 Sarah Siddons dominated the London stage, giving highly emotional performances that proved capable of evoking an equally dramatic response from her captivated audiences.

Like Garrick himself, Siddons was quick to appreciate the importance of publicity in reinforcing her fame; her portrait was painted by artists ranging from GAINSBOROUGH to Fuseli; perhaps the most famous of these images was the 1784 canvas by REYNOLDS depicting 'Sarah Siddons as the Tragic Muse'. Self-promotion could prove a double-edged sword, however, and it was unfortunate for Siddons that her career coincided with the heyday of those masters of caricature, GILLRAY and ROWLANDSON, who found a ready target in her stage antics and increasingly matronly figure.

Siddons played a range of tragic heroines, but was best known for her powerful interpretation of Lady Macbeth; it was the role she chose for her farewell performance at Covent Garden. The spellbinding quality of Siddons's acting was not easily forgotten: her funeral at Paddington Church attracted 5000 mourners.

Sidmouth, Henry Addington, 1st Viscount.
See ADDINGTON, HENRY, 1ST VISCOUNT SIDMOUTH.

Simeon, Charles. *See* EVANGELICAL REVIVAL.

sinking fund, scheme devised by Sir Robert WAL-POLE to reduce the NATIONAL DEBT. The rise in the national debt alarmed many in the early 18th century to whom the new phenomenon of making money make money seemed to be hazardous, especially after the SOUTH SEA BUBBLE. Before that event Sir Robert Walpole, as chancellor of the exchequer, had devised a scheme in 1715 to reduce or 'sink' it by setting up a fund specially earmarked, not just to pay off the interest, but also to reduce the capital. This was implemented by Earl STAN-HOPE in 1717. It was not, however, until the late 1730s under Walpole that any serious inroads were made into the level of the national debt. In 1733 it stood at £50 million, and by 1739 it was down to £46.9 million. This had more to do with Walpole's pacific foreign policy, however, than with the efficacy of the sinking fund. Indeed the fund was too often raided for other purposes than debt reduction, such as augmenting the CIVIL LIST. The younger PITT launched a new sinking fund in 1786, but the onset of war with France after 1793 made it a forlorn gesture. The whole idea of a sinking fund fell into disrepute and was abandoned in 1828.

slave trade. Given the 18th-century Englishman's concern for the liberty of the individual, it was deeply ironic that Britain should play a leading role in perpetuating an institution that denied such freedom to others. Indeed, in the years between the Restoration and the abolition of the slave trade in 1807, it has been estimated that British merchants were responsible for the shipment of some 3.5 million enslaved Africans. This figure equalled the combined total of slaves carried by the rival European participants in the trade – the French, Dutch and Portuguese. The vast majority of such slaves were destined for Britain's Caribbean colonies of Jamaica, Barbados and the Leeward Islands, where their labour was crucial for the production of sugar. Others played an important role in the more varied economies of the North American continental colonies or were exported to Spanish America. A small number of slaves were brought to England for employment as servants of the fashionable; for all its humiliations, such a life remained preferable to the back-breaking toil of the Caribbean field-hand.

Britain's involvement in what the historian Richard Hofstadter characterized as a 'far-flung fraternity of the unfraternal' originated in the free-lance activities of Elizabethan sea dogs and the chartered merchant bodies of the Stuart era. However, organizations such as the Royal Africa Company proved unable to maintain their monopolies in the face of competition from private traders. Such encroachment was perhaps surprising considering the high risks involved in slaving. The arduous voyages that constituted the so-called 'triangular trade' often lasted for more than a year. With hellish conditions below decks, slave mortality during the notorious 'middle passage' between Africa and the Americas sometimes reached 20%, while unseasoned crews also suffered heavily from the tropical illnesses they encountered from Senegambia to the Bight of Biafra.

Despite the heavy overheads involved, slaving plainly commanded sufficient returns to render it an attractive investment for many. Although suggestions that such profits provided crucial capital for Britain's industrial growth during the 18th century are now discredited, the African rulers who fought each other to control the supply of slaves represented a ready market for a wide range of British manufactures. It has been argued that Liverpool's role in the British trade, which easily eclipsed that of both Bristol and London, stemmed partly from Merseyside's proximity to the textiles of Lancashire.

Throughout Britain's American colonies slaves endured a far harsher regime than the white indentured servants whom they replaced from the late

17th century onwards. Slavery as an institution was often characterized by brutality and degradation. Denied the most fundamental political and legal rights, slaves were regarded as little more than chattels. Conditions were harshest in those areas, such as the Caribbean and South Carolina, where slaves outnumbered the white populations and were therefore deemed to pose a threat. The planters' dread of slave revolt was voiced in 1736 by the Virginian landowner William Byrd of West-over when he pondered the ever-growing number of slaves in the province. Byrd feared that if 'there should arise a man of desperate courage among us, exasperated by a desperate fortune, he might with more advantage than Cataline kindle a servile war ... and tinge our rivers wide as they are with human blood'.

Despite such foreboding, slave insurrections – such as South Carolina's Stono uprising of 1739 and the Tacky revolt in Jamaica in 1760 – were rare. A more common response to enslavement was to flee the plantation. In Jamaica, where dense interior forests offered refuge for runaways, communities of escaped slaves, or 'Maroons' defied all efforts to crush them, and in 1739–40 forced the authorities to recognize their autonomy. For most slaves resistance took a less dramatic form: duties were shirked and tasks bungled, while concerted efforts to preserve African traditions provided slaves with a supporting culture of their own. In contrast to the slave societies of the West Indies – where a lethal disease environment, harsh conditions and a skewed ratio of males to females necessitated frequent imports to maintain manpower levels – those of the southern mainland colonies proved capable of reproducing themselves successfully.

Although many British merchants and manufacturers benefited from slavery, its evils did not go unnoticed in an age when the spread of EN-LIGHTENMENT values was prompting a new humanitarianism. Antislavery sentiment in Britain began to gather momentum in the second half of the 18th century; it gained impetus during the AMERICAN WAR OF INDEPENDENCE, when men like

Samuel JOHNSON noted that the colonists who made the loudest appeals for liberty were themselves guilty of the brutal oppression of slaves. The Virginian George Washington owned 135 slaves, while the French aid that proved so vital to the success of the patriot war effort was largely purchased from the profits of tobacco cultivated by slave labour. The cruelties of the slave trade were denounced through pamphlets and propaganda tracts, but the continuing importance of the Caribbean sugar plantations for Britain's economy ensured that any moves towards abolition would meet vociferous opposition from a powerful merchant lobby.

The initial onslaught upon the trade was spearheaded by the EVANGELICAL movement (in particular by the CLAPHAM SECT), and a national committee headed by Granville SHARP was established in 1787. In the following year, the cause gained a significant ally when the Yorkshire MP William WILBERFORCE, a friend of the younger Pitt, provided vocal leadership in Parliament. Despite growing support in the provinces, Wilberforce's bid to ban the trade in 1789 foundered upon predictable economic objections, while subsequent efforts were hampered by a conservative reaction to the excesses of the FRENCH REVOLUTION. However, by the onset of the new century it was apparent that the West Indies were declining in importance for Britain's trade. Much entrenched resistance to abolition was thereby removed, and in 1807 Lord GRENVILLE secured his government's backing to an abolition bill, which ended Britain's involvement in the slave trade. The 1820s witnessed a further campaign to end slavery itself throughout the British empire, and this bore fruit in an act of 1833. However, the 'peculiar institution' lingered in Britain's former American colonies until it sparked a bloody civil war in the 1860s.

SEE ALSO CLARKSON, THOMAS; EQUIANO, OLAUDAH; MACAULAY, ZACHARY; SHARP, GRANVILLE; WILBER-FORCE, WILLIAM.

FURTHER READING K. Morgan, *Slavery, Atlantic*

Trade and the British Economy, 1660–1800 (2000); R.B. Sheridan, *Sugar and Slavery: An Economic History of the British West Indies, 1623–1775* (1974).

Smeaton, John (1724–92), the first Briton to adopt the title of 'civil engineer'. Smeaton was born in Leeds, where his father had a successful legal practice, and where he attended the grammar school. He demonstrated an early aptitude for mathematics and engineering. Apprenticed to an instrument maker in London, Smeaton rapidly established his own reputation in the trade; in 1750 he read a paper on the mariner's compass to the Royal Society and was soon after made a fellow. He published several papers in its *Philosophical Transactions*, mainly on hydraulic engineering, which he had studied closely in Holland.

Smeaton's growing fame as a versatile engineer gained him the commission that was to make his name. In 1755 he was chosen to construct a new lighthouse on the Eddystone Rock, some 24 km (15 miles) off Plymouth. The existing wooden lighthouse had been destroyed by fire, and Smeaton replaced it with a revolutionary tower of dovetailed blocks that was embedded into the rock itself. Completed in 1759, Smeaton's design proved a resounding success and inspired many other offshore lighthouses. 'Smeaton's Tower' remained in service for more than a century; in 1877 it was partially dismantled and reconstructed on Plymouth Hoe, where it remains as a tourist attraction.

Capitalizing upon his new-found celebrity, Smeaton established a consultancy business, calling himself a 'civil engineer' – a deliberate distinction from the existing profession of military engineer. Like many of his contemporaries, Smeaton was expected to grapple with diverse engineering problems. He dabbled with steam, and sought to improve upon NEWCOMEN's engine. However, Smeaton remained unconvinced that such power could be transferred into the circular motion required to operate machinery, and instead concentrated upon refining the water mills that

long continued to play an important role in Georgian industry. Smeaton was also prominent in the era's CANAL-building programmes. Between 1758 and 1765 he overcame difficult terrain to construct the Calder and Hebble Navigation through West Yorkshire; this achievement was soon after surpassed by his contribution to the crucial Forth–Clyde Canal. Smeaton also constructed several notable masonry bridges, including those at Perth and Coldstream. That which he built over the Tyne at Hexham in 1777 was destroyed in a storm in 1782. Smeaton founded the Smeatonian Society in 1771 to discuss engineering problems, and this provided the foundation for the subsequent Institute of Civil Engineers established in 1818.

Smith, Adam (1723–90), economic theorist, and one of the leading figures of the SCOTTISH ENLIGHTENMENT. Smith became professor of logic at Glasgow University in 1751, and was elected to the chair of moral philosophy there in 1752. He published the *Theory of Moral Sentiments* in 1759. While today this work is relatively unknown and unread in comparison with the *Wealth of Nations*, at the time it made him internationally famous. It is important to bear in mind that Smith had addressed the question of what led men to describe some actions as virtuous and others as vicious before he theorized about economics. Otherwise it can erroneously be concluded that he accepted the untrammelled operations of the market without regard for their moral consequences. Nothing could be further from the truth. He maintained that the criteria of right and wrong rested on 'sentiments'. Feelings of sympathy for the victims of the actions of others were what led to their being defined as evil. In 1763 Smith resigned his chair to go to France as tutor to the duke of Buccleuch. He returned to Scotland in 1767 via London, where he was elected a fellow of the Royal Society. His celebrated *Inquiry into the nature and causes of the Wealth of Nations* appeared in 1776. This is now generally accepted as the most compelling argument for free trade ever to be propounded. Smith accused governments in general, and the British government in particular, of regulating commerce in the interests of the distributors of goods rather than in those of the consumer. Such regulation he regarded as restrictive. To him 'the uniform, constant and uninterrupted effort of every man to better his condition' was much more conducive to economic expansion than an economy regulated by the state. Restrictions on these activities were 'most unnecessary'. He showed how demand for goods led to improvements in their production, for instance in the division of labour, which he famously illustrated with the example of pin making. But in the end the market was not left to its own devices, since a 'hidden hand' regulated it to maximize its benefits to society. *The Wealth of Nations* had an immense influence in the late 18th century and in the 19th and early 20th centuries, providing justification for Britain's own free trade policy and its adoption in other countries.

FURTHER READING R.H. Campbell and A.S. Skinner, *Adam Smith* (1982).

Smith, Sydney (1771–1845), liberal clergyman. Smith was 'a Wykehamist of both foundations' – he went to Winchester School and New College, Oxford. Although after ordination he became a minister in a remote Wiltshire living, he kept abreast of current affairs towards which he adopted a liberal stance, welcoming the French Revolution and advocating reform in Britain. While conscientious in his parish duties, he yearned for sophisticated company and conversation, which he found in Edinburgh. There he was one of the original contributors to the *Edinburgh Review* which he helped launch in 1802. The following year he moved to London where he became a regular guest at the dinner tables of the leading Whig politicians, his witty conversation being much appreciated by his hosts. Some of his observations, such as that heaven would be like eating paté de foie gras to the sound of trumpets, have become widely known. His income from his writing for the *Edin-*

burgh Review, to which he contributed for 28 years, and lectures at the Royal Institution, failed to provide sufficient means to sustain an extravagant lifestyle, and in 1806 he accepted another remote living at Foston-le-Clay in Yorkshire. Again he was dutiful towards his parishioners, from whom he escaped for two months every year to London. He later moved to a rectory in Combe Flovey, Somerset, but when the Whigs came to power in 1830 he was rewarded with a canonry at St Paul's and spent the rest of his life in the capital he loved.

FURTHER READING A. Bell, *Sydney Smith* (1980).

Smollett, Tobias (1721–71), novelist, dramatist, historian and surgeon. Smollett was born in Scotland and studied medicine at Glasgow University. In 1739 he went to London to try his hand as a playwright as well. He was however more successful initially as a surgeon, for his tragedy *The Regicide* was a flop, whereas he used his surgical skills aboard a ship on the expedition to Cartagena in 1741. He remained in the West Indies where he found himself a wealthy wife, which enabled him to practice medicine on his return to London in 1744.

Smollett proved more successful as a novelist than as a dramatist, and his *Adventures of Roderick Random*, which drew heavily on his own experiences, was widely acclaimed on its appearance in 1748. *The Adventures of Peregrine Pickle* followed in 1751, and *The Adventures of Ferdinand Count Fathom* in 1753. Smollett then undertook the editorship of *The Critical Review* from 1756 to 1763.

During his editorship Smollett began work on *The Complete History of England*, which was published in nine volumes between 1757 and 1765. This is often described as a 'Tory' work, but in fact was more inspired by the views of opposition Whigs. Thus he deplored the treaty of UTRECHT of 1713, although it was negotiated by a Tory government, since in his view it betrayed British interests. He dedicated the work to 'the patriot' William PITT the Elder, admiring 'that integrity which you have maintained in the midst of corruption'. He felt that a tidal wave of corruption and 'LUXURY' had swept through the country since the Glorious Revolution of 1688, a view that also informs his novels.

After the accession of George III, Smollett supported the new king's favourite, his fellow countryman Lord BUTE, in *The Briton*. This earned for him the savage attacks of John WILKES in *The North Briton*. These so wounded him that he left England in 1763, as he put it, 'traduced by malice, persecuted by faction, abandoned by false patrons'. After spending two years abroad he returned, describing his experiences in his *Travels* (1766). Failing to settle down he left again in 1768 to live in Tuscany, where he died. It was in Italy that he wrote his last and best novel, *The Expedition of Humphrey Clinker* (1771).

FURTHER READING A. Bold (ed.), *Smollett: Author of the First Distinction* (1982).

social structure. *See* CLASS.

Society for Constitutional Information. *See* CARTWRIGHT, JOHN; CORRESPONDING SOCIETIES; PARLIAMENTARY REFORM.

Society for the Promotion of Christian Knowledge (SPCK), organization that cooperated with local associations of clergymen to distribute bibles and tracts and to encourage the establishment of charity schools. It was founded by Thomas Bray in March 1699. Bray, rector of Sheldon in Warwickshire, was convinced that the defences of Christianity had been overwhelmed by DEISTS, freethinkers and other infidels until by 1696 they had 'enter'd through our breaches into the very heart of our City'. The SOCIETY FOR THE PROPAGATION OF THE GOSPEL was an offshoot of the SPCK.

Society for the Propagation of the Gospel in Foreign Parts (SPG), missionary organization established in 1701 as an offshoot of the SOCIETY FOR THE PROMOTION OF CHRISTIAN KNOWLEDGE (SPCK) by its founder Thomas Bray.

Previously the SPCK had been responsible for proselytizing overseas as well as in Britain. Now the SPG took over that function, principally aiming its efforts at the British colonies in North America and the West Indies.

Society of Supporters of the Bill of Rights (SSBR), organization formed in February 1769 with the avowed aim of settling the debts of John WILKES. It also sought to 'defend and maintain the constitutional liberty of the subject'. As its name suggests, its main aim was not to reform the constitution but to restore the REVOLUTION SETTLEMENT. Thus they claimed that corruption was the 'monster' that had undermined it, and campaigned for the restoration of triennial, and even annual, Parliaments and the elimination of PLACEMEN from them. Its schemes for redistributing parliamentary seats and to extend the franchise with a view to making the House of Commons more representative anticipated more radical demands for PARLIAMENTARY REFORM.

In April 1771 HORNE TOOKE and others seceded from the SSBR, complaining that the goal of clearing Wilkes's debts, which had already raised £20,000, was interfering with its constitutional objectives. They set up a rival Constitutional Society. The remnant of the SSBR met in the London Tavern on 23 July and issued a manifesto. Among other demands it advised electors to require from candidates a pledge to 'promote ... a full and equal representation of the people in Parliament'. The SSBR survived to field candidates in the general election of 1774, but folded soon afterwards.

Society of the Friends of the People, organization that sought a greater representation of the people in Parliament. It was set up in April 1792 by Charles Grey, the future Earl Grey of the 1832 Reform Bill, and Richard SHERIDAN. Its name was unintentionally ironic, given the aristocratic connections of its members, since it implied that they were not themselves of 'the people'. A Scottish society founded at the same time was less elitist.

It organized a convention of CORRESPONDING SOCIETIES in Edinburgh in 1793, which provoked a judicial backlash resulting in the dissolution of the society.

SEE ALSO PARLIAMENTARY REFORM.

Somers, John, Lord (1651–1716), lord chancellor and member of the Whig JUNTO. After attending Trinity College, Oxford, Somers pursued a legal career, entering the Middle Temple in 1669. He became prominent as counsel for the Seven Bishops in 1688. The following year he was returned to the CONVENTION PARLIAMENT for his native city of Worcester. His contributions to the Convention's proceedings were vital, especially his chairmanship of the committee which drew up the Declaration of Rights. His advance up the legal ladder was rapid. In May 1689 he was appointed as solicitor general, three years later he was promoted to the attorney generalship, in 1693 he became lord keeper of the great seal, and in 1697 reached the top of the legal profession as lord chancellor. This final move earned him a peerage as Baron Somers of Evesham. His appointment to the lord keepership was the first sign that William III was turning to the Junto for support. By the time Somers became lord chancellor, all his Whig colleagues were in office. They presided over the establishment of the BANK OF ENGLAND in 1694, the passing of the TRIENNIAL ACT of 1694 and the RECOINAGE of the currency in 1696. These measures were resented by the COUNTRY PARTY, who were opponents of the Junto; they successfully reduced the size of the armed forces in the STANDING ARMY CONTROVERSY despite the Junto's efforts to keep a larger force on foot, efforts in which Somers was prominent.

Somers's political enemies found him vulnerable to attack for his support of the pirate Captain Kidd (*see* PIRACY), and in 1700 put pressure on the king to dismiss him from his counsels. William reluctantly accepted his resignation in 1700. This did not appease his opponents, who attempted to impeach him in 1701 for putting the great seal to

the first Partition treaty in 1698 before it had been finalized, leaving the king to complete it. Although impeachment proceedings were begun by the Tories in the Commons, the Whig majority in the Lords prevented them from being successfully completed, saving Somers from humiliation. The king was urged by the 2nd earl of SUNDERLAND to turn again to the Whigs, and especially to Somers, whom he called 'the life, the soul and the spirit of the party'. William III was making moves in that direction when he died in March 1702. The accession of Queen ANNE reversed them in favour of the Tories. Somers became effectively leader of the Whigs in opposition, opposing the OCCASIONAL CONFORMITY bills and upholding the rights of electors in the case of VS. WHITE. The Junto earned Anne's respect, however, by opposing a Tory motion to invite the elector of Hanover to reside in England during her lifetime and by supporting the UNION OF ENGLAND AND SCOTLAND. Eventually the queen was persuaded to part with Tory ministers and to appoint members of the Junto, Somers returning to office in 1708 as president of the council. Anne, who had previously found him personally objectionable, was won over with a charm offensive. Somers opposed the impeachment of Dr SACHEVERELL and the duke of MARLBOROUGH's bid to be captain general for life. Robert HARLEY wanted to retain his services in his plans for ministerial reconstruction in 1710, but in the event Somers fell along with his Whig partners in September. During the last four years of Anne's reign, when the Whigs were again in opposition, ill health caused his powers to fail and the leadership of the party was taken over by the 1st marquess of WHARTON. On the accession of George I, Somers was too unwell to accept high office, but was offered a place in the cabinet, though he rarely attended its meetings before his death in 1716.

Somersett case (1772), an important early victory in the protracted war against slavery. James Somersett was a black slave whose American master attempted to remove him from England for sale.

In response, antislavery campaigners including Granville SHARP mounted a legal campaign to secure his freedom. Britain's leading expert on the common law, Sir William BLACKSTONE, had already stated that slavery did not exist under English law. The Somersett case resulted in a cautious but momentous ruling from the century's greatest British judge, William Murray 1st earl of MANS-FIELD: he observed that slavery was 'so odious that nothing can be suffered to support it but positive law'; as the case in question was not 'allowed or approved by the law of England', he had no option but to discharge Somersett.

Mansfield's hesitancy can be explained by the continuing support for slavery among those powerful men possessing connections with West Indian commerce and the SLAVE TRADE. However, the outcome of the Somersett case was nonetheless interpreted as a statement that slavery was illegal in England itself and therefore represented a crucial psychological victory for the abolitionists.

Sophia, electress of Hanover. *See* HANOVERIAN SUCCESSION.

Southcott, Joanna (1750–1814), the most famous millenarian of the 1790s, a decade marked by the emergence of extreme messianic movements. Although her creed now appears bizarre, at the peak of her influence the former domestic servant attracted some 100,000 followers.

Originally an enthusiastic METHODIST, Southcott was first 'called' in 1792 at the age of 42. Southcott's religious experiences prompted her to write prophesies that were then 'sealed' to await the coming of the events she had predicted. Her influence grew after 1800 with the publication of her first book *The Strange Effects of Faith*, and increased when her writings were subjected to critical scrutiny in a so-called trial at Exeter. Moving to London in 1802, Southcott embarked upon a programme of 'sealing' the faithful. According to the Book of Revelation, the 'faithful' were to number 144,000; by 1805 Southcott had already received 10,000

applications for her sealed certificates, and a chapel for her disciples was established at Southwark.

Styling herself 'the Lamb's wife', Southcott believed that she would give birth to a 'second Christ' – the 'Almighty Shiloh' – in 1814. Southcott fell ill that year, and medical experts diagnosed symptoms that would suggest pregnancy in a younger woman, so plunging her followers into a frenzy of excitement. In fact, she died of a brain disease without producing the anticipated saviour-child. Southcott's devotees kept her body warm for four days in the hope of a resurrection, and their belief that she would ultimately rise again endured for many years. At her death Southcott left a mysterious box with instructions that it be examined after the passage of a century. When finally opened in 1927, it was found to contain nothing more than a handful of mundane items.

FURTHER READING J.K. Hopkins, *A Woman to Deliver Her People: Joanna Southcott and English Millenarianism in the Era of Revolution* (1982).

Southey, Robert. *See* LAKE POETS.

South Sea Bubble (1720), major financial crisis that turned into a political scandal. The origin of the 'Bubble', or 'confidence trick' as the term meant at the time, can be traced back to the foundation of the South Sea Company in 1711. This was launched in order to consolidate some £9 million of NATIONAL DEBT that was not secured against the proceeds of taxation; this unfunded debt was changed into South Sea stock. The Company was thus from the start primarily a financial corporation, and was only marginally concerned with trading activities. Although it had been set up in anticipation of considerable trading concessions from Spain at the signing of the treaty of UTRECHT in 1713, the actual terms negotiated with the Spanish government were disappointing. As a financial corporation, however, it was modestly successful and the debt conversion exercise of 1711 worked. In 1719 the experiment was repeated when holders of 1710 lottery orders valued at £1,084,790 converted them into South Sea stock. This was a prelude to the much more ambitious scheme undertaken the following year.

In 1720 the national debt stood at about £50 million. The scheme was to convert into Company stock that part of it, some £31 million, that was held in the form of annuities, leaving the rest to the BANK OF ENGLAND and the EAST INDIA COMPANY. Annuitants were to be encouraged to transfer their annuities into the South Sea Company's stock, on which the government would pay 5% interest until 1727 and 4% thereafter. At first the Company proposed to lend the government some £3 million at the time of the conversion, but the Bank got wind of it and insisted that the scheme should be put out to tender. The Company outbid the Bank, but by then was pledged to advance £7.5 million when the annuities were converted. Instead of insisting that the conversion should be at par, the government allowed the Company to convert the annuities into the market value of its stock. Thus if £100 of its stock sold for £200, it need only assign £15.5 million to the holders of the annuities and could sell the rest on the exchange. The difference between what the stock raised on the market and the sum of £31 million owed to the government would be the Company's profit from the scheme. It therefore used all means, both fair and foul, to drive up the market value of its stock.

Prospects of glittering profits from trade with Spanish possessions across the Atlantic were held out as inducements to annuitants to convert their annuities into stock. Some of the promised gains were highly exaggerated given the modest concessions granted by Spain to the Company in 1713. It also used questionable means to eliminate rivals by persuading the government to pass the BUBBLE ACT, whereby companies without a charter were declared illegal. This act closed down many such companies that had mushroomed at a time when the financial world seemed to have gone mad with speculation. Downright corruption was also employed, with the allocation of stock valued at over £500,000 for the bribery of politicians, including, among others, the earl of SUNDERLAND, first lord of the Treasury, and John Aislabie, chancellor of the exchequer.

These measures worked beyond the wildest dreams of even the Company's directors. South Sea stock began the year 1720 above par, £100 of stock selling for £128. By the end of June it had reached £745, and in July it peaked at over £1000. Then big investors, headed by foreigners, saw that the market had reached its zenith and sold. This precipitated the crash. By mid-September £100 of stock was selling for £520, and by October it was down to £290. Many were ruined by the collapse in its value. There were a few spectacular bankruptcies. One city magnate, Sir Joseph Beck, was left owing £347,000. Many lesser investors, country gentlemen as well as merchants, lost heavily.

The political fallout was heavy too. There were demands that the directors of the Company should be brought to trial, and that those politicians who had benefited fraudulently should also be prosecuted. There were even accusations that members of the royal household, if not of the royal family, had been beneficiaries. The situation was so tense that some observers thought the exiled Stuarts could have exploited it to secure their restoration. The Hanoverian dynasty was saved from disaster when GEORGE I hurried back from Hanover while James Francis Edward STUART, the Old Pretender, did little except publish a proclamation. Some £2 million of the Company's assets were confiscated to compensate ruined creditors. The chancellor of the exchequer was expelled permanently from Parliament. But beyond that very little happened. WALPOLE, for whom the Bubble was a political opportunity, was determined to limit the damage, and 'screened' politicians from the demands for an investigation. He also helped to restore confidence in the country's financial institutions, getting the Bank to put the South Sea Company's affairs back on a sound basis. When the fever of speculation died down people with spare capital to invest were cautious about investing in paper securities, and there was to be no repetition of the Bubble in the 18th century.

FURTHER READING J. Carswell, *The South Sea Bubble* (1960); L. Neal, *The Rise of Financial Capitalism; International Capital Markets in the Age of Reason* (1990).

Spanish Succession, War of the (1702–13), global conflict arising from a disputed succession in Spain.

It was the death of Charles II of Spain in 1700 that precipitated war between the Bourbon powers headed by Louis XIV of France and the Grand Alliance of Britain, the Dutch Republic and the Austrian Habsburgs. It had long been apparent that when the childless, deformed and mentally ill 'Carlos the Sufferer' died there would be hostilities to try to prevent the whole of his vast inheritance on both sides of the Atlantic passing to either the Bourbon or the Habsburg claimant, Philip of Anjou (grandson of Louis XIV) and the archduke Charles of Austria respectively. Attempts to divide the Spanish empire in partition treaties came to naught, however, when the dying Spanish monarch made a will leaving all his territories to Philip. Louis promptly recognized his grandson as Philip V, declaring 'now there are no Pyrenees'. The French king's recognition of James II's son – James Francis Edward STUART – as king of England when his father died in 1701 played into the hands of WILLIAM III, the architect of the Grand Alliance. William recognized the Austrian candidate as Charles III of Spain, and declared war on his behalf just before his own death in 1702.

Queen ANNE respected her predecessor's wishes and appointed the duke of MARLBOROUGH as captain general of the forces abroad. Marlborough took over the late king's role as the leader of the allies, taking them to victory in 1704 at the battle of BLENHEIM. Meanwhile the alliance had been strengthened by the addition of Portugal (*see* METHUEN TREATY) and Savoy in 1703. The Portuguese joined on condition that the acquisition of Spain and its possessions in America should be

made a war aim of the Grand Alliance. This led to the capture of GIBRALTAR by the British navy in 1704, which gave a foothold in Spain that enabled the allies to capture Barcelona for 'Charles III' in 1705.

There was now a European war on three fronts: the Low Countries, Italy and the Iberian peninsula. The year 1706 seemed to be an *annus mirabilis* for the allies. The war in the Low Countries went well for them with the expulsion of the French from most of the Spanish Netherlands after the battle of RAMILLIES. In Italy, too, allied forces under Prince Eugène of Savoy gained a victory over the French at Turin. In Spain Philip V was expelled from his capital in Madrid. Thereafter, however, in the southern theatre the war went badly for the allies. Their forces were dealt a severe blow at the battle of ALMANZA in 1707, while an attempt to capture Toulon from the French that year was abortive. Marlborough's victory at the battle of OUDENARDE in 1708 offset allied defeats in the south, and carried hostilities onto French soil with the successful siege of Lille. However, after the Pyrrhic victory at the battle of MALPLAQUET in 1709 it seemed as though allied attempts to beat France into submission would be unavailing.

Negotiations with the French were opened at the Hague in 1709, but were called off by Louis XIV when the allies insisted that he should help them to remove his grandson from the throne of Spain. Although Louis made much capital out of this 'unnatural' demand, it made sense to insist on his helping the allies since he had shown repeatedly that he could not be trusted to honour his treaty obligations. Thus his recognition of James II's son as James III was in flagrant breach of his commitments in the treaty of Ryswick of 1697 (*see* NINE YEARS WAR). To allow France to be at peace while the allies fought on in Spain was to invite a refreshed French army to come to Philip V's assistance after the forces of Charles III had exhausted themselves.

Nevertheless, Louis managed to attain the moral high ground, and there was a reaction to the Hague preliminaries by the war-weary subjects of the allies. The British were particularly resentful of them, accusing Marlborough and Anne's Whig ministers of seeking deliberately to prolong the war for their own benefit and to the impoverishment of the taxpayers. Such sentiments helped in the process of removing the Whig ministry in 1710; it was replaced with a largely Tory administration under Robert HARLEY (*see* BARRIER FORTRESSES).

Harley's ministry abandoned the war aim of placing Charles III on the throne of Spain, which became militarily unrealistic after the allied defeat at Brihuega in 1710. Terms of peace dropping the requirement were negotiated and submitted to Parliament in 1711. When the duke of Marlborough voted against them with the Whigs in the House of Lords he was dismissed as captain general and replaced by the duke of ORMONDE. Ormonde was issued with 'restraining orders' in 1712 prohibiting him from engaging with the enemy, and in 1713 Britain signed the treaty of UTRECHT with France. The Dutch and the Austrian Habsburgs refused to sign, and fought on for another year before agreeing to the peace of Rastatt.

FURTHER READING, D. Chandler, *Marlborough as a Military Commander* (1970); G.M. Trevelyan, *England Under Queen Anne* (3 vols., 1930–34).

Spectator, the, periodical produced every weekday between 1 March 1711 and 6 December 1712. It usually comprised a single essay, written either by Joseph ADDISON or Richard STEELE. In the characters who made up the membership of the 'Spectator Club' they created a fictional world that in many ways anticipated the novel. Their sympathetic characterization of the Tory country gentleman Sir Roger de Coverley is often cited as evidence that they did not adopt a partisan stance in these essays, but genuinely strove to reduce PARTY tensions by discounting politics. While blatant partisanship is indeed at a discount there can be no denying the underlying Whig ideology of the *Spectator*. It is much more sympathetic to the city merchant Sir Andrew Freeport than to the Tory squire. And the commitment to Whig finances is explicitly upheld in the essay on public credit, which was a barely disguised appeal to support the Whig candidates in the elections to the directorships of the Bank of England in 1711. Yet the civilizing mission of the journal is upheld in the urbane measured prose, quite lacking the shrill invective of contemporary political pamphlets. The *Spectator* was the most celebrated and influential periodical of the 18th century, its fame spreading to Europe and North America.

Speenhamland system, system of poor relief. During the closing decade of the 18th century the long-established parish system of relief for the poor (*see* POOR LAW) proved inadequate to cope with the demands of a rapidly expanding population. The crisis was exacerbated by the widespread economic hardship resulting from the onset of war with revolutionary France. In 1795, when the price of bread reached record levels, the Berkshire magistrates meeting at Speenhamland sought to tackle rural poverty by introducing a system whereby the families of rural labourers received financial assistance on a scale linked to the cost of a loaf. The Speenhamland system was widely imitated but soon proved controversial on grounds of expense; as the poor rate was effectively used to supplement workers' income, it also provided an excuse for farmers to cut wages. In consequence, when the Poor Law was amended in 1834 relief was restricted so far as possible to those who could be accommodated within the harsh regime of the workhouse.

Spence, Thomas (1750–1814), radical reformer. Spence was born in Newcastle upon Tyne and taught in a school on the quayside. His experience as a teacher informed his *Grand Repository of the English Language* (1775) based on phonetic spelling. He became involved in disputes concerning the rights of the freemen of Newcastle on the Town Moor. This led him to the radical conclusion that property should be redistributed to give the inhabitants of every parish an equal proportion. The land was not to be freehold but leased from a corporation representing the parishioners. This scheme, which amounted to the nationalization of land, was debated in the Newcastle Philosophical Society in 1775. When Spence published his views in *The Real Rights of Man* later that year he was expelled from the Society. His expulsion was not because members disapproved of his ideas – they had after all expressed a preference for a republic over a monarchy in one debate – but because he had broken their rules by printing the tract 'in the manner of a halfpenny ballad and having it hawked about the streets to the manifest dishonour of the society'.

Spence went to London and set up a bookstall where he sold his radical tracts. The most notorious of his publications was *Pig's Meat: or lessons from the Swinish Multitude* (three volumes, 1793–5), a riposte to BURKE's disparaging reference to the mass of the people. His radical views brought him into conflict with the authorities, and he was imprisoned without trial for seven months in 1794, and for a year following a trial for seditious libel in 1801. He also attracted considerable support from 'Spenceans', who continued to uphold his ideas on land after his death.

Spencer, Charles, 3rd earl of Sunderland.
See SUNDERLAND, CHARLES SPENCER, 3RD EARL OF.

Spencer, Robert, 2nd earl of Sunderland.
See SUNDERLAND, ROBERT SPENCER, 2ND EARL OF.

Spithead naval mutiny. *See* NAVAL MUTINIES OF 1797.

sport. At the onset of the 'long 18th century' the sports and recreations of Britons would have remained familiar to their medieval forbears. Popular pastimes were closely linked to the calendar of established feasts and festivals. Occasions such as 'Plough Monday' – the hiring fair for agricultural workers held on the first Monday of the new year – Shrove Tuesday, May Day, hay-making and parish feasts all prompted gatherings that provided an excuse for celebrations and recreations ranging from innocent dancing to violent communal football matches. By the 1830s this traditional picture was undergoing a transformation as a predominantly rural world gave way to an urban and industrial society.

In 1700 sport remained essentially informal and uncodified. Popular recreations varied from region to region, lacked regulation and frequently involved mass participation by the community as a whole. In part, this reflected the influence of customs communicated orally rather than written in a rule book. Long-established sports included football, which embraced both casual street matches and large organized festival games between villages. There were also various recreations based upon fighting: wrestling was popular, with variations in technique ranging from Cumberland to Cornwall. Other sports involved duelling with sticks or cudgels. Provincial newspapers regularly carried advertisements for 'single-stick', or 'backsword' bouts, with the purse going to the 'gamester' who 'broke most heads while saving his own'. Such bloodletting usually went hand in hand with betting: indeed, foreign visitors were shocked to note that when quarrelsome Englishmen resorted to their fists, spectators invariably formed a ring and placed wagers upon the outcome of the clash instead of seeking to part the combatants.

When not inflicting pain upon each other, sportsmen all too often tormented animals instead. Particularly popular were bull, badger and bear baiting, during which tethered beasts were attacked by dogs; cock-fighting, involving deadly contests between cockerels wearing metal spurs; and also 'cock-throwing', where missiles were flung at pinioned birds. Less vicious entertainments included dancing around the maypole, chasing after rolling cheeses, and attempting to catch a greased pig. Such plebeian pursuits enjoyed the patronage of the wealthy. Lords and labourers mingled as spectators at prize fights and cricket matches: as

Hogarth's famous engraving *The Cockpit* (1759) demonstrates, a shared passion for sport and gambling united all classes of society.

By the final quarter of the 18th century this traditional sporting culture was under attack from several quarters. Evangelical religious movements such as the Methodists frowned upon the misuse of leisure time, while factory and mill owners sought to impose stricter work-discipline upon their employees. In addition, such environmental factors as the spread of enclosure (*see* AGRICULTURE) restricted traditional football, where players had previously rambled wherever the game took them. Growing urbanization also eroded the seasonal rhythms of the countryside that underlay traditional popular culture. Both central and local government enacted legislation to control fairs, HORSE RACING and prize fighting. Especially prominent was an attack upon inhumane animal sports. Attempts to ban 'throwing at cocks' began in the 1750s, and by the end of the century bull baiting was becoming increasingly rare. This trend culminated in the 1820s with the foundation of the Royal Society for the Prevention of Cruelty to Animals (RSPCA).

Such developments were accompanied by a gradual change from informal to formal sporting events. For example, there were concerted efforts to curb the excesses associated with old-style football matches. Horse-racing was also subject to regularization: the Jockey Club was established in the 1750s, and several of the classics of the racing calendar – the St Leger, the Oaks and the Derby – date from 1778–80. In cricket, a progressive development of rules, first written by the 2nd duke of Richmond in 1727, led to the establishment of the Marylebone Cricket Club (MCC) in 1787. The 18th century had witnessed a progressive weakening of the traditional links between popular and elite culture: at its beginning all classes participated in communal recreations; by its close, local magistrates and landowners who had once encouraged such events were now more concerned to restrict and control them.

FURTHER READING R.W. Malcolmson, *Popular Recreations in English Society, 1700–1815* (1973).

squadrone or **squadrone volante,** name given to the group in the last Scottish Parliament connected with Lords Marchmont, Montrose, Roxburgh and Tweeddale. It was also known as the New Party. Their alliance with the court was crucial in getting the Edinburgh Parliament to approve the Articles of Union (*see* UNION OF ENGLAND AND SCOTLAND).

Stair, John Dalrymple, 2nd earl of (1673–1747), soldier. Dalrymple inherited a name with a grim resonance in Scotland: as secretary of state for Scotland, his father had implemented the notorious GLENCOE massacre. Dalrymple's early life was also marred by personal tragedy: at the age of eight he killed his elder brother in a shooting accident. He was subsequently sent to join his exiled grandfather in the Netherlands, where he gained the friendship of William of Orange, the future WILLIAM III. In 1692 Dalrymple began an extensive military career when he served as a volunteer at the costly battle of STEENKIRK during the NINE YEARS WAR. Upon the outbreak of the War of the SPANISH SUCCESSION, Dalrymple returned to Flanders as aide-de-camp to the duke of Marlborough, and served under the duke as a brigadier general at RAMILLIES. As the 2nd earl of Stair he won such acclaim for his gallant conduct at the battle of OUDENARDE that he was sent home with the victory despatches. Promoted to major general in 1709, Stair saw further hard service at MALPLAQUET.

After the electoral triumph of the Tories in 1710 Stair was recalled with Marlborough. As a leading Scottish Whig, he favoured the accession of the elector of Hanover. When George I assumed the throne in 1714 Stair was rewarded with honours and appointed ambassador in Paris. At the Bourbon court Stair's diplomacy contributed to the establishment of the lasting Anglo-French peace that followed the death of Louis XIV; his presence was likewise important in monitoring the activities of the exiled JACOBITES, and ultimately secured the removal of the Old Pretender, James Francis Edward STUART, from Paris.

Recalled in 1720, Stair busied himself in managing his Scottish estates. He took a keen interest in agricultural improvement and pioneered the large-scale planting of cabbages and turnips in his homeland. Stair became a staunch opponent of Sir Robert WALPOLE and his leading Scottish manager, Archibald Campbell (the future 3rd duke of Argyll). In 1742, following Walpole's fall from office, Stair was made a field marshal and appointed to command Britain's contingent during its opening continental campaign of the War of the AUSTRIAN SUCCESSION. George II soon joined the so-called Pragmatic Army and at the victory of DETTINGEN in 1743 commanded in person. When the king subsequently rejected Stair's advice on the conduct of operations the old campaigner tendered his resignation. He nevertheless retained the royal favour and commanded the troops in England during the Franco-Jacobite invasion scare of 1744.

Stamp Act (1765), revenue-raising legislation applied to the American colonies requiring that a wide range of written and printed items use officially stamped paper, dispensed upon the payment of specified taxes. The act and the resistance to it in America were significant milestones on the road to American independence (*see* AMERICAN COLONIES 1763–1776).

Looking back on the loss of his prized North American colonies, GEORGE III traced the trouble to what he regarded as a crucial error of parliamentary judgment – the repeal of the Stamp Act in 1766. George GRENVILLE's attempt to increase revenue from the American colonies had been under discussion for a year when it became law in March 1765. Stamp duties had long been a fact of English life; however, in America they were seen as an unconstitutional attack upon property. The Sugar Act of 1764 had already stirred the colonists to consider means of retaliating against unpopu-

lar British measures. Faced with the Stamp Act, American merchants agreed to impose a boycott on the importation of all British goods until it was repealed. Meanwhile, mobs staged demonstrations to intimidate those men selected to distribute the stamps.

Organizations dubbed the 'Sons of Liberty' emerged, vowing to resist the Stamp Act at all costs. Delegates from nine colonies gathered in New York to hold the Stamp Act Congress. They argued that Parliament had no right to tax men who were not represented in it; further, the colonists saw no distinction between internal taxes imposed within America – such as the Stamp Act – and external taxes like the Sugar Act that aimed to regulate trade. In their eyes, Parliament had no right to tax them at all; that was the exclusive privilege of their own elected assemblies. This wave of protest took Britain's politicians by surprise. The tax was not seen as particularly onerous; indeed, many of the stamp duties were lower than those already operating in Britain.

By the time news of American resistance reached Britain, the Grenville ministry had been replaced by another headed by the marquess of ROCKINGHAM. While it was clear that it would be impossible to impose the Stamp Act in the face of such opposition, some form of face-saving compromise was necessary if repeal was to be made palatable to British political opinion. The Rockingham ministry clinched repeal of the act through the introduction of a compromise measure: this was the Declaratory Act of 1766, which maintained Parliament's right to legislate for the colonies 'in all cases whatsoever'. However, the vagueness of the Declaratory Act rendered it dangerously ambiguous, and both sides were left believing they had won their case.

While the Stamp Act crisis appeared resolved on the surface, the deeper issue raised – the question of Britain's sovereignty over its American colonies – remained unsettled. In Britain the row hardened attitudes towards America; across the Atlantic it saw the rise of new popular leaders who

365 Stanhope, James, 1st Earl Stanhope

now looked upon all government policy with suspicion. Despite the surface return to normality, the Stamp Act crisis fundamentally changed the imperial–colonial relationship.

FURTHER READING P.D.G. Thomas, *British Politics and the Stamp Act Crisis: The First Phase of the American Revolution, 1763–1767* (1975).

standing army controversy, fierce debate during the reign of WILLIAM III – and for many years thereafter – as to whether a large peacetime standing army should be allowed. Suspicions regarding the alleged tyrannical tendencies of James II had been reinforced by his decision to expand England's regular army from 8500 to 40,000 men. After he was ousted by William of Orange the BILL OF RIGHTS ruled that a permanent, or 'standing', army was illegal in time of peace without the consent of Parliament. At the height of his conflict with France in the NINE YEARS WAR William maintained an army far larger than that of his predecessor. He believed that the peace of Ryswick that ended the war in 1697 was unlikely to represent more than a brief lull in the fighting, and he therefore sought to retain a sizeable peacetime army that could be rapidly expanded when war resumed.

In the years 1697 to 1698 opponents of a standing army in peacetime aired objections that were to resonate for another half century. The crux of their fears was encapsulated in the very title of the most celebrated tract of the controversy, John TRENCHARD's *An Argument showing that a standing army is inconsistent with a free government and absolutely destructive of the Constitution*. To COUNTRY PARTY politicians such as Robert HARLEY a standing army threatened not only to introduce absolutism but also crippling taxation to sustain it. By contrast William's defenders denied that the army threatened liberty; on the contrary, they asserted, it was needed to defend English liberties from threats posed by JACOBITES reinforced by foreign assistance. William's ministers failed to persuade Parliament to approve a peacetime establishment of 30,000 men, the majority in the

Commons cutting it to 10,000 before the general election of 1698 and to 7000 after it. William threatened abdication, but found a way of circumventing Parliament's intentions by maintaining some 12,000 additional troops in Ireland.

The granting of parliamentary approval through the MUTINY ACT permitted annual discussion of the standing army issue, but in the course of the 18th century such debates became increasingly ritualistic. Although the army's police role continued to provoke criticism, other factors combined to defuse the Englishman's ingrained fear of military despotism. The Jacobite invasion of 1745 drew attention to the paucity of Britain's regular forces, whilst the MILITIA ACT of 1757 was prompted by the army's inability to defend a growing empire. In addition, the exploits of British soldiers at QUEBEC and MINDEN, and the heroic leadership of able generals such as WOLFE and GRANBY, gained the army a share of the plaudits previously reserved for the Royal Navy. Growing acceptance of the army as a permanent national institution was reflected in the allocation of numbers to regiments in 1751, followed by the introduction of county affiliations in 1782.

However, like other issues that had disappeared from Britain's political agenda, the standing army debate continued to smoulder in British America; there, the decision to impose a substantial peacetime garrison after 1763 fuelled fears of ministerial tyranny that contributed to the subsequent rift between mother country and colonies.

FURTHER READING L. Schwoerer, *No Standing Armies* (1974).

Stanhope, James, 1st Earl Stanhope (1673–1721), soldier and Whig politician; chief minister (1717–21). Stanhope entered the army after attending Oxford University. He had a distinguished military career in the War of the SPANISH SUCCESSION, taking MINORCA in 1708, until he was captured at the battle of Brihuega in 1710. He also made his mark as a Whig member of Parliament, playing a key role in the tactics of the 'whimsical

Whigs' designed to maintain a broad proscription of PLACEMEN from the Commons in the Regency Act of 1706 (*see* PARLIAMENTARY REFORM). In 1710 he was one of the Commons' managers in the impeachment proceedings against Dr SACHEVERELL, whom he described as 'an inconsiderable tool of a party'.

Although Stanhope's homosexuality aroused public comment in the general election of 1710, it did not impede his political advancement. After his release from being a prisoner of war he became a leading figure in the Whig opposition to the ministry of Robert HARLEY. When Harley fell in 1714 and BOLINGBROKE sought to form a ministry Stanhope told him bluntly that he had 'only two ways of escaping the gallows. The first is to join the honest party of the Whigs; the other to give yourself up entirely to the French King and seek his help for the Pretender.' On the accession of George I, Stanhope became secretary of state, in which post he displayed, in Horace WALPOLE's words, a 'fruitful and luxurious genius in foreign affairs'. He showed that he was prepared to accept the Tory treaty of UTRECHT as the basis of Britain's foreign policy, negotiating alliances with France that included the Netherlands in 1717 and Austria in 1718. He also stood up to attempts by Spain and Sweden to support the Stuart claimant to the throne, getting the British fleet to destroy the Spanish at Cape Passaro in 1718 and to threaten to sink the Swedish fleet in the Baltic.

In domestic politics Stanhope worked with the earl of SUNDERLAND to outmanoeuvre 2nd Viscount TOWNSHEND and WALPOLE, and when they went into opposition in 1717 he effectively became prime minister. The Stanhope ministry adopted a liberal stance towards dissent, repealing the OCCASIONAL CONFORMITY ACT and the SCHISM ACT and even considering the repeal of the Corporation and Test Acts. Although the resistance of Anglicans thwarted the lifting of the requirement to take communion in the Church of England in order to hold office, Stanhope protected DISSENTERS from the threat of prosecution for breach-

ing it by passing indemnity acts, which set a precedent for indemnifying them for the rest of the century. He even contemplated giving Catholics some relief from the penal laws, but this was doomed to failure.

Stanhope's enlightened religious policy stands in sharp contrast to his proposals for dealing with Parliament, where he planned nothing less than the deliberate creation of a permanent majority for his ministry in both houses. His Peerage Bill of 1719 (*see* LORDS, HOUSE OF) was designed to prevent any addition to the number of lords, closing the door after he had entered as viscount in 1717 (he became an earl in 1718). When this measure was introduced in February 1719 it created such a furore that Stanhope deferred it until the next session, and meanwhile endeavoured to make it more acceptable to the Commons by offering to repeal the SEPTENNIAL ACT, thereby extending indefinitely the date of the next election. This failed to defuse the opposition, which defeated the bill when it was reintroduced in December.

Although Sunderland rather than Stanhope was responsible for the scheme that led to the SOUTH SEA BUBBLE, Stanhope nevertheless defended the government against its critics in the House of Lords so vehemently that he suffered a stroke in the debate, from which he died in February 1721.

FURTHER READING B. Williams, *Stanhope: A Study in Eighteenth-Century War and Diplomacy* (1932).

Stanhope, Philip Dormer. *See* CHESTERFIELD, PHILIP DORMER STANHOPE, 4TH EARL OF.

Steele, Sir Richard (1672–1729), playwright, essayist and Whig politician. Steele was born in Dublin but educated in England at Charterhouse and Oxford. He began a military career, becoming a captain in the Life Guards. His career as an author commenced with the poem 'The Procession' published on the occasion of the death of Queen Mary. It was dedicated to Lord Cutts, as was his tract

The Christian Hero (1701). Cutts for a time employed Steele in his household. Steele's acquaintance with Joseph ADDISON, which began at school, led them to collaborate in Anne's reign. Addison wrote a prologue to Steele's play *The Tender Husband* in 1705. Steele had already written two plays, *The Funeral* in 1701 and *The Lying Lovers* in 1704, which were both examples of the new, more refined 'sentimental' comedy that arose as a result of the strictures against Restoration comedy made in Jeremy Collier's *Short View of the Profaneness and Immorality of the English Stage* (see DRAMA).

In 1707 Steele was appointed as gazetteer, or editor of the *London Gazette*, a government-sponsored publication that carried official news. As a Whig he lost the post when the Tories came to power in 1710. Steele meanwhile launched his own paper, the *Tatler*, which appeared three times a week from 1709 to 1711. The first volume was largely Steele's, but the next three were written in collaboration with Addison. The *Tatler* was succeeded by the more famous SPECTATOR, which came out daily from March 1711 to December 1712. Addison contributed more essays than his co-author. Whereas the *Tatler* and the *Spectator* purported to be neutral in politics, Steele entered the lists overtly on the Whig side in 1713. He launched the *Guardian* in March to attack the Tory government's appeasement of France, and in August became a member of Parliament. When he took his seat in 1714 he was accused of writing seditious libels, particularly *The Crisis*, which charged the Tories with JACOBITE inclinations. After a heated debate he was expelled from the House of Commons.

When George I succeeded later in the year Steele was rewarded, obtaining among other preferments the lucrative post of supervisor of the Theatre Royal, Drury Lane. In 1715 he was knighted. Following the suppression of the 1715 JACOBITE RISING he was made one of the commissioners of forfeited estates in Scotland. But his good fortune ran out in 1718. In that year a scheme to bring salmon from Ireland to England failed, and

his second wife died. The following year he quarrelled with Addison over the merits of the Peerage Bill (*see* LORDS, HOUSE OF). Addison supported the measure but Steele opposed it in the *Plebeian*. For his opposition he was deprived of his patent at the Theatre Royal in 1720, though WALPOLE restored it to him in 1721. In 1722 he dedicated his comedy *The Conscious Lovers* to the king, who gave him 500 guineas. His growing debts led him to retire from London in 1724. He finally settled in Carmarthen where he died.

FURTHER READING R. Dammers, *Richard Steele* (1982).

Steenkirk, battle of (3 August 1692), an extremely hard-fought but indecisive engagement in Flanders during the NINE YEARS WAR. Following the French capture of Namur, Louis XIV's leading general, Marshal Luxembourg, manoeuvred as if to threaten Brussels. He was followed by WILLIAM III, commanding an Allied army composed of British, Dutch and Danish troops. On 2 August 1692, Luxembourg adopted a strong position at Steenkirk that was screened by broken and wooded terrain. More French troops, under Marshal Boufflers, were encamped 11km (7 miles) away.

At his own camp at Hal, William unearthed a French spy who, with a pistol held to his head, was obliged to write a letter reassuring Luxembourg that any enemy troop movements detected upon the following morning would be nothing more serious than a foraging party. The ruse came close to success. On 3 August, when William's leading troops began threading their way through the woods towards the French position, Luxembourg initially ignored the intelligence sent by his patrols. It was only after the third report that the Marshal realized the danger of the situation, raised the alarm and sent a messenger requesting Boufflers' assistance. The Allied advance guard awaited support before attacking, a hiatus that gave Luxembourg time to organize his defences. Fierce infantry fighting ensued amongst the thickets and hedges but, although the Allied assault penetrated

Luxembourg's camp, it was stemmed by the counter-attack of the French and Swiss Guards.

The British and Danish troops in the firing line made repeated calls for reinforcements, but the Dutch commander Count Solmes proved either unable or unwilling to send forward more men. In response he allegedly growled: 'Damn the English. If they are so fond of fighting, let them have a bellyful.' With the arrival of Boufflers, the allies were obliged to withdraw under cover of a rearguard action. Having seen the chance of victory slip through his fingers, the mortified William was left regretting the loss of 7000 men. The French also suffered heavily and the inconclusive campaign drew to a close as Luxembourg retired to winter quarters.

Sterne, Laurence (1713–68), novelist, known principally for *Tristram Shandy*. Sterne was born in Clonmel, Ireland. He managed nevertheless to obtain a scholarship at Jesus College, Cambridge, which was reserved for poor boys from Yorkshire. The fact that his great-grandfather, an archbishop of York, had established it has been cited to accuse Sterne of wrongly benefiting from it. Yet, since his father Roger was a soldier at the time of his birth, he could claim the right of settlement in the paternal parish of Elvington in Yorkshire.

After graduating from Cambridge Sterne was admitted into deacon's orders in 1737, and a year later became vicar of Sutton-in-the-Forest, north of York. This was to be his home until Lord Fauconberg obtained for him the living of Coxwold, also in Yorkshire, in 1760. He married Elizabeth Lumley in 1741. She was committed to a private lunatic asylum in York in 1759, allegedly becoming distracted after finding him in bed with a maid. Certainly he was involved with other women. His wife subsequently agreed to a formal separation and went to live with their daughter Lydia in France.

Sterne's first venture into publication was to write electoral propaganda in *The York Gazetteer* on behalf of a COURT Whig candidate in a by-election for the county seat in 1742. During the '45 JACOBITE RISING he contributed £10 to the subscription raised by government supporters in Yorkshire. In 1747 he wrote a letter to the *Protestant York Courant* proclaiming 'as for my political principles, I have the highest opinion of the constitution of my country and think it very safe in the hands of our present Governors'.

Indeed, Sterne dedicated the second edition of his novel *Tristram Shandy* to the elder PITT. The novel is suffused with Whiggish, even Lockean, principles. When the first two volumes appeared in 1759 Sterne became famous. He was lionized in London in 1760, and received advanced royalties of £850 for the remainder of the novel. These advances enabled him to return to his new living at Coxwold in style. There he rented from Lord Fauconberg the house that has ever since been known as Shandy Hall. Sterne missed the excitement of London, and was back there in 1761 for the publication of the third and fourth volumes of *Tristram Shandy*. Whereas the first and second volumes had been ecstatically received, these met with a mixed reception.

At the end of the year Sterne went to France, where he met David HUME and John WILKES. On his return he gave up preaching, installing a curate in Coxwold. He apparently experienced a crisis of faith in France. The continued success of his novel, and advanced subscriptions for two volumes of sermons, raised enough to finance another journey to the continent in 1765. This time it was for the sake of his health, for by then Sterne was constantly spitting blood. His account of his travels, *A Sentimental Journey through France and Italy*, was published just before he died. On his return to England in 1766 he wrote the last volume of *Tristram Shandy*. Early in 1767 he went to London as usual to be present for its publication. There he met Mrs Elizabeth Draper, the young wife of an East India Company official who was resident in India. His relationship with her was recorded in his *Journal to Eliza*, much of which he wrote in Coxwold over that summer. In January 1768 he returned to London where he died on 15 March.

Sterne's reputation now rests on *Tristram Shandy* rather than on the sentimentality of *A Sentimental Journey* or the maudlin *Journal to Eliza*. In his innovative novel he virtually invented the subjective narrator, breaking with the objective narratives of previous novels. Thus there is little or no chronological development, the focus shifting rapidly backwards and forwards from object to object. This makes it at once bewildering and refreshing. Readers cannot be indifferent to the novel – they either love it or loathe it.

FURTHER READING A.H. Cash, *Laurence Sterne: The Early and Middle Years* (1975); A.H. Cash, *Laurence Sterne: The Later Years* (1986); M. New, *Laurence Sterne as Satirist: A Reading of Tristram Shandy* (1969).

Stewart, Robert. *See* CASTLEREAGH, ROBERT STEWART, VISCOUNT.

Stourhead, mansion in Wiltshire, the grounds of which represent a remarkable statement of the world view of their creator, the banker Henry Hoare (1705–85). After 1741 Hoare embarked upon a programme of landscaping that created one of the best-known gardens in Britain. Centred upon an ornamental lake, the resulting garden was so extensive that 18th-century visitors were obliged to undertake its outer circuit by coach.

Unlike the gardens at STOWE, which alluded to 18th-century politics, Stourhead was rich in literary references. Above all, Hoare's vision was dominated by a fixation upon the *Aeneid*. It has been argued that the circuit's features deliberately mirror the travels of Aeneas in Book IV of Virgil's epic – for example, the grotto represents the underworld. The inscription over the door of the first building to be encountered upon the garden circuit, the Temple of Flora, comes directly from the *Aeneid*: in translation it reads 'Be gone all you who are uninitiated.' The quotation not only advertised an intimate knowledge of classical literature, it also indicated Hoare's kinship with that exclusive band of gentlemen connoisseurs whose outlook was coloured by the idealized conception of the Roman Campagna encapsulated in the paintings of Claude Lorrain. A gentleman-amateur who oversaw much of the work at Stourhead, Hoare was a patron of the landscape designer and architect William Kent (*see* LANDSCAPE GARDENING). The mansion at Stourhead was the work of Colen Campbell, himself a leading figure in the PALLADIAN movement.

Stourhead offers the most famous example of the Georgian 'pictorial circuit garden'. The grounds consist of a sequence of artfully arranged views that unfold as the visitor follows the route around the lake. Stourhead's walks are screened with trees until vantage points provide the opportunity to reveal vistas such as that across the lake to Henry Flitcroft's Pantheon of 1754. The view from the portico of the Pantheon was similarly contrived, embracing the village and church of Stourton, complete with a medieval cross transplanted from Bristol in 1765 to add further interest to the vista.

Like those at Stowe, the gardens at Stourhead ultimately became overcrowded with buildings that detracted from their 'natural' beauty. When Henry Hoare's grandson, Sir Richard Colt Hoare, returned from touring Italy in 1791 he weeded out structures ranging from a Gothic greenhouse to a Chinese temple. For all their artificiality, the gardens at Stourhead have never lacked admirers: Horace WALPOLE believed that Hoare's efforts had created 'one of the most picturesque scenes in the world', and today the gardens continue to attract visitors who echo his words.

Stowe, mansion near Buckingham, whose gardens can be appreciated both for their outstanding beauty and as an elaborate expression of distaste for the political regime of Robert WALPOLE.

Landscaping at Stowe continued throughout much of the 18th century; it originated with Sir Richard Temple, Viscount Cobham (1675–1749), who inherited the estate in 1697. Cobham's vision transformed Stowe and obliterated the nearby village as the gardens spread to cover more than 160 ha (400 acres).

The gardens at Stowe underwent distinct stages of development. The first, undertaken by Charles Bridgeman in the opening decades of the century, conformed to prevailing tastes by emphasizing formality: an area sloping away from the house itself was characterized by straight walks and canals. Bridgeman contained the whole complex within a boundary 'ha-ha'(concealed ditch) that offered uninterrupted views of the open countryside beyond the estate, while keeping straying cattle at bay. VANBRUGH contributed to this phase of the landscaping by designing buildings including the Rotunda and pavilions alongside the lake.

During the 1730s the grounds at Stowe began to reflect changing attitudes toward LANDSCAPE GARDENING. As with the architectural cult of PALLADIANISM, the trend embodied political overtones: rigid and symmetrical gardens now evoked the authoritarian regime of Bourbon France; by contrast informal, naturalistic grounds expressed Whig concerns with liberty and freedom. At Stowe the strict regularity of the original layout was slowly transformed. For example, an area known as the Elysian Fields was created and divided by a stream dubbed the river Styx. With time, the grounds became increasingly naturalistic. The master of the genre, Lancelot 'Capability' Brown, served his apprenticeship at Stowe in the 1740s, and was married in the parish church – the last vestige of the village – in 1744. At this period Brown's reputation was already growing, and Lord Cobham lent him to neighbours who wished to remodel their own estates.

Buildings and sculpture within the gardens at Stowe reveal the political ideology of Lord Cobham and his circle (COBHAM'S CUBS), who were increasingly associated with Whig opposition against the Walpolean hegemony. For example, William Kent's Temple of Ancient Virtue, which was based on Palladio's drawing of the Temple of Vesta at Tivoli, contained statues of a number of celebrated figures from classical times; in stark contrast, the neighbouring Temple of Modern Virtue was a ruin containing a headless statue of the hated Walpole. Similarly, the Gothic Temple was originally known as the Temple of Liberty; this carried an anti-Roman motto that once again attacked an administration that was colourfully compared to Rome at its most decadent. A curving gallery known as the Temple of British Worthies contained the busts of 16 distinguished figures, including Inigo Jones, Shakespeare and Newton; prominent among these past heroes was Alfred the Great, a king believed to epitomize the traditional English freedoms that now appeared to be endangered by a corrupt regime. Again, the Temple of Friendship, which housed busts of Cobham's allies, promoted both fraternity and anti-government solidarity.

Later structures, such as the Temple of Concord and Victory, renamed in order to commemorate the successful conclusion of the SEVEN YEARS WAR, lacked these political overtones, while Kent's Temple of Venus was erected in simple celebration of erotic love. In commissioning so many temples the masters of Stowe had more than justified their own surname, and some visitors felt that such a proliferation of buildings detracted from the true splendours of the gardens. Indeed, in 1744 the duchess of Portland complained that Stowe was positively cluttered with them. Despite such criticisms, Stowe's gardens continued to prove a popular attraction: their delights were promoted in published guides and Cobham's successor, Earl Temple, was obliged to maintain an inn to provide accommodation for genteel tourists.

Strawberry Hill, Horace WALPOLE's GOTHIC mansion, which was among the most original, celebrated and influential buildings of the Georgian era.

A key figure in 18th-century England's 'Gothic revival', Walpole had acquired a modest house at Twickenham on the Thames in 1749. In the following year he embarked upon an extensive rebuilding programme in the Gothic style that was beginning to find favour among a small group of gentlemen aficionados. Walpole's return to the medieval past was probably influenced by his association with the gifted architect and landscape designer William Kent (*see* LANDSCAPE GARDENING). Not only had Walpole spent his boyhood in a house built by Kent, but he had also expressed his admiration for the irregularity characteristic of Kent's landscape gardening; Walpole sought to apply a similar asymmetry to the design of Strawberry Hill.

Enlisting the help of his friend and fellow amateur architect John Chute, Walpole began designing his new home in 1750. The house that gradually emerged from their plans was characterized by the battlements, pinnacles, arches and quatrefoil windows that had been included in Batty Langley's illustrated manual of Gothic architectural features. Although the Gothic style was employed on several British houses in the mid-18th century, at Strawberry Hill the Middle Ages were recreated with an unrivalled thoroughness; Gothic features characterized both the exterior and the interior decoration.

The evolution of Strawberry Hill was governed by a 'Committee of Taste' originally composed of Walpole, Chute and the illustrator Richard Bentley. Walpole was primarily concerned with creating authentically Gothic surroundings, and the faithful designs of Chute were increasingly preferred to Bentley's more imaginative interpretations. The second phase of work at Strawberry Hill between 1758 and 1763 saw the completion of the lavish Gallery: the room's ceiling featured elaborate mock vaulting based upon the much admired chapel of Henry VII in Westminster Abbey. Walpole was delighted with the result, which he proudly described as 'richer than the roof of Paradise'.

Bentley departed from the Committee of Taste in 1759, to be replaced by Thomas Pitt. Over the next three decades the ongoing work at Strawberry Hill would employ the talents of such leading architects as James Wyatt and Robert ADAM; indeed, while Adam is invariably linked with NEOCLASSICISM, his contribution to Strawberry Hill provides a reminder of his parallel ability in the Gothic style. Although the first phase of work had relied heavily upon Langley's drawings of Gothic architecture, the later central section of the mansion – which employs authentic lancet windows and stepped buttresses – was consciously based upon existing Gothic structures.

Walpole's home generated immense interest, not least because he wrote and published a detailed *Description of Strawberry Hill* (1774–84), which illustrated and described the architecture and interiors in loving detail. Naturally enough, when Walpole produced his ground-breaking Gothic novel *The Castle of Otranto* in 1765, Strawberry Hill provided the ideal backdrop for several key scenes. A further wing, also in the Gothic style, was added to Strawberry Hill during the 1860s – a tribute to the enduring appeal of the architectural movement that Walpole and his 'little Gothic castle' had done so much to promote.

Stuart, Charles Edward (1720–88), the 'Young Pretender', enshrined in Jacobite lore as 'Bonnie Prince Charlie', who instigated one of the most dramatic, and tragic, episodes in British history: the '45 JACOBITE RISING.

Charles was born in Rome, the eldest son of the Old Pretender, the exiled Stuart claimant 'James III' – James Francis Edward STUART – and his frail Polish wife, Clementina Sobieska. When his father grew increasingly pessimistic about regaining the British throne, the energetic and charming Charles became the focus for JACOBITE hopes. Charles assumed a sense of heroic mission, subjecting himself to a punishing regime designed to toughen his body for the impending challenge of ejecting the Hanoverians.

In late 1743, during the War of the AUSTRIAN SUCCESSION, Charles believed that his chance had finally come. Chafing from defeat at the hands of the British at DETTINGEN, Louis XV of France approved plans for an invasion of England. An excited Charles donned disguise, bid farewell to his anxious father, and embarked upon a break-neck journey to Brest. There his hopes were soon shattered when the fleet appointed to escort the invading force was dispersed by storms in the spring of 1744. Marshal Maurice de Saxe, the able commander appointed to lead the invaders, soon adopted a safer strategy of campaigning in Flanders. Charles meanwhile dallied in France, growing increasingly impatient with his host's failure to mount a fresh invasion.

The exasperated Charles eventually decided to take the initiative. Raising a loan from a Jacobite banker in Paris, the prince hired two warships, filled them with arms and ammunition, and promptly embarked for Scotland, where he expected enthusiastic support. By ill luck the tiny squadron was intercepted en route by a British warship. In the ensuing engagement one of Charles's ships was so badly damaged that it was obliged to turn back – taking crucial supplies and trained officers with it. It was an inauspicious start to Charles's bid to regain the throne of his forebears. Nothing daunted, Charles continued his hazardous journey in the remaining vessel.

On 22 July 1745, the prince and his small band of followers sighted Scotland. They were put ashore on the remote Outer Hebridean island of Eriskay, from where Charles summoned the clans he believed to be ripe for rebellion. The response was disappointing: the powerful MacDonalds told Charles to turn back, while other local Jacobites proved equally lukewarm. Once again, the prince's own commitment proved crucial; despite his discouraging reception he insisted upon proceeding to the mainland, landing in Moidart in the western Highlands. Posing as smugglers, Charles and his motley entourage of adventurers – the 'seven men of Moidart' – again awaited the verdict of the local chiefs. Although moved by the arrival of their hereditary prince, the clan leaders remained adamant that a rising was unthinkable without the backing of French troops. A combination of Charles's charisma and his clear determination to proceed alone if necessary finally shamed the sceptical chiefs into pledging their aid. The ill-fated rebellion of the '45 had begun.

By 1 August news of the landing reached London. The government responded by offering a £30,000 reward for the Pretender's capture. Events now moved quickly. On 19 August, as more than 1000 Highlanders looked on, Charles raised the Stuart standard at Glenfinnan, declaring his father 'King James III' and himself 'Prince Regent'. The administration of George II proved unable to nip rebellion in the bud; many British regiments were preoccupied in Flanders, while those in Scotland were ill-trained. With the poor material at his disposal, the government's commander, Sir John Cope, proved reluctant to risk a confrontation in the Highlands. Cope's withdrawal left Edinburgh unprotected. Charles's little army marched rapidly southwards, its progress expedited by General George WADE's fine new military roads.

Charles's new recruits included James Drummond duke of Perth and Lord George MURRAY: each was given the rank of lieutenant general in the growing Jacobite army. Both men enjoyed enormous prestige, although Lord George's blunt manner ultimately sparked a damaging rift with the prince. As Charles consolidated his position, encouraging messages arrived promising support from France and Spain. Although Glasgow rebuffed the prince's demands for assistance, and the garrison of Stirling Castle advertised its defiance with gunfire, the pro-government city of Edinburgh was captured by surprise on 17 September. The Castle held out, but the glamorous 'Young Chevalier' received an enthusiastic reception from curious crowds. News soon arrived that Cope had landed at Dunbar and was marching on the capital. Following a council of war, the prince resolved to seek battle. Exchanging his fine clothes for the coarse plaid and blue bonnet of the humble Highlander, Charles led his men to Prestonpans where Cope had arrayed his force in a strong defensive position. On the night of 20 September a local sympathizer indicated a route by which Cope's army could be taken by surprise. On the following morning the

Highlanders attacked at dawn. Their broadswords made short work of Cope's raw redcoats: as Charles reported to his father, victory was complete. Elated at his success, Charles was nevertheless shocked at the carnage inflicted upon his own 'subjects'.

Ironically, the triumph at Prestonpans exposed a worrying rift in the Jacobite army. While Charles now coveted London, his Highlanders believed their obligations ended with the restoration of Stuart fortunes in Scotland. Rival factions were exposed during daily meetings in Holyroodhouse, the royal palace in Edinburgh. Perth clashed with Murray, while Charles's Irish favourites were despised by the Scots. The young prince proved resentful of any advice from his elders that contradicted his own opinions. While at Edinburgh the prince became a major social attraction: his gallant bearing charmed females of all political persuasions; but their white cockades and tartan dresses symbolized a sentimental allegiance that was no substitute for genuine mass support. Despite romantic legends, Charles remained more interested in battles than balls. His ambition to march on London was encouraged by news that France had finally sent concrete aid for the rebellion; a small force of troops had arrived in Scotland, but large-scale assistance was promised.

The government's response to the crisis was now gathering momentum. Troops were recalled from Flanders, while an army under the elderly General Wade was despatched to Newcastle. Charles sought an encounter with Wade, but the clan chiefs remained reluctant to leave Scotland. Lord George Murray's compromise suggestion of a strike into England via Carlisle eventually carried the day. In a remarkable campaign, the Jacobite army evaded government forces to penetrate as far as Derby, within 160 km (100 miles) of London: there, on 6 December, the absence of significant English support for the Jacobites prompted withdrawal.

Thwarted in his desire to march onwards, Charles adopted his father's fatalism. Under the leadership of Murray, the Jacobite army conducted a skilful retreat to Scotland. At Falkirk, on 17 January 1746, the Highlanders inflicted a reverse on government forces under General Henry Hawley. Despite this success, Murray and the clan chiefs were for retiring to the Highlands, and the prince proved unable to dissuade them. Government forces under the duke of CUMBERLAND advanced steadily. Against the advice of his field commanders, the prince opted to seek battle at CULLODEN Moor near Inverness. A projected night attack on Cumberland's camp miscarried. On the following morning, 16 April, the outnumbered and dispirited Highlanders were crushed by superior firepower. While Cumberland's troops exacted a bloody vengeance on the defeated rebels, their erstwhile prince was led away in shock. The remnants of the Jacobite army rendezvoused at Ruthven, only to receive the prince's orders to save themselves.

The Young Pretender was now a hunted fugitive. During the tense months that followed the prince recovered his old spirits; cold, hunger and the constant danger of betrayal during a perilous odyssey around the Western Isles all failed to dampen them. Charles surprised his companions with his gaiety, which came increasingly from the brandy bottle. After Flora MACDONALD ferried him from Benbecula to Skye, Charles hid on the mainland; he was eventually rescued by a French vessel in September near to where he had first landed.

The prince's wanderings in the heather subsequently became clouded in romance, and they guaranteed a hero's reception upon his arrival in Paris. For all his popularity, Charles soon became a political embarrassment to Louis XV. In December 1748 Charles was arrested; his freedom was dependent upon leaving the country. He now embarked upon a nomadic existence, spending years roaming Europe in disguise and under a succession of fake identities. Such precautions were prompted by a genuine fear of British agents, but also reflected an inability to settle after the excitements of the '45. Charles continued plotting his return to Britain; in 1750 he actually visited London and formally renounced his Catholicism.

A subsequent conspiracy, purportedly with Swedish backing, was abandoned after infiltration by a government spy.

By his mid-30s Charles's private life was in the doldrums: bitter and disappointed, he bickered with his mistress Clementina Walkenshaw, by whom he had a daughter, Charlotte, and lapsed into alcoholism. Jacobitism no longer counted in international politics: upon the Old Pretender's death in 1766, no European power recognized his eldest son as 'Charles III'. Charles married Louise of Stolberg in 1772; she left him eight years later after he attacked her in a drunken rage. Charles's final days were comforted by his daughter and haunted by memories of his year of fame.

FURTHER READING F. McLynn, *Charles Edward Stuart: A Tragedy in Many Acts* (1988).

Stuart, Henry Benedict (1725–1807), the second son of James Francis Edward STUART, the Old Pretender. Henry Benedict Stuart was born in Rome. More serious than his boisterous elder brother Charles Edward STUART – the future 'Bonnie Prince Charlie' – the young Henry was clearly his father's favourite. Henry did not participate in his brother's attempt to recover the Stuart throne in 1745. In 1747, Henry left Charles fuming after he took holy orders to become Cardinal York (his father had named him duke of York shortly after his birth). Charles had good reason for his anger, as Henry's surprise decision had damaging repercussions for the JACOBITE cause. Catholicism was regarded as the root of Britons' objection to the Stuarts, and both James and Charles had emphasized that a Stuart restoration would involve no interference with Britain's established Protestant religion. Now Henry's open acceptance of Catholicism suggested that this stance had been no more than a cynical front. In consequence, Charles wanted little more to do with his brother.

When Charles died without legitimate issue in 1788, the Cardinal York adopted the title of 'Henry IX', although the declining Stuart fortunes meant that it had long since lost any meaning. When the victorious armies of the French Republic invaded Italy in 1796, Henry's palace was sacked and his property confiscated. Learning of the cardinal's distress, the British government aided his passage to Venice, and George III granted him a pension. 'Henry IX' died at Frascati in 1807, and lies buried in St Peter's, Rome, alongside his father and brother. Henry had bequeathed the house of Stuart's remaining crown jewels to George prince of Wales (the future GEORGE IV); as prince regent, George reciprocated by erecting an impressive marble monument over the tomb of the three exiled Stuarts.

Stuart, James Francis Edward (1688–1766), the son of the ousted James II of England. 'The Old Pretender', as he was known – or James III by his JACOBITE followers – was destined to endure a gloomy life of exile.

By his birth James had unwittingly triggered the events that culminated in WILLIAM of Orange's successful coup in the GLORIOUS REVOLUTION of 1688. Despite his Catholicism, James II had been tolerated by his subjects because his acknowledged heir was a daughter by his first marriage, MARY – and she was a Protestant. The arrival of a male heir by James's second wife, Mary of Modena, heightened those fears of a Catholic succession that underpinned the Glorious Revolution. Indeed, gossip spread the falsehood that the baby was an impostor smuggled into Mary's bedchamber in a warming pan. Before James reached his first birthday, his mother had whisked him away to refuge in France.

James matured within the insecure world of the Stuart shadow court at St Germain, near Paris. Upon the death of James's father in 1701, Louis XIV of France recognized him as 'James III'. Bourbon support for the Old Pretender contributed to the onset of the War of the SPANISH SUCCESSION. As the figurehead of the Jacobite cause, James participated in the abortive attempt to invade Scotland in 1708; seven years later he took a belated role in the '15 JACOBITE RISING. Although he was crowned 'James VIII of Scotland' at Perth, the rebellion was already defeated and he was soon obliged to flee for France.

These repeated disappointments, combined with the unsettled existence pursued by the exiled Jacobite court, left James depressed and frustrated. In 1719, the year that a Spanish-backed Jacobite invasion of Scotland encountered failure, James married Clementina Sobieska, a granddaughter of John III Sobieski of Poland. The couple were ill matched, but Clementina nonetheless produced two sons, Charles Edward STUART – the future 'Bonnie Prince Charlie' – and Henry Benedict STUART, who became a cardinal in the Roman Catholic Church. Although Henry was James's clear favourite, it was Charles who embodied Jacobite hopes. In 1745, when Charles landed in Scotland, James was initially horrified at his son's rashness, although he soon confessed pride at the boldness of the venture. James remained at Rome while the bloody drama of the '45 unfolded, signifying his readiness to abdicate in favour of his son if the rebellion succeeded. James suffered a stroke in 1762 and died four years later, his life time having embraced the birth and demise of Jacobitism as a political force.

Stuart, John, 3rd earl of Bute. *See* BUTE, JOHN STUART, 3RD EARL OF.

Stubbs, George (1724–1806), painter. Although renowned as a painter of horses, Stubbs proved equally adept as a portraitist and chronicler of rural life.

The son of a Liverpool currier, Stubbs learned his trade travelling in northern England, followed by a brief stint in Rome. Stubbs possessed an inquiring mind: by his mid-20s he had embarked upon the methodical study of anatomy that was to culminate in the publication of his monumental engraved work *The Anatomy of the Horse* (1766) – still a standard work on the subject. Such meticulous research ensured that Stubbs's animal studies possessed an originality and realism that set them apart from the stilted efforts of his predecessors and rivals. He likewise avoided the sentimentality that was to characterize the work of many subsequent animal painters.

Based in London from the early 1760s, Stubbs deployed his unique skills in depicting the prized horseflesh of England's gentry and aristocracy; more exotic subjects included the zebra brought from South Africa for the royal family in 1763. Often, as in the magnificent life-sized *Whistlejacket* (1762), the beasts themselves took centre stage; however, Stubbs frequently incorporated proud owners and humble grooms in his striking compositions. In other works Stubbs turned his attention to country pursuits, producing convincing scenes of the upper classes at sport, and more idealized images of the rural workforce labouring in the fields.

Between 1761 and 1774 Stubbs was a regular exhibitor with the Society of Artists, and was elected president in 1773. During the 1770s Stubbs turned his knowledge of animal anatomy to the depiction of more deliberately dramatic themes, notably his *Horse Frightened by a Lion*. Despite his versatility, Stubbs was dogged by his reputation as a lowly 'horse painter', and his appointment as a Royal Academician in 1781 was never ratified.

FURTHER READING B. Taylor, *Stubbs* (1971).

Sunday schools, schools for poor working children that operated on their only day off. During the closing decades of the 18th century such schools made a dramatic impact upon the education of the 'lower orders', by teaching reading and writing as well as religious education.

A movement destined to spread rapidly throughout Britain was kindled by Robert Raikes (1735–1811), the owner of the *Gloucester Journal*. Raikes was shocked by the poverty and idleness of the children he saw in the streets of his home city. In 1780 he established a school, and the idea was soon copied across the country. By

1783 John WESLEY was encountering the new Sunday schools wherever he travelled. Their growth was especially pronounced in traditional mining areas and the manufacturing districts of south Lancashire. The correlation between Sunday schools and concentrated industrial activity was no mere coincidence; it reflected the fact that they provided schooling for humble children without distracting them from the work that occupied their weekdays. As the bishop of Chester remarked, such classes therefore achieved 'that most desirable union ... of manual labour and spiritual instruction'.

In its early days the Sunday-school movement enjoyed phenomenal growth: as early as 1788 Manchester alone had 5000 pupils, and by 1800 the national total may have been as high as 100,000. Both children and adults attended classes. The extraordinary popularity of the Sunday schools may be partially explained by the incentives that their sponsors offered in the form of free meals and clothing. In addition, a degree of compulsion was often present: parents who refused to send their children for instruction might risk exclusion from the list of those deemed to be proper objects for parish charity under the provisions of the POOR LAW.

While Sunday schools offered an opportunity to increase learning among the working classes, this was not seen as their primary purpose. Like the existing charity schools (see CHARITY), the Sunday schools gained the support of magistrates and employers because they were viewed as an effective method of indoctrinating the children of the poor with religious piety, habits of work-discipline and a spirit of deference towards their masters. In consequence, there was a growing reaction against the use of the Sabbath for the teaching of writing as opposed to instruction of a purely religious nature.

Although Sunday schools had originated as a non-denominational movement, by the end of the 18th century the established church was adopting an increasingly cautious attitude towards them. Anglican clerics feared that the literacy they promoted not only encouraged METHODISM but also gave the 'lower orders' access to subversive 'JACOBIN' literature capable of breeding the radical views that such lessons were intended to stifle. During the course of the 19th century increasing restrictions upon the use of child labour, combined with the growth of day schooling, ensured that Sunday schools became concerned with religious education alone.

FURTHER READING P. B. Cliff, *The Rise and Development of the Sunday School Movement in England, 1780–1980* (1986).

Sunderland, Charles Spencer, 3rd earl of

(1674–1722), Whig politician who became the fifth member of the JUNTO. He held high office from 1706 to 1710, and again from 1715 to 1721.

Spencer was taken by his father, the second earl of SUNDERLAND, to Holland in 1688, but was back at the family home at Althorp in Northamptonshire by 1691. In 1695 he married the daughter of the duke of Newcastle. Following her death in 1698 negotiations were begun that led to him marrying Anne Churchill, the daughter of the earl and countess of MARLBOROUGH in 1700. This alliance with her favourites ensured that when Queen Anne came to the throne in 1702 he had the backing of the most powerful politicians in the land. Although the queen objected to his politics, which were so extremely Whig that he had the reputation of being a republican, he was the first of the Whig Junto to obtain office under her, becoming secretary of state in 1706. His fellow secretary Robert HARLEY intrigued against his appointment and following it tried to wrong-foot him until his intrigues led to his own downfall in 1708. Thereafter the animosity between the two was mutual, and in June 1710 Sunderland was the first of the Junto to be dismissed in the ministerial revolution engineered by his rival.

Sunderland became one of the leaders of the opposition to the Harley ministry in the House of Lords. When he was appointed lord lieutenant of Ireland by George I in 1714 he felt that his efforts had not been adequately rewarded, and still entertained ambitions for higher office when he became lord privy seal the following year. His chance came when the king went to Hanover. Sunderland went abroad ostensibly on health grounds, only to make a beeline for the royal presence. There he intrigued against 2nd Viscount TOWNSHEND and WALPOLE, and was instrumental in their leaving the ministry in 1717. He became secretary of state while STANHOPE was appointed first lord of the Treasury, a distribution of offices that was reversed the following year. Despite becoming first lord, Sunderland accepted the dominance of Stanhope in the ministry. Thus the latter was held responsible for the Peerage Bill (*see* LORDS, HOUSE OF). Sunderland, however, was responsible for the scheme to get the South Sea Company to take over the unfunded debt, which led to the SOUTH SEA BUBBLE in 1720. Despite his involvement he was sheltered from investigation by Walpole, who replaced him as first lord in 1721. Sunderland would have been a formidable rival to Walpole had he not died suddenly in 1722. He left one of the finest libraries in England at the time.

Sunderland, Robert Spencer, 2nd earl of

(1641–1702), politician who played a leading role during the reigns of Charles II, James II and William III, successfully managing to survive the upheavals of the GLORIOUS REVOLUTION.

Spencer succeeded to the earldom as an infant, which was to mean that, unlike many politicians of the period, he never served as a member of the House of Commons. Sunderland's first involvement in high politics was to bring dissident elements, including Shaftesbury, leader of the first Whigs, into government in an attempt to buy them off. This scheme failed to resolve the Exclusion crisis, brought on by the attempt to exlude James duke of York, Charles II's brother and heir, from the throne. Nevertheless, it gave him valuable experience in wheeling and dealing with politicians ostensibly opposed to the court. Sunderland then persuaded the king to dissolve Parliament and hold

fresh elections. Throughout 1680 the ministry laboured to try to offset the results of the parliamentary elections, which had gone again in favour of the exclusionists. The ministry persuaded the king to keep proroguing Parliament to avoid an early meeting, which would play into the hands of the Whigs. It was Sunderland's determination to demonstrate his commitment to William, and to dish Whig support for the duke of Monmouth, which apparently lay behind his otherwise inexplicable decision to support the second Exclusion Bill. For on the face of things it was to commit political suicide. Charles marked the secretary down for destruction, but waited until he dissolved Parliament on 18 January 1681 before dismissing him on the 24th.

Within two years Sunderland was to be restored to favour. In September 1682 he was readmitted to the privy council and on 31 January 1683 he again became secretary of state. In the closing weeks of Charles II's reign, therefore, Sunderland came close to being the chief minister. He survived the crisis of James II's accession, and remained at the very centre of his affairs until just before the GLORIOUS REVOLUTION, because he was more sympathetic to the king's religious aims than other close advisers. In 1686 he converted to Catholicism.

Sunderland was aware that a government that rested solely on Catholic support was too narrowly based to be viable. Having broken with the Anglicans he advised the king to make a conciliatory gesture to Protestant DISSENTERS. James issued the Declaration of Indulgence, granting toleration to all non-Anglicans.

Sunderland went along with the policy of appointing Catholics to the point of approving Father Petre's admission to the privy council in November, to the alarm even of moderate Catholics. Then in December Sunderland assured James that he would make his own conversion public whenever it seemed to be advantageous for the king. The campaign to pack Parliament led to tensions in the council early in 1688. James, egged on by the Catholic cabal, was eager for an election as soon as possible. Sunderland, realizing that the outcome would be disastrous, advised postponing the polls as long as possible. In March he persuaded the king to put them off until after the summer.

This victory for common sense was soon offset, however, by James's fateful decision, on reissuing the Declaration of Indulgence in April, to require the clergy to read it from their pulpits – 'of which I most solemnly protest,' Sunderland claimed later, adding, 'I never heard one word till the King directed it in Council.' He was present at the birth of a son to James and his queen – a Catholic heir in the form of James Francis Edward STUART – and a few days later he publicly announced his earlier conversion to the Catholic faith.

When William invaded England, Sunderland fled to Holland. There he published a *Letter to a Friend in London, plainly discovering the designs of the Romish Party and others for the subverting of the Protestant Religion and the Laws of the Kingdom*. This was an attempt to gain a sympathetic audience for his version of events. Thus he sought to demonstrate that he had tried to restrain the more extravagant schemes of the king. He also sought to mend fences with William, praising 'the miracles he has done by his wonderful prudence, conduct and courage, for the greatest thing which has been undertaken these thousand years'.

Sunderland's political instincts could be invaluable for the survival of the post-Revolution regime, and his advice was increasingly sought from the spring of 1692. He urged William to drop his policy of offsetting Tory and Whig ministers in order to achieve a balanced ministry, and instead to swing the balance decisively in favour of the Whigs. Sunderland's scheme paid dividends in the parliamentary session of 1693–4. For, though the king had to accept the TRIENNIAL ACT (after vetoing such a bill the previous year) as the price of Whig cooperation, he also gave his assent to the bill creating the BANK OF ENGLAND. This Whig measure showed William that the party meant business when it claimed to support his war effort more wholeheartedly than did the Tories. But they began

to demand more ministerial posts as the price of their continued support, and this challenged Sunderland's control.

In 1696 these divisions in Whig ranks temporarily closed in response to the issues raised by the JACOBITE Sir John FENWICK. Fenwick, who had been implicated in a plot to assassinate William, accused members of the government of plotting to restore James II. Sunderland, whose loyalty to William was undoubted, conducted the government's answer to Fenwick's charges. But whereas Sunderland wanted Fenwick to be repudiated, the JUNTO that dominated the government wanted him to be eliminated. They introduced the bill of attainder against Fenwick that eventually resulted in his execution, a procedure that Sunderland opposed.

At that time Sunderland held no ministerial post, being regarded as a minister behind the curtain. In 1697, however, he was appointed to the office of lord chamberlain. His appointment was attacked in Parliament, where his role in the previous regime as an instrument of despotism was recalled. Sunderland panicked and resigned. However, he did not retire completely from politics, his advice being frequently given and occasionally sought, so that he was still thought of as a grey eminence behind the turbulent ministerial changes between 1698 and the death of William III. He himself died shortly after the accession of Queen Anne.

FURTHER READING J.P. Kenyon, *Robert Spencer, Second Earl of Sunderland* (1956).

Swift, Jonathan (1667–1745), clergyman, poet and satirist. Swift was born in Dublin and educated at Trinity College. On the outbreak of the Glorious Revolution in 1688 he went to live with his widowed mother in Leicester. Sir William Temple invited him to his house at Moor Park in Surrey to act as his private secretary. Swift spent the next ten years there, apart from a brief spell in Ireland to be ordained as an Anglican clergyman. He took up the living of Kilroot, but resigned it in 1696.

At Moor Park he met Esther Johnson, whom he immortalized as 'Stella'. The dispute as to whether or not they later married is still unresolved.

While in Temple's employ Swift also began to write poems and started his *Tale of a Tub*, although it was not published until 1704. This satire on what he described as 'the numerous and gross corruptions in religion and learning' was provoked by the great flood of what Swift regarded as heretical, irreligious and seditious literature released on the expiry of the Licensing Act in 1695. Together with the *Tale* Swift published 'an account of a Battle between the Ancient and Modern books in St James's library'. 'The Battle of the Books' was his contribution to the quarrel between his patron Temple and the Hon. Charles Boyle on one side, and Richard BENTLEY and William Wotton on the other, over the relative merits of classical and contemporary authors (*see* BATTLE OF THE BOOKS). In Swift's mock epic, books by Homer, Plato and Aristotle rout works by modern writers such as Descartes, Bentley and Wotton.

When Temple died in 1699, Swift again went to Ireland to seek preferment, becoming vicar of Laracor and prebendary of St Patrick's Cathedral, Dublin. In 1701 he published his first political tract, *The Contests and Dissensions of the Nobles and Commons in Athens and Rome*, which took the side of the Whig peers then being impeached by the Tory House of Commons in England. Thus his entry into politics was on the Whig side. He hoped to get favours from the Whigs, and in 1707 went to England to try to negotiate the extension of QUEEN ANNE'S BOUNTY to the clergy of the Church of Ireland. The Whig ministers, however, would only approve of the scheme if the Irish Anglicans agreed to the repeal of the Test Act passed by the Dublin Parliament in 1704. Since this act barred DISSENTERS from office in Ireland, Swift, a HIGH-CHURCH Anglican, refused to accept these terms and wrote a pamphlet defending the Test. He therefore failed to get the concession while the Whigs were in power.

When the Whigs were replaced by a Tory government led by Robert HARLEY in 1710, however, Swift found a much more sympathetic response to his request, which was granted in 1711. His rapport with the Harley ministry was such that he became its chief propagandist. Thus he contributed to the *Examiner* between 1710 and 1711. In it he voiced the passions and prejudices of the Tories: their devotion to the Church of England and hatred of dissenters; their conviction that the Whigs had deliberately prolonged the War of the SPANISH SUCCESSION for their own ends; and their suspicions of foreigners that verged on xenophobia. Swift played on these themes not only in the *Examiner* but also in *The Conduct of the Allies*, which appeared in November 1711.

Swift's favour in high places ought to have obtained for him a comfortable living in England. But he was not favoured in the highest place, for Queen Anne took against him. Anne disliked the *Tale of a Tub*, but was infuriated by a poem, *The Windsor Prophecy*, which attacked her favourite the duchess of Somerset. Thwarted by 'the royal prude' as Swift called her, all that his ministerial friends were able to obtain for him was the deanery of St Patrick's, Dublin, in 1713.

In the last year of Anne's reign Swift found himself torn between Harley, now earl of Oxford, and his rival BOLINGBROKE. By then their rivalry reflected the torment of the Tories as they contemplated their prospects when the queen died. The future George I had made no secret of his dislike of their negotiation of the treaty of UTRECHT, and leaned towards the Whigs. Oxford was a staunch Hanoverian, while Bolingbroke was prepared to consider the possibility of a restoration of the Stuarts. Swift like Oxford was never a JACOBITE, and the option of restoring the Old Pretender – James Francis Edward STUART – was ruled out. But whereas the prime minister seemed incapable of decisive action to try to ensure that the Tory party would be a force to be reckoned with in the new reign, Bolingbroke proposed measures to consolidate its natural majority, and to undermine the Whigs by filling all post with Tories.

Swift, frustrated by Oxford's moderation, was swept along by Bolingbroke's visionary schemes. Anne's death in the summer of 1714, however, scotched both their prospects. Swift fled the Whig vengeance by moving to Ireland, arriving in Dublin before George I landed in London. Apart from brief visits to England in 1726 and 1727 for the publication of *Gulliver's Travels* he spent the rest of his life in Ireland.

For a while Swift lay low until the storm against his English Tory friends subsided. By the 1720s, however, he felt that he could lift his head above the parapet, not as a Tory but as an Irish patriot. The issue that most roused his wrath was the patent given to William Wood in 1722 to supply Ireland with copper coins. Swift adopted the persona of a Dublin shopkeeper in the *Drapier's Letters*, which not only attacked WOOD'S HALFPENCE but questioned the whole basis of England's claim to govern Ireland. His bold stance on this issue, particularly in the fourth letter addressed to 'the whole people of Ireland', ensured for him the title of 'Irish patriot'. When Wood's patent was withdrawn in 1725, just a year after the publication of the first letter, Swift became a popular hero. A year later, when he came back to Ireland from England after delivering *Gulliver's Travels* to a London publisher, he was given an enthusiastic civic reception in Dublin.

Twelve months after that, when Swift made his last journey from England to his native country, the inhabitants of Ireland were less inclined to celebrate. On the contrary there was widespread famine, largely brought about – so Swift believed – through the refusal of the Irish to manage their economy efficiently. These views are implicit in his greatest and most biting satirical tract, *A Modest Proposal for preventing the children of the poor in Ireland from being burdensome, and for making them beneficial* (1729). Ostensibly this was a monstrous scheme to breed babies as delicacies for the tables of the wealthy.

Swift continued to write poems and pamphlets until he was incapacitated by a stroke in 1742. Then he was declared incapable of looking after himself, and had to be cared for by friends during the last sad three years of his life. He had suffered for many years from Menière's syndrome, or labyrinthine vertigo, a disease of the inner ear that made him dizzy. But he had never been mad, as legend still sometimes perversely has it. Then again, he had never been 'normal', as some even more perverse scholars claim. His writings show that he had many inner demons that made him a deeply disturbed man, but which also inspired works that are still in print. Undoubtedly the greatest of these is *Gulliver's Travels*, one of the most widely read books in the English language. Suitably expurgated it is a popular children's story. To contemporaries it was obviously a satire on party politics and a critique of Walpole's regime. At a more serious level it is a profoundly disturbing investigation of human nature. Swift challenged the definition of man as a rational creature, claiming he was only capable of reason. He was pessimistic about the ability of men to control their passions, and showed how they tended to be governed by all seven deadly sins.

FURTHER READING I. Ehrenpreis, *Swift: The Man, His Works, the Age* (3 vols., 1962–83).

T

Talbot, Charles, 1st duke of Shrewsbury. *See*
SHREWSBURY, CHARLES TALBOT, 1ST DUKE OF.

Talents, Ministry of All the. *See* MINISTRY OF
ALL THE TALENTS.

***Tatler,* the.** *See* STEELE, SIR RICHARD.

textiles. Woollen and worsted cloths dominated
English manufacturing through much of the 18th
century, only to be usurped by 'King Cotton' in
the era of the Napoleonic Wars. The ascendancy of
wool dated to medieval times; the stout broadcloth
of the Cotswolds was as English as roast beef itself,
and in 1776 Arthur YOUNG could still describe
woollen manufacture as 'the sacred staple and foundation of all our wealth'. Woollen textiles remained
Britain's major manufacturing industry in terms of
employment, output and exports until the opening decade of the 19th century; thenceforth, cotton
textiles rapidly assumed the crown of leading industry and export earner (*see* INDUSTRY).

The Georgian woollen industry was both
widely scattered and diversified, with products
ranging from high-quality serges to cheap 'ker-
sies'; it was also subject to internal competition
that often rendered the life of the weaver precarious. For example, over the course of the 18th century the long-established woollen industries of the
West Country were overtaken by East Anglia's
worsted products; that industry, which in the reign
of Queen Anne employed some 70,000 weavers,
was itself eclipsed after 1770, when it proved
incapable of competing with the cheaper cloths
produced in Yorkshire's West Riding. These developments fall within what economic historians have
identified as a broader tendency for manufacturing to forsake the southern and eastern regions for
the north and Midlands.

The cotton industry was the most affected by
changes in manufacturing techniques in the late
18th and early 19th centuries. The first major
change was in the spinning process, where mechanization enabled mass production of cotton yarn
for weaving. Where James Hargreaves's spinning
jenny could be used in the home, ARKWRIGHT's
water frames required to be accommodated in
mills, employing several hundred carders, rollers,
drawers and spinners. Later, the application of
steam power also necessitated the introduction of
the factory system. Despite improvements in hand-
loom weaving, such as John Kay's flying shuttle,
cloth making remained largely a domestic industry until Edmund CARTWRIGHT's power loom was
perfected and widely applied in the early 19th century. The result of these developments was a vast
increase in the import of raw cotton, principally
from the United States, a substantial fall in the

price of cotton goods and the eclipse of woollen cloth by cotton as England's main export.

Unlike the pioneers of the cotton industry, who were quick to harness contemporary innovations, the more conservative woollen manufacturers proved sluggish in their adoption of technological advances: John Kay's flying shuttle, which had been evolved in 1733, was initially applied only to the weaving of fustian – a mixture of cotton and linen – rather than woollens and worsteds. It was not until the 1780s that the spinning of worsteds was first mechanized using Richard Arkwright's water frame; wool-spinning followed in 1810 after the growing adoption of CROMPTON's mule. With the coming of mechanization, woollen manufacturing was increasingly concentrated in the West Riding. The factory system remained exceptional in the Georgian woollen industry; as late as 1830 most mills averaged less than 50 employees. Despite the slow pace of technological change, new machinery nonetheless sparked outbreaks of machine smashing; the cloth croppers whose livelihoods were menaced by such advances as the shearing frame were to prove dedicated adherents of 'King Ludd' (*see* LUDDITES).

Cotton textiles offer the prime example of the rapid transformation of manufacturing associated with the concept of 'industrial revolution'. From a position of little significance before the 1780s, within a generation cotton manufacturing became Britain's leading industry and major export earner, employing thousands in the factories of Lancashire. However, modern economic historians emphasize that cotton's contribution to Britain's economy should not be exaggerated; although spectacular, its growth stemmed from a very small base. Introduced into Britain from the Netherlands in Tudor times, by 1750 small-scale cotton manufacture was already established in areas where it would later dominate, particularly Lancashire and the west of Scotland. The fashionable and expensive cottons imported from India were imitated in cheaper cotton mixtures. Before the shift to factory production, the fledgling cotton industry could there-fore already draw upon an experienced labour force and established business contacts. The burgeoning cotton industry is intimately linked to the rise of the factory system, with social consequences evoked in William BLAKE's memorable condemnation of 'dark satanic mills'. In 1774 Arkwright's cotton factories in Nottingham and Cromford already employed some 600 workers – many of them cheap child labourers; within a decade, Arkwright's own establishments and those of others using his machinery were propagating the classic factory concept whereby varied production processes were concentrated in one building and relied upon a single source of power. Before the end of the Napoleonic Wars, the workers in Britain's cotton factories already numbered 100,000.

theatre. On the evening of 10 January 1763, James BOSWELL joined the expectant audience at Drury Lane Theatre. From his bench in the 'pit' Boswell soon fell under the spell of the great actor-manager David GARRICK in a performance of Shakespeare's *Henry IV: Part Two*. Boswell recorded in his journal how 'the pathetic scene between the old King and his son drew tears from my eyes'. The main attraction was followed by James Love's pantomime *The Witches*: this lighter fare was less to Boswell's taste, being 'but a dull thing'.

Boswell's laconic entry says much about the mid-Georgian theatre: it reveals the impact of Garrick's naturalistic approach to acting, his revival of classic works from the past, and the common practice of including a brief farce, masque, pantomime or 'entertainment' after the main drama. Boswell's choice of a seat in the 'pit' represented a compromise between the cheaper galleries and the more expensive boxes; places in the gallery or pit could not be reserved, but had to be claimed by physical occupation when the theatre doors opened. In an age in which queueing was an alien concept, scuffles and injuries were common as theatre-goers struggled to secure the prime seats. As a result of Garrick's theatrical reforms, from 1763 onwards wealthy patrons no longer occupied boxes on the stage itself; as can be seen in Hogarth's paintings of John GAY's *The Beggar's Opera* of 1728–9, such spectators could crowd in upon the players themselves.

Gay's satirical ballad-opera remained the runaway success of the 18th-century stage, and its reliance upon song indicates the central importance of music to the Georgian theatre. Performances did not begin until two hours after the doors had opened, so the orchestra played a crucial role in pacifying restless audiences. In addition, as Boswell's outing reveals, theatrical evenings typically offered a varied programme of full-length plays and shorter musical 'entertainments'. Indeed, many members of the audience were more interested in seeing the 'after-piece' than the main drama. In consequence it was customary to offer half-price seats towards the end of the play for the benefit of these latecomers. When an effort was made to abolish 'second price' in January 1763, the audience vented its outrage by wrecking benches and chandeliers. Boswell was otherwise engaged on the night in question, but the incident was by no means isolated: in 18th-century England 'audience participation' often went beyond mere applause or heckling. It was not for nothing that the stage was fortified with a forbidding row of iron spikes. Physical invasion of the stage was just one way in which an audience could register disapproval of a performance; sometimes hostile crowds 'damned' new plays into oblivion by shouting down the efforts of managers and actors to announce further performances.

Just as the accession of the Hanoverians had seen musical performance shift away from the restricted circles of the court towards a 'popular' audience in both London and the provinces, so the same trend was apparent in the theatre. In addition, the bawdy and cynical Restoration comedies that had delighted Charles II and his clique of courtiers had little relevance for a very different Georgian audience. During much of the 18th century drama was overwhelmingly concerned with sentimental and moral themes calculated to appeal

to the emerging middle class. Playwrights were obliged to cater carefully for such tastes: GOLD-SMITH's *She Stoops to Conquer* (1773) and SHERIDAN's *The School for Scandal* (1777) represented a more spirited reaction to such bland and formulaic offerings, although even authors capable of creating such witty social comedies attracted accusations of vulgarity. Popular expectations could not be ignored, and revived classics were altered to suit prevailing tastes: Shakespeare's *King Lear* was given a happy ending in line with audience expectations. (*See also* DRAMA.)

In Boswell's day, Drury Lane was one of just two London theatres possessing royal patents to stage spoken drama; the other was Covent Garden. Musical performances were given at the Royal Opera House in the Haymarket. In marked contrast to the press, the Georgian theatre became subject to rigorous government regulation and censorship. This crackdown on culture was a reaction to the widespread independence that the theatre had acquired during the opening decades of the 18th century. Plays frequently carried a scurrilous political message: *The Beggar's Opera* itself was widely interpreted as a thinly disguised attack upon the regime of Robert WALPOLE, while other critics believed it to glamorize crime. Indeed, Gay's sequel *Polly* was banned by the lord chamberlain. Concern about the baleful influence of the theatre mounted in the 1730s. Henry FIELDING's ballad drama, *The Welsh Opera, or the Grey Mare the Better Horse*, which was staged at the Haymarket Theatre in 1731, attacked ministry and opposition alike; other works in similar vein eroded sympathy for the theatre and eventually provoked a draconian response.

Legislation to outlaw all plays not licensed by the lord chamberlain gained royal assent on 21 June 1737. Besides confirming the monopoly of the two patent theatres, the Licensing Act authorized the lord chamberlain to act as censor, and decreed that the smaller unlicensed theatres were illegal. Actors operating outside the licensed theatres could now be regarded as vagabonds and punished accordingly. The act fell heavily upon informal companies of wandering players: Hogarth's print *Strolling Actresses in a Barn* (1738) shows one such band assembled together 'for the last time of acting before the Act commences'. Outside London, the act effectively rendered all theatre illegal, although it failed to stop regular performances in the provinces and the construction of theatres in many towns and cities. Old established centres already had theatres that could be licensed under the act, but the growing industrial towns were obliged to gain special acts of Parliament before they could establish them. This could lead to protracted wrangling with pressure groups who believed that the theatre posed a threat to morals and deflected the 'lower orders' from work. Even such fashionable resorts as BATH, which attracted wealthy Londoners who expected theatrical entertainment, could face problems in catering for their needs. The city's original theatre was closed down on religious grounds, to be replaced by a stop-gap establishment within one of the assembly rooms. Bath only acquired a purpose-built theatre in 1749; it was there that Sarah SIDDONS recovered her nerve after her disastrous debut at Drury Lane, while the city also formed the backdrop for Sheridan's 1775 dramatic hit *The Rivals*. The growth of theatre outside the metropolis was recognized by the 1788 Enabling Act, which gave local magistrates the power to issue licences for performances. By 1800 theatre was flourishing throughout the provinces.

In London the patent holders clung on to their monopolies throughout the Georgian era. With no new theatres opening, increasing public demand was instead met by a dramatic expansion of existing venues: by the 1790s, Covent Garden had more than doubled its capacity to 3000. Not everyone approved of the cavernous new theatres, and their daunting size has been seen as contributing to the development of the melodramatic and declamatory style of acting that Mrs Siddons made her own. Between June and September the patent companies toured the provinces; in their absence, the London audience patronized such suburban theatres as Sadler's Wells. Although banned from presenting straight drama under the Licensing Act, such establishments catered for popular tastes by offering dances, comic ballets, musical pieces, harlequinades and circus-type acts. By the closing decades of the century, many unconventional acts had penetrated the portals of the patent theatres. For example, in 1789 the legendary boxer Daniel Mendoza graced the stage at Covent Garden during an interlude in the pantomime *Aladdin*; his pugilistic display was mounted in response to the demands of 'many persons of distinction'. Through such sheer variety of performance, the late Georgian theatre increasingly anticipated the attractions of the Victorian music hall.

FURTHER READING J. Brewer, *The Pleasures of the Imagination: English Culture in the 18th Century* (1997); R.D. Hume (ed.), *The London Theatre World 1660–1800* (1989).

Thelwall, John (1764–1834), radical. Thelwall was born in London and grew up in the capital, where he turned to radical politics after the outbreak of the FRENCH REVOLUTION. His tract *Politics for the People* (1793) brought him to the attention of the authorities, the printer being prosecuted for publishing seditious literature. As a member of the London Corresponding Society (*see* CORRESPONDING SOCIETIES) Thelwall was indicted along with Thomas Hardy and HORNE TOOKE for treason, and like them was acquitted. Thereafter he became an itinerant lecturer, overcoming his stammer to deliver passionate harangues against Pitt's government. He also wrote poetry, and became acquainted with Coleridge and Wordsworth. By 1800 he had abandoned politics and devoted himself to promoting the cure of speech impediments such as he himself had overcome.

Thomson, James (1700–1748), poet. Thomson was born in the Scottish Borders and attended Jedburgh Abbey school and Edinburgh University. In

1725 he went to London where he published his poem 'Winter' the following year. Its success encouraged him to add 'Summer' in 1727, 'Spring' in 1728, and in 1730, with the addition of 'Autumn', he completed *The Seasons*. He continued to make changes to these poems until the final version appeared in 1746.

The success of Thomson's poems was due to his evocation of natural phenomena exerting an influence on human activity. Thus the opening lines of 'Winter' depict how the season 'comes to rule the varied year ... with all his varied train, vapours, and clouds, and storms ... that exalt the soul to solemn thought, and heavenly musings'. Such sentiments have been seen as an anticipation of Romanticism. But the anthropomorphic device of personifying the inanimate was an Augustan conceit, rather like Johnson's 'Let Observation with extensive view survey mankind'. It did not foreshadow Romantic pantheism. On the contrary Thomson's last poem, *The Castle of Indolence*, published in 1748, was often castigated by the Romantics for its elevation of industry over imagination. Indolence was a wizard who enchanted visitors to his castle, situated in 'a fairy land'. There they were lulled into deep sleep, to be awakened by the Knight of Industry.

Thomson was a Whig who advocated commercial activity to promote economic growth. In 1727 Sir Robert WALPOLE gave him £50 for dedicating to him his *Poem sacred to the memory of Sir Isaac Newton*. Two years later, for reasons that remain obscure, he attacked the ministry in *Britannia*, which warned of LUXURY eating out the heart of Liberty and narrow selfishness 'sapping the very frame of government' until 'the whole state of broad corruption sinks'. Thomson was ideologically more inclined to the COUNTRY than to the court. In *The Seasons* he contrasted

> The happiest he! who far from public rage
> Deep in the vale, with a choice few retired
> Drinks the pure pleasures of the rural life

with courtiers who

> Wreathe the deep brow, diffuse the lying smile,
> And tread the weary labyrinth of State.

His poem *Liberty* (1736) encapsulated the Country ideology in verse. In 1737 he joined the group of 'patriots' round FREDERICK PRINCE OF WALES, who had gone over to the opposition. His 'Rule Britannia', first performed in 1740, became their anthem. It was written for a patriotic play *Alfred*, one of several that he wrote against the Court. His *Edward and Eleanora* was regarded as so offensive that the lord chamberlain banned its production. After Walpole's fall Thomson was rewarded with the post of surveyor general of the Leeward Islands. He never went there, living in Richmond from 1736 until his death.

FURTHER READING J. Sambrook, *James Thomson 1700–1748: A Life* (1991).

Thornhill, James (1675–1734), England's leading decorative painter of the early 18th century, who employed his talents to brighten the vast BAROQUE mansions of VANBRUGH and his rivals.

Thornhill was born in Dorset, but his spendthrift father sent him to London where he trained under his relative, the king's sergeant-painter, Thomas Highmore. The youthful Thornhill demonstrated precocious gifts, and was greatly influenced by a European tour that gave him access to works by some of the most acclaimed artists of the era. Upon returning to England Thornhill produced decorative paintings that won the admiration of Queen Anne, and her patronage brought commissions at Hampton Court and Windsor Castle. After the completion of the dome of St Paul's Cathedral, Thornhill was chosen to decorate its interior. Sir Christopher WREN had opposed the plan as unsuited to his structure, and Thornhill's capable designs featuring scenes from the life of St Paul were indeed rendered insignificant by the sheer scale of the dome.

Although his skills were in great demand, relatively little of Thornhill's decorative work remains today: such large-scale mural paintings were especially vulnerable to decay or replacement as they fell out of fashion. Survivals include the paintings at Greenwich Hospital that occupied Thornhill over two decades. Besides the decorative painting that dominated his output, Thornhill also executed competent portraits of prominent figures including Sir Isaac NEWTON. In 1720 Thornhill succeeded Highmore as sergeant-painter to the king, and soon after became the first native painter to receive a knighthood.

Thornhill was among the earliest proponents of an academy to encourage British artists. Although Thornhill's own efforts to establish such a school proved stillborn, this quest was inherited by his son-in-law William HOGARTH, who established an academy of his own in St Martin's Lane. As one of the most celebrated artists of his age, Thornhill's abilities permitted him to redeem the family seat in Dorset that had been lost through his father's extravagance.

Ticonderoga, strategic fort in what is now New York state. Built on a peninsula guarding the crucial waterway connecting the Hudson and St Lawrence rivers, the fort became a key objective during the American wars of the later 18th century.

The site was first fortified by the French in the autumn of 1755, the year before the official outbreak of the SEVEN YEARS WAR, when hostilities had already erupted between the French and the British in North America. Named Carillon, the fort was situated between Lakes George and Champlain in the no-man's-land dividing Canada from the colony of New York. Originally constructed of logs and earth, it was subsequently rebuilt in stone. During the summer of 1758 a large force under Major General James Abercromby tried to storm Carillon's outer defences, but was rebuffed with heavy casualties by troops commanded by the marquis de Montcalm. In the following year when AMHERST began methodical siege operations the French withdrew after detonating the powder magazine. Amherst rebuilt the fort and renamed it Ticonderoga.

When the AMERICAN WAR OF INDEPENDENCE broke out Ticonderoga became a strategic priority for both sides. In May 1775 the British garrison fell to a surprise attack by Ethan Allen and Benedict Arnold, so providing the rebel cause with an early morale-boosting victory. The fort was recaptured by BURGOYNE in July 1777 during his advance from Canada. News of the fort's fall caused a delighted George III to exclaim: 'I have beat them! I have beat the Americans!' The king's celebrations proved premature; Burgoyne marched on to disaster at SARATOGA, and Ticonderoga was ultimately restored to the victorious republic. It fell into ruin in the early 19th century, but has since been reconstructed as a tourist attraction.

Tindal, Matthew. *See* DEISM.

Toland, John. *See* DEISM.

Toleration Act (1689), statute that allowed Protestant DISSENTERS who believed in the Trinity to worship separately from the established Church of England in licensed meeting houses, and to conduct schools. This was a much less generous measure than James II's Declarations of Indulgence, which had extended toleration to Catholics. It also specifically upheld the Corporation and Test Acts requiring office holders in boroughs or under the crown to take communion in the Anglican church, as well as the duty of non-Anglicans to pay tithes to maintain the ministers of the established church. It was nevertheless a real relief from persecution for nonconformists. In practice its scope was much wider than its stated purpose. No unitarian was prosecuted for breach of the Toleration Act in the 18th century, while the duty of attending church or chapel remained unenforceable.

Tone, (Theobald) Wolfe (1763–98), Irish patriot. Despite his niche in Irish republican iconography as a martyr to the armed struggle for independence during the IRISH REBELLION OF 1798, Tone originally sought change through constitutional methods.

Born into a middle-class Protestant family, Tone was educated at Trinity College, Dublin, and trained as a lawyer. Tone quickly became concerned with the cause of Catholic relief, and spread his views through his influential *Argument on Behalf of the Catholics of Ireland*, published in 1791. Tone was closely linked with the emergence of the radical and non-sectarian United Irishmen, originally based in Dublin and Belfast. In the early 1790s Tone's views became increasingly militant. He believed that Ireland's political ills could only be cured if his countrymen ignored their religious differences and concentrated upon severing the connection with Britain.

By 1795 Tone had become a marked man and was forced into exile in the United States of America. He subsequently served as the United Irish emissary to the revolutionary regime in France and proved himself a highly effective advocate of military assistance for Irish republicanism. It was largely owing to Tone's pleading that a major invasion flotilla reached Bantry Bay in 1796, only to be dispersed by storms. The death of the great revolutionary commander General Hoche in 1797 robbed Tone of his most influential ally in Paris. Bonaparte preferred to damage Britain by striking at Egypt rather than Ireland (*see* REVOLUTIONARY AND NAPOLEONIC WARS). However, further French forces were despatched to Ireland in 1798; General Humbert's veterans actually landed and routed government troops at Castlebar, but proved too late to change the course of that summer's bloody rebellion.

Tone was finally captured by the Royal Navy while participating in another French expedition to Lough Swilly in Donegal in October 1798. He was convicted of treason by court martial and sentenced to hang. Rather than undergo the ignominy of public execution, Tone cut his own throat with a penknife. Although relatively unknown in his own lifetime compared with other leaders of the 1798 rebellion, Tone was subsequently elevated

to the ranks of Ireland's revolutionary heroes. **FURTHER READING** M. Elliot, *Wolfe Tone; Prophet of Irish Independence* (1987).

Tooke, John Horne. *See* HORNE TOOKE, JOHN.

Tories, one of the two main political PARTIES of the 18th century. 'Tory' was a name first given to Catholic bandits in Ireland, and was applied by their opponents to the supporters of Charles II in the Exclusion crisis. The implication that they were Catholic sympathizers because of their support of the right of the king's Catholic brother to succeed was a libel. They were in fact staunch Anglicans, and committed to the doctrines of the Church of England. These included the notion of indefeasible hereditary right and the principle of passive obedience and non-resistance to the sovereign power.

When James II made incompatible demands on their loyalties to crown and church most Tories chose the latter, albeit with guilty consciences, and acquiesced in the GLORIOUS REVOLUTION of 1688. Those who could not accept the abandonment of the hereditary principle became JACOBITES. The extent of Jacobitism among the Tories is impossible to gauge accurately, which makes it hard to substantiate claims that it was widespread. That Jacobitism did appeal to many Tories cannot be denied – but that a majority were seeking to restore the direct Stuart line can. Had the Old Pretender, James Francis Edward STUART – the so-called James III – renounced Catholicism and become an Anglican things might have been very different. Most Tories showed where their first allegiance lay by not joining in the JACOBITE RISINGS of 1715 and 1745.

The Tories' defence of the church led them to oppose any erosion of its rights and privileges by DISSENTERS, a stance adopted most vigorously by their champion Henry SACHEVERELL. Thus they abhorred the practice of occasional conformity and in Anne's reign vigorously supported the OCCASIONAL CONFORMITY ACT. They also pressed for the SCHISM ACT of 1714. These measures were passed in the last four years of Anne's reign when they had a majority in the House of Commons. Under the early Hanoverians they were condemned to be a permanent minority in Parliament and these Acts were repealed. Tories were also denied office in national or local government until the 1740s. After Walpole's fall, however, the proscription was lifted. Tories joined in the 'BROAD-BOTTOM ADMINISTRATION' and in the counties were admitted into the commissions of the peace. By the accession of George III the ideological distinctions between Tories and Whigs had virtually disappeared, and even the name 'Tory' was used mainly by opposition Whigs as a pejorative term to describe such ministers as Lord NORTH and the younger PITT, who repudiated it. It was not until the 1820s that self-styled Tories were again in power.

towns. The extent of urbanization in the 18th century, and the degree to which it expanded during that period, is difficult to measure. This is because historians disagree about what actually constitutes a 'town'. Contemporaries clearly used the term to describe communities that would today be considered mere villages. There have been attempts to distinguish between agricultural villages and towns with more complex economies by analysing the occupations of their inhabitants. But this still begs the question of size, and some historians have arrived at a minimum population of 2500 as the basic criterion of a town; while others believe that a population of at least 5000 is necessary to qualify for town status.

By 1700, some 67 English towns possessed populations of more than 2500; about half of these topped the 5000 mark. The biggest by far was LONDON, a giant with more than 500,000 inhabitants – about 10% of England's total population. At this time, no other English town could count its population in six figures. Next in rank below the capital were Norwich and BRISTOL, numbering about 30,000 and 20,000 respectively. Another four urban centres (Newcastle, Exeter, York and Great Yarmouth) boasted populations of between 10,000 and 16,000.

In 1801 the number of urban centres with populations in excess of 2500 had risen to 187. In addition, there were now no fewer than 27 towns with populations of 15,000 or more. Whilst London maintained the clear lead that it had demonstrated a century before, and continued to absorb the same proportion of the country's population, its three nearest rivals were now MANCHESTER, LIVERPOOL and BIRMINGHAM. This reflected a major shift in the urban population from the south to the industrial cities of the north and Midlands.

Whereas in 1700 approximately one in six of the total population lived in towns of at least 2500 inhabitants, a century later the ratio had changed to about one in three. Urban growth took various forms. Many older county towns became centres for the local gentry, who stimulated LUXURY trades and devoted themselves to concerts, balls and HORSE RACING. Such leisure activities supplied towns with ASSEMBLY ROOMS, racecourses and theatres, providing amenities for affluent visitors, while some local gentry also built themselves town houses. This gave towns such as BATH, Beverley, Bury St Edmunds, Northampton, Preston, Shrewsbury, Warwick, Winchester and York a core of 18th-century buildings, which are among their more striking visible remains of the past.

In other towns commerce and industry rather than leisure stimulated urban growth. For a brief spell in the 18th century Whitehaven enjoyed prosperity due to overseas trade, and its surviving stock of Georgian architecture rivals that of more celebrated towns. As the pattern of urban growth already noted above indicates, manufacturing also stimulated expansion. The poet John Dyer observed in *The Fleece* (1757): 'Th'increasing walls of busy Manchester, Sheffield and Birmingham whose redd'ning fields / Rise and enlarge their suburbs.' Dyer was drawing attention to burgeoning manufacturing areas such as the metalworking districts of the Midlands and south Yorkshire and the textile towns of Lancashire and the West Riding of Yorkshire.

The rapid expansion of such industrial centres

was fuelled by steady immigration from elsewhere in Britain. This influx of humanity led to overcrowding, with poor workers accommodated within damp cellars and 'back to back' housing. Advances in sanitation failed to cope with booming urban populations, resulting in high mortality from illness. In many urban slums, clean water supplies and sewage removal facilities remained inadequate into the 20th century.

FURTHER READING P. Borsay, *The English Urban Renaissance* (1989); R. Sweet, *The English Town 1680–1840. Government, Society and Culture* (1999).

Townshend, Charles, 2nd Viscount (1674–1738), Whig politician. Townshend was brother-in-law to Sir Robert WALPOLE, whose sister Dorothy ('Dolly') he married in 1713. The two worked together in local and national politics, both serving in the Whig administration of 1708–10. Thus Charles was employed in negotiating the Barrier Treaty of 1709 (*see* BARRIER FORTRESSES). Both went into opposition in the last four years of Queen Anne's reign, to be rewarded with office at the accession of George I, Townshead becoming SEC-RETARY OF STATE for the north. When the Whig schism occurred in 1717 it was largely brought about through rivalry between Townshend and Walpole on the one hand and Earl STANHOPE and the 3rd earl of SUNDERLAND on the other. The dispute was over the degree to which George I showed a preference for the interests of the Electorate of Hanover in his foreign policy, with Townshend and Walpole objecting that he did, and Stanhope and Sunderland supporting the king. One sure sign that the king sided with the latter was shown when Townshend was transferred to the post of lord lieutenant of Ireland in 1716. After a short spell in Dublin he resigned and joined Walpole in opposition to the Stanhope ministry. Their unscrupulous tactics in allying with Tories to discomfort the ministry paid dividends, especially in their successful attack on the Peerage Bill (*see* LORDS, HOUSE OF). They exploited their nuisance

value until the king agreed to take them back into office in 1720, Townshend becoming president of the council. When Stanhope died the following year he became secretary of state for the second time. Until 1724 he was the junior secretary to CARTERET. When Carteret was sent to Dublin as lord lieutenant of Ireland, however, and was replaced by the duke of NEWCASTLE as secretary, Townshend became the senior. He was therefore mainly responsible for foreign policy for the rest of the 1720s.

In 1725 the diplomatic pattern of Europe, which had been settled since the treaty of UTRECHT of 1713, was seriously disturbed when the king of Spain, a Bourbon, and the Holy Roman emperor, a Habsburg, were reconciled in the treaty of Vienna. Until then, the main threat to European peace had been the possibility of hostilities between these two powers. Now peace appeared to be precarious, with the possibility that they would combine against the other major powers in Europe. They seemed above all to threaten Britain, since the Spanish king, Philip V, granted trading concessions to an East India Company based at Ostend in the Austrian Netherlands, a territory under the control of the emperor. This appeared to challenge the British EAST INDIA COMPANY. In return, Emperor Charles VI agreed to help Spain to retake Gibraltar and Minorca from the British. Townshend's response to the treaty of Vienna was to isolate the empire by constructing a system of alliances, starting with the treaty of Hanover in 1725 between Britain, Hanover, France and Prussia, and eventually involving the Dutch, the Swedes and the Danes. The treaty shocked Walpole, however, because of the costly commitments which Townshend had made to the allies. Among them was an agreement that Britain should take 12,000 Hanoverian troops into its pay. The threat of war with Spain forced Walpole to increase the land tax to the maximum rate of four shillings in the pound for the first time since becoming prime minister. Townshend's foreign policy, therefore, produced serious friction between the two. Walpole had previously left foreign affairs to his brother-in-law; now he decided to take the initiative in foreign policy. His solution to the threat to peace was not to isolate the empire but to buy off Spain. In 1729, therefore, he negotiated the treaty of Seville behind Townshend's back. The secretary took umbrage at this, and resigned in May 1730. As the prime minister put it, 'as long as the firm of the house was Townshend and Walpole the utmost harmony prevailed; but it no sooner became Walpole and Townshend than things went wrong.' After his resignation he retired from politics to became celebrated as 'Turnip Townshend' for his interest in AGRICULTURE.

FURTHER READING S. Wade Martins, *'Turnip' Townshend. Statesman and Farmer* (1990).

Townshend, Charles (1725–67), politician. Townshend was the son of the 3rd viscount, who brought him up after the age of 15 when he separated from his wife. After studying at the universities of Cambridge and Leiden, and at Lincoln's Inn, he entered Parliament in 1747 as a member for Great Yarmouth. His advancement as a Whig supporter of the court with family connections to the leading ministers was assured. On becoming president of the BOARD OF TRADE in 1748, the 2nd earl of HALIFAX appointed Townshend to serve on it with him. During his time on the Board he acquired considerable knowledge of the American colonies. In 1754 he was moved to the Admiralty Board, but resigned in 1755 and went into opposition, where he attached himself to the elder PITT. Pitt obtained for him the post of treasurer of the chamber when he formed his own administration. In 1759 there was talk of promoting him to the chancellorship of the exchequer, but the duke of NEWCASTLE came out against it, saying 'there is no depending on him, and his character will not go down in the City or anywhere else'. Townshend had acquired a reputation for emotional volatility and a flamboyant debating style. His renown as a speaker led the Select Society in Edinburgh to disregard its own rules and elect him as a member so

that he could address it when visiting Scotland in 1758. Townshend stayed in office when Pitt resigned in 1761, becoming secretary at war. The following year he was made president of the Board of Trade, but his volatile temperament became increasingly erratic and he spoke against the ministry of George GRENVILLE, of which he was a member. Though he resigned his post on the Board of Trade, Grenville retained his services despite his unreliability in debate, appointing him as paymaster general, a position he held through Lord ROCKINGHAM's first administration.

When Pitt, now earl of Chatham, formed a ministry in 1766 he appointed his old follower to the chancellorship of the exchequer. It was in this role that he introduced the ill-fated 'Townshend duties' on imports into the colonies of tea, glass, lead, paint and paper in 1767. His immediate justification was that he needed to raise revenue urgently since his proposal to keep the land tax at four shillings in the pound had been defeated, the rate being reduced to three shillings. He also felt that American objections to the STAMP ACT had been due to its being a direct tax, whereas the colonists had indicated that they accepted indirect taxes on trade. Townshend's insistance on this distinction was unfortunate, since the dispute had gone beyond the right to tax to the issue of sovereignty, but he was also implementing a policy which had been devised by Halifax at the Board of Trade, of which he had been a member of in the early 1750s. The onset of the SEVEN YEARS WAR had frustrated the Board's intentions at the time, but now, as Chancellor, Townshend was in a position to realize them. He died suddenly, however, before the fateful reactions to his duties could be ascertained.

Townshend will always be remembered as the original 'Champagne Charlie' for a speech he made in the Commons shortly before introducing his duties. Delivered after drinking copious quantities of champagne, it was by all accounts one of the most brilliant, if incoherent, speeches ever made in Parliament.

FURTHER READING C.P. Forster, *The Uncontrolled Chancellor: Charles Townshend and His American Policy* (1978).

trade. *See* COMMERCE; EMPIRE; NAVIGATION ACTS; SLAVE TRADE; SMITH, ADAM.

Trafalgar, battle of (21 October 1805), decisive British naval victory during the REVOLUTIONARY AND NAPOLEONIC WARS that ended Napoleon's plans to invade Britain. NELSON's great triumph over the combined French and Spanish fleet off Cape Trafalgar in southwest Spain represented a classic encounter of the age of sail.

Goaded by Napoleon's jibes about his caution, the French Admiral Villeneuve left the safety of Cadiz on 20 October commanding 33 ships of the line and 7 smaller vessels. Nelson waited to intercept the combined Franco-Spanish fleet with 27 line vessels and 4 frigates: 'the Nelson touch' envisaged an attack in two parallel columns aimed at the centre and rear of the enemy line. Nelson in the *Victory* would lead the windward column, while his devoted friend COLLINGWOOD led the leeward squadron. As the rival fleets drew closer Nelson hoisted his famous signal 'England expects every man to do his duty.' The message reflected the confident mood of the British fleet. In contrast, the pessimistic Villeneuve knew only too well that his own crews had spent months confined in harbour and were poorly trained by the standards of the Royal Navy.

The battle commenced at noon on the 21st when Collingwood's *Royal Sovereign* engaged the Spanish three-decker *Santa Ana*. Nelson's *Victory* soon joined the action and a fierce close-range encounter ensued. Despite their inexperience the Franco-Spanish crews fought bravely. After more than an hour of fighting Nelson was felled by a sharpshooter aboard the French *Redoutable*; taken below, he died later that afternoon. Nelson lived long enough to learn the outcome of his decisive victory. Fifteen enemy vessels had surrendered, while the British lost not a single ship. The clash resulted in thousands of killed and wounded, and many others drowned during the week of gales that followed the battle. Casualties ultimately included Villeneuve, who was captured aboard his flagship *Bucentaure*: upon returning to France in 1806 he committed suicide. In Britain celebration of a great victory was balanced by the news of Nelson's death. As Collingwood predicted in his dispatch to the Admiralty, Nelson's name would 'be immortal and his memory ever dear to his country'.

transport. *See* CANALS; ROADS.

transportation, system of punishment for convicted felons, who were shipped in their thousands to the American colonies, and, after the loss of those territories, to AUSTRALIA. The system evolved in response to the limitations of Britain's existing criminal code. During the early 18th century, sentencing judges had little choice between the ultimate penalty of execution, or the contrasting sanction of discharge following a short, sharp dose of corporal punishment. There was plainly a need to vary the repertoire of retribution. Transportation offered just such a compromise measure against those criminals who boasted insufficient notoriety to warrant the hangman's noose, but who remained too dangerous to be released into society unpunished.

Enforced exile had initially been employed to rid the state of political undesirables: for example, Scottish royalists captured during the Third Civil War and West Country dissidents rounded up in the wake of the Monmouth Rebellion of 1685 had been despatched to toil amidst the tobacco and cane plantations of England's unhealthy Caribbean possessions. However, during the 18th century, transportation was increasingly employed as a punishment for a broad range of criminal offences, overtaking whipping and branding as Britain's leading mode of 'secondary' punishment.

The 1718 Transportation Act empowered courts to send convicts overseas as indentured labourers. The terms imposed ranged from 7 to 14 years depending upon the seriousness of the offence. Under the act, premature return from exile would warrant a further period of transportation, or, in the case of those banished for the most serious offences, death. The rapid adoption of large-scale transportation had a dramatic impact upon patterns of sentencing. The force of the law now fell more heavily upon those petty criminals who would previously have escaped with lesser punishments, while mitigating the worst excesses of the 'BLOODY CODE'. For example, between 1736 and 1753 some 179 men and women in Surrey were sentenced to death for offences against property; 100 of these cases were commuted to transportation. Owing to the spread of transportation, the death penalty was increasingly restricted to those crimes regarded with particular horror – murder, highway robbery, horse theft and burglary.

For the merchants appointed as government agents to handle the transportation of felons, the system could yield handsome profits. However, transportation faced criticism on several counts. Many felons, especially those with gang connections, returned before their allotted time, and as such criminals often faced death if apprehended they had little to lose by committing further serious offences. Some opponents of transportation doubted whether it represented a deterrent to criminals; after all, free passage to the booming colonies might be viewed as a desirable consequence of conviction. Other critics believed that the system drained dwindling manpower and encouraged poverty and crime by robbing families of their fathers and principal breadwinners.

Understandably enough, the most vociferous opposition to transportation came from the American colonists who were obliged to absorb Britain's undesirables. Attempts to halt the practice had predated the Transportation Act, and in the early 1730s Virginia made an unsuccessful bid to prevent the settlement of transported felons who had completed their stints of servitude. Colonial newspapers blamed British felons for transferring their unwanted skills from the Old World to the New. In 1751 the *Virginia Gazette* complained about a crime wave in the colony, caused by 'the most audacious robberies, the most cruel murders, and infinite other villainies perpetrated by convicts transported from Europe'. The newspaper proceeded to castigate the British authorities for allowing such unwholesome exports: 'Thou art called our Mother Country, but what good mother ever sent thieves and villains to accompany her children. In what can Britain show a more sovereign contempt for us than by emptying their jails into our settlements, unless they would likewise empty their privies onto our tables?' Benjamin Franklin urged his countrymen to retaliate against the transportation system by sending the British consignments of American rattlesnakes.

American desires to end the influx of old-country convicts were realized in 1775 at the outbreak of war with Britain. The rupture of Britain's Atlantic empire obliged the authorities to consider the alternatives to transportation. Large numbers of minor felons were crammed within floating prison 'hulks' moored on the Thames at Woolwich, but the hulks proved an unsatisfactory substitute. It was the need to find a viable replacement for America as a destination for transportees that encouraged the cabinet to back proposals for a penal colony at Botany Bay in Australia in 1786. Although the Australian settlement provided the harsh environment for a new generation of 'delinquents' in the decades that followed, the very concept of transportation as the primary mode of 'secondary' punishment was gradually eclipsed by the emergence of the PRISON system.

SEE ALSO CRIME AND PUNISHMENT.

FURTHER READING R. Ekirch, *Bound for America: The Transportation of British Convicts to the Colonies 1718–1775* (1987); R. Hughes, *The Fatal Shore: A History of the Transportation of Convicts to Australia, 1787–1868* (1987).

Trenchard, John (1662–1732), political pamphleteer. Trenchard was educated at Trinity College,

Dublin, and began to study law until marriage to an heiress and a legacy from an uncle made him financially independent. He began a career as a political pamphleteer with *An Argument showing that a standing army is inconsistent with a free government ...* (1697), which was the most effective contribution to the STANDING ARMY CONTROVERSY. He also contributed to it the following year with *A Short History of standing armies in England.* Apart from a tract on superstition little was heard of him again until 1719, when he cooperated with Thomas Gordon on *The Independent Whig*, a virulently anticlerical journal. They collaborated in writing CATO'S LETTERS for the *London Journal* between 1720 and 1722. At the general election of 1722 Trenchard was elected as member of Parliament for Taunton, but died the following year.

Triennial Act (1694), statute governing the frequency of general elections. It replaced an earlier act with the same name passed in the reign of Charles II.

Whereas the earlier act had only required a session of Parliament to be held at least once every three years, the 1694 act necessitated triennial elections of a new Parliament, thus requiring a dissolution and general election to occur at least every third year. Since it did not curtail the royal prerogative of dissolving Parliament earlier, in the event ten general elections were held between 1695 and 1715, an average of one every two years. In 1716 this unique run of elections came to an end with the passing of the SEPTENNIAL ACT.

Tucker, Josiah (1712–99), writer on religious and commercial matters. The son of a Welsh farmer, Tucker went to St John's College, Oxford, was ordained and after holding several livings in Bristol became dean of Gloucester in 1758. Tucker was a noted controversialist, his first tract published in 1742 being a critique of METHODISM. He justified the JEWISH NATURALIZATION ACT in 1753. While several of his later tracts addressed religious themes,

notably the debate over clerical subscription to the Thirty-nine Articles in 1771, many were concerned with commerce. Of these the most famous were those that argued that it was pointless to try to force the American colonies to remain within the British empire from an economic point of view, since transatlantic commerce would continue to flow between them and Britain even if they became independent. Although this stance was much criticized at the time, his views were vindicated by trends after the American War of Independence.

Tull, Jethro (1674–1741), agricultural improver. Although long regarded as one of the founding fathers of the so-called 'Agricultural Revolution', Tull is today viewed primarily as a propagandist for improved farming techniques rather than a genuine innovator.

Tull's popular fame rests upon the horse-drawn seed drill that he introduced on his farm near Wallingford during the opening years of the 18th century. However, this machine, which offered an alternative to the wasteful broadcast method of sowing, was actually a refinement of a model first developed more than half a century before. Although Tull publicized his ideas through his book *The Horse-Hoeing Husbandry* (1733) they were slow to take root; indeed, as late as 1813 Arthur YOUNG recorded the adoption of Tull's methods by a farmer in Suffolk as a distinct novelty.

Like Young after him, Tull travelled widely in an effort to broaden his knowledge of farming methods, and he sought to disseminate the information acquired in this way through a series of publications. Again in common with Young, Tull enjoyed more success as a writer than as a practical farmer. The careers of both men serve as a reminder that change within Georgian AGRICULTURE was far from 'revolutionary', with mechanization remaining an overwhelmingly Victorian phenomenon.

Tullibardine, William Murray, marquess of.
See MURRAY, LORD GEORGE.

Turner, Joseph Mallord William (1775–1851), painter regarded as one of the most innovative of all British artists. Turner's dramatic handling of light and colour and an overwhelmingly emotional response to natural phenomena placed him at the very forefront of the ROMANTIC MOVEMENT. His lifetime embraced both the Georgian and early Victorian eras – born in the year which saw war erupt with the American colonies, he died in that of the Great Exhibition. The rapidly changing times in which Turner lived were reflected in one of his most poignant and powerful canvases, *The Fighting Temeraire* (1838): this depicted a stately wooden-walled veteran of NELSON's navy being towed to the breaker's yard by a dark and ugly steam tug.

The son of a London barber, Turner began his artistic career as an engraver's copyist. In 1789 he started attending classes at the ROYAL ACADEMY. He developed an expertise in watercolour depictions of ancient buildings and exhibited his first painting the following year. Soon after, Turner visited the mountains of Wales on the first of many sketching tours that were to provide him with the raw materials for his studio paintings. Turner was remarkable for his mastery of both watercolour and oil painting. His watercolour technique drew heavily upon that pioneered by his friend Thomas Girtin (1775–1802); indeed, Turner later remarked that if 'Tom Girtin had lived, he [Turner] would have starved'. In fact, by the year of Girtin's death Turner had already demonstrated his own exceptional talents and was a full member of the Academy. The peace that followed the treaty of AMIENS that same year provided Turner with an opportunity to visit continental Europe. This not only introduced him to the spectacular scenery of Switzerland, but also allowed him to inspect those works of the Italian old masters that had been carried to Paris by Napoleon's victorious army of Italy.

Turner's versatility embraced an interest in both landscape and 'history' painting, the two genres being combined to spectacular effect in such works as his *Snow Storm: Hannibal and His Army Crossing the Alps* of 1812. The many influences that shaped Turner's varied output included the work of the 17th-century Frenchman Claude Lorrain, which inspired his *Dido Building Carthage* (1815). Turner was strongly influenced by the poetry of his age, and frequently attached quotations to his exhibited works. In 1819 Turner visited Italy, a journey that introduced him to the quality of light so apparent in his later works: paintings such as *Snow Storm: Steamboat Off a Harbour Mouth* (1842) reveal an abstract approach unparalleled in his own times. Turner's revolutionary contribution was not always appreciated by his contemporaries, although he lived long enough to hear his work extolled by the great Victorian art critic John Ruskin.

FURTHER READING J. Lindsay, *Turner: The Man and his Art* (1990).

Turpin, Dick (1705–39), highwayman, whose reputation as 18th-century England's most notorious criminal rests upon an amalgam of fact and fiction. While undoubtedly a prolific and daring highwayman, Turpin was raised above the ranks of his fellows largely because he managed to evade the hangman's noose for longer than most. By the time of his execution in 1739, Dick Turpin was already celebrated in anecdotes and ballads that cast him in a Robin Hood role. He was subsequently credited with other exploits – notably the famous ride from London to York – previously linked with earlier folk heroes. The reality of Turpin's life was less glamorous and more violent.

Born at Hempstead, Essex, in 1705, the teenage Turpin was apprenticed to a butcher in Whitechapel, and by the late 1720s he was established in the same trade back in his native county. Turpin first turned to crime in 1733: with business flagging, he resorted to cattle rustling. Discovery of the hides led to Turpin's detection, but he escaped arrest. Following short stints with local smugglers and deer stealers, Turpin joined the infamous Gregory Gang, participating in its brutal campaign of house-breaking throughout the southeast.

The vicious crimes of the Gregory Gang attracted extensive press coverage, and prompted the first description of Turpin's appearance. In April 1735 the *London Gazette* reported Turpin to be 'a Tall Fresh Coloured Man, very much marked with the Small Pox, about 26 years of age'. With each member now carrying a reward of £50 on his head, the Gregory Gang was soon dispersed. Turpin now began a busy career on the highway. Teaming up with another highwayman, 'Tom' King, he preyed upon riders and carriages in a zone spreading from London to East Anglia. The pair's favourite targets included patrons returning from Newmarket races. However, when they stole the racehorse White Stockings their luck turned bad; the thoroughbred was traced to the Red Lion pub in Whitechapel, and in a confused night-time shoot-out King sustained a mortal wound.

Turpin, who may have been responsible for the accidental shooting of his accomplice, once again avoided capture. Traced to his hideout in Epping Forest, the cornered Turpin shot and killed Thomas Morris, the servant of one of the forest keepers, before seeking refuge in Huntingdonshire and London. Despite his growing notoriety, Turpin continued to prowl the highways and defy the law until the bounty for his arrest rose to £200. By 1738 Turpin was living at Welton, Yorkshire, using the assumed name of John Palmer and posing as a respectable livestock and horse dealer.

Turpin's true identity emerged that autumn after he was arrested for threatening a labourer who objected when he shot a cockerel. Subsequent investigations pointed to illegal activities in Lincolnshire, and Turpin was imprisoned in York Castle. His fate was sealed by a fluke when his handwriting was recognized by a former teacher. Along with John Stead, Turpin was convicted for horse stealing and hanged at York on 7 April 1739. The *York Courant* reported that while Stead appeared penitent, an unrepentant Turpin assured the admiring crowd that he was indeed the infamous highwayman who had proved such a persistent scourge to the authorities.

FURTHER READING D. Barlow, *Dick Turpin and the Gregory Gang* (1973).

U

Union of Britain and Ireland. The union was enacted in 1800 and implemented in 1801. Although the Irish Parliament was given legislative independence in 1782 this did not satisfy the aspirations of Catholics, who continued to be disfranchised. In 1793 the Dublin Parliament passed a Catholic Relief Act that allowed them to vote but not to sit as MPs. The pressure for direct representation alarmed British politicians who could not contemplate a Catholic majority in the Irish legislature. After the abortive IRISH REBELLION OF 1798, which the French encouraged, the younger PITT decided that the only safe solution was to incorporate Ireland into the United Kingdom. The Act of Union of 1800 added 100 Irish seats to the 558 seats for England, Scotland and Wales. Since 64 of these were for the counties, this left only 36 borough seats for Ireland. Previously there had been 117 borough members in the Irish Parliament, so many lost their representation. Proprietors of disfranchised boroughs were compensated, which cost the British taxpayer £1.4 million.

Union of England and Scotland (1707). The union was more the result of deteriorating relations than a genuine rapprochement. Many Scots resented English resistance to the DARIEN SCHEME in the 1690s. When the English Parliament passed the ACT OF SETTLEMENT in 1701, placing the succession to the crown of England in the house of Hanover, there was no similar move in the Edinburgh Parliament. Both WILLIAM III and Queen ANNE sought the union of their two kingdoms. One of William's last communications with the English Parliament was to tell the members 'that there was nothing that he desired more than an union with Scotland'. Anne repeated these sentiments in her first speech to the Lords and Commons. They responded by approving the appointment of commissioners to negotiate terms with Scottish commissioners.

These negotiations collapsed in 1703, partly on the issue of compensation for losses made by Scots in the Darien debacle. There were also reservations about the constitutionality of the Scottish Parliament that had appointed the Scottish team of commissioners. To get round this difficulty Anne dissolved the Edinburgh Parliament and fresh elections were held. The Parliament that met after the elections, however, proved to be very prickly on the subject of relations with England and the succession to the crown of Scotland. It proceeded to pass the Security Act, which declared that the successor to the crown of Scotland would not be the elector of Hanover unless the Scottish Parliament was first satisfied with guarantees for the Presbyterian church and the trade of the country. Anne refused her assent to this act and the following year put pressure on the Edinburgh Parliament to accept the succession to the Scottish crown of the house of Hanover. Instead the members renewed the Security Act, and this time Anne felt she had no choice but to accept it in August 1704.

The English Parliament retaliated with a stick and a carrot. The stick was the Aliens Act, which threatened to lay an embargo on Scottish trade with England if the Scots did not accept the Hanoverian succession by Christmas 1705. The carrot was the appointment of new commissioners for a union. The Scottish Parliament responded by appointing its own commissioners. The two commissions began to negotiate in April 1706. By August terms could be submitted to the queen. The separate Scottish Parliament was to disappear, and the Scots were to be represented in a new Parliament of Great Britain.

The fact that the Scots were only allotted 45 members when England and Wales had 513 has always raised questions. Had the representation been based on population, Scotland should have been granted about 100 seats. But nobody seriously discussed that at the time. Not only was there no official CENSUS until 1801, but in the 18th century seats were allocated on the basis of the proportion of taxes paid. And on that basis the Scots were treated quite generously, since the ratio of their contributions to the exchequer indicated no more than 28 seats. Instead of all Scottish peers being admitted to the House of Lords they were to elect 16 of their number to represent them.

The establishment of the CHURCH OF SCOTLAND and the independence of the Scottish legal system were recognized and safeguarded. The national debt of Scotland – estimated at £398,085 10s. – was to be paid from the English Treasury, a payment known as the EQUIVALENT. Scottish merchants were to be allowed access to the markets of the new British empire where before England had kept them out of its imperial commerce.

These were the main terms of the treaty, which was communicated to the two Parliaments for ratification. The Scottish Parliament took from October 1706 to January 1707 to ratify them, due to steady opposition from a group of anti-union members. The fact that public opinion was also hostile to the treaty in Scotland led to accusations that the pro-union members of the last Parliament to meet in Edinburgh were bribed. Certainly some of the money paid to them allegedly to cancel debts owed by the crown, or as their share of the Equivalent, can be construed as bribery. As one English minister cynically said, 'We bought them.' But that Scots sold their independence wholesale cannot be proved.

Once the Scottish Parliament had approved the terms they were submitted to the English Parliament on 20 January 1707. There they met comparatively little opposition, and a bill to ratify the treaty sailed through both Houses to be given the royal assent on 6 March. The union was inaugurated on 1 May. It brought into being the new kingdom of Great Britain.

FURTHER READING W.A. Speck, *The Birth of Britain: A New Nation 1700–1710* (1994).

Unitarians, Christians who reject the orthodox beliefs in the Trinity and the divinity of Christ, instead regarding God as a single being.

Unitarians were not strictly speaking tolerated by the TOLERATION ACT of 1689, which was confined to Protestants who believed in the Trinity. It was not until 1813 that a Unitarian Relief Act was passed officially granting them toleration. Nevertheless they flourished without prosecution during the 18th century. The bulk of the Presbyterians represented in the synod at Salter's Hall in 1719 adopted Unitarian beliefs (see DISSENTERS). In 1770 when the General Baptist New Connexion was established many Baptists who refrained from joining it joined the Unitarians instead.

The first avowed denomination of Unitarians was formed in 1774 by Theophilus Lindsey, who had resigned from the Church of England following the rejection of the FEATHERS TAVERN PETITION. Lindsey opened a Unitarian chapel in

London in 1778. In 1791 a Unitarian Society was established, one of its founder members being Joseph PRIESTLEY.

universities. There were six universities in the 18th century, five of which had been founded in the Middle Ages: Oxford (12th century), Cambridge (13th century) and St Andrews, Glasgow and Aberdeen all in the 14th century. The sixth university – Edinburgh – was established in the 1580s. No new universities had been created in Britain since then, though degree-awarding institutions had been introduced into the American colonies: at Harvard in the 1630s, William and Mary in Virginia in 1694 and Yale in 1701. These, however, were based more on the model of Trinity College, Dublin, an Elizabethan foundation, than on that of Oxford and Cambridge.

Although no new institutions were chartered in Britain there was considerable investment in building in the established universities. Thus at Cambridge the Senate House was built, at Edinburgh the new quadrangle was added, and at Oxford the Radcliffe Camera was constructed. Some colleges, like Queen's at Oxford, were completely reconstructed. Student numbers, however, fell in the two English universities, though they increased in the four Scottish universities from about 1000 in 1700 to 2700 in 1800. Oxford and Cambridge recruited overwhelmingly from the aristocracy and gentry, and served mainly to qualify clergymen for ordination in the Church of England. Clerical careers seem to have become less attractive to the younger sons of the landed classes in the course of the century. The Scottish universities had always had a wider entry, attracting many more middle-class students than did Oxbridge This was partly because they were much less expensive, costing between £5 and £20 a year compared with £50–£100 at Oxbridge. The English universities were also confined to Anglicans, and many DISSENTERS sent their sons to Edinburgh instead.

Traditionally Oxford and Cambridge have been regarded as intellectually stagnant in the 18th century, compared with their counterparts in Scotland. There have been some attempts to revise these assessments. Thus the dismissal of Oxford as moribund has been attributed to undue reliance on the jaundiced memoirs of Edward GIBBON. While the Oxford curriculum remained traditional, with an emphasis upon medieval subjects of logic and classical literature, there were some changes: a readership in chemistry was established there in 1704, and the chairs of astronomy and botany later; while at Cambridge chairs of anatomy, botany, chemistry and geology were all added in the 18th century. There was also informal instruction in contemporary academic developments. Thus LOCKE's philosophy was available to undergraduates at both English institutions.

At Cambridge, the 18th century saw significant changes, with an emphasis upon Newtonian natural philosophy. Mathematics became central to the curriculum, and the mathematical examination emerged as the favoured method of assessing undergraduates; while the mathematical tripos became the sole route to a fellowship. Cambridge thereby pioneered the concept of the competitive examination and, by 1800, Oxford had followed its example.

Despite this revisionism, however, it can hardly be denied that Oxford and Cambridge lagged behind the Scottish universities. Certainly in the field of medicine Edinburgh took the clear lead, where of a student body of 1279 in 1800 no fewer than 600 were studying medicine. By contrast, there were no medical – or legal – schools at Oxbridge. While Oxford and Cambridge became intellectual backwaters, the universities in Scotland played host to the SCOTTISH ENLIGHTENMENT (*see also* EDUCATION).

FURTHER READING J. Gascoigne, *Cambridge in the Age of the Enlightenment: Science, Religion and Politics from the Restoration to the French Revolution* (1989); R. O'Day, *Education and Society: The social foundations of education in early modern Britain* (1982); W.R. Ward, *Georgian Oxford* (1958).

Utrecht, treaty of (1713), treaty that ended the War of the SPANISH SUCCESSION. Louis XIV recognized the Protestant succession in the house of Hanover and undertook to expel James Francis Edward STUART from France. France also returned to Britain the North American territories of the Hudson's Bay Company, together with Newfoundland and Nova Scotia, and the West Indian island of St Kitts. Spain ceded GIBRALTAR and MINORCA to Britain and granted British merchants the *ASIENTO*, whereby they were permitted to engage in the SLAVE TRADE to Spanish America. Britain recognized Philip V as king of Spain and its empire, to the disgust of the Habsburg claimant, the Emperor Charles VI, who refused to recognize the treaty and fought another campaign before negotiating the peace of Rastatt in 1714. The treaty of Utrecht was controversial in Britain and only got through the House of Lords as a result of the creation of peers. It was long remembered as a betrayal of its allies by 'Perfidious Albion'.

SEE ALSO BARRIER FORTRESSES.

V

vaccination. *See* JENNER, EDWARD.

Vanbrugh, Sir John (1664–1726), soldier, playwright and architect, one of the most versatile men of his age. Vanbrugh's grandfather was a Fleming who established himself as a merchant in London; his father relocated to Chester in the wake of the Great Fire of 1666. Although the details of Vanbrugh's early life remain obscure, he served as an army officer during the NINE YEARS WAR, and while on a visit to France he was arrested and jailed as a spy.

Back in England, Vanbrugh rapidly established a reputation as a dramatist. In 1696–7 he wrote the comedy *The Relapse, or Virtue in Danger*, swiftly followed by another, *The Provok'd Wife*. Both plays remained favourites with theatre audiences through much of the 18th century. Vanbrugh's literary talents earned him admission to the select ranks of the KIT CAT CLUB and thereby brought access to influential Whig politicians.

In 1699 Vanbrugh revealed fresh gifts when the earl of Carlisle chose him to supersede William Talman as architect of his vast country house of CASTLE HOWARD in Yorkshire. Vanbrugh was soon joined by Nicholas HAWKSMOOR: it was the foundation of a firm friendship that only ended with Vanbrugh's death. In professional terms the partnership proved equally happy, resulting in some of the masterpieces of English BAROQUE architecture, including Vanbrugh's finest work, the monumental BLENHEIM PALACE undertaken for the duke of MARLBOROUGH between 1705 and 1720.

Vanbrugh's achievements brought him the influential post of comptroller of the Office of Works in 1702. Upon the accession of George I he gained a knighthood and was selected as architect for the Royal Hospital at Greenwich. Although invariably associated with the baroque, Vanbrugh also revealed a precocious appreciation of the GOTHIC and picturesque: the gardens he created at Castle Howard possessed a highly unusual informality, while the 'castle' he built himself at Blackheath includes the asymmetrical medieval-style features that would challenge the ascendancy of classical architecture during the second half of the 18th century.

SEE ALSO STOWE.

FURTHER READING K. Downes, *Sir John Vanbrugh, A Biography* (1987).

Vauxhall Gardens, pleasure gardens in Lambeth. Throughout much of the 18th century Vauxhall Gardens remained at the very heart of London's social scene, rivalled only by RANELAGH GARDENS in Chelsea. Vauxhall's recreational delights offered a feast for the senses. Although aimed primarily at the rising 'middling classes', they nonetheless attracted a vibrant mix of visitors ranging from the royal family to pickpockets and prostitutes.

Originating in the aftermath of the Restoration, the New Spring Gardens were subsequently upgraded by Jonathan Tyers and formally reopened in 1732 in the presence of FREDERICK PRINCE OF WALES. Tyers won praise for improving the moral tone of what had reputedly degenerated into a 'rural brothel'. His more genteel vision embraced scenic walkways, secluded supper boxes, exotic pavilions, large-scale paintings and ROUBILIAC's much-praised statue of Handel. Vauxhall provided a perfect setting for strolling, dining, gossip and dalliance; its devotees included James BOSWELL and Horace WALPOLE.

Musical performance was a key factor in Vauxhall's enduring appeal. The Gardens' finest hour came in 1749, when 12,000 spectators paid half a crown each to attend a rehearsal of Handel's *Music for the Royal Fireworks*, staged to celebrate the treaty of Aix-la-Chapelle; the throng was so dense that it blocked London Bridge. As Thomas ROWLANDSON's teeming watercolour of 1784 indicates, Vauxhall retained its social cachet and crowd-pulling power for many years; the characters depicted include the prince of Wales, Dr Johnson, Oliver Goldsmith and the duchess of Devonshire. Foreign observers were amazed by its scale and the social mixing it permitted. During the 19th century Vauxhall entered a steady decline as Tyers's sophisticated social centre degenerated into a tawdry and rowdy amusement park. Vauxhall Gardens finally closed in 1859.

Vernon, Edward (1684–1757), admiral and politician. He became a national hero when he commanded the expedition that captured Porto Bello during the War of JENKINS'S EAR. He was nicknamed 'Old Grog' because of his distinctive coat of grogram – a coarse fabric of wool and silk.

Vernon was the second son of William III's secretary of state, James Vernon. He entered the navy as a teenager, served during the War of the SPANISH SUCCESSION and had reached the rank of rear admiral by the age of 24. Vernon entered Parliament in 1722, where he became an increasingly outspoken critic of the pacific WALPOLE administration and helped to fuel the growing popular clamour for war against Spain.

Upon the outbreak of hostilities in 1739, Vernon was promoted to vice admiral and placed in command of a fleet bound for the Caribbean. In an exploit reminiscent of the Elizabethan sea dogs, Vernon took Porto Bello by storm, so winning much loot and widespread acclaim back in England, where he was treated as a hero. Despite Vernon's encouraging lead, the major expedition for the West Indies that was finally assembled early in 1741 met with dispiriting defeat at Cartagena, Santiago and Panama after military and naval commanders quarrelled and tropical disease ravaged the force. Vernon was recalled in late 1742.

Vernon played a prominent role among the opponents of Sir Robert Walpole in the general election of 1741, being put up as a candidate in no fewer than six constituencies. As member of Parliament for Ipswich, Vernon proved himself a vocal member of the opposition. Vernon gained promotion to admiral in 1745, but was dismissed in the following year after he published his letters to the Admiralty.

The outspoken Vernon was an ardent advocate of sea power. Upon returning from the Caribbean in 1742 he told George II – an experienced soldier who took a great pride in his army – that his security depended upon 'being master of the sea'. Alongside his belief in a 'BLUE-WATER POLICY', Vernon expressed a deep interest in the service conditions of those ordinary seamen who manned Britain's 'wooden walls', deploring the violence of the press gangs that raised recruits in wartime and the harshness of shipboard discipline. As a health measure Vernon introduced the custom of diluting the fiery rum ration with water, thereby creating the drink named 'grog' in his honour. After leaving the navy Vernon demonstrated a continuing concern for social improvements by helping to found an innovative 'House of Industry' at Nacton in Suffolk.

Versailles, treaty of (1783), peace treaty that formally ended the AMERICAN WAR OF INDEPENDENCE, and by which Britian recognized the independence of the United States of America.

Following just two decades after the triumphant 1763 treaty of PARIS, the treaty of Versailles appeared to confirm Britain's eclipse as an imperial power. In fact, the outcome of the global conflict that had snowballed from the American War of Independence was less damaging to Britain than it might have proved. Above all, Britain's hand at the peace table had been strengthened by Admiral RODNEY's timely victory over the French fleet at the battle of the Saints early in 1782. The success demonstrated Britain's ability to continue the fight at a time when its adversaries were nearing exhaustion.

Britain had likewise maintained a dogged defence of its Mediterranean bastion of GIBRALTAR; despite the clamourings of Spain, Britain refused to relinquish it at the peace. Thanks to the arrival of badly needed reinforcements, the critical situation in INDIA had also been stabilized.

Against this, Britain had been obliged to bow to the inevitable and recognize the independence of her rebellious 13 colonies. In addition, Florida and MINORCA were returned to Spain, and Tobago and Senegal to France.

The SHELBURNE ministry foundered during the negotiations over its handling of peace terms with the new United States. Besides relinquishing large swathes of territory that had been included within the province of Quebec, the ministry failed to secure adequate protection for those Americans who had remained loyal to George III during the war. Shelburne himself had hoped that his conciliatory approach would help to salvage the wreck of Britain's transatlantic empire by maintaining a commercial connection. However, the FOX–NORTH coalition that succeeded Shelburne in power proved incapable of obtaining any significant improvement in the terms of the treaty. Britain recovered from its humiliating defeat with remarkable speed. For France on the other hand, the price of victory was a growing financial crisis that would soon pave the way for revolution.

W

Wade, George (1673–1748), general and road builder. Wade was the grandson of a Cromwellian officer. He joined the army as a teenager and continued soldiering into his 70s. Wade first saw action in Flanders in 1692 when his regiment fought at the bloody battle of STEENKIRK during the NINE YEARS WAR. At the outbreak of the War of the SPANISH SUCCESSION he returned to the Low Countries and distinguished himself at the siege of Liège. Having established his reputation and reached the rank of lieutenant colonel, Wade volunteered to join the expedition destined for Portugal under the earl of Galway. As a member of Galway's staff, Wade accompanied the allied army when it entered Madrid in triumph in June 1706. In the following year Wade commanded an infantry brigade at the disastrous battle of ALMANZA, but he escaped with his reputation intact and gained promotion to brigadier general. Wade's impressive combat record led to his selection as second in command to General James Stanhope's expedition against MINORCA in 1708; the campaign succeeded, resulting in the acquisition of a key British naval base in the Mediterranean. Returning to Spain, Wade participated in the allies' victory at Saragossa, a triumph that failed to stave off ultimate defeat in the peninsula.

At the accession of George I in 1714, Wade was promoted to major general and appointed commander of the troops in Ireland. Upon the eruption of the '15 JACOBITE rising, the veteran Wade was despatched to deal with suspected Jacobite sympathizers in Bath and discovered concealed weapons. In 1717 Wade was once again employed in a counterinsurgency role, helping to foil a Jacobite conspiracy to purchase military aid from Charles XII of Sweden. Wade's service on the victorious expedition to Vigo during the hostilities with Spain in 1719 was followed three years later by election as MP for Bath; he represented the borough until his death, forging a powerful alliance with the city's influential postmaster, Ralph Allen (see BATH).

In 1724 Wade was appointed to investigate the state and resources of the rebellious Scottish Highlands. A comprehensive intelligence report to George I, which advocated reforms aimed at bringing the region under government control, earned Wade appointment as commander of the forces in 'North Britain'. Wade's proposals included a remarkable programme of road building designed to improve communications between the Highlands and Lowland garrisons, and from 1725 to 1735 the general's soldier-labourers built more than 380 km (240 miles) of such 'military ways', plus 30 bridges. Although representing an impressive feat of civil engineering through difficult terrain, Wade's roads proved a double-edged weapon, which actually helped to speed the movement of Jacobite rebels during the '45 rebellion.

Wade's military career was crowned in 1743 during the War of the AUSTRIAN SUCCESSION when he was promoted to field marshal and given command of the British contingent in Flanders. Wade, who was now aged over 70 and sickly, was obliged to cooperate with truculent Austrian and Dutch allies against the brilliant French commander Maurice de Saxe. Unsurprisingly, the 1744 campaign failed to secure any victories to place beside DETTINGEN, while Wade became a popular scapegoat for the allies' poor showing.

During the 1745 JACOBITE RISING Wade was sent to Newcastle to block Prince Charles Edward STUART's advance into England. The Highlanders sidestepped Wade's army, which became bogged down in snow drifts at Hexham, and proceeded unmolested into Lancashire. Wade likewise failed to intercept the Highland army on its retreat from Derby. Pleading that his age excused him from further campaigning, Wade finally retired from active military service.

Wade's last campaigns proved an inglorious end to a glittering career of service to the state, through which 'he rose under four succeeding princes to the highest honours of his profession'. His exploits earned him a resting place in Westminster Abbey and a monument that the sculptor ROUBILIAC considered his finest work.

Wake, William (1657–1737), Whig cleric. Wake was educated at Christ Church, Oxford, of which he became a canon. In 1682 he went to Paris as chaplain to the English ambassador and there became acquainted with clergymen involved in the Gallican movement. This aroused in him an interest in the reunion of the churches that lasted all his life. In 1685 he returned to England where James II had just succeeded as king. James's policies alienated Wake, who consequently became a leading Whig ecclesiastic. He was particularly effective in London during William III's reign where he had pulpits at Gray's Inn and St James's, West-minster. His definitive *State of the Church and Clergy of England in their Councils, Synods, Convocations, Conventions and other their Assemblies historically deduced* (1703) effectively settled the CONVOCATION CONTROVERSY. In 1705 he became bishop of Lincoln and voted steadily with the Whigs in the House of Lords throughout Anne's reign. His loyalty to the Protestant succession was rewarded with his translation to the archbishopric of Canterbury in 1716.

Walpole, Horace, 4th earl of Orford (1717–1791), man of letters who pioneered both GOTHIC architecture and the Gothic novel. WALPOLE was the fourth and youngest son of Sir Robert Walpole. Like his father he was educated at Eton and King's College, Cambridge. Sir Robert obtained for him three sinecures in 1738 that brought in about £1200 a year, giving him an income fit for the leisured lifestyle of a gentleman dilettante. Thus from 1739 to 1741 he went on the GRAND TOUR with the poet Thomas GRAY, whom he had known at Eton and King's. They visited Italy where Walpole started his collection of antiquities. He also struck up a friendship with Sir Horace Mann, the British resident in Florence, with whom he began to correspond on his way home. This was to become the most substantial correspondence of a letter-writing career that eventually involved over a hundred regular correspondents. Many of his letters were intended for publication and now form the greatest part of his published works. They are written with sparkling wit and are among the most entertaining and instructive letters to have survived from the century.

While Walpole was abroad he was elected a member of Parliament, and was returned at each general election until 1768, representing successively Callington in Cornwall and Castle Rising and King's Lynn in Norfolk. The only mark he made in the House was a spirited defence of Admiral BYNG in 1757. Otherwise he was a nondescript Whig MP. When his father died in 1745 he left him a legacy that included a house in Arlington

Street and enough money to make a comfortable standard of living opulent.

The legacy allowed him to move in 1747 to Twickenham, where over the next 25 years he had built what he called 'a little Gothic castle', STRAWBERRY HILL. In it he lodged his collections of paintings and antiquities, which he described in his *Description of the Villa of Horace Walpole*, published in 1774 at his private press on the premises. His first publication was of his old friend Gray's *Odes* in 1757. The press became famous for his own works, such as *Anecdotes of Painting in England* (four volumes, 1762–71), and those of others, such as Hannah MORE's *Bishop Bonner's Ghost* (1789). Curiously his own most famous work, *The Castle of Otranto* (1765), widely regarded as the first Gothic novel, was published elsewhere. His *Memoirs of the Reign of George II* and *Memoirs of the Reign of George III* were published posthumously.

FURTHER READING W.S. Lewis, *Horace Walpole* (1960).

Walpole, Sir Robert, 1st earl of Orford (1676–1745), Whig politician, traditionally recognized as Britain's first prime minister, although the term had been used previously, being applied, for instance, to Robert HARLEY. Walpole's premiership is usually dated from 1721, and continued until his fall in 1742.

Walpole was the son of a Norfolk country gentleman, and entered Parliament for the family borough of Castle Rising in 1701. His interest there was so strong that he returned two members for it in the general election of 1702, at which he himself was elected at King's Lynn, a borough he represented for the rest of his political career. He served his political apprenticeship in Anne's reign as a protégé of Lord GODOLPHIN, the lord treasurer, whose financial acumen he appreciated. His own talent led to his early promotion: in 1705 he was made a commissioner on the Admiralty council headed by Anne's husband, GEORGE PRINCE OF DENMARK; in 1708 he became secretary at war; and

in 1710 treasurer of the navy. In Parliament he voted with the Whigs, and was so closely identified with that party that he was appointed by the Commons as a manager of the impeachment of Dr SACHEVERELL in 1710.

When the Tories ousted the Whigs in the general election of that year Walpole was targeted by them as a major opponent. He was expelled from the Commons in 1712 for alleged bribery during his time as secretary at war, and spent six months in the Tower. At the accession of the house of Hanover in 1714 the tables were turned as the Whigs replaced the Tories in office and Walpole was rewarded with the post of chancellor of the exchequer. His association with his colleague and relative 2nd Viscount TOWNSHEND – a fellow Norfolk man – led to his resignation along with Townshend in 1717, when they were outmanoeuvred by Lords STANHOPE and SUNDERLAND for the favour of George I. The ensuing Whig schism saw Walpole siding with Tories in Parliament to discredit the ministry. He also supported George prince of Wales (the future GEORGE II) in his quarrel with his father, which became public in 1717. Walpole's chief victory in opposition was the defeat of the Peerage Bill in 1719, a measure designed to give the ministers a permanent majority in the Lords by restricting the royal prerogative of creating peers (*see* LORDS, HOUSE OF). When the prince was reconciled with the king in 1720 Walpole was too, becoming paymaster general.

The bursting of the SOUTH SEA BUBBLE shortly afterwards was the making of Walpole, for he had not been in office when the deal was made between the government and the South Sea Company to convert annuities into its stock. He was thus not part of the hue and cry for ministerial culprits by those who had been ruined in the crash. Instead of encouraging it – as might have been expected – Walpole rather tried to stave off the full force of the attacks. Joining in the demands for ministerial scalps might have made him popular with backbenchers in the Commons, but it would have alienated the king, whose closest friends and mistresses were involved in the shady transactions under investigation. Since the way to win power was not to court popularity but to gain the confidence of the crown, Walpole alienated popular support by defending the ministers. He thereby earned himself the contemptuous nickname of 'the screen master general' because he tried to protect the court from charges of corruption. He even screened the earl of Sunderland, his deadly rival within the ministry. On 15 March 1721 Sunderland was acquitted in the Commons by 233 votes to 172.

A few days later Walpole got his reward when he was made chancellor of the exchequer and replaced Sunderland as first lord of the Treasury. He did not become prime minister, however, until he had eliminated other rivals. These included Lords CARTERET and Townshend. Carteret was eliminated in 1724, when he was sent to Ireland as lord lieutenant to take care of the crisis caused by WOOD'S HALFPENCE. Townshend resigned as secretary of state in 1730 in protest at Walpole's interference with his conduct of foreign policy.

Yet, although Walpole was not effectively prime minister until 1730, it is conventional to date his premiership from 1721. His unrivalled stint of 21 years in that position was due to a unique combination of circumstances. First and foremost he retained the confidence of the crown throughout. With the later Stuarts and again with George III the accession of a new monarch heralded major ministerial changes. In contrast, although Walpole faced a crisis in 1727 when George II came to the throne, he survived it. The new king's choice of Sir Spencer COMPTON to replace him saw a temporary waning of support for Walpole, but he managed to outsmart Compton by showing more political dexterity and by exploiting his friendship with Queen CAROLINE. It is also possible that George II merely sought to impress upon the prime minister that his support was indispensable.

Another contributory factor to Walpole's long premiership was the relative quiescence of political PARTIES compared with the rage of party under William and Anne and the partisan politics of George III's reign. Political conflict under the later Stuarts had taken the form of a contest between rival Tory and Whig parties. These had oscillated in power to the extent that a two-party system seemed to be emerging. After Anne's death, however, the Tories never again achieved anything like a majority in the Commons, being reduced to less than a quarter of the House. The main threat to Walpole came not from the Tory party but from dissident Whigs who went into opposition to him, especially if they could join the Tories to form a COUNTRY PARTY. Walpole worked assiduously to prevent such a combination by harping constantly on the JACOBITE element among the Tories to scare Whigs from combining with them. Despite attempts of opponents such as the Tory BOLINGBROKE and the Whig William PULTENEY to combine Tories and dissident Whigs into a single party, one was not formed during Walpole's ministry. The nearest the opposition came to forming a party was in 1733 when Walpole's excise scheme provoked a crisis (*see* EXCISE CRISIS). In the ensuing general election Country candidates stood in some constituencies against the COURT, and in those where public opinion counted the ministerialists were defeated. But the ministry survived with a parliamentary majority because of the imperviousness of the larger number of parliamentary boroughs to public opinion (*see* ELECTORAL SYSTEM).

The growth of oligarchy in the boroughs was another process that helped to keep Walpole in power so long. It was assisted by the1716 SEPTENNIAL ACT, a measure supported by Walpole that extended the statutory interval between general elections from three to seven years. It was also helped by government secret-service money, which under Walpole ensured that the oligarchy became overwhelmingly Whig. He also used government resources to build up parliamentary support more directly by rewarding members of Parliament with places in the administration (*see* PLACEMEN).

The opposition's chief journal, *The Craftsman*, never tired of complaining that this policy gave Walpole a built-in majority based on corruption.

But this was not the case. In any vote his ministry had to rely for a majority on the support of some of the independent members, who amounted to over 200. Walpole tried to retain their allegiance by offering them both stability and prosperity. He understood the backbench mentality as well as anybody, and he knew that the country gentlemen were weary of the political upheavals of the last fifty years and yearned for stable government without any excitement. They therefore welcomed a politician who boasted that he let sleeping dogs lie. He offered no threat to the Protestant succession, left the church alone and above all kept the country at peace. A pacific foreign policy allowed him to keep direct taxes low.

Walpole's foreign policy paid off until the late 1730s when his appeasement of Spain led his opponents, now styled 'the patriots', to attack him for undermining the country's interests by not resisting Spanish harassment of British merchants trading with South America. Their criticism played a role both in the breakdown of diplomatic efforts to reach an agreement and in the outbreak of the War of JENKINS's EAR in 1739.

The war played a part in the general election of 1741. Admiral VERNON, a popular 'patriot' hero, stood in several constituencies to great public acclaim. As in the previous contest, Walpole could ignore public opinion in the open constituencies, but he was vulnerable to defection in the smaller boroughs by supporters of FREDERICK PRINCE OF WALES, who had gone into opposition in 1737. Frederick's electoral interest in the small boroughs of Cornwall was extensive and was employed against the ministry. Walpole had also alienated the duke of ARGYLL, whose influence was great in several of the tiny Scottish constituencies. The results were much closer than in 1734. Everything depended upon control of the Committee of Privileges and Elections, which was set up by the Commons to decide the fate of petitions from defeated candidates (*see* CONTROVERTED ELECTIONS). In the event the ministry lost control of this crucial committee, which normally used its powers blatantly to 'weed' the Commons of opposition members and thereby to increase the government's majority. On this occasion it employed them to oust ministerial supporters. Walpole saw power slipping away from him and resigned.

Walpole survived another three years, dying in 1745 at the age of 67. George II had made him earl of Orford in 1742, and he could find some consolation for the loss of power in the role of elder statesman. But he also suffered a sad decline. The death of Queen Caroline in 1737 had affected him badly, but not so much as that of his second wife, Maria Skerrett, his former mistress, in 1738. Now advancing years and incapacity also took their toll. He had never enjoyed excellent health despite his apparently robust constitution. Although his massive bulk led to him being dubbed 'the Great Man', he was seriously overweight, weighing some 130 kg (20 stone). The result was kidney stones, which afflicted him with chronic pain. The attentions of his doctors seem rather to have aggravated than relieved his distress, yet he bore their treatments stoically. As he said to one of them, ''Tis impossible not to be a little disturbed going out of the world, but you see I am not afraid.' These were the dying words of a brave as well as a great man.

FURTHER READING J. Black, *Robert Walpole and the Nature of Politics in Early Eighteenth-Century Britain* (1990); J.H. Plumb, *Sir Robert Walpole: The Making of a Statesman* (1956); J.H. Plumb, *Sir Robert Walpole: The King's Minister* (1960).

Warburton, William (1698–1779), cleric, religious writer and controversialist. Warburton was the son of the town clerk of Newark, where he was apprenticed to an attorney before being ordained as a deacon in 1723 and a priest in 1727. He held various livings, including the chaplaincy to FREDERICK PRINCE OF WALES and a deanery at Bristol, before his appointment as bishop of Gloucester in 1759. In 1745 he married a niece of Ralph Allen, one of the leading citizens of BATH, where the couple subsequently settled.

Warburton, an abrasive controversialist, was described by BOLINGBROKE as 'the most impudent man living'. He also published substantial works such as *The Alliance of Church and State* (1736) and *The Divine Legation of Moses* (1737–41). The *Alliance* argued for the interdependence of the established church and the state, taking a middle road between the HIGH-CHURCH view of the supremacy of the church and the Erastian position of LOW-CHURCH Anglicans (*see* ERASTIANISM). The *Divine Legation* asserted – against the principles of DEISM – that there was a divine authority for the system of eternal rewards and punishments implied in the Old Testament.

In the 1740s Warburton became acquainted with Alexander POPE, to whom he was to act as literary executor. Warburton also published an edition of Shakespeare in 1747, which literary scholars have dismissed as worthless. Warburton renewed his controversial writings in the 1750s with a posthumous attack on Bolingbroke and a critique of David HUME. After his elevation to the bishopric of Gloucester he took on the METHODISTS in *The Doctrine of Grace* (1762). In the 1760s he became involved in an acrimonious controversy with Robert Lowth about the Book of Job.

War of 1812, conflict between Britain and the United States of America that coincided with the closing phase of the REVOLUTIONARY AND NAPOLEONIC WARS. The frictions that would lead to war had their roots in American anger at Britain's interference with international trade through its naval blockade of Napoleonic Europe. Tensions were exacerbated by the Royal Navy's policy of 'pressing' American merchant seamen to serve aboard its own ships. In addition, some hawkish American politicians saw war with Britain as a chance to acquire new territory at Canada's expense. Heavily embroiled in the PENINSULAR WAR and facing increasing unrest at home, the British government was prepared to make concessions. These came too late, however, to avert the American declaration of war.

Despite its name, the War of 1812 lasted into 1815. American invasions of Canada led to heavy fighting and pitched battles including Queenstown Heights in 1812 and Lundy's Lane in 1814. The American efforts were uncoordinated and further hampered by poor leadership, bad weather and logistical problems. Britain's troops in Canada also enjoyed the backing of the French Canadian population and Native American tribes, both groups being determined to oppose American expansion. The abdication of Napoleon in 1814 allowed Britain to reinforce Canada with veterans of the Peninsular campaigns, although these troops would be badly missed by WELLINGTON when the emperor's return from exile led to the close-run WATERLOO campaign.

Whilst heavily armed American frigates worsted their British counterparts in several celebrated ship-to-ship duels, and the Republic's vessels scored notable successes on the Great Lakes, the Royal Navy's superior resources nonetheless permitted the landing of amphibious forces at points along the eastern seaboard of the United States. One such army occupied Washington in August 1814 and burned buildings in revenge for American depredations at York (Toronto), and it was the subsequent efforts to paint over the scorch marks that gained the 'White House' its name.

Although the Royal Navy retained overall superiority at sea, Wellington opposed any escalation of the conflict into a bid to reconquer Britain's lost American possessions, and on his advice the British government sought a negotiated settlement. Talks at Ghent led to a peace that reaffirmed the pre-war territorial situation. News of the settlement only arrived after a final bloody confrontation at New Orleans in January 1815, a British force under major general Sir Edward Pakenham suffering heavy losses after it launched a misguided frontal assault against an entrenched American army led by the future American president Andrew Jackson.

FURTHER READING R. Horsman, *The War of 1812* (1969).

Waterloo, battle of (18 June 1815), the final and decisive victory of Britain and its Prussian allies over the French in the REVOLUTIONARY AND NAPOLEONIC WARS. It also marked the end of the 'Second Hundred Years War' that had seen Britain and France in almost constant conflict since the late 17th century.

Napoleon Bonaparte's 'Hundred Days' of freedom came to a bloody close at Waterloo, near Brussels. The emperor's advance into Belgium sought to engage WELLINGTON's motley Anglo-Dutch army and Blücher's Prussians before the two forces could unite to oppose him. Both of the allied armies were embroiled in heavy but inconclusive fighting with the French on 16 June, the Prussians at Ligny and Wellington's army at Quatre Bras. After sending a substantial force under Marshal Grouchy in pursuit of the retreating Prussians, Napoleon and the bulk of his army followed Wellington to Waterloo, where the latter took up position on a ridge.

On 18 June Napoleon subjected Wellington's positions to a succession of frontal assaults. Denied most of the veterans he had commanded in the PENINSULAR WAR, Wellington nonetheless employed the careful defensive tactics perfected during the Iberian campaigns. The battle included episodes that remain among the most celebrated in military history: the stubborn defence of the château of Hougoumont; the costly charge of the Scots Greys; Marshal Ney's frenzied cavalry assaults upon the immovable squares of British infantry; and the final attack of the emperor's famed Imperial Guard.

During the day's fighting Napoleon displayed none of his former genius: his tactics were unimaginative and the battle disintegrated into a brutal slogging match. From mid-afternoon Napoleon's right flank came under increasing pressure from the Prussians who had evaded Grouchy; by early evening Blücher's men were streaming onto the field to complete the rout of the emperor's army and to bring more than twenty years of warfare to a dramatic finale. Writing from Brussels on the day after the battle, Wellington gave his verdict upon a close-fought encounter that had proved costly to victors and vanquished alike: 'It was the most desperate business I ever was in. I never took so much trouble about any battle & never was so near being beat.'

Watson Wentworth, Charles, 2nd marquess of Rockingham. *See* ROCKINGHAM, CHARLES WATSON WENTWORTH, 2ND MARQUESS OF.

Watt, James (1736–1819), engineer whose improvements to the steam engine eventually revolutionized industry. Watt was the son of a Greenock merchant. He had no academic training, and began his varied career as a maker of mathematical instruments. According to legend, Watt first became obsessed with the potential of steam as he watched his mother's boiling kettle. It was in 1764, however, while Watt was following his trade at Glasgow University, that he was inspired to improve the steam engine. He had been asked to repair a model NEWCOMEN engine, and realized that its inefficiency was principally due to a loss of latent heat – a concept discovered by his friend Joseph Black, then professor of medicine at Glasgow.

When Watt began his experiments, steam had already been harnessed for industrial use: indeed, Newcomen's steam-powered beam engines had been pumping water from mine workings since 1715. However, these early engines remained slow, inefficient and limited in their application. Watt's own efforts to improve upon John SMEATON's refinements of Newcomen's engine initially failed to impress; his suggested modifications were too complex and costly to gain widespread support. In 1769 Watt entered into partnership with John Roebuck of Falkirk's Carron ironworks. Roebuck's mining ventures soon left him bankrupt, but not before he had persuaded Watt to take out a patent for his innovations: these included the double-action engine capable of employing the piston on both the upward and downward strokes and a separate condenser, thereby improving efficiency and conserving fuel.

Watt's significant breakthrough came in 1775 when he partnered Matthew BOULTON of Birmingham's famous Soho factory. During the following quarter-century the Watt–Boulton alliance lay behind the invention, production and promotion of engines that would ultimately prove profitable. During this time Watt and Boulton both became members of the Birmingham LUNAR SOCIETY. After a foundry was added to the Soho manufacturing complex in 1795 it produced a wide range of steam-engine components in what has been described as 'the first heavy engineering plant'. Watt continued to secure patents for a succession of improvements, including the key ability to transfer reciprocal into rotative motion, thereby enabling steam to power machinery.

Despite such advances, the full potential of steam power remained unexploited in Watt's lifetime. Although Whitbread's brewery bought a Boulton and Watt engine in 1786, this was untypical: Watt's engines made little impact outside the coal- and tin-mining industries, and even mine owners proved reluctant to replace their existing Newcomen engines with expensive new machinery. Watt's development of steam power would eventually revolutionize the TEXTILE industry, but at the time of his death waterwheels still dominated production. For all his own important innovations, in some respects Watt remained remarkably conservative: he was sceptical of high-pressure systems, and opposed experiments to evolve a steam-powered carriage.

Like his contemporary Smeaton, Watt was an engineer of great versatility. It was Watt who planned the successful and lucrative Monkland Canal and evolved the principle of the marine screw. He also developed a chemical method of copying letters and drawings, and redefined the unit of 'horsepower' to measure the capability of engines; the modern unit of power, the watt, was named after him. A fellow of the Royal Society, Watt was also a distinguished scientist who conducted experiments upon the properties of air. Despite his lack of formal training, he was a man whose vision reflected the highest values of the Enlightenment. As the mathematician John Robison observed of their first meeting at Glasgow: 'I saw a workman and expected no more; but was surprised to find a philosopher.'

FURTHER READING E. Robinson and A.E. Musson, *James Watt and the Steam Revolution* (1969).

Watts, Isaac (1678–1748), hymn writer. Watts was born in Southampton and educated at the dissenting academy at Stoke Newington. He subsequently became pastor of an independent chapel in London. In 1707 he published *Hymns and Spiritual Songs*. Among his best-known hymns are 'O God our help in ages past, our hope for years to come' and 'When I survey the wondrous cross on which the Prince of Glory died'. He also published *Divine Songs in Easy Language for the use of Children* (1715). Watts sided with the UNITARIANS in the dispute among DISSENTERS at Salter's Hall in 1719, and published tracts on the doctrine of the Trinity.

Wedgwood, Josiah (1730–95), potter and industrialist. Wedgwood was born in Staffordshire, at the heart of England's pottery industry, and was to earn his county's traditional craft an international reputation. Wedgwood came from a family of potters; as a child he began working for his brother, gaining valuable practical experience at the potter's wheel.

When his apprenticeship expired Wedgwood went into partnership with one of the era's outstanding potters, Thomas Whieldon. Wedgwood's instructions to improve the body, glazes, colour and shape of Whieldon's wares allowed considerable scope for his talents. However, he soon grew frustrated and in 1759 established his own Log House works. With the assistance of the modeller William Greatbatch, Wedgwood began to experiment with naturalistic forms: the fruits of this alliance included the so-called 'Pine Apple ware', employing green and yellow glazes.

With growing confidence, Wedgwood now turned to the difficult challenge of refining the creamwares. An astute businessman, Wedgwood appreciated the value of publicity; when he had achieved a lighter and more consistent colour he presented his creamware to Queen Charlotte. As 'potter to the Queen', Wedgwood obtained permission to adopt the term 'Queen's Ware', thereby boosting his sales both at home and abroad. Wedgwood's foreign commissions included two major orders, in 1768 and 1775, from Catherine the Great of Russia. The second order was a dinner service that consisted of no less than 952 pieces, each decorated with English landscapes and marked with a frog within a shield.

Wedgwood prospered through a combination of hard-headed business acumen, creative flair and an inspired feel for a market in which the spread of tea drinking had increased demand for china ware. Like his friend Matthew BOULTON – the proprietor of Birmingham's Soho manufacturing complex – Wedgwood appreciated the importance of both production and promotion, and established showrooms in London to advertise his wares. Wedgwood also remained alive to the possibilities offered by contemporary improvements in transport. In conjunction with his future business partner, the Liverpool merchant Thomas Bentley, Wedgwood promoted the Trent and Mersey Canal, and the resulting waterway not only expanded markets but also spared his fragile products from a prolonged jolting on rutted roads.

By 1769, when Wedgwood formalized the successful partnership with Bentley, production of his wares had begun at the custom-built canal-side factory of 'Etruria' near Burslem, the very epicentre of the Staffordshire potteries. As at Boulton's Soho factory, the workforce was divided into specialized gangs, and Wedgwood hoped to make 'such machines of men as cannot err'. The adoption of more systematic 'mass' production techniques did not signal a decline in quality; on the contrary, the Etruria years saw Wedgwood at his most creative. The pottery of the ancient world, as illustrated in archaeological works, provided the inspiration for popular NEOCLASSICAL designs. In 1775, years of experimentation culminated in Wedgwood's production of medallions based upon classical cameos; when set against coloured grounds this 'jasper' ware proved immensely popular and versatile, especially after the noted sculptor John FLAXMAN was enlisted as a Wedgwood modeller.

Having begun his own career as a journeyman potter, Wedgwood was a paternalist who maintained a keen interest in the working and living conditions of his employees. Wedgwood held liberal and radical views. During the 1770s he sympathized with the cause of American independence; he later greeted the onset of the French Revolution with enthusiasm, and proved a staunch opponent of slavery. He was also a member of the progressive Birmingham LUNAR SOCIETY, whose members included Erasmus DARWIN. Darwin's son married Wedgwood's daughter, and their younger son was the naturalist Charles Darwin.

FURTHER READING R. Reilly, *Josiah Wedgwood, 1730–1795* (1992).

Wellesley, Arthur. *See* WELLINGTON, ARTHUR WELLESLEY, 1ST DUKE OF.

Wellesley, Richard, 1st Marquess Wellesley. *See* INDIA.

Wellington, Arthur Wellesley, 1st duke of (1769–1852), general who is ranked alongside MARLBOROUGH as one of the most gifted of all British soldiers. Wellington crowned an unbroken record of victories when he defeated Napoleon at WATERLOO in 1815. Wellington's military services earned him immense prestige. He subsequently followed a more controversial political career – he was Tory prime minister from 1828 to 1830, and again, very briefly, in 1834 – before ending his days as respected elder statesman.

SEE ALSO PENINSULAR WAR.

Wellesley was born into an old and impoverished Anglo-Irish family. He proved a lonely boy, and made little impression at Eton, where his elder brother Richard had already achieved a glittering reputation. It was as a cadet in a French military college at Angers that Wellesley first found a niche and began to shake off his shyness. In 1787, at the age of 18, he was commissioned ensign in the 73rd Highlanders; having finally decided upon a career, he now determined to master all its details. Family influence secured a posting as aide-de-camp to the lord lieutenant of Ireland, and frequent exchanges between regiments followed. While in Dublin he fell in love with Catherine 'Kitty' Pakenham, the third daughter of Lord Longford. However, her powerful brother opposed a match to an officer who still lacked prospects. In an effort to improve his chances Arthur resolved to progress in the army; he studied hard and borrowed the money necessary to buy his way up the promotion ladder. By 1793 – the year that war erupted with France – he had purchased the lieutenant-colonelcy of the 33rd Foot.

Wellesley's first experience of fighting came during the duke of YORK's unlucky Flanders operations of 1794–5. Britain's army was inexperienced and unprepared for a grim winter campaign against the massed revolutionary forces. Yet, despite the humiliating withdrawal, young Wellesley absorbed valuable lessons about 'what one ought not to do'. In 1796 his regiment was ordered to INDIA, where his brother Richard had been appointed governor general of Bengal. Successive campaigns to break the power of those local rulers who defied British empire-building provided Arthur with a chance to demonstrate his abilities. The favour granted to the young Wellesley initially sparked jealousies. For example, when Tipu Sultan of Mysore was finally defeated at Seringapatam in 1799, command of the captured city was given to Colonel Wellesley, even though he had not participated in the actual assault. Yet whatever the advantages afforded by his name, Wellesley soon proved himself through military and administrative capacities and his flair

for handling Indian troops. By 1802 he had risen to major general. At the battle of Assaye, in September 1803, Wellesley's exhausted soldiers overcame heavy odds to smash the military power of the French-backed Maharattas. During the battle Wellesley had two horses killed under him; looking back on his military services in later life, he considered Assaye to be his best-conducted fight. Further victories followed on the plains at Argaum and in the mountains at Gawilghur.

By the time he left India in 1805, Wellesley was an experienced commander capable of leading men on the battlefield, dealing tactfully with allies from alien backgrounds, and orchestrating the complex logistics of a sprawling campaign through inhospitable territory under a searing sun. Wellesley's success was founded upon a minute knowledge of soldiering; as his voluminous despatches reveal, few matters were too small to escape notice. In consequence Wellesley usually possessed the information he required to respond swiftly to events. The arduous Indian campaigns had also demonstrated his physical toughness and habitual coolness under fire.

Upon his return to Ireland Arthur married his old sweetheart Kitty Pakenham, even though they had exchanged no letters during his lengthy absence in India. They proved an ill-sorted pair, and the marriage was not a happy one. Wellesley remained hungry for active service. He interrupted a spell as chief secretary of Ireland to command a brigade during the 1807 expedition against Copenhagen, which succeeded in its aim of preventing the Danish fleet from falling into French hands. A better opportunity for advancement came with the Spanish revolt against French rule of May 1808, which marked the opening of the PENINSULAR WAR.

Wellesley had been assembling a 9000-strong task force for use against Spanish America. It was now decided that these men should be diverted to Portugal instead. The first objective was the removal of the French from Lisbon, but the ultimate goal was their ejection from the entire Iberian peninsula. Wellesley knew that he was a stop-gap appointment who would be replaced by higher-ranking officers, Sir Harry Burrard and Sir Hew Dalrymple. Before they arrived to assume command he inflicted sharp defeats on the French at Rolica and Vimeiro. Wellesley's successors threw away much of what he had won, although his reputation survived the inquiry into the humiliating convention of Cintra. Following the evacuation of Sir John MOORE's expedition in 1809, Wellesley was chosen to re-establish the British presence in Portugal.

During the course of the protracted Peninsular War, Wellesley applied all his Indian expertise to support and maintain the Iberian peoples' struggle against the French invaders. Although Napoleon dismissed him as a mere 'sepoy general', Wellesley's hard-won talents were put to good use against a succession of French commanders. In 1809 he won an important battle at Talavera, a success that gained him the title of Viscount Wellington. Although often obliged to act defensively, Wellington proved equally adept on the attack, as his great offensive victories at SALAMANCA (1812) and Vitoria (1813) demonstrated. By this stage Wellington had been made both a marquess and field marshal; following his invasion of southern France in 1814 and the abdication of Napoleon, he was made a duke.

Confident in the fighting abilities of his soldiers, and always frugal with their lives, Wellington frequently despaired of the army's discipline on campaign. Although justified by events, his withering criticisms of officers and men alike caused widespread resentment. Indeed, Wellington never enjoyed the widespread popularity afforded to his naval contemporary Horatio NELSON. Although far from emotionless, the intelligent, aristocratic and hook-nosed Wellington sometimes exhibited a surface coolness and brusqueness that discouraged intimacy and led to accusations of insensitivity. Unlike Nelson, Wellington cared little for public acclaim; his lack of ostentation was epitomized by his habitual dress of cocked hat and plain blue riding coat devoid of any decoration.

Napoleon's escape from Elba obliged Wellington to thwart the emperor's ambitions at Waterloo – the first occasion upon which the two commanders had been pitted against each other. Wellington was characteristically terse about his final victory. He reported to his friend Marshal Beresford: 'Never did I see such a pounding match. Both were what the boxers call gluttons. Napoleon did not manoeuvre at all. He just moved forward in the old style, in columns, and was driven off in the old style.' Wellington had little patience with budding authors who approached him for more detailed recollections of Waterloo, believing that such accounts must inevitably reveal incidents of misbehaviour alongside the episodes of glory. His own feelings about his costly victory are expressed in a despatch he sent from the battlefield: 'Nothing except a battle lost can be half so melancholy as a battle won.'

Following his decisive victory over Napoleon, 'the Peer' commanded great respect on the European diplomatic scene. Wellington became prime minister in 1828; conservative by background and nature, he resigned two years later after having reluctantly bowed to the clamour for CATHOLIC EMANCIPATION. Wellington's instincts likewise led him to oppose parliamentary reform, although once again he recognized the futility of resisting the inevitable. In old age Wellington acquired genuine popularity as the true scale of his achievements as a soldier and untiring servant of the state were recognized.

FURTHER READING E. Longford, *Wellington: The Years of the Sword* (1969).

Wesley, Charles (1707–88), clergyman and hymn writer. Charles was educated at Westminster School and Christ Church, Oxford. While at Oxford he was associated with a group of students who acquired the name of 'Methodists' from their method of studying according to the university statutes. Wesley was ordained in 1735 just before going with his brother John to Georgia, where he had been engaged as OGLETHORPE's secretary. Charles disliked the task and returned to England in 1736, though he did not resign the secretaryship until 1738. That was the year in which he felt himself to be reborn, and began his Methodist ministry. From 1739 to 1756 he was an itinerant preacher in England and Ireland. In 1771 he settled in London, where he preached frequently at the City Road Chapel. Charles was an ardent member of the Church of England throughout his life, and disagreed with John's ordaining of ministers for America. He is best remembered as a hymn writer, having written over 6000 hymns. Some, like 'Hark! the herald angels sing' and 'Love Divine, all Loves excelling', are still sung today.

Wesley, John (1703–91), clergyman and religious reformer who was one of the leading founders of METHODISM. Wesley was educated at Charterhouse and Christ Church, Oxford. He was ordained in 1725 and the following year he became a fellow of Lincoln College. Wesley began to attend meetings of his brother Charles WESLEY's group of 'Methodists', which became known as the 'Holy Club'. At this time John was much influenced by William LAW, and especially by the latter's *Serious Call* (1729). In 1735 he went on a mission to Georgia, and was much impressed by the calm resignation of some MORAVIANS on board when they encountered a storm. On arriving in the colony he stayed with one of them, who persuaded him to correspond with the Moravian leader Count Zinzendorf, whom he visited in Herrnhut after his return to Europe. He was later to say that 'William Law begat Methodism but Count Zinzendorf rocked the cradle.' His experience of Georgia was not a happy one and he returned to England in 1737.

On 24 May 1738 Wesley recorded in his journal that at a service in Aldersgate Street, London, he felt his heart 'strangely warmed' and knew that he was saved. This rebirth launched him on his life-long career as the leading Methodist. In 1739 he established chapels in Bristol and at the Foundry in London. Later he opened the orphan house at Newcastle upon Tyne. Bristol, London and Newcastle formed the points of a triangle for his Methodist societies. He himself journeyed constantly between them, frequently preaching in the open air to vast crowds. He was also a frequent visitor to Ireland and Scotland. It was estimated that he travelled 400,000 km (250,000 miles) and preached 40,000 sermons. He was a charismatic preacher, often whipping up his hearers to hysteria and even convulsions. Wesley was a prolific publisher, not only of religious tracts but of treatises on a whole range of topics, including history, languages and medicine. The income from his publications made him 'unawares become rich'.

Although Wesley was adamant that his societies were part of the Anglican communion, relations between them and the Church of England became strained. There was pressure from some of his followers for him to break with episcopal ordination and ordain his own ministers, especially those bound for America. He resisted this until 1784, when he agreed to ordain an American ministry, and later a Scottish one. Yet he insisted that 'whatever is done in America or Scotland is no separation from the Church of England'. The final rift between Methodism and the established church was delayed until his death.

FURTHER READING H. Abelove, *The Evangelist of Desire: John Wesley and the Methodists* (1990); S.J. Rogal, *John and Charles Wesley* (1983).

West, Benjamin (1738–1820), American-born painter who emerged on the London art scene as a leading exponent of the prestigious 'history painting'.

West was born in Pennsylvania; later biographers enjoyed depicting him as an artistic 'noble savage' who manufactured brushes from his cat's tail and was taught the use of pigments by neighbouring Native American warriors. Whatever the truth of such stories, West's precocious talents persuaded a group of influential Pennsylvanians to subscribe sufficient funds to send him on a three-year study trip to Italy. West arrived in London in

1763, and rapidly won notice by producing moralistic history paintings that caught the fancy of George III. Such works as *Cleombrutus Ordered into Banishment by Leonidas II* (1768) harked back to the dramas of classical times.

In contrast, West's greatest success, his 1770 canvas depicting *The Death of General Wolfe*, applied the concepts of history painting to an event from the recent past. West broke with tradition by portraying the protagonists in modern garb instead of the customary neoclassical togas, and when exhibited at the Royal Academy in 1771 the painting caused a sensation. Although not the first artist to paint the scene in contemporary dress – George ROMNEY and Edward Penny had already produced their own interpretations – West invested the moment with a pathos and drama that won widespread acclaim and obliged some female spectators to take to their smelling salts. An engraving of the painting enjoyed healthy sales.

King George III had initially been shocked by West's innovations. However, he subsequently changed his mind and appointed him as his official history painter. West's commissions included paintings for the royal residences at Buckingham House and Windsor Castle. Despite the success of his *Wolfe*, West failed to produce further outstanding 'heroic' paintings on modern themes, instead returning to the religious, historical and mythological subjects that appealed to the king. It was West's fellow countryman John Singleton COPLEY who went on to realize the full potential of the 'modern heroic history painting' through such dramatic works as *The Death of Major Pierson* of 1783. A founder member of the Royal Academy, West succeeded as president upon the death of Sir Joshua Reynolds. Alongside 'history' paintings, West's prolific output also included portraits, landscapes and stained glass.

FURTHER READING H. von Erffa and A. Staley, *The Paintings of Benjamin West* (1986).

Wharton, Philip Wharton, 1st duke of

(1698–1731), JACOBITE politician. Wharton was the only son of Thomas WHARTON, the JUNTO Whig. At his christening he was sponsored by William III and Princess Anne, the future queen. He was brought up as a Whig, and his father, who died in 1715, would have been dismayed by his son's subsequent adherence to Jacobitism. While on the GRAND TOUR with a Huguenot tutor in 1716 Wharton made his own way to the court of James Francis Edward STUART, the Old Pretender, and pledged support to his cause. On his return Wharton played the part of a loyal subject of the house of Hanover both in Ireland, where he was returned to the Irish Parliament as marquess of Catherlough, and in England, where he was elevated to a dukedom in 1718.

When Wharton took his seat in the House of Lords on reaching his majority the following year, however, he went into opposition. In 1723 he defended the Jacobite Francis ATTERBURY, bishop of Rochester. He also began a Jacobite journal, *The True Briton*, which lasted until 1724. By then Wharton was overwhelmed with debt, and he left the country in 1726 to enter the service of the exiled 'James III', who made him a knight of the Garter and duke of Northumberland. He was sent as the Pretender's ambassador to Spain, where he discredited himself with his master by his drunken appearances in public. Although he announced his conversion to Catholicism he remained *persona non grata* in Rome, and spent his last years as a penniless adventurer wandering around Europe. He died in Spain at the age of 32.

Wharton, Thomas Wharton, 1st marquess of (1648–1715), Whig politician and member of the JUNTO. Wharton was the son of a Presbyterian peer who employed dissenting teachers to educate him. In 1663 he went to France accompanied by his tutors, and spent three years abroad. He entered Parliament in 1673 as member for Wendover, and in debates he emerged as a critic of the court. During the Exclusion crisis he was returned as a Whig knight of the shire for Buckinghamshire. In 1680 he joined with Shaftesbury in presenting

James duke of York to the Middlesex Grand Jury as a recusant. His desecration of the pulpit at the parish church of Great Barrington, Gloucestershire, in 1682 was held against him by his political opponents for years afterwards.

Wharton was one of the few Whigs to be returned to Parliament in 1685. He spoke against the retention of Catholic officers in the army raised by James II to defeat the duke of Monmouth. After James prorogued Parliament in November Wharton took part in the conspiracies of the 'Treason Club'. This helped to undermine the morale of James's army during the GLORIOUS REVOLUTION, as did the song 'Lilliburlero' written by Wharton, which he boasted 'whistled a king out of three kingdoms'.

Wharton was the first peer to join WILLIAM after his landing at Brixham. In the CONVENTION PARLIAMENT he nominated William and Mary as joint sovereigns. Shortly after their acceptance he was appointed comptroller of the household. When William moved towards the Tories and dissolved the Convention in 1690, Wharton accused him of being ungrateful to the Whigs who 'had made him king'. With his Whig colleagues who became known as the Junto, Wharton kept up sustained opposition to the Tories in the new Parliament, and eventually the earl of SUNDERLAND persuaded the king to bring them into the ministry. Where his colleagues obtained major posts, however, Wharton remained as comptroller of the household. The general election of 1695 consolidated the Whig hold on power. Wharton was in his element at the polls, having influence in constituencies scattered as far afield as Buckinghamshire, Yorkshire, Westmorland and Cumberland. He fielded candidates in them all and backed them with money and in person. His achievements in this field made him one of the greatest electioneers of the period. In 1696 his father died and he entered the House of Lords.

On the accession of ANNE, Wharton was stripped of the comptrollership and even removed from the privy council, an unusual gesture that

reflected her utter detestation of his principles. In opposition to the Tory government appointed by the new queen, the Junto exploited the Whig majority in the House of Lords to defeat measures such as the OCCASIONAL CONFORMITY bills. Wharton was also involved in the heated partisan debate over the case of ASHBY VS. WHITE. The Junto supported the UNION OF ENGLAND AND SCOTLAND and the allied cause in the War of the SPANISH SUCCESSION, for which they sought their reward. Wharton obtained a promotion in the peerage to an earldom in 1706 and the lord lieutenancy of Ireland in 1708. He went to Dublin and was an energetic and efficient lord lieutenant.

Unfortunately Wharton earned the enmity of Jonathan SWIFT, who was to castigate him in *A Short Character of his Excellency Thomas earl of Wharton*. It libelled him as a totally unscrupulous and corrupt politician, a liar and a womanizer. He was in fact a man of integrity, who had refused to be bought off by the court and who was known to his allies as 'Honest Tom'. While his infidelities to his two wives were notorious, at the age of 60 his days of spectacular debauchery were long over. Even Swift conceded that he was no drinker, his only addiction being to the turf, where his racehorses were famous for their victories.

Wharton went to England in 1709 to play a leading part in the impeachment of Dr SACHEVERELL. In the ministerial revolution of 1710 he lost his post of lord lieutenant. He was indefatigable in the House of Lords, opposing the HARLEY ministry's peace negotiations, leading the attack on the preliminary articles in December 1711. This produced a defeat for the government that was only reversed when the prime minister persuaded the queen to create twelve new peers. When these appeared in the Lords Wharton asked sarcastically if they voted by their foreman. At the next election the Tories were so triumphant that Wharton lost the Buckinghamshire election at the heart of his electoral empire. The Whigs were thus driven back more on the upper house, where Wharton led their opposition. A motion that the succession was in danger under the Tory ministry was lost there by only twelve votes: 'Saved by your dozen,' Wharton commented to the prime minister.

When George I arrived in London Wharton was given the office of lord privy seal, and at the polls in 1715 he recovered the ground lost at the previous general election. His efforts were rewarded with a promotion in the peerage to a marquessate and a pension of £2000 a year. Shortly afterwards he died. He was variously remembered: a Jacobite described him as 'another great atheistical, knavish, republican villain', while Whigs revered him as being 'so constantly right in all things that concerned the true interests of England'.

Whigs, one of the two main political PARTIES of the 18th century. The word 'Whig' originated in Scotland as an abbreviation of 'Whiggamore', which referred to the militant Presbyterians who were regarded as rebels by the supporters of the Stuarts. The latter thus applied it pejoratively to their opponents in the Exclusion Parliaments of 1679 to 1681 who sought to exclude Charles II's brother James from succeeding him. The name stuck and the Exclusionists became the first Whigs.

What characterized the Whigs was a political philosophy enunciated by John LOCKE, whose two *Treatises of Government*, though not published until 1690, circulated in manuscript during the Exclusion crisis. Essentially Locke upheld the right to resist a monarch who did not protect his subjects' rights but invaded them. Such a monarch could be set aside and replaced by one who would uphold the 'natural' rights to life, liberty and property. A Catholic by definition would threaten the rights of Protestant subjects, and therefore James, as a Catholic, should be barred from the succession. When they failed to exclude him by passing a bill in Parliament some Whigs were prepared to plot against his life. The leader of the first Whigs, the earl of Shaftesbury, fled to Holland after having charges of treason dropped by a London grand jury consisting of Whigs. He died in exile in 1682. Others, including Algernon Sidney and Richard

Hampden, were arrested for complicity in the Rye House plot of 1683 and were brought to trial, found guilty and executed.

The association of Whigs with violence led to their being associated also with republicanism. Although some undoubtedly were republicans, Whiggism was never incompatible with monarchy. Indeed to some thinkers a limited monarch responsible to Parliament was almost the equivalent of a republic. Certainly when Whigs, who had had to lie low in the reign of James II, found themselves able to influence the debates in the CONVENTION PARLIAMENT held after the GLORIOUS REVOLUTION in 1689, the majority supported the BILL OF RIGHTS. This placed limitations on the crown, but also showed that Whigs were committed to the Protestant succession. Thus in 1701 they supported further limitations on the power of the crown in the ACT OF SETTLEMENT, which placed the succession in the house of Hanover.

In addition to their opposition to Catholicism, Whigs were also champions of the DISSENTERS. They supported the TOLERATION ACT passed by the Convention in 1689. They also defended dissenters from Tory attacks upon occasional conformity in the first years of the reign of Queen ANNE. In 1711, however, they acquiesced in the passage of the OCCASIONAL CONFORMITY ACT. While they could plead political necessity, it demonstrated that support of dissent could be seen by some Whigs as expedient.

During the reign of William III a significant split had occurred in the Whig party. The first Whigs had been essentially in opposition. After the Revolution an opportunity arose for their successors to be in office. Their leaders, who collectively became known as the JUNTO, took this opportunity and by 1695 were leading a Whig ministry. Backbench Whigs retained their opposition or COUNTRY mentality and remained opposed even to a ministry dominated by the Junto, whom they criticized as Court Whigs. Among the leading Country Whigs was Robert HARLEY. After the treaty of Ryswick that ended the NINE YEARS WAR in

1697, Harley led the attack upon the maintenance of a standing army, which the Junto sought to sustain. According to the Bill of Rights this required the sanction of Parliament in peacetime. The resulting STANDING ARMY CONTROVERSY opened up the gap in the Whig party.

The outbreak of the War of the SPANISH SUCCESSION made the issue redundant, and Whig ranks closed again behind the war effort. Only in the parliamentary session of 1705–6 did the split temporarily reopen over the repeal of the PLACEMEN clause in the Act of Settlement. But after the treaty of UTRECHT the divisions emerged again. To some extent this was due to the fact that the TORIES were no longer in a position to offer serious opposition to Whig hegemony. They had so offended the elector of Hanover by their support of the peace in 1713 that he determined not to employ them. The result was the proscription of the Tory party, which was not fully lifted until 1760. Consequently Britain became governed by the Whig party.

With the demise of the Junto, rival Whig factions struggled to replace them as leaders, resulting in the Whig schism of 1717 when 2nd Viscount TOWNSHEND and Robert WALPOLE went into opposition to a ministry dominated by Lords STANHOPE and SUNDERLAND. That there was very little principle behind this schism was demonstrated by Walpole's cynical alliance with Tories and exploitation of the Peerage Bill of 1719 (see LORDS, HOUSE OF). Further rifts can also be attributed to a struggle between ins and outs, such as William PULTENEY's departure from the ministry in 1724 because of frustrated ambition. But there was more to it than that.

As Walpole's long ministry endured he came to be perceived as a betrayer of Whig principles by the devious means he use to stay in power. His use of the king's patronage to build up a body of supporters in Parliament was regarded by his opponents, Whig as well as Tory, as a gigantic system of corruption. The old Country attacks on placemen and standing armies were revived. Demands for more frequent elections and hence the repeal

of the SEPTENNIAL ACT were raised. Underlying these demands were ideological differences between the Court and Country Whigs over the location of sovereignty. Traditionally Whigs had placed this ultimately in the people, and the Country Whigs maintained this tradition. The Court Whigs, however, had come to argue more and more that it resided in the king in Parliament. Again Whiggism was held to defend liberty and property. But the Country Whigs tended to stress liberty while the Court Whigs stressed property. Country Whigs also accused Walpole of sacrificing dissenters to the need to placate the Church of England. Although the Occasional Conformity Act had been repealed in 1719, the Test and Corporation Acts, which required aspirants for office in boroughs or under the crown to take communion in the Church of England, were still on the statute book. Country Whigs campaigned to repeal them, which Walpole resisted, preferring to pass annual acts giving dissenters immunity from prosecution under them.

By the accession of GEORGE III, therefore, Whig differences were such that it is hard to see any fundamental issue on which Whigs were united except the Protestant succession. On the other hand, after the failure of the JACOBITE RISING of 1745 it was clear that the Tories also accepted the Protestant succession, and after their proscription was lifted by George III it becomes difficult to discern any ideological differences between the two parties. It was almost as though the politicians of the time could say 'We are all Whigs nowadays.' It was of the early years of George III's reign that the historian Sir Lewis Namier (1888–1960) claimed that 'the words Whig and Tory explain little and require a great deal of explanation'. Although the ROCKINGHAMITES asserted that they were the heirs of the Whig tradition and accused the ministers they opposed of being Tories, the label did not stick. All prime ministers considered themselves to be Whig until Lord LIVERPOOL, who became the first to accept the name Tory since the reign of Queen Anne. Yet there was a clear difference between the

'Pittites' – the supporters of the younger PITT – and the 'Foxites' – the followers of Charles James FOX. The distinction became especially clear after 1792 when many Whigs went over to the government, leaving a remnant loyal to Fox who claimed to be upholding the true Whig tradition.

Whitbread, Samuel (1720–96), a founding father of the British brewing industry, who poured the profits from his popular beers into a wide variety of charitable causes. Of Bedfordshire yeoman stock, Whitbread was apprenticed to a London brewer in 1736. Within six years he had entered into partnership with Thomas and Godfrey Shewell, and the trio pooled sufficient funds to buy a brewery. Whitbread emerged as the driving force behind the business and by 1750 the partnership's brewery in Chiswell Street was the leading producer of the dark and well-hopped 'porter' style beer that had recently revolutionized a market previously dominated by more traditional ales. Within a decade Whitbread had gained complete control of the enterprise. He proved keen to take advantage of the era's technological advances, and ultimately installed one of James WATT's new steam engines in his brewery. Through such large-scale methods of production Whitbread transformed brewing in Britain and accumulated a substantial personal fortune.

Whitbread's wealth made him one of the most influential landowners in Bedfordshire, and his popularity in the county of his birth made him a natural parliamentary candidate for the borough of Bedford, which he won in the election of 1768 and represented until 1790. Whitbread had stood in his own interest, and assumed the same fiercely independent stance throughout a parliamentary career that was to continue with scarcely an interruption until his death in 1796. Voting with the government or opposition as his conscience dictated, Whitbread usually restricted his parliamentary speeches to financial affairs: in 1782 he highlighted the costly corruption surrounding naval victualling contracts and demanded a com-

mittee of investigation. A noted philanthropist, Whitbread was among those entrepreneurs who backed the campaign to abolish the SLAVE TRADE.

White, Gilbert (1720–93), clergyman and naturalist. White was born in Selborne in Hampshire and, after education at Oriel College, Oxford, where he was ordained, returned there in 1761, following brief curacies elsewhere, to become curate of nearby Faringdon. There he made the acute observations of nature which resulted in *The Natural History and Antiquities of Selborne*, published in 1788. Its detailed and affectionate observation of wildlife and nature was to make it one of the best-loved books in the English language. White's life, though uneventful, was not totally spent in provincial obscurity, since he attended meetings of the ROYAL SOCIETY and the Society of Antiquaries. In 1784 he became curate of Selborne where he died in 1793.

Whitefield, George (1714–70), clergyman who played an important role in the development of METHODISM. Whitefield was educated at Pembroke College, Oxford, where he was a member of the Holy Club along with John and Charles WESLEY. He commenced preaching in the open soon after he was ordained in 1736. His enthusiastic style was at complete variance with the fashionable sermons based on the reasoned prose of John Tillotson, of whom Whitefield said that he 'knew no more of true Christianity than of Mahomet'. Instead of stressing morality he emphasized regeneration, one of his first published sermons being on *The nature and necessity of a new birth in Jesus Christ in order to salvation*. In 1737 he went with John Wesley to Georgia, the first of many evangelizing voyages to the American colonies.

Although Whitefield and Wesley worked together in Bristol after their return, they had a serious theological disagreement in 1739, with Wesley insisting upon free will and that Christ had died for all, while Whitefield maintained predestination and the salvation of the elect. In 1747

Whitefield became chaplain to Selina countess of Huntingdon and her exclusive 'Connexion'. Perhaps the elite were more responsive to his Calvinism than they were to Wesley's Arminianism because they could more readily accept the notion that they were also the elect. At all events, the Wesleys were much more popular, at least in England.

In America, however, where the 'Great Awakening' stressed predestination and denounced free will, Whitefield swept all before him. His evangelical movement surmounted colonial borders, so that some historians see it as the first American phenomenon and its leader as the first American. FURTHER READING H.S. Stout, *The Divine Dramatist: George Whitefield and the Rise of Modern Evangelicalism* (1991).

Wilberforce, William (1759–1833), a leading evangelical opponent of slavery and the SLAVE TRADE. He drew upon a close friendship with the younger PITT to further the abolitionist cause in Parliament.

The son of a prosperous Hull merchant, Wilberforce was elected MP for the port in 1780. He soon made his mark in Parliament, where he formed an early association with Pitt; he backed the SHELBURNE administration in which Pitt served as chancellor of the exchequer, and supported Pitt's motion for the reform of Parliament. In 1784 Wilberforce was elected to represent the county of Yorkshire. The same year saw his religious conversion; he emerged as leader of the influential CLAPHAM SECT and became involved in a wide range of societies aimed at promoting Christian values and improving the lot of the poor. A popular and fluent member of the House, Wilberforce used his political position chiefly to further such causes, writing in 1787 that God had set him two great tasks – 'the suppression of the slave trade and the reformation of manners'.

Since the 1750s opposition to slavery had been spearheaded by the evangelical movement. By the time Wilberforce adopted the antislavery cause it had been decided to concentrate upon the abolition of the slave trade as a first objective. An avowed independent, Wilberforce nonetheless remained a firm ally of Pitt and exerted considerable influence over him; in return, Pitt gave the antislavery campaign his blessing, leading to the establishment of vocal committees in Manchester and other provincial cities.

In 1789 Wilberforce put forward a parliamentary motion to end the trade. Despite the backing of 100 petitions, the economic interests vested in slavery proved too influential and the motion was defeated. A further attempt to end the trade in 1791 foundered amidst the general backlash against the slave revolts unleashed by the upheavals of the French Revolution. It was only in 1807, when the economic importance of Britain's Caribbean colonies had dwindled, that the GRENVILLE government passed a bill to abolish the slave trade. Wilberforce retired from Parliament in 1825, and died in July 1833 – just days before the institution of slavery was abolished throughout the British Empire.
FURTHER READING J.C. Pollock, *Wilberforce* (1977).

Wild, Jonathan (1683–1725), criminal who, during a well-publicized career, dominated London's underworld. Anticipating the systematic techniques associated with present-day 'organized crime', Wild gained the unofficial title of 'thief-taker general' before ending his days on the gallows at Tyburn. He inspired the character Peachum in John GAY's theatrical success *The Beggar's Opera*, and was later the eponymous antihero of Henry FIELDING's novel.

A native of Wolverhampton, Wild worked as a buckle-maker before succumbing to the lure of London. It was while he was in prison for debt in 1710 that he found his true calling. He became friendly with a prostitute, Mary Milliner, who became his common-law wife, and they joined forces to run a brothel in Lewkener's Lane. Upon such foundations Wild's genius was to build a sprawling empire of crime. From unsophisticated extortion and protection rackets he evolved more subtle techniques calculated to exploit yawning gaps in the existing law-enforcement process.

Wild's breakthrough came when he refined the business of receiving stolen goods by eliminating the middle man, or 'fence', and dealing directly with the thieves themselves: he undercut the fences by paying a higher price for the stolen goods, then recouped his outlay by charging still more to the original owners for the return of their property. To avoid prosecution under the Receiving Acts, Wild never handled stolen goods himself; instead he contacted the owners, mentioned that he knew the location of their missing property, and offered to return it – at a price. Carefully worded newspaper advertisements proved equally effective. Stolen items were returned at meetings between the thieves and their victims. Wild became so confident in his methods that he established lost-property offices – one of them audaciously located in the yard of the Old Bailey itself.

Through his system of receivership, Wild gradually assumed a position in which he straddled both sides of the law: not only did he control many of the capital's criminals, but he also became the first point of contact when their prey sought redress. Wild's ambiguous stance was reinforced by his growing reputation as a 'thief-taker': this derived from his policy of arresting prominent highwaymen and footpads for the rewards on their heads, and periodically betraying his own gang members. As an account written in 1735 reported, Wild brought 'a vast number' of felons to the gallows, 'even though he himself had bred them up in the art of thieving, and given them both instructions and encouragement to take that road which was ruinous enough in itself and by him made fatal'. Such methods did not go unresented. When Wild 'shopped' one of his protégés, Joseph 'Blueskin' Blake, the latter responded by inflicting a near fatal gash across the thief-taker's throat.

A fearless brawler, whose twice-fractured skull was patched with silver plates, Wild continued to deal ruthlessly with those criminals who refused to conform to his regime. Between 1720 and 1723 Wild and his henchmen launched a violent campaign that smashed a succession of underworld fraternities, including the notorious Spiggott, Hawkins and Carrick gangs. Wild's failure to abide by the unwritten code of 'honour among thieves' had long since alienated the 'lower orders', and when his network of informers secured the arrest and execution of Jack Sheppard, a cockney housebreaker whose spectacular escapes from Newgate Prison had made him a popular hero, he incurred their undisguised hatred. Despite his useful role in apprehending criminals, Wild's activities had also exhausted the patience of the authorities. The wily gangster was eventually convicted of receiving. At his execution the usually supportive spectators were so hostile that they threatened to lynch the hangman when he offered Wild time to prepare himself for death.

FURTHER READING G. Howson, *Thief-taker General: The Rise and Fall of Jonathan Wild* (1970).

Wilkes, John (1725–97), journalist and politician who became a persistent irritant to GEORGE III and his ministers in the 1760s. Through his involvement in a series of well-publicized constitutional disputes, Wilkes came to personify the struggle of the freedom-loving Englishman against a 'tyrannical' state. To his exasperated monarch he was 'that devil Wilkes'; however, in the eyes of ordinary Londoners Wilkes was a popular hero, and 'Wilkes and Liberty!' became a familiar rallying cry when the 'mob' vented its feelings on the street.

The son of a successful London distiller, Wilkes acquired a substantial income after marrying the wealthy Aylesbury heiress Mary Meade in 1747. Wilkes rapidly gained a reputation for debauchery and proved an enthusiastic participant in the depraved activities of the locally based HELL-FIRE CLUB. Leering and squint-eyed, Wilkes compensated by wit and charm for what he lacked in looks. His first attempt to enter Parliament as member for Berwick-upon-Tweed in 1754 was unsuccessful, even though he bribed the captain of a ship ferrying his rival's supporters from London to land them in Norway instead. Three years later Wilkes deployed his wealth more effectively to secure election as the member for Aylesbury.

From 1762 Wilkes employed his barbed journalism to mount vociferous campaigns against the ministries of the king's Scottish favourite, Lord BUTE, and his successor George GRENVILLE. Through his political newspaper *The North Briton* Wilkes had already cast aspersions upon Bute's relationship with the king's mother, when on 23 April 1763 issue number 45 of the paper questioned the veracity of ministerial statements incorporated within the king's speech. The outraged administration resorted to a general warrant to assemble evidence leading to Wilkes's arrest and imprisonment in the Tower of London. Wilkes was released within a week after Lord Chief Justice Pratt (later Earl CAMDEN) ruled that his arrest infringed parliamentary privilege. A jubilant Wilkes proceeded to secure damages and establish the illegality of GENERAL WARRANTS.

Wilkes's triumph was transitory. The government now launched a more thoughtful attack led by Wilkes's old friend Lord SANDWICH. In November 1763 Sandwich read to the House of Lords Wilkes's obscene *Essay on Woman*; their lordships deemed it a libel and breach of privilege, while the Commons simultaneously backed a government motion to declare the infamous 'number 45' a seditious libel. While recuperating after a serious wound sustained in a duel provoked by a government henchman, Wilkes visited his daughter in Paris and decided to remain in France rather than face prosecution back in England. Wilkes was soon after expelled from the Commons, and in his absence he was found guilty of publishing seditious and obscene libels and declared an outlaw.

For more than four years Wilkes dallied in Paris while awaiting an opportunity to mount his political comeback. In early 1768 mounting frustration and dwindling funds encouraged him to take the reckless step of contesting the London election.

Trounced in the City, Wilkes soon rode a wave of anti-ministerial sentiment to top the poll in Middlesex. That April Wilkes surrendered himself to the authorities. During his sojourn in the King's Bench Prison Wilkes attracted massive popular support, which led to bloodshed when protesters clashed with troops during the so-called ST GEORGE'S FIELD MASSACRE. Although his outlawry was reversed on a technicality, Wilkes received a fine and a two-year gaol sentence on the charges for which he had been convicted in 1764. Nothing daunted, Wilkes maintained his attacks upon the ministry and in February 1769 was again expelled from Parliament. However, his stand against the unpopular government guaranteed his re-election in February, and again in March and April following further expulsions. In a controversial development, the Commons eventually declared that Henry Lawes Luttrell, who was defeated by Wilkes in the final contest, should be duly elected.

Wilkes's role as the martyr of English liberty won him widespread sympathy, and a SOCIETY OF THE SUPPORTERS OF THE BILL OF RIGHTS bolstered his cause and shouldered his debts. Although excluded from Parliament, Wilkes pursued his political career in the City of London: in 1774 he became lord mayor and was re-elected MP for Middlesex. In Parliament once more, Wilkes adopted a radical programme and voiced support for the rebellious American colonists. Wilkes's anti-government stance was widely believed to be nothing more than a cynical ploy to maintain his credibility with the mob. In fact, despite his debt to the ordinary Londoners who had rallied to his cause in their thousands, the *nouveau riche* Wilkes had little sympathy with their grievances; in 1780 he took a conspicuous role in defending the Bank of England against the GORDON RIOTERS composed of just such elements. Although Wilkes was re-elected in both 1780 and 1784, by the end of the American war the issues that had once made Wilkes the darling of the Middlesex electors were no longer relevant, and his popularity waned to the extent that he did not risk electoral humiliation in 1790.

While many contemporary observers believed Wilkes to be insincere in his political beliefs, the agitation that he fomented nonetheless raised basic constitutional issues. In addition, his career was crucial in establishing the freedoms of a rapidly growing press, while the mass support that the Wilkesite movement attracted helped to lay the foundations of popular English RADICALISM.

FURTHER READING G. Rudé, *Wilkes and Liberty: A Social Study of 1763 to 1774* (1962); P.D.G. Thomas, *John Wilkes: A Friend to Liberty* (1996).

William III (1650–1702), king of England, Scotland (as William II) and Ireland (1689–1702), prince of Orange and stadholder of the United Provinces of the Netherlands (1672–1702). He was joint monarch with his wife Mary until her death in 1694.

William was already a soldier and statesman of European stature when he accepted an invitation from the opponents of James II to intervene in English affairs. William's successful invasion during the autumn of 1688 provoked James's panic and flight, and, in conjunction with his wife Mary, William subsequently accepted the vacant throne and the terms of the BILL OF RIGHTS. From this so-called GLORIOUS REVOLUTION until his death William worked to consolidate Britain's Protestant succession and win its recognition throughout Europe.

The only child of William II of Orange and Mary Stuart, eldest daughter of Charles I, William was born shortly after his father's death in an era of upheaval in Dutch politics: strife between the house of Orange and its opponents led to two decades of republican rule associated with the de Witt brothers. During this time the prince of Orange and his descendants were barred from holding state office by the Act of Seclusion (1654). William nevertheless received a broad education and gave early signs of qualities that would ultimately transcend republican hostility towards his family.

In 1670 William was received with honour by Charles II, but remained suspicious that his English uncle would join Louis XIV in an assault upon the Dutch Republic. In fact, when it came in 1672, the anticipated Anglo-French attack triggered a dramatic rise in William's fortunes. The looming threat of conflict had already secured his appointment as captain general of the republic's troops, and the crisis posed by the subsequent French invasion resulted in the downfall of the de Witts and his own elevation to the position of stadholder, or lieutenant, of most of the Dutch provinces. Despite his youth, William constructed an anti-French alliance that ultimately forced the withdrawal of Louis XIV's troops from the United Provinces. William's leadership of the resistance to France brought international prestige. Returning to England in 1677 William married his teenage cousin Mary, the staunchly Protestant elder daughter of the Catholic James duke of York. As next in line to the throne after her father, Mary offered William the tantalizing prospect of enlisting England's resources in his struggle with France.

During the closing years of Charles II's reign William grew convinced that the accession of the king's brother James would dash his hopes of Anglo-Dutch cooperation against Louis XIV. Certainly when James II came to the English throne in 1685 he showed more inclination to side with the French king. William accepted the invitation to invade England not only to secure English liberties, for which he was invited, but also to take England out of France's sphere of influence and attach it to his anti-French alliance.

William's chance came in the autumn of 1688 when Louis was preoccupied with campaigning in the Rhineland. After an abortive expedition that had to turn back because of storms at sea, he made a successful landing in Torbay on 5 November. James advanced to Salisbury prepared to do battle with the invading forces, but lost his nerve and retreated to London. He sent his wife and newborn son – James Francis Edward STUART – to France and planned to join them there. Unfortunately for William, who found the way to London unhindered by James's retreat there, the king bungled his attempt at flight and was brought back to the capital. William made sure that a second attempt was successful, and took over the administration of the government in the absence of the departed monarch at the invitation of several peers and gentlemen. He then summoned a CONVENTION PARLIAMENT, which met early in 1689. After prolonged debate it offered the crown jointly to William and Mary. The king, however, insisted upon, and obtained, the sole executive authority. In Edinburgh a Convention of Estates issued the CLAIM OF RIGHT, which, among other things, offered the crown of Scotland to William and Mary.

Not since 1066 when William I had launched the last successful invasion of England had the monarchy undergone such an upheaval. In all respects William III offered a dramatic contrast to his Catholic, insular and absolutist predecessor. In religion William's personal preference was for the Calvinism of the Dutch Reformed Church, and his closest friends were Dutch like himself, while his political interests extended far beyond the limited horizons of most Englishmen. Although he was no natural champion of representative institutions he lacked James's undisguised hostility towards them. Indeed, his lengthy apprenticeship as a soldier and statesman in the constitutionally complex Dutch Republic proved invaluable for his role as monarch of England and Scotland.

In its early years the Revolution monarchy weathered JACOBITE revolts in Scotland and Ireland which amounted to WILLIAMITE WARS OF SUCCESSION. William's reputation in his northern kingdom was tarnished in 1692, when his representatives orchestrated the massacre of the Macdonalds in GLENCOE after they had proved sluggish in pledging allegiance to the new regime. In Ireland the decisive defeat of the Jacobites established an overwhelming Protestant ascendancy that was destined to blight future relations with the Catholic Irish. Following his victory at the BOYNE in July 1690 William turned to his overriding objective – the war against Louis XIV in Europe. The NINE YEARS WAR was indeed 'King William's War'. Although his dogged generalship produced no spectacular victories, the gruelling operations in Flanders helped to lay the foundations for the successes of the British army under the duke of MARLBOROUGH during the War of the SPANISH SUCCESSION.

William's expensive continental warfare – together with the honours he lavished upon Dutch favourites such as William Bentinck earl of PORTLAND and Arnold Keppel earl of ALBEMARLE – cost him the esteem of many of his leading English subjects. Some did not scruple to claim that the king had a homosexual relationship with Portland. This negative image was at first balanced by the genuine popularity of Queen Mary, whose obvious devotion to the Church of England was crucial in maintaining the support of Anglican Tories. Her death in 1694 was a blow to the Revolution monarchy and rekindled Jacobite hopes of invasion. However, the involvement of the exiled James II in the FENWICK conspiracy to assassinate William unleashed a wave of revulsion against the Stuarts. The discovery of the plot marked a turning point for William: it prompted the formation of a Whig-backed 'Association' pledged to defend the king and his government.

The last years of his reign, however, saw renewed tension between William and an increasingly vocal opposition in Parliament. The end of the war in 1697 gave rise to the STANDING ARMY CONTROVERSY. After that William's grants to his favourites in Ireland came under resumed attack. The passage of the ACT OF SETTLEMENT in 1701 was taken as an opportunity to score points off the king. But as the international situation deteriorated that year, especially when Louis XIV recognized James II's son as James III on the death of his father, there was a rallying of support for William's efforts to construct a 'Grand Alliance' to contain French expansion. William's death in March 1702 from injuries sustained by a fall from his horse was variously greeted by his subjects. Jacobites rejoiced, while Whigs were apprehensive, and anxious to keep alive William's reputation as England's 'Great Deliverer' from 'popery' and arbitrary power.

SEE ALSO REVOLUTION SETTLEMENT.

FURTHER READING S.B. Baxter, *William III* (1966).

Williamite Wars of Succession (1689–91), conflicts between the JACOBITE supporters of the exiled James II and the supporters of the new king, WILLIAM III. Although in England the GLORIOUS REVOLUTION was implemented with little bloodshed, in Scotland and Ireland enforcement of the new regime required heavy fighting.

In Scotland James's standard was raised in April 1689 by John Graham of Claverhouse, Viscount Dundee. He captured Perth before retreating to the Highlands in search of recruits. Dundee's force was pursued by a Williamite army under Hugh Mackay, and the rival armies clashed at the Pass of Killiecrankie on 27 July. With just 2000 men Dundee was outnumbered two to one, but his Highlanders broke the royal government line with a devastating broadsword charge. Jacobite victory came at a high price: the 1000 casualties included Dundee himself. Mackay's discomfiture attracted fresh recruits to the Stuart cause, but the campaign soon lost momentum under Dundee's lacklustre replacement, Colonel Alexander Cannon. Refusing to engage Mackay on ground favourable to the Highlanders, Cannon instead led them into the constricted streets of Dunkeld, where they were repulsed by a stubborn garrison of Cameronians. Cannon's replacement, Major General Thomas Buchan, was no more fortunate; on 1 May 1690 his command was cut to pieces by Mackay's cavalry on the exposed Haughs of Cromdale. Buchan fell back to Lochaber, where his remaining forces melted away. Armed resistance to the REVOLUTION SETTLEMENT ended in Scotland.

In Ireland Jacobite resistance proved more protracted. The exiled James arrived from France in March 1689 and established himself in Dublin. James enjoyed greater popularity in Catholic Ire-land than in Protestant England, and he soon recruited some 30,000 local men to bolster the 5000 who had landed with him. Although his infantry was raw and ill-equipped, James's cavalry represented a formidable force. Jacobite troops under Richard Talbot duke of Tyrconnel swiftly swamped much of Protestant Ulster, although Enniskillen and Londonderry both defied him. Londonderry endured a half-hearted but celebrated siege (*see* APPRENTICE BOYS) that ended when English ships brought relief on 28 July. Such sea power provided William III with an invaluable asset throughout the Irish campaign, permitting the transport of troops and supplies. On 13 August 1689 a force of 10,000 Englishmen, Dutchmen and French Huguenots under Marshal von Schomberg landed in County Down. Despatching some of these to seize Belfast, Schomberg secured the surrender of the port of Carrickfergus. Having failed to bring James to battle, Schomberg dug in at Dundalk, where his command passed a sickly winter.

Unimpressed by Schomberg's inactivity, William decided to take personal command of the 1690 campaign and reinforced his polyglot army to 35,000 well-armed men. Landing at Carrickfergus on 14 June, William marched south. Against the advice of his French officers James decided to contest William's advance on Dublin, and arrayed his outnumbered troops behind the natural barrier of the river BOYNE. The armies met on 1 July. Duped by a diversionary flanking attack, James withdrew units to counter the threat, thereby allowing William to cross the Boyne. Fearing encirclement, the Jacobite army retreated. James fled to France, though his army regrouped at Limerick. William's attempt to storm the town's defences was repulsed with heavy losses, and his bloodied forces withdrew to winter quarters.

In 1691 William turned his attention to Flanders, leaving the Irish theatre to his countryman Godard van Reede van Ginkel. The Jacobite position in Ireland had been weakened by Louis XIV's decision to withdraw the French contingent to the

Low Countries. The decisive engagement in the Irish war was fought at Aughrim on 12 July, after the marquis de St Ruth decided to block Ginkel's advance on Galway: St Ruth was killed amidst fierce fighting, so prompting the collapse of the Jacobite army. In the wake of Aughrim, Galway and Sligo fell. A substantial Jacobite force remained at Limerick, which Ginkel pounded until the defenders requested a cease-fire. Under the treaty of Limerick of 3 October, the garrison surrendered. Most sailed off to uphold the Jacobite cause as the so-called 'Wild Geese' in the ranks of the French army. Limerick's fall ended both the Irish war and James's chances of recovering his throne.

FURTHER READING J. Childs, 'The Williamite War, 1689–1691' in T. Bartlett and K. Jeffery (eds.), *A Military History of Ireland* (1996).

Wilmington, Spencer Compton, 1st earl of.

See COMPTON, SPENCER, 1ST EARL OF WILMINGTON.

Wilson, Richard (1713–82), landscape painter, often regarded as the founding father of a genre in which Britons were soon to become pre-eminent. Born in Wales, Wilson studied portrait painting in London. He concentrated upon portraiture until his mid-30s, when an extended visit to Italy and meetings with Zuccarelli and Vernet prompted a dramatic change of direction in favour of landscape. Wilson's decision was probably a mistake in financial terms; however, the principles he established proved far-reaching and prepared the ground for the emergence of CONSTABLE and TURNER. Indeed, the critic John Ruskin credited Wilson as the originator 'of sincere landscape art founded on a meditative love of nature'.

Identifying a potential market for landscape among classically minded connoisseurs, Wilson initially drew inspiration from the idealized views of the Roman Campagna produced in the previous century by Claude Lorrain and Gaspard Poussin (Dughet); the Dutch landscape tradition may have contributed further influences, particularly on Wilson's distinctive treatment of light. Wilson returned from his Italian trip with a large collection of drawings, which provided the raw material for many subsequent paintings.

A founder member of the Royal Academy, Wilson produced spectacular mythological landscapes, views of the countryside surrounding London, and paintings reflecting the natural grandeur of the Welsh mountains. *Mount Snowdon* (*c*.1762) offers a fine example of Wilson's contribution to the development of landscape as an atmospheric art form rising above mere topography. Ironically, the very realism of Wilson's landscapes contradicted the taste of contemporary patrons, who preferred to see their paintings inhabited with classical nymphs, fauns and satyrs.

Wilson's work was frequently copied and forged. In 1776 he succeeded Francis Hayman as librarian at the Royal Academy. Suffering from ill health, he retired to his native Wales in 1781.

Wolfe, James (1727–59), general who became one of the British empire's first popular heroes after dying of wounds sustained in his dramatic victory at QUEBEC. The son of a general, James was prevented by illness from joining the expedition against Cartagena during the War of JENKINS'S EAR; given that force's heavy losses from tropical diseases, it is unlikely that the sickly youngster would have survived to earn a glowing military reputation. Wolfe remained tormented by ill health throughout his short life. Gangling and redheaded, with a pointed nose and receding chin, he possessed an unmilitary appearance. His dedication and professionalism nonetheless earned him a reputation as one of the army's most promising officers.

Wolfe gained a lieutenancy after fighting at DETTINGEN in 1743 during the War of the AUSTRIAN SUCCESSION. Three years later he campaigned against the Jacobites in Scotland, tasting defeat at Falkirk and victory at CULLODEN. He was reputed to have refused to join in the atrocities that earned for the duke of CUMBERLAND his reputation as 'the Butcher'. In January 1747 Wolfe rejoined his regiment in Flanders, where he was wounded at the battle of Laffeldt. At the peace of 1748 he was based in Scotland and subsequently visited Ireland and France before commanding a regiment in England.

In 1757, during the first phase of the SEVEN YEARS WAR, Wolfe was appointed quartermaster general of the expedition against Rochefort in the Bay of Biscay; unlike other officers he emerged from that inglorious episode with his reputation intact. When Amherst was picked to lead the attack on Louisbourg in 1758 Wolfe went as one of his brigadiers. He played a conspicuous part in the waterborne attack on Cape Breton, and distinguished himself throughout the subsequent siege. That September he led an expedition that destroyed the French fisheries in the Gulf of St Lawrence, but when his hopes of proceeding further upriver were disappointed he returned to England. Wolfe acquainted both PITT and Lord LIGONIER of his willingness to serve against Quebec, and in January 1759 he was duly promoted to major general and given command of the troops despatched against that city.

By the end of June a powerful fleet under Vice Admiral Sir Charles Saunders had landed Wolfe's army of 8000 redcoats near Quebec. For more than two months Wolfe grappled with the problem of engaging with his opponent the marquis de Montcalm. On 31 July Wolfe's amphibious landing at Beauport was beaten back with heavy casualties. His plans frustrated and his health failing, Wolfe was reduced to bombarding the city and burning outlying hamlets. He was also at loggerheads with his brigadiers over strategy: they believed that the key to Quebec's defences lay above the city and that a landing there would sever its supply line, so obliging Montcalm to emerge and fight. Wolfe accepted their advice, but decided to land much closer to Quebec than suggested, choosing a cove just 3 km (2 miles) upriver from the city. In the early hours of 13 September he coolly implemented his modified version of the brigadiers' plan. Through a combination of careful

planning and amazingly good luck the boats transporting his troops reached their objective unopposed. Wolfe's advance guard then scrambled up a scrubby cliff while their comrades negotiated a rough path.

With the coming of dawn Wolfe had assembled 4500 men on the Plains of Abraham facing the city. An incredulous Montcalm decided to attack them before they were reinforced. The battle that followed was brief but bloody, as the disciplined firepower of Wolfe's redcoats shattered the French advance. During the action Wolfe received three wounds, the last proving fatal. Montcalm was also mortally wounded as his army was routed and Quebec surrendered on 18 September. News of the victory took Britain by surprise, as Wolfe's last despatch to Pitt had suggested failure – so the spectacular climax to the siege, with the young general slain in the hour of victory, created a sensation. Wolfe became the subject of countless odes, while his death was depicted by leading artists: Edward Penny and George Romney had already tackled the subject when Benjamin WEST secured Wolfe's permanent place in the pantheon of national heroes through his vastly popular depiction of the scene.
FURTHER READING R. Reilly, *The Rest to Fortune: The Life of Major-General James Wolfe* (1960).

Wollstonecraft, Mary (1759–97), feminist writer and novelist. Although remembered chiefly for *A Vindication of the Rights of Woman* published in 1792, Mary Wollstonecraft wrote many other works, including conduct books and NOVELS. Her most famous work was a sequel to her *Vindication of the Rights of Man*, which she published in 1790 to defend Richard PRICE from the attack made on him by Edmund BURKE. She received little in the way of a formal education, being the daughter of a weaver who had set himself up as a farmer. However, she read voraciously, not only in English but also in Dutch, French, German and Italian – languages which she taught herself. In addition to her own writings she translated the works of several continental authors. After teaching in a school that she herself established in Newington Green, she travelled abroad, visiting France in 1792 where, like so many English radicals who had greeted the French Revolution with enthusiasm, she became disillusioned with its violent progress. Her disillusion found expression in *An Historical and Moral View of the Origin and Progress of the French Revolution* (1794). In Paris she met an American, Gilbert Imlay, by whom she had a daughter in 1794 and with whom she travelled through Scandinavia. Her grim experiences on these travels, during which Imlay was unfaithful to her to the point where she contemplated suicide, were chronicled in her *Letters written during a short residence in Sweden, Norway and Denmark*. After breaking with Imlay she renewed her acquaintance with William GODWIN, whom she married in 1797 when she found herself pregnant. Their union invited ridicule, because both had condemned the institution of marriage. The pregnancy ended fatally for her: she died of complications shortly after giving birth to a daughter, the future Mary Wollstonecraft Shelley, who was to become celebrated as the creator of *Frankenstein*. Although she is rightly celebrated as an early feminist, the thrust of most of Mary Wollstonecraft's writing was not to advocate independence for women but to argue that they should acquire a level of education to enable them to become intellectual partners for their husbands.

FURTHER READING J. Todd, *Mary Wollstonecraft* (2000).

women. The lives and expectations of 18th-century women from the highest ranks through the lower classes differed significantly from those of their male counterparts. As strict notions of position and role continued to dominate 18th-century society, so women were also expected to adhere to the traditional concepts of duty and responsibility that defined their lives. Religious strictures – and, later in the century, the philosophical and scientific ideologies expressed by ENLIGHTENMENT

thinkers – assisted in defining the position of women throughout the era.

Writers and philosophers of both sexes such as John LOCKE, Jean-Jacques Rousseau and Hester Chapone continued to agree that nature intended women to occupy a position of dependence upon men due to their smaller stature, their physical weakness and their unstable and emotional temperaments. Whereas men were thought to possess the qualities of reason, intellect, courage, independence and strength, it was believed that, as Lord Camelford wrote to his daughter, 'Meekness, tenderness, patience, constancy, love and beauty' were the 'ornaments' of the female sex. Endowed with such characteristics women were viewed as society's softening influence, better able to superintend over families, devote attention to the interests of others and render the home delightful through charm and affection, while men occupied themselves in the public sphere.

Historians have suggested that the 'separate spheres' of women and men, one private and one public, were regarded by both sexes with equal esteem during the 18th century. However, recent scholarship has begun to question the relevance of separate spheres and the notion that the domain of the woman was exclusively in the private realm. Nevertheless, historical evidence generally suggests that women's lives revolved principally around the home. As a woman's role was predominantly a domestic one, her marriage and her ability to mother children became the two most important aspects of her life. Her greatest achievement would be to forge an advantageous and 'companionate' union, ideally founded upon mutual affection and friendship, with a socially and financially suitable partner. In response to demand, instructive literature and didactic novels geared towards a female readership and offering advice on courtship, marriage and the choice of a husband rolled off the era's printing presses in vast numbers. Some of the more popular – including those composed by Wetenhall Wilkes, John Gregory and James Fordyce – suggested that a woman's success as a wife depended primarily on the preservation of her virtue (or chastity) and on her modesty, 'sensibility' and obedience.

The cultivation of these characteristics – in addition to the rudimentary skills of reading, writing and simple arithmetic – formed the basis of a woman's education during the 18th century. If her family was wealthy enough to afford formalized schooling, their choice of girls' educational institutions would have grown significantly by the end of the century. As one observer in 1759 commented, '2 or 3 houses might be seen in almost every village with the inscription "Young Ladies Boarded and Educated"'. Although the quality of education was not always of the highest order, most schools offered instruction in 'accomplishments' such as music, dancing, needlework, French and Italian. Ultimately, however, the most important lesson a young unmarried woman could learn would be to 'know ever so little well', lest the brilliance of her mind render her undesirable to prospective suitors.

Unlike their male counterparts, women were not educated with a view to pursuing careers. In theory, women throughout their lives would remain dependent upon men for their maintenance. A girl would pass from the care of her father into the home of her husband and eventually be provided for by her sons in her widowhood. In practice this was not always the case. Although very little historical evidence survives to document the lives of middle- and lower-class women, there is much to indicate that many worked to support themselves and their families. In cities and urban centres women could typically earn low pay as laundresses, milliners, seamstresses, domestic servants and food sellers, while in rural locations women worked alongside men bringing in harvests and hauling coal. PROSTITUTION was always a reliable method of supplementing poor wages; in the 1780s Sophie von la Roche, a visitor to London, estimated the existence of 50,000 'light girls' in the capital alone. However, it was not an absolute impossibility for a woman to earn a decent living

through her skill or talent. It was not unknown for wives, daughters and sisters of tradesmen to assume or assist in the running of affairs at various times, while women such as Fanny BURNEY, Angelica KAUFFMAN, Sarah SIDDONS and Elizabeth Linley were able to become successful writers, artists, actresses or musicians in their own right.

By modern standards a woman's lot in life was not a pleasant one. Women of all classes were unable to vote, hold property in their own name if married or divorce their husbands. Lack of medical knowledge ensured that childbirth remained life-threatening, and effective contraception was virtually unknown. Women were legally expected to tolerate their husbands' infidelity, as well as beatings or rape received within the bounds of marriage. However, on the whole women generally accepted their positions within society's very explicit framework, and voices of female discontent, such as that of Mary WOLLSTONECRAFT at the end of the century, were in the minority.

The era was not altogether void of the intellectual, scientific and political influences of women: the intellectually active Lady Mary Wortley MONTAGU and the politically vocal Georgiana duchess of DEVONSHIRE left their individual marks on the pages of the century's history. But the social and gender restrictions of the age left very few others with similar access to such opportunity.

SEE ALSO ASTELL, MARY; BARBAULD, ANNA; BLUESTOCKING.

FURTHER READING L. Stone, *The Family, Sex and Marriage in England: 1500–1800* (1977); A. Vickery, *The Gentleman's Daughter: Women's Lives in Georgian England* (1998).

Wood's halfpence, issue of copper coinage that caused a political crisis in Ireland. In 1722 the Treasury granted a patent to the duchess of Kendal, one of George I's mistresses, to issue copper coins to the value of £100,800 to meet the chronic shortage of small change in Ireland. She sold the patent to William Wood for £10,000, so the coins were called 'Wood's halfpence'. As far as the Irish were concerned it was a licence for Wood to make money *from* rather than *for* Ireland. All sections of Irish society, from the Anglo-Irish establishment to the Catholic peasantry, were up in arms against the scheme, their indignation brilliantly captured in Jonathan SWIFT's caustic *Drapier's Letters*. The uproar led to a recommended reduction in the face value of the copper coinage from £100,800 to £40,000. This, however, did nothing to disarm criticism, and Lord CARTERET, who replaced the duke of Grafton as lord lieutenant of Ireland in 1724 because of the furore, recommended that the scheme be dropped. Wood's patent was then recalled in 1725.

wool. *See* TEXTILES.

Wordsworth, William. *See* LAKE POETS.

workhouses. *See* POOR LAW.

Wren, Sir Christopher (1632–1723), architect. Wren was still active at the beginning of the 18th century, although his heyday had been earlier, especially with the commissions for rebuilding churches destroyed in the 1666 Fire of London. Nevertheless, he still exerted enormous influence on English architecture. Indeed his greatest work, St Paul's Cathedral, started in 1675, was not completed until 1710. He kept his post of surveyor general of the Board of Works throughout the reigns of WILLIAM III and ANNE, to be deprived of it in 1718, when he was 86 years old.

Wright, Joseph (1734–97), painter, now invariably linked with his native Derby. Wright is best known for his original and atmospheric images inspired by Britain's industrial and scientific 'revolutions'. His choice of subject matter stemmed both from his decision to remain outside the established London art scene, and from the patronage of some of the key figures behind economic developments in the Midlands, including Richard ARKWRIGHT and Josiah WEDGWOOD.

A pupil of Thomas Hudson, Wright developed a distinctive style featuring a mastery of lighting effects. Although drawing upon the traditions of the 'conversation' piece, many of his works reflected weightier themes that placed them in the category of the more prestigious 'history' painting. Among the best known of Wright's paintings inspired by contemporary developments in science is the candlelit *An Experiment on a Bird in the Air-Pump* of 1768. Wright thrived as a portraitist in the booming port of Liverpool between 1769 and 1771. Two years later he travelled to Italy, where he remained until 1775. While at Naples, Wright witnessed an eruption of Vesuvius, and the spectacular sight left a deep impression and inspired future canvases. Wright's fascination with light embraced both the natural and artificial; quirks of the former lend distinction to the Derbyshire landscapes he painted during the 1780s. An interest in the natural world characterized Wright's influential portrait of Rousseau's first British editor, Sir Brooke Boothby (1781), who was depicted deep in thought and sprawled full-length in a glade.

Although Wright achieved popular acclaim, his determination to remain in the provinces denied him the recognition of the elitist metropolitan art world; he was only given associate membership of the Royal Academy in his twilight years.

FURTHER READING B. Nicolson, *Joseph Wright of Derby: Painter of Light* (2 vols., 1968).

Wyndham, Sir William. *See* JACOBITES.

Wyvill, Christopher (1740–1822), campaigner for PARLIAMENTARY REFORM. Wyvill was educated at Queens' College, Cambridge, and after ordination obtained a living in Essex. His scruples about subscription to all Thirty-nine Articles led him to support the FEATHERS TAVERN PETITION in 1772. Its defeat and his inheritance of an estate at Constable Burton in the North Riding of Yorkshire from a branch of his family led him to put a curate into his Essex living and retire to Burton Hall. There he organized the Yorkshire Association, launched with a petition to Parliament from the county gentry who met at York in December 1779. They sought to gain extra representation for their class by adding to the number of county seats. They also sought to reduce the influence of the executive over Parliament by measures of 'economical reform', the abolition of rotten boroughs, and annual general elections.

The 'association movement' made some progress in 1780, but apart from some economical reforms made by the ROCKINGHAM ministry failed to realize its objective of parliamentary reform. Wyvill attached himself to the younger PITT in hopes of achieving some redistribution of parliamentary seats, and supported the prime minister in the general election of 1784. But Pitt's reform bill of 1785 was soundly beaten. Thereafter Wyvill fell out with Pitt and gravitated into the orbit of Charles James FOX. He became a keen advocate of CATHOLIC EMANCIPATION in his declining years.

Y–Z

York, Frederick Augustus, duke of, soldier and army administrator. Long ridiculed as the hapless 'Grand Old Duke of York', Frederick Augustus, Duke of York and Albany (1763–1827) has more recently received recognition for his role in reforming the British army that was to emerge victorious during the REVOLUTIONARY AND NAPOLEONIC WARS.

The second son of GEORGE III, York was elected bishop of Osnabruck before he had reached his first birthday; this lucrative appointment, which continued until 1803, reflected the king's influence as elector of Hanover. He served with Hanoverian forces in Germany before the outbreak of war with France in 1793, experience which won him the leadership of the British expeditionary force sent to Flanders. His raw and outnumbered troops performed as well as could be expected against the armies of revolutionary France, although the indecisive operations that followed inspired the nursery rhyme accusation that the duke had done nothing more than march his men up hill and down again. Although his generalship was far from inept, York came under increasing pressure from the advancing French. Abandoned by their allies, the British contingent withdrew to Germany and was evacuated from Bremen in the spring of 1795.

That year, York replaced the aged and ineffective AMHERST as the army's commander in chief.

At the time of York's appointment the British army was in dire need of reform. The duke capitalized upon his prestigious royal background to tackle this task with methodical vigour. Besides curbing the most notorious abuses of the system, by which officers purchased promotion regardless of ability, York oversaw the introduction of a unified drill and encouraged the light infantry tactics pioneered by John MOORE. York also sought to improve the army's health, and instigated educational initiatives that underpinned the establishment of the Royal Military Academy at Sandhurst.

During 1799 York returned to active service in joint command of the combined Russian-British army despatched to Holland; like the one sent to Flanders six years before, the expedition made little headway and was soon forced to withdraw amidst logistical problems. In 1809 York was obliged to resign as commander in chief after his former mistress, Mary Anne Clarke, became the focus of a scandal; she claimed to have accepted bribes from officers seeking promotion, and that York had benefited from the proceedings. York returned to the Horse Guards two years later at the height of the PENINSULAR WAR and resumed the programme of reforms that were to contribute to the final defeat of Napoleon at WATERLOO.

FURTHER READING A.H. Burne, *The Noble Duke of York* (1949).

Yorke, Philip, 1st earl of Hardwicke. *See* HARD-
WICKE, PHILIP YORKE, 1ST EARL OF.

Yorkshire Association. *See* PARLIAMENTARY RE-
FORM; WYVILL, CHRISTOPHER.

Yorktown, surrender at (19 October 1781),
capitulation of more than 6000 royalist troops
under CORNWALLIS to the Americans in Virginia.
The defeat destroyed Britain's resolve to continue
the AMERICAN WAR OF INDEPENDENCE.

Following his Pyrrhic victory at Guilford
Courthouse in March 1781, Cornwallis had
marched from North Carolina into Virginia. In
the hope of maintaining communications with the
Royal Navy he entrenched his troops at Yorktown,
situated towards the end of a peninsula between
the York and James rivers on the western shore of
the Chesapeake Bay. Unfortunately for the British,
when a French fleet from the West Indies under
de Grasse blockaded the entrance to the bay,
Cornwallis had no way to escape from the advance
along the peninsula of 16,000 American and
French troops under Washington and Rochambeau. Washington himself dug the first spadeful of
soil in the siege batteries, and the British defences
were soon subjected to heavy bombardment.
As casualties from gunfire and disease mounted
steadily, the beleaguered Cornwallis warned
General CLINTON at the British headquarters in
New York, 'if you cannot relieve me very soon you
must be prepared to hear the Worst'. A relief
expedition was assembled but could not break
through the French blockade of the Chesapeake.
Cornwallis surrendered on 19 October: he tried
to surrender to Rochambeau, but the French
general obliged him to capitulate to Washington.
Nevertheless, his sullen force of redcoats, Hessians
and American loyalists were accorded the honours
of war in recognition of their stubborn defence.
In London news of the disaster heralded the
downfall of Lord North's ministry. Although the
British still retained important bases along the
eastern seaboard of North America, the defeat at

Yorktown ended concerted efforts to contest
American independence.

Young, Arthur (1741–1820), prolific journalist
whose writings – despite his own early failure as a
farmer – helped to propagate the techniques of
Britain's 'agricultural revolution'.

After contemplating a career in business, Young
began farming on the family estate at Bradfield,
Suffolk. By the late 1760s Young was experi-
menting with new agricultural ideas and seeking
to spread them through his *Farmer's Letters to the
People*. Neither the practical nor the theoretical
approach proved successful; Young was obliged to
pay another farmer £100 to take over his founder-
ing farm in Essex, while his writings likewise failed
to make an impact.

Young's tenure of a holding in Hertfordshire
proved equally fruitless, although this did not discourage him from making extensive tours of other
farms in England and Wales. Young published his
observations, and produced a steady stream of
pamphlets on a wide range of topics; in the early
1770s, when times grew particularly hard, he supplemented his income by writing newspaper reports
of parliamentary debates for the *Morning Post*. In
1784, after a stint as estate agent for Lord Kings-
borough in County Cork, Young began publication of his influential *Annals of Agriculture*. Over
the next quarter of a century Young's *Annals*
showcased the latest experiments in farming, and
provided a forum for debate that drew contributions from such notables as COKE of Holkham and
'Farmer George' III himself.

Young was given an opportunity to contrast
English with continental agriculture when he
embarked upon protracted tours of France and
Italy between 1787 and 1790. He was in Paris
when the Revolution began, and the published
account of his *Travels* provides a vivid impression
of both its underlying causes in the countryside
and the dramatic events that followed its eruption.
By this time Young's writings on agriculture had
gained him considerable fame. The younger Pitt

consulted him on farming matters, and in 1793 appointed him secretary of the newly created Board of Agriculture (*see* AGRICULTURE). The post brought an annual salary of £400 and served to consolidate Young's role as a leading exponent of Georgian Britain's 'improved' agriculture.

Zoffany, Johann (1733–1810), painter. Zoffany was born at Frankfurt am Main and studied at Regensburg and Rome, before seeking his fortune in London in 1760. Zoffany's background was in history painting, although his first English commissions were mere hack work. However, with the encouragement of the great actor-manager David GARRICK, Zoffany embarked upon a series of paintings depicting dramatic highlights from his patron's stage career; unlike previous portrayals of the theatre, which had included members of the audience and stilted stage scenery, these placed the incidents in realistic settings. The alliance was both successful and lucrative: Zoffany's lively paintings were reproduced as popular engravings and helped to bolster Garrick's reputation as the most distinguished and versatile actor of his age.

From the mid-1760s Zoffany enjoyed the favour of GEORGE III and created informal images of the royal family. He produced life-sized portraits capable of rivalling REYNOLDS, and proved a master of the complex multi-figured conversation piece: his *Royal Academicians at the RA* of 1772 is a spectacular example of this genre. Based in Florence for much of the 1770s, Zoffany returned to England to find that his style was no longer in demand. Undeterred, he sought fresh markets in India, where the appetite for the conversation piece remained undiminished; his lively renderings of European colonists and native princes provide a remarkable record of the racial integration that characterized the era. Returning from India in 1789, Zoffany subsequently painted few pictures of note. He died in 1810, having abandoned painting a decade before.

Subject index

Chronology

1688	November	WILLIAM of Orange lands in Torbay
	December	James II flees to France
		General election
1689	January	CONVENTION PARLIAMENT meets in London
	February	Declaration of Rights (*see* BILL OF RIGHTS): Parliament offers English crown to WILLIAM and MARY
	March	James II lands in Ireland
		Convention of Estates meets in Edinburgh
	April	Convention of Estates issues CLAIM OF RIGHT, offering William and Mary the crown of Scotland
		Coronation of William and Mary
	May	William III declares war on France, formally marking England's entry into the NINE YEARS WAR (to 1697), although hostilities began the year before
		TOLERATION ACT grants a degree of religious freedom to DISSENTERS
	July	Siege of Londonderry raised (*see* APPRENTICE BOYS)
		Battle of Killiecrankie: Scottish Jacobites defeat government forces (*see* WILLIAMITE WARS OF SUCCESSION)
		Battle of Dunkeld: Scottish Jacobites defeated by government forces (*see* WILLIAMITE WARS OF SUCCESSION)
	December	Parliament changes Declaration of Rights into BILL OF RIGHTS
	~	LOCKE's *Two Treatises of Government* and *Letter on Toleration*
1690	February	General election
	June	William III lands in Ireland
		Battle of Beachy Head: French gain control of the English Channel (*see* NINE YEARS WAR)
	July	Battle of the BOYNE: victory in Ireland of William III's Anglo-Dutch army

1690		over James II's Franco-Irish army
	~	LOCKE's *Essay on Human Understanding*
1691	July	Battle of Aughrim in Ireland: further WILLIAMITE victory over Jacobite forces
	October	Treaty of Limerick dictates the terms of the Jacobite surrender in IRELAND, ending WILLIAMITE WARS OF SUCCESSION
1692	February	Massacre of GLENCOE
	May	Battle of La Hogue: Anglo-Dutch naval victory over a French fleet
	~	First Boyle lecture
1693	~	LOCKE's *Some Thoughts concerning Education*
1694	July	BANK OF ENGLAND established
	December	TRIENNIAL ACT: general elections to be held at least every third year
	~	Mary ASTELL's *A Serious Proposal to the Ladies*
1695	May	Licensing Act expires followed by torrent of tracts against the established church (*see* CENSORSHIP; CONVOCATION CONTROVERSY; PRESS, THE)
	October	General election
	~	LOCKE's *The Reasonableness of Christianity*
1696	February	Assassination plot against William III (*see* FENWICK)
1697	September–October	Treaty of Ryswick ends NINE YEARS WAR
1698	~	Scottish expedition to DARIEN on isthmus of Panama
	July	General election
	October	First partition treaty (*see* SPANISH SUCCESSION, WAR OF THE)
	~	TRENCHARD's *Short History of Standing Armies* (*see* STANDING ARMY CONTROVERSY)
1700	~	Second partition treaty (*see* SPANISH SUCCESSION, WAR OF THE)
	~	Failure of Scottish DARIEN SCHEME; Darien abandoned
1701	January	General election
	June	ACT OF SETTLEMENT establishes HANOVERIAN SUCCESSION
	August	Treaty of Grand Alliance signed by Britain, the Dutch Republic and the Austrian Habsburgs; basis of anti-French alliance in the War of the SPANISH SUCCESSION
	September	Death of James II; His son James Francis Edward STUART becomes, for Jacobites, James III
	December	General election
1702	March	Death of William III
		Accession of Queen ANNE
	May	War declared on France; beginning of War of the SPANISH SUCCESSION (to 1713)

1702	July	General election
	December	DEFOE's *Shortest Way with the Dissenters*
1703	August	Scottish Parliament passes Security Act (*see* UNION OF ENGLAND AND SCOTLAND); act vetoed by Queen Anne
1704	July	Capture of GIBRALTAR
	August	New Scottish Security Act given royal assent (*see* UNION OF ENGLAND AND SCOTLAND)
		Battle of BLENHEIM: Marlborough defeats Franco-Bavarian army
	~	Test Act restricts officeholding in IRELAND to Anglicans
	~	SWIFT's *Tale of a Tub*
1705	March	English Parliament passes Aliens Act (*see* UNION OF ENGLAND AND SCOTLAND)
1706	April	Queen Anne chooses commissioners for UNION OF ENGLAND AND SCOTLAND
	May	Battle of RAMILLIES: Marlborough defeats French
		General election
	July	Anglo-Scottish treaty of UNION concluded
1707	January	Scottish Parliament ratifies treaty of UNION
	March	Anne gives royal assent to Act of UNION
	October	First Parliament of Great Britain meets
1708	March	Abortive JACOBITE attempt to invade Scotland
	May	General election won by Whigs
	July	Battle of OUDENARDE: Marlborough defeats French
	September	Capture of MINORCA
1709	September	Battle of MALPLAQUET: Marlborough defeats French
	November	Dr SACHEVERELL preaches sermon in St Paul's; regarded as subversive by Whig government
	December	Dr Sacheverell impeached
1710	February–March	Trial of Dr Sacheverell
	April–September	Ministerial revolution engineered by Robert HARLEY, who returns to power, presiding over a largely Tory ministry
	September	General election won by Tories
	~	SWIFT contributes to *The Examiner*
1711	December	Peace preliminaries defeated in House of Lords
		OCCASIONAL CONFORMITY ACT penalizes DISSENTERS who take Anglican communion to qualify for offices
	~	SWIFT's *The Conduct of the Allies*

1711	~	Addison and Steele launch the SPECTATOR
1712	~	Duke of MARLBOROUGH replaced by duke of ORMONDE as commander of allied forces
1713	March–April	Treaty of UTRECHT ends War of the SPANISH SUCCESSION
	August–September	General election increases Tory majority
1714	June	SCHISM ACT seeks to eliminate the separate education of DISSENTERS
	July	Queen Anne dismisses the earl of Oxford (Robert HARLEY)
	August	Death of Queen Anne; Accession of GEORGE I
		George dismisses BOLINGBROKE, who flees to France; Whig ministry appointed
	~	MANDEVILLE's *The Fable of the Bees* separates economics from ethics
1715	January–February	General election won by Whigs
	April–July	Anti-Hanoverian riots
	June	Bolingbroke flees to France
	July	RIOT ACT
	September–December	JACOBITE RISING
	November	Battle of Sheriffmuir: government forces halt Jacobite advance
	~	ADDISON's *The Freeholder*
1716	May	SEPTENNIAL ACT extends the maximum interval between general elections to seven years
1717	March	BANGORIAN CONTROVERSY over the power of the church
	April	TOWNSHEND dismissed from the ministry; WALPOLE resigns; STANHOPE and Charles SUNDERLAND head ministry
1718	March	SUNDERLAND becomes first lord of the Treasury
	August	STANHOPE negotiates Quadruple Alliance: Austria joins Triple Alliance of Britain, the Dutch Republic and France to stop the Spanish changing the terms of the treaty of UTRECHT
1719	January	Repeal of OCCASIONAL CONFORMITY ACT and SCHISM ACT against DISSENTERS
	February–April	Debates on Peerage Bill, which aims to restrict the monarch's power to create new peerages (*see* LORDS, HOUSE OF)
	June	Spanish and Scottish JACOBITE force defeated at Glenshiel
	~	DEFOE's *Robinson Crusoe*
1720	~	TOWNSHEND and WALPOLE return to the ministry
	~	DECLARATORY ACT: Westminster Parliament asserts Irish Parliament is subordinate to it

1720	August– September	SOUTH SEA BUBBLE crisis
1721	April	WALPOLE replaces SUNDERLAND as first lord of the Treasury and also becomes chancellor of the exchequer
1722	March–April	General election won by Whigs
	May	Atterbury plot: Bishop Francis ATTERBURY accused of promoting a Jacobite rising; Atterbury exiled, BOLINGBROKE returns
	~	DEFOE's *Moll Flanders*
1723	June	ATTERBURY exiled
1724	February	First of Swift's *Drapier's Letters* against WOOD'S HALFPENCE
1725	June	Malt tax riots in Glasgow
	September	Wood's patent for Irish coinage annulled (*see* WOOD'S HALFPENCE)
1726	December	*The Craftsman* launched by opposition leaders Lord BOLINGBROKE and William PULTENEY
	~	SWIFT's *Gulliver's Travels*
1727	June	Death of George I; Accession of GEORGE II
	July	General election
1728	December	FREDERICK (prince of Wales from 1729) arrives in England
	~	GAY's *Beggar's Opera*
	~	POPE's *Dunciad*
1729	October	TOWNSHEND negotiates Treaty of Seville with Spain
	~	SWIFT's *A Modest Proposal*
1730	May	TOWNSHEND resigns as secretary of state
1731	March	Treaty of Vienna with Holy Roman emperor
	~	*The Gentleman's Magazine* launched
1732	June	Report of committee on frauds and abuses in the customs service reveals widespread intimidation of officials and smuggling, WALPOLE responds with Excise scheme
1733	April–June	EXCISE CRISIS: Walpole's excise scheme provokes resistance in Parliament and the country until withdrawn
	~	POPE's *Essay on Man*
1734	April–May	General election sees opposition gains
1735	~	BOLINGBROKE returns to France
	~	HOGARTH's *Rake's Progress*
	~	Act against piracy of PRINTS

1736	September	PORTEOUS RIOTS in Edinburgh
1737	September	FREDERICK PRINCE OF WALES breaks with his parents
	November	Death of Queen CAROLINE, wife of George II
	~	Licensing Act censors plays (*see* CENSORSHIP; THEATRE)
1738	April	Reporting of parliamentary speeches declared a breach of privilege
	~	BOLINGBROKE's *The Idea of a Patriot King*
	~	JOHNSON's *London*
1739	October	War of JENKINS'S EAR with Spain begins
	November	Admiral VERNON captures Puerto Bello
1740	March	Vernon lionized when news of Puerto Bello reaches England
	~	War of Jenkins's Ear merges into War of the AUSTRIAN SUCCESSION (to 1748)
	~	Thomas Arne's 'Rule Britannia'
	~	RICHARDSON's *Pamela* (to 1742)
1741	April	Unsuccessful British attack on Carthagena
	May	General election removes WALPOLE's majority
	~	HUME's *Essays*
	~	FIELDING's *Shamela*
1742	February	WALPOLE resigns
	~	HANDEL's *Messiah* first performed
	~	FIELDING's *Joseph Andrews*
1743	June	GEORGE II leads allied army to victory over French at DETTINGEN
	August	Henry PELHAM made first lord of the Treasury
1744	March	France formally declares war on Britain
	December	NEWCASTLE and PELHAM form the BROAD-BOTTOM ADMINISTRATION
1745	May	Anglo-Dutch army defeated by French at FONTENOY
	July	Charles Edward STUART lands in Scotland to lead the last JACOBITE RISING (to 1746)
	September	Jacobites win battle of Prestonpans
	December	Jacobite army reaches Derby, then retreats
1746	February	Jacobites win battle of Falkirk
	April	Jacobites routed by CUMBERLAND at CULLODEN; end of Jacobite rising
	~	French capture British trading post at Madras, INDIA
1747	June–July	General election gives ministry of NEWCASTLE and PELHAM a huge majority
1748	October	Treaty of AIX-LA-CHAPELLE ends War of the AUSTRIAN SUCCESSION

1748	~	RICHARDSON's *Clarissa*
1749	~	FIELDING's *Tom Jones*
1750	~	JOHNSON's periodical, *The Rambler* (to 1752)
1751	March	Death of FREDERICK PRINCE OF WALES
	May	CALENDAR REFORM: act of Parliament abolishes Old Style (Julian) calendar and introduces New Style (Gregorian): change to be made in 1752
	~	CLIVE reopens hostilities with French in INDIA
	~	GRAY's *Elegy*
1752	September	CALENDAR REFORM: day after 2 September numbered the 14th
	~	FIELDING's *Amelia*
1753	June	HARDWICKE'S MARRIAGE ACT, aimed at stopping clandestine marriages
1754	March	Henry PELHAM dies; duke of NEWCASTLE becomes prime minister
	April–May	General election
1755	July	Braddock's expedition defeated by French and Native Americans at Monongahela River, Pennsylvania (one of several encounters prior to the formal declaration of the SEVEN YEARS WAR)
	~	JOHNSON's *Dictionary*
1756	May	Britain declares war on France; formal beginning of SEVEN YEARS WAR (to 1763)
	June	French take MINORCA from British
		British prisoners die in Black Hole of Calcutta, INDIA
	November	DEVONSHIRE-PITT ministry formed
1757	June	CLIVE's victory at PLASSEY secures British control of Bengal, INDIA
	July	PITT-NEWCASTLE ministry formed
1758	June	Amphibious expedition under command of AMHERST and BOSCAWEN captures Louisbourg on Cape Breton
	December	HALLEY's correct prediction that a comet observed in previous centuries would return; thereafter named Halley's comet
	~	Magdalen Hospital for penitent prostitutes founded
1759	~	*Annus mirabilis*: year of British victories
	May	British take Guadeloupe
	August	British–German army defeats French at battle of MINDEN
	September	British take QUEBEC
	November	British naval victory over French fleet at QUIBERON BAY
	~	JOHNSON's *Rasselas*
1760	January	Sir Eyre COOTE defeats the French at Wandewash, INDIA

1760	September	British take Montreal
	October	Death of George II; Accession of GEORGE III
	~	STERNE's *Tristram Shandy* (to 1767)
1761	March	Lord BUTE becomes a leading minister
	March–April	General election
	October	PITT resigns
	December	Spain declares war on Britain
	~	In INDIA, COOTE takes Pondicherry from the French
1762	February	British take Martinique
	May	BUTE replaces NEWCASTLE as first lord of the Treasury (prime minister)
1763	February	Treaty of PARIS ends SEVEN YEARS WAR
	April	George GRENVILLE replaces BUTE as prime minister
	November	Parliament resolves that WILKES's paper *The North Briton* number 45 is a seditious libel
1764	January	Wilkes expelled from the House of Commons
1765	March	STAMP ACT passed; causes outrage among American colonists
	July	ROCKINGHAM replaces GRENVILLE as prime minister
1766	February	Repeal of the STAMP ACT
	April	GENERAL WARRANTS declared to be illegal by House of Commons, following case brought by John WILKES
	July	Lord Chatham (the elder PITT) replaces ROCKINGHAM as prime minister
	~	GOLDSMITH's *Vicar of Wakefield*
1767	June	'TOWNSHEND duties' on imports into the colonies enacted; duties cause uproar in America
1768	March–April	General election; WILKES returned for Middlesex
	May	ST GEORGE'S FIELDS 'massacre' of demonstrators supporting Wilkes
	October	GRAFTON replaces Chatham (the elder PITT) as prime minister
1769	January	WILKES expelled from the Commons
	April	Wilkes's return as MP for Middlesex after victories at three by-elections over ruled in favour of his opponent
	~	*Letters of* JUNIUS
1770	January	NORTH replaces GRAFTON as prime minister
	March	'TOWNSHEND duties' on imports into the colonies repealed, except for the duty on tea
	April	Captain COOK lands at Botany Bay, AUSTRALIA, and claims New South Wales for Britain

1770	~	GOLDSMITH's *The Deserted Village*
1771	March	Reporting of parliamentary debates permitted
	~	SMOLLETT's *Humphry Clinker*
1772	March	Royal Marriages Act prohibits royal marriages without the king's consent
	~	FEATHERS TAVERN PETITION drawn up by clergymen unhappy with the Thirty-nine Articles
	~	*Encyclopaedia Britannica*
1773	May	EAST INDIA COMPANY given monopoly to supply tea to American colonies
	December	Boston Tea Party demonstrates the opposition in the AMERICAN COLONIES to the import duty on tea
	~	GOLDSMITH's *She Stoops to Conquer*
1774	March–May	Parliament passes the 'INTOLERABLE ACTS' in response to the crisis in the AMERICAN COLONIES
	October–November	General election gives NORTH a big majority
1775	April	British troops harassed by American militia at Lexington and Concord; marks outbreak of AMERICAN WAR OF INDEPENDENCE (to 1783)
	June	Battle of Bunker Hill; British achieve a narrow and costly victory over the Americans
	~	SHERIDAN's *The Rivals*
1776	July	Declaration of American Independence
	~	GIBBON's *Decline and Fall of the Roman Empire*
	~	Adam SMITH's *Wealth of Nations*
1777	September	British commander William HOWE captures Philadelphia
	October	Battle of SARATOGA, followed by BURGOYNE's surrender to the Americans
	~	SHERIDAN's *The Rivals*
1778	February	France allies itself with the Americans
	June	France declares war on Britain
	~	Fanny BURNEY's *Evelina*
1779	June	Spain declares war on Britain
	~	JOHNSON's *Lives of the Poets* (to 1781)
1780	April	DUNNING's MOTION in Parliament attacks 'the influence of the crown'
	June	GORDON RIOTS in London, directed against Catholics
	September–October	General election reduces NORTH's majority
	~	Hyder Ali begins his campaign against the British in INDIA

1781	October	CORNWALLIS surrenders to Americans at Yorktown; it ended Britain's efforts to subdue America
1782	March	ROCKINGHAM replaces NORTH as prime minister
	April	Battle of the Saints: RODNEY defeats French fleet
	July	SHELBURNE becomes prime minister on the death of Rockingham
	~	Repeal of Poynings Law and DECLARATORY ACT, 1720, gives virtual legislative autonomy to IRELAND
1783	February	Shelburne resigns after defeat of peace preliminaries in House of Commons
	April	FOX and NORTH form government
	September	Treaty of VERSAILLES formally ends AMERICAN WAR OF INDEPENDENCE; Britain recognizes USA
	December	Defeat of FOX's India Bill in House of Lords; bill proposed that the Commons, not the crown, should control patronage in India; Fox–North ministry dismissed, and replaced by William PITT the Younger
1784	March	General election: PITT obtains majority
	~	Pitt's India Act establishes BOARD OF CONTROL
1785	~	PITT introduces private bill proposing PARLIAMENTARY REFORM; bill is defeated
	~	Warren HASTINGS resigns as governor of Bengal and returns to Britain
	~	COWPER's *The Task*
1786	September	EDEN trade treaty signed with France
	~	BURNS's *Poems in the Scottish Dialect*
1787	April	Warren HASTINGS impeached (to 1795)
	January	First fleet carrying convicts arrives in AUSTRALIA
	November	GEORGE III shows signs of mental instability
1788–9	~	REGENCY CRISIS over whether the prince of Wales (the future GEORGE IV) should take over as regent
1789	July	Storming of the Bastille symbolizes outbreak of FRENCH REVOLUTION
	~	BLAKE's *Songs of Innocence*
1790	June	General election
	~	BURKE's *Reflections on the Revolution in France*
1791	July	'Church and King' riots destroy PRIESTLEY's house and laboratory in Birmingham
	~	Formation of Society of United Irishmen; presses for complete independence for IRELAND
	~	Thomas PAINE's *Rights of Man*, Part One
	~	BOSWELL's *Life of Johnson*

1792	January	Foundation of the London Corresponding Society, a radical political organization (*see* CORRESPONDING SOCIETIES)
	~	PAINE's *Rights of Man*, Part Two
	~	Mary WOLLSTONECRAFT's *Vindication of the Rights of Woman*
1793	February	Britain declares war against France, marking the beginning of the REVOLUTIONARY AND NAPOLEONIC WARS (to 1815)
	~	Irish Parliament passes Catholic Relief Act, allowing some Catholics in IRELAND to vote
	~	William GODWIN, *Enquiry concerning the principles of political justice*
1794	April	PITT clamps down on radicalism: suspension of habeas corpus
	June	GLORIOUS FIRST OF JUNE: Richard HOWE defeats French fleet
	July	PORTLAND Whigs join Pitt's ministry
	~	Suppression of Society of United Irishmen, who go underground
	~	PAINE's *Age of Reason*
1795	April	Acquittal of Warren HASTINGS
	October	Treasonable Practices Act and Seditious Meetings Act: aimed at crushing the politically radical CORRESPONDING SOCIETIES
1796	June	General election
	~	French attempt invasion of IRELAND
	~	Fanny BURNEY's *Camilla*
1797	February	Nelson defeats Spanish fleet at battle of CAPE ST VINCENT
	April, May	NAVAL MUTINIES at Spithead and the Nore
	October	Battle of CAMPERDOWN: British defeat Dutch fleet
1798	May	IRISH REBELLION
	August	Battle of the NILE: Nelson defeats French fleet
	~	MALTHUS's *Essay on the Principle of Population*
	~	Wordsworth and Coleridge, *Lyrical Ballads* (*see* LAKE POETS)
1799	April	PITT introduces income tax
	May	Tipu Sultan defeated and killed by British at Seringapatam, INDIA
1800	March	Act of Union brings about UNION OF BRITAIN AND IRELAND (implemented 1801)
1801	March	ADDINGTON replaces PITT as prime minister
	April	British defeat Danish fleet at battle of COPENHAGEN
	~	First CENSUS
1802	March	Treaty of AMIENS brings brief lull in the REVOLUTIONARY AND NAPOLEONIC WARS
	July	General election

1802	~	Launch of *Edinburgh Review*
1803	May	War with France resumes
1804	May	PITT replaces ADDINGTON as prime minister
1805	October	NELSON defeats French and Spanish fleets at TRAFALGAR
1806	January	Death of PITT
	February	Formation of MINISTRY OF ALL THE TALENTS
	September	Death of FOX
	November	General election
1807	March	PORTLAND becomes prime minister, replacing MINISTRY OF ALL THE TALENTS
	May	General election
	~	Abolition of the SLAVE TRADE in the British empire
1808	~	Start of PENINSULAR WAR (to 1814)
1809	January	British defeat French at CORUNNA, northwest Spain
	July	British defeat French at Talavera
	October	PERCEVAL succeeds PORTLAND as prime minister
1810	October	GEORGE III's mental illness recurs
1811	February	Regency declared: the future GEORGE IV becomes prince regent
1812	May	PERCEVAL assassinated; LIVERPOOL succeeds as prime minister
	June	Outbreak of WAR OF 1812 with USA (to 1815)
	July	British defeat French at SALAMANCA
	October	General election
1813	June	British defeat French at Vitoria
	~	Jane Austen's *Pride and Prejudice*
1814	April	Napoleon abdicates
	December	Formal end of WAR OF 1812, although fighting continues into 1815
	~	Walter Scott's *Waverley*
1815	June	Battle of WATERLOO: final defeat of Napoleon by WELLINGTON

Further reading

The following works are intended to complement the 'further reading' appended to individual entries.

General

Christie, I.R., *Wars and Revolutions. Britain 1760–1815* (1982)

Holmes, G., *The Making of a Great Power. Late Stuart and Early Georgian Britain, 1660 1722* (1993)

Holmes, G., and D. Szechi, *The Age of Oligarchy. Pre Industrial Britain 1722–1783* (1993)

Hoppit, J., *A Land of Liberty? England 1689–1727* (2000)

Jones, J.R., *Country and Court. England 1658–1714* (1978)

Langford, P., *A Polite and Commercial People. England 1727–1783* (1989)

Lenman, B., *Integration, Enlightenment and Industrialisation: Scotland, 1746–1832* (1981)

Mitchison, R., *Lordship to Patronage: Scotland, 1603–1746* (1983)

O'Gorman, F., *The Long Eighteenth Century. British Political and Social History 1688–1832* (1997)

Porter, R., *English Society in the Eighteenth Century* (rev. edn, 1991)

Prest, W., *Albion Ascendant. English History 1660–1815* (1998)

Rule, R., *Albion's People. English Society 1714–1815* (1992)

Speck, W.A., *Stability and Strife. England 1714–1760* (2nd edn, 1980)

More specialized studies

Barrell, J., *Imagining the King's Death: Figurative Treason, Fantasies of Regicide 1793–1796* (2000)

Berg, M., *The Age of Manufactures, 1700–1820* (1985)

Black, J., *A System of Ambition? British Foreign Policy 1660–1793* (1991)

Black, J., *Britain as a Military Power, 1688–1815* (1999)

Brewer, J., *The Sinews of Power: War, Money and the English State 1688–1783* (1989)

Brewer, J., *The Pleasures of the Imagination. English Culture in the Eighteenth Century* (1997)

Christie, I.R., *Stress and Stability in Late Eighteenth-Century Britain* (1984)

Clark, J.C.D., *English Society 1660–1832. Religion, ideology and politics during the ancien regime* (2nd edn, 2000)

Colley, L., *Britons: Forging the Nation, 1707–1837* (1993)

Conway, S., *The British Isles and the War of American Independence* (2000)

Cookson, J., *The British Armed Nation, 1793–1815* (1997)

Daunton, M.J., *Progress and Poverty: an economic and social history of Britain, 1700–1815* (1995)

Devine, T.M., *The Scottish Nation, 1700–2000* (1999)

Dickinson, H.T., *Liberty and Property. Political Ideology in Eighteenth-Century Britain* (1977)

Dickinson, H.T., *The Politics of the People in Eighteenth-Century Britain* (1995)

Earle, P., *The Making of the English Middle Class. Business, Society and Family Life in London, 1660–1730* (1989)

Emsley, C., *British Society and the French Wars 1793–1815* (1979)

Hitchcock, T., *English Sexualities, 1700–1800* (1997)

Holmes, G., *Augustan England. Professions, State and Society 1680–1730* (1982)

Hunt, M., *The Middling Sort; Commerce, Gender and the Family in England, 1680–1780* (1996)

Jones, J.R., *Britain and the World, 1649–1815* (1980)

Langford, P., *[Modern British Foreign Policy] The Eighteenth Century 1688–1815* (1982)

Langford, P., *Public Life and the Propertied Englishman, 1689–1798* (1991)

Mathias, P., *The Transformation of England: essays in the economic and social history of England in the eighteenth century* (1979)

McDowell, R.B., *Ireland in the age of Imperialism and Revolution, 1760–1801* (1979)

Murdoch, A., *British History 1660–1832: National Identity and Local Culture* (1998)

Pittock, M.G.H., *Inventing and Resisting Britain. Cultural Identities in Britain and Ireland, 1685–1789* (1997)

Pocock, J.G.A., *Virtue, Commerce, and History: Essays on Political Thought and History, chiefly in the Eighteenth Century* (1985)

Porter, R., *Disease, Medicine and Society in England 1550–1860* (2nd edn, 1993)

Rogers, N., *Whigs and Cities. Popular Politics in the Age of Walpole and Pitt* (1989)

Rose, C., *England in the 1690s. Revolution, Religion and War* (1999)

Rule, J., *The Labouring Classes in Early Industrial England 1750–1850* (1986)

Rule, J., *The Vital Century. England's Developing Economy, 1714–1815* (1991)

Scott, H.M., *British Foreign Policy in the Age of the American Revolution* (1990)

Speck, W.A., *Literature and Society in Eighteenth-Century England. Ideology, Politics and Culture 1680–1820* (1998)

Stone, L., *The Family, Sex and Marriage in England, 1500–1800* (1977)

Summerson, J., *Architecture in Britain: 1530–1830* (1983)

Szechi, D., *The Jacobites* (1994)

Thomas, P.D.G., *Politics in Eighteenth Century Wales* (1998)

Thompson, E.P., *Whigs and Hunters. The Origin of the Black Act* (1975)

Thompson, E.P., *The Making of the English Working Class* (new edn, 1980)

Thompson, E.P., *Customs in Common* (1991)

Waterhouse, E., *The Dictionary of British 18th Century Painters in Oils and Crayons* (1981)

Wilson, K., *The Sense of the People. Politics, Culture and Imperialism in England, 1715–1785* (1998)

Young, B., *Religion and Enlightenment in Eighteenth-Century England: Theological Debate from Locke to Burke* (1998)

Collections of essays

Black, J. (ed.), *Britain in the Age of Walpole* (1984)

Black, J. (ed.), *British Politics and Society from Walpole to Pitt, 1742–1789* (1990)

Black, J. (ed.), *Culture and Society in Britain, 1660–1800* (1997)

Blanning, T.C.W (ed.), *The Eighteenth Century* (2000)

Cannon, J. (ed.), *The Whig Ascendancy: Colloquies on Hanoverian England* (1981)

Devine, T.M., and J.R. Young (eds.), *Eighteenth Century Scotland: New Perspectives* (1999)

Dickinson, H.T. (ed.), *Britain and the French Revolution* (1989)

Dickinson, H.T. (ed.), *Britain and the American Revolution* (1998)

Ford, B. (ed.), *The Cambridge Cultural History of Britain. Vol. 5: Eighteenth-Century Britain* (1992)

Ford, B. (ed.), *The Cambridge Cultural History of Britain. Vol. 6: The Romantic Age in Britain* (new edn, 1992)

Hay, D., P. Linebaugh and E.P. Thompson (eds.), *Albion's Fatal Tree: Crime and Society in Eighteenth-Century England* (1975)

Israel, J.I. (ed.), *The Anglo-Dutch Moment: Essays on the Glorious Revolution and its world impact* (1991)

Jones, C. (ed.), *Britain in the First Age of Party* (1987)

Marshall, P.J. (ed.), *The Oxford History of the British: Vol. II, The Eighteenth Century Empire* (1998)

McKendrick, N., J. Brewer and J.H. Plumb (eds.), *The Birth of a Consumer Society: The Commercialization of Eighteenth Century England* (1982)

Moody, T.W., and W.E. Vaughan (eds.), *A New History of Ireland IV: Eighteenth Century Ireland (1691–1800)* (1986)

Taylor, S., R. Connors and C. Jones (eds.), *Hanoverian Britain and Empire: Essays in Memory of Philip Lawson* (1998)

Thompson, F.M.L. (ed.), *The Cambridge Social History of Britain, 1750–1950* (3 vols., 1990)

Walsh, J., C. Haydon and S. Taylor (eds.), *The Church of England, c.1689–c.1833: From Toleration to Tractarianism* (1993)

Other Media

The Royal Historical Society Bibliography on CD-ROM: The History of Britain, Ireland and the British Overseas (1998) ISBN 019 268573 2